The Wines of the Rhône

FABER BOOKS ON WINE
General Editor: Julian Jeffs

Bordeaux (new edition) by David Peppercorn
Burgundy by Anthony Hanson
French Country Wines by Rosemary George
German Wines by Ian Jamieson
Italian Wines (new edition) by Philip Dallas
Port (new edition) by George Robertson
Sherry (new edition) by Julian Jeffs
Spirits and Liqueurs by Peter Hallgarten
The Wines of Australia (new edition) by Oliver Mayo
The Wines of Greece by Miles Lambert-Gócs
The Wines of Portugal (new edition) by Jan Read
The Wines of the Rhône (new edition) by John Livingstone-Learmonth
Drilling for Wine by Robin Yapp

THE WINES OF THE RHÔNE

JOHN LIVINGSTONE-LEARMONTH

new edition

faber and faber
LONDON · BOSTON

First published in 1978
by Faber and Faber Limited
3 Queen Square London WC1N 3AU
New revised edition published 1983
This third new and revised edition first published in 1992

Phototypeset by Intype Ltd, London
Printed in England by
Clays Ltd, St Ives plc

A CIP record for this book is available from the British Library

ISBN 0–571–15111–6
0–571–14622–8 (pbk)

1 3 5 7 9 10 8 6 4 2

Contents

Maps

Foreword

The current edition of *The Wines of the Rhône* is intended to provoke thought and reflection by its readers on some of the issues facing the wine world in the early 1990s, as seen from a Rhône standpoint.

I am happy to say that I am more traditionalist than modernist, if 'traditionalist' means sticking to a regional identity and authenticity for the wines, and harnessing new techniques behind this first premise.

While I hope that the book contains information which will prove useful for wine buyers when they go to their local supplier, there has been neither time nor budget for a freelance writer on a specialized subject to carry out an investigation that is totally comprehensive – alas, the days of patronage are no more.

One background point I would like to make is that I have no commercial links with the wine trade, so any opinions or comments are made entirely without commercial bias.

I hope the book provides some stimulating reading and perspective on this great wine region over the past twenty years.

John Livingstone-Learmonth,
Putney, London, May 1992

Acknowledgements

Round up the usual suspects. For this third edition and continuing help and support over the years, thanks to the Paris mafia – Tim Johnston and Mark Williamson – who have the first and second *arrondissements* well sorted out with Willis and Juvenales. Parisians at last know and appreciate the true taste of the mighty Syrah. Thanks also to Robin and Judith Yapp for their hospitality and generosity over the years and for their ability to offer up tracts of their wine list for tasting. On overseas patrol, the *meilleur sommelier* of Norway, Christopher Moestue, has been a great enthusiast for the Rhône and its *cépages*. It is also good to know that the original inspiration, Melvyn Master, has returned from his ventures in the United States to live again in Provence – which he should never have left.

Obviously my continued thanks go to the Rhône growers themselves, several of whom I feel I can now genuinely call friends.

Mary Treherne kindly produced new line drawings of the Rhône growers, characters and views, and thanks to her for doing this and giving the reader an impression of some of the principal personalities.

Lastly, thanks and love to my wife Fiona for putting up with an invisible husband at weekends while expecting Marina. She must have felt like Scott saying goodbye to Oates as I trudged off through the snow to write in the den at the bottom of the garden. Thank you, Zu.

1991 *Vintage Review*

The run had to end. After three top-class vintages in a row, the Rhône growers were given extra work and worry in 1991. While the northern Rhône succeeded in delivering some attractive, elegant wines, the south had a vintage that compares with 1987 as being below par. Depending in part on what 1992 delivers, it is possible that the 1991 northern reds and whites, if well selected, will provide good buying opportunities for those seeking a healthy rapport between price and quality. Remember that 1991 was widely regarded as a moderate year in Bordeaux; this often sets the tone for the other regions of France, and the Rhône is sure to suffer from this association. The northern reds are lighter than the generally dense wines of 1988, 1989 and 1990, but possess an attractive fruitiness on top of a discreet structure that indicates an effective evolution over the course of perhaps a dozen years. The whites are superior – really well balanced, complete wines that will develop great dimension and appeal.

Climatically, the northern Rhône escaped the worst of the excesses experienced by France during 1991, although there were pockets of drama such as frost at Crozes-Hermitage in the fourth week of April: this reduced the crop of Jaboulet's Thalabert by 30 per cent, for example. There was some decent rainfall during the spring, and a generally very dry summer, with only a little hail at the end of July. Ripening quickened noticeably in the second half of August, and hopes were high for a very successful vintage until the onset of rains in the second half of September. Between the last days of September and the 8 October there were severe rainfall and warm winds, which provoked rot in the vineyards of those who delayed harvesting. As a result, buyers will have to select carefully because there were uneven levels of ripeness within the same *appellations*.

Côte-Rôtie delivered charming, quietly substantial wines that will show well over around a dozen years providing the *vigneron* selected both crop and *cuvée*. There are some wines that are a bit green and lack intensity, but the best will be aromatic and very pleasing around 1997–2000. The reds of Hermitage – again, when at their best – hold some good fruit with discreet tannic support. They are sometimes a little raw, and will need about half a dozen years to settle down. They have a quiet richness in them, and are superior to the 1987s by some way, with alcohol levels naturally around 13°. The year was more irregular at Crozes-Hermitage, where it will be best to select the top *cuvées* of the best growers. Some of the standard *cuvées* are a little raw, with a precarious fruitiness, but the top wines have an elegance and gentle richness that will make them drink well for up to eight years or so.

Selection is also necessary at St-Joseph, with the top *cuvées* providing more secure, better-integrated wines than the standard bottles. This is a mid-weight year, as in the whole region. The vintage was generally successful at Cornas, where most of the harvesting had been completed before the onset of the late, heavy rains. Good colour extract, and sound flavours mark the wines, which have greater keeping potential than many in the northern Rhône this year.

1991 was extremely successful for the white wines of the north. The harvest at Condrieu was at least one-third smaller than 1990, and had been brought in before the rains, with sugar levels that gave wines of 13° to 14°. They promise well on the bouquet, have attractive richness and are very long on the finish. The white Hermitages are very good indeed; they, too, have good levels of natural alcohol, are well perfumed and promise to develop really well during the 1990s. The whites of Crozes-Hermitage, St-Joseph and St-Péray also bear a quiet strength, with potential on the bouquet and very good length on the palate.

The southern Rhône suffered more violently and persistently from the weather in 1991. The spring was cold, and while the worst of the frost that ravaged Provence was avoided, *domaines* were afflicted, notably around the eastern Vaucluse – parts of Gigondas and towards Vaison-la-Romaine, as well as the Mont Ventoux and Lubéron areas. The next trouble came at flowering, with *coulure* quite frequently present on the Grenache, inhibiting a successful fruit formation. By now the growers were looking down the barrel of a gun regarding their quantity, and the 29–30 July brought further calamity. In the space of four hours there was 230 mm (9 inches) of torrential rain (amounting to 30 per cent of the annual average rainfall). Some vineyards at Châteauneuf-du-Pape were partly washed away and growers spoke of it being the worst storm since 1929. The heavy rain and hail were widespread – Gigondas received 140mm (5½ inches) in the one night, while the pattern in the Gard *département* (Lirac, Tavel) was for the hail to follow the course of the Rhône, resulting in the loss of a further ten per cent of the harvest. To cap it all, hot, humid weather in September encouraged grape-worm and rot.

Unfortunately quantity and quality are both low. The Grenache did not ripen well in some cases, and those who waited were then hit by October rains. Châteauneuf-du-Pape's crop was below 30 hectolitres a hectare, and it remains to be seen how much of that will end up in bottle. The reds are low on colour, as they are at Gigondas and in most of the southern Rhône. They are also short on genuine extract, their lightness all the more resounding since they follow three very big vintages. They are low in alcohol, and this is really a vintage that most growers would prefer to forget. Gigondas, Vacqueyras and the Villages are in much the same boat, with growers having to chaptalize even to reach the minimum required degree in some instances. The Syrah and Mourvèdre crops were healthier than the Grenache, so that those growers with a high proportion of these vines have made some atypical but quite medium-weight wines from carefully selected *cuvées*.

Similar comments apply to the reds of the Gard, where growers who wanted to defend their reputations had to make two or three journeys through the vineyards. The wines are somewhere around the standard of the 1987s and will not keep at all long.

The rosés of Lirac and Tavel have more acidity than the often vastly over-alcoholic 1990s, and show decent early aromas and fair substance.

As with many off-vintages for Rhône reds, the 1991 southern whites are quite successful. Harvested before the onset of rot, the grapes gave wines whose fresh fruitiness was an immediately striking aspect. Many of them are very aromatic, and from *appellations* like Lirac and Laudun they will provide very good drinking over five years or so.

Introduction

1975

The Rhône Valley possesses some of France's most remarkable and distinguished wines, and its vineyards are probably the oldest in France. It is therefore quite amazing that even today it should still be a comparatively unexplored, little noticed wine region. Magnificent wines like Côte-Rôtie and Hermitage have been made for over 2,000 years but have strangely never become widely known as two of their country's best red wines. Wines like St-Joseph and Cornas, only marginally lesser, have themselves existed for over 1,000 years, yet are practically unheard of outside the immediate Rhône Valley area. These are by no means the only really good wines of the region: there are the exceptional white wines of Château-Grillet and Condrieu, made from the rare, highly perfumed Viognier grape. There is the sturdy, strongly flavoured red wine of Châteauneuf-du-Pape, which, when genuine, is almost certainly the best red wine from the South of France. And there is of course the rosé of Tavel, generally recognized as the leading rosé in France, and most probably the world.

Quite apart from the extremely high standards of these wines – and there can be little doubt that *marques* such as Côte-Rôtie's La Mouline and Hermitage's La Chapelle are some of the best red wines in the world – there exists enormous variety in the Rhône Valley. Reds, whites and rosés of many different styles are made near the river between Vienne and Avignon, and there are even additional local specialities such as the excellent Muscat de Beaumes-de-Venise.

Despite all this, much of the Rhône Valley wine region remains an unknown quantity. 'Côtes du Rhône' implies to most people a medium-quality, low-priced and highly alcoholic red wine.

Traditionally, wine merchants have never looked to the Rhône as a source of their finest wines and have preferred to turn to Bordeaux and Burgundy. The euphoric wine-buying days of the 1970s changed this, however. Bordeaux and Burgundy reached such unattainable price levels that interest naturally started to focus more intently on the Rhône. The northern part of the Valley, containing the finest wines, was by and large unappealing owing to its limited production, but the southern part suited the market admirably. The mixture of panic buying and natural greed that followed, however, thrust wines like Châteauneuf-du-Pape and Gigondas firmly into the limelight, and the old disease of high prices struck yet again. As a result, Châteauneuf-du-Pape and Gigondas became two of the least sought-after wines from the Rhône. To illustrate: on 31 August 1972 stocks of wine held at the property in Châteauneuf-du-Pape amounted to 58,910 hectolitres. On 31 August 1974 the figure had risen to 112,505 hectolitres. At Gigondas the respective holdings were 17,440 hectolitres in 1972 and 33,903 hectolitres in 1974. The growers could see their cellars practically overflowing with wine and in 1975 very slowly started to realize the error of their ways. A fall in price was the only solution to their problem.

This is an important story because it shows that many merchants' first experience of the Rhône was an unhappy one. The more adventurous who persevered with their search, however, were amply rewarded. Underneath all the full *appellation* wines – there are fourteen of them – is a series of very good, little explored wines from all over the southern part of the Valley. For instance, there are seventeen Côtes du Rhône Villages, communities making good, and sometimes very good, wines: leading names here are Cairanne, Chusclan, Laudun and Vacqueyras. Then there is the less strictly regulated Côtes du Rhône *générique* wine, the main reason for the area's fame and its prosperity. Even in this category there are some agreeable finds to be made, generally in the small barrel-lined cellar of a private grower. Some of the Co-opératives also make good wine and, as wine-making techniques become more professional, the standard can only rise.

In the vineyards the march of the Syrah continues. Its plantation in the southern Rhône has increased extensively, but the most widely planted vine of all is still the Grenache, which like the rest of the Rhône Valley 'regulars' is relatively unknown outside its region. A vine of Spanish origin that may have originally entered the Roussillon area of France, it gives wines characterized by their ruby-red colour and by their high alcohol degree; they have a marked tendency to fade after about eight years, however, which is one of the reasons why the Grenache-based Châteauneuf-du-Pape cannot be considered a really long-lived wine.

Meanwhile the origin of the Syrah merits close inspection, for it provides possible evidence that the Côtes du Rhône is by a long way France's oldest wine-producing region. Some people believe that the Syrah originates from Syracuse, the connection being founded on the linking of names, but the authors do not subscribe to this. They believe that the Syrah came originally from around Shiraz, which is today the capital of the state of Fars in Iran. About 850 kilometres from Tehran, and 50 from the ruins of Persepolis, Shiraz was, until recent Islamic developments, the wine-growing centre of Iran. At Persepolis, founded in c. 518 BC, stone tablets have been found bearing inscriptions that mention wine and vintners. Such evidence would seem to suggest that the wine of Shiraz was already quite famous around that time.[1] Furthermore, the likeness between the words Syrah and Shiraz is evident, and M. Paul Gauthier of Hermitage, a leading négociant, once found in a book published in 1860 six different spellings of the word Syrah: Syra, Sirrah, Syras, Chira, Sirac and Syrac. Their common denominator would appear to be the word Shiraz.

An obvious question arises, however. How did the Syrah vine arrive in the Rhône Valley, which is more than 5,000 kilometres from Iran? The answer could be that it was the Greeks of Phocaea, the founders of Marseille, who brought it with them. Phocaea was on the west coast of Asia Minor, about 50 kilometres south of the Aegean island of Lesbos. According to Herodotus, the Phocaeans were the first Greeks to undertake distant sea journeys and, around 600 BC, opened up the coasts of the Adriatic, France and Spain: Marseille was founded by them in 600 BC under the name of Massalia.

No connection between Phocaea and Shiraz can be established until the middle of the sixth century BC, so it seems that it was not the actual founders of Marseille who introduced the Syrah vine into France but some later Phocaean generation. The reasons for this supposition are as follows: in 546 BC the Persian King Cyrus I roundly

---

[1] William Culican, *The Medes and Persians* (London: Thames and Hudson, 1965), p. 115.

defeated the Lydian Croesus, and the western capital of the Persian Empire became established at Sardes, only 120 kilometres south-east of Phocaea. The Lydian Empire, which bordered on Phocaea, was, incidentally, a rich vine-growing country.

The defeat of the Lydians by Cyrus opened up the western seaboard for Persia, and Phocaea continued thereafter under Persian rule. Then, some time after 546 BC, a large group of Phocaeans reportedly tried to escape by sailing west towards the Mediterranean and their own city of Massalia. Many are known to have turned back after reaching Chios, but a few boats continued to Marseille. With their country then under Persian rule, it is therefore not improbable that it was these Phocaean voyagers who brought the Syrah vine to France, and not those who founded Marseille around 600 BC.

As Persian domination continued in Phocaea, links between Marseille and its mother country naturally receded, and trade had to be sought within France itself. The natural route towards the interior was the Rhône Valley, and Massaliote coins, dating from 500–450 BC, have been found along it as far as the Alps, near the river's source in Switzerland. At that time wine was a fairly major element of trade, and old Greek amphorae have been found in both Marseille and Tain-l'Hermitage, about 240 kilometres farther north. This could indicate that it was at Hermitage that the Syrah was first planted: no similarly ancient amphorae have been found around the other northern Rhône vineyards. As if to support this contention, it is also interesting to note the naming of the Syrah vine in Australia today; there it passes under one of two names, either 'Shiraz' or 'Hermitage'.

The Roman invasion of Gaul naturally secured the continued cultivation of the hillside vineyards in the northern Rhône, and the area around the important Roman town of Vienne – today the Côte-Rôtie – became particularly famous for its *vinum picatum*, or resinated wine. Terraces were carefully structured into the hillside slopes and their basic form remains the same today as it was 2,000 years ago.

The Roman era was in many ways the Golden Age of the Rhône Valley south of Lyon, and its legacy has been both striking and long-lived. Vienne is distinguished by its splendid Temple of Augustus and Livia, similar in style to the famous Maison Carrée in Nîmes, its theatre, not excavated until the 1930s, and its Pyramide, once the finishing-post for chariot races and now the name of one of France's most eminent restaurants. The Roman influence continues all the way down the Valley, most notably at Orange, where there is an antique theatre with a marvellously preserved front wall ('the finest wall in my kingdom', according to Louis XIV), and a fine Arc de Triomphe that makes the Paris version look very junior indeed.

The Romans' departure from Gaul was accompanied by a decline in wine-making. The peasant farmers and small Gallic communities had not the resources to maintain extensive vineyards, and wine therefore lost much of its utility value. As a means for barter or exchange it became more localized, and most cultivators were content to make just enough for their own consumption.

Then, around the ninth century AD, the Church emerged as the most prolific owner of vineyards. Well-disciplined and well-organized, its members possessed the resources to produce wine on a scale not seen since the expulsion of the Romans. Wine had always been needed for their religious services and it slowly evolved as a useful source of income. Complex deals were often drawn up with the region's nobility and cultivation became more widespread. Its scale was probably very limited by comparison with today's, however, as can be judged from local documents found at Cornas, Rasteau and other places. All vineyards were strictly defined according to their size and were generally mentioned by a specific name – the Coteau St-Martin at Rasteau, for instance.

As wine became more accepted as an everyday drink, so more was made. In the fourteenth century the country surrounding Avignon seems to have been quite widely planted with vines – encouraged, no doubt, by the imposing needs of the Papal Palace. Demand remained largely localized at this time, although visiting monarchs or royal emissaries would take back their favourite discoveries to the Court of France; there was then just as much pleasure to be derived from finding a 'new wine' as there is today. Favour could also be curried by introducing the king to a fine country wine, and aristocratic families were not slow to realize this. The Grignan family at Chusclan was a case in point.

Slowly, individual wines started to be known and recognized in their own right, and enterprising owners would put out legendary stories concerning their wine's life-giving properties, general excellence and so on. All this helped to raise the price, and little by little export came to be considered a worthwhile undertaking. The *vinum picatum* of Vienne had been the very first wine export from the

Côtes du Rhône region, being regularly sent to Rome in the first century AD.

Until the eighteenth century the wines from near the Rhône bore a mixture of different names, based on the name of the vineyard owner, or of the vineyard, or of the nearest village or town. Respective examples of this were the *vin de Mure* from Crozes-Hermitage, the *vin de la Nerte* from Châteauneuf-du-Pape, and the *vin d'Avignon* – also probably Châteauneuf-du-Pape – that was bought by the Earl of Bristol in 1704, according to P Morton Shand in his *Book of French Wines* (London: Penguin/Jonathan Cape, 1964).

In 1731 the first official grouping of wine villages was made in what is now the Gard *département*, and the title chosen for the group was 'La Côte du Rhône'. This represented the wine from many small communities on the west banks of the Rhône opposite Avignon; the most important villages were Orsan, Chusclan, Codolet, St-Victor and Tavel. In 1737 it was decided to mark the letters 'CdR', along with the vintage, on all barrels coming from member communities, and this agreement lasted into the early twentieth century.

The Gard *département* grouping marked a significant advance in relations between the various Rhône Valley wine villages, since earlier local decrees are all full of protectionist laws and regulations. Many villages, notably Tavel, had previously completely forbidden the entry of any 'foreign' wine or grapes within their community boundaries. The purpose was probably twofold: to ensure that all the village wine was drunk, and the vineyards therefore well kept up; and to eliminate the possibility of blending with any inferior local wines.

The need for strict, well-defined laws in order to preserve standards of quality emerged very strongly in the twentieth century, by when the world market for wine was growing very quickly. The *vignerons* of Châteauneuf-du-Pape, led by the Baron Le Roy, therefore instituted a series of quality controls over themselves, so that only sound, honest wine would be made there. Unfortunately they did not, and could not, legislate for what happened to the wine once it had left its place of origin. This is still a pressing problem today.

The Châteauneuf-du-Pape rules were drawn up in 1923, the first of their kind in the world, and by 1936 the French had made them broadly applicable to the whole country. High-grade wines were obviously the most restricted, with regulations governing which grapes could be used, how much wine per acre could be made, and so on, and it was decided that these were to possess their own *Appellation d'Origine Contrôlée*. Beneath them, the lesser wines were subject to less rigid stipulations.

The first *appellations* in the Côtes du Rhône were divided into three groups. There was a northern group, consisting of Côte-Rôtie, Château-Grillet and Condrieu; a middle group, consisting of Cornas, St-Péray, Hermitage and Crozes-Hermitage; and finally a southern group, made up of Tavel and Châteauneuf-du-Pape. The additions to this list, now generally regarded as being split on a purely north–south basis, have been Muscat de Beaumes-de-Venise in 1943, Rasteau *vin doux naturel* and Lirac in 1945, St-Joseph in 1956 and Gigondas in 1971.

1982

The above words were written in 1975, and in the seven years since some changes have obviously occurred in an area that, although old by origin, is young and relatively unsophisticated in practice. Many *appellations* are now better known; several are at a crossroads in their development; and some are teetering on the edge of a sorry decline. New influences, particularly on cellar work and vinification, have filtered into the more avant-garde *domaines*, and attitudes towards wine-making have certainly become less parochial.

Many of the progressive influences have reached the open-minded growers through visits to California rather than through encouragement from within France. In the northern Rhône the best *vignerons*, such as Guigal and Chave, are also the ones who show most interest in seeing how other people make their wine. Not that they will necessarily change their technique – Chave is the most thoroughly old-fashioned and competent grower in the Valley – but they are better able to evaluate the worth of their equipment, their methods of vinification and the manner of their wines when they have seen parallel cases a long way from home. Marcel Guigal keeps some of Joseph Phelps's Syrah wine in his cellar at Ampuis to remind himself how the cuttings taken from the vines at Côte-Rôtie and transplanted to California are performing.

In the south of the Valley Châteauneuf-du-Pape is where the most exciting things are happening. Growers such as Henri Brunier at Domaine du Vieux Télégraphe, MM. Abeille and Fabre at Domaine de Mont-Redon and M. Boisson at Père Caboche have set up very sophisticated and well thought-out installations, where a premium is put on logic, cleanliness and efficiency. Their wine is not made in a clinical, offhand manner, as this might imply; it just means that they are reducing the various elements that can make up into a failed vat and indifferent wine.

Contrast their enthusiasm, their search to make their red wine more elegant and less clumsy than some of the old Châteauneufs, and to make a refreshing, well balanced white Châteauneuf as well, with the state of affairs in one of the most famous *appellations*, Côte-Rôtie. Here the good name is being upheld by no more than four or five growers; the vineyards are being inexorably expanded, off the slopes and up on to the mediocre soil of the ill-exposed plateau above them. The maximum permitted yield per hectare has been increased from 35 to 40 hectolitres, while the growers seem to be as becalmed as the Ancient Mariner's boat on its painted ocean: very few have modernized any of their cellar equipment but feel the need, derived partly from fashion and partly from economic necessity, to make a lighter wine. The result is evident in some *cuvées* of Côte-Rôtie that are disgracefully pale and wishy-washy. There is no zest in the *appellation*, no firm leadership, and the resulting inertia is a bitter pill to swallow for those such as the author who is a confirmed addict of good Syrah wines. May the growers of Côte-Rôtie remember that quality will always sell, that their wine is undoubtedly better known today than it was ten years ago and that they are in danger of slipping out of the top bracket.

This view about Côte-Rôtie is reinforced when one sees the depth of good quality wines that exist at Hermitage, for instance. There the name of the wine is not founded on just one or two outstanding *cuvées*; several growers are making quite exceptional wine without any recourse to lowering their standards or to enlarging the vineyard.

Elsewhere in the Rhône there are areas of hope and pockets of gloom. Hope at Crozes-Hermitage, where the number of private *domaines* bottling their own wine has risen substantially; the general quality of their wine is not yet irreproachable, but standards are rising and the future looks good. Hope, too, in the Gard *département*, where there has been a massive increase in the number of *domaines* undertaking their own wine-making, bottling and selling of ordinary Côtes du Rhône; their wines are admirable, concentrating on fruitiness and drinkability without necessarily sacrificing the depth and backbone whose absence would render them much less interesting.

Some gloom exists, however. Growers at St-Péray and Cornas are depressed about the future of their vineyards, as few young men are showing an interest in looking after these steep hillside vines. At thirty-five, Robert Michel is the youngest *vigneron* at Cornas, and there are no enthusiastic teenagers in sight – they have all gone to seek work in the neighbouring towns.

Then there are problems that have arisen from the authorities' tampering with the laws, with the result that growers are foregoing the chance of making superior Côtes du Rhône Villages wine and electing to make more simple Côtes du Rhône *générique*, which is already a very crowded category. This means that villages like Cairanne are unlikely to progress to full individual *appellation* status, as did Gigondas in 1971, if their leading growers are all settling to make ordinary Côtes du Rhône – hardly the best-quality advertising for the community, which will remain stuck in its Côtes du Rhône groove.

Overall a tendency has arisen to try to make lighter wines that carry less overriding tannin; in some ways this strips the area of one of its main characteristics, but in others it is a positive development – especially for wines that previously suffered from over-extensive ageing. Often those growers who use casks for really prolonged periods of ageing seem unsure about just why it is wood that should be ageing their wine. They fall into the trap of acting on blind instinct, on customs handed down from father to son, and fail to realize that casks need just as much treatment, just as much maintenance and cleanliness, as do concrete or stainless steel vats. The contradiction is that while many growers in the New World are turning to the use of wood, but ensuring that their casks are replaced with great regularity, some growers in the Rhône are tending to move away from it, without grasping that well-cared-for casks can make a valuable contribution to a wine's development.

Lighter wines are also resulting from the move away from crushing and destalking the grapes prior to fermentation. The *raisin entier* technique leaves the grapes to macerate and subsequently commence fermentation mostly within their skins. The process extracts the fruitiness from the grapes without all the accompanying tannins and is proving very beneficial when well applied. It does not involve the use of carbonic gas and should not be confused with the *macération carbonique* process, which strips many wines of their intrinsic character.

Important white grape vines include the Viognier and the Roussanne. The Viognier is extremely rare, and its cultivation in France is limited mainly to Condrieu and Château-Grillet in the northern Rhône, although lately one or two experimental plantings have been undertaken in the southern Rhône. A tender plant, its grapes are small even when fully ripe, so that its yield per hectare is never large. Its wines are generally excellent and are marked by their very strongly scented bouquets. The origin of the Viognier is disputed, although some of the Rhône growers believe that it came from Dalmatia around the third century AD.

The Roussanne is the other good white-wine grape in the Côtes du Rhône, but grafting of its root-stock over the years has changed the characteristics of its wines, so that they now do not work well on their own. Like the Viognier, it is not a hardy vine, being susceptible to oïdium in particular, and needs frequent sulphur treatments. Jean-François Chaboud of St-Péray has experimented with the making of *cuvées* of Roussanne on their own but is happy with the wine only when it is blended with that of the Marsanne grape, for instance. Otherwise the Roussanne wine is too delicate and starts to decline and to lose its length of finish after as little as a year. The Marsanne is a higher-yielding vine that is also more resistant to the diseases of the vineyard and is therefore more widely favoured by the white wine-makers of Hermitage, St-Joseph, Crozes-Hermitage and St-Péray.

In the southern part of the Rhône Valley other important red wine grapes are the Mourvèdre and the Cinsault. The Mourvèdre, which has always enjoyed a certain fame as the grape that makes the south-coast wines from Bandol, ripens late because it has a large second growth around the month of July. In Provençal it is known as the 'strangle-a-dog' grape, a rather harsh assessment based on its hardness of style. With its dark colour and its backward style of wine, it is often useful as a prop to the weaker Grenache.

The Cinsault is a grape that does not always enlist great support from the growers. Although its colour can be an attractive, even red, it is a little thin on both bouquet and palate and has a tendency to fade very quickly within three or four years. Of course, no pure Cinsault wine is ever made, and it acts in a constructive way to soften the sturdier Mourvèdre and Syrah, as well as being a crucial element in the southern Rhône rosés.

Finally, the Syrah vine is the one that gives the Rhône's best red wines and which holds the key to the region's viticultural history. Syrah wines are always well coloured, rich in tannin and flavour and very long-lived. The only red wine grape included in the red wines of the northern Rhône, it has recently become extremely popular in the southern Côtes du Rhône, where it is regarded as capable of bringing extra finesse to the slightly coarser, more alcoholic wines made from the Grenache. Its nature was altered during the 1970s by what is known as 'clonal selection'; this refers to the attempt to purify the strain by selecting for the vines better root-stock and shoots. These derive from studies of the soil and climate, with the result that a less mixed strain of Syrah has been developed, one that better resists the disease of *coulure*, or the dropping off the vine of its fruit in the early stages of its ripening.

This represents an advance for some growers, who are happy with their increased yields, but doubt persists in the minds of several traditional growers. They point to this new Syrah vine's propensity to produce larger and more numerous grapes, which dilute the plant's fruit. Nor need the new Syrah be trained in the old Guyot manner, the three-stemmed Gobelet training sufficing. A lower degree and less colour result in the wine from such grapes, and the cloning is evidently not to everyone's satisfaction.

On the periphery of the Côtes du Rhône region there are some local country wines that use some of these grapes – Coteaux du Tricastin, Côtes du Ventoux, Châtillon-en-Diois, Côtes du Vivarais and Clairette de Die. The first four make red, rosé and white wines of no great pretension and have for a long time been barely known beyond their immediate area of production. Suddenly, however, the French National Institute of Appellations of Origin (INAO) has promoted the first three to full *appellation contrôlée* status – a move that seems to set a dangerous precedent.

Certainly the respective areas are now growing better-quality vines, but, with the exception of Tricastin, the wines have barely advanced their quality so as to merit the highest accolade in French viticulture. It is not easy, but it is possible, to alter growers' attitudes towards the way they look after and run their vineyards; it is much less easy to change the casual, haphazard mentality that many possess when it comes actually to making their wine. The author's experiences with some of these wines (excepting also the good sparkling Clairette de Die) have strongly suggested that full *appellation contrôlée* status is today being won too easily; it is no use having a hierarchy if everyone is at the top of it, and such a situation is also downright misleading for the average consumer.

The importance of the central *appellation contrôlée* policy is emphasized by the increasing role played by the Côtes du Rhône in the French wine export field. It is a story of constant development. In 1965 Rhône exports, in bottle and cask, came to 122,278 hectolitres; in 1970, 191,416 hectolitres; in 1975, 418,025 hectolitres, in 1980, 516,282 hectolitres, and in 1981, 602,182 hectolitres. The Rhône is now exporting more wine than Burgundy, having overtaken that area for the first time in 1979, and more than Beaujolais, which it overtook in 1976. It is now second only to Bordeaux in volume of exports, and while the world feels the effects of a steady, uncompromising recession, that is a fortunate position to be in.

Apart from its wine, the Rhône Valley is an important industrial and commercial artery for the rest of France. The River Rhône runs for 808 kilometres altogether, from its torrential source in the east of the Swiss canton of the Valais all the way down to the Mediterranean, west of Marseille. South of Lyon it extends for 370 kilometres and is joined by several fair-sized rivers, all of which help to boost its imposing flow. These rivers include the Isère, the Drôme, the Ardèche, the Aigues, the Ouvèze and the Durance.

The area is therefore naturally suitable for hydroelectric projects, which have brought an influx of both money and skilled labour into the surrounding countryside. Important schemes exist at Pierre-Bénite near Lyon, at Donzère and at Valence, for instance. Along the river other heavy industries have sprung up during the last fifty years, including large cement works near Montélimar and some of the country's leading metallurgical industries at Givors, near Vienne, and at Ardoise, near Roquemaure. In the south, at Pierrelatte and Marcoule, the French atomic system has its centre.

In some cases, notably in the northern part of the Valley, these factories have brought problems for the owners of vineyards. Young men derive considerably greater financial benefit from entering their local industry than from continuing to work the land. Where all the vineyard cultivation must by necessity be manual, the fall in the total size of the vineyards has been most marked: this is the case with the lesser-known *appellations* that lie between Vienne and Valence – Cornas and St-Péray.

The Rhône Valley is extremely fertile, however, and its agriculture, although diminished, has broadly remained on a sound level. North of Montélimar the main fruits are peaches, pears, apricots and cherries; to the south there are pears, apples, cherries, plums, melons and peaches. The main vegetables are artichokes, asparagus, cabbages, lettuce and tomatoes. All are grown on an extensive scale and are sold both inside and outside France, with a particularly large proportion going to Paris.

In addition to these staple fruits and vegetables, the surrounds of the Rhône produce other fine local specialities. The *département* of the Isère is rich in walnuts, while the *département* of the Ardèche grows plentiful raspberries, bilberries, blackcurrants and chestnuts. On either side of the river between Lyon and Montélimar a variety of local goat and cow cheeses are made – notably the Rigottes of Condrieu and the St-Marcellin of the Isère. In the north of the Vaucluse *département*, around Valréas, there are widespread lavender plantations, as well as a steady production of olive-oil, especially around Nyons and Beaumes-de-Venise. South of Montélimar, in the Tricastin country, high-grade black truffles are another important local speciality.

The countryside around the river is also rich in poultry and game, and the regional cooking is shaped accordingly. Favourite dishes are the *poulet aux écrevisses* (chicken cooked in a crayfish sauce), *quenelles de brochet* (a sort of pike soufflé), *agneau grillé aux herbes* (lamb roasted in herbs), *perdrix aux choux* (partridge cooked in cabbage) and *charcuterie*, or selected pork meats. The *gratin dauphinois* (potato gratin) and the *lièvre en pouvrade* (hare cooked in pepper sauce) are other favourites. To finish any meal there is the celebrated nougat of Montélimar.

1991

The 1980s were a good decade for the Rhône. Prosperity came to the region. Its best wines became equated in price and quality with the best French and international wines. Vineyards of the steep terraces of the northern Rhône were reclaimed and replanted. Growers modernized and completely rebuilt their cellars. Young faces appeared, eager to put into practice theories learned at wine school. The value of exports grew remarkably, while the quantity of exports increased only slightly, confirming the Rhône's position as the third French quality region, now only a touch behind Bordeaux and Burgundy, and some would say carrying more potential than the other two for the future.

The challenge for the 1990s is to maintain prosperity and quality. Here the regional and national legislators carry great responsibility. There has been a marked increase in crop yields during the 1980s with the march of clonally selected vines and more intensive working of the vineyards, so that the Syndicat des Vignerons at Cornas can actually request a permitted yield for 1989 of over 55 hectolitres per hectare, up from a previous level of 35 hectolitres. Put another way, about 7,500, instead of 4,650, bottles of Cornas would come from a hectare of vines. The 'more is less' syndrome is at work here – more quantity, less quality – which is very bad news for the wine drinker. The tragedy would be if the Rhône became a producer of commercial wines, which would strip the region of its hallmark and of its appeal. Cosy rulings rather than long-sighted decisions are therefore perils facing the Rhône in the 1990s.

Individual *appellations* have flourished, however, and the northern Rhône is now humming with activity and ideas. Côte-Rôtie has a new lease of life, the words written in 1982 appearing to come from another epoch. The *vignerons* have slowed down the advance of plateau plantations in poorer locations. Marcel Guigal has burst on the world stage as the maker of highly intense, top-class wines which have captured people's imaginations at a time of some doubt as to how good Bordeaux wines really are. There is a tight group of young wine-makers who have either taken over family vineyards or set up from scratch on their own. They differ from the previous generation in their seriousness – for them, wine-making is more of a science than an art, and they are meticulous in their attention to detail, both in the vineyards and in the cellars. Their presence has raised the quality of many of the wines, and it is to be hoped that in the coming years they will gain increased confidence to express themselves more freely in their wine-making, away from the edicts of wine school and the advocacy of *œnologues*, whose hovering presence sometimes seems to parallel the role of the shrink in modern society.

Condrieu has taken a turn for the better. One only has to drive along the N86 on the west bank of the Rhône to spot fresh plantations on formerly abstract-looking hillsides. But a word of caution here – there are plenty of fruit cultivators or small *agriculteurs* ready to 'try their hand' with a spot of Viognier, and the quality of some of the wine that now sells for nearly £12 or US$20 out of the cellars is poor. It is up to conscientious merchants to select carefully or to reject a Condrieu listing, if the *appellation*'s name is to be protected.

The cornerstone of the northern Rhône remains Hermitage, where top-quality red wine is produced every year by some of the growers. Gérard Chave remains utterly committed to quality and is a shining example for many of the region's *vignerons*, especially the younger ones, who understandably hold him in some reverence.

Great progress has been made with the reds at Crozes-Hermitage, where more elegant, better-balanced and just plain classier wines are now being made. A bold new star here is Alain Graillot, whose reds are superbly succulent and serve to set a yardstick, along with Jaboulet's irreproachable Domaine de Thalabert.

Cornas has recovered from a pervading gloom apparent in the late 1970s. While there are several growers on the threshold of retirement, there are also younger *vignerons* coming through, either to maintain family tradition, as with the excellent Auguste Clape vineyard, or to revise their wine-making methods completely, as in the case of Jean Lionnet, whose great success has been to bring greater finesse to his Cornas without sacrificing its robust nature.

Also on the west bank of the Rhône, St-Joseph has to a certain extent fallen prey to the legislators, whose decision radically to extend the vineyard has brought forth a lot of moderate wine, the quality of which is far removed from that of the main villages such as Mauves and the main producers such as Grippat. At least measures are now being taken to halt this, although as it is the reversal of vineyard plantations that we are talking about, thirty years have been set aside for their accomplishment. In this case, it is the consumer who suffers, since unless he or she reads a book like this, there is little knowing what is good and what is bad.

In the southern Rhône, Châteauneuf-du-Pape remains a worthy centrepiece. There is great variety of choice here, with the number of *domaines* bottling their own wine approaching 120. Quality is strong, and styles of wine range from the tannic and intense to the aromatic and refined. The Mourvèdre has been a beneficial influence here, and its presence has grown during the 1980s to give wines of greater structure and length on the palate. The *vignerons* have stepped up their collective commitment to quality and to spreading the word about Châteauneuf, and prospects seem set fair. Any *appellation* that can reject the use of harvesting machines in order to uphold the compulsory pre-vinification discard of poor grapes is certainly working on the right lines.

Elsewhere in the south, Vacqueyras has received sole *appellation* status, following on from Gigondas back in 1971. Here the authorities have shown admirable restraint in making sole *appellation contrôlée* status hard to win. Future candidates for this are Cairanne, Beaumes-de-Venise and the improving Sablet, where there are now several very good private *domaines*.

The 1980s also brought great advances for white wines made in the southern Rhône. Châteauneuf-du-Pape, Lirac and Laudun are three places now giving some excellent whites. These are vinified at low temperatures, but unlike wines from more northerly climes, they possess enough depth to emerge with greater complexity beyond the fresh, racy fruitiness apparent at the outset. Between two and six years old, the wines of good producers provide excellent drinking at sound prices for those sated on a regime of ubiquitous Chardonnay or modest Sauvignon. The pity is that most importers report that, outside a few notable exceptions like the Château de Beaucastel white wines, white Rhônes are very hard to sell. All the same, with growers planting Viognier, Roussanne and Marsanne on their Côtes du Rhône *domaines*, there could be some very interesting developments in the quality and appeal of white wines during the 1990s. If global warming continues, white wine-making which produces refined and elegant wines will become all the more necessary.

The climate was a major theme of the 1980s in the Rhône. It was a decade when harvesting dates fell earlier and earlier. First notes for this book made around 1973 show the growers quoting the end of September or early October as the normal date for the *vendanges*. By the late 1980s, the first week of September was a regular occurrence. In 1982 few growers were equipped to cope with the intense day and night temperatures at harvest-time, which is why many of that year's wines tasted stewed and jammy. Cellar equipment, with touch-of-a-button temperature control, has been vastly updated and is now ready to work alongside the crop that nature delivers.

Vineyard care also edged away from the unquestioning use of

herbicides, pesticides and fertilizers produced by large multinational chemical companies. These are topics about which one hears *vignerons* talking and reflecting more now, but marching in the opposite direction is the issue from most local nurseries or *pépiniéristes* of clonally grafted vine-stock, with such prolific results that one hears stories about young Grenache at Châteauneuf-du-Pape yielding 80 hectolitres per hectare – against a theoretical, historic level of 35 hectolitres. Responsible growers like the Baron Le Roy of Château Fortia and François Perrin of Château de Beaucastel are quite rightly alarmed by such developments, since they recognize the dilution in quality that such mass production can bring. A few growers still take their young vine cuttings from old stock in their vineyards, but this is a time-consuming task, and requires both dedication and numbers of people – which is why the three members of the Marsanne family of St-Joseph can still manage to do their own grafting.

The main evolution in the style of red wines during the 1980s has been towards greater elegance and more sophistication of taste. Harsh tannins are strictly out; long ageing in old casks is yesterday's game. Less fining is done, and fewer growers filter their wine. Colour extraction is more pronounced through temperature-controlled macerations; intra-cellular fermentations have been used to encourage greater fruitiness. And something of an obsession with new oak has developed in certain quarters – a lot of it, one cannot help but feel, fuelled by whizz-kid wine journalists who have taken it on as their international *cause célèbre*. Fashions come and go in wine-making as much as they do with hemlines, and wry amusement is sometimes afforded by the sight of a *vigneron* grappling with offers of oak casks from different origins that have received different degrees of prior smoking. I wonder where their enthusiasm for this new product will be in ten years' time?

Overseas, the Rhône has caught the imagination of wine-makers keen to experiment and to stretch their skills. This is nowhere more apparent than in California, where it is now estimated that 8 per cent of the vines under plantation (those not attacked by phylloxera) are Rhône varieties. The two major challenges come from the Syrah and the Viognier. Joseph Phelps was a pioneer for the former, with occasional bottles of his Syrah circulating in forward-looking Rhône *domaines* in the 1970s – Guigal's, for example. Now there are other serious producers of Syrah like Qupé (Syrah/Mourvèdre), the Tolmachs' Ojai vineyard and Meridian – bottles of all three even penetrated Jacques Reynaud's Chateau Rayas in 1991 as the search for comparison and improvement continues to be international. While Syrah transplants have started to produce wines of a genuine, proximate substance to those of the Rhône, not surprisingly the Viognier has proved more brittle off its natural habitat. Some sound efforts have been made by vineyards like Calera, whose Viognier dates back to 1984, and Joseph Phelps. Such interest and enthusiasm, personified by the exotic Randall Grahm of Bonny Doon, are a great compliment to the Rhône and its new-found stature.

For the wine drinker, the Rhône still presents uncertainties that reflect the relative innocence of the area. Growers often still like to do several bottlings of any given vintage. There may be an interval of fifteen months between the first and last bottling, so one wine can have spent markedly longer, for instance, in cask, or another wine can drink with markedly greater freshness. No indication is given on the labels about this. *Vignerons* are also coy about telling drinkers about the grape blends in their wine: for a region where multiple grape use is the norm, such information on the front or back label would provide a simple, useful service. In matters of marketing, a certain naïvety is shown by some producers, who tag their wines with all sorts of descriptions about foot of the slopes, high hills, young vines or very aged old gentlemen vines, all of which detract from getting across the *appellation* name and yardstick quality in a clear, easy way.

But these are minor quibbles beside the satisfaction of reading words recorded in 1975 and thinking how irrelevant they are today. The Rhône has reached a level of recognition in keeping with the quality of its wines and the talents of its growers, and while it may be absurd to pay £283 or US$500 for a bottle of Guigal's La Turque, it is most certainly not absurd to pay just £17 or US$30 for a Château de Beaucastel Châteauneuf-du-Pape red or £8.50 or US$15 for a Domaine de Thalabert Crozes-Hermitage red – these are some of the great-value buys in French wine today.

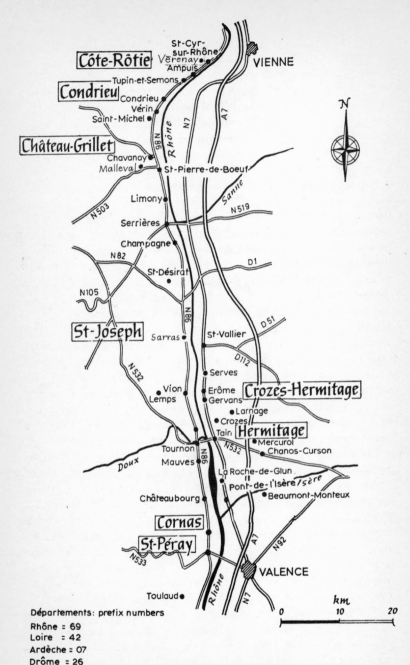

Northern Rhône

I

Côte-Rôtie

———

Côte-Rôtie, one of the world's foremost red wines, bears a splendidly evocative name. The 'Roasted Slope', the 'Burnt Hillside': an exact translation is not required to call to mind very precisely the dark intensity of this majestic, voluptuous wine. As the northernmost vineyard in the Côtes du Rhône, Côte-Rôtie accomplishes with ease the awkward transition between Burgundy and the 'hot South', where the wines are often thought to be blowzy and overbearing.

The very best of Côte-Rôtie merits inclusion in any roll call of the world's great red wines. Yet ordinary wine drinkers have rarely come across this startling wine. While in the late 1980s its name received wide press coverage, largely due to an intense spotlight on the activities of Marcel Guigal, its limited production still leads the average wine buyer unerringly towards Bordeaux, French regional wines, Rioja or exotic Cabernets. Côte-Rôtie remains more the province of specialist importers than of large retail chains.

Even taking into account a recent surge in planting and the reclamation of abandoned vineyard slopes, the surface area under production at Côte-Rôtie in 1991 was 140 hectares, with a further 20 hectares or so filtering through into the production of full *appellation* wine by 1994. As a comparison, all *cru classé* wine from Margaux is taken from around 725 hectares, that from St-Julien from around 560 hectares. In 1971, when Côte-Rôtie and the whole area were struggling for both recognition and survival, the total vineyard came to just under 70 hectares; by 1982, as prospects gradually improved, it had risen to 102 hectares.

The *appellation*'s vineyards are just south of the old Roman town of Vienne, lodged among five wholly inconspicuous communities on the west side of the River Rhône. There is a hard, no-frills aspect about the Rhône and its surrounds here. The river runs with sheer power, its semi-industrial backdrop giving it a masculinity that city rivers like the Seine and the Thames do not possess: more New York with an abrasive edge than London plus charm. Its river traffic is also large and menacing – hundreds of yards of dark, low working barges rather than brief, angular pleasure-craft.

The centre of Côte-Rôtie is at Ampuis. Entering from the north on a rainy day, mist and urban smog brood oppressively over the Valley, which is dark, dank and even *looks* smelly. The tough urban tone carries itself down here – the view is metal, solid textures, pylons, electrical power-lines, warehouses, concrete river constructions. Sitting on the main road from Lyon to Nîmes, Ampuis doesn't have a lot of middle-class chic about it. The hotels on the main road may have the odd coat of fresh paint and a quick flash of new canvas awning, but the shops remain as small-store local as ever – the simple *épicerie, charcuterie*, baker, pharmacy and anonymous post office. The cars parked in the sombre car park are ordinary and downbeat, and populate what amounts to the village square. On Sunday morning there are flurries of activity here as locals meet to chat and drink and the Ampuis rugby bus collects its players. For the rest of the time the sense of a community at work prevails, with the back streets given up to ferociously barking dogs that howl at the occasional passer-by. Around Ampuis the hamlets of Vérenay, Tupin, Semons and St-Cyr-sur-Rhône complete the picture of shabby anonymity: majestic the name, hardly majestic the place.

Côte-Rôtie is a wine that dates back to Roman times. After the local Allobroges tribe was defeated by the Romans at Bollène in around 121 BC, the colonization of the area further north was confirmed by Julius Caesar's conversion of Vienne into a divisional depot for his army in 58 BC. Thereafter Lyon and Vienne vied for favour from Rome, and Vienne's early golden period occurred during the reign of Augustus from 27 BC, when it was the chief commercial centre for the trade in flax and hemp supplying the western part of the Roman Empire. It was then that many of its lasting monuments were built – theatre, temple, circus with its pyramid obelisk.

Much of the Côte-Rôtie cultivation still takes place on the original steeply graded Roman terraces that overlook the Rhône. Some researchers, however, believe the wine to be even older than this. For instance, Professor Claudius Roux, the author of a detailed monograph on Ampuis and Côte-Rôtie, has stated that the vineyard probably dates from the sixth century BC, the time of the Phocaean

Greeks' arrival in southern France, as outlined in the Introduction. This view has been disputed by local growers with an interest in ancient Greek history. They claim, to the contrary, that the Phocaeans were a predominantly seafaring race who liked to establish their colonies and restrict them to the edge of the ocean. If the vine shoots were brought up the Rhône Valley at such an early date, it was more probably by traffickers or pirates.

By the early years after Christ, Vienne and its wine had risen to exalted eminence within the Roman Empire. Vienne was then the thriving capital of mid-Gaul and its local wine, the *vinum picatum*, had become famous as the first Gallic wine to reach Rome. According to the writings of Roman authors of the time, such as Lucius Columella in his *De re rustica* (*c.* AD 60), the *picatum* seems to have been a deeply coloured wine with a certain 'pitchy' taste – hence the description *picatum*.

Both Pliny the Elder, who was born in AD 23 and died in the destruction caused by the eruption of Vesuvius in AD 79, and Martial (AD 40–105) had encountered the *picatum*, which was apparently quite a snob wine in their day. In his *Epigrams*,[1] Martial boasted to his doubting friends that he had been sent the wine from the vine-growing area of Vienne by a friend of his called Romulus. Martial appears to have visited Vienne and seen the vineyards himself, since he had a circle of friends living there.

Pliny discussed the wine with more reverence,[2] as befits probably the world's first wine chronicler. In the thirty-seven books that comprise his *Natural History*, he refers to more than forty different wines with an expertise undoubtedly acquired from frequent tasting. Pliny was drawn by the very 'pitchiness', or coarseness, of the wine from Vienne and found it to be a good example of a country wine – one that was better appreciated in its native place than overseas. Pliny solemnly concluded that one could not know what real *picatum* was like unless it had been drunk in Vienne itself: a handy let-out for a host in Rome if his *picatum* was found to be disappointing!

Vienne started to decline in importance around the second century AD, when the Emperor Marcus Aurelius (AD 121–180) conferred his favours on his preferred Gallic town of Lyon. At the same time the Viennois wine disappears from all chroniclers' records and does not

[1] *Epigrams*, XIII, 107.
[2] *Natural History*, XIV, 26 and 57.

re-emerge until the mid-nineteenth century, when the French authors Jules Janin and Cochard praised it under the name of Côte-Rôtie.

The scourge of phylloxera hit Côte-Rôtie around 1880 and most of the vineyard was destroyed within two years. By 1893 it had been built up again, but not on the same scale. Many farmers had turned swiftly to fruit-growing as a more immediate means of remuneration. They could not afford to wait the four years before the Syrah vines yielded their first worthwhile fruit. Another blow was dealt the vineyard by the First World War, for the loss of young men needed to tend the slopes meant that many growers gave up their plots for want of labour: the long lists of Great War fallen in the local churches and village squares serve to emphasize this. Meagre prices during the Depression further compounded Côte-Rôtie's difficulties, and during the Second World War the wine was sold mainly as *vin ordinaire*. By 1949 Côte-Rôtie was fetching only about 1 franc a litre – a ridiculous price in view of the work involved and the quality of the wine.

Times were lean for the wine growers through the 1960s and early 1970s. In those days it was still uncommon for a small producer to bottle all his wine: the market for it was too localized and the task was made easier by the existence of merchants who could distribute the grower's lesser *cuvées* further afield.

There was the additional problem of working these steep vineyards. France was entering a period of prosperity when its manufacturing base moved ahead, leaving seemingly decadent, strike-ridden countries like Britain behind in a wake of smart cars, Chanel and other designer clothes and secondary residences. Prosperity and the prospect of an enhanced life-style filtered into the rural communities. Only the most dedicated were prepared to sweat it out on the hillsides while their contemporaries went for the easy wage in a factory, with extra social cachet and shorter, less strenuous hours. Local industry in Vienne and Lyon served as a big counter-attraction to wine-making at this time.

It was only in the late 1970s and early 1980s that Côte-Rôtie firmly caught the eye of foreign importers rather than pioneers, people who felt confident they could sell the wine to a wider audience. Then the Parisian market, driven along by the capital's raucous publicity machine, woke up to the wine as well, and even Lyonnais restaurants started to lean southwards in their wine lists.

Nowadays the January Ampuis Wine Fair is no longer a cosy, local celebration of the new vintage, a time for the growers to take a quiet

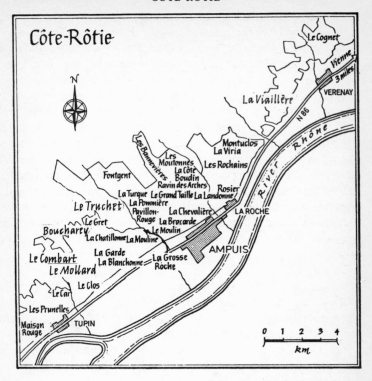

peep sideways at their neighbours' work in between drinks. The hall is overwhelmed by visitors from Lyon, Paris, Marseille and overseas; the doors are shut when necessary to avoid people being crushed, and the growers seem relieved when the two-day marathon is over. But what they are now obtaining is much higher prices and steady demand for their wine, which in turn are financing the extensive replanting and expansion of the vineyards.

The hillside vineyards themselves are among the steepest in France; in places their incline is as much as 55°. There are other European vineyards – notably along the River Mosel – that may possess a more startling abruptness, but few can lay claim to such ancient traditions as well. The packed stone walls that form the terraces have not changed substantially since the days of the Romans and are still generally held together without the aid of cement. Under the joint attack of wind and rain, these walls need annual maintenance; they are often higher than a man, and only skilled hands can perform the delicate task of repairing them.

Along the narrow escarpments and short slopes are planted two different vines, the red-grape Syrah and the white-grape Viognier. Although it is a tenacious plant that thrives in modest conditions, the Syrah is usually specially trained at Côte-Rôtie by the Guyot method in order for it to produce well: four support sticks of different lengths are hammered into the ground around the foot of the plant, and the vine shoots are then led outward along the sticks so as to achieve the greatest possible exposure. The job of hammering these sticks into the rocky ground is arduous indeed and is repeated every year when the growers plant their new vines. The hammer and the pickaxe used to be the only tools for this operation, but now mini-caterpillar bulldozers do some of the clearance, angled precariously on the inclines. Otherwise a spot of dynamite – artistically termed 'agricultural explosives' – does the trick. This is not always as time-saving as it should be since the blast often affects the terrace walls as well. When this happens, passers-by on the main road below can encounter some rude shocks from falling debris!

Since the late 1960s the general nature of the vineyards has altered as the area under vines has grown, first through planting on untilled ground on the plateau above the top slopes and then by the grubbing out of overgrown patches on the high slopes or in the nooks and gulleys that lead off the front hillside towards the plateau.

By the mid-1980s replanting fever had become rampant, encouraged by the soaring prices being charged and paid for the wine. The younger breed of growers, mostly educated at eminent wine schools like Beaune, are still busy acquiring or renting small plots on or near the Côtes Blonde and Brune and running up to the plateau at Le Champin. Even those who have never cultivated a vine in their lives, but who own small plots on the hillsides through family inheritance, are now planting vines in order to sell their grapes to *négociants*.

Traditionally most of the growers have maintained a small sideline in fruit cultivation – cherries, apricots and apples principally – but now, with increasingly proficient market-gardening methods, with the hillside crop further and further behind the ripening elsewhere, and with cheap produce coming in from Common Market countries like Spain, they are accepting that it is more worthwhile to be single-minded about growing vines. As a result the attractive rows of cherry trees and apple trees that frame some of the vineyards, providing a lush Mediterranean perspective down to the valley below, are disappearing. Only the gentle shade of blue provided by the banks of wild irises breaks up the colours in early summer.

One of the problems of this take-off in planting to a total of 140 hectares by 1991, will be the overall amount of wine from young vines in circulation in the next few years. Only on the fifth crop can the wine first be called 'Côte-Rôtie', while for another five years or so it is lighter, less coloured and more subdued on the palate than the wine from older vines. The acidity levels can be higher, too, especially if the young vines are sited on the topmost slopes like Boucharey near the plateau, which is subject to the cooling wind known as the *vent du nord*.

As President of the Syndicat des Vignerons, Gilles Barge has an important job at a crucial time in Côte-Rôtie's development. In the mid-1980s price rises for the wine provoked a stampede of requests for new plantations: 13 hectares asked for in 1985 alone, and 16 new hectares allowed in 1984 and 1985. The INAO, which in 1985 actually granted 8 hectares, is obviously guided by the growers' wishes, so self-discipline by the Syndicat is critical if quality is to be upheld. After 12 hectares of new surface were requested in 1989, Gilles Barge and his fellow Syndicat committee members have restricted the increase of the vineyard to at most 5 hectares a year in future; their task is then to decide who gets what among the *vigneron* community.

'This will allow us to bring along a progressive increase and not have the market flooded with wine made from young vines,' comments M. Barge, who took over as President of the Syndicat from Albert Dervieux in the summer of 1989. The younger generation is stamping its mark on the Syndicat in a positive way, trying to encourage planting by younger growers; they are also content that the French wine authorities have, from the 1992 harvest, terminated the 10 per cent top-up or *dérogation*; so the maximum permitted yield will be 40 hectolitres per hectare.

'There's no reason why we shouldn't stop at a final total of 40 hectos,' says M. Barge, 'because with our economic situation much more satisfactory now, we must go for quality above all.' In the meantime it is to be hoped that the *appellation* does not sink too far into a morass of marketing techniques whereby Côte-Rôtie is sold at several different price levels with sobriquets like *jeunes vignes, vieilles vignes, vin de coteau* paraded on the labels.

Reclamation and new planting have occurred on both the full slopes and the plateau above. It is hard to believe the local claim that 95 per cent of the new planting between 1985 and 1990 has been on the slopes – slopes that had lain abandoned since the First World War. However, the growers are now able to use mini-excavators to clear the hillsides and help prepare the rebuilding of the containing walls. Up on the plateau the vines are planted 2.5 metres apart to allow tractor-working, but on the steep slopes there is only half the distance between the vines, space being so precious and one worker requiring so little room for manoeuvre. Unlike the plateau and the more shaded gullies, the full slopes have the combination of shale, a high mean temperature and admirable exposure that enables the vines to provide the very intense grape juice that is the hallmark of good Côte-Rôtie.

Another beneficial development since 1990 has been the spraying of the hillside vines for basic treatments from the air, by helicopter. 'One man can spray just 0.7 hectare in a day, with the machine on his back,' commented Jean-Michel Gérin, one of the younger growers, 'whereas in 1990 the helicopter treated 100 hectares in a day at three times less the price. We had to have guided tours to Hermitage to see what Philippe Jaboulet had achieved there with the helicopter, to overcome the doubters, though.'

The Syrah forms nearly 95 per cent of the total plantation. The growers refer to it as the 'Sérine', a local name that means little to a grower at Hermitage, for example. Although Côte-Rôtie can be made with up to 20 per cent Viognier in it, many *vignerons* have completely forsaken the white grape. It is a much less consistent producer than the Syrah and seems very particular about where it will grow. One of the best parts of the vineyard is the Côte Brune, for instance, but the Viognier has never shown very well in its clayey soil, and the veteran Marius Gentaz is perhaps the only grower with any Viognier vines on his Côte Brune holding. As these vines are over sixty-five years old, the grapes from them are few but generally well formed and go some way to matching the quality from the more commonly found Viognier vines grown extensively on the lighter, limestone-based ground of the Côte Blonde next door. A young supporter of the Viognier, with sizeable plantations on the Fontgent and Viaillère plots, is Pierre Gaillard. 'It acts to soften the Syrah', he comments simply.

The Côtes Brune and Blonde, two adjacent hillsides above Ampuis, are Côte-Rôtie's most famous denominations. Indeed, in a 1909 showcard made for the Paris Concours Agricole, the Brune and the Blonde were stated to give 'the *premiers grands crus*', while 'the various other slopes give the *grands crus classés*, the *crus classés* and the *crus bourgeois*' – terminology which is very rarely used today, although Guigal's La Mouline calls itself a *premier cru de la Côte Blonde*, a self-styled epithet.

Much Côte-Rôtie is subtitled 'Brune et Blonde'; this has nowadays become really a catch-all and often inaccurately used subheading on a bottle of Côte-Rôtie. If correctly titled, a blend of the two slopes' wine is said to provide the most attractively balanced wine of all the *appellation*. Among the best vineyards figure La Mouline, La Chatillonne, La Côte Boudin, La Landonne, La Chevalière, Fontgent and La Turque, the first two on the Côte Blonde, the last five on or hard by the Côte Brune. Also well known are La Viria and La Viaillère a little to the north towards Vérenay.

The Brune and the Blonde are the subject of Côte-Rôtie's most often-repeated legend, which runs essentially as follows. In dusky, feudal days an all-powerful aristocrat named Maugiron is said to have inhabited the Château d'Ampuis. His two daughters were ravishing beauties, one possessing fair, golden hair, the other long, dark tresses. Whether out of simple kindness, or out of a desire to evade his tax commitments, Maugiron decided to bequeath the two slopes to his daughters; they in turn were christened according to the colour of the girls' hair.

Such are the bare bones of a story that appears in some form or other in most textbooks on wine. Sometimes it is the similarity between the girls' characters and the wines of the two slopes that is said to have prompted the choice of names: the Blonde being bright and lively when young, but fading quickly, the Brune starting off quiet and reserved, but growing into a splendid eminence. This corresponds in part to the style of two of the principal wines made by the House of Guigal, La Mouline and La Landonne. The La Mouline wine is always extremely rich, almost lush in texture, and superbly balanced, but it has an added delicacy that makes it a little less long-lived than some Côte-Rôties; after about its tenth birthday a touch of the damp, almost herbaceous aromas of age has entered the bouquet, even though the fruit on the palate still seems compressed and very intense. Thereafter the purple colour starts to fade gracefully, and the most powerful vintages of La Mouline, such as the 1969,

1978 and 1983, are best drunk before they are twenty to twenty-five years old. Vintages like the 1985, 1986 and 1989, with their open aromas and softer edge on the palate, will be in top form around nine to fifteen years old.

The Guigal La Landonne wine, by contrast, starts life extremely backward, with a black-purple colour and a bouquet that for its first five years reveals a solid wall of stewed berried fruits – the extraction is utterly intense and tight-knit. Possessed of a deep and tannic concentration of flavours, the wine has a slightly spicy finish that promises to develop into a glorious complex richness in later years. Marcel Guigal and his late father only started to make La Landonne in the 1978 vintage, but M. Guigal readily gives this *cuvée*, his 1983 and his 1988 a life-span of up to thirty-five years, considering the 1983 to be the longest-lived of the three.

Since acquiring the House of Vidal-Fleury in 1984, the Guigals have added a third special wine, the site of which is wholly owned by them, to their illustrious line-up – La Turque. This small plot is situated on the Côte Brune, and was formerly a holding of the Maison Vidal-Fleury. Its first wine came in 1985, from vines that were then only five years old. A tasting note of mid-October 1986 on this wine runs: 'La Turque 1985 – brand new *pièce* 225 litres. Racked 30 July 1986. Good, brilliant colour, good density, not much sign of Viognier, is very solid purple rather than black. Bouquet is violent – musky, heavy with some raspberry aromas. Palate starts in a lively way, has soft fruits on the *attaque*. Is already accessible despite being very solid indeed. Has the makings of a smile out of the corner of its mouth.'

For a wine issued from such novice vines, these are extraordinary observations. The only seeming explanation for the wine's intensity and depth of extraction comes from the low yield harvested from this 0.95 hectare plot – 25 hectolitres in 1985. Like La Mouline and La Landonne, La Turque spends a very precise forty-two months in new oak casks (*pièces*). Subsequent tastings of different vintages of this exemplary wine show it to have a darker hue than La Mouline, to carry firm berry and stewed fruit aromas and to be very well put together on the palate, with immense concentration and tremendous elegance. Its tannins are firm but fit in well with the wine's structure. Perhaps some of the elegance is the result of the quite high percentage of Viognier present in the wine – 6 to 7 per cent.

Since the 1970s, when only Guigal, Vidal-Fleury and Albert

Dervieux designated their wines with a place name, several of the growers have attached specific vineyard site names to their bottled wine. M. Dervieux, now retired and in his seventies, always had a leaning towards this practice, which is only really possible if the *vigneron* has a sufficient size of single-holding to justify a particular name. M. Dervieux's 3.2 hectares, now worked by his son-in-law René Rostaing, are divided into ten separate plots, for instance, but until 1990 his wine was sold under three single titles – La Viaillère, La Garde from a site on the Côte Blonde, and Fontgent from the top of the Côte Brune. M. Rostaing has stopped the separate bottling of La Garde and Fontgent, perhaps to make life easier for wine buyers.

Otherwise outside plain Côte-Rôtie, the split is mostly Brune-Blonde. Bottling under Côte Brune are Marius Gentaz-Dervieux and Joseph Jamet, while under Côte Blonde are René Rostaing, Vidal-Fleury (called La Chatillonne) and Chol et Fils.

Beyond the specific vineyard site-names come *les marques* – the brand names that are registered and allow the grower or merchant to use grapes from different areas within the *appellation*. Examples here are Jaboulet's Les Jumelles, Guigal's La Mouline, and both Chapoutier's non-vintage Grande Cuvée (now terminated), and from 1989, the La Mordorée, which is a blend of some *parcelles* between the Côtes Brune and Blonde. Obviously, in this status-conscious world, growers have an interest in putting before the public single-vineyard identities rather than brand names, since the latter smack more of mass marketing and less of bespoke produce.

The average date of harvesting at Côte-Rôtie reflects pretty directly what appears to be happening with the world's climate. In the early 1970s the *vendanges* started around the end of September, but during the 1980s there has been a significant advance in date. There is always a difference of perhaps a couple of degrees in the mean temperature between Côte-Rôtie and Hermitage further south, the latter being favoured by a quite exceptional local *micro climat*. None the less, average dates for the *ban des vendanges* at Côte-Rôtie during the 1980s run like this:

1980	8	October
1981	6	October
1982	15	September
1983	17	September
1984	8	October

1985   12 September
1986   2 October
1987   8 October
1988   18 September
1989   15 September
1990   15 September

Conversely to what one might think, the string of hot summers has served to restrain the picking habits of some of the shrewd growers. In the last couple of years an expert like Guigal has not actually started his harvesting until 29 September (as in 1990), has employed extra personnel and has had the whole crop in by 5 October – measures taken very professionally to improve the level of maturity of the parched fruit and to reduce to a minimum weather risks late on. The earliest harvest that growers can remember remains that of 1947, which started on 7 September. Such an early date gives the clue to what the climate 30 kilometres south of Lyon is capable of : suddenly there is a warmer tone, the light is brighter and the sun has an intensity that is not apparent further north, in Burgundy, for example.

With the Côte-Rôtie hillsides perfectly angled towards the south-east, the vineyards receive the firm impact of the sun from dawn to dusk, and the grapes can ripen well accordingly. Extra heat is also generated in the sloped vineyards through the enclosing effect of the terrace walls or brief rockfaces, and particularly in the hot years of the late 1980s the harvest has been taken in by people working in a serious state of undress – shorts and sometimes bikinis.

The harvesters' day is made more arduous by the tiring steepness of the slopes and by the fact that in places one can never be sure of a firm foothold. The *vendange* has to be taken to pick-up points which are sometimes uphill; in the old days – up until the 1970s, anyway – there were neither pick-up points nor light plastic containers for the grapes. Now some approach tracks have literally been hewn across the hill to provide vehicle access, and the old wooden *beneaux*, which used to be carried on one shoulder with a counter-weight such a sandbag resting on the other, have largely disappeared.

The growers attempt to complete their harvesting as quickly as possible to keep the whole crop under control. One of the potential pitfalls is the sudden rain that comes up the Rhône Valley, driven by the south wind, the *vent du midi*. Such was the case in 1991, with some preliminary rain on 29 September and then two days of ferocious rain on 6/7 October. Thus a grower with around 3 hectares of vines will finish in four or five days, with a team totalling about twenty-five pickers. Such stop-gap labour for the harvest is often provided by Spanish and Portuguese women whose husbands work in local factories, although greater ecological enthusiasm has brought more young French people back to full- or part-time employment in the vineyards. There is also often a sprinkling of students – who frequently disgrace themselves by going to sleep among the vines after a winy lunch-break – and a few *exotiques*, like the *meilleur sommelier* of Norway and his band of immaculate northern beauties all lending a hand.

The growers organize the delivery of many small loads to the cellars rather than leave the picked grapes out for too long, and upon arrival the roughly 25-kilogram boxes are emptied so that the harvest can be crushed. Very few growers now tread down the grapes in the traditional way, and the tendency is towards crushers that can be finely programmed to give a light bursting of the skins with part of the crop often intact. Some young growers who lack large amounts of capital work with well-maintained wooden equipment, but, like the young married couple of Clusel-Roch, they worry about not being able to control the potential damage to the grapes at this stage. For the 1992 vintage, this enterprising couple had moved into new premises.

Over the years the tradition at Côte-Rôtie has been not to destalk the grapes before fermentation, and this school of thought remains predominant. As Gilles Barge puts it: 'The stalks provide a tannic advantage; they also prevent the pips sticking together and so help the circulation in the fermenting vat – the result being a better distribution of the good elements and a better extraction.' There are a few dissidents to this thinking – Bernard Burgaud and Pierre Gaillard, both in their thirties and so somewhat 'new-wave', and René Rostaing, a man always open to ideas. Burgaud's comment is both succinct and provocative: 'All that is interesting in the wine comes from the skin.' In 1987 he destalked 75 per cent of his harvest, and since 1988 has destalked the whole crop.

Gaillard, encouraged by the ubiquitous *œnologue* Jean-Luc Colombo, has been doing experiments, but confesses that destalking may well serve to rob the different wines of the northern Rhône of their different local nuances. He is also someone who likes to cool the grapes for two to three days at 10°C to control the take-off of the fermentation and to extract some fruit aromas. Here again he is in a minority, but his end wine is very successful, showing that there is room for anyone who is bright and conscientious.

Several of the growers now use stainless steel vats for the fermentation of their musts. The most compelling example of this new technology within the previously staid cellars of Côte-Rôtie comes from Marcel Guigal's battery of stainless steel vats housed in what was an old Vidal-Fleury cellar across the road from Guigal's building. The Vidal-Fleury family kept 400 barrels there, which used to be looked after by Étienne Guigal until he left the House of Vidal in 1946 after fifteen years' service with them. Apparently the key to the cellar was lost in 1974, so no one properly used it until Guigal *père* and *fils* put their new *cuvage* there in 1986. And with Marcel doing nothing by halves in his search for perfection, he had a tunnel bored out underneath the N86 main road to connect the two cellars. The work took five months and was supervised by an engineer who had worked on high-profile projects like the TGV fast train and the Ariane rocket-launcher. The tunnel is 1 metre beneath a road that nowadays has 12,000 vehicles using it per day, and there is not a trace of vibration from the traffic.

M. Marcel Guigal

Guigal's fermenting cellar here is where he vinifies all his own production of Côte-Rôtie: there are two lines of eight *inox* vats in which he can practise his *pigeage* under modern techniques at the press of a button – that is, without calling in a few lads to beat the *chapeau* (cap) down in an open fermenting vat. Guigal does about two *pigeages* a day, to compress the top matter within the vat in much the way that certain coffee-making machines punch down the grains in the water to gain full extract. 'For me,' comments Guigal, 'the *pigeage* brings a gain of about six-tenths of a degree, and provides more bouquet plus colour and tannin through more polyphenols (anthocycans and tannins mainly). I find this can also help to obtain a lower pH level, taking about 0.2 or 0.3 off the acidity level to drop it to around 3.5.'

The *pigeage* demands vigilance and more continuous work from growers like Bernard Burgaud who ferment in open enamel-lined vats – he does his *pigeage* eight times a day, aiming for the absolute maximum extract from his maceration.

The temperature of the fermentation vats at Côte-Rôtie can run high, up to 32–33°C for Guigal, or 34°C for Burgaud. But most *vignerons* have their little tweaks on this, with Burgaud for example then letting his temperature cool down to around 25°C to extend the alcoholic maceration to around eight to ten days. Gilles Barge, for instance, aims for 20°C within the first forty-eight hours, with a subsequent increase to 25–30°C. After a density of 1010 has been reached, he is not worried by an acceleration to 30–32°C to obtain maximum extraction for a short time – in his view colour, tannin and secondary aromas all come from this. As a traditionalist, Robert Jasmin works with concrete vats, and in these he keeps his fermentation around the 30°C mark.

In the early 1970s the majority of growers at Côte-Rôtie worked with open wood fermenting tuns, massive broad objects into which the cellar workers would lower themselves to budge the *chapeau*. Now, with most cellars equipped with closed vats, and plenty of switch-controlled stainless steel about, changes have occurred at a faster and more widespread rate than could have been envisaged. Likewise the task of pressing the pulp at the end of the primary fermentation was once carried out on the old vertical wooden presses that had to be turned by men straining on the stout wooden bars. Now the pulp is set in an automatic press and the press wine is run off without sweat and tears, usually to be added to the main wine, the *vin de goutte*.

The young Côte-Rôtie is then put in wood, around the month of November at the earliest, with the growers liking the malolactic fermentation completed beforehand. Then starts the Great Debate. Where should the oak come from – the Allier (seemingly favoured by many growers), or the Nevers, the Vosges, the Radoux, the Tronçay or parts of Cognac? What size of cask should be used – the local 225-litre *pièce*, 600-litre *demi-muids* or larger *foudres* that run up to 20 hectolitres or more? Should the wine be switched from one size of cask to another to provoke different development in its aromas or flavours? How smoked should the cask be when first brought into the cellar? Should it be smoked or steamed? What age of wood should be used – brand new, with therefore a more blatant influence on the wine than that from wood that is several seasons old?

With so many variables, and so many growers frequently changing their policy on oak as they learn more about the subject, it is hard to define the general approach within the *appellation*. Smallholders like Marius Gentaz-Dervieux rely on the traditional Rhône small cask, the 225-litre *pièce*, which they have in the main inherited from previous generations. Then there are those growers like Robert Jasmin and René Rostaing who use a combination of *pièces* and 600-litre *demi-muids*. Robert Jasmin has just started to use a little brand new wood, but in a very restrained way: out of 120 hectolitres of his wine, only around 16 hectolitres will have been exposed to first-season oak. A similar line is taken by Jean-Paul and Jean-Luc Jamet, who use seasoned *foudres* and *demi-muids*, plus new 225-litre *barriques* (about 15–20 per cent) for their two-year ageing process.

Again, there are *vignerons* like Gilles and Pierre Barge and Louis de Vallouit who age their wine in large *foudres* that can range in size from 10 to 40 hectolitres. The Barge wine is aged for two years or so, with two-thirds of it in *foudres* of 10–30 hectolitres and the other one-third in *pièces*; de Vallouit, whose wines are noted for their appealing aromas and pleasant fruit, puts his Côte-Rôtie for the first third of its ageing in *foudres* of around 40 hectolitres, then for the final two-thirds of the process the wine is in *demi-muids*.

Those most keen on new oak are the younger wave of growers like Burgaud, Clusel-Roch, Pierre Gaillard and Jean-Michel Gérin, plus of course Marcel Guigal. Burgaud is nevertheless restrained with its application: after his wine has completed its malolactic in *foudre*, he passes 20 per cent of the new wine into new oak *pièces*. He therefore replaces 20 per cent of his casks every five years. 'I leave my wine to age in wood for fifteen months. The question of new wood is neither here nor there – the wood is just a means to an end – the end for me being to obtain the finest possible tannins in as concentrated a form as possible. I also avoid assembling the different *pièces* until bottling time to eliminate the chance that my wine will have too woody a character.'

Guigal is the arch-exponent of wood at Côte-Rôtie – indeed, part of his world fame is based on respect for him as a tactician when it comes to wood. His Côte-Rôties bear an imprint that sets them apart in style from many others in the *appellation*. This imprint is due to Guigal's cellar methods, which have been developed over the past twenty years. For example, during visits around Côte-Rôtie in the early 1970s, Marcel Guigal would be the only grower to raise the subject of barrel care and, more importantly, the regular replacement of barrels. In those days there was still a fully understandable pride in and allegiance to the methods and equipment of previous generations. In this sense Guigal's intelligence, which borders on the quest for intellectual solutions to problems, and his open-mindedness to new versions of an old art gave him an edge over his fellow *vignerons*.

Guigal is extraordinarily hard-working and given to great concern over detail. His meticulous approach has therefore eliminated some of the risks inherent in the wine-making process, and brought a certain science to his work. That is why he is able to produce good wines in lesser vintages. While an expert like Gérard Chave at Hermitage achieves success in poorer years through flair, Guigal achieves similar success through method.

Such application of method means that there is a steady turnover of barrels every year – around 140 of the 225-litre *pièces* are traded in. All Guigal's top three wines – La Landonne, La Mouline and La Turque – remain in these small casks for forty-two months. While he first used new oak for La Mouline in 1971, he varied the barrel size between 225 litres and 5,000 litres until 1983. On his Brune et Blonde *cuvée* of Côte-Rôtie Guigal varies the treatment according to the year – tannic years like 1983 or 1988 were mostly raised in *pièces*, while a more tender year like 1987 was mostly raised in *foudre*. As for length of time in cask, the Brune et Blonde has just under three years before its first bottling, with another four bottling runs over the subsequent months.

Guigal maintains that the use of a *pièce* develops the wine's bouquet more than a large *foudre*. The new oak also invests the softer wine like La Mouline with an initial smokiness on the nose and vanilla hints on the palate; while the richness and dense, crushed fruit flavours of La Landonne and La Turque are well able to stand the extra effect of the young oak. There is also a purely commercial consideration at work here; a much cheaper wine like the Guigal Côtes du Rhône red will be put in *foudres*, where the larger part of the crop spends six to eighteen months. Streams of small new oak casks have to be paid for through a suitably costed asking-price, and on lesser wines the sums do not add up.

Côte-Rôtie's recent success has had another effect on old customs – nowadays growers (Guigal is a marked exception) do not keep their wine in cask for nearly as long as they used to. Marius Gentaz-Dervieux admits that under pressure of demand from clients he is now bottling within fifteen months of the harvest. Thirty years ago the family allowed three years before bottling, and only ten years ago he still left his wine for two years in cask. In the early 1930s Côte-Rôtie *vignerons* would have five or six vintages of their wine on offer for sale at any one time.

When first put into cask, young Côte-Rôtie is thoroughly 'green', or coarse, and the lower the percentage of Viognier grapes, or the higher the percentage of fruit from young vines or plots on the top plateau above the steep hillside, the greener it is. The task of rounding out the wine and completing its complex structure through cask-ageing demands vigilance and fineness of touch. The vigilance comes through attention to tasks such as racking or transferring the wine between casks and topping up the casks or *l'ouillage*. A wine aged for three years in wood, for instance, would have to be topped up on more than 150 occasions. The fineness of touch comes from combining the laboratory or chemical analysis with the tasting skill of knowing when the wine or the different *cuvées* are ready for bottling.

Once bottled, a Côte-Rôtie is not in possession of all its powers. Its grace or finesse, and notably its bouquet, are still underplayed. On the palate its diverse elements struggle for ascendancy, marked by firm berry fruit, strong tannins and a lurking warmth on the finish derived from the ripeness of the grapes harvested in these southerly climes. Leaving the wine quietly in bottle is a necessity if Côte-Rôtie is to show its true worth, the duration depending on such factors as the relative hardness or roundness of the tannins, the depth of extract that the growers have achieved during vinification, and the degree of natural (non-chaptalized) alcohol. In firm vintages like 1976 and 1986 a stay in bottle of at least six years is desirable if the wine is to develop and soften well, and in the years of strong, harder tannins, like 1978, 1983 and 1988, it is better to allow six to twelve years in bottle if the wine is to show the harmony of which it is eventually capable. Years whose tannins are rounded and more elegant – like 1985, 1989, 1990 and 1991 – benefit from a wait of around five to seven years. Lighter vintages like 1979, 1982 and 1987, which in the best *cuvées* gave attractively scented, rather feminine and very approachable wines, are excellent to have been drunk before they are five to eight years old or so.

Deep purple when young, a good Côte-Rôtie only starts to fade towards red and ruby colours after ten to fifteen years, but in the meantime its bouquet gains an enveloping warmth and soft fruitiness, more like ripe garden fruits than the more acid, tangy berry fruits found in hedgerows. Where growers use some Viognier, the wine emerges softer and more aromatic, a touch sweeter on the nose. It is interesting that the *appellation* rules dictate that the Viognier must be fermented with the Syrah rather than added to the wine afterwards – this derives from the haphazard planting of the vineyards in previous generations, which means that the varieties tended to be mixed up together on the narrow terraces.

With or without the Viognier, Côte-Rôtie's style is softer and more rounded than that of its neighbour, Hermitage. Although granite is a predominant constituent of the soil in both places, the greatest difference between the two areas probably comes from the local climate which provides Hermitage with a Mediterranean-type average temperature in the vineyards of nearly 14°C. When discussing the harvest with growers from the two *appellations*, more often than not it is the Hermitage faction which is more content with the year's weather. It seems to be simpler to bring in healthy, well-ripened grapes at Hermitage than at Côte-Rôtie, and this may account for the greater sturdiness and strength of the Hermitage reds, which prompt the dictum that Côte-Rôtie is the Queen of the Rhône, Hermitage the King.

On the palate Côte-Rôtie is rich but elegant. Its full-blooded flavour makes the drinker think he is almost 'eating' his wine, but the long, supple aftertaste will persuade him to raise his glass again, and again. . . Drinking Côte-Rôtie from *vignerons* such as Guigal,

Jasmin, Gentaz-Dervieux or Rostaing is a vivid experience, which should instantly convert anyone to an unqualified enthusiasm for wine: Côte-Rôtie of this high standard can certainly be rated as one of the world's most striking and totally enchanting red wines.

Côte-Rôtie does, of course, come from a small vineyard, so it is all the more surprising to note that there are over eighty-five individual growers in and around Ampuis. The number of those making and selling their own wine has risen from around thirty to forty during the 1980s as the wine's fame and price have increased. The rest harvest their grapes and sell them to the local *négociant* houses, such as Guigal and Vidal-Fleury in Ampuis, Delas at Tournon and Chapoutier and Jaboulet at Hermitage. These small cultivators sometimes own less than one-fifth of a hectare of vines and also grow fruit and vegetables on the narrow stretch of flat land between the hillsides and the Rhône. Some of the more recent bottlers still sell part of their crop to the big houses – Bernard Burgaud has always sold about one-fifth of his wine *en gros*, and has a steady working relationship with Delas for this.

The oldest *maison du vin* in the northern Côtes du Rhône is the House of Vidal-Fleury, dating back to 1781. From the mid-1970s onwards its wines suffered a decline in quality until the whole operation, prize vineyards and all, was bought by the House of Guigal in 1984. Marcel Guigal has injected badly needed capital into the Vidal-Fleury business, with a thorough upgrading and replanting of the vineyards and a complete revitalization of the dingy, old-fashioned cellars and their equipment.

The slide in quality was connected with the death in 1976 of the company's patriarch, Joseph Vidal-Fleury, who had run the business for an incredible sixty-eight years, and so had experienced the changing work methods and attitudes of three generations. An hour spent with Joseph Vidal-Fleury was a wonderful education, for he possessed a Pandora's box of knowledge and anecdotes that was impossible to rival. He had seen wine-making evolve before his eyes: in his later years he saw in cellars around him metal fermenting vats, pneumatic presses, experiments with chestnut instead of oak casks and so on, but throughout it all his confidence in the old methods had remained unshaken. As he would frankly admit: 'It is difficult for me to talk about new things. I am a believer in ancient processes, which I esteem to be the best, the most honest and the most efficient. Wine just needs a lot of care, cleanliness, racking and a minimum of chemical products. Like that, one makes very good wine.

'The company has always been like a family and I have been repaid with a cohesion and team effort that would be difficult to match. I have 7 hectares of well-sited vines on the Côtes Brune and Blonde, vineyards such as La Chatillonne and Le Clos on the Blonde, and La Turque, La Pommière and Pavillon-Rouge on the Brune.'

Much of the appeal of this business for Marcel Guigal and his late father Étienne undoubtedly lay in these 7 hectares of prime-site vineyards, which brought Guigal's total holding to 12 hectares with another 3 hectares gradually coming into production in 1992–5. The latter 3 hectares are at the summit of La Viria on the north side of La Landonne. The principal Vidal-Fleury wine remains La Chatillonne from the Côte Blonde, while the House of Guigal has taken over the cultivation and vinification of the new celebrity plot of La Turque, their one single vineyard.

Until the mid-1970s, Vidal-Fleury produced strong-bodied, slow-maturing and classically made Côte-Rôtie La Rolande as well as an excellent red Hermitage. Any red Vidal-Fleury dated before 1971 can make a first-class buy if found at auction.

Quality at this old house started to rise once more, starting with the 1983 vintage, vinified in spotless cellars opposite the Guigal premises. The head of the company, Jean-Pierre Rochias, used to work first at Châteauneuf-du-Pape, then at the House of Cordier in Bordeaux, and he has tightened up the working practices and vinification methods. By 1992 he had embarked on an essential development – that of replacing all the old Vidal-Fleury casks.

The whole Guigal–Vidal story contains ingredients that would have screenplay writers scrambling for their word-processors. Étienne, the father and founder of the business, died in 1988 aged seventy-nine, having worked during the course of his life on sixty-five harvests. He started out in a modest way, employed by the local grandee Vidal-Fleury and rising to become their cellar master and then their head *vigneron*. After fifteen years of work *chez* Vidal-Fleury he left in 1946 to set up his own company, Ets Guigal, which progressed steadily from a solid northern Rhône business combining its own vineyard produce and purchased wine until given extra momentum in the 1970s by Étienne's son, Marcel.

The two Guigals brought off their lifetime coup with the purchase of the House of Vidal-Fleury, beating off potential foreign buyers and multinationals, and so gaining control of around 35 per cent of the Côte-Rôtie harvest. In part Guigal buys grapes from around fifty small cultivators, the largest of whom tends 2.5 hectares, in part he uses the crop from his 12 hectares of choicely sited vineyards. Guigal's Côte-Rôties, while blessed with a house style that makes them untypical of classic Côte-Rôtie, are undoubtedly the most sumptuous, the most lush offerings from the *appellation*. Their depth and complexity are rarely found in the Rhône Valley. Behind them there is an array of excellent, ever-improving white wines, notably a powerful Condrieu and a firm Hermitage, and a sound set of red wines led by the Hermitage and the top-rate Côtes du Rhône red which is tremendous value for money.

An unpretentious man, rarely parted from his cloth cap, Étienne Guigal's forte was caring for the vineyards. He left the commercial side and the cellar developments to Marcel and his capable wife Bernadette, and even as they enjoy heady success and acclaim in the early 1990s, Marcel's average night's sleep is still around five hours. Two of his few concessions to personal materialism are a larger, smarter Mercedes car and a shiny red Porsche – red sports cars have had particular appeal for Marcel since he was a boy, and his house and offices contain several model cars – all red. The family might also slip off to the Nile for a few days' cruise, but the work ethic at this extraordinary house remains largely unimpaired.

Marcel Guigal is now one of the most sought-after growers in France, let alone the Rhône. Press coverage, notably from the United States, has sent his *côte* dizzily into orbit; the curious, the enthusiastic, the greedy all beat a path to his door from all around the world. Gare de Lyon conditions prevail in his cellars on any given day as Marcel tries to take round a group of visitors, line up a tasting for a restaurateur and his friends, answer questions over the tannoy about which wine should be drunk with a local fish, and keep an eye on dispatches out of the cellars. Such pandemonium must exert its pressure, and as with many newly acclaimed heroes, Guigal's challenge now is to cope with this, while getting on with the job of making excellent wine. In the early 1970s, when the wines were already consistently good, visitors French or foreign were rare, and major amounts of his time and thought were allocated to the making and the raising of the wines. Now there are distractions away from these prime activities, and as the number of bottles sold out of the House of Guigal clicks inexorably up, past the 1.5 million bottles and on towards the 2 million landmark, so the scrutiny on quality will grow.

A slight man whose glasses, already greying hair at the age of forty-eight and wiry frame bely a stamina for manual cellar work running late into the night, Marcel Guigal talks cautiously but clearly about his wine-making. In stripping out the old Vidal-Fleury cellars opposite his buildings he allowed himself greater flexibility of approach to his three big-name wines. La Mouline, of which there are just under 5,000 bottles on average, is crushed and fermented in a closed vat in the original cellars, with a *remontage* or pumping over of the must 'to add finesse'. La Turque, of which there were 2,200 bottles in its first 1985 crop and now 4,300 bottles, is fermented in the new cellars in a closed vat with a *pigeage* or beating down of the cap in the morning and evening, over fifteen to twenty days. La Landonne, of which there are around 8,500 bottles, is crushed, then fermented in two vats, one of which he waits to close only when its density has fallen considerably.

Guigal likes to obtain as much concentration of taste and flavour from the grapes' raw materials as possible. He harvests later than nearly everyone – in 1990 with its sustained heat he waited until 29 September, against 15–20 September for his neighbours. He likes high-temperature fermentations; while he may restrain the starting temperature so as to extract bouquet gradually, once his musts have reached an undisclosed density Guigal increases the vat temperature by 2–3°C to extract colour.

In cask Guigal continues to be in no hurry, and his fidelity to new oak extends firmly to his two leading whites, the Condrieu and the Hermitage. One-third of his Condrieu goes into new oak, with bottling taking place after the malolactic has been done around the end of March or early April. The white Hermitage, made up of 93 per cent Marsanne, 7 per cent Roussanne, then spends one year in the newly vacated Condrieu casks before bottling around midsummer eighteen months after the harvest.

When talking about his white procedures, Guigal's short college haircut and darting glances indicate a student's enthusiasm for his subject: 'Whites are now an important part of our work. They're fermented at 16–18°C in stainless steel, and just for the Condrieu I use a *macération pelliculaire* to obtain more richness or *gras*, providing the crop is healthy enough. In 1990, for instance, I did a total *macération pelliculaire*, with different lengths of contact – three, six and nine hours. In 1991, by contrast, the harvest wasn't healthy enough to permit such a *macération*. I'm doing some tests with moistened jute to see if one can control temperatures in cask, so we could have some interesting developments coming up.'

The Condrieus from Guigal are immense wines, really powerful and full-blown, the sort that jolt white wine drinkers out of a Chardonnay-only rut. Recent harvests like 1990 have produced very ripe Viognier, with alcohol levels ranging from 13–14.5°. But once wines like the 1989 or the 1985 have had a couple of years to settle down, they reveal both swirling Viognier aromas on the nose and a tightness of structure on the palate that keeps the ample fruit and volume of flavour within a fine balance. Years like the 1988 are altogether very heady and perhaps lack a little of the appealing delicacy and elegance found in years like 1991. These wines are good to drink for up to six years or so if their bold fruitiness and richness are to be most strongly appreciated, but there is little doubt that they would please traditional British palates after that.

Alongside Guigal's leading whites comes the ever-improving Côtes du Rhône *blanc*; in 1989 Guigal bought 100 hectolitres of Viognier from the Gard *département* to include in this wine, whose main *cépages* are the Roussanne, the Bourboulenc and the Clairette. The Viognier proportion is increasing all the time – towards 13 per cent by 1992, while the Roussanne accounts for around 35 per cent. Guigal varies the Clairette's presence according to the vintage – 'more in a fat year, less in a lean year,' he comments; 'the Clairette serves to cool the wine.' This white sees no oak and is bottled over several months from February onwards. It has shown marked improvement recently, and the 1990 carried greater style and freshness than any of the previous years. Again, the hand of Guigal is directing this wine surely into a category above that of many Rhône *blancs génériques*.

Guigal's most successful southern Rhône red is his Côtes du Rhône, ahead of a Gigondas and Châteauneuf, which while they are plump, attractive wines, have had their local *terroir* definitions subdued under the prevailing house vinification and style, plus carrying a reliance on more Mourvèdre and less Grenache (40–45 per cent for the latter). The Côtes red can contain between 40 per cent (1986, 1989) and 55 per cent (1988) Grenache, backed up by 'the two important grapes – the Syrah and the Mourvèdre' – and tiny amounts of Cinsault and Carignan. Eighteen *domaines* currently supply this wine, which comes mostly from the Vaucluse, some from the Gard and, in the case of the Syrah, from the northern Rhône. Eighty per cent of the wine is reared at Guigal's cellars in *foudres* of around 35 hectolitres for about a year, the rest at the *domaines* before assembling and bottling two to three years after the harvest. The popularity of this wine – 500,000 bottles produced in a year – means that it is being released earlier. And the popularity is well deserved: it has a class and quality superior to its mere name, firm tannins keeping it together when young, with a rounded appeal on the palate which runs through to a peppery finish. The 1986, 1988 and 1989 have been very good, the 1988 holding sound fruit with some firm tannic support, the 1989 being a more open, succulent wine with greater early appeal. The 1988 is capable of showing well towards 1998.

With Guigal now controlling the top Vidal-Fleury Côte-Rôtie, La Chatillonne, he now has a nap hand of styles for his own Côte-Rôties. La Chatillonne comes from the Côte Blonde only, about 3,000 to 4,000 bottles are made each year, and it is the most delicate of the collection. Its colour is purple to plum, rather than tinged with black, it typically carries a complex, leathery bouquet, and on the palate its gentle fruit overrides some restrained tannins. In lighter vintages like 1987 it is fine to drink around five years old; otherwise, in years like 1988, it is good to drink around the six- to ten-year mark. Like all the Vidal-Fleury reds, this is fined before bottling, whereas the Guigal reds receive no fining.

Guigal's Brune et Blonde can be forgotten amid all the publicity for his brand or single-vineyard wines, but now provides the best access for those not living on champagne incomes. Since the 1988 vintage, one quarter has been raised in new oak, with an overall predominance of the *pièce* size in strong vintages like 1983 or 1988. Later bottlings of the 1986, with five months' more oak, were more striking and longer *en bouche* than the wine of that vintage first bottled in October 1989, while the 1987 was not as tightly knit as usual, lacking a little in balance and clearly defined taste. Unlike most Guigals the 1987 is not a wine to search out or to keep for long. This is in contrast with Guigal's success in earlier difficult years like 1975 and 1977, when the Brune et Blonde were very successful, gentle wines that developed quietly and well over ten or more years. The 1988, however, is back on full form, with great warmth on the bouquet and very persistent fruit and depth on the palate. In mainstream vintages like 1985, 1988 and 1989, the Brune et Blonde *cuvée* provides good drinking over ten to fifteen years – at accessible prices.

Guigal's famous Côte Blonde wine, La Mouline, was first made by him in 1966. It had been the property of Joannes Dervieux and already held a high reputation, selling for double the price of other Côte-Rôties. Dervieux had cherry trees growing within the vineyard, but Guigal took his time to replant, working in half-ledges of new vines little by little. Most notably, he brought the amount of Viognier up to about 10 per cent.

With its cellophane and wire wrapping, La Mouline was the first of Guigal's specially packaged wines and its sale was directed at the good restaurants of Lyon and Vienne. Always very full and opulent, this is a fantastically elegant wine whose harmony in a vintage like 1988 is breathtaking. Possessing a powerful berries and fruit-extract bouquet even when only four years old, the La Mouline style has continued much the same over its first twenty-five years. Tasting notes over the past eighteen years consistently refer to a deep, red-black colour that turns towards ruby after six to eight years, an intense raspberry and highly scented nose, and always supremely classy, well-rounded flavours on the palate. This wine is not a real long liver, however; even a memorable vintage like La Mouline 1969 has started to move off the summit of its development after twenty years, while the 1978 – tremendously round and long on the palate – is now showing very well, and the magnificently balanced 1985 will be superb to drink by the mid-1990s. The 1989, likewise, shows signs from cask tasting of being approachable after eight to ten years while the 1988, tasted just before bottling in early 1992, showed firmer flavours that may need until 1998–2000 to settle down.

In 1978, not content with the high standards achieved by La Mouline, Guigal launched another blockbuster wine, La Landonne. 'You can't imagine the trouble we went to in order to buy up the Landonne vineyard. The Mouline wine is made from 0.9 hectare, but La Landonne's vineyard is 1.8 hectares, which involved the ownership of seventeen smallholders, and I'm sure I shall never have to be so patient again when it comes to buying a single vineyard. It took more than ten years, buying each small plot individually, but it has proved well worthwhile.'

La Landonne is a bruiser of a wine, showing off the Syrah in its most massive form. It always carries an intense colour centred on deep purple and black with some dark red at the top, while its young bouquet has a firm, wild berry fruit combined with new cask aromas, liquorice and a bit of spice. The palate is marked by the early surge of a wall of tannin covering the underlying fruit, and a persistent length that runs on to an amazing aftertaste in which there is a massive extract of fruit. A wine like the 1988 is extraordinarily sustained on the palate and is one of the best red wines made in the northern Rhône in recent years – an immense, solid *cuvée* that will live for many years. But close behind it come both the 1986 and 1987, the probably underestimated latter wine being slightly finer than the 1986 and exciting through its really crunchy fruit; the 1986 showing a true Landonne concentration of intense flavour *en bouche*. Meanwhile, the 1989 carries a very strong fruit extract, immense length, and is less of a big hitter than the 1988.

The 1988 shades the others in alcohol – 13.3° against 13.1° for the 1987 and 13° for the 1986 (there was a small amount of chaptalization in the latter two wines). Like the Mouline and the Turque wines, the Landonnes are not fined or filtered, and between one vintage and the next, the main variable is the number and type of rackings: in a faster-maturing year Guigal will leave the wine for up to eighteen months without a racking, and it will be transferred out of contact with the air. In more tannic vintages rackings may occur on an eight- to nine-month basis with some exposure to the air.

The Landonnes live a long time: the more refined years like 1987 and 1982 are likely to drink very well around twelve to fifteen years old, while the 1978, 1983, 1986 and 1988 are all twenty-plus-year wines, rising to thirty years or more, perhaps. The 1989 and the 1985 are a little softer and more approachable than this last group.

Guigal's marketing sense has been astute with La Landonne. Its packaging is lavish, with shipment in wooden cases and a label reproducing a Roman mosaic found close to Vienne that depicts grape-crushing at harvest-time. Guigal also works the marketplace's thirst for the wine by offering importers or distributors an allowance of just six bottles . . . if they buy 100 cases of his Côtes du Rhône. If there is an unseemly scramble for his Big Three wines around the world, then some of the reason for this starts with the house policy out of Ampuis.

Joining the galaxy of star wines, whose idolization and cult following are symptomatic of the gross side of 1980s' consumerism, is La Turque, a true single-vineyard wine. Marcel Guigal tells the story of a Canadian offering him the use of his helicopter, his water-ski power-boat and his Ferrari if Guigal came to Canada – with one mixed case of the top three Guigal wines for him.

The slope on La Turque is extremely steep – about 60° – and its vines had been cultivated until the early 1960s by a smallholder who was regarded by the locals as '*un peu fou*'. For twenty years it had remained an overgrown patch, next to holdings of Marius Gentaz-Dervieux and Vidal-Fleury. M. Gentaz did not wish to take it over, so it became part of the Vidal-Fleury holding. One of those who helped to clear and replant it was Pierre Gaillard, now a *vigneron* with his own holdings. 'La Turque is so steep that we had to take out some terrace walls to make a regular slope and to allow some mechanical working. We could use winches when clearing it in 1981, which made life a bit easier.'

First made in 1985, La Turque's colour tends towards a dark purple and always has a good sheen or lustre on it. There is about 7 per cent Viognier in it, and perhaps partly as a result, the bouquet is heavy and musky, showing more earthy, open aromas than the more tucked-up La Landonne, aromas that are reminiscent of stewed fruits and dark berry jams, while the palate shows imposing richness and structure. A strong but elegant wine, its tannins are less raw than those of La Landonne, and in style La Turque fits neatly between the Mouline and Landonne wines: it has less of the sheer power and regionality of La Landonne and fewer early charms than La Mouline. But its balance, weight and elegance make it a wine of great breeding, not a word usually associated with the Rhône, one more at home with assessments of *grand cru* wines from St-Julien – on the Léoville-Lascases lines, for example.

The 1985 La Turque is an extremely rounded wine, with solid but very well balanced flavours. Like all the Turques, the bouquet is very ripe and full of deep, cooked-fruit aromas. The 1986 is rich and well structured – a strong but elegant wine with great persistence of flavours on the palate. The 1987 is not as big as the 1986, and the aromas and flavours, while very sustained, are not as complex. The 1988 has great depth and roundness on the bouquet, with an intense, dark fruit surge on the attack; the fruit in style is quite clean and modern, while the bouquet has a touch of earthiness to make the wine a bit more regional, a bit less pristine. The 1989 exudes harmonious aromas and taste on the palate. There is a lovely balance in it and a very sustained aftertaste. The 1988 promises to show well towards 2007/2012, the 1986 towards 1998/2002, and the 1985 in between. The 1989 should drink well at ten years, the 1987 at eight years.

Around the corner from the Maison Guigal live a family that make a classically styled Côte-Rôtie, one that is more representative of the *appellation* than the wines that carry Guigal's own style in them. The Jasmins have been at Côte-Rôtie since the time that M. Robert Jasmin's grandfather came down from Champagne to work as chef at the Château d'Ampuis. Developing an eager interest in the village's principal activity, he bought the vineyard that went with the *château*: this is well situated at one end of the Côte Brune.

The Jasmin family have continued from there, with first the late Georges Jasmin, then his son Robert and then Robert's son Patrick looking after the vineyards and working stoically in the cellars. With Patrick aged thirty and Robert fifty-four, the Jasmins have had the incentive to increase their plantation to 3.6 hectares. They have recently reclaimed two plots, one called Les Moutonnes, of 1.2 hectares, the other Le Baleyat, a hectare near Boucharey; the former is high up on the hillside at the top of the Côte Brune, the latter faces towards the south of the village. This replanting was hard work. At Le Baleyat an apple orchard had grown up, the spot is high up and exposed to the *vent du nord*, and the Jasmins had to blast the overgrown rock-face to carve out a short approach track to the site, across slopes with a 20–30 per cent incline.

The best sites on the Côte-Rôtie hillsides have never fallen out of cultivation, but with the progress made by the *appellation* it is now the inner nooks and gullies that are being reclaimed as the authorities try to stem the advance of the plateau plantation. The plateau is thought to have a mean temperature one degree lower than the full *coteau*, while some of these newly hewn sites do not receive sun much after mid- or late afternoon and suffer from extra exposure to the *vent du nord*. Ripening is therefore harder and growers like Jasmin recognize that they will have to balance artfully the intake from their oldest vines of thirty to fifty years of age on sheltered *parcelles* like La Garde and La Chevalière with the crop from the younger vines on more open sites like Le Baleyat.

Robert Jasmin is a jovial man, full of chuckles and good humour, who likes nothing more than a long gastronomic evening after a full tasting of seven or eight vintages. The recent prosperity of the vineyard has translated into a new porch and doing-up of both his house and his cellars, a neat sort of his-and-hers allocation of funds. But only now, with the price of Côte-Rôtie much stronger than its late-1960s level, does one feel that he has a sound chance of supporting his family properly. His wife Josette has worked in a local factory for several years to supplement their income so that the two of them and their two children could live more comfortably.

One of the prized photographs in the Jasmin home, which sits modestly beside the local railway and is shaded on one side by a generous cherry tree, shows the three generations together in the vineyards – Georges, Robert and Patrick. Georges died in 1988 aged eighty-three, but his hardiness was salutary. He no doubt exercised the fine twinkle in his eye to great effect with the local *demoiselles*, and even after suffering from hepatitis when he was seventy-six, carried on the strong-man approach to life by continuing to wheel his bicycle up to the hillside to do some pruning on even the coldest winter days, and then would console himself from the doctor's orders of no Côte-Rôtie by lustily blowing on the trombone for the village band.

The Jasmin Côte-Rôties have always been among the most aromatic and wonderfuly scented wines from the *appellation*, although they only have very small amounts of Viognier planted. Robert did once conduct an experiment with a cask of his 1983 Côte-Rôtie which he filled with 20 per cent Viognier. The Viognier effect was very pronounced on the bouquet and the early palate, and such a high percentage, which might sound an appealing idea in theory, in fact robbed the wine of some of its guts and potential for development.

The wines are made in the old way, with fermentation in closed concrete vats for fifteen to twenty days, and all *cuvées* assembled at the time of the second racking, around May the year after the harvest. Jasmin proceeds cautiously with new oak; around 13 per cent of his wine is passed through new casks, with Robert desperate not to conceal the true Syrah *typicité* through an overlay of the wood effect. Robert and Patrick's annual production is around 10,000 to 12,000 bottles, and because they have to maintain a positive cash flow, the bottling of an entire vintage will occur on three to four different occasions, starting about fifteen months after the original harvest. This means that different styles of their wine will be available: there will be a 1983 which has an exuberant, rich fruit-and-spice flavouring as opposed to the chewy, mature, drier flavours of a later bottling. There is no way of spotting which is which from looking at the label, and the best advice is to book an early or late delivery of the wine from the importer.

Of recent vintages, the 1988 shows in full measure what Jasmin is capable of: a sound, light plum colour; amazing sustained fruit aromas supported by a firm extract, and on the palate a strong, potentially delicious flavour whose texture and plump ripeness is akin to that of a top Burgundy. In style it is a long way from the more upright issues of growers like Burgaud and Guigal – there is more direct and innocent Syrah fruit in a very sensuous wine that will show extremely well aged seven to ten. In general Robert Jasmin considers that his wine should be drunk between eight and fifteen years old. The 1989 was a less succulent wine, reflecting some of the dry tannins generated that year. There was fair warmth on the bouquet and the palate requires a few years to settle, soften and throw off some raw elements; meanwhile the first bottling of the 1987 produced a sound, reasonably scented wine for early drinking.

Sometimes Robert Jasmin leaves certain *cuvées* in cask for two and a half to three years, using some old family casks, but the effect is to bring forward the more astringent, drier tannins that seem to override the usual light garden fruit flavours that make his wine so appealing.

Of other recent years, Jasmin's 1978 is outstanding for its sheer guts and surging richness, in part derived from the low yield he took from his top vineyards that year. It is a heady, old-fashioned Rhône wine which should now be settling down. By contrast, his well-made 1980, from a difficult year, is likely to drink well until around 1995 – it contains mature fruit flavours and chewy tannins and has developed good complexity on the nose. His top issue of 1983 from the best hillside vineyards and his Brune et Blonde of 1985 are both very good wines, the former having a massive structure with lots of firm fruit, while the latter is a gentler ten-year wine, rather on the lines of the 1988, with riper tannins in it than the 1983. The 1986 is a medium weight wine, showing well by 1992. Its delicate aromas and roundness on the palate once again recall the affinity of style between the Jasmin Côte-Rôtie and good Burgundy.

The Jasmin wines can be idiosyncratic from one year to another, but that has always been the appeal of going to a small producer whose work is authentic and an extension of his personality. A man and his wife who are prepared to live in a caravan in Ampuis for six months while their house is being done up, whose work in the meantime takes them either to a dank cellar or a windy hillside, deserve to be reckoned with.

Another eminent *vigneron* of the old school over many years has been Albert Dervieux, who in 1991 took a well-earned retirement and handed over his vineyard interests to his son-in-law, René Rostaing. He was President of the Syndicat des Vignerons for over thirty-five years from 1953 and in his later years of office expressed concern over the advance of the plateau and the *appellation*'s yield rising to 40 hectolitres. Another concern expressed by other *vignerons* is that newly planted areas of the vineyard, particularly around the area of Le Mollard to the south of the village, are not being built with retaining walls, and any heavy rains will sweep away what in that area is mainly sandy topsoil. New, neat mechanical excavators just 1.3 metres wide are an advance, but man's thinking has to go in step with such progress.

Small, wiry and always on the move, M. Dervieux spent much of his official time dealing with government rulings and local land deals. One of his more regular tasks became the handling of abundant harvests, something that is now much more frequent through the use of disease-resistant Syrah clones. In such events M. Dervieux and his fellow committee members had to taste the wine and decide whether to apply to Paris for an extension in excess of the *appellation* production limit (5,310 bottles per hectare). Otherwise the excess would be sold off as *vin* not quite so *ordinaire*.

M. Dervieux's holdings are typical of many northern Rhône growers in that the 3-plus hectares are spread out, but for his successor, M. Rostaing, they represent a priceless portfolio of good names. There are four separate plots on La Garde, near the Blonde, totalling 0.9 hectare; three plots on Fontgent at the top of the Brune amounting to 1.09 hectare, and three plots on La Viaillère north of Ampuis near Vérenay coming to 1.2 hectares.

Each of these wines was aged until 1991 according to its different characteristics: the more floral, fine La Garde would be bottled after twelve to fifteen months in cask: the stronger, more blackcurrant- and raspberry-fruited Fontgent was bottled in different batches from fourteen months after the harvest, and the dark, concentrated and initially very closed La Viaillère, which M. Rostaing has kept as a separate wine, will still be bottled around two years on. The vineyards at Fontgent and La Garde date from the early 1970s, whereas the La Viaillère holding comes from old family vines going back to the 1930s. This fact gives it the edge over the other two *cuvées* – it bears impressive depth in years like 1983, 1985 and 1988 and requires at least ten years' ageing in bottle. It is also the most travelled of the wines, with bottles seen in the United States and in country hotels in Japan.

M. Dervieux, surprisingly, is one of the few people at Côte-Rôtie to have an anciently stocked personal cellar. Until quite recently this included 1929, rated the 'year of the century', and he holds all the best vintages since – 1945, 1947, 1955, 1961, 1969, 1971, 1978 and the main years from the 1980s. 'I drank one of my 1929s in 1969, and it was still in marvellous condition. The colour had turned almost brown, I grant you, but the wine had kept much of its strength and all its character. Normally I would say a Côte-Rôtie can live between twenty and thirty years, but they should be good to drink after ten or twelve years. As for my 1947s, they're still in perfect order, and I'm quite looking forward to drinking them,' he adds drily.

M. Dervieux's holdings are passing into capable hands, for René Rostaing is a sound wine-maker, despite an appearance and activities that suggest otherwise. For a start his neat good looks and trimly cut clothes don't quite add up – answer, for most of his life he has worked in real estate in Condrieu. But his vinous pedigree – through marriage to M. Dervieux's daughter – has become impeccable. His wine work used to be done in the evenings and at weekends, but with a brand new cellar since August 1990, and the working of M. Dervieux's 3.2 hectares, he now spends two thirds of his time on wine and one third on residential lettings – and is clearly pleased as punch about the change. He is kept even busier by now looking after 0.6 hectare – half the holding – belonging to his wife's uncle Marius Gentaz-Dervieux; at a total of 5.5 hectares, M. Rostaing now has enough land to produce four *cuvées*, a straight Côte-Rôtie, a Côte Blonde, a La Landonne and a La Viaillère. His cellar is equipped with the latest stainless steel, but he remains faithful to extended cask ageing over one and a half years or more 'so as to give the client a wine that is not far off ready to drink'. M. Rostaing is also one of the few growers to markedly favour the *demi-muid* size of cask (600 litres) over *pièces*, saying very logically that even when new they do not stamp the wine with a wood effect because of their much higher ratio of wine to wood.

Rostaing's Blonde *cuvée* is excellent: it is made from sixty-year-old vines whose yield can be as low as 20 hectolitres, and contains about 8 per cent Viognier. Of recent vintages the 1988 and the 1990 are outstanding. The former's colour and bouquet have started to evolve after four years, and there is great depth in the wine, both on the bouquet and the palate. Similarly intense fruit and length of finish are shown by the 1990, which has tremendous class – *grand vin*, indeed. Both will drink well over the course of ten years or more but M. Rostaing does not consider his Côte Blonde wines to be long livers. The 1991 and the 1989 are both elegant, charming wines with lovely persistent flavours and should drink very well after six to eight years. Previous years to note are the 1983 (elegant) and the 1985 (good depth). M. Rostaing also has vines on the Landonne site, and these produce a firmly structured wine that is very representative of good, solid Côte-Rôtie made in the traditional way. The 1990, for instance, will show well around 1998, while the 1991 is likely to be a seven- to eleven-year wine.

During the 1980s there were many changes for the better at Côte-Rôtie, not least the emergence of a band of younger, highly dedicated growers whose presence gave the *appellation* extra stimulus. Notable among this group are Bernard Burgaud, the husband-and-wife team of Gilbert Clusel and Brigitte Roch, Jean-Paul and Jean-Luc Jamet, Jean-Michel Gérin, Pierre Gaillard, Didier Chol and Joël Champet. The wine from all these growers is worth investigation.

Bernard Burgaud is definitely a man to watch. He took over the 3.5–hectare family vineyard when his father Roger died in 1986. He has a strong Mediterranean aspect, with curly, jet-black hair, dark eyes and a solid frame, and he works an immaculate cellar high above Ampuis on the Champin plain. His vines lie in three different places: a hectare on the high slopes near Les Moutonnes which is worked only by human labour; 1.75 hectares on the *tête de coteau* near Le Boudin, which are worked by machine; and 0.7 hectare on the plateau opposite his house. This last area, Burgaud says, contributes positively in a very hot year like 1989, since its grapes bring extra and needed acidity to the rest of the harvest taken from the hot high slopes. Equally, in 1990 he found it difficult to achieve maturity with his slope vines – mainly for reasons of drought – while the plateau ripened more easily. Half the vineyard was planted in the early 1980s, the rest is about twenty to thirty years old, and there is a tiny holding of forty-year vines.

Roger Burgaud originally sold the entire crop before progressing to making wine and selling it in bulk himself. He was joined by his son in 1980 and they started off bottling 1,500 bottles a year; Bernard Burgaud still sells off his less-flavoured wine to *négociants*, which also helps cash flow. He keeps his wine in *foudre* for its malolactic and transfers to *pièces*, 20 per cent of which are new every year, until bottling in February, fifteen months after the harvest. He uses open enamel-lined vats for the maceration of the grapes, and is an enthusiastic practitioner of the *pigeage*, which he does eight times a day to keep the *chapeau* involved in the full maceration. He aims systematically for a temperature of 34°C which he then lets fall to 25°C.

'I think that wood and *terroir* must go arm in arm,' he states emphatically when discussing his methods. 'I sense a snobbishness against new oak, which is silly. I use it in a very controlled way – rotation of 20 per cent a year and a very fine heating of my Allier casks before I get them in – so that above all I obtain the presence of the finest tannins possible.'

On the grape varieties Burgaud has some firm comments. 'I planted Viognier in the beginning, but I don't use it in my red wine any more. I don't think it adds anything special – it may well have come into Côte-Rôtie because it produces wines of a degree or two more alcohol than the Syrah if grown in the same conditions. But once it has been vinified in the same vat as the Syrah, at a high temperature of 30°C or more, you've probably rid it of most of its aromas anyway.

'With the Syrah I'm obliged by the authorities to plant clones. I'd like to have the true Sérine since it allows wines to age better and its grapes have a better rapport between the juice and the dry materials in them. For me, all that is interesting in the wine comes from the skin. Another feature of the new clone is that it is more susceptible to rot than the Sérine.'

Burgaud's wines are very good, with a lot of elegance but also a solid amount of power within them that at times makes them very upright, if not austere. They are not wines that put on a flashy show and impress easily, and his 1989 and 1990 seem more awkward and reserved when young than previous vintages. His Côte-Rôties are well crafted in good and difficult years, the sign of a skilled wine-maker, so that his 1984, for example, was one of the best wines from Côte-Rôtie with a fine balance between fruit and firm, chewy after-flavours. His first vintage, the 1983, is now showing well, with some interesting mint and liquorice flavours residing inside a solid wine. Its slight lack of fruit was not repeated in 1985, which compensated for a lack of tannin with an easy charm on the palate – in this case there was 3 per cent Viognier in the wine, but its style was not the one desired by M. Burgaud.

Burgaud's excellent 1988 carries an extreme dark colour and its densely packed fruit is sufficient to edge above the firm tannic underlay. Although restrained on the bouquet as a young wine, it gives every indication of developing and softening over the next fifteen years. The 1989 is marked by drier tannins and while it has a lot of extract on the palate, is rather an angular, stern wine. It is already showing fruit early on the palate, however, and may work itself out given time. The 1990 has rather a hard bouquet, which is not fully typical of a Côte-Rôtie, and the flavours are solid. It is difficult to judge where its power centre lies, and so where and how it may develop. The 1991, by contrast, leans towards a more compact mix of fruit and weight of extract, and should make an elegant wine by about 1998/2001. Judgment on Burgaud's wines when they are young is not straightforward since they have a complex structure, and the diverse elements are not well joined together. Because of this they are unlikely to age and soften in an uncomplicated straight line.

Gilbert Clusel is another Beaune-educated *vigneron* just into his thirties. His 3 hectares are all on La Viaillère which is formed of two slopes split by a stream above Vérenay to the north of the village. The soil is decomposed schiste or *arzelle*, and as a sign of the times he prunes his younger vines by the Gobelet method, even though it carries fewer shoots than the Guyot and so gives a lower yield. Many of his vines are old – thirty years half-way up the slope and around sixty years at the top. About half a hectare dates from the mid-1980s, from reclaimed land.

As with many of the younger generation, Clusel-Roch are concerned to treat their vineyards as naturally as possible. They leave their cuttings to rot on the soil, and last used chemical products in 1984. Now the vines receive a dung in powder form every three years, which they claim has the same effect as the real, smelly thing. They are also working on recycling their *Sérine de pays* cuttings with the *pépiniériste* at nearby Limony so that they can replant new vines with them in the future. Although they have been using the clone for five years and its yield is much higher, they are not yet ready to write it off or cast definitive judgment on it. 'It's a mixture of influences, you see: take our sixty-year vines – they give 30 hectos, but I know this is helped by the Guyot pruning on them. We'd face possible commercial problems if we used the Gobelet on old Sérine, which is what you might call the ideal solution in theory,' comments Brigitte Roch.

Clusel-Roch are glad to have moved to new premises in 1992. In the past, they have vinified with open vats and are one of the few *domaines* to use a thoroughly overhauled ancient wooden press. After a ten-day fermentation at around 28–30°C (and no prior destalking) the wine is aged in Burgundian casks of 228 hectolitres from Nuits-St-Georges, an innovation since the 1989 vintage. Two-thirds of the wood is Allier, the remainder splits between Nevers and Vosges. Clusel-Roch first used one cask of new oak in 1984, but lack of finance meant that the sorting out of their barrels took a total of five years. 'The *cuverie* is next – we've done the vineyards, which are mainly my husband's responsibility, and the casks. Little by little . . .' adds Brigitte Roch determinedly.

The Clusel-Roch wines are very conscientiously made, and during the 1980s have shown a development towards an elegance without quite hitting the bull's-eye. The 1983 was aged in cask for two years and held solid mature fruit and tannins with a good length. The fast-maturing 1984 was a bit lean, while the 1985 was a charming ten-year wine, but short on tannic support. With the three years of 1989, 1988 and 1987, their skill has emerged more. The 1987's dark flavours and extract were successful, and the wine shows signs of being able to develop with age, perhaps through to 1996 at least. The 1988 carries a lot of *mâche*, a real chewiness and excellent depth with a sustained follow-through on the finish. There is a *cuvée* of old vines called Les Grandes Places which, bottled in May 1990, will be released around early 1992 and is well worth looking out for. Meanwhile the 1989, like several of its year, needs time to settle. It has a steady purple colour, nothing very dark, and a pleasant balance *en bouche*. Perhaps more aromatic than the 1988, it doesn't quite have the class of the latter.

Two brothers with a local reputation of being almost workaholic are Jean-Paul and Jean-Luc Jamet. On either side of thirty years old, they took over the running of their 4-hectare vineyard from wily, *sympathique* father Joseph with the 1991 harvest. They have 15 different plots altogether, with another hectare due into production by 1995. Father Joseph started in 1950 with just 0.35 hectare, and only did his first bottling in 1976. 'Up here on the plateau of Champin we grew peaches, apricots and nectarines because the wine didn't pay enough. We've kept our apricot trees to this day, since their pruning and picking fit in neatly with the wine cycle.'

Joseph comes from the old school, and it is clear that he has no qualms about his two sons not having done formal wine school training – certainly, experience of the land built up over the years has not hurt many a skilled winegrower in the past.

The crop receives a light crushing, with plenty of pumping in vat before ageing in wood – *foudre*, *demi-muid* and *pièce* size – for at least two years. Perhaps 20 per cent is exposed to new oak. The Jamet wines carry a medium to firm weight; the 1991, for instance, is likely to come together very well by about 1995–7 – a charming, well scented wine. The 1990 is a bit fuller, and shows definite promise on the bouquet and well sustained flavours that indicate likely good drinking around 1997–2001. The 1989's fruit is a little hidden and needs time to integrate, while the 1988 is very firm and well balanced – a very successful year. Up until 1990, Joseph Jamet used to amuse himself with the tiny production of his 0.4 hectare Côte Brune holding. This is superb wine, particularly in a year like 1988, but is not commercially available. So solid is this wine that it is easy to mistake it for a Hermitage – an exceptional one. In a very good year like 1988, it will live for twenty years or more.

Working away tucked out of sight on the plateau south of Ampuis above the Ardèche stone village of Malleval is one of the *appellation*'s most promising wine-makers, Pierre Gaillard. A Lyonnais, his parents worked in the SNCF – French railways – but he wanted to work in agriculture or viticulture, and with his studies taking him to Beaune and Montpellier, during which he became a friend of Gilbert Clusel, he turned to Côte-Rôtie. A sturdy, open-faced man who is a little shy until the talk turns full-square on to wine-making, when he reveals a passion and a strict attention to detail, M. Gaillard spent seven years at Vidal-Fleury and Guigal, first on the vinification and then the vineyards, until setting up on his own in 1986. He has been buying or renting vineyards since the early 1980s, starting with 2.3 hectares on the Clos de Cuminaille, a St-Joseph vineyard above Chavanay, south of Côte-Rôtie. He now has the full 5 hectares of the Clos de Cuminaille, where a sandy topsoil covers the granite slope, as well as just over 2 hectares at Côte-Rôtie, spread over the Côte Blonde, Viaillère, Fontgent and Rozier. To show how hard it is to break into a vineyard like this if the grower does not possess limitless funds and heavyweight contacts, M. Gaillard started off at Côte-Rôtie with just 0.25 hectare.

Pierre Gaillard's talent and thoughtful approach have produced some promising wines. While he is experimenting with destalking, he is not convinced that this allows the red wine to express its local character properly. He likes to wait at harvest time to achieve a thorough maturity, having pruned the vines short to restrict production from what are mostly clones. His Côte-Rôtie is exposed to new oak for one year of its eighteen months wood *élévage*, and his Fontgent and Côte Blonde *cuvées* are both unusual for containing as much as 15 per cent Viognier. Tasted separately in cask, the Fontgent impresses with attractive weight and charm, while the Blonde is a lighter, more aromatic wine. These both go into his Côte-Rôtie Brune et Blonde, a wine which in 1988 was solid and stylish, with enough power to run towards 2000 or so. The 1989 was well balanced, with a reticent bouquet as a young wine, and sufficient length to indicate a good showing over slightly less time than the 1988. The 1990 is well scented and stylish, and promises to provide attractive drinking over the next eight years or more.

M. Gaillard's St-Joseph Clos de Cuminaille is a wine that balances the influence of young cask with lots of solid extract when young. The wine carries a heady, potent Syrah bouquet, and after settling in bottle over a couple of years fuses its elements very successfully. The 1990 and the 1989 were both wines capable of developing well over a period of seven to ten years. M. Gaillard also makes a sound, improving St-Joseph *blanc* (two-thirds Marsanne, one-third Roussanne); so struck by the Roussanne wines of Château de Beaucastel at Châteauneuf-du-Pape was he that he intends to switch this ratio in the next five years. There is also a well-worked Côtes du Rhône *blanc* Viognier, made from vines planted in 1982; this has a firm texture on the palate, and an oily, vinous bouquet that make it interesting. This bodes well for the wine from M. Gaillard's one hectare plot at Condrieu, above Chavanay, which will make its first *appellation* wine in 1993.

With young *vignerons* now bringing fresh ideas to the *appellation*, it is heartening that there is still a band of seasoned growers making traditionally long-lived and full wines. In this category comes Marius Gentaz-Dervieux, who keeps a very low profile, living in a little house above his cellars not far from the Château d'Ampuis and year-in, year-out producing a wine that is the embodiment of top-flight Côte-Rôtie. His 1.2 hectare vineyard is on the Côte Brune, the wine is vinified with an immersed *chapeau* in concrete vats and then stored in wood (no razzmatazz like new oak for M. Gentaz) for fifteen months or a little longer. A wine like the 1988 will be bottled on several occasions, for example, running over a period between April and October 1990. Like the young breed, who use egg whites when they fine, M. Gentaz fines with four egg whites per *pièce* before bottling.

M. Gentaz considers his 1989 as his wine of the decade, followed by his delicious 1985 and solid 1988. On tasting from cask the 1989 seemed more nervous and a bit more aggressive, with its various constituents barely joined together. It shows good ripe fruit on the palate, while the 1988 is a thorough wine with a firm grip and a chewy finish. The structure and balance of the 1988 indicate a life of fifteen years or so, with good drinking starting from eight years of age. The 1989 may take longer to settle. A 1987 bottled in October 1989 – the last bottling of its year – seemed a little stale on the palate, but possessed decent weight for its vintage and an appealing richness on the bouquet. M. Gentaz is now sixty-nine years old, and it is worth snapping up bottles made by this craftsman before he takes his retirement; by 1991 he was only tending half his vineyard to have a quieter life.

One of the peculiarities of Côte-Rôtie in the 1970s was the ownership by a group of American investors of an 8-hectare vineyard run by the local Senator and Mayor of Ampuis, M. Alfred Gérin. This Franco-American alliance was set off in the 1960s, as M. Gérin explains: 'In 1961, confident about Côte-Rôtie's future and anxious to see more wine produced here, I approached a number of local friends with the idea of buying some of the then many untilled plots of land, with a view to putting them to the vine. We started absolutely from scratch and regrouped many of the plots into better-sized, more workable units. Once we had begun producing and selling our wine in France and abroad, some Americans from New York expressed a desire to import more Côte-Rôtie than we were able to give them. We decided therefore to go straight to the source of the problem and to expand our holding. Some of them, including a chocolate merchant and a lawyer, entered the concern in 1971 and the Domaine de Bonsérine, since 1990 the name for the old Domaine Alfred Gérin, now works 8 hectares of vineyards.'

Meanwhile M. Gérin's son Jean-Michel struck out on his own in 1990; his pedigree is good, for the 5 hectares he cultivates go back in places three generations – notably at Vérenay, with the 1-hectare

Les Grandes Places plot, whose vines are between thirty and fifty-five years old. M. Gérin's wife is also the sister of Vignerons Syndicat President Gilles Barge, and with a brand new cellar making the 1991 wine, this will be a *domaine* in the forefront of experimentation at Côte-Rôtie.

M. Gérin's wine from his 4 hectares of main holdings is called Champin le Seigneur, reflecting the presence of grapes from the Champin plateau. He likes to harvest late but very fast and in the cellars is happy to follow much of the thinking of northern Rhône *œnologue* and mentor, Jean-Luc Colombo from Cornas. This can mean borrowing ideas from other *œnologues* such as Michel Rolland in Bordeaux about at what stage to take the wine out of its fermentation vat, for instance. With a smart ageing cellar filled with 110 young *barriques*, M. Gérin's wines carry a modern style.

The Champin le Seigneur and Les Grandes Places both spend about twenty to twenty-two months in the young oak. The Champin in years like 1989 and 1991 is a polished wine, carrying agreeable fruit and elegant length on the palate – a wine to drink between perhaps six and nine years old. It shows more local character and a firmer stamp in a year like 1988, where its fullness will see it drinking very well around 1996–2000.

Wines from Vérenay are considered to be very robust, so M. Gérin's grandfather planted Viognier there to soften the Syrah; Jean-Michel Gérin's Les Grandes Places is a success, for it has a welcome complexity and in lighter years like 1989 and 1991 – good to drink at eight to ten years old – benefits from the oak's contribution. The 1988 Les Grandes Places is very well scented, and has plenty of tannin and depth to ensure a protracted and well balanced development.

Like several of the young growers, M. Gérin also makes a Condrieu, from 2 hectares on the Coteau de la Loye, next to the prime site of Chéry. His uncle abandoned this vineyard after the 1956 frost, and first indications in 1990 and 1991 are of a powerful, quite earthy wine with blatant rather than delicate aromas.

Côte-Rôtie Vintages

1955   An excellent vintage, with harmonious wines of long-lived charm.

1956   A mediocre year, with light wines.

1957　A very good year. The wines were sturdy, yet attractive. They are now in decline.

1958　A mediocre year, with acid wines that faded early.

1959　An excellent vintage of extremely high-class wines. Tannic when young, they were noted for being exceptionally well balanced. This harmony has helped them to keep going and carefully stored bottles should still drink well enough during the early 1990s, providing allowances are made for some loss of colour and fruit.

1960　A poor vintage. Wines of little distinction.

1961　A tip-top year. The wines were more powerful than the 1959s, and perhaps lacked a little of that vintage's striking finesse. They have mellowed superbly, have acquired interesting spicy and plum fruit flavours and should now be drunk as they are losing some of their richness.

1962　A good year. The wines were soft and well structured. They have shown ample charm and length of finish with ageing, but decline is beginning to set in.

1963　Poor. Frost hit the harvest, and the wines were light and unmemorable.

1964　An excellent year. Well-coloured wines that combined strength and elegance. A little fuller than 1962, this is a vintage to drink up and enjoy for its well aged flavours while there is still some richness left.

1965　A poor vintage. Light wines.

1966　A very good year. Dark-coloured wines of good balance that took some time to round out. They are now drinking very well and have scant room for improvement: these are wines that were most enjoyably drunk before they were twenty-five years old.

1967　A very good vintage, although lighter than 1966. The wines lacked a little colour, but their bouquet has opened out to reveal full, herbaceous aromas. Their fruit is well softened and they are good to drink now on the threshold of old age.

1968　A mediocre year, although there were some good bottles made by the best vinifiers – notably Guigal's La Mouline.

1969　A truly memorable vintage. A tiny crop gave wines that were on a parallel with 1961, with perhaps even greater finesse. Very full-bodied, these wines still display vigour and richness of flavour and are delicious to drink now before the elements of old age creep in. An outstanding La Mouline wine whose balance has kept it showing splendidly into the 1990s.

1970   A very good year of well balanced wines that started to drink well early on. Their colour is turning, and their flowery bouquet is gently losing the fullness of its aromas. On the palate there is an extensive finish behind the soft garden fruit. The wines are declining slowly; for best enjoyment, drink them up. A wonderful La Mouline from Guigal showed up very well in late 1988. This wine will drink superbly until past 1995.

1971   An excellent vintage. Big, strong-bodied wines with a classic Rhône 'warmth' about them. Deeply coloured, they are now very elegant and are still good to drink in the early 1990s.

1972   A disappointing, mediocre vintage. The wines were high in acidity and lacked harmony. They have now faded.

1973   A good year. A huge crop yielded some well-coloured wines of good balance. They are a little light, however, and it is recommended that they be drunk up.

1974   A mediocre vintage. An abundant crop for the second consecutive year took its toll on the vines. The wines were often light and lacking in colour and guts. In general these wines should have been drunk by now.

1975   A mediocre vintage from a fairly small crop. Light wines and even the best *cuvées* – Jasmin and Guigal Brune et Blonde – have lost most of their fruit and colour by now.

1976   A very good vintage indeed. The wines have retained their dark colour well, and the bouquet remains powerful and concentrated. They are very full-flavoured, and the best *cuvées* from growers like Guigal are likely to show well into the mid-1990s.

1977   An average year with wines that, despite their even colour, were rather acidic and astringent at first. As their acidity wore off, some attractive bottles emerged to provide easy drinking with delicately flavoured foods. Drink up any survivors.

1978   The vintage that has most excited growers in the last fifteen years. Immense, almost black colour, a gradually unfolding bouquet of infinite promise and a powerful surge of dense, raw fruit and thick tannin on the palate – what more could a grower wish for? A hot month of September helped the ripening, and growers such as Guigal, Gentaz-Dervieux and Jasmin made wines of such balance and depth of extraction that they will live on and retain their richness for many, many years. An exceptional year for Guigal's La Mouline and La Landonne; both have outstanding class, and the latter will live for over thirty years .

1979   Quite a good vintage. From the start the wines were softer than in the big vintages, with many of the middle-weight-style growers – Émile Champet, Jasmin for example – making wine that hit its peak around 1989. The more closed-up wines of Guigal – a magnificent, fruit-packed Brune et Blonde and La Landonne, for instance – will run for at least twenty years. The extract and density of this Landonne are showing off more exuberantly than the Mouline.

1980   Another quite good vintage. The wines held a little more colour than the 1979s and although they are short on tannin have an easy, uncomplicated charm about them. They are now very striking on the palate, showing a rounded, protracted fruitiness, and will be best drunk before around 1992/3. The Jasmin is developing well and Guigal's La Landonne is a very concentrated wine. The La Mouline has lovely depth of bouquet and lingering flavours, and will show well towards 2000 or so.

1981   An average year. Some of the wines are correctly coloured, but many show the effects of the rain that fell during harvesting, being pale and unimpressive. A vintage that sorted out the good and bad vinifiers; a slow, extended fermentation was necessary along with careful crop selection. Wines from Jasmin and Rostaing were successful for drinking before 1988, while the splendid, concentrated wines of Gentaz-Dervieux and La Mouline will run into the 1990s.

1982   A very dry, hot summer and intense heat during the harvest made life difficult for the growers, with problems of overheated vats during fermentation. The year can be rated good, with a few very good *cuvées*: the wines have a respectable red-purple colour, and a bouquet that is already opening up well. The best wines have more finesse than full-blown flavour and their decent composition will allow them to unfold well into the mid-1990s. Notable wines were made by Jasmin (early bottling), Gentaz-Dervieux and Guigal – both the Brune et Blonde and La Mouline. The La Landonne is the most robust and backward of Guigal's 'Big Three'. Wines made by smaller growers should often be drunk sooner since they are prone to a jamminess of flavour and lack of fresh fruit.

1983   A very good vintage which produced powerful, chewy wines whose severe tannins will take at least ten years in most cases to soften and integrate. As in 1982, harvesting took place in extreme heat, around 25 September, and further problems of overheated vats occurred for the less-equipped. However, the wines have much greater depth than the 1982s, with notable concentration in the best *cuvées* and a solid structure promising long life. Notable wines were made by Gilbert Clusel, Gentaz-Dervieux, Pierre Barge and Guigal with his La Mouline and La Landonne – the former wine being very good, very typical Mouline with lovely length and a fine balance of fruit, tannins and liquorice-inspired chewiness, the Landonne bearing great balance and intense, cooked fruit concentration; its tannins are well packed into the wine, which will take until 1998 to emerge properly from its shell.

1984   A moderate vintage, with a late flowering and no consistently sunny weather in August and September to save the day. High rainfall meant that the growers waited and waited for the grapes to ripen, but eventually had to start at the end of the first week of October. Lacking the full-blown richness of the 1982 and 1983 grapes, the wines from this small crop are lean and often rather astringent on the palate. Colours are light, reds rather than purples predominating, and there is noticeably more acidity than usual. Many *cuvées* finish short, and apart from honourable exceptions such as Burgaud, Jasmin (best drunk before 1992) and Guigal's well weighted La Mouline, this is a vintage to avoid.

1985   Excellent. A vintage of great all-round appeal, combining the merits of fleshy, succulently fruited wines with firm but not hard tannins and a delightful balance. The spring was quite dry, the summer very dry, and having been a month behind at the end of a very hard winter, the vines were only a week behind the schedule of a normal year when harvested. The colours are generally really strong purple, especially on wines like Guigal's La Landonne and La Turque and on those of Gentaz-Dervieux and Pierre Barge, and while still withdrawn, the bouquets promise development of fruit-and-spice complexity, given eight to ten years. On the palate the early attack is vigorous, backed by good depth, and the presence of some acidity alongside the fruits and tannins ensures a balanced future lies ahead. Exemplary wines have been made by Guigal, with his La Mouline and La Landonne possessing remarkable length. The other leading growers were successful to a man, and it was a crime of the highest order for any *vigneron* to fail to deliver the goods in this vintage.

1986   A large crop, which had to be carefully selected owing to rot, produced some good to very good wines which with time may improve beyond people's first expectations. There is a marked divergence in the alcohol levels, with some *cuvées* low. Some of the wines lack a concentration of flavour and contain rather astringent tannins; where rigorous grape selection was applied there is a chance of sound future development. Jasmin's wine bears good fruit and is now showing well. More solid wines were made by growers like Burgaud and Gentaz-Dervieux, while the Guigal trio of La Landonne, La Mouline and La Turque are all excellent in their own different styles: the Landonne is perhaps the winner of the trio and may live for twenty years or so. The other two are ten- to fifteen-year wines.

1987   A difficult year for the growers, with a variable summer, below-average temperatures and more rain than desirable. Those growers who exercised a careful selection have made some middle-weight, elegant wines with enough tannic support to keep them going for ten years or so. Choose carefully. There were well-crafted wines from Émile Champet, Joseph Jamet and Jean-Michel Gérin, and the Guigal

Landonne and the Vidal-Fleury La Chatillonne were both successful.

1988 An excellent vintage, with a restricted crop – even smaller than the rot-affected 1987. There was some *coulure* before an exceedingly dry summer. Harvesting for the majority started around 21 September and results from most growers were impressive. The wines have a natural fullness and strength capable of fending off intrusions by wine-makers tinkering with the vinification process. Well balanced, with a nice call between the fruit and tannic extracts, these are old-fashioned, direct wines likely to age well over the next eighteen to twenty-five years. *Vignerons* like Gilles Barge, Burgaud, Joseph Jamet, Gentaz-Dervieux, Robert Jasmin, Rostaing and, of course, Guigal all delivered excellent wines. Of Guigal's 'Big Three', the most solid and upright is La Landonne; there is greater complexity and regional flavour in La Turque than its previous three vintages and it will do well over fifteen or twenty years or more. La Mouline has the potential to show superb finesse by around 1998 or so.

1989 Another very hot and dry year, the drought hurting the vines until a welcome spot of rain on 10 September. The *ban des vendanges* was called on 15 September, the earliest in forty years for Marius Gentaz-Dervieux. A larger crop than 1988 gave some very good wines, but their overall quality does not match growers' first hopes and announcements. While generally well-coloured the wines can lack intensity and their often appealing fruitiness is not always supported by a firm extract. The best *cuvées* have very ripe aromas that show signs of evolving quite quickly; on the palate the best are complex, with their fruitiness still to settle down with some firm, sometimes angular tannins. These are wines that may well age in stop-go phases, as opposed to the deeper, more roundly balanced and generally better 1988s. Note the wines of growers like Rostaing (La Côte Blonde), J-M Gérin (Les Grandes Places), Gentaz-Dervieux, Pierre Gaillard and Chapoutier (standard wine and La Mordorée) – their most selected, top *cuvées* will please.

1990 Another year of drought, when a full ripening was not

always easy to achieve. Flowering was a shade earlier than usual, but harvesting passed the '100-day' rule in many cases with the slow pace of ripening. The wines are of medium weight, and will provide pleasant drinking in their first ten years or so. Colour levels are generally good and the wines are capable of providing some attractive bouquets with a little bottle age. Their fruit is not always clear-cut, however, and some growers certainly faced problems in extracting a tight, clean flavour from their Syrah crop. When successful the wines have a bit more depth than the 1991s, but overall 1991 has a greater and more discreet class. A top wine like Rostaing's Côte Blonde – very stylish, with lovely, persistent flavours – will show well towards the turn of the century; the best *cuvées* from growers like Guigal, Chapoutier and Jasmin are also worth noting.

Earlier Exceptional Vintages   1953, 1952, 1949, 1947, 1945, 1929

Leading Growers at Côte-Rôtie

The nucleus of growers and producers of Côte-Rôtie capable of providing wine that can range from the sound to the spectacular is:

Barge, Gilles and Pierre	
Burgaud, Bernard	69420 Ampuis
Champet, Émile and Joël	
Chapoutier, M.	26600 Tain-l'Hermitage
Chol et Fils	42410 Chavanay
Clusel-Roch	69420 Ampuis
Dervieux-Thaize	
Gaillard, Pierre	42860 Malleval
Gentaz-Dervieux, Marius	
Gérin, Jean-Michel	69420 Ampuis
Guigal, E.	
Jaboulet Aîné, Paul	26600 La Roche-de-Glun
Jamet, Joseph, Jean-Paul and Jean-Luc	
Jasmin, Robert and Patrick	69420 Ampuis
Rostaing, René	
Vidal-Fleury	

Other producers:

Bernard, Guy
Blanc, André
Bonnefond, Gérard
Bonsérine, Domaine de
Chambeyron, Marius and
    Bernard   69420 Ampuis
Champagneux, André and
    Christian
Clusel, Jean
David, Bernard

Delas Frères (why does their   07300 St Jean-de-Muzols
    spelling of Côte-Rôtie on
    their Seigneur de Maugiron
    lack a circumflex on the
    'Rotie'?)

Drevon, André and Louis
Duclaux, Edmond
Duplessy, Joseph
Fernandez, René
François, André
Gasse-Lafoy, Vincent   69420 Ampuis
Gérard, François
Levet, Bernard
Niéro, Robert
Ogier, Michel
Remiller, Louis

Royer, Adolphe   69420 Tupin
de Vallouit, Louis   26240 St-Vallier
Vernay, Georges and Daniel   69420 Condrieu

2

Condrieu

Condrieu sees the Rhône át its most inviting. The river runs past the village in a gently curling arc, prompting its early name of *Coin du Ruisseau* (Corner of the Stream). Bounded by lush green under-growth, the swirling waters here appear to possess little malice: there is no torrent, no crash of water on rock, just the oscillating patterns of its steady tow gliding across the surface.

Such apparent calmness is reflected on the riverside. The quiet air is disturbed only occasionally – perhaps by chugging barges, a train hastening along the eastern bank, by the barking of a tethered dog, or even by a game of *pétanque*, with the 'clink-clink' of the *boules* resonating in the unhurried stillness.

The village itself is crammed into a brief stretch of flatland between the river and the broad, gently rising slopes that build steadily up towards the Massif Central. It has more bustle, more character than Ampuis; it is more obviously a market centre than a wine community, partly because there are few signs indicating wine growers' cellars or *domaines*. A quick scan of the hillsides shows new patches of vineyards, their modern stake-poles intruding into what was pre-viously lush and often overgrown vegetation.

Condrieu's brightest days as a wine community were before the First World War, and the dim form of old, well-ordered terracing arising out of the clumps of scrub and bramble serves as a ghostly reminder of that time. Famous slopes like the Coteau de Chéry were then fully covered by vines, splendidly delineated, with spare land just for the occasional tool shed. But by 1949, under 200 hectolitres of wine were being made. Although there were as many as fourteen growers bottling their wine, the sums were tiny – 1500 bottles here and there – and the wider wine trade had little interest in such a small *appellation*. By the 1960s the hillside of Chéry was a rundown, gloomy vineyard, with only a very few outcrops of Viognier growing on its steep slope. During the 1970s a minor revival occurred, with a little land reclaimed for the vine. In the 1980s there was extensive replanting, with forty-year-old ash trees and magnolias bulldozed away, retaining stone walls repaired and the soil cleared of ivy and thick growth. Now, in the 1990s, there is greater confidence.

The main reason for this is financial. For years there had been only limited return from a plot of Viognier, after labour and cultivation costs, vinification and bottling costs had been taken into account. Not many people were prepared to endure the rigours of an outdoor life conducted in an old-fashioned way – always outdoor work to be done by hand and on foot, perched up on the side of a steep slope covered in a slippery topsoil, exceedingly hot in summer, bitingly cold in winter. So when Condrieu's name and price were languishing, little incentive existed for the young or middle-aged to leave their comfortable indoor occupations. Only a few old-timers or persistent, dyed-in-the-wool *vignerons* with long local connections continued to work the slopes, often doubling up with fruit and vegetable cultivation. The sunny southern exposure of the slopes meant that their fruit was always ripened some time ahead of anything grown on the plain – just right for the early summer market in Paris.

But then covered cultivation, often under large strips of plastic, started up. The hillsiders saw their fruit and vegetable market disappear. They also saw the price of the local wine creep slowly upwards during the late 1970s as foreigners became interested in it. Word spread about the qualities of this rare, singular white wine, and even larger vineyard owners like Vernay, Multier and Delas were seen to be reclaiming land for the vine. From that point came the return towards wine-growing.

A miserable 8 hectares were cultivated in 1965; only 12 hectares were under vine in 1971; by 1982 a minor rise to 14 hectares indicated a trend which by 1986 had gathered speed to reach 20 hectares. The figure in 1990 was up to 40 hectares, and by 1992 had shot up to 60 hectares, with another 20 hectares due to come into production by 1995. As St-Joseph found out, such 'plantation fever' is only beneficial if the *viticulteurs* know how to look after well-sited vineyards and how to make sound wine even in awkward vintages.

The Viognier grape is the only one allowed in the making of Condrieu, and indeed the wine is often referred to as 'Viognier'. It is a vine of obscure origin, one that sets off instant and animated discussion between fellow *vignerons*, all anxious to flaunt their own theory of where it came from. Some say that it was brought up from Marseille by the Phocaean Greeks around 600 BC. This is dubious, for it is more generally assumed that the Phocaeans – if they carried any vine with them – brought only one variety, the Syrah. The other leading theory relies heavily on legend and local history books record it as hearsay. According to this, it was the Emperor Probus who imported the Viognier from Dalmatia in AD 281, after the total destruction of the Condrieu vineyards by his predecessor Vespasian. The latter seems to have been an austere figure, and it is suspected that he ordered the total clearance of the vines as retribution for a local uprising, fomented, it was claimed, by too much drinking of Condrieu's wine by the Gallic natives. Although this story is shrouded in parochial gossip, the most learned *vignerons* tend to plump for Dalmatia as the source of their vine.

Whatever the exact origin of the Viognier (and no precise history of it has ever been put forward), it is certain that wine was made at Condrieu during the Roman occupation. In the third century the poet Martial sang the praises of the 'violet perfume of the wines of Vienne', and today's hillside terraces date back at least as long. Whether the wine was red or white, or whether it was similar to the *vinum picatum* of Côte-Rôtie, is not known.

The expulsion of the Romans from Gaul in the fifth century constituted a severe setback, and it is thought that the vineyards went uncultivated until the ninth century. Even then only very little wine was probably made, the local peasants being content to drink it all themselves. Slowly the wine's reputation grew, and by the fourteenth century it was being shipped down to the Papal Palace in Avignon from the ports of Condrieu and St-Pierre-de-Boeuf. The fact that more than one port of embarkation was used would indicate that the wine was perhaps ordered several times.

Condrieu was exported to England by 1714. P. Morton Shand relates that the Earl of Bristol then introduced it into his already well-stocked home cellar.

However, despite such early shipment abroad, Condrieu remains unknown to most wine drinkers. It used to be well publicized by the late Fernand Point, one of France's most famous chefs this century and precursor of the Bocuse–Troisgros school of cooking; he considered Condrieu to be one of the country's three best wines, and his restaurant, the Pyramide, introduced it to many French and foreign

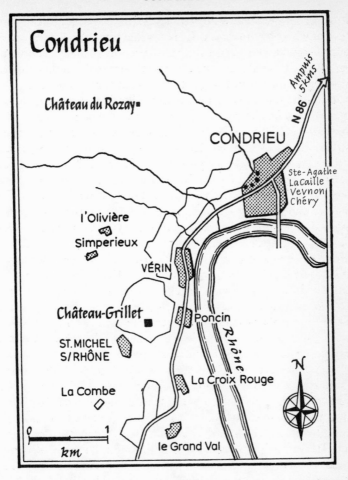

gourmets. Now that both he and his wife are dead, the role of local propagator of the wine has gone to Jacques Pic, whose restaurant in Valence is the most consistently enjoyable eating-place in the Rhône.

Condrieu now turns up on the shelves of cut-price New York wine stores, London wine warehouses and out-of-the-way country hotels in Europe, but the fact remains that there simply isn't enough of it to become well known. The Viognier vine is restricted principally to a 22-kilometre stretch above the western banks of the Rhône and, despite being currently fashionable in the southern Rhône, has rarely prospered to its full, opulent extent when transplanted away from this restricted environment. The *appellation*'s principal grower, Georges Vernay, explained some of the reasons why the Viognier remains one of France's rarest vines:

'I think first and foremost it's a case of soil. We have this curious top soil, 40 centimetres deep, of *arzelle*' – it's decomposed rock, mica and schist, under which there can be some clay, as I have on the Coteau de Vernon. This is the vine's natural home – it simply doesn't settle down elsewhere, even not far away in the Rhône Valley. In the past I've organized cuttings for a variety of growers – the late Lord Gray at Hermitage, Guy Steinmaier at Domaine Ste-Anne in the Gard, Paul Avril at Châteauneuf, the Mas de Daumas in the South-West and Domaine Ste-Apollinaire in the Vaucluse. Lord Gray was probably the first to plant, around the mid-1960s, and his wine has been the nearest in style to mine, though some way off the full aromas and depth that the wine achieves here.

M. Georges Vernay

'The Viognier is also a difficult plant. It's full of caprice and never wholly predictable. Some years we will have a really successful flowering in June and expect a large crop as a result. The weather may remain healthy right up to the time of the *vendanges*, and yet for some unknown reason the grapes will be shrivelled and undeveloped. You can't use fruit like that for your wine, and it's at times like that I start thinking – well, only half-thinking – what on earth am I doing here at Condrieu making wine?'

In its defence the Viognier can prosper outside Condrieu – if handled by a grower of exceptional talent in small quantities. 'I wanted to achieve the sort of Viognier I remembered from the 1960s', stated Gérard Chave, who took over Lord Gray's Viognier at the top of Hermitage hill during the 1980s. He makes 200 bottles for personal consumption in a good vintage like 1990, and the result is extraordinary. His 1990 'Viognier' (no *appellation contrôlée*) weighed in at 15° or more, and possessed a very floral bouquet of great width. Most impressive of all was the delicious depth on the palate – there was a very opulent, slightly sweet texture which was perfectly expressive of this unusual grape. The real pity is that more people can't taste this; it would stop them crooning over the modern, taut, steely Viogniers and make them realize that they have little to do with the real taste and aroma of this extraordinary grape.

Also in its defence, the Viognier vine lives a long time: M. Vernay has plants of around fifty-five years old on his Coteau de Vernon vineyard, which help produce the best Condrieu of all. While the vine can live till seventy, its best fruit is borne between the ages of thirty and fifty, and never in great quantity: the average yield for the period 1962–78 was approximately 17 hectolitres per hectare, just over half the total amount permitted. The 1978 crop was disastrously small – only 96 hectolitres – while the trend for the 1980s with the new plantations coming into the reckoning has been set by 1983 with 426 hectolitres, 1984 with 622 hectolitres, 1986 with 894 hectolitres and 1989 with 1,183 hectolitres. Three factors have contributed: the first is the jump in the permitted yield per hectare from 30 to 37 hectolitres, permitted from the mid-1980s, the second is the extra area under cultivation, and the third is the use of disease-resistant strains of Viognier that boost average production. Growers do not talk freely about clonal selection in the Viognier, but it is apparent that the younger plantations are composed of strains that differ from the stock planted in Condrieu in the years leading up to the 1970s.

The Condrieu *appellation* extends in a very straggling way over seven communities altogether: Condrieu and to the south, Vérin, St-Michel-sur-Rhône, St-Pierre-de-Bœuf, Chavanay, Malleval and Limony. Apart from six vineyard owners and cultivators – Vernay, Delas, André Perret, Dézormeaux, Multier at the Château du Rozay and Niéro – the plots are tiny, spread out and often grown around and in the middle of lines of fruit trees that cast unwelcome shade over the vines and divert water from their roots. These old-fashioned smaller *viticulteurs* are delighted if they have a half-hectare of Viognier to look after; they come from families that have traditionally worked in mixed agriculture, with greatest emphasis being placed on the rearing of cherries, plums, apricots and apples. These have in the past provided a rapid and ready source of income, as the growers set their wives, nieces and nephews (the children being in the vineyard) to man the impromptu fruit stalls that they establish beside the main road in summer.

Now that Condrieu is fetching such high prices – by 1982 it had risen to over £6 or US $11 a bottle in the grower's cellar, by 1987 it stood at over £8 or nearly US $14, even with a 30 per cent depreciation of the franc against the dollar, and by 1992 around £20 or US $36 – the mixed *agriculteurs* and even local tradesmen and skilled artisans are doing their sums and finding it worthwhile to start planting Viognier on whatever plots they can find on the hills above and around Condrieu. Something approaching Klondyke fever has taken over, since some of the new plots are ludicrously poorly situated, facing the east and a cold wind, or suffer from a northerly slope siting.

Such seemingly good news for the locals is not necessarily such good news for the drinker, however. It is clear that some of the recent arrivals to viniculture, with backgrounds as diverse as electricians or carton manufacturers, may have underestimated the immense physical work involved in keeping up a slope vineyard, and then watchfully minding the vinification of its fruit. There has always been a hard core of reliable, seasoned wine-makers at Condrieu, and in future it will be essential to stay with these or choose a dedicated newcomer like Patrice Porte, who worked with his father *chez* Vernay, when selecting the wine. Otherwise Condrieu risks being tainted by Burgundian connotations of high price and unreliable wine. The combination of young vines and confused wine-making is a pretty lethal one.

The slopes at Condrieu tend to be less steep than those of Côte-Rôtie and, although rock-based, by and large carry a very fine topsoil of decomposed mica. This very powdery *arzelle* is said to contribute much to the wine's usually flowery and refined bouquet, which is quite unlike that of the most commonly encountered white wines – those based on Chardonnay, Sauvignon, Riesling, or Chenin, for instance. The soft floweriness often resembles the scent of violets, and so persistent is it that it can dominate a sturdy Côte-Rôtie when up to 20 per cent of it is mixed in. Robert Jasmin of Ampuis experimented by including 20 per cent Viognier in a cask of his 1983 Côte-Rôtie, and while the colour remained solid, the bouquet bore a pronounced Viognier aroma which continued on to the start of the palate. The flavours were appealing, fine and aromatic, but the wine's development was likely to be restrained by this influence: its guts and finish had been diminished.

The soft rock is highly vulnerable to heavy rains or extremes of temperature, however, and remounting the fallen soil is an annual task. M. André Dézormeaux of St-Michel recalled that in 1972 he had had to retrieve 100 cubic metres of soil from the bottom of his 1.25-hectare vineyard: 'I had to carry it all up on my back, and it makes me wonder what I did wrong to deserve such a severe penance,' he remarked ruefully.

Being part of a small *appellation*, the growers naturally fear all adverse weather that may in any way restrict their total crop. Only 19 hectolitres of Condrieu were made in 1969 after a disastrous storm in July: even tiny Château-Grillet next door made more wine that year. It is when a quarter of an hour's hail can destroy a year's work that the *vigneron*'s heart is well and truly broken.

Most Condrieu is now dry, but over the years it has also been made as a sweet and sometimes slightly sparkling wine. When M. Vernay first joined his father in the family vineyard in 1944 the prevailing taste was just changing from a sweet and sparkling wine to a drier version. Prominent names in the *appellation* around that time were Dézormeaux, Perret, Marthoud, Vernay, Lagnier, Pinchon, Multier, Corompt and the producer of the most reputed wine, Pierre Berry. It is interesting that Berry is the only name no longer involved in wine-making at Condrieu, and that those who have continued the tradition of making some *demi-sec*, or sweeter – *liquoreux* – still wine into the 1990s include Lucien Dézormeaux, the Marthoud Frères, Lucien Lagnier, Pierre Corompt and the estate of the late Jean Pinchon, run by his son-in-law, M. Niéro.

Generally the sweet wine is now called *demi-sec*, and is often reserved in lots of around 300–600 bottles for friends and family. For instance, Gilles Barge at Côte-Rôtie makes an excellent *demi-sec* which serves to demonstrate in vivid measure the fresh flower aromas and peach- and apricot-style flavours of the Viognier on the palate. Lucien Dézormeaux is another capable maker of the *demi-sec*, and indeed his father André made nothing other than a sweet wine until the late 1960s. However, some growers' *cuvées* can be afflicted by excessive use of sulphur during vinification, which serves to halt the fermentation and retain unfermented sugar in the wine. 'I gave up our *demi-sec* in the 1970s,' commented Georges Vernay, 'because you had to put quite a lot of sulphur in to keep the wine stable. It's at the end of the fermentation that you extract most perfumes, and you're acting to block it – so the two aren't in synchronization. I suppose the way round it really, to get a similar effect, is to do a sort of *vendange tardive* and ferment it all the way through to maybe 14° or more – but there's a lot of competition in the world of *liquoreux* wines these days.'

Much of Condrieu's vinification follows broadly similar lines from one cellar to the next. The greatest divergences occur over the composition of the fermenting vats – stainless steel, wood or sometimes still concrete – and over whether to store the wine in stainless steel, old oak or new oak before bottling.

To avoid the hottest sun, harvesting will start around seven in the morning, the grapes being collected in 30-kilogram boxes and most usually emptied into the press the moment they enter the cellar. Recently some growers like Guigal and Vernay have been evolving their fermentation towards the use of intracellular maceration techniques before the pressing, providing the harvest has been healthy, as in 1990 but not in 1991. Here the grapes are left whole for between three and fifteen hours in either the press or a vat whose temperature is controlled at around 15°C. Where applicable, they are then put in to the press. The aim is to macerate the juice in contact with the skin and the pips, while it is not yet fermenting. This is to help the perfumes and fruitiness of the wine, but more importantly the process is considered to bring what Marcel Guigal describes as 'extra richness and dimension' to the wine.

Guigal varies the duration of his pre-press maceration between three and twelve hours, the longer time serving for grapes that come in cool from an early morning picking. He feels that this process is ideally suited to the Viognier, and doesn't exercise it on his white Hermitage which he says is already a big wine: 'Blindfolded and served a white Hermitage, I think you'd be quite likely to call it a red wine,' he claims provocatively.

When harvests like 1988, 1989 and 1990 turn in perfectly ripened grapes without a trace of rot, no destemming takes place. Any sorting of the harvest occurs late on at the conveyor belt *chez* Vernay, for instance, where the speed can be set to ensure that cellar staff can remove odd leaves or the like.

After pressing, the new juice is left to settle down – the *débourbage* – for about a day. Generally a little sulphur is added to stop the development of unwanted bacteria, but from 1989 Vernay has exposed the juice to a cold temperature of 4–5°C for around twelve hours, so avoiding the use of sulphur at this stage.

The juice is run into 225 or 650 litre oak casks, stainless steel or enamel-lined tanks to commence fermentation. Several growers split the fermentation between cask and stainless steel. Vernay ferments around 35 per cent of his crop in 20-hectolitre barrels, and the remainder is divided between 225-litre casks, one-fifth of which are new, and stainless steel. Perret and Guigal ferment one-third in new oak and two-thirds in stainless steel, Jean-Michel Gérin is a half *barrique*, half stainless steel man, and Delas stick to enamel-lined vats.

With his usual thorough rationale about the use of wood, Guigal believes that there is a very delicate balance in the Viognier between keeping its fruit and still producing a wine that is typical of the region – hence the use of intracellular maceration and new oak. 'The fruit leaves a Viognier wine quickly in my opinion,' comments M. Guigal, 'which is why I seek to make full-bodied, firm-tasting Condrieus that still have a touch of lively fruit on the palate. By using around one-third new oak I am adding to the wine's fullness – don't forget that it's common to harvest Viognier which measures over 14° alcohol naturally, and you're setting yourself against nature if you try to make a fresh, lively little wine from such ingredients.'

The alcoholic fermentation, referred to locally as the 'tumultuous fermentation' is conducted at a controlled temperature varying from 15–18°C. Generally it ends at the higher figure, with the Vernays for example looking for less than 2 grams of residual sugar in the wine. At this stage the difference in resources between the front-line growers and those with small plots and perhaps a part-time interest in wine becomes marked, for the smaller group often lacks the equipment to control the fermentation in very hot years like 1982 and 1989: a runaway fermentation can easily result in a blowzy, flabby wine lacking the acidity and balance to survive long.

The alcoholic fermentation can last for about three weeks, and the next decision to tax the growers is whether they wish to let the malolactic fermentation occur. The issue here is that in a very well-ripened year like 1989 the wine may undergo a threatening loss of acidity if the 'malo' is allowed to take place. Opinions clearly differ on this; for instance Guigal, Perret and Multier at the Château du Rozay always bottle their wine with the 'malo' done, while the Vernays let it take place in 1988 and 1991, but blocked it in 1989 because of lower acidity levels in the latter year.

The date of bottling is governed by the style of wine produced by the growers. An early bird is Georges Vernay with his regular *cuvée* of Condrieu; the various vats are assembled in stainless steel after fermentation, with one-third spending six months in cask. Then instead of several bottlings between February and May, the regular *cuvée* is bottled all at the same time in April. For his special Coteau de Vernon, Vernay again leaves about a third of the wine in one- to five-year old casks for a year before bottling at Christmas time.

Of other leading growers, Guigal bottles his Condrieu around Easter following the harvest, Jean-Yves Multier bottles in April or May, as do Lucien Dézormeaux and Delas, while the Domaine Niéro, Yves Cuilleron and André Perret all rely on traditional practice in waiting a year before bottling.

With so many families steeped in the customs of generations at Condrieu, it is no surprise that the approach to ageing in wood, and what age of wood should be used, differ substantially. Guigal and Pierre Boucher use new oak, the latter for one year, while André Perret and Jean-Yves Multier use two-year- and four-year-old casks respectively. There is a solid feeling of mistrust towards new oak on the part of several growers, which used to be summed up by the late Jean Pinchon thus: 'The wine is already well scented, so I don't want an intrusion that the new casks would bring to it.' A recent about-turn has been taken by Luc and Georges Vernay in the early 1990s, no doubt because they are being advised by Jean-Luc Colombo, the *œnologue* based in Cornas. Having adamantly rejected new oak, they now replace their *pièces* on a one year in five basis. The Vernays also have larger *foudres*, which are under ten years old. With the Viognier producing such florally scented wines – a characteristic not possessed by other white vines, with the possible exception of the Muscat – it is encouraging that most growers have not fallen for a new oak blitz on their Condrieus.

The finished wine of Condrieu possesses a wonderfully fine combination of powerful fullness and flowerlike delicacy, its aromas evoking a highly singular series of scents and smells that carry very direct, immediate appeal. When young, the wine is often a firm yellow which accedes to pale gold within about five years. At this stage its intrinsic richness is but partly developed, manifesting itself more as a sort of spicy earthiness. The often-heard phrase *goût de terroir* is perhaps the nearest French description: the wine has a firm backbone behind all the superficial fruit and aromas.

Condrieu's main difference in style from Château-Grillet is primarily this clean and frequently remarkable fullness of fruit and exotic flavours such as dried peach and apricot, which make it a more instantly striking, direct wine. For most of the 1980s, the greater flamboyance of flavours and secondary aromas that developed during the first six years of a good Condrieu were due to the later harvesting of the Viognier at Condrieu. During most of this time Château-Grillet pursued a policy of early harvesting, which made it difficult to achieve a richness suitable to carry the wine along with a good foundation of alcohol and musky Viognier flavours. The 1989 vintage marked a possible turn towards later harvesting there, however.

Young Condrieu displays a compelling fruitiness on the bouquet, giving the impression of slightly under-ripe pears or of eating the fruit near the pear skin. As the years advance, the golds become more prominent in the wine's *robe*, and the early soaring fruit settles down into a complexity of rounded flavours, among which the sensations of honey and apricots are sometimes mentioned by the growers. Condrieu is not a real staying wine, though, and after about eight to ten years its fruitiness and bouquet naturally start to fade.

'I personally like to drink my wine within two or three years,' says M. Georges Vernay, basing his preference on the experience of more than forty-five years' wine-making. M. Vernay has been the kingpin of Condrieu for the last twenty-five years, through which time he has steadfastly maintained his determination to keep wine-making going in the community. Condrieu's debt to him is a big one.

A strong-voiced, big, ruddy man in his early sixties, he is a true countryman. He doesn't give a lot away when sitting talking in the confines of his shaded tasting-room, but the moment he is up the hillside tending and discussing his vines, he reveals an animation and sure instinct for his craft that one only finds in those whose wine-making has been carried out across the same land for several generations, with many hours of personal toil attached. It's not a feeling that owners of large estates give, and a direct parallel to M.

Vernay comes from Gérard Chave further south at Hermitage, whose family have been *vignerons* there for over 500 years.

Georges Vernay has been working the vines since he was fifteen, and he has the large hands and broad shoulders that go with the activity. On the steep hillside of his top-grade Vernon holding, he trains the young vines against their posts, deftly attaching them with brief lengths of straw and swiftly moving with a lightness of foot over the slippery topsoil, despite an increasing problem with his eyesight. His explanations are delivered in deep tones, while his bushy eyebrows work up and down when he comes to the more contentious points, a steady chuckle helping them across.

M. Vernay is the major vineyard owner at Condrieu and has 7 hectares in production; a large single plot is his 2.5 hectares at the top of the Vernon slope, separated from the Chéry hillside by the stream of Vernon. This is just south of Condrieu, roughly facing the Beau Rivage Hotel, and is the heart of Condrieu's vineyard. Immediately next to Vernon in a northerly direction are the slopes of La Caille and Ste-Agathe and the transformation in their appearance – now chock-a-block with vines – has been startling since the 1970s. The Vernays also have 2.4 hectares of Syrah at Côte-Rôtie, on the Côte Blonde and at Tupin, and a small area of Syrah at Chavanay, which gives a red St-Joseph.

Georges now works with his switched-on son Luc, who has an impeccable pedigree for the job of vinification and cellar responsibilities, having been sent to wine school at Beaune and around numerous overseas vineyards to cut his teeth. The family holding has been gradually increased over the years, as Georges has fought to keep the *appellation* from sliding into obscurity.

As President of the Syndicat du Vin, M. Vernay has been closely involved with Condrieu's future. One of his recent developments was to instigate the spraying of parts of the vineyard by helicopter; five flights are made between June and September and serve to give the vines a general protection. This eliminates the need for five treatments painstakingly done on foot, leaving Vernay's seven permanent staff to spray by hand only for oïdium treatment.

Over the years M. Vernay has also seen too much potential wine land go towards the building of weekend homes for residents of Lyon, a trend that only slowed down in the late 1980s as the price of the wine rose. 'As growers get old it's obviously tempting for them to sell their vineyards for development; by and large they can't use machinery to tend the vines, which makes it a profession for a young man with a very supportive bank manager. What I would like to see created is something like a Protected Wine Zone, given over to viticulture and nothing else. In this way the Wine Syndicate would rent vineyards from older growers and pay them extra according to the size of the crop, the state of the market and so on. It's been a little more encouraging lately to know that people like the *négociant* house of Delas have increased their property under vine, so that their 3 hectares at Clos Bouché at Vérin is now the second largest single-holding. And well-established growers like Multier, Perret and Niéro are also increasing their active cultivation of prime sites like the Coteaux de Chéry and Corbéry that used to hold vines fifty to sixty years ago. I estimate that there are now around fifty *viticulteurs* throughout Condrieu; maybe twenty-five do some bottling and about ten what I call serious bottling. What you have to remember, though, is just how much time and money it takes to plant vines on these hillsides: it takes my full team of seven about four hours, even using drills, just to make a 20-feet-long trench on a steep hillside like Vernon. For the small grower on his own it can mean employing someone to help, but there's always a risk of the grape harvest being so limited as to make this completely uneconomic. *Voilà notre problème!*'

M. Vernay dominates the *appellation*, and the total size of his vineyards justifies his extending the cellars and buying the latest equipment to make his wine. There is no doubt that his new equipment has contributed to a change in the style of his wine since the late 1970s, towards a lighter, fresher wine which the French would term *nerveux* when young. Tasting vintages like 1986, 1989 and 1990 within their first year reveals a taut style of wine, especially on the palate, with green apple aromas on the bouquet and only a light sense of the usual luscious Viognier extracts running through the wine. These wines are very clean, very 'technological', and a touch of dirt under their fingernails would not hurt them. They show more if given time to settle, with a little generosity entering the bouquet, and in a year like 1990 will provide correct, if not inspirational drinking within their first five years.

The Vernay Coteau de Vernon, which at around 5,000 bottles a year forms 15–20 per cent of his total production, is a triumphant wine, one that epitomizes the richness and opulent essences of its grape. A firmer straw colour than the standard *cuvée*, it has oily and floral aromas whose density is matched on the palate, and comes over as a very well-knit and complex affair with refined flavours that end in a satisfyingly chewy finish. The wine has an international elegance about it, making it different from the direct, typical Viogniers made by others in the *appellation*. It is made from vines of forty to fifty years of age, which contribute to the density of texture; vinified in wood, a third of the wine receives twelve months in wood before its bottling: the rest is stored in stainless steel.

Over the years Georges Vernay has acted as something of a guru for small growers in the region, giving them advice and lending them equipment. Up until the late 1970s he also vinified all the wine from one of the larger properties, the Château du Rozay, then owned by the late M. Paul Multier.

M. Multier was one of those *vignerons* who stand out by their zany enthusiasm for what they are doing in life. He would stride around the château and its cellar, dispensing information on Rozay or its wine or even Lyon and its traditions, clad in a jauntily angled cloth cap and wearing large green wellington boots that seemed set to gobble up his small frame. When he died in the early 1980s his son Jean-Yves, just twenty-five, had to take on the property and guide it ahead on his own – in an *appellation* where there were few young growers, and even fewer motor-bike riders and part-time one-man-show actors among the *vignerons*. Jean-Yves has a taste for the latest model in heavy-duty German '*motos*', certainly never less than 1,000 cc; these he is able to exercise thoroughly on the many curves that lead up to the pink family château, which stands on the plateau 300 metres above Condrieu. He is also game enough to perform a single-handed show at a café-theatre in Lyon, involving recitals, sketches and singing.

The family connection with Rozay, whose three turrets give it a slightly lopsided look, was explained by Jean-Yves: 'We've been here since 1898, a Lyonnais family who used Rozay as a secondary residence. My great-grandparents manufactured braided uniforms and gilded vestments for the military and the Church – keeping good company, you might say – and it wasn't until the 1940s that they started seriously to replant the vineyard, which had become largely abandoned. Our vines on Chéry date from then, and now that they're forty-five years old, they're bearing excellent fruit.

'My father's real passion was agriculture, and he was never that keen on lugging around textile samples to his clients, especially as he had only one lung and a deformation of the spinal cord, which made it all very hard work for him. He had no grounding in wine, so taught himself, read a lot and started having our crop vinified at the Co-opérative in Tain-l'Hermitage. At the time it was merely a complement to 40 hectares of corn, maize and a few sheep. The wine was bottled and sold through an intermediary under the title Château du Rozay until about 1968 when some young Co-opérateurs managed to mix our precious Viognier with some Marsanne. That put us off them, even though the wine actually became rather good after about four years: Robin Yapp in England took it, as a Côtes du Rhône.

'From 1969 to 1978 Georges Vernay vinified and bottled our wine, on average 1,500 litres from under 1 hectare, with the third that we kept sold to Yapp. Georges Vernay always helped my father tremendously, and by 1979 we were vinifying and bottling here, ready to spread our wings.'

Jean-Yves has replanted since his father died, taking extra space on the well-exposed Chéry hillside. By the early 1990s his vineyard had reached 2.5 hectares, held in five plots headed by 1.4 hectares on Chéry and by the Corbéry vineyard next to the house. His wine is fermented in stainless steel, and two *sélections* are made – a straight Condrieu and the Château du Rozay. The latter spends around six months in cask, the former a little less.

With the fine summers of the late 1980s, Jean-Yves has been harvesting earlier than in his father's day – 10 September in 1989 – but as he waits strictly for each plot to ripen correctly, the whole process may run over two weeks or more. He fines with bentonite before bottling over a sustained four-day period in April or May, the Château du Rozay wine providing about 3,500 bottles of his total 10,000 bottle production.

With a high proportion of vines dating from between 1946 and 1956, the Château du Rozay is invariably marked by temendous richness and vinosity on the palate. In its best years like 1979, 1982, 1986 and 1989, it starts to show its true worth after about two years – a flowery, ample bouquet, great depth and a balanced richness that ends with a notable aftertaste. These Rozay wines are best drunk between two and six or seven years, since there can be a low residual acidity in them which will hinder their achieving old age past ten years – the 1989 with 3.6 grams is a case in point, but its great balance and complex structure serve to mitigate against this.

Of other recent vintages, the 1990 held a potent bouquet, with considerable depth. When young, its flavours were a little raw and the wine had not integrated itself with its young oak, fading a bit towards the finish. By 1993 it may show greater authority and a clearer extract. The 1988 seemed to lack a genuine richness, and was a bit hard; whether time would open up its rather tense construction is open to question. Both the 1987 and the 1986 were successful, holding good length and elegance, while the 1985 was rather light and restrained on the bouquet.

Like the Vernays, Jean-Yves has also been working with Jean-Luc Colombo, the *œnologue*-wine-maker from Cornas, since the 1988 harvest, so the style likely to emerge in the next years is a finer, more elegant version of the old robust, voluptuous Rozay wines.

Rozay exports 80 per cent of its wine, mainly to the United States and Britain, and those who like their wine fully mature and have old bottles hidden away will be comforted by an experiment that Paul Multier conducted in early 1982 with a bottle of 1951 Condrieu. It was in correct shape, despite the start of a gentle oxidation, and was still offering a rounded Viognier style. The late M. Multier's summary: 'I would never set out to keep my wine that long, and would really advise drinking it before about six years old.'

At Rozay it was fortunate not only that Jean-Yves was interested in continuing wine-making but also that the size of the vineyard could justify his full-time attention. Not as lucky was M. Pierre Dumazet, whose father Marc made a very good wine from a little more than a quarter of a hectare on the most precipitous hillside imaginable, near Limony. M. Dumazet *père* was an inspiration to the young, for when in his seventies he would still look after the vineyard, make the wine and sell it – all by himself. The Dumazets have been making wine at Limony for over 110 years, but the vineyard was not large enough to support Pierre full-time. He therefore left to work in Lyon, and when his father died in 1978 he was only lightly versed in the art of wine-making. He is a very careful and thorough man, however, and his wines have become some of the most regularly successful at Condrieu. They are marked by an intense concentration of flavour, a good old-fashioned Viognier power, with a welcome opulence on the nose. In difficult years like 1987 the wine is very carefully selected, and drinks well before it is five years old; otherwise these wines can usually keep going for around eight to ten years.

The Dumazets used to grow fruit as well as vines, and Pierre's grandfather would make spectacular journeys all the way to London in his 1930 truck to sell the fruit at the Covent Garden market. The family still like to hold a big reunion at the time of the *vendanges*, with all the grandchildren eagerly helping – and hindering – the collection of the grapes. Marc Dumazet always picked his grapes early in the morning before the sun rose high, and Pierre has maintained this system. When his grapes go into the press, they are cold to the touch and so avoid the danger of a premature fermentation breaking out.

Another family recently to face the problem of keeping their long-established vineyard going has been the Pinchons. Émile Pinchon was a respected grower at Condrieu, but his holding was too small to keep him and his son Jean in gainful work. Accordingly Jean became a cheese specialist, running a mobile cheese shop on the square of Condrieu, so being in a prime position to observe all the goings-on of the community. He was a reserved man, which was no doubt a relief for some of Condrieu's more racy residents.

When his father died in the early 1970s the late Jean Pinchon took over the 1.5-hectare vineyard; he himself died in his mid-sixties in 1990, having brought in his son-in-law Robert Niéro, who was whisked away from life in a bank in Lyon to join him. The vineyard has been enlarged to just over 2 hectares, and the future is happily secure, since the wine is close to the best at Condrieu. It is never released until over a year after the harvest and some exposure to wood that is *not* young, and settles down to show great richness and profound, rounded flavours. Notable wines from this *domaine* in the 1980s were the 1983, 1985, 1987 and 1989 – all bearing typically persistent Viognier characteristics.

Another of the younger growers to be making his mark in the *appellation* is André Perret, who with his father Pierre works 4 hectares of Condrieu. André looks after the wine-making side, and takes full advantage of the total of 3 hectares planted on the Coteau de Chéry: of this, half belongs to his family and half is worked on behalf of Robert Jurie des Camiers, a Lyonnais who used to have a silk factory which was forced to close in the face of Far Eastern imports. The Jurie des Camiers vineyard on Chéry goes back five generations, and the wine was made by Jean Pinchon until 1982. It has a prime southerly exposure, with a steep 35° incline. Perret also has a 1–hectare plot at Chavanay where the twenty-five-year-old vines are half the age of those on Chéry.

On these steep slopes the work is awkward and arduous. There are between just two and thirty plants on any of the terraces, and these have to be tended and treated – largely against oïdium – on foot. Perret's vineyards do not yield large crops either; in 1989 25 hectolitres per hectare, and in 1988 just under 20 hectolitres. Perret puts this down to the age of his vines, to the fact that in some years, like 1988, a rainy spring leads to a poor flowering, and to the fact that he is conservative in his pruning and working of the vines. He would also pick a little later than Multier, for example – about a week – which can serve to strengthen the extract in his wine.

A controlled 18–20°C fermentation lasts for fifteen to twenty days. In 1989 one-third was fermented in cask, two-thirds in stainless steel. The 'steel' wine then spends six months in wood, while the cask-fermented wine returns to steel. Like the majority of growers, Perret waits for the malolactic to occur, and bottles between September and November the year following the harvest. As his young vines come on stream Perret will make around 12,000 bottles a year which he sells as Coteau de Chéry – the more expensive wine – and Clos Chanson. Meanwhile, Robert Jurie des Camiers continues to sell his part of the Chéry crop under his own name.

The Perret family's first home-bottled vintage was 1969; André's grandfather worked at the Tain l'Hermitage Cave Co-opérative before coming to Condrieu, and André's path into wine was via a biology degree at Lyon University after which he very sensibly moved on to a specialization in viticulture at the Mâcon wine school.

A reticent, shy man of thirty-four, André is modest when discussing the merits of his wines. The Chéry is certainly marked by its *terroir*. It has a firm, almost earthy taste, some way removed from the soft fruits associated with most Condrieu. On the nose it can show a herby, complex smell which develops fullness with three years' or more age. There is a lot of extract and power on the palate, and the wine's complexity makes it very interesting.

The Clos Chanson is a pure charmer; a direct wine, it offers the floral appeal of good Viognier on the nose, and while there is some heat on the palate, the wine shows great harmony and good balance, making it delightful to drink a bit earlier than the Chéry – perhaps at two or three years old.

As a mark of his growing ability, Perret also makes an excellent St-Joseph *rouge*, with his old vines' *cuvée* called Les Grisières. The

1987 was outstanding for its year, while the richly concentrated 1989 will live for around ten years. Of his past Condrieus, Perret describes his 1983 as very good keeping wine, his 1985 as a little short in acidity (like several of that vintage), and his 1987 as sound, given the difficulties of the year. His 1988 Chéry showed great promise for drinking between 1991 and 1993, while the powerful 1989 wines may just lack a touch of acidity, which will encourage relatively earlier consumption.

Three more of the young lions of Condrieu are Lucien Dézormeaux, whose family vineyards are near Château-Grillet at St-Michel-sur-Rhône, Yves Cuilleron, who has taken over from his father Antoine, and Patrice Porte, who now produces around 4,000 bottles from his cellars at La Maladière, on the N86 just south of Condrieu. Lucien Dézormeaux took over from his fairly eccentric father André in the latter half of the 1980s. André used to tend vines and fruit trees, with the peach trees often gaining the better of the argument for space on the Coteau du Colombier that rises steeply behind the back door of his house – to such an extent that in the abundant year of 1973 he produced a mere 891 litres of wine; as a comparison, Georges Vernay, whose vineyard was then four times bigger, came up with over twelve times as much. The peach trees have now been removed.

One of the Dézormeaux family traditions that has persisted with the arrival of a new generation is the making of a sweet Condrieu, called Coteau du Colombier *demi-sec*. When carefully made by a man like Lucien Dézormeaux, the *demi-sec* can really strut the Viognier in all its panoply of sumptuous appeal: there are genuinely few vines that can yield such luscious, ripe flavours and aromas. The dry Condrieu from him is also very successful, and, as with Cuilleron and Porte, this is now a *domaine* to watch for the future.

Condrieu Vintages

Condrieu is not a wine that repays long keeping if its full, sumptuous taste is to be most clearly and powerfully enjoyed. The *vignerons* believe it is best drunk around two to five years old, and the only grower who used to talk openly of drinking his wine at more than seven years old was Jean Pinchon. According to him, his wine's perfumes were floral up till then, thereafter changing to a more quince, apricot or peach style. The Niéro wine, along with occasional *cuvées* from Guigal, the Château du Rozay (pre-1985) and Perret's

Coteau de Chéry should drink well with heightened complexity and variety of flavour until around ten or twelve years old. Thereafter the wines will show definite traces of drying out or decline.

Recent vintages have been as follows:

1959   Very good.

1960   Poor.

1961   Very good. Rich, attractive wines that with age developed tremendous bouquet.

1962   Mediocre.

1963   Mediocre.

1964   Excellent. Very complete wines.

1965   Mediocre.

1966   Very good. Full-bodied wines.

1967   Very good.

1968   Mediocre. Light, often acidic wines.

1969   Very good, although the tiny crop meant that few people ever saw the wine.

1970   Very good. Strongly perfumed wines that were rich and well balanced.

1971   Excellent. The wines were full and possessed a good colour and alcohol content. A vintage that has aged well, but one that should be drunk without delay.

1972   Good, although a few of the wines were disappointingly acidic.

1973   Good. A large crop, but one that produced wines of pleasant balance.

1974   Very good. Well-balanced, agreeably perfumed wines.

1975   Very good. The wines came round to achieve good balance after a difficult vinification hindered by a slow malolactic fermentation. They are now tiring and showing their age.

1976   Good to very good. There was a lack of rain during the summer which left the wines short on acidity. They developed quite rapidly and are now losing their fruit and vigour. Vernay's Coteau de Vernon was very successful.

1977   A light year, with the wines tending to be acid. They lacked the substance to maintain themselves and are now in decline.

1978   Excellent, very richly flavoured wines with bouquets that blossomed in fine style. They are so well structured and concentrated that they gained interesting secondary aromas and flavours with age: their great inherent richness means that several of the main growers' wines could still show respectably.

1979   Good. Although rather pale initially, the wines quickly shrugged off their early acidity and showed fantastically well after about four years. Behind the balanced richness there was a touch of residual acidity that provided a lovely clean finish. The wines are now tiring, their bouquets have damp aromas, and they seem to be on their last lap. Vernay's wine evolved more rapidly than the Château du Rozay, which was the star of this vintage.

1980   A reasonable vintage. The quality was uneven from one grower to the next, as it was difficult to achieve a satisfactory balance between the fruit and acidity. The best wines were soundly perfumed and in the case of Château du Rozay and Delas showed strongly until around 1988. Not a vintage to sit on.

1981   A very good vintage, with plenty of robust elements to it. The wines were strongly scented, rich in alcohol and flavour. They evolved quite rapidly to show a broad range of fruit and honeyed flavours. Of note were the wines of Vernay and Château du Rozay, but they are now tired.

1982   Good, but an old Viognier failing – lack of acidity – occurred, due to the intense protracted heat of the summer and early September. The wines' most striking feature was the ample range of aromas on the bouquet. Some wines were full-bodied, others – often from small, less well-equipped growers – were overblown, almost in the manner of dessert wines. They should be drunk up. Vernay made a quite exceptional Coteau de Vernon.

1983   A very good vintage, with full-bodied but well-integrated wines that carried their high alcohol content well. Dry conditions prevailed from midsummer to harvest-time, giving a very well-ripened crop. With high heat during vinification, some wines became flabby after about four years. The most balanced offerings – such as the excellent Coteau de Vernon and the Château du Rozay – now need drinking. Pinchon's showed superbly for its first three years, but fell in a heap after that.

1984   A variable vintage. Late flowering and lowish summer temperatures gave the wine more acidity, but harvesting took place in rainy, south-wind conditions. As a result the wines were finer than usual, with the best *cuvées* delicately fruited. Perret and Vernay produced agreeably fine wines, while Guigal's Condrieu was heavier, new-oak-inspired and very good – pure class. Ideally the wines should have been drunk by now.

1985   Good, sometimes very good. Another hot, dry summer gave heady, full-blown wines that in some cases held more balance than the 1983s, thanks to some late rain. Both bouquet and flavours were strongly accentuated. The wines are now at or past their peak. An excellent year for Pinchon, Delas and Dumazet, whose wines were very rich but early-maturing. The Vernay and Rozay needed longer to settle and are still showing well, while Guigal opted for an overtly woody style, a little to the detriment of fruit.

1986   An uneven vintage, where the wines were noticeably less alcoholic than the 1985s. A combination of drought, August hail which hit the best vineyards in Vérin, St-Michel and Condrieu, and a slow malolactic gave the growers a hard time. Several of the wines lacked the usual Condrieu generosity, and were green on the palate and subdued on the nose. Leading wines were made by the Château du Rozay, Delas Frères and Pinchon. They were fuller than most, but should not be specially cellared.

1987   A fair, if difficult, vintage. The summer weather was variable, part cloudy, part hot and humid; excessive rain in September was also a problem for those who waited to pick. All the wines lack a little of the usual *gras* or substance, shown by a restricted finish on many of them. Guigal, Rozay and Dumazet all made sound wines, which should be drunk before about 1993, while Perret's Coteau de Chéry, with an impressive, earthy bouquet and reasonable depth on the palate, may live towards 1995.

1988   Excellent. A rainy spring led to some lower than usual yields. A really healthy crop was brought in around mid-September. The wines have great depth and power on the palate – a year of great fullness. Perret's wines were led by a very promising, complex Coteau de Chéry and a well-balanced Clos Chanson which was a bit marked by young oak. Vernay's Coteau de Vernon was splendidly rich and oily, while the Guigal mixed the classic strong Viognier nose and power with a discreet touch of new oak. These wines will show impressively for at least six to eight years, and are already delicious.

1989　A very good, potentially long-lived year. The weather behaved strangely, giving 25°C heat in March and flowering three weeks early at the end of May. A hot, dry summer led to some low levels of acidity in the wines. A well-scented Rozay has notable length, a still latent richness and should progress very well, with sufficient balance to keep it going towards 1999. The Guigal is very rich and well structured and will live for several years. Alain Paret's Ceps du Nébadon was very successful, marked by a striking depth of fruitiness and concentration on the palate. It has enough grip to run for six or more years. Vernay's standard *cuvée* is very clean and its structure is taut in the modern way – it needs to be looked at around 1993 to show more than an initially understated Viognier character. His Coteau de Vernon held discreet, lasting flavours on the palate, and a bouquet with some latent promise; it is an attractive, classy wine to drink enjoyably towards 1996. Perret's Coteau de Chéry has a lot of extract, but could be flabby, while the Vidal-Fleury has been slow to develop its bouquet and shows traces of new oak. Dézormeaux's Coteau du Colombier is rich and should be drunk within four or five years.

1990　A generally good vintage, although yet another very dry summer and autumn furnished wines that can lack crispness. The large harvest was brought in with no sign of rot, but because of an absence of rain from July to October some bunches were slow to ripen. The wines carry a heady level of alcohol – often between 13° and 14° – and need time to open up and show their power. This is a beefy vintage where the palate is initially more impressive than the bouquet.

Earlier Exceptional Vintages　1949, 1947, 1929

Leading Growers at Condrieu

The nucleus of growers and producers of Condrieu capable of bringing out wine that can range from the sound to the spectacular is:

Barge, Gilles	69420 Ampuis
Cuilleron, Yves	42410 Chavanay
Delas Frères	07300 St-Jean-de-Muzols
Dézormeaux, Lucien	42410 St-Michel-sur-Rhone
Dumazet, Pierre	07340 Limony
Guigal, E.	69420 Ampuis
Jaboulet Aîné, Paul	26600 La Roche-de-Glun
Multier, Jean-Yves Château du Rozay Niéro, Robert	69420 Condrieu
Perret, André	42410 Chavanay
Vernay, Georges and Luc	69420 Condrieu
Vidal-Fleury	69420 Ampuis

Other producers:

Boucher, Pierre	42520 St Pierre-de-Bœuf
Chanal, Roger	42410 Pélussin
Chapoutier, M.	26600 Tain-l'Hermitage
Chirat, Gilbert	42410 St Michel-sur-Rhône
Clusel-Roch	69420 Ampuis
Corompt, Pierre	69420 Condrieu
David, Émile	42410 Vérin
Faury, Philippe	42410 Chavanay
Gangoff	69420 Condrieu
Gérard, François Gérin, Jean-Michel	69420 Ampuis
Lagnier, Georges et Lucien Maisonneuve, Jean Marthoud, Frères Montez, Antoine	42410 Chavanay
Mouton, Père, et Fils	69420 Condrieu
Paret, Alain	42520 St-Pierre-de-Bœuf
Pichon, Philippe	42410 Chavanay

Porte, Patrice	69420 Condrieu
Richard, Martial	42410 Chavanay
Rouvière, Marc	42410 Chavanay
de Vallouit, Louis-Francis	26240 St-Vallier
Villano, Gérard	69420 Condrieu

3

Château-Grillet

Château-Grillet is an unusual, curious white wine. It represents the quirkiness of mankind – our liking for rarity, for exclusivity – and yet our naïvety – how we believe fables, how legend can confuse us and hide the truth. Yes, it is unusual – it *is* its own *appellation*: no one other than André Canet and his family have any say or influence on making the wine, on what style it should be, and indeed how much it should cost. Yes, it is curious – here is a famous wine tucked away right slap bang in the middle of an industrial corridor of the Rhône Valley, somewhere on the way between Paris and the Côte d'Azur. Did the travellers of old alight from the local train, or steer their heavy motor cars towards this hillside château – it's not the sort of location that one can imagine was frequented by the *beau monde* of yesteryear? And it's very small – 3.8 hectares, although it has got bigger between 1971 and 1991. Oh yes, two last *petits points*: it's expensive (a case of the 1988 in Britain was on regular sale at around £440, or over US$70 a bottle, with the bottles containing 70, not 75 centilitres) and it's not worth the money.

But history and legend are fine companions for a *vin de curiosité*, and Château-Grillet has its fair share of tales from the past. The real tragedy with this property is simply that it could be making outstanding wine, for the vineyard, in its conformation, grape variety and soil, bestows a marvellous advantage into the hands of the wine-maker. But the last fifteen years have brought commercial policies that override considerations of quality, and many of the wines have been depressingly dull and humdrum, easily outpointed by any number of their fellow Viognier-based white wines from next-door Condrieu, even taking into account differences of style in the wines.

Writers of different nationalities and different times have praised Château-Grillet with zeal. The French gastronome Curnonsky, writing in *Lyon et le Lyonnais gastronomique* in the 1920s, was moved to rank Château-Grillet as one of France's three best white wines. Curnonsky wrote:

> But of all the white wines made from the Viognier around Condrieu, the palm must go to a very great, exceptional, marvellous and suave white wine: the most rare Château-Grillet, a golden and flamboyant wine cultivated in a vineyard of less than 2 hectares, a wine above commercialization, just about untraceable and jealously guarded by its one owner. . . . This wine is quite simply the third (and rarest) of the five best white wines of France (and therefore the world). The wine of Château-Grillet is lively, violent, changeable like a pretty woman, with a flavour of the flowers of vines and almonds, with a stunning bouquet of wild flowers and violets, and reaching up to 15° alcohol. In short, *un très grand seigneur!*

Beat that! Well, Maurice Healy, an Irish barrister and wine connoisseur, had a try in 1940:[1]

> I once drank a Château-Grillet that was over seventy years old, and delicious. . . . I think the vintage was 1861. . . . it had preserved its vinosity, and the clean, pebbly taste was quite remarkable. It appeared to me to be of a majesty greater than that attained by Chablis, or any Burgundy except Montrachet.

So there has indeed been a glorious past for the wine. The château itself stands next to the the village of St-Michel-sur-Rhône, a little to the south of Condrieu. Backed against a sheltered hillside, it carries a mixture of architectural styles. The château records date back to the reign of Louis XIII (1610–43) and indicate that it was then a small lodge or dower house. In subsequent years successive owners built on as the fancy took them, their main criterion seemingly being size rather than charm.

Up until the French Revolution in 1789 the château stood on uninterruptedly royalist territory, looking across the Rhône towards the Dauphiné, the home of Republicanism. As such, the rent had to be paid to the Church, who were clearly liberal with their granting of planning permission. While the façade dates from the Renaissance, the cellar below, with its blocked-in window, is considered by the

[1] Maurice Healy, *Stay Me with Flagons* (London: Michael Joseph, 1940).

owner, M. André Canet, to date from the Middle Ages. In places the outer walls suddenly become as much as a metre thick, and judging by such defences, it is clear that possession of the property was hotly contested when the Neyret-Gachet family, today's owners, moved in.

Thereafter the wine became well known in select circles, particularly outside France. In the 1830s Château-Grillet was sent on several occasions to both Moscow and Odessa, the price of 4 francs a bottle being charged to the Russians, while the home French price was only 3 francs a bottle. And in 1829 the Court of St James's ordered two cases of seventy-two bottles each for King George IV; James Christie, the Lord Steward, wrote the following letter to the Wine House of Faure in St-Péray to secure the order:

> Gentlemen, I beg you will have the kindness to forward immediately the undermentioned wine for the use of His Majesty the King of England with directions to your agent at Bordeaux to ship it by the very first vessel for this Port, the Bill of Lading to be enclosed to me; the Invoice I request you will send to me and for the amount you may draw a Bill at thirty days Sight on the Lord Steward of His Majesty's Household, St. James's Palace. In selecting this wine I trust you will be careful that it is of the very first vintage and such as may be fit for immediate use.[1]

Certainly, two things have changed little in over 150 years: the method of arranging for an importation of wine and the thirst of people for Château-Grillet – hence the declaration that the wine was wanted 'for immediate use'. Who would blame King George for that?

Only 100 metres away from the château is the site of an ancient Roman community, traces of which were discovered at the turn of the century. One can only imagine that the Romans enjoyed a better view than that which now extends before the château, for across the river at St-Clair-du-Rhône there have been factories, including a large Rhône-Poulenc, since around 1920. An ICI chemical plant built in 1971 did not help, and streams of steam and smoke curl slowly south, aided by the light north wind. Below the château trains rumble past at regular intervals. From the shaded terrace of the old house, its splendid wistaria sprouting a sustained pale mauve in early

[1] R. Bailly, *Histoire de la Vigne et des Grands Vins des Côtes du Rhône* (Avignon: Imp. F. Orta, 1978).

summer, all this makes an incongruous, curious scene.

As at Condrieu, the Viognier is the only grape variety permitted, and the irregular rows of vines crouch up above and all around the château in the form of an amphitheatre. It is a conveniently exposed amphitheatre, too, for the vines, facing full south, benefit from great sunshine and warmth and are perfectly protected from the *bise* wind by their encircling hillside, which mounts steeply to a height of 240 metres.

All vineyard care remains manual: the depth of many of the ledges is only about 1 metre, and the vines run across them at intervals of 90 centimetres. The retaining walls are dry-stone, and need upkeep to stop erosion and soil slippage. When defending the high price of his wine, M. Canet is quick to point out that in Burgundy there are no terrace walls to keep and repair, and that his fixed costs are therefore much higher. This assumes that one is comparing like with like.

The vines are all trained in the Guyot way, and grow on surprisingly light and powdery soil that makes movement on the hillside a slippery operation. In bright sunshine tiny particles can be seen glinting here and there; these are little pieces of decomposed mica, also found in the Condrieu vineyards.

Since the 1960s M. André Canet has gradually increased the size of the vineyard by restoring a series of little terraces adjoining the property, as well as managing in the mid-1970s to buy the well-sited Régis Campo Viognier vines that stood below the château on the left of the approach road. M. Campo was a producer of Condrieu and one of his regular clients was the late Fernand Point at his restaurant La Pyramide in Vienne, a noted promoter of the wines of Condrieu. M. Canet (born in 1912) married into the Neyret-Gachet family, and came to live at Château-Grillet in 1961. He was clearly a man of action, for a lot of planting took place in 1962, and while this distinguished old gentleman does not like to talk about such unseemly subjects as expansion and pushing for a higher production, the figures speak for themselves. The vineyard has been enlarged from 1.7 hectares in 1971 (when it was indeed France's smallest *appellation*, behind Romanée-Conti's 1.8 hectares), to 2.3 hectares in 1977, to 3.01 hectares in 1982, to 3.8 hectares in 1991.

The wine taken from this tiny vineyard is even more revealing. As an average for several five-year periods, the figures are:

1966–70	4,455 litres per annum
1971–5	5,663 litres per annum
1976–80	7,840 litres per annum (including the tiny 1978 crop of 2,900 litres, the smallest since the 2,600 litre harvest of 1969)
1981–5	10,000 litres per annum
1986–90	9,602 litres per annum

A combination of intensive plantation, pruning that left many buds per plant, early picking to avoid the least chance of late damage from rain, extensive use of clonal disease-resistant cuttings of the Viognier and liberal use of fertilizer brought this vineyard metaphorically to its knees in the years of 1983 and 1984. 'Never mind the quality, what's the quantity?' must have been the cry to produce consecutive harvests of 13,700 litres and 14,400 litres. On an *appellation* whose yield per hectare was then set at 32 hectolitres (from 1984 it was formally raised to 37 hectolitres), we're still talking about an average of about 45 hectos in 1983 and 47 hectos in 1984 – absolutely scandalous, and a seeming mockery of the French *appellation* laws, designed, one might have thought, to protect the interests of the consumer rather than feather the nest of the producer.

When asked about this, M. Canet admits that there was too much fertilizer used, *c'est tout*. Well, nature has a way of saying 'enough', and in 1985 when early wet weather hampered the flowering, the vines, probably largely spent, produced only 5,300 litres in total, an average of under 18 hectolitres per hectare. During the remainder of the 1980s yields thankfully did not hit the earlier heights, and it is to be hoped that some sense of propriety was restored to the *domaine*. One recalls that in the mid-1980s there were rumours of the estate being up for sale, with the family allegedly looking for a way out, so the yields of 1983 and 1984 may have helped increase a bargaining hand. Those days have happily passed, and M. Canet now runs the estate in association with his two daughters and sons-in-law, with vinification advice from sources in Beaune, further north in Burgundy.

Harvesting does not take long in this tiny vineyard. Three days in September or occasionally early October are sufficient to clear the rugged terraces of their fruit. The château has a reputation among the growers of Condrieu of being an early harvester – up to two weeks ahead has been cited – but M. Canet says that he applies the rule of thumb of 100 days from the flowering. This may be so, but there is little doubt that he is quick on the draw, touched with what Gérard Chave of Hermitage describes as a common Rhône complaint – 'harvest fever'. What this means is that his Viognier has a reduced chance of achieving 12° natural alcohol, extra body and, most importantly, the musky, opulent Viognier flavours that accompany extra maturity. One can put this down to style, but under such a system the Viognier is shorn of the chance to show what it can really do.

M. Canet brings in a team of two dozen cutters and carriers to work with his five permanent staff, and the harvesters demonstrate laudable agility in bringing down the grapes from the sometimes highly restricted ledges. There is only one narrow and awkward approach stairway from the vines to the cellars, and this presents one final challenge to the flagging *porteurs*.

Upon receipt at the cellars the harvest is crushed in a pneumatic press that was brought in to replace the château's old cast-iron vertical version in the mid-1970s. The juice is then left for up to forty-eight hours to settle in 20-hectolitre enamel-lined vats before fermentation. The increases in vines and production have put pressure on space in the cellars under the château, and the enamel vats are a more economical use of space than any smaller wooden receptacles.

Fermentation temperature is controlled around the 25°C mark – still some 5–7°C above most Condrieu these days – with the vats cooled in the old-fashioned way by circulating water over them. According to the maturity of the vintage, the fermentation lasts for fifteen to twenty days. At this stage, says M. Canet, the wine is not dry – it becomes so after a further six months. The young wine remains in vats to complete its malolactic fermentation and is then transferred into *pièces* for ageing. These are old casks and the wine will remain in them for six months or so: this is less than the one-year stay quoted to the author by M. Canet in the mid-1980s.

M. Canet is emphatically a member of the old school in his outlook. 'I like to leave the wine alone,' he says. 'I won't even do a racking during the pre-"malo" and post-"malo" phases. The wine is on a fine lees in cask, but that doesn't fuss me – it allows the wine to evolve normally.'

Bottling takes place around fifteen to sixteen months after the harvest, and is done by hand in lots of 2,000 bottles at a time. The whole process, therefore, will run over the course of three months. The wine is fined and lightly filtered beforehand. M. Canet feels that the wine should then be allowed at least two years in bottle to settle and start to show its qualities.

In recent years these qualities have become more elusive. Looking back through tasting-notes, the most impressive bottles of Grillet drunk in the past few years have been the 1966 (drunk in 1986), the 1969 (drunk in 1989), the 1971 (drunk in 1985), the 1974 (drunk in 1987), the 1976 (drunk in 1985) and the 1982 (drunk in 1987). Until some welcome progress was noted in 1988 and 1989, many of the vintages of the 1980s simply do not hold out the likelihood of similar development, being marked by a blurred quality of fruit, a sometimes sticky texture and a lack of the typically potent Viognier aromas. Not that Grillet was ever a flamboyant wine – its ace card was a discreet elegance, a classy finesse unusual in wines of this region.

At its best, Château-Grillet presents itself with a very pale straw colour, one that is more marked than in most modern-day white wines. In a strong, well-made vintage the bouquet carries varied aromas, some of which are described as apricot, truffle and honey. With age – eight years or more – the aromas turn more floral, a welcome difference of evolution from the fat honey smells of older Chardonnay, for instance. On the palate a mixture of apricot and exotic fruits (orange, tangerine) can be called up, but the interesting observation is that they are different from the fruit connotations – pears, for example – generally attached to Viogniers made at Condrieu up the road. The ageing in cask may have some impact on this, as well as the attachment to a fine lees for perhaps as long as a year. As a dry wine these days, Château-Grillet carries with it a rich underlying fullness and undoubted depth of flavour. But all its notes are subtle, underscored and therefore all the more intriguing when the wine truly is on song.

With age the wine intensifies its colour towards gold and both the bouquet and the palate gain in opulence. Of course such development presupposes sound raw materials at the outset, and sadly many recent vintages have lacked the extract and breeding necessary for this. Set against wines like the magnificent 1969 and 1976, the 1985 and 1983 are pale indeed. At least more hope is offered by the 1989.

Château-Grillet is now the only Côtes du Rhône *appellation* to use distinguished dark yellow and brown Rhine bottles of 70-centilitre content (most wine is sold in 75-centilitre bottles). In days gone by the Viognier growers of Condrieu also used flute-shaped bottles, which were specially blown for them at a glass factory in St-Étienne. The custom may have died out in Condrieu, but Château-Grillet continues with its long-established *domaine*-bottling tradition, started in 1830 by the Neyret-Gachet family. Before this date the wine had always left the property in cask.

Today M. André Canet has ceded some of the running of the vineyard to his daughter after thirty years in charge. Despite recent illnesses he still presents an imposing, austere personality, drawn more from Victorian times than anything more recent. He would be many people's idea of the distinguished Gallic gentleman with his strong features, darkly tanned face and confident, almost stern bearing. To his ten grandchildren he probably seems fierce and forbidding when they come to stay in the château for Easter holidays.

He defends his vineyard stoutly, as would only be expected. 'When I arrived, my first challenges were to reclaim the vineyard and keep its good name going. Some of the terraces had been long abandoned, and we were only making around 40–45 hectolitres per year. Between 1965 and 1970 we got on with this *défrichage*, clearing the terraces of plants like acacia, whose roots go incredibly deep. This was the area right at the top of the hillside above the château. We still replace about 250 vine plants a year.

'My main work perhaps has been to try to maintain the perfumes of the wine. My personal taste is to drink it when it's about ten years old, and I think it goes very well with meat – beef, veal or a leg of lamb. Even though it's dry today, it still has richness underneath it. I consider it probable that when Curnonsky was writing, he was describing a semi-sweet or sweet Château-Grillet, which was the old style. That's also why he called it a poor traveller as its sweetness made it less stable.'

Tracking down bottles of Château-Grillet calls for sound sleuthing. M. Canet works with one importer per country, and keeps them all on tenterhooks over their annual allowance. Most of the overseas wine goes to Europe and the United States – that means Robin Yapp in Britain in 1988 received just ten cases, while the New York allocation is generally around twenty cases. So that exclusive tag sticks firmly to this wine, and does little harm to its price. If curiosity is not to kill the cat, make friends with the importer or tap Aunt Agatha for a few bob – but buy one bottle and choose your vintage carefully to avoid disappointment.

Château-Grillet Vintages

1965   A medium-quality vintage that lived a surprising time – into the 1980s. When young, the wine was light and fruity: it is now past its best.

1966   A very good year. A richly scented wine of great style and finish. Some bottles are tiring, showing marked signs of oxidation; others still retain an imposing dried fruit richness on the palate. Drink up. (24 hectolitres)

1967   A sound, heavy wine that possessed more body than finesse. It has turned a deep gold and is tasting old, with an end dryness creeping in. (42 hectolitres)

1968   A light-coloured year that needed time to develop its full bouquet. Unusually successful for a generally poor vintage in the northern Rhône, the wine became very agreeably fruity but is now fading. (67 hectolitres)

1969   An excellent year, one that combined remarkable fruitiness with sound body. The wine possessed great length and elegance on the palate – Château-Grillet at its best. 1,730 bottles (46 per cent of the tiny crop) were made into a special Cuvée Renaissance. The supreme balance of the wine has helped to conserve it, but its richness has started to thin and bottles should be drunk within an hour of opening. (26 hectolitres)

1970   A good year, with the wine possessing much of the fruitiness of the 1969s. A little lacking in body and style, this wine has now lost its cohesion on the palate, and should be drunk. 6,360 bottles (67 per cent of the crop) were made into the Cuvée Renaissance. (66 hectolitres)

1971   A wine that has developed its aromas and strength on the palate with ageing. Initially it was refined but unimpressive. Good, full flavours are beginning to wither, and there is a loss of length *en bouche*. Well-cellared bottles, particularly of the Cuvée Renaissance (3,670 bottles or 55 per cent of the crop) can still show signs of the opulence of old age. (47 hectolitres)

1972   Similar to 1969 in that a small vintage of some 3,680 bottles produced an excellent, highly concentrated wine. It has developed very well, but should now be drunk as its richness fades. (28 hectolitres)

1973 An extremely large crop for its time resulted in a fine, rather light wine. At this stage of the 1970s the wine would be in cask for its 'malo' and would be bottled between eighteen months and two years after the harvest, so there was longer contact with wood – eighteen months – than in the 1980s. This vintage has now passed its best and needs drinking up. (84 hectolitres)

1974 Another large crop, despite which the resultant wine bore a good combination of fruit and depth. With age it has developed good length on the palate, and its finish is commendably clean. Needs drinking as it loses its grip. (87 hectolitres)

1975 A small crop whose wine was unexceptional. Only lightly scented, it is now thin and in the process of oxidizing on the palate. (40 hectolitres)

1976 A wine of good bouquet and lots of complex spice and dried fruit aromas that have appeared with age. It possesses good balance and is now showing very well, with great width on the palate and a long follow-through. Drink now to 1995 to catch some of this wine's enticement. (87 hectolitres)

1977 A limited crop gave a light but attractive wine. It has evolved rapidly and for an off-year has surprising depth. It needs to be drunk soon. (63 hectolitres)

1978 A tiny crop, but a successful wine. It holds great richness and, as opposed to many Château-Grillets of the later 1980s, is very thorough – the palate is very dense, the length exemplary. It has opened up very well. For best results drink now to 1994 or so. (29 hectolitres)

1979 An even yellow colour with touches of gold, this wine displays richness but has always lacked a little freshness. It has aged quite quickly, lightening in the process, and needs to be drunk. (97 hectolitres)

1980 At the time, the largest harvest ever. The wine was somewhat hard and dull-tasting, with little evidence of the refined aromas and fruit extract of the Viognier. An inauspicious start to what turned out to be a poor decade. A woodiness always showed up on the nose. Drink now; the wine has nowhere to go. (116 hectolitres)

1981 A good wine marked by sound Viognier depth on the

bouquet and the palate. With age it has gained a certain refinement but is already starting to tire – the richness is less extreme and a little of the flesh has gone. Drink now to 1993. (75 hectolitres)

1982 Mediocre. The wine is light without compensating through a refined southern grip. Many Viogniers of this vintage showed splendid depth of fruit, but Grillet has gone the other way – early harvesting must be to blame. Difficulties during vinification added to the problem. The wine is very supple and needs to be drunk. (91 hectolitres)

1983 Rain in early September stampeded the owner into early harvesting; the sun came out afterwards to reward those of greater patience. Blatant overproduction resulted. The wine is pallid without being interesting. Faintly scented, there was some reasonable fruit on the attack, and the style was that of a quiet, rounded wine. For those who love the Viognier it is innocuous, boring. Short on the finish, it should be drunk before around 1993. (137 hectolitres)

1984 Harvesting took place in good weather after some rot had started to appear. The wines were an attractive pale colour and were finely structured. There are refined Viognier aromas on the nose, but a lack of richness on the palate means the wine is now going nowhere. It is a weak wine; it lacks the guts needed to give it a future, and is very much in the vein of the Grillets of the 1980s. Simply not worth the money. (144 hectolitres)

1985 Later harvesting – thank goodness. Greater substance than the two previous years, but once again there is a lack of thoroughness in this wine. The nose is discreet and has opened further with age, but will never be opulent and striking. The palate contains soft fruit flavours and reasonable length. It won't age like the wines from the 1960s and 1970s; one can find no reason why this should not happen in a favourable year like 1985. (53 hectolitres)

1986 A difficult year to vinify, with quite a high level of acidity. The wine is palely coloured, and on the palate its flavours are firm, a little lacking in rich extract. The wine's balance is a little unsteady. The bouquet may evolve and open further around 1992, and drinking of this finely styled wine is recommended before 1996. (91 hectolitres)

1987   Pale yellow, the wine has an indistinct bouquet; it seems to have matured early, but the aromas are not decisive and floral – a bit damp and mushroomy. Once more, a wine that lacks thoroughness on the palate – the flavours are light and uninteresting and ill-defined. The aftertaste drifts into anonymity. No particular future; it's hard to see how this pale offering can improve. (97 hectolitres)

1988   This is one of the best recent vintages of Château-Grillet. The wine is pale, with a hint of lime. The bouquet holds ripe, almost over-mature fruit aromas. There is sound depth on the palate, and much more heat and follow-through than in recent years. The balance is sound, there is greater extraction of ripe flavour than in past years, and this wine should show very well around 1993 to 1995, although it will satisfy before then. (57 hectolitres)

1989   Very good indeed. Perhaps a return to previous standards is starting to occur. The colour is light, and, similar to the 1988, the bouquet is pungent, musky. A hint of light flowers is there, but the prevailing sensation is of over-ripe smells. On the palate the wine is like some of the ripe, full Château-Grillets of the past, where the expression of the Viognier is more traditional and different to that achieved at Condrieu. There are good length and breadth on the wine, which is drinking very well at the age of three. It should be capable of going along for another six to nine years. (78 hectolitres)

Grower at Château-Grillet

Neyret-Gachet
   Château-Grillet   42410 Vérin

4

Hermitage

The Hermitage hillside is a truly spectacular home for a vineyard. Curved to follow the course of the Rhône, the roughly hewn hill mounts forcefully towards the skyline. Its vines trace an irregular pattern, seeming to zigzag across the hill's contours until they reach their summit near the tiny chapel of St Christopher.

In summer the hillside, resplendent in its green mantle, loses its customary severity. In winter the dour granite colours and the long lines of oddly contorted vine plants lend an air of lunar austerity. It is then hard to imagine that here is the home of such a magnificently rich wine.

In the lee of the hill, wedged between it and the strong-flowing Rhône, is Tain-l'Hermitage, the unofficial capital of the Rhône wine industry. A small, busy town through the centre of which runs the N7, the old main highway going south, Tain shares with Tournon on the opposite bank the privilege of housing some of the Valley's larger *négociant* companies, and certainly those with most prestige. Houses like Chapoutier, Jaboulet and Delas have traditions dating back to the early nineteenth century, and Jaboulet's office and bottling operations move in the early 1980s down the road to La Roche-de-Glun was the first major severance by any company of their full, close ties with Tain. The town is still a noisy place, a convenient exit off the nearby autoroute for traffic heading north–south, and it can hardly be called charming. However, these defects are more than compensated for by the glorious wine maturing slowly underneath its streets. As the local people say, there is only one reason to go to Tain, but that's a good one!

Tain is acknowledged as having been a wine-producing community in Roman times, when it went by the name of Tegna. In their works, the *Natural History* and the *Epigrams*, both Pliny and Martial

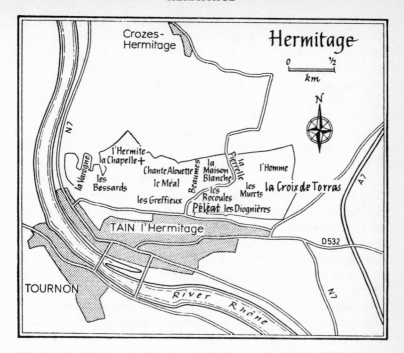

mentioned the wine of Tegna, which would suggest that it enjoyed a certain fame. Indeed, Hermitage is thought by some regional historians to be the oldest vineyard in the Rhône Valley and, therefore, in the whole of France. They are joined by local growers in believing that the famous hillside was first planted with vines around 600 BC – Syrah vines, that had come up the river from Marseille with the first band of invading Phocaean Greeks. The accuracy of this view is difficult to assess, for the evidence (see Introduction) is obviously somewhat circumstantial.

Tain still displays a relic from its Roman days – an ancient altar called a taurobolium that was used for the sacrifice and offering of bulls to the god Mithras. It dates from about AD 180 and is the town's most jealously guarded possession, as the following story illustrates.

In 1724 a British traveller arrived in Tain expressly to buy the altar, claiming that its sale to England would help promote the *entente* that was noticeably lacking between the two countries. The town officials refused his request out of hand, however, and to make absolutely sure, took advantage of a dark night to carry off the taurobolium and hide it in the cellars of the Town Hall. The next day the British visitor was informed by grief-stricken, angered officials that the taurobolium had been scandalously stolen. The poor man took pains to console them and, as some sort of amends bought a small barrel of their wine: to have kept the taurobolium and to have exported some of their wine in the process proved an eminently satisfactory outcome for the locals!

There are several legends surrounding the origins of vine-growing and the name Hermitage, whose old style was 'Ermitage'. These legends tend to vie with one another in romanticism but are none the less worth recounting. One is the work of the Irish writer James Joyce, who claimed that it was St Patrick who planted the first vines on the slopes of Hermitage, taking a quick break there on his way to convert Ireland. This is beautiful storytelling and a fine piece of national trumpeting from a people known for their endearing art of exaggeration; there is absolutely no evidence to uphold Joyce's theory. In fact, one of the few written references to this tale does indeed come from another Irishman, Maurice Healy, in his *Stay Me with Flagons*. In 1940 Healy wrote, with broad Irish charm, as follows: 'Hermitage has an Irish link; there is a Clos Saint-Patrice there, which is supposed to be the site of a resting place of St Patrick on his way to Ireland . . . it is producing a red wine that would almost convert Hitler to Christianity.'

The Irish tale must in all honesty take second place to the much better-known, oft-quoted legend that concerns the holy knight Gaspard de Stérimberg. This gentleman's name now appears on the labels of the House of Jaboulet's white Hermitage. Returning wounded in 1224 from a crusade against the Albigensian heretics, Stérimberg was making his way home when he came upon the Hermitage hillside; he climbed it, found it quite enchanting and decided to stay – but, of course, had no roof over his head. As befits a knight, he dutifully applied to the then Queen of France, Blanche of Castille, for permission to build a retreat. This was granted, and he is said to have lived there for thirty years until his death. His chapel still stands in solitary splendour near the top of the Hermitage hill.

A final local legend, attributed to Brother Benedict – of whom nothing else is known – dates from the time of the Roman persecution of the Christians, when a hunted priest is said to have taken refuge on the Hermitage hill: his basic source of nourishment, bread and cheese, was brought by the wild animals all around him. Nothing could be found to drink, however, and the holy man was on the point of death when the timely intervention of the good Lord saved him. As is well known, all *vignerons* eventually find their way into Paradise, and so there suddenly appeared a band of angelic growers ready with fruit-bearing vines which made wine overnight. The priest drank and was saved.

Between Roman times and the seventeenth century Hermitage surprisingly disappears from the history books, but in 1642 it acquired a royal connection that eventually spanned three centuries. In that year King Louis XIII was touring the Rhône Valley, which at Tain reaches one of its narrowest points. The king's travelling companions advised him to descend from his carriage and be carried over the most dangerous part of the river, a large protruding rock. Of course, Louis's itineraries always allowed for impromptu glasses of wine, so when a subject offered him some of the local wine, he was quite happy to accept it and appreciate it at his leisure. The rock where he was forced to descend is known as the King's Table, for it was there that Louis decided that in future he would serve the wine at the Court of France – a decision that did much to advance the fame of Hermitage.

The grandson of a former French President records that the Court of Russia was equally drawn to the wine. When his grandfather, M. Émile Loubet, visited Tsar Nicholas in 1903, he was served red and white Hermitage at the imperial banquet. M. Loubet took this as a friendly sign of recognition that he came from Hermitage's Drôme *département*, but the Tsar said, no, the wines of Hermitage had in fact been regular Romanov favourites since the time that Nicholas Boileau wrote his satire *Le Repas ridicule* in 1663. True to form, the cynic Boileau had commented not on the wine's worth but on its apparent falsification:

Un laquais effronté m'apporte un rouge bord
D'un auvergnat fumeux, qui, melé de lignage,
Se vendait, chez Crénet, pour vin de l'Hermitage.[1]

Since Boileau's time, Hermitage has been a source of inspiration to a wide variety of writers. The Frenchman Jean-François Marmontel

[1] A cheeky flunkey brings me my red wine brimful
With a heady Auvergnat, which, mixed with dregs,
Was sold at Crénet's as wine from the Hermitage.

stopped in Tain in 1755 to buy half a dozen bottles of the white wine; they cost him only 50 sous each, but he was quite entranced by their 'nectar bouquet' (*Memoires d'un père*). The English novelist Henry Fielding (1707–54) obviously had a soft spot for the wine, for it crept into several of his works, *Tom Jones* included; while the Scottish author Walter Scott held no doubts about Hermitage's ability to charm: in *Charles the Bold* (1831), he wrote: 'I shall have a snack with you, and I shall satisfy you with a flask of old Ermitage.'

The Hermitage that Scott knew may well have been that of the House of Bergier, prominent at the time in making and selling the wine, always with flair. M. Bergier himself had been an artist and lawyer when young, and made a flamboyant impression on the people of Tain when he designed and had built a six-windowed pavilion, exactly on the lines of one of the smartest villas of Pompeii, which was located slap bang in the centre of his Hermitage vineyards. From here M. Bergier could watch the river and town below, plus of course his vineyard workers.

M. Bergier's vineyard was centred on the *climat* known as Le Méal, and he further distinguished himself by putting up an enormous signboard painted red and white marked 'HERMITAGE, CUVÉE BERGIER'. This was the forerunner of the large Hollywood-style wall announcements that today carry the names of 'Paul Jaboulet Aîné' and 'Chapoutier et Cie' – free publicity in the heart of the vineyards.

Bergier was a keen promoter of his wines, and in 1862 presented both white and red Hermitage at an exhibition in 'the Palace of the Cromwell road' in London. Curiously, the oldest wine on show was a white 1822, which along with other whites from 1834 and 1848 was said to have become *liqueur* – evidently a prized taste at the time, for the younger 1850 and 1859 were commented upon as having a nutty, slightly bitter taste, 'special to the Bergier wines'. This *goût de noisette* is what we nowadays regard as typical of, and essential to, good white Hermitage. One of the most notable reds shown, the oldest being the 1830, was the 1834, which had been harvested in very hot weather. A remarkably healthy crop apparently gave a wine that was still fermenting in the summer of 1835, much to the desperation of the Bergier cellar archivist.

Hermitage was at the time well known in its own right, as the famous French novelist Alexandre Dumas, author of *The Three Musketeers*, recorded in 1834. Travelling around the Midi region of

France with his friend Jadin, he arrived one night at Tain-l'Hermitage.

> The next morning [he wrote] I was up first and went for a walk.
> On returning to the hotel, I took Jadin to the window and invited
> him to salute the hill that dominated the town. Jadin hailed it
> wholeheartedly, but when I told him that it was the hill of
> Hermitage, he immediately repeated his action quite of his own
> accord; . . . we both considered Hermitage to be one of the best
> wines of France.

Despite such praise, Hermitage was a regular supplier to the
merchants of Bordeaux from the second half of the eighteenth century
for nearly 100 years, until the advent of phylloxera, its role being to
strengthen the finer wines of Bordeaux. H. Warner Allen, in his
History of Wine,[1] quotes from The Letter Books of Nathaniel
Johnston, written between 1799 and 1809 to his partner Guestier in
Bordeaux.

> I was averse to using Roussillon on our best wines, unless it be a
> gallon or two, and that if you could get a sufficient quantity of
> good Hermitage to put a couple of Cans of it, it would be better.
> The Lafitte of 1795, which was made up with Hermitage, was the
> best liked wine of any of that year.

In the Bergier cellar book, we find that the July 1830 Revolution
hindered the sale of their wine, but that none the less Bordeaux
bought some later on: Hermitage had obviously become pretty
indispensable in providing all the best châteaux with superior staying
power. Edmund Penning-Rowsell, in his *Wines of Bordeaux*,[2]
mentioned a Château Ausone 1880 he had drunk, 'without much
hope', in 1967:

> It was surprisingly good. The colour, though pale, was much truer
> than the previous bottle [of Ausone 1880], the nose was fruity,
> and the body had a fullness that did actually suggest a St-Émilion.
> It had been *château*-bottled, and perhaps was *hermitagé*.

That year was certainly quite late for Hermitage still to be boosting
the great *châteaux*, for the practice seems to have reached its peak
around the 1860s, when, according to the late M. Paul Gauthier of

[1] H. Warner Allen, *History of Wine* (London: David and Charles, 1961)
[2] Edmund Penning-Rowsell, *Wines of Bordeaux* (London: International Wine &
Food Society, 1969)

Tain-l'Hermitage, labels like Margaux would proclaim with some pride that they were 'Château Margaux – Hermitage'.

Hermitage held its renown until near the end of the last century, with a following in Britain, if silver decanter labels of the period are any yardstick. However, the early part of this century signalled a sharp downturn in fortunes; young men failed to return from the Great War, and the vineyards suffered from the same lack of interest and manpower that affected Condrieu, for instance.

By the 1960s Hermitage held a connoisseur's following, both in France and elsewhere. Demand never greatly exceeded supply, and prices lagged a long way behind the Bordeaux *crus classés* and all the main Côtes de Nuits and Côtes de Beaune red wines. In the 1970s, press coverage and reporting on the wine increased, as did international awareness of the Rhône and the value it offered, and Hermitage started to be bought by a wider audience. Single-vineyard growers suddenly found themselves visited by foreign buyers, and the media spotlight swung heavily on to the easy name, the one that could offer any sort of quantity with good quality attached – Paul Jaboulet Aîné. Utterances from this house served as a definitive vintage summary on the whole Rhône Valley for stay-at-home wine journalists, and all the while prices pushed steadily ahead.

By the mid-1980s futures in Hermitage red wines had become a commonplace offering from mainly British and American wine merchants. The play here is to create in front of the consumer the view that the opening is the one chance of obtaining access to these prized, rare wines. An early scramble ensues, speculation develops as Hermitage becomes 'the latest thing', and prices at the retail end soar.

There is a runaway-train momentum at work here, what the controversial but punchy writer Andrew Barr calls 'the Falernian syndrome': 'In a natural progression, high quality is followed by a good reputation, which leads to abuse and consequently to downfall.'[1] Falernian was the most celebrated of Roman wines, and fell out of favour because more attention was paid to quantity than quality (Pliny the Elder, *Natural History*, AD 77, Book 14, Chapter 8).

What Andrew Barr omitted was the stage that occurs between enhanced reputation and the drive for both greater quantity and a

[1] Andrew Barr, *Wine Snobbery* (London: Faber and Faber, 1988)

more homogeneous product: the heating of demand by intermediaries, so that in-bond offers on strictly limited quantities occur. Take the spring 1987 offer from British wine merchant Henry Townsend: 'The worldwide demand for these wines is such that they are now only available in restricted quantities' (referring to Paul Jaboulet's Crozes-Hermitage, Gigondas, Cornas, Châteauneuf-du-Pape, Côte-Rôtie and Hermitage). 'Quantities are limited and the quality excellent; the simple Côtes du Rhône offers exceptional value' (referring to Guigal's Côtes du Rhône, Côte-Rôtie and Hermitage). How anybody in their right mind could put up front good money to order any red Côtes du Rhône, however good, in advance of its shipment from France is beyond comprehension.

Opening offers and in-bond orders for Rhône wines now include the basic table wine of the region – Côtes du Rhône – the sound northern wine of St-Joseph, Crozes-Hermitage – the workhorse in terms of volume – plus all the other northern *appellations* from Cornas up to Côte-Rôtie. The writer is approached by merchants asking for a few hot tips with a view to getting some opening offers going, and refuses to become involved in this speculative brokerage activity that ultimately does nothing for the interests of the true enthusiast consumer.

The speculators have one ace card – at Hermitage they know that there will never be too much – there is no risk of over-supply. They focus their speculation on the big-name producers, while most traditional country growers still offer their wine ex-cellars at around £10 or US$18 per bottle. Is Guigal's La Turque Côte-Rôtie 1986 really worth £172.50 retail (offered by T & W Wines, *Decanter*, January 1991)? The question is intended to be rhetorical. Even a committed Rhône man can see the triumph of money over sense here.

Over-supply of Hermitage is impossible because production is severely limited, both by law and by the sheer physical layout of the famous hillside. Whereas the *vignerons* of nearby *appellations* like St-Joseph and Côte-Rôtie can alter their vineyard size and allocation by local rulings, both Hermitage and Cornas are restricted by national legislation. This serves as an excellent quality control and acts to avoid the sort of plateau expansion or riverside flatland cultivation that has made some wines from Côte-Rôtie or St-Joseph unworthy of their increasing prices.

The Hermitage vineyards cover only 126 hectares, and the first increase in their area for many years occurred in 1984, when Gérard

Chave cleared 2.5 hectares around L'Hermite. The hillside acts as its own natural boundary. It is convex in shape, and rises abruptly away from the centre of Tain to reach a natural point of focus near its summit with the chapel of St Christopher, at night-time an incandescent glow perched on a looming dark shape. Down-river of this central site runs a spur, half the height and the home of the most easterly vineyards, those *mas* known as Les Diognières, L'Homme and La Croix de Torras. The vines throughout enjoy a sunny, near full-south exposure.

The gradients are a little less steep than Côte-Rôtie's, but many of the problems such as awkward access, a loose topsoil and maintenance of retaining walls remain. Much cultivation is still manual, although in the 1980s the vines started to be sprayed by helicopter, bringing a considerable freeing-up of labour. Otherwise the pattern is still much the same as it ever was – work runs from dawn to dusk, and under the early morning sunshine little bands of *vignoble* workers weave their way slowly up the hillside, where they spend the rest of the day. These specialized vineyard workers often belong to the large *négociant* companies like Chapoutier and Jaboulet, and traditionally pass down their expertise and their anecdotes from father to son.

The soil that they must work on is granitic and, in places, quite unyielding. The rock base is sprinkled with a fine layer of decomposed flint and chalk, which after heavy rain escapes the bonds of the retaining walls and slides steadily down the hillside; carrying it back and tightly repacking the terrace walls is therefore a difficult but regular task.

The unusual fact that the Hermitage hill, on the east bank of the Rhône, should be granite is explained by a geological transformation which took place many thousands of years ago. Then the Rhône flowed past the other, more easterly, side of the hillside; Hermitage was consequently a part of the granitic Massif Central mountain range which lies behind Tournon. At some indeterminate date the river changed its course and burrowed out today's beautiful valley.

Hermitage red wine is made principally from the Syrah grape, although because most vineyards have been planted – normally with Syrah as well as Marsanne – in a rather unplanned way over the years, a maximum of 15 per cent white grapes from the Marsanne and the less popular Roussanne are permitted to enter the fermenting vats with the Syrah. This is a decree designed to make the *vigneron*'s life easier – so that he can harvest a whole vineyard instead of having to return later to one or two *souches* of white grapes – but as the Marsanne has quite a high glycerine content, it is thought that its presence can give the red wine a little extra richness and profundity. Apparently, few growers ever use much more than 5 per cent Marsanne in their red Hermitage, although they can be tempted to add more in years of Syrah losses from setbacks such as *coulure* or malformation of the fruit.

The exposed Hermitage hill is an ideal home for the Syrah, since sun and wind are abundant, while the granite acts as a useful heat-retainer. Temperatures on the top of the hill on a sunny summer's day are surprisingly high, with so many terraced walls all around absorbing and radiating the sun's heat. It is similar down at the foot of the vineyards, for there a low stone wall provides shelter as it runs along the curve of the hillside and is broken only every 45 metres or so by iron gates that indicate the entrance to a new *clos*.

A meteorological study conducted at the end of the last century revealed an average temperature in the vineyards of 13.9°C, a figure more normally associated with Mediterranean France: what it would reveal after the run of scorching summers in the 1980s is anybody's guess. Under such conditions the Syrah has every chance to produce well, and in a more consistent way than it does at Côte-Rôtie.

Between one-quarter and one-third of all the wine is white, a surprisingly high percentage since there are many enthusiasts who know the red well but who have never tried or even seen the white wine. As a quality white with the most interesting ageing possibilities, it still has trouble obtaining a following. In price it is around the level of a *premier cru* Chablis, a little below a Meursault, and there is no doubt that consumers naturally lean towards a well-publicized Chardonnay rather than this more obscure wine.

White Hermitage is made principally from the Marsanne – Chapoutier, who have the excellent, and until the late 1980s old-fashioned keeping *cuvée* Chante-Alouette, back it 100 per cent, as do smaller proprietors like Jean-Louis Grippat and Philippe Desmeure, while Gérard Chave's whites are 85 per cent Marsanne. The exception to the rule is the House of Jaboulet, whose Chevalier de Stérimberg, a finer style of white Hermitage, is made up of only 55 per cent Marsanne, with the Roussanne taking 45 per cent. The two white grape vines are generally planted across the hillside in small patches of clay-topped ground.

The Marsanne is the more favoured of the two since it is considerably less prone to disease and so not only regularly produces more
fruit, but is also cheaper to look after. It a vine vilified unfairly by
wine writers such as Jancis Robinson, who in her entertaining *Vines,
Grapes and Wines* says that the Marsanne, alas, seems to be winning
the territorial dispute against the Viognier in the north of the St-
Joseph *appellation*, and that it produces wines of perhaps too much
substance.[1] Such an assessment does not stand up when wines like
Chave's 1985, Grippat's 1983 (both tasted in 1990) are considered,
or the utterly delicious pre-Roussanne wines of Jaboulet – their 1961
or 1967 Chevalier de Stérimberg (tasted in 1991). And even when
transplanted to Australia at Château Tahbilk in Victoria, the 80 per
cent Marsanne, 20 per cent Chardonnay white certainly carries
greater depth on the bouquet than would a pure Chardonnay. Bonny
Doon in California is another estate whose Marsanne blend shows
this underestimated vine in its true colours.

The Roussanne experienced an upsurge of popularity during the
1980s in the Rhône, but results from the southern Rhône have in many
ways been more successful. The excellent Château de Beaucastel at
Châteauneuf-du-Pape makes probably the classiest white Châteauneuf with Roussanne, whereas offerings from the north of the Valley
– be they from the singular version that exists at St-Péray or through
blends with other grapes – have often shown a disappointing tendency
to be thin rather than fine and to oxidize more quickly than one
would expect from a fairly acidic wine. Despite *vignerons* taking
more interest in this vine – Jean Lionnet uses 20 per cent in his St-
Péray, Bernard Gripa 10 per cent, for example – it is still a stubborn
producer, susceptible to oïdium and slow to ripen.

Some Hermitage *vignerons* have followed modern marketing
devices by putting a sub-name on their labels – Marc Sorrel sells Le
Gréal, a blend of Le Méal and Les Greffieux, and Michel Ferraton
La Cuvée des Miaux, a blend of Le Méal and Beaumes. But the major
suppliers, like Chave and Jaboulet, have not succumbed to this recent
temptation of subdividing their production – indeed, the former is
steadfastly opposed to such moves.

Every year Chave blends the wines made from his multiple holdings
spread over the hillside. His intention is to make one definable style
of wine, and he regards his greatest challenge as being precisely the

---

[1] Jancis Robinson, *Vines, Grapes and Wines* (London: Mitchell Beazley, 1986).

successful integration of all the different *cuvées* from his plots: he positively licks his lips at the prospect of a little alchemy each year. So a thorough tasting in his musty cellars in Mauves covers as many as eight *climats*, whose wines in cask individually reveal widely differing characteristics. In a similar way the House of Jaboulet concentrates its blend that finally becomes La Chapelle on grapes from two *climats*, Le Méal and Les Bessards.

One of the traps awaiting the drinker of northern Rhône reds is the fact that the growers like to spread out the bottling of a single vintage over a period of twelve months. If the next harvest has suffered early setbacks from severe frost or poor flowering, for instance, the *vignerons* will already look to cover their stocks of cellared wines, and will deliberately hold back a last *tranche* from an earlier vintage. Space constrictions in the usually small Rhône cellars have traditionally made it easier to hold wine in cask or tank than in bottle: for example, even a *vigneron* like Gérard Chave, with a large holding, only built a bottle extension in the early 1980s.

There will therefore sometimes be differences in what is ostensibly the same wine from the same grower in the same vintage. A case in point is Chave's 1978, which has shown differently on several of the eight occasions when it has been tasted (and drunk) between 1982 and 1990. The earliest bottling holds more of a fruit underlay and shows itself more vigorously and freshly than the sometimes subdued later bottling, which is firmer, less flamboyant and, for most people, less impressive.

A source of endless fascination is the different styles of wine produced from the different sites on the Hermitage hill. Back in the 1866 edition of *Topographie de tous les Vignobles Connus*, A. Jullien listed his three outstanding vineyards: Les Bessards, at the western limit of the hill, producing a deep-coloured, sturdy wine; Le Méal next to it, with very small stones, chalky soil and a fine, perfumed wine; Les Greffieux, below Le Méal, producer of generous, supple wine. It was Jullien's claim that the ideal bottle of Hermitage was formed through a combination of these three growths.

Chave's Hermitage is the most exotic of current-day offerings, with its composition of wine from eight growths. They run the range from single-*climat* wines that show elegance, a bright colour and open aromas even when young, to wines that have solid purple colours, good richness and length and a firm tannic backing behind their berried fruit, to wines that are a monstrous dark colour when young, very closed on the bouquet and running with tannin almost to the point of severity.

In the first group are the light, aromatic and charming wines of Les Beaumes (clay–sandstone soil), Les Diognières (sandy soil) and L'Hermite (clay–limestone). In the second group are Péléat (Chave is the sole owner of this hectare that he bought off the late Terence Gray; its soil is *poudin* or clayey), whose wines are very concentrated and show great flair on the finish; and Les Rocoules (clay-topped) whose wines are blessed with strong fruit extracts and good, complex structure. In the third group, fully corresponding to George Saintsbury's 'manly' quote, are Petits Bessards and Grands Bessards (granite and decomposed granite) and Le Méal (clay–sandstone and chalk with small stones).

Of the other *climats* that figure prominently, Les Greffieux, on which Chapoutier has a large holding, as well as the smaller *viticulteurs* Bernard Faurie and Marc Sorrel, produces wine that is firmer than that from Les Rocoules – bright purple and vigorous, with strong tannins on the finish. The soil here is mainly stony.

The best-known finished red over the years has been Paul Jaboulet Aîné's La Chapelle, which is a registered title that they use for their most select wine. There is not actually a vineyard called La Chapelle, but the Jaboulet family own the tiny chapel that stands near the top of the hill on the *lieu-dit* of L'Hermite. Meanwhile, the most famous wine sold under its *vigneron*'s name alone is Gérard Chave's – his red and white are both superb.

For white Hermitage, the most celebrated growths are the romantically named Chante-Alouette, which sits just above Le Méal in the centre of the hillside, Les Rocoules and Les Murets. The last two are split by the road from Tain to Larnage, Les Rocoules standing nearer the centre of the hill than the Murets. The Rocoules white invariably reveals the classic nuttiness or peach-stone scent given by white Hermitage. Wine from Les Murets tends to be a little finer and very well balanced, while Chante-Alouette gives the most robust wine of the three.

From such innocuous-sounding vineyards comes the mighty wine of Hermitage, a wine that displays abundant strength and massive depth of flavour, be it red or white. Hermitage red is still capable of being one of the world's longest-lived wines, which in a concentrated, tannic vintage and vinified along traditional lines will last for a good forty years: 1978 is a good example.

When young, it is robust, rich in dark fruits – sometimes berries, sometimes more stewed fruit flavours. Tannin runs around the edges and often down the middle, searing an unsuspecting palate with its closing severity, while there is generally a firm alcoholic backing to the wine which, because of the power of its other constituents, is rarely very noticeable. The colour is a dazzler – brilliant purple, with traces of jet-black in it. The bouquet is closed, initially difficult to draw out; the main aromas are often those of under-ripe blackcurrants or raspberries. Such a wine excites simply through the inordinate promise that all the diverse elements and aromas display, and for anyone seeking the best, most classic example of young Syrah to be found anywhere, he or she can do worse than to seek out a bottle of Chave, the 1983 perhaps, for this is wine in the grand old manner.

With all but the lightest vintages – years like 1975, 1977, 1984 and 1987, which are great to drink between five and ten years old – it is a crime even to contemplate touching a bottle of red Hermitage before its sixth or seventh birthday. The bouquet can start to loosen up by its eighth or tenth year, as the precocious wild fruit aromas soften out and develop a more plum-like aspect, accompanied by the odd pepper and spice touches. The palate remains backward and tannic for a long time, however, since the Syrah at Hermitage needs ample time to develop and unfold all its potential and complexity. Middle-weight years like 1979, 1982, 1986, 1989 and 1991 start to show their true worth between eight and twelve years old, although they can be drinkable for easily twenty years as the tannins loosen and the wine loses some of its grip.

With age, red Hermitage acquires an uncommon equilibrium and a finesse that would have been bet against early in its life. The full-bodied constituents demand time and patience to integrate and develop a rich, enveloping harmony. Unlike wines from Bordeaux or old-fashioned Burgundies, an aged Hermitage still has an impressive and succulent richness at its centre – the fruit of its southern climes never deserts it, so that it dries out less obviously than many other great French reds. Great Hermitage twenty to thirty years old, from the best vintages and the best makers, stands alongside the best wines of Bordeaux, or of anywhere on earth for that matter: save up and try to find the La Chapelle 1961 or the Chave 1952, both of which were still going strong in 1991, and see.

One of the main reasons why Hermitage lives for so long is that it is still usually vinified by traditional methods that have just gently been revived through the use of modern cellar equipment. Few attempts are made to over-hasten the early development of the wine. One of the reasons for this is that the pool of growers at Hermitage has remained remarkably stable over the past twenty-five years. There have been almost no new entrants of note; generally succession goes from father to son, or brave smallholders like Dard and Ribo leave the Co-opérative to have a go on their own.

Harvest-time is always one of excitement at Tain, for that is what the town lives for. Teams of pickers, between fifteen and thirty strong, are dispatched up the hillside, and their progress can be easily monitored from across the river in Tournon, so prominent is the Hermitage hillside and so colourful the harvesters' clothing. As in most of the northern Rhône vineyards, the work is exacting; the full grape boxes, the lightest of which are made of plastic and weigh around 25 kilograms, have to be brought to tracks running alongside the vineyards, where tractors or the occasional donkey and cart are waiting to take them down to the cellars in the town.

Since the early 1970s it seems that some growers are more actively driven by a conscious philosophy over their date of harvesting: whereas there used to be evident variations according to nature's work during the year, nowadays certainly Chave and Chapoutier like to pick late as a regular matter of policy, while Jaboulet are earlier with their *vendanges*. Michel Chapoutier comments, 'We've always been about the last harvesters at Hermitage since we're seeking a really thorough extract of ripe fruit from the grapes. It's a large operation for us, with maybe eighty people up on the hill, and a tractor leaving with ten boxes of grapes every five minutes or so.' By way of contrast, Jaboulet are seeking more *nervosité* for their whites, for example, and so like to pick their white crop when there are higher levels of acidity in it.

After a light treading – still practised at Chapoutier – or a gentle pump-crush, the grapes are loaded into the fermenting vats, all of which used to be stout open wood containers until ten years or so ago. Now Jaboulet, Delas and Desmeure use closed concrete vats, Sorrel a mix of stainless steel and open wood, Chave enamel-lined and stainless steel, and Chapoutier, Bernard Faurie and Grippat open wood. Louis Jaboulet puffs and dismisses open fermenting vats as being something 'from the Middle Ages': as this house seeks and obtains a more commercial style of wine, his remark is not surprising.

The open vats, stained purple with accumulated years of holding fresh Syrah juice, give the wine-maker like Chapoutier or Grippat extra hard work when he wants to keep the fermentation temperature under control. At this stage Grippat reaches for his *pichet*, a short wooden stump on the end of a handle that resembles a croquet mallet, in order to immerse and moisten the *chapeau* and cool off the vat. This work of striking down the *chapeau* while leaning over the top of the vat is strenuous and takes at least twenty minutes for each vat. Once in the morning and once in the evening for up to a week means a lot of time spent on this one task, but it is an indication of the desire to seek what the grower regards as perfection.

Views are mixed on destalking. Chapoutier and Jaboulet both destalk their entire harvest: Louis Jaboulet says, 'We've destalked entirely since 1987 or so, and find that we get finer tannins, finer and more elegant wines.' Grippat and Fauries do not destalk, however, and Chave and Delas only destalk if the harvest is under-ripe; in 1991 Delas destalked half their crop, in 1990 none of it.

Those vinifiers who have turned to glass-lined closed concrete vats for their primary fermentation – Paul Jaboulet Aîné, for instance – are therefore able to control and vary the temperature during fermentation without undue difficulty. Jaboulet allow their *cuves* to rise towards the 30°sC before falling back to 28°C, to obtain decent colour extraction. As Chapoutier now reach for just a little less robustness, something that some used to describe as an almost rustic style, so they have eased back the average temperature of the fermenting must in their open vats from 30°C to 27°C; this, they hope, obtains a little more fruit flavour – raspberry, perhaps – in the wine. The other tactic they are using in the 1990s to obtain greater extract from their grapes is a simple one – lower yields per hectare from severely pruned vines that are fed and treated only in a natural way.

Unless the harvest has delivered grapes in absolutely tip-top condition, it is at this stage that much of the wine's style, and therefore the *appellation* style, is determined. There is no doubt that today the House of Jaboulet is less consistently capable under its present methods and policy of coming up with a massively layered and structured, backward red Hermitage that could live and blossom for many years as the 1961 La Chapelle has. Of the last fifteen years, only the 1978, 1982 and 1990 have the full, fleshy southern intensity that marked out many La Chapelles of the 1960s.

The debate about wines reflecting their *terroir* – about faithfully representing their grape variety when grown in favourable soils and conditions – seems irrelevant if a house policy is to homogenize the wines through a series of measures that ultimately combine to chip away the regionality. Apart from 1990, most recent tastings of La Chapelle have rarely set the pulses racing as they did in the 1970s: by the vintages of the late 1980s the consumer has often been presented with a safe, technically sound product whose taste contains reflections of the current fashionable methods prevalent in wine-making anywhere in the world: drink La Chapelle 1989 and you are cruising down the Rue du Faubourg St Honoré in Paris – no mysteries, lots of gloss; drink La Chapelle 1964, 1966, 1969 or 1971 and you're in the side streets of *vieux* Lyon – robust kitchen aromas in the air, broader accents carried on the breeze, intrigue around the corner.

The primary fermentation lasts for between two and three weeks, and the red wine subsequently spends at least one year ageing in wood. Like most places in the Rhône, there are mixed views on the ageing process. Jaboulet use only 225-litre *pièces*; around February their wine is taken off its large lees, the different vats are assembled then placed for eighteen months into casks whose age varies from brand new (28 per cent of the 1988 La Chapelle, for example) up to three years old. Gérard Chave uses a mixture of *pièces*, 600-litre *demi-muids* and *foudres* of around 15 hectolitres. His softer *cuvées* like L'Hermite and Les Diognières go into *foudres*, while sterner *cuvées* like Le Méal are expected to calm down in *pièces*. M. Chave says he uses brand new oak 'with great parsimony', and tasting from a new *demi-muid* of his 1989 red off Les Bessards, one notices that some of the Bessards nuances fail to appear – there is a little flavour of *cassis* but notably a strong dryness on the finish, an imposition rather than a naturally integrated element. Overall, his reds receive fifteen to eighteen months' ageing in wood.

Until 1991 Chapoutier was one of the last producers still using chestnut casks, and indeed only started to use oak in the mid-1980s. Chestnut is the traditional wood of the region, supplies being drawn from the Ardèche. Michel Chapoutier is not hesitant in declaring his total aversion to the use of chestnut, which he thinks helped hold back quality at Chapoutier in the past. 'Chestnut casks are lovely for barbecues', he states in trenchant tones. The new wood coming in from Burgundy is either brand new or one year old. The Chapoutier method is to start the wine off either in *demi-muids* or in *pièces* and to leave it for fifteen to eighteen months, with rackings every three months before bottling. The bottling process may run over a certain period, so that the first *tranche* of 1988 Hermitage was bottled around April 1990 after a final stay of six months in *pièces*. The last *tranche* received around a year longer in cask.

Delas maintain a flexible approach with the use of their old *foudres* and young *pièces*. 'In good years like 1990 we leave the wine around eighteen months, in lesser years like 1987 only twelve months', states chief wine-maker Antoine Fuchs. 'If the wine is exposed to young wood, it may spend twelve months there, and then be put in the older *foudres* to balance it. Our main change at this stage is that since 1990 we haven't filtered the wine before putting it in cask – only racked it.'

The smaller cultivators vary their approaches. Marc Sorrel ages his wine for around sixteen months in Burgundy and Bordeaux casks, with the emphasis on young wood, and runs his bottling programme from sixteen months to over two years after the harvest. Bernard Faurie's tiny cellar is lined with *demi-muids* on three of its sides, old oak being the order of the day, with bottling around fifteen to twenty months after the harvest. Jean-Louis Grippat places his young wine in either vats or *pièces* for four to five months – while it does the malolactic – and then in *demi-muids* for a maximum of twelve months. He has one new *pièce* for every seven old ones on average: he says that for him, 'The old casks bring a *patine* – a polish – to the wine, not an addition or intrusion.'

Of course cost determines much of what the growers do, so that while as a group they are far more conscious than before of the need to keep their barrels spotless and to replace them more frequently than in their fathers' time, they cannot generally effect wholesale changes in their cellars. That is why Marc Sorrel, for instance, uses a mix of second-growth Bordeaux *barriques* and Burgundy *pièces* with the ten- to twenty-two-year-old casks introduced by his late father.

During its stay in wood, Hermitage's early rough edges slowly wear off, but even when bottled after eighteen months in cask the wine demands at least a further five years if it is to have a chance to develop a rounded harmony. As it advances towards middle and old age – anywhere from ten years up – it is inclined to throw a substantial deposit, and decanting is therefore an advantage before drinking it.

White Hermitage is credited in many books with almost the same remarkable keeping qualities as the red wine; this definitely holds true in outstanding vintages, made by traditional vinifiers like Chapoutier and Chave or by Jaboulet before the mid-1960s: a 1929 white made by Gérard Chave's grandfather was astoundingly rich and still very long on the palate when drunk in the summer of 1986. Its vigour held after opening, with a warm variety of honeyed, dried fruit and floral aromas emerging on the bouquet, and a classic white Hermitage nuttiness on the palate. Similarly a 1961 white from Chapoutier tasted in April 1990 still held a good lustre to the eye, showed a lovely depth of nutty aroma on the nose, and on the palate possessed excellent finesse around a powerful, rich structure. The wine was still a bit closed. Michel Chapoutier offers his opinion that the malolactic fermentation must be done if his whites are to age well – which, of course, opposes the more modernist school like Jaboulet who like to obtain freshness and what they call style from a systematic blocking of the malo. Overall the realistic length of life for a traditionally made white Hermitage is thirty years or more, and the wine's evolution over that time delivers a stream of pleasant surprises.

As an example of a white Hermitage made by traditional instincts that have been pepped up by some innovative thinking, Chapoutier's Chante-Alouette is made from a crop that is harvested after those of other growers. Since 1988, the wine has been fermented at three different temperatures; one-third ferments in new Tronçay oak casks at a natural 23°; one-third in enamel-lined vats at 19–20°, and the final third in stainless steel vats at 17°. 'The cask brings spice aromas, the enamel vat mostly flower aromas and the stainless steel mainly fruit aromas', declares Michel Chapoutier. Once assembled, all the wine spends four months in young oak with bottling a year after the harvest.

'We seek a wine that has the potential to develop over ten years at least, and the process starts with our relatively delayed harvesting, where we obtain more glycerol', adds Chapoutier, who emulates his father Max by dint of his bouncy walk, his lack of inches and his ability to make a statement like 'Hermitage *blanc must* be 14° alcohol – without that it's not Hermitage at all.' The Chante-Alouettes of the mid-1980s – 1984 and 1985 – support this comment, running with big aromas, fat, rich flavours and excellent, chewy length. The Chante-Alouette of 1988 shows a slightly lighter approach but still retains the essential Hermitage richness – the difference is that it will drink well around 1994. The 1989 is very well-measured on the palate, and may take eight years or so to show in an open way, while the 1990 gains momentum on the palate, a dry attack leading to a lasting, rich finish. These wines are a little more tight and less full-blown than previous Chante-Alouettes.

For *vignerons* like Sorrel and Bernard Faurie, fermenting in cask is the best method for the white. Sorrel uses wood aged up to ten years and runs a steady fermentation at about 18°C for as long as four or five weeks while Faurie has rejected stainless steel for his fermentation after using it for two harvests: 'I want more than primary perfumes from my wine,' he comments. 'The stainless steel brings lots of early fruit and aromas, but I don't think there is much behind them afterwards, later on.'

Chave uses half enamel-lined vats, half wood, while Grippat ferments wholly in enamel-lined vats. Jaboulet's thinking in using stainless steel or glass-lined vats at the start of the process is partly governed by their desire to prevent the malolactic taking place. Since 1987 they have left the wine briefly in new oak before bottling – two months in 1987 and six months in 1988–1991. 'With our 45 per cent Roussanne content, the wine has an acidity that can take the new oak', comments Gérard Jaboulet.

M. Gérard Jaboulet

Gérard Chave is after a compromise from the differing influences of cask and vat, so he assembles a final wine whose parts have been exposed to two-year oak, old oak and enamel vats. His bottling occurs fifteen to eighteen months after the harvest, just like Grippat's and Chapoutier's, and by then the malolactic has been completed.

Jaboulet adjusted their white Stérimberg vinification away from an overtly lightweight style in the late 1980s, and in 1990 succeeded in making one of the best, most full-tasting Stérimbergs of recent times. Only time will indicate how their use of young wood will affect these wines' development. Gérard Jaboulet, as befits a younger wine-maker who is good friends with Olivier Leflaive and Marcel Vincent who make modern white burgundies with a very marked influence of new oak, in 1988 used 50 per cent Jura oak and 50 per cent Vosges oak. 'The Vosges imparts finesse and elegance, while the Jura brings a more marked wood taste', comments Gérard. 'We don't have fixed rules, since each year's fruit is different. Accordingly in 1989 we used the same ratio of Jura and Vosges, but half the casks were brand new and half one year old. In 1990 we used only brand new oak.'

Jaboulet's adjustments to their white Hermitage have now taken place over nearly thirty years. They first started to block the malolactic in 1963 and 1964; they first planted large numbers of Roussanne in 1970; they turned to fermenting in stainless steel in the late 1970s, and they first used new oak in 1987. At least they are not hidebound by their own rules: they allowed the malolactic to take place in 1984, a year marked by above average acidity due to the poor summer and early autumn weather, while in 1983 they picked their Marsanne crop late, so as to give the wine a high alcohol content and the sort of guts that it used to possess in the late 1970s

The wine is therefore shifting its style on a fairly regular basis, but the overall effect of lightening it seems most obvious in its impact on the flavours once they have a certain age – four to seven years, say. Prominent citrus aromas are not generally associated with white Hermitage – Gérard Chave talks of acacia or hazelnuts but never citrus fruit, for example – while the residual vanilla finish left by new wood places the wine in a bland, cosmopolitan category.

A review of Stérimbergs of the 1980s makes interesting reading, since there is no fixed pattern to them. The 1983 and 1985 are likely to develop well over about ten years, the former showing very well after only two years, the latter being richer and more reticent. The 1987 was a subtle-tasting wine, although the new oak is marked in this fairly light vintage, while the 1988 possesses a solid bouquet, and medium weight on the palate – this wine may live for around seven years, or it may just run a little further, perhaps up to twelve years: the prominent new oak overlay makes a judgment difficult.

The 1989 is a disappointment in that its flavours are neutral and lack definition. Fortunately, the 1990 is altogether a more convincing, fuller and better balanced wine. In the meantime it is well worth looking out for Stérimberg wines dated from the start of the 1970s or earlier, to see how they can grow into a splendid complex fullness over the course of ten to twenty years. The 1971 is a prime example of a wine that after twenty years gained greater complexity and a delicious line-up of different flavours. It will be equally interesting to see whether the 1980s wines can achieve a similar complexity, diversity of flavour and staying-power in the course of their development.

The best white Hermitage made in the traditional way starts life a pale yellow, with sometimes a trace of a darker straw colour present. In really fat vintages like 1985 this can be a very pale gold even by the age of six. The wines are always strongly scented ('peaches or apricots, also acacia', say certain growers) and noticeably southern on the bouquet, with a warmth and ripeness absent from other high-class French whites. The generally high share of Marsanne gives great richness and roundness. Some tasters detect a *goût de noisette* on the long aftertaste – a sort of nuttiness that lurks at the back of the throat. After around eight years the wine has taken on a firm golden colour, and its extraordinary richness is more than ever apparent. Some wines, however, have a tendency to pass through a 'dumb' phase at between about three and six years old; this sounds strange, but is also observable with certain traditionally made white wines at Châteauneuf-du-Pape. One finds the colour correct – showing rich yellows – but both the bouquet and the palate fail to reveal the full extent of the aromas and the flavours, almost as if they were being held back by a magic hand. Returning to the same wine when it is eight years old, one is often bowled over by its all-round appeal and complexity of taste, both elements acquired with age. Perhaps these wines do not like being middle-aged and would rather pass straight from being quite young to quite old!

By the age of about twenty-five white Hermitage has nearly run its race, and only the greatest vintages, if well kept, will live for much longer. Because of its happy balance of power and elegance, most white Hermitage is the ideal accompaniment for chicken, veal, wild mushroom dishes, fish with heavy sauces and, very particularly, poached Scotch salmon. And when around eight years old, it is excellent to drink with game pâtés and terrines.

Until the turn of the century another white wine was regularly made at Hermitage by another method – the *vin de paille*, which today is found in the Jura region of France, east of Burgundy, although the Hermitage growers still possess the right to make it. Recently Gérard Chave, the House of Chapoutier, Michel Ferraton, Jean-Louis Grippat, the Cave Co-opérative de Tain and Guigal have all satisfied their curiosity about this legendary wine. Chave led the way, starting with an experiment in 1974, and more recently made a couple of *pièces* in 1986 and a little more in 1989: this turns out now in a special half-bottle he found in Italy, with a natural alcohol degree of 16°, made entirely from Marsanne . . . and the lads simply cannot get enough of it. Chave is besieged by all France's best chefs to sell them just a little of this legendary wine, but he plays a tight game of poker, and the wine is virtually *hors commerce*. Greater, more commercial quantities are very successfully made by Chapoutier – 15 hectolitres in 1990 and 7 hectolitres in 1991 – still not much!

M. Chave tells the tale of his *vin de paille* very well, especially when all present are seated with a glass of this extraordinary wine in their hands. 'I had been thinking of trying this experiment for several years, and eventually selected the 1974 crop. I didn't leave the grapes on the vines particularly late, choosing to pick them at the end of normal harvesting. I then separated them one by one and laid them out individually on straw on the floor of the attic above the *cuverie*; I used the straw that ties up the vines against their support stakes in the vineyards.

'The grapes stayed in the attic for a month and a half, and I was careful not to let them dry out since this would have robbed them of their remaining concentrated juice. I remember that my parents always used to give us dried raisins on Christmas Day, having let the grapes completely dry out. Anyway, I then pressed the grapes and started off the fermentation. Normally I estimate that to make a bottle of my white Hermitage I need to use 1.3 kilograms of grapes; with the *vin de paille* I needed 4 kilograms for each bottle.

'The straw wine fermented in cask on and off for two years. I did no racking during this drawn-out fermentation, mainly because the must was entirely clean – the grapes had been especially healthy at the time of pressing so that there seemed no need to disturb the wine. Once the *malo* had taken place, I bottled the wine, and here it is.'

The delivery is not quite deadpan, for there is a tiny wry smile right at the end, as is permitted men who know that their experiment has been a glorious success. Chave's *vin de paille* has the writer scrambling for his thesaurus as he seeks the correct array of adjectives to put such a brilliant, extraordinary wine in perspective. A bottle of 1974 drunk in 1982 presented a lustrous dark gold *robe*, with a soaring bouquet of concentrated richness, the aromas being most reminiscent of flowers and honey. Then the surprise – the incredible richness continued on to the palate and through to the aftertaste, but left a crystal-clear, bitingly clean finish. The flavours, similar to honey and fresh fruit jams, such was the concentration, ended with a winning dryness. Alcohol degree 14.5° – no sense of this at all.

As a comparison, a 37.5-cl bottle of 1986 *vin de paille* drunk in 1990 showed a firm gold colour; the bouquet held a fine raisin smell; the palate was very well balanced, with a delightful attack and very rich, explosive flavours – nuts, dry cheese and some almost essence of greengage, with the nut flavour returning on the finish. The bouquet had plenty of development in it, and the whole wine was very striking. Alcohol degree 16°.

Probably the oldest bottles of Hermitage still in existence are of *vin de paille*. The Chapoutier family of Tain have an 1848 *vin de paille*, decanted in 1910, 1948 and 1977, in their personal cellar, while M. Max Chapoutier, the former head of the family firm, once recalled that until only quite recently, they had two even older bottles. Producing from the sideboard of the company's reception room a thickly blown old bottle with a faint, blurred label saying 'Hermitage 1760', he related the following story.

'This bottle of Hermitage *vin de paille* was drunk by my father Marc in 1964. There were two other bottles of this wine, but in the late 1970s they were given back to the Cambourg family, who had originally made the wine, and they have since been drunk. The bottles had certainly moved around, as we had earlier given them to the Sizeranne family after buying a leading Hermitage vineyard from them some years ago. When my father drank this particular bottle, the wine, whose degree was around 17°, was in an impeccable state, showing plenty of full-bodied flavour, even though there was a little ullage.'

Chapoutier is the oldest and largest wine house in Tain. The story goes that the first Chapoutier came down to the Rhône from a village up in the Ardèche some time before the French Revolution, and worked his way up from a simple *caviste* at a firm called Voselgesang until he was in a position, with a partner called Delphine, to buy out

Voselgesang in 1808. Shades of the Guigal story from the 1980s.

The company is a typical family affair, with different generations involved in it. The patriarch today is Marc *père*, in his nineties and a survivor of many rigours during the Second World War, including the arrest of his wife by Klaus Barbie and his torturers in Lyon. He ran the firm from 1937 until 1977, and his son Max was head from 1977 until 1990, when he retired due to ill-health. The company has let youth have its head, and is now run by Max's two sons Marc and Michel, both in their twenties, with the export director, Gilles Charrière, similarly aged. The two boys are full of the usual Chapoutier energy and zest; Michel looks after vinification and the technical side, and Marc is in charge of exports. Michel, slim and dressed in black, looks more the artist; Marc, one year older at twenty-nine and more solidly built, looks the businessman.

Chapoutier's holding at Hermitage is enviable. The company increased its ownership from 23.5 to 26 hectares in the early 1990s and cultivates under *fermage* another 5.5 hectares of the famous hill – just about one quarter of it in total – with 10 hectares of Marsanne spread between Chante-Alouette and Les Murets, and the remaining Syrah plantations sited on Le Méal, Les Greffieux and Les Bessards. Elsewhere in the northern Rhône they own 2.7 hectares at Côte-Rôtie, 5.5 hectares at St-Joseph (including the select St-Joseph hillside vineyard right at the centre of the *appellation*) and 8 hectares at Crozes-Hermitage. *Fermage* accounts for a further 2 hectares at Crozes, 3 at St-Joseph, and just under 1 at Cornas. They also own the 27-hectare estate of La Bernardine at Châteauneuf-du-Pape – red-grape *cépages* only planted on it – which was bought up in the mid-1930s, much to the dismay of Marc *père*'s father Marius. His indignation was extreme when he heard of the family proposal to own a vineyard at Châteauneuf-du-Pape, his memorable utterance being that he would never stoop to selling simple *vin ordinaire*!

Such an impressive array of vineyards was regarded as an economic burden by previous company head Max Chapoutier, who in the early 1980s told the author that Chapoutier had lost money at Côte-Rôtie and St-Joseph every year since 1973. One of the problems cited was the need to employ two full-time vineyard workers on the small but labour intensive Côte-Rôtie holding.

The fact is that the firm lost its way during the 1980s. At a time when quality in the Rhône progressed steadily, under the joint impetus of talented *vignerons* and good vintages, Chapoutier's wines remained stuck in a '*négociant* of yore' groove. There was a general house style – normally big, alcoholic wines – and little individual expression of what each Rhône *appellation* had to offer.

Michel Chapoutier does not hesitate in discussing this. 'We have no more non-vintage wines – not since 1988. I like to work from the vineyards, plot by plot; my father preferred to work by the vintage. We now no longer buy through intermediaries – *courtiers*. We act as a consultant if you like to *vignerons* who are often younger than before – we go and see them, we advise them, we guide them. One of the most significant changes is that we pay them by the hectare, not by the wine they produce. Imagine that – now they can believe in vineyard work like short pruning, restricting the amount each plant produces.' He pauses for breath, his declaration of philosophy moving into top gear: 'For me, the key is restricted production. If you want to really make a wine 'sing', you must get the yields down – only then will the *terroir* express itself ahead of the grape varietal. The grower must be a subordinate to the *terroir* – at all costs.'

The presence of Michel Chapoutier, who has an agricultural training, and his brother Marc at the helm of Chapoutier et Cie has given a lift to the company's reputation, and, more importantly, to its wines. During the 1980s, the House had certain very good *cuvées*, such as Chante-Alouette and the special blended fifteen- to twenty-year wines like the excellent red Hermitage Le Pavillon, the white Hermitage La Cuvée de l'Orée (wines from five or six vintages, average age twelve years – outstanding) and the red Châteauneuf Barbe Rac (delightful, Grenache-driven wine), but suffered from an inability to present a clear set of wines to the consumer. There were so many different versions of Chapoutier wines, with vintage, non-vintage and local bottlings in Britain, for example, that it was very hard to know what one was getting. Now, as an example of the new policy, the Barbe Rac from Châteauneuf, Le Pavillon from Ermitage (old spelling) and La Mordorée from Côte-Rôtie are the House's top red wine selections from each vintage from these leading *appellations* – and are bottled as such. One of the other factors during the late 1970s and much of the 1980s was that, as used to be the case with many Spanish and Chilean wineries, the wine tasted fresh in the cellars, full of promise and bursting with fruit, but rarely seemed to hit those heights when tasted later on in bottle. One suspects that Michel Chapoutier is inclined to blame poor chestnut barrels for much of this drawback.

Recent evidence in tasting the Chapoutier wines points to a definite tick-up in quality and style, and the future for this family affair in the 1990s seems hopeful – the family appear to have a concerted policy and belief in working together, the company is not marked by murky internal politics, and youth is centre-stage.

The Syrah harvest at Hermitage is given an old-fashioned reception – treading down by foot – although about 95 per cent of it is destalked. 'We are actually considering reducing the proportion destalked', comments Michel Chapoutier. 'It may take a little bit of *typicité* from our wines, especially the Côte-Rôtie.' Fermentation and *macération* last for fifteen to twenty days in 12,000-litre open wooden vats, with a twice daily *pigeage*, and temperature ending at 35°C, before being brought back in a controlled way to 25°C for the last seven to ten days. Since 1988 no press wine has been added, and Michel Chapoutier now feels that they are able to take out the first, least stable tannins by this entire process.

The red Hermitage then goes mostly into *pièces*, with a few *demi-muids*, for fifteen to eighteen months, with a racking every three months, before bottling. Like all Chapoutier reds these days, it is neither fined nor filtered. The other *appellation* reds mostly spend a year in cask – all new oak – with the Côtes du Rhône Villages staying just six months and the Côtes du Rhône remaining six to twelve months in larger *foudres*. This is quite different from the past when a flexible ageing policy gave a firm Hermitage vintage like 1983 three years in cask before its last bottling.

Attention to detail, such as passing through the vineyards two or three times when harvesting, is evident. Commenting on how the Châteauneuf-du-Pape harvest can be cleanly and safely brought in from 130 kilometres away, Michel Chapoutier makes the salient point that journey time – about one and a half hours – is very much the same as used to be the case for a donkey and cart leaving the top of Hermitage hill in the old days, when vineyard care was less systematic. The Chapoutier vineyards are still weeded by hand, while the pruning and cutting back of the vines is severe, in pursuit of maximum yields of 30–32 hectolitres in most vineyards, including Crozes.

The first crop to be vinified with the help of the Chapoutier sons was 1984, and throughout the rest of the 1980s the white Hermitage Chante-Alouette showed well, with the 1984, 1985 and 1986 all likely to develop well over ten or more years. Since 1988 the wine has become more stylish, more reserved and less opulent than in the past. In a vintage like 1990, it still carries around 14° alcohol, but shows fine, discreet aromas that suggest just a gradual opening during its ageing process. There are early hints of young oak in the 1989, which is a more measured wine than the 1990, while the 1988 is built around a firm framework, without quite the depth of the two later years. These wines will age successfully over twelve to fifteen years.

The red Hermitage, La Sizeranne – now called Monnier de la Sizeranne – was, as usual, more varied during the 1980s: well-extracted 1982, dense and well-balanced 1983, a finer 1985, a solid 1986, a chewy, strong-brew 1988 and a finer, well-structured 1989 with plenty of intense fruit in it. Like the white, the wine has become a bit more 'swish', more polished than in the past: the 1990 took advantage of that excellent vintage in showing a strong dark purple colour, leathery, almost prune aromas on the bouquet and profound extract on the palate, with the cask influence initially uppermost over a rounded fruitiness. The change of policy in cask ageing – young, oak barrels now used – was particularly noticeable in the rasping wood tannins on this wine; the vintage is sufficiently well balanced to indicate a successful fusion of the elements given several years. The Sizeranne wines are likely to gain in quality and consistency in the future, while if coming across a good Sizeranne from the past twenty or thirty years, the advice is to buy it, since its rapport between price and quality when on form has been one of the best at Hermitage over the years – a tribute to Max Chapoutier.

All the Chapoutier wines age in the maze of cellars at Tain in long, neatly stacked rows of casks that sometimes rise right up to the ceiling. Visiting the cellars with Max Chapoutier was always an entertainment, part theatre, part snappy dialogue. Surveying the barrels with obvious pride, he would rock back and forth on his heels, the ever-buttoned jacket of his suit puffing out. Always keen for everyone to love his wines, and visibly disappointed when the visitor had the ill grace to mention a small grower who perhaps was making better wine, Max would leap from his seat in the boardroom with a 'Well, if you like small growers so much, what about me?' – and would dart round the side of the desk to reveal his diminutive frame.

Of the House's wine from other *appellations*, the St-Joseph red and white Deschants are very good and representative of their region, the red carrying an interesting, reserved fruitiness when young. Their authenticity is commendable, while the red Crozes-Hermitage Les Meysonniers, also bottled after about twelve months in wood, is more obviously a *vin de négoce*. The red St-Joseph in strong vintages like 1988 and 1989 is good to drink between five and ten years old, but the Crozes red is a lighter, easy fruit offering that lacks the dimension of the St-Joseph and of the Cornas, the last-named a rich, insistent wine with ageing potential of around a dozen years in a vintage like 1989.

The Chapoutier Côte-Rôtie generally has a soft style, but in the best vintages before 1989 often lacked a little of the thorough substance of the best producers' wines: there can be around 8 per cent Viognier in this wine. The 1989 marked a turning point, however. Possessing excellent, almost floral aromas with plenty of future potential, the wine had a stylish, lovely fruit surge on the palate. It held good depth and was truly a typical, *vigneron* wine, one that would drink very well around 1997–9. This was a marked improvement on previous Chapoutier Côte-Rôties, and curiously, contained no Viognier. The 1990 was also a rich wine, rounder than the 1989, and confirmed this progress.

The La Bernardine from Châteauneuf-du-Pape is usually a very middle-ground wine, the red being sound and quite representative without fireworks attached. The 1989, however, was very complete and is worth looking out for. The white Châteauneuf is bought in wine form and marketed discreetly by Chapoutier – again a middle-range offering.

Chapoutier's new-found confidence is most evident in their three flagship *cuvées*, which are likely to become high-priced, sought-after wines in years to come. In some ways, the Châteauneuf-du-Pape, Barbe Rac, is the most extraordinary of the three, given the House's traditional lower profile in the southern Rhône. The 1989 was an excellent expression of the Grenache, containing really delicious fruit, a lovely aftertaste and great, chewy warmth all over it. It has great promise for a stylish, elegant development. It comes from a 3-hectare plot of seventy-year-old Grenache which yields just 15 hectolitres a hectare. Watch out, Chateau Rayas!

Le Pavillon from Ermitage, as the label says, is another excellent wine that always gave great pleasure in its non-vintage days. The 1989 was taken from a 3.5 hectare plot of seventy-year-old Syrah on the bottom of the Bessards *lieu-dit*, and was a very dark, black cherry toothcrusher with enormous intense flavours and tremendous potential over at least twenty years. The bouquet carries brooding, dark fruit smells, and the wine possesses great balance.

The La Mordorée Côte-Rôtie lags a little behind the other two exceptional wines, but the 1989 carried plenty of power and substance. It promises to be very aromatic and to show well around 1997 or so.

Max Chapoutier's father Marc still keeps an eye on matters, but the most active doyen of the Hermitage scene is Louis Jaboulet. Born in 1912, he still interviews well – a bit of a joust takes place; answers are snapped back, suspicion about the validity of the whole exercise is not hard to detect. But his presence keeps this rather disparate family grouping together. His sons are Jacques, who deals with vinification and the buying-in of wines, and the cosmopolitan Gérard, a familiar face in the tasting rooms of both London and New York as well as on the river banks of leading salmon rivers in Ireland when he is not overseeing the export function. Louis's brother Jean, born in 1914, has two sons, Philippe, who looks after the *vignoble*, and Michel, who works mostly on the commercial side within France. This is altogether a more complicated ship to keep tight as regards commercial policy and the approach to wine-making.

For many years Paul Jaboulet Aîne have been the international quality standard-bearers for the best Rhône wines: even in the early 1970s they possessed an active overseas network, running across some forty or more countries, with their wines turning up in places as far apart as Caracas, Hong Kong and San Francisco. Founded in 1834, the company has always produced some of the best and best-known Rhônes – the red Hermitage La Chapelle, the red Crozes-Hermitage Thalabert, the southern reds Châteauneuf-du-Pape Les Cèdres and Vacqueyras. Their vineyard holdings are restricted to Hermitage and Crozes-Hermitage – 19 hectares of Syrah and 5 hectares of Marsanne and Roussanne at Hermitage, and 46 hectares of Syrah and 5 hectares of Marsanne and Roussanne within the Crozes *appellation* – with the addition of 2.5 hectares of an old, abandoned Condrieu vineyard in 1992. Their sites at Hermitage are choice, as one would expect – a full 7 hectares on Le Méal, along with plots on Les Bessards, Les Greffieux and Les Diognières for the red, and on Les Murets and Les Rocoules for the white.

The average age of their vineyard is twenty-five years, with some replanting occurring every year. The training of the vines is by the crouched Gobelet method, with support from wooden stakes that have to be bored into the rocky ground. The Jaboulets have been innovators in their vineyard upkeep, and were one of the first producers to advocate the use of helicopter spraying, back around 1978.

At Crozes-Hermitage, Jaboulet own a complete 45-hectare vineyard in and around the Domaine de Thalabert on the reputed Les Chassis and their red wine from here is the best at Crozes, and the best-value wine made by them. The vineyard is split into 38 hectares Syrah, 7 hectares Marsanne-Roussanne in nearly equal proportions. Jaboulet also sell a second Crozes brand name, Les Jalets, which is made from a mix of the harvest from their 6-hectare holding near their Roche-de-Glun offices and from grapes bought in from outside cultivators, as well as a simply denominated 'Crozes-Hermitage'. These do not possess the stature of the Thalabert.

Paul Jaboulet Aîné work with all the wines of the Rhône except St-Péray – a vote of little confidence in the commercial relevance of that *appellation*. Mainly they buy wines from carefully selected *vignerons*. At Châteauneuf-du-Pape, for instance, they have a very long-standing relationship with their supplier. The Jaboulet Les Cèdres from there is dominated by Grenache, with, according to the year, Syrah, Mourvèdre and Cinsault in it as well. Their red Côtes du Rhône 45ème Parallèle always has 20 per cent Syrah or Mourvèdre in it to give it more staying-power, the Syrah sometimes rising to 40 or 50 per cent. 'We seek colour, tannin and longevity in the wine, and always take Syrah from the southern Rhône,' states Louis Jaboulet. In 1990 they found 6,500 litres of Syrah that so pleased them that it was set apart, raised for three months in cask and bottled as a Syrah Cuvée Personelle. Their well-known and successful Muscat de Beaumes-de-Venise comes in grape form from growers, but is vinified and bottled at the Cave Co-opérative under the supervision of son Jacques. In all, 50,000 bottles are produced every year.

Where suitable, these wines are aged in their premises and can carry a brand name as well as a vintage – Les Jumelles at Côte-Rôtie for example – while some of their best straight *appellation* wines, with no branding, comes from places like Cornas and Vacqueyras.

Quite rightly, it is on their Hermitage wines that most interest centres. The red La Chapelle is a consistently high-grade wine, but, the 1990 vintage apart, is undoubtedly less striking and less expressive of its origins than it used to be up to around the early 1980s. Much sought after by buyers from around the world, it is therefore interesting to chart this wine from tasting notes over the past twenty years. Extracts follow, with size of bottle (b = bottle, m = magnum) and date at last tasting given in brackets.

La Chapelle

1969   Colour very dark, just a hint of brick. Bouquet has great, lurking richness, some damp leaf, prune smells and capable of greater complexity. Palate has a lovely, lasting richness, and great depth, very thorough flavours, showing some evolution. Delicious – everything an old Hermitage should be and in stronger shape than a bottle drunk in Feb. '91. (b Jan. '92)

1970   Brick colour; burnt aromas, some residual warmth; a 'quiet' vintage – some rounded fruit still, but lacks substance. Drink towards 1998. (b May '92)

1971   Bit of brown in colour; many rich coffee, vegetal aromas; rich, developed flavours on palate; tiring, but still very good. Drink 1990–4. Largest yield ever (46 hectolitres). (b Apr. '90)

1972   Colour garnet now; nose very rich, well marked by its origins – coffee, *sous bois* smells; palate rich, some alcohol emerging; runs on with good intensity; will become more interesting and well drinkable 1998–2002. Old-fashioned style, similar to Hermitage of the 1950s being drunk in the 1970s. Smallest yield (15 hectolitres). (b Oct. '90)

1973   Dark purple; bouquet closed; good fruit and balance; faster maturer than the 1974. (b Oct. '78)

1974   Sound colour; tannins and fruit on nose; complex, youthful structure on palate; promises well. (b Oct. '78)

1975   Pale, colour thinning; nose has only light fruit. Palate lacks depth and aftertaste. Lightweight wine. Drink by 1985–7. (b Mar. '80)

1976   Colour red to ruby. Bouquet was vegetal by '82 – has some gentle fruit left and a slight mineral smell. Palate is now a bit 'stringy' – lacks a core, the tannins are abrasive. Has not developed as well as first expected. A nervous wine, drink soon. (b May '92)

1977   Pale colour; fruity, up-front bouquet; light, lacks complexity and balance uncertain. (b Oct. '78)

1978   Dark *robe*, some black still there; bouquet currently withdrawn – fruitiness still red or blackcurrant in style. Lovely
finesse of fruit on palate with sleek tannins closely attached
– really good harmony. Hasn't loosened much over last six
years – still reserved. Very long finish, great promise to live
until 2012+. Half normal crop. (b May '92)

1979   Some purple in good, well-sustained colour; Fair depth on
bouquet – mature fruit, but a touch of a drier, mineral side
emerging. Palate starts a little mustily, quite intriguing
combination of cooked fruit and drier, more resinous
flavours. Ends with some dry tannins. Have never been
sure about its balance, or how well integrated. Drink now
or wait for development on bouquet, plus risk of greater
dryness on finish. (b Mar. '92)

1980   Fair plum colour, touch of ruby. Bouquet is on the turn,
coppery, mineral aspects. Palate has old, maybe dried
prune flavours, its grip is precarious, the dryness of age
coming to the fore. Was never a big wine, now finishes a
little dustily. Drink now to 1997 according to taste. (b
Mar. '92)

1981   Dull colour, purple, some red; lacks some fruit on nose;
agreeable fruit on palate, some tannic support. Lacks a bit
of harmony. Not bad for year. Drink before 1992. Only
6,000 bottles made in this very rainy year, mainly sold to
French and American collectors. (½ b Sept. '84)

1982   Decent plum colour, some lightness, plenty of glycerine.
Bouquet taking on a ripe, damp evolution, some *gibier* and
overall a lovely southern warmth. Very fleshy fruitiness
on palate, depth under it with a little residual tannin.
Resounding, lasting aftertaste. A full succulent wine, much
more thorough than the fairly similar 1985. A real crowd-
pleaser, can't see it slipping unduly during its evolution.
Will drink well another ten to fifteen years. (b Mar. '92)

1983   Solid, thorough colour, looks younger than its nine years.
Masses of potential in still largely hidden bouquet – dark
berried fruit and leathery extract, has lost the oak influence
that lasted about five years. Still very much in formation
on the palate, the fruit has a compelling intensity but is still
enveloped by masses of tannins; striking balance, notably
long finish. Stylish but full. Delicious, well worked wine –

likely to live towards thirty years. Twenty-day *cuvaison* here. (b Mar. '92)

1984   Dark plum, a hint of lightening. Bouquet rather resinous, has a tarry edge alongside cooked fruit aromas. Palate's fruit has evolved to a more stewed taste in the last year. Fair depth, pretty sound length, tendency to finish dry. Pleasant, very drinkable and good rapport price-quality. Won't improve. Drink towards 1998. (b Jan. '92)

1985   Decent cherry/plum colour. The nearly over-ripe fruit smell on the bouquet has developed with age – is now creeping towards a more musky, damp phase – stylish. Flavours are rounded, still vigorous. Quite chewy tannins more prominent than expected, the wine may lack a little body to keep it going on an even keel. Likely to develop in fits and starts, may be difficult to catch on the right day. Could drink decently towards early 2000s, but danger of loss of grip on palate. Eight-day *cuvaison* here. (b Mar. '92)

1986   Pretty, bright colour – dark, cherry aspects. Early warmth on bouquet, still carries a bit of oak. Discreet richness, reveals some promise of showing southern traits. Decent depth and richness on attack, has a gentle fullness and tasty fruitiness with a touch of softening tannin overriding. Likely to taste more openly in three to eight years, may live towards or past 2004. Could be a bit of a sleeper that will flourish quietly with age. Vines lower down the hill suffered from rain at harvest, one-third of crop declassified, so selection rigorous. (b Mar. '92)

1987   Dark plum, quite sound colour. Bouquet a bit precarious and narrow – tarry, black jam, lacks depth and clarity. Palate starts quite spicily, a shade aggressive and austere. Finish is rather hot, tarry. Some oak presence helps to soften, could settle if given maybe another two to five years. I suspect they had their work cut out to make this. Should drink towards 2000 or so. (b Mar. '92)

1988   Solid, deep colour, some black with the purple. Quite striking, berried fruit warmth on bouquet – stylish, promising. Decent depth of dark fruit on palate, has shaken off young wood overlay, though overall the wine is taut rather than fleshy. Decent persistence on aftertaste, chewiness helped by the oak. Has less *terroir* than the Chapelles of old at this stage, but a good vintage, likely to hold together until 2006–2010. (b Feb. '92)

1989   Colour pretty solid, purple/black. Sappy, cooked fruit aromas on bouquet, has shaken off last year's raw, evident oak influence. Fair substance, quite ripe elements on palate, but it somehow just misses a beat – it seems to lack a convincing thoroughness; it's almost too sleek for its own good. Probably in an interim phase right now. Upsurge of liquorice chew and tannins at end – still sorting itself out. Still don't think it's greatly typical of its *terroir*. Likely to run for fifteen to twenty years. (b Feb. '92)

1990   Extremely dark, inky colour, good hue. Big aromas of almost overripe grapes, lots of potential variety and complexity – no coyness here. Palate starts with surge of ripe, deep tasting flavours that are impressively moulded together. Some fine tannins burst from cover on the lasting finish – they're generally well enveloped by the fruit and fleshy extract, which is the great success of the wine. Reticent still, has brooding power. Perfect harmony, strong, generous, long-lasting. Grand Vin. Will run for at least twenty-five years, no problem. (pre-bottling sample Feb. '92)

The comments above, which in many cases are compilations, covering several tastings of the same wine, the date mentioned being the last occasion, are intended to serve as a running view of the famous La Chapelle wine over twenty years – from one man's perspective. One hopes that the excellent, deeply concentrated 1990 will act as a spur to Jaboulet, but leaving this vintage aside, some idea of the trend in style of this wine may perhaps be detected – the move towards greater elegance, less flesh and substance and less pure dependence on fruit and soil to provide a gloriously full-bodied wine, the likes of which cannot be found elsewhere. Surely substance *is* Hermitage – reduce substance and local stamp and you have robbed the wine of part of its core.

Of the other red Paul Jaboulet wines, the Thalabert is their year-in, year-out winner. This top-end Crozes is always endowed with great fruit extraction, and a healthy purple Syrah colour. Throughout the 1980s this wine was consistently good, be it in lesser years like 1987, beautifully fruited years like 1985 or full-blown years like 1983 and 1988. The 1988 appears to be a nine- to twelve-year wine, and in the current Jaboulet way was initially very marked by new oak (28 per cent first year, 72 per cent second crop). The Syrah fruit re-emerged after four years, and this chunky, solid wine which holds greater elegance than past Thalaberts is reminiscent of the 1983 in its composition. The 1989 Thalabert is a more mid-weight wine suitable for drinking towards 1997. Dark purple, it has quite an earthy, almost burnt bouquet, and while it carries fair fruit, it is not very sustained on the palate. The excellent 1990 Thalabert, 35 per cent of which was exposed to brand new oak, the rest to young oak for the usual year, is smashing – *Grand Vin* at a tiny price. Very darkly coloured, it holds a very pleasant hint of over-ripeness on the bouquet and there was tremendous harmony of ripe, sustained flavours on the palate. Delicious, ample-tasting wine, it will start to show well around the age of five or six, and will do well towards 2014.

Of their other *négociant* wines, the Cornas (very successful in 1990, a fifteen-year wine) is usually robust and honest and is bought in wine form from sometimes as many as eighteen small cultivators, while the Côte-Rôtie Les Jumelles sparkles in a top year like 1983, but can be uninspiring – unfortunate in an *appellation* where there are sufficient go-ahead small growers to ensure the issue of authentic, interesting wines each year. This is bought in grape form from twelve to sixteen small cultivators and may contain 5 per cent Viognier. From the South, the Châteauneuf-du-Pape Les Cèdres comes in red and white: again, Les Cèdres can be memorable, as in 1967 and in 1989, but can also miss the mark in strong vintages like 1981 and 1983. It is representative of mainstream Châteauneuf, with a correct depth of flavour in it and the potential in a year like 1990 to show well after seven years or so.

The Gigondas and Vacqueyras from Jaboulet have risen in quality recently; the Gigondas, bought as wine from two *domaines*, showed well in both 1989 and 1990. The former, a big, dense wine, is very full-bodied but its flavours are fresher than many Gigondas wines of old – it needs eight years or so to settle down. The 1990 is also full of dark flavours and plenty of tannins which have been beneficially tamed by the wine-maker. It will drink very well from around 1996. The Vacqueyras, from two or three suppliers, was very successful in 1990, with good, warm, earthy aromas on the bouquet and such obvious balance that it will drink well throughout its evolution – maybe for ten years.

The main house whites, the Hermitage Chevalier de Stérimberg and the Crozes Mule Blanche, are fermented at low temperature – 14°C – with the 1989 Hermitage done on a one-off basis in cask and the Crozes in stainless steel. Both are raised in brand new oak, the Crozes for four months, the Hermitage for six or seven months. The Crozes is bottled in February or March, the Hermitage in June after the harvest, and no fining or filtration occurs after the first racking. For extra freshness, the malolactic is always blocked. The 1990 Chevalier de Stérimberg was thankfully one of the biggest and best of recent years. The bouquet was full, the palate loaded with rich matter, and the young oak support worked very well, bringing a delicious wine. It knocked previous recent Stérimbergs like 1989 and 1986 into the shadows. The 1989 was a pale wine, short on substance and on local character, and was readily upstaged by the 1988, which held an attractive richness on the palate despite being a short-term wine, one to drink successfully before around 1996.

The Mule Blanche is a dependable wine, that in 1991, 1990 and 1989 was very successful. The 1991 initially held an oily, oak-influenced bouquet and showed fair depth on the palate. A cleanly made wine, the cask influence is beneficial and by 1994 or so it should have settled and integrated well. The 1990 is fuller and richer and more immediately striking, while the 1989 had just five weeks in one-year Jura oak, and had a fruity elegance, the Roussanne bringing extra *nervosité* or edge to it. At Crozes one of the defects of several of the whites is an excessive oiliness or flabbiness brought on by a combination of working with ripe Marsanne fruit and vinifying in only a partly modernized way. It is the greater breeding of the Hermitage vineyards that produces Marsanne more capable of showing its true worth on its own – one of those strange quirks that cannot be quantified with mathematical precision, but which make the subject of wine all the more intriguing.

Since 1988 Jaboulet have listed a Condrieu, the grapes being bought from a cultivator at Limony, with enough to make 4–5,000 bottles. In 1990 the wine carried a genuine, earthy bouquet, with a fullness similar to that of Pierre Dumazet's wine, also from Limony. Clean and long on the finish, this is vinified only in stainless steel, and is bottled at the end of April. In early 1992 Jaboulet advanced a stage further, buying 2.5 hectares of vineyards abandoned for thirty years on a site next to their supplier, the sixty-year-old M. Bèze. Wine from this new vineyard will come on stream just before the end of the century.

The third, but smaller, merchant house based on this part of the Valley was until 1977 a family enterprise, Delas Frères. Founded in 1835, they own 10 hectares at Hermitage – split between 8 hectares of Syrah (mostly Les Bessards, some L'Hermite and Les Grandes Vignes and 0.5 hectare on Le Méal) and 2 hectares of Marsanne (65 per cent) and Roussanne (35 per cent), which are mostly on L'Hermite, with a little on Les Grandes Vignes. Now owned by the Champagne House of Deutz, who rescued them from possible bankruptcy and who are working to upgrade the overall house quality, they also have direct access to vineyards at Condrieu (3 hectares on the Clos Bouché near Château-Grillet, whose crop is sold to them by Michael Delas's son-in-law), at Côte-Rôtie (an old Michel Delas vineyard of a bit under 3 hectares, mainly Côte Brune) and at St-Joseph (2 hectares in two sites above St-Jean-de-Muzols). In the northern Rhône, they buy grapes and wine from around twenty different *domaines* at Crozes-Hermitage for their red and white, they buy grapes amounting to around 250 hectolitres of wine from about ten suppliers at Côte-Rôtie, they buy an equal mix of grapes and wines at Cornas, having sold their vineyards there in the early 1980s, and lastly at St-Péray they buy the princely amount of 10 hectolitres a year from several growers like Balthazar and Teysseire. In the southern Rhône they buy only wine, and work with all the leading *appellations*, including Muscat de Beaumes, Tricastin and Ventoux.

By 1992 the making of the principal reds and whites was in a state of flux, with efforts made to continue improvements started in the 1980s. The 1988s benefited from being raised in a new *chai*, while a series of new 50-hectolitre vats for the 1992 harvest will allow the Hermitage grapes to be harvested and vinified separately on a *parcelle* by *parcelle* basis, only being assembled just before bottling. This will bring the wine greater polish in the view of technical director Antoine Fuchs. The Delas preference is also to omit a full crush of the red grapes, with just a light breaking of skins that may occur during the partial destalking of the crop. The policy of wood ageing is very much on a case by case basis: there is plenty of young wood in their cellars, but again, in some vintages they like to mix its use with older, larger *foudres*. The top red Hermitage Marquise de la Tourette, for instance, was aged in Burgundian *pièces* of one to three years in

1988; exactly the same casks were used for the Tourette's first year in 1989 and 1990.

The Marquise de la Tourette from 1982 onwards has shown an improved quality and, most importantly, better consistency. Hence more difficult years like 1984 were very sound through having decent depth of flavour, while the 1982 and 1983 were interesting wines, with a fair amount of fruit extraction and definition coming through.

Of recent vintages of Tourette, the best appear to be 1988 and 1990, the former, a wine with a dark matt colour, a spicy, leathery, warm bouquet and a firm feel for the *terroir* on the palate: this is a wine that will keep well. The 1989 is a more approachable wine which will drink well around 1996–7; there is promising fruit on the bouquet and some rounded tannic support on the palate. The 1990 is vigorous and intense, and has the great, ripe fullness of its vintage. It will run for perhaps fifteen years. The 1991 will be an earlier wine, with plenty of berried fruit and some chewy tannins. The Tourette wine is mainly composed of grapes from Les Bessards, while the Hermitage *cuvée normale* has a greater presence of crop from L'Hermite and Les Grandes Vignes in it. In 1989 this was an early wine with warmth on the bouquet and decent length on the palate and in 1990 it was quite sweet and succulent – a plump wine which needed time to settle into its young oak overlay.

Generally the Delas style is lighter than Chapoutier, less flamboyant than Chave, and less elegant than Jaboulet – which makes these good, middle-division wines capable of ageing around fifteen years or so. They have less staying power than in the past if old bottles are any yardstick: for instance, a bottle of 1950 drunk in 1986 still showed some Hermitage sweetness and fullness, despite a fading colour and being a wine from a light vintage.

Of the other House reds, the Côte-Rôtie and the special Côte-Rôtie, the Seigneur de Maugiron (there really is only one circumflex on the label) are correct wines which improved in the late 1980s. The 1988 Maugiron was quite firm, held some berried fruit but lacked a beat or two of authenticity. The 1989, a softer wine, with some friendly fruitiness, was a touch less commercial than the 1988. The standard Côte-Rôtie, made from younger vines, also carries a pleasant fruit and these are wines to drink around the age of six or seven. The Cornas Chante-Perdrix in the past has been a firm, sometimes austere wine, but one with greater distinction than the soft, overtly commercial Crozes-Hermitage. An easier, more approachable style of Cornas was sought with the 1990 vintage, however. In the southern Rhône, a very genuine, Grenache-inspired Gigondas dominated proceedings in 1990.

The two leading whites are the Condrieu and white Hermitage Marquise de la Tourette. The Condrieu is not exposed to any cask – past wood experiments showed that overly dry tannins were brought into the wine. It is fermented at 18° in enamel vats, and bottled the following April with the malolactic completed. The 1991 was successful, with some sustained flavours on the palate, good length and complexity, and the promise of an aromatic bouquet given a year or two. In 1990 the harvest was enormous, and the wine lacked depth and genuine extract; the 1989 was a fatter wine than the 1991, but a good representative of the Viognier *appellation*.

Delas reverted to a cask-fermentation for part of their white Hermitage in 1991. 'I'm seeking an older style of Hermitage, one that is capable of ageing well and progressing well over time', commented Antoine Fuchs enthusiastically. 'Until 1976 Delas fermented their white Hermitage in *demi-muid* barrels, so this is really a return to those days.' About one-fifth of the wine receives young oak rearing of a couple of months, and the results with the 1991 vintage indicate a wine with a sound expression of the Marsanne in it – quietly solid, almost oily texture with length and a final flourish provided by the young oak. It may be a little more elegant than the more full-blown 1990 Marquise de la Tourette *blanc*, and now resembles a reduced version of Chapoutier's extremely good Chante-Alouette, which is a sign of its recent progress.

While Delas are likely to continue to seek improved quality during the 1990s, there is one family affair whose wines are superb and have been so over many generations. M. Gérard Chave's family has owned vineyards in the area since the far-off time of 1481, which in all probability makes them the oldest wine family in the Rhône. M. Chave is a well-known figure all around Hermitage and has a confirmed band of followers outside France, particularly in Britain and the United States. However, he is a private man; he lives in a modest house where the family has always been based in the west-bank village of Mauves, and he holds old-fashioned principles on quality and commercial behaviour. His delight is to be left alone to think out his outstanding wines to the last detail, and then to be sociable over them with a close circle of regular friends.

'Thinking out' wines may not be a pastime commonly attributed to *vignerons*, but in M. Chave's case the phrase is relevant. Since the early 1970s it has been fascinating to observe the development of M. Chave's skills and how he has managed to raise his family business on to a broader, more extensive commercial footing without sacrificing all-important quality. During the 1980s he acquired the late Terence Gray's site of L'Hermite, built a new bottle extension, installed an updated *cuverie* and yet maintained a meticulous approach to making his wine. Not only is he fully master of the requirements of his vineyards, but in his cellars he appears to practise a form of wizardry in the vinification and assembly of his wines. For example, part of the L'Hermite plot had not, in Chave's estimation, held vines since phylloxera, which is just the sort of challenge he relishes, setting to work on this long untilled land with a caterpillar-tracked cultivator.

M. Gérard Chave

Likewise underground in his family's old cellars at Mauves. Chave's famous *vin de paille* has already been mentioned, and in 1989 'for amusement – strictly not commercial' he made his first vintage of 150 litres of Viognier *demi-sec* off the Hermitage hill. This 18° wine showed floral aromas within a surround of dense weight and alcohol on the bouquet; on the palate there were dried fruits and extreme length – the wine was very big, in an apéritif style, with the Viognier showing the extraordinary opulent roundness which is its hallmark. M. Chave added that this wine had had very little sulphur mixture applied to it to obtain the residual sweetness. In 1990 a slightly drier, even more successful Viognier was made and bottled earlier, in July 1991.

At Hermitage, M. Chave owns 10 hectares of Syrah vineyards and 5 hectares of Marsanne (85 per cent) and Roussanne (15 per cent). He also has 2 hectares of Syrah at St-Joseph, mostly above Tournon. There can be no more educative exercise than to accompany M. Chave around his intimate, intriguingly musty cellar and to taste the wines from his different plots on Hermitage hill. The line-up for the red is as follows: Les Bessards (Grands and Petits), Le Méal, Beaumes, Péléat, Les Rocoules, Maison Blanche, L'Hermite and Les Diognières. For the white it is L'Hermite, Maison Blanche, Péléat and Les Rocoules. Tasting the issue of these various *climats*, it becomes clear just how varied their styles can be, from the thick, almost hard Péléat to the finer and delicately scented Rocoules. To know how to bring these different styles together into a well-knit unity – that is the real art, one that is admitted by growers to be among their hardest tasks every year.

M. Chave does this with refreshing modesty. The man has flair, and is lucky to be blessed with a natural talent of the sort that audiences love, whether they are listening to a virtuoso violinist or watching sport – his touch is McEnroe's, not Lendl's, at the net, or Gower easing the cricket ball to the boundary rather than Boycott methodically working it there. The joy of the man is his ability to surprise with personal wisdom and interpretations.

For example, on vinification: 'I change my vinification according to what I taste. The white may be made about one-third in wood, two-thirds in vat, but I'm ready to change this. The wood brings some more finesse, but I'd rather work with the different elements available. If the wood intrudes too much in a certain year, I'll switch to the vats. I'm not very in favour of the wood – you know, the first-year stuff.'

Racking: 'Vat or large barrel (*foudre*) wines should be racked two to three times more than a *pièce* wine. The latter might be racked three to five times over about eighteen months.'

Fining: 'For the whites I fine with bentonite; if I use egg whites on them, I'll take out their tannins. I use egg whites on my reds since they have more and heavier tannins.'

Yeasts: 'I very rarely add yeasts. I had to in 1982, when it was so hot both by day (35°C) and by night that I had to cool the wine. The

Gérard Chave's Cellar

yeasts then became tired, so they needed pepping up.'

When to rack and taste: 'With the *vent du nord* you have higher atmospheric pressure here, so the lees are more suppressed – further down. That's why I'll rack and do my tasting by preference when there's a *vent du nord*. When there's a *vent du midi* from the south, I smell the lees more. And I like to bottle the wine by preference when there's an old moon.'

Cooking: 'It's close to what I do. I've attended courses in Lyon with the *grands chefs* to improve my cooking – Monique approves! I managed to make a wine, a *cuvée* of red, that suited a lamb dish of the late Alain Chapel's.'

One of the clues to M. Chave's expertise is that he can make good wine in a generally poor vintage. Of his neighbours in the north, only Guigal at Côte-Rôtie and Clape at Cornas are consistently able to make good wine in poor vintages and excellent wine when the harvest has been good. Nicknamed the 'Trio' by the author, they are the three men in the northern Rhône who come closest to complete mastery of their art. In the southern Rhône their peers are Jean-Pierre and François Perrin of Château de Beaucastel at Châteauneuf-du-Pape.

Gérard Chave is a good-looking man, with a rather Pinocchio-styled nose, a rugged, ruddy face and a delightful smile. His explanations given in his cellars are accompanied by chortles and cackles of delight – his enthusiasm at the age of fifty-seven is that of a man half his age. His bright, intelligent wife Monique is a shrewd businesswoman who runs a tight ship on the commercial side, and their son Jean-Louis, named after his grandfather, has studied in the United States for a business degree which will stand him in good stead when he takes over from his parents, as well as spending time at Davis University, California. Their nineteen-year-old daughter Géraldine also takes an active interest in the wine, so 500 years of wines and vines are in capable and committed hands.

M. Chave's red and white Hermitages are among the longest-lived of the *appellation*, in big vintages the red sustaining its enormous depth of intricate flavour for at least thirty years, and the white obtaining a really big, apricot-inspired aftertaste after eight or ten years. Some tasting notes over eighteen of the past nineteen vintages serve to show his skill under a variety of different and difficult conditions.

Gérard Chave, red Hermitage

1972   Plum colour, lightening to rust at top; with air bouquet thickens and gains depth, has prune and smoky aromas. Very attractive, soft richness on palate, and very good length. Elegant, fine wine, style is like a rich but still upright claret. Near its peak. Will keep going towards 2000. (b Mar. '92)

1974   Some rust alongside the red; fine, has become elegant and long. Bouquet has softened, palate has *sous-bois* dampness. Very good in a difficult year. Drink now to 1988 for best results. (b June '84)

1975   Trace of ruby in colour, slight age; marvellous bouquet – like wild strawberries, very fruity. Light on the palate, finishes a bit early. Delicate wine, drink before 1987. (b July '80)

1976   Colour starting towards garnet, some red traces left. Damp leaves smell, but quiet richness, some dark fruit also on the bouquet. Delicate, elegant on the palate; some richness on the attack, a fairly pebbly finish. Could continue until 1996–8, but will show signs of decline if not well cellared. (b Jan. '92)

1977   Orange has entered colour; excellent raspberry aromas on bouquet, maturing although richness behind them. Fine, approachable style on the palate. Very good in this light year, but needs drinking before 1989. (b Jan. '86)

1978   Mat colour, dulling, lots of glycerine; nose has some reticent berry aromas, not very generous. Better on the palate – but lacks thoroughness. Tannins present, quite hot ending. Not sure where it's going. (b Oct. '90)
Very dense colour still, purple and plum, lot of glycerine. Plum, prune aromas, some spice, has moved on from first berried bouquet. Palate starts with a whoosh of flavours, an extraordinary explosion of taste like few wines ever – very rich, wonderful balance, great harmony, lasting flavours. The tannins are so well absorbed into the richness that it is difficult to judge its longevity – 1996–2002? (b Oct. '86)
(This wine has been tasted a total of eight times between July 1980 and October 1990. Two sets of comments are

given because over the course of this ten-year period, the above split pattern has regularly shown up, for reasons at which one can only surmise – perhaps late versus early bottling, the early bottling being the better?)

1979   Colour pretty well held together. Some rust above the dark plum. Bouquet gains in richness with air and shows a gamey, *gibier* side. The palate was gutsy six years ago but is now showing fine, evolved almost mineral flavours. Progressing quietly and attractively, this is now a *vin de finesse*. Will live on gently for another six to eight years. (b Jan. '92)

1980   Colour turning towards pale red, top is a little see-through. Quite warm bouquet, start of the damp, *sous-bois* aromas – but still has the richness to evolve further. Palate has become well-rounded, pretty broad and long with some nice tannic resurgence at the end. Drinking well and fully now, a quietly plump wine which can still run to 2002 or past. (b Feb. '92)

1981   Colour quite pale, hint of brick. Bouquet a touch musty, sweetens and shows some berried fruit with air. Only a medium-weight wine, but it has good fruit extract with some drier tannin underneath. A wine to surprise people – can develop further and longer (another eight to eleven years) than expected. Only risk is the tannins drying out and getting on top in that time. (b Feb. '92)

1982   Sustained, pretty plum colour, touch of lightness. Rich, brooding warmth on the bouquet, plenty of development still there. Palate has striking, delicious fat early flavours, lots of intense fruit. Fills out well *en bouche*, and has quiet tannic support holding it together. Has always been a plump, ripe wine of great appeal and exceptional balance. Lasts very well on the aftertaste. Will keep going for another eight to fifteen years at least. (b Feb. '92)

1983   Intense purple-black colour, still has great lustre; lots of glycerine. Bouquet still locked up, but great promise with crushed fruits and lots of extract. Palate intense, solid; lots of tannin and alcohol busy driving it along. Breathtaking, one of the best Hermitages of recent years. A thirty-year wine, no problem. (b Nov. '90)

1984 Colour a fragile, pale plum, fading at top. Quite pleasant, but precarious bouquet – some cooked fruit/jam aroma, sweet, typical of year. Agreeable, sappy texture on start of palate – cooked fruit flavours and some final heat. Lacks intensity and its hold is fragile. Well made in a difficult year – under-ripe stalks meant 100 per cent destemming, whereas in ripe years, the stalks are left. Some unevenness emerging on palate – drink it up, though could run for five years or so. (b Feb. '92)

1985 Dark *robe*, blacks there, matting a little. Excellent deep berry aromas, lot of potential. Palate very impressive – very well-knit, strong, chewy wine with nicely rounded tannins. Very profound, its balance gives it a life of over twenty-five years. (b Apr. '90)

1986 Solid plum colour. Bouquet just starting to show some good depth and potential for rich development. Well-knit flavours on the palate, good fruit extract. Bit of a dark horse, this could develop above the vintage's reputation, there are some sound tannins and good weight. Will be more approachable around 1995, but will certainly live for twenty years or so. (b Nov. '91)

1987 Middling colour; fruity, typical Syrah bouquet. Palate has sound fruit and vigour, a middle-weight wine that should drink really well within ten or twelve years. Made half his usual amount of wine, with severe crop selection to obtain concentration. The tannins are quite firm in it. Well made under difficulties. (b Apr. '90)

1988 Dark, purple-black colour. Major potential on the bouquet, great width, great warmth. Superb surge of intense fruit on start of palate, cracking Syrah wild fruit, firm and sustained. Plenty of tannins circulating – quite strong ones – but the whole is very well-knit. Excellent balance, long and lingering finish. A harder hitter than the 1989, and very true to type. Grèat keeping possibilities – this will drink fabulously between fifteen and thirty years. (b Jan. '92)

1989 Good attractive purple, lighter than 1988. Plenty of berry fruit aromas waiting to emerge on the warm bouquet – a hint of development here. Palate shows early fruit but there is more strength here than is first apparent. Tightly closed flavours end with a sound tannic chew – good length. Complex, reserved right now. Drink over course of fifteen to twenty years, will 'sing' around age of eight to twelve. (b Jan. '92)

1990 Extraordinary potent fruit and concentration in the Bessards; Le Méal bouquet bit more open than Bessards, lovely depth and delicious fruit attack. Rocoules more floral nose, great finesse, complexity and length – this wine will be a good 'team player' come *assemblage* in June '92. Steely, upright bouquet on Péléat, wild, hedgerow fruit and great length – this is a real provider of structure. Lot of dark, berried fruit aroma on Diognières – is very darkly coloured, and harmonious, tasty on the palate – could please on its own. Soft, beguiling, ample bouquet on Beaumes, very nice fruit with quiet, sustained tannin on finish. L'Hermite sound colour, has some *terroir* on bouquet, almost a touch of pepper; intense, lovely fruit on palate, agreeable final tannins. These will make up into a memorable wine. Gérard Chave puts it alongside 1952 and 1961. (Tasted from casks, the only new one containing the Bessards, in Jan. '92)

Meanwhile M. Chave's white Hermitage is thoroughly representative of what the traditional vinification can bring. His Marsanne grows in four places – Rocoules, Péléat, Maison Blanche and L'Hermite – and his Roussanne in two – Rocoules and L'Hermite. His wines hold great depth of flavour, and their strength of taste and power are a revelation to drinkers reared on the orthodox varieties like Chardonnay and Sauvignon. There is often a flowing, grapey bouquet that moves towards a later nuttiness. M. Chave also does not succumb to what he terms 'harvest fever', so a lateish picking contributes to the firm straw colour that his whites usually display. In 1989 he recalls that he started to harvest the Marsanne and Roussanne when those around him were already at the stage of distilling their grape *marc* – they started around 12 September, he finished on 10 October.

Excellent white wines have been made in 1982, 1984, 1985, 1986, 1987, 1988, 1989, 1990 and 1991 – it's a question of style for the drinker. By the age of nine, the 1982 was showing interesting dried fruit aromas (apricots, figs) and nutty, complex flavours; very fine, it had plenty of living still to do. After seven years, the 1984 was being pushed along by its gutsy, firm alcohol extract. Opulent but stylish on the bouquet, it, too, had several years left in it. The 1985 white has an immense straw colour, an unctuous, ripely-aromatic bouquet, with great concentration and length on the palate – it is delicious in a restrained way, will run towards 2000–2003 and needs to be set against a richly flavoured dish. The 1986 is also extremely rich, very long, the flavours are almost honeyed – this would go well alongside meat or rich fish and still has some opening up to do after six years – it could run towards 2004. The 1987, bottled in January 1990, is a little lighter; it has a certain lush extract and a profound bouquet, and will go well with poultry.

The 1988 is a firm, tightly knit wine that will take longer than the others to emerge – lots of dried fruit flavours and excellent balance. The 1989 may be at least 13.5°, but it is more delicate than the 1988, and shows some musky aromas. It is taking time to sort itself out. The 1990 is excellent, with plenty of fat aromas, and a welcome firm layer on the palate that stops it being too corpulent. It has masses of flavour and potential and could do well over twelve to sixteen years. The 1991 has a rich bouquet, good middle weight and balance, and will be very attractive around six to eight years old.

These are all wines that will age better than most commercial whites made these days, and the beauty of them is that their evolution contains surprises as they show flamboyantly and then retreat, show well again and so on. Chave considers his 1987 a twenty-year wine, for instance; that may be looking a little far out, but overall we're talking an easy ten or twelve years for all these wines: the trouble is that they can be so delicious and striking when they're five years old that bottles do not remain hidden away.

There are only a few private growers like M. Chave at Hermitage. Their *domaines* are very much father-to-son affairs, which has lent great stability to wine-making from the hillside. In the case of the Sorrel family, for instance, the third son, Marc, left a business post to take up the running of the vineyard that had been left in equal portions to his brothers after the death of their father Henri, who was the *Notary Public* at Tain for many years. Henri admitted that he always preferred being a *vigneron*, but that time was against him. Until the early 1970s the Sorrel harvest from their 3.4-hectare total holding was sold as grapes to local *négociants*, but during that decade Henri progressed to making an excellent red and white – the red Le Méal of 1978 and 1979 being wines of great breeding and appeal.

Marc is a hard-working man in his early forties, and has had to learn about wine-making and vineyard care at speed. He joined his father in 1982, his father died in January 1984, and he then learnt his trade with the help first of a local *vigneron* and then an *œnologue* consultant. He personally looks after 2.5 hectares, while his brothers have 0.9 hectare, the wine from which they sell mainly abroad labelled as made by J. M. B. Sorrel.

Marc has slightly increased his planting of white vines – he has 0.8 hectare split between Les Rocoules and Les Greffieux. He leads with the Marsanne, although he has 5 per cent Roussanne on Les Rocoules, where the vines are around forty-five years old. They therefore bring low yields – around 25 hectolitres per hectare, but well-concentrated juice.

His Syrah holdings are 1 hectare on Le Méal (including 5 per cent Marsanne), with the remainder made up of plots on Les Greffieux (giving the derivative name of his main wine Gréal), Les Bessards and the *lieu-dit* known as Les Plantiers, right on the flatland between Les Greffieux and the railway line. He is gradually replanting older portions of the vineyard, and certainly regards his role as a *vigneron* as a thoroughly commercial one – lower-yielding vines are taken out, and the ethos of quantity is nowadays king at this property.

The white is fermented in casks aged two to ten years at around 18°C, and after a brief stay in wood is bottled around ten months after the harvest. The top red wine, Le Gréal, is made from post-war vines whose crop has not been destalked; it is fermented for a little over two weeks, three parts in stainless steel, one part in open wood vats. It stays in 225–litre *pièces* for around sixteen months and is neither fined nor filtered. Bottling runs over an eight-month span.

The Sorrel white fits in style between the densely-extracted Chapoutier and the more modern Jaboulet. It leans towards the classic approach, being a sound wine of middle weight, with a dry, clean finish, and representative of its *terroir*. M. Sorrel likes to harvest his white crop quite early, and is seeking extra refinement. Recent quietly successful years have been the 1985 and the 1988.

The red crop is harvested shortly after the white, making it one of the earlier pickings. Le Gréal has been a bit disappointing recently. If one thinks back to the superb efforts from this *domaine* of the late 1970s, the late 1980s wines are subdued and lack character in comparison. The 1987 held a fair substance, given the difficult year, but the 1988 was a very middle-of-the road wine, with a slightness that was surprising in such a strong year. There was a little richness on the palate – not a lot – and the wine lacked depth. The ordinary Hermitage *cuvée* was also a middle-weight wine, with no special true power in it. The 1989 held more promise, with a darker colour, better extract and livelier fruit. Its tannins are well rounded, and it should drink well around eight to ten years old. But it lacked the intensity that should be present in an exciting vintage. The 1990 is a deeper, darker wine, with a richness that was compulsory in such a good vintage. It will age well over twelve to fifteen years, but one is still left wondering if M. Sorrel will permanently regain the great grip and firm local stamp of his wines made in 1985 and 1983. M. Sorrel has the perceptible accoutrements of the modern cellar – the Bordeaux *barriques*, the stainless steel – but just at this moment they aren't guaranteed to bring home the bacon quite as one would wish.

During the 1980s one small grower has worked with great persistence to build up his *domaine* – Bernard Faurie. Until 1980 he worked in a factory near Tournon, while his father worked the family cherry and apricot trees and their 0.56 hectare of Hermitage vines. He then started to learn to vinify the wine for his father and for his relation Jean Bouzige in nearby Mauves. Between them, the three elder members of the family each held 0.56 hectare: 'It simply wasn't big enough for me to work when I came out of school,' comments M. Faurie. The Faurie family used to be the large local *pépiniériste* before the Second World War, when they would supply around 200,000 vine plants a year up and down the Rhône Valley. 'My family has owned vines on Hermitage since 1935, and my aunt, Mme Bouzige, says that nowadays it's the *grosse* Syrah – the Syrah 3309 – which is the enemy vine. This is the one with fatter pips which gives enormous crops, and it's been particularly in evidence at Crozes-Hermitage since the mid- to late 1970s.'

M. Faurie is now in his early forties. An enthusiast, he takes his wine-making very seriously, and perhaps borders on the hyperactive. He darts around his small cellar, talking at speed with a marked southern twang, but his zeal hides a shy personality. He now exploits 1.7 hectares at Hermitage, of which he has two-thirds and his cousin one-third. His plots are on Les Greffieux and Le Méal, and he has also built up nearly 2 hectares of St-Joseph vineyards and 0.7 hectare of a rented holding at Crozes. In line with this expansion he now has one full-time worker to help him.

Small at Hermitage is just that: M. Faurie buys precisely one new

225-litre *pièce* every year to help ferment in wood the 600 litres of white wine he usually turns out. He bottles the white, which is pure Marsanne from Les Greffieux, after a cask stay of around twelve to fourteen months. His attitude towards the malolactic varies according to the levels of acidity of the vintage. In the ripe year of 1988 he blocked the malolactic, for instance; in 1986, a difficult year, he allowed it to occur. The 1990 as a young wine had an oily, almondy bouquet, which like the palate was marked by the young wood. The wine was clean, quite full and possibly a little short on acidity. His 1989 had a nice, gentle length, is already open on the bouquet, and is finer than the concentrated, chewy 1988. The latter is certainly more an old-style white Hermitage. M. Faurie finds his white wines a considerable personal challenge, and during the 1980s their quality has improved from a rather rustic beginning.

His red is always a very thorough wine, one that well expresses the true qualities of good Hermitage. His policy is to harvest relatively late, and in comparison with M. Sorrel's wines made from earlier pickings in 1989, the Faurie wine is certainly richer, more robust and more sustained on the palate. He does not usually destalk, ferments for about eighteen days in open wood and, after storage in 660-litre *demi-muids*, bottles the red without filtration from seventeen months to two years after the harvest. His recent vintages show him moving into the league of consistently sound producers. The 1991 Greffieux from *demi-muid* had a sweet, quite aromatic bouquet, a pure purple colour and middle weight texture on the palate. Like Le Méal, it suggested good drinking around 1997–9, with the Méal's tannic support likely to help the wines along if they are blended. The 1990 was very good, dark wine, with a firm quality about it. It needs plenty of time to open on the bouquet and to yield a little on the palate. The 1989 was less solid than the 1988, but it has a complex structure where the early fruits and tannins are still at war with one another. The colour is a bright purple, the bouquet is rounded, and the tannins build to an intense finish. The 1988 is a tub-thumping sort of wine, a heavy-weight on the palate, with thick tannins and great chewy extract. It will take a long time to open, and lovers of silky, fine, modern mainstream reds will find it hard. Lovers of Syrah will lick their darkened lips and call for more ... around the year 2002 onwards. It is comparable to his 1983, which when tasted in June 1984 elicited the description 'an old-fashioned whopper of a wine on the palate – immense depth and vast tannins'.

Bernard Faurie's 1987 was also successful. He made a Bessards-Méal *cuvée* which contains good Syrah extract, with correct balance. This will drink well around 1993–5. There was also a Greffieux *cuvée* which is lighter, pleasant, and more representative of its generally awkward vintage. Of his other recent vintages the 1985 was better than the 1986. It contained very pleasant fruit, and there was an underlying vigour on the palate sustained by some solid but not hard tannins. It is holding together well, and is likely to drink well until at least around 1998.

In the ranks of smaller growers, who are made up of people like the Fayolle brothers (1.5 hectares), Michel Ferraton (4 hectares), Philippe Desmeure (3 hectares), Jean-Louis Grippat (1.5 hectares), François Ribo and René-Jean Dard (0.8 hectare), Alain Graillot and Albert Belle, Bernard Faurie is the king of the reds and Jean-Louis Grippat the king of the whites.

The Fayolle holding on Les Diognières was abandoned and overgrown when bought in 1965, so the whole plot dates from then. Only red was made until 1988, in which year a solid white was introduced; the red is sound when conditions suit – the 1985 was a firmly rounded wine and, like the 1982, will be best drunk when it is seven to eleven years old.

The volatile Michel Ferraton is like his wines – some days one catches him on song, other days not. Rustic is how some describe his wine-making and his attention to his vineyards, but in the late 1980s his red Cuvée des Miaux has shown greater consistency and a cleaner, snappier quality. Perhaps his son's presence has tightened things up.

Philippe Desmeure's vineyards are mostly in Crozes, but his red Hemitage is a quality wine which has gained in distinction in the past few years. It has an interesting, upright composition that requires ageing to soften and show more open appeal. All the vintages from 1988 to 1991 have been successful, both in red and white, and this is a name – the Domaine des Remizières – to look out for.

Jean-Louis Grippat's excellent white Hermitage has been mentioned under St-Joseph, but it is one of the consistently best whites in the whole *appellation*; the red is made from just 0.3 hectare on Les Murets, and in a year like 1988 shows as a keeping wine, with quite extreme tannins but good material surrounding them. In a year like 1990, it is a refined, harmonious wine.

François Ribo and René-Jean Dard are two young men striving to make a smallholding pay. They have 1.7 hectares of red and white

St-Joseph and red Crozes, and just the 0.8 hectare of red Hermitage. Most of their vines are rented, and they work from some old Delas cellars in the back streets of Tain. They split the river neatly – Dard, who studied at the Beaune wine school, is from Tournon, and Ribo from Tain. They have been making wine together since 1980 and bottle their whole crop. Early tastings of their Hermitage show wines of a solid purple-black colour, a strong extract but an accompanying woodiness – something they obtain from an eighteen-month stay in *demi-muid*. When visiting two men like these, shy, tousle-haired and obviously totally dedicated to their chosen craft, the analogy of young musicians comes to mind – the gaunt, serious saxophonist, all intensity and commitment, whose artistic streak finds expression in the choice of shoe, the choice of shirt. With Ribo and Dard it's the choice of car – a black Citroën 15, famous as Inspector Maigret's conveyance.

In the past their families were subscribers to Tain's Cave Co-opérative, of which there are 450 members. This makes it one of the really big local enterprises. Its production of red Hermitage is 80,000 bottles (from two bottlings a year) and of white Hermitage 12,000 bottles (one bottling). As with the small *domaines*, there is family continuity at work here, for director Michel Courtial's father was director before him from the Cave's foundation in 1933. Michel joined in 1968 and comments wryly that he hasn't ever had to travel far to work – his family lived at the Cave and he was born two rooms away from his current office.

The white Hermitage is mostly Marsanne. About 60 per cent of the crop is fermented in new oak *pièces* at around 19°C, stocked in stainless steel and bottled one year after the harvest. The red undergoes a seven- to eighteen-day fermentation, and the best selection is aged one-third in stainless steel vats, one-third in first-year *pièces*, and one-third in three- to five-year casks. Along with Jaboulet and Chapoutier, the Cave is the last large wine entity in the northern Rhône to have its own barrel-maker, or *tonnelier* – a West Indian who gives displays of his virtuoso skills and who rejoices in the simple nickname of Chocolat. The red Hermitage, whose ageing process is the same as that for the Cornas and red St-Joseph, receives nine months in wood overall, although the duration can vary according to the state of the harvest.

1987 was the first year that the Co-opérative used wood in the making of their white Hermitage, and the move appears to have been successful. There was a nice freshness and vigour in the wine, it was well balanced and had a good fruit extract. The red in 1987 also showed up as an improved wine, one that was more interesting and contained more character than past offerings – not a heavyweight wine, it was well scented, but like some of the other wines from here had a slightly hot ending.

The Co-opérative holds the key to much of the northern Rhône's reputation if one realizes how much of the total production it controls in either bottle or bulk wine form. At Cornas 300 hectolitres (all bottled), or 12 per cent of the total; at Crozes-Hermitage 30,000 hectos (of which 5,300 are bottled by them), or 60 per cent; at Hermitage itself 1,450 hectolitres, or 25 per cent; at St-Joseph 2,000 hectolitres (mostly sold in bottle), or 11 per cent; at St-Péray 1,000 hectolitres (one-third sold in bottle), or 35 per cent. So whether an *appellation* has a good or bad name with consumers is in many cases down to the Co-opérative.

Of recent tastings the whites can be variable: the Hermitage is definitely top of the range, and totally overshadows the modest offerings of white Crozes (1989 – not very clear tasting, fair richness, OK), St-Péray (1989 – banal, balance not certain) and St-Joseph *blanc* (1989 – decent bouquet, but not that clean on palate, lacks substance). The reds are generally superior: Crozes (1988 – sound colour, fair bouquet but not that fresh; middle-weight wine, some decent tannins, finishes a little hotly) or the Cornas (1987 – old, slightly woody nose, a middling wine on the palate, lacks the thorough guts one expects from Cornas, but more cleanly made than in the past).

By the early 1990s, one senses that the Co-opérative is working hard to reconcile the fact of an enormous production – boosted in 1986 when it took on the local St-Donat Co-opérative that makes mostly table wines – with a leading edge of quality at the top end. It is very much to be hoped that the accountants do not triumph to the banishment of the purists.

Hermitage Vintages

1955   A very good vintage. The whites lived for at least twenty years, while the reds, latterly very charming, are now fading gracefully.

1956   Mediocre. Many of the wines were disappointingly light.

1957   A very good year which produced full-bodied wines. A

little 'harder' than 1955, they have begun to dry out.

1958 Mediocre. Variable wines that tended to be light in colour and body.

1959 A very good year, with some *cuvées* of excellent quality. The wines attained great elegance and harmony with age; although they have lost some of their vigour, well-kept bottles could still be very interesting, with the classic Rhône warmth helping to preserve them.

1960 A generally mediocre year, with wines lacking in strength.

1961 An excellent vintage, which ranks with 1929 and perhaps 1990 as being the best of the century. Both the reds and the whites were laden with rich extract and despite their enormous flavours have a remarkable finesse that is asserting itself increasingly after thirty years. The colour of the reds has eased, turning with orange hints in them, and the bouquets have opened up a hoard of rich, dense coffee and plum aromas. On the palate the reds are ample, with full, lush flavours that have moved on to damp, *sous-bois* aspects. A memorable La Chapelle from Jaboulet, which is now showing a little age (just a touch of spicy dryness on the finish as it shortens up a little), but also a stunning complexity of flavour. The best reds are so rich that they are likely to continue in good drinking shape past the year 2000. The whites also possess extreme depth and are sometimes even younger than the reds, their bouquets displaying a ripe nuttiness with air, but enormous potential and warmth on the palate. A memorable white Hermitage from Chapoutier – a wine of greater strength than most of its contemporaries, it will live easily for forty-five years.

1962 Very good. Not surprisingly lighter than the 1961s, the wines were nonetheless quite full and very well balanced. They have passed their peak, but are still capable of showing the interesting aromas and residual sweetness of well-matured Syrah. The white wines are becoming oxidized.

1963 A poor year. Wishy-washy wines.

1964 An excellent vintage. The red wines have been slow to shake off their tannin, but have retained a dark plum colour with some traces of orange. They have very strong bouquets which still need a little aeration. Firm and well put together on the palate, the best reds, like a still potent La Chapelle, can live until at least 2005. The white wines were very full, and the odd well looked after bottle could provide excellent drinking.

1965   Disappointing. Some good *cuvées* were made, but the wines were generally weak-bodied.

1966   A very good year. The strongly scented red wines are still holding a steady colour and showing a true Rhône richness. They are very well balanced and in the case of a tremendous, powerfully aromatic La Chapelle are still vigorous – likely to drink well throughout the 1990s. The whites were extremely full-bodied, but are tending to dry out, and need drinking up.

1967   A very good vintage. The wines had good colour and richness of flavour. The reds are proving excellent for drinking now, with soft fruit and a lovely richness present, but a slight loss of grip is apparent. Note Chapoutier's La Sizeranne. The whites have turned a golden colour, but have developed striking dried fruit aromas and the complex nutty flavours of old white Hermitage. Note Jaboulet's Chevalier de Stérimberg. Both the reds and the whites will give pleasure past 1995.

1968   A disaster. Very light wines, many of which were never bottled.

1969   Very good indeed. The red wines were rich and well balanced. They have achieved great style and complexity with ageing. The colour has slipped, but their bouquets are very attractive and on the palate they show richness and exemplary length. Both the Chave and the La Chapelle were very successful, and seem likely to continue to show well towards the end of the millennium. The white wines have held up surprisingly well after their early evolution. They are rich, oily wines with admirable finesse, and well-kept bottles will continue to show well until at least 1997.

1970   Very good. Initially, the deeply coloured red wines were perhaps marginally superior to the 1969s, with just a little more body to them. They have reached a state of great equilibrium, with the fruits and tannins well softened out, and in so doing display great length of aftertaste. They may be tiring a little faster than the 1969s, though the best growers' wines have sufficient grip still to show well past 1995. The whites have held up well; less full-bodied, they now show great complexity and distinction – the best, like Grippat's, are very fine to drink before 1994 or so.

1971 A very good vintage whose reds are starting to tire a little. They have become very harmonious despite losing colour, and the bouquets are showing the damp, coffee aromas of old age. Finely structured, their initial richness on the palate is yielding to a hint of final dryness. Drink before 1996 to enjoy the richness they still retain. The whites have aged very well and have kept some of their early depth. A straw-gold colour, they have an impressive warm elegance that sets them apart from the big, voluptuous vintages. A wine like the Jaboulet Chevalier de Stérimberg is very appealing now and can run into the late 1990s.

1972 An excellent vintage for the best wine-makers. The crop was small and the quality of the wines correspondingly high. Initially very full in colour and flavour, several of the reds have advanced more quickly than expected and are now a little wobbly – their colour contains orange, the noses have burnt cocoa and coffee aromas, and the alcohol is starting to show through. The fruit on the palate can be fading in some cases. The Chave has held together well, and shows discreet depth and an impressive finesse. The bouquet is still rich and while the wine may drink well towards 2000 or so, it may lose a little grip by around 1997. A notable La Chapelle which held sensational fruit in its youth, and which has similar ageing potential to the Chave. The whites were fruity and quite rich and are now beginning to taste their age.

1973 Generally a very good year, even if, as with 1972, parts of the vineyard were affected by hail. The reds, initially quite sturdy and driven along by sound underlying tannin, have softened out, and do not possess further scope. They should ideally be drunk before around 1994. The whites were very well scented and well balanced, but need drinking up.

1974 The best growers made quietly agreeable wines in only a fairly good vintage. The reds have lost much of their colour and now show the damp, leafy aromas of old age on the bouquet, while a little light fruit remains on the palate. The

Chave now shows great finesse, but should be drunk. The light, fruity white wines have developed a tenuous and rather wobbly honeyed appeal on the palate, but are slipping. Guigal possesses an extraordinary white made by the late Terence Gray and left in oak for ten years. Guigal bottled two of the four casks he bought from Gray, and when last tasted in October 1990, notes were: clear gold; rich, ripe nose, lovely depth, touch of dried fruits. Palate has the immediate dryness or oxidizing effect of the wood. Clean, rather short finish. Needs food – delicious with sardines.

1975   A small crop produced some light reds. Deficient in colour and depth of flavour, their early fruitiness has largely faded and they are (for Hermitages) a bit thin. Drink them up, they lack any potential. The whites have held together better – well-developed bouquets are very appealing, and they can provide good drinking for a few years yet.

1976   A good to very good vintage that fell victim of the growers' early hue and cry that it was quite exceptional. The red wines have progressed more rapidly than first anticipated, and their colour has started to turn, the bouquets show the mellow but drying aromas of old age and there is a thinning of the middle-aged richness on the palate. Drink them up. The whites are golden now, but they have done very well thanks to above-average levels of acidity. Well-kept bottles will show great balance and refinement, and are delightful to drink now.

1977   A light vintage where the reds lacked a little colour and extract. They were drinking with great appeal after eight to ten years, but the best has been seen of them. The whites have held together better; rich aromas and dried fruit flavours abound and they can be drunk with pleasure past 1992.

1978   An excellent vintage that approached 1961 in dimension. A small harvest, very healthy grapes, and wines that are therefore notable for their power, richness and balance. The reds have held a dark purple hue well, while the bouquets are crammed with berry, pine and essential oil aromas which will undoubtedly show very well by the late 1990s. Very firmly structured on the palate, the tannins still have a solid grip, and these are thirty-plus-year wines. The La Chapelle is sensational, a full-blooded offering from Jaboulet, while Chave's red seems split into a more vibrant *cuvée* and a rather, hard, subdued *cuvée*. Chapoutier was successful with La Sizeranne, Sorrel's red Le Méal had an extraordinary bouquet and remarkable construction, and the Guigal was richly balanced, while most other growers came up trumps – those from smaller *domaines* will continue to show very well around 1996–2000. The whites are very good, full and succulent on the palate now: they should be drunk over the next four or five years. Jaboulet's white Stérimberg did not live up to its name this year.

1979   Very good. The reds were not in the same powerful league as the biggest years, and developed very good fruit flavours during the 1980s; they are showing their age, with spices and coffee flavours coming through now. They should ideally be drunk before around 1995 to obtain the best of their richness. The whites have developed tremendous apricot-inspired aromas, and are long, full and simply delicious now. They can live for a few years more. Note the excellent red and white of the late Henri Sorrel, the reds of Chave and Guigal and the white of Grippat.

1980   A fair vintage, where the harvest was interrupted by rain. The reds are middle-weight wines. Their colour was a firm red initially, but it now has distinct traces of orange-brown. They have developed soft fruit bouquets and an easy elegance on the palate, but by and large should be drunk now as they risk having passed their best. The Chave red has done well in bottle and is likely to be an unsung hero of this vintage – it will live past the end of the century. The whites were excellent – very aromatic, very long *en bouche* and full of early appeal. They, too, have mostly hit the top, but well-cellared bottles could still show well towards 1994. Note Jaboulet's white Stérimberg and Chapoutier's white Cuvée des Boys.

1981   An uneven vintage, from a very rainy year, better for the whites than the reds. The colour of the reds was middling, quite close to the 1980s, but they lacked sufficient extract to round up into a typically thorough Hermitage – partly the result of heavy rain at harvest. These light wines are drinking *à point* now; they are short on the finish and should not be kept for anything other than anniversaries. The whites set off with good early aromas and lively fruit and are now just starting to tire – drink before around 1994.

1982   The first of the scorching summers of the 1980s produced very good wines from the leading, best-equipped growers, a suitable forerunner to the remarkably distinguished quintet of 1983, 1985, 1988, 1989 and 1990. The crop was large but gave wines of great richness and colour. Smaller growers had problems with cooling their fermentation vats, so some wines are rather jammy on the palate. The best reds are very ripe, very lush, with well-balanced flavours. They have started to show well, with delicious, appealing softness; they are likely to drink well out towards 2000–2007. The whites were sustained by high alcohol and dense flavours; a little short on acidity, they are now very unctuous on the palate, and their impressive richness is driving them along. They will drink superbly throughout the 1990s with so much to sustain them. Note the reds of Chave, Bernard Faurie, Guigal and La Chapelle; also the whites of Guigal and Chave (both very powerful) and the white of Grippat (elegant).

1983   Excellent. A tremendously strong, dark vintage of deeply concentrated wines with great prospects of long ageing. Early summer rain and a touch of *coulure* on the Syrah were succeeded by prolonged heat and drought, making the harvest very strongly flavoured. The wines are still full of black in their colour, and the bouquets show great berry and pine or cedar aromas that will fan out into generous and complex offerings after fifteen years or so. Very firm still on the palate, the reds have a tight-knit structure, and it is a pity to open them now when they are suggesting only a part of what they can offer. Chave and Jaboulet with their La Chapelle excelled themselves this year – yardstick Hermitage. The wines of growers like Alphonse Desmeure will run towards 2000. In general, the harder tannins of 1983 give it a much longer life in prospect than 1982 – thirty-five years for the best. The whites were excellent as well. They held more acidity than the 1982s, they have a delightful balance and are very long on the palate. They are drinking very well now, but will continue to show supreme quality towards the turn of the century. Very good Chevalier de Stérimberg, Guigal and Chapoutier whites.

1984 Lack of heat during the summer and rains in August and September affected the quality of this vintage, which is only middling. The reds' colour was below its usual depth, and the bouquets were not well extracted – the lesser *cuvées* tended towards astringence. Those growers who picked late and selected their harvest carefully – Chave, Bernard Faurie and Delas with their Marquise de la Tourette, for example – succeeded in making wines whose soft fruitiness was very attractive. These wines do not have the balance and depth to live long and should be drunk before around 1995. The whites were lighter than the 1983s and 1982s, but their fruit and vitality were appealing. Some *cuvées* were dull, but the best – Chave, Grippat, Chapoutier's Chante-Alouette – were stylish, elegant wines likely to show well towards 1996.

1985 Very good indeed. *Coulure* affected the size of the crop, and the white harvest was almost half the size of the 1984. The summer was hot, but interspersed with welcome bouts of rain; the reds are darkly coloured, but while the 1983s were marked by severe tannins, the 1985s were marked by rounded, well-ripened tannins – no need for Chave to destalk his 1985 as opposed to the 1983. The bouquets are generous, and by the mid-1990s will start to open and blossom out. The palates are marked by exuberant fruit and a good length at the finish. A very good Le Gréal from Marc Sorrel, likewise a successful red from Bernard Faurie – both ten- to fifteen-year wines. Good but not startling La Chapelle, a Chapoutier La Sizeranne chock-full of fruit, and an immaculately balanced red Chave which has the longest life in prospect – up to twenty-five years or so. The whites are superb – excellent balance, good depth and luscious flavours. Some of these wines will drink well over the course of twenty years. Note Chapoutier's Chante-Alouette and Chave for the longest-lived *cuvées*; the Jaboulet Stérimberg, Sorrel and Grippat wines are all drinking well now.

1986   A vintage where there are variations in quality and where the competence of the growers was tested. The best *cuvées* are becoming very good. Rain and warm temperatures at harvest-time upset the work of a hot, sunny summer and gave the growers rot to contend with. Those who sorted the harvest severely made soundly coloured red wines whose bouquets are starting to unfold already. But they are solid on the palate, with good length and can age successfully towards the year 2004 or so. The Chave was very well made and the Guigal has excellent length and firm tannic support: both will be worth seeking out as value for money. The La Chapelle is developing well in bottle, and further improvement is likely in the coming years. The whites were good, the best – like Grippat – holding a combination of acidity and *gras* or substance. They will drink well for around twelve years or so. The Jaboulet Stérimberg white missed out.

1987   A difficult vintage with the summer short on heat. The reds are a bit better than popularly assumed; their colour is middling, and some *cuvées* suffer from rather hot, uneven bouquets. But there are wines with pleasant berried fruit on the nose and some lurking residual tannins pushing along on the palate. These are ten-year wines for great, uncomplicated drinking. The whites have emerged as very good – full-blown bouquets and lush flavours on the palate – they have good prospects for keeping over fifteen years or more. Note the red of Chave and Marc Sorrel, and delightful whites from Chave (full), Guigal and Desmeure (both elegant) and Vidal-Fleury.

1988   Excellent. A vintage of classically full-blooded, solid red wines whose depth and concentration will ensure a long life ahead. A very healthy harvest was brought in after a long, dry and hot summer. The reds are very darkly coloured, and some possess extreme tannins: these are offset by the richness of the extract on the palate. The bouquets will take time to emerge, but this fine, upstanding vintage has given wine-makers every chance to produce thorough, traditional Hermitage. Several of the reds will live for twenty-five years or more. Note Grippat, Chave, Chapoutier (fifteen to twenty years), La Chapelle (eighteen-plus years) Delas Marquise de la Tourette (fifteen years) and Desmeure (ten to fourteen years). The size of the white harvest was affected by *coulure*; the wines show great finesse and are backed by enough substance on the palate to end with a satisfying chewiness. They hold good fruit and their balance indicates sound development over at least a dozen years. A finer Chante-Alouette than usual from Chapoutier (will drink well from the mid-1990s), a new oak-fashioned Stérimberg from Jaboulet (not typical of its *terroir* – may regain its authenticity after four or five years), a fine, middle-distance wine from Grippat (excellent after six to eight years) and an elegant Chave (will drink well after five years, great fruit; but will live on).

1989   Excellent, and only history will fully reveal the relative standing versus 1988. The 1989 reds are fleshier wines, and more complex, with more sensual fruit in them. They are darkly coloured, rich in extract and have good length. They are likely to show more on the bouquet at an earlier stage than the more reticent, backward 1988s, and this vintage appears like a superior, more all-round version of 1985. Marc Sorrel's Gréal showed some return to form this year; an excellent wine from Bernard Faurie, a medium-weight La Chapelle (marked by new oak) – certainly less robust than the 1988; a middle-weight, solid but well-structured Sizeranne and an intense, captivating Le Pavillon from Chapoutier, and a complex, rich and long Chave. These wines have sufficient balance of tannin and acidity to live and blossom well over twenty to thirty years – they will stay further than most people might expect. The whites are strongly scented, bear good fruit and finish with very good depth of flavour. They look like developing steadily over twelve or more years.

1990   Excellent, if not superb; a vintage that approached the majesty and delicious depth of 1961. Yet another drought summer hit the growers, but this year the rainfall, although slight, came at just the right moments, notably in August. The harvest was a regular size and really ripe grapes were brought in. The red wines bear a characteristic of very well-ripened aromas on some of the bouquets; there is a tremendous amount of extract present and all the constituents are extremely well balanced. These are exciting wines, which in the hands of growers like Jaboulet (La Chapelle), Chave and Chapoutier will become classics of great long life and enormous pleasure. They are more complete than the 1988s and 1989s, and the odds (and the Gods) must dictate that such a stunning trio of vintages will not be seen together for several years or even decades. The whites were powerful, initially subdued wines, whose richness will drive them along for perhaps twenty years. The Chave and the Jaboulet Stérimberg were both full but well-integrated wines; some growers' *cuvées* risk being a little too corpulent, however, and may lose their grip by the second half of the 1990s.

Earlier Exceptional Vintages 1953, 1952, 1949, 1947, 1945, 1943, 1933, 1929. Any of these wines could be quite marvellous, but their well-being depends very much on where and how they have been kept. The 1953 red La Sizeranne from Chapoutier, for example, may carry a brown colour, but there is still an impressive, sweet richness on the palate: it has become very winy, is losing its grip, but was still remarkable to try in 1990. The 1952s tasted are excellent – both a Chapoutier and a Chave, the latter holding more depth than the former. These need drinking to catch their exquisite roundness. The 1929 Chave red is also still very well scented and full for its age on the palate – this is a wine that will never quite fade away. A 1947 Chave red drunk in 1986 showed increasingly well on the bouquet with air, which brought out spice and pepper aromas alongside the coffee-bean smell. It was becoming a bit hot *en bouche*, but still displayed a lovely plum richness on the palate. And a 1942 Chave red tasted in 1984 was still lively on the early palate; like all these old wines its calling card was a lingering southern sweetness on the nose – very attractive. Old whites can provide similar pleasure. The Chave *blanc* 1929, tasted in 1984 and 1986, was still opening and revealing greater nuttiness of flavour on the palate after exposure to the air, and possessed an incredible length – the most remarkable white Rhône ever tasted by the author. A 1952 Chave *blanc* was still elegant and chewy when tasted in 1984. Old white Hermitage is well worth keeping an eye out for around the auction rooms.

Leading Growers at Hermitage

The nucleus of growers and producers of Hermitage capable of bringing out wine that can range from the sound to the spectacular is:

Belle, Albert	26600 Larnage
Chapoutier, M.	26600 Tain-l'Hermitage
Chave, Jean-Louis	07300 Mauves
Delas Frères	07300 St-Jean-de-Muzols
Desmeure, Philippe	26600 Mercurol
Faurie, Bernard	07300 Tournon
Graillot, Alain	26600 Tain-l'Hermitage
Grippat, Jean-Louis	07300 Tournon
Guigal, E.	69420 Ampuis
Jaboulet Aîné, Paul	26600 La Roche-de-Glun
Sorrel, Marc	26600 Tain-l'Hermitage
Vidal-Fleury	69420 Ampuis

Other producers:

Cave Co-opérative des Vins Fins	26600 Tain-l'Hermitage
Faurie, Pierre	07300 Mauves
Fayolle, Jean-Claude and Jean-Paul	26600 Gervans
Ferraton, Michel	26600 Tain-l'Hermitage
Michelas, Robert	
Ribo, Francois and Dard, René-Jean	} 26600 Mercurol
Sorrel, J. M. B.	26600 Tain-l'Hermitage
de Vallouit, Louis-Francis	26240 St-Vallier

5
Crozes-Hermitage

For many years Crozes-Hermitage bumbled along in the lee of Hermitage, a rather dowdy relation in name, producing red and white wines of a lesser stature and only moderate interest value. The first paragraph of this chapter in the 1983 edition did the then orthodox thing – took a quick swipe at Crozes as follows:

> In 1846 the tasting panel of the Lyon Wine Congress had this to say about the wines of Crozes-Hermitage and Hermitage: 'If they are not brothers, then they are certainly first cousins.' This is a slightly flattering overall evaluation of the comparatively unknown wines of Crozes-Hermitage.

Well, things have changed for the better. During the 1980s a movement continued, started by a few hardy souls about fifteen years ago, to make fresh, appealing and still vigorous wines from the northern Rhône's one large open space. And while in most cases the wines cannot remotely compare with Hermitage, then that is no bad thing – they are beginning to gain some sex appeal of their own, some style that makes them a little bit New Worldy, especially with the reds. Wine-making techniques have tightened up, fresh young bloods have started up their own *domaines*, and from being a worthy but dull *appellation*, this is now one place where wise wine merchants should patrol in search of finds.

The *appellation contrôlée* area is made up of eleven villages around Tain-l'Hermitage and derives its name from one of them, a tiny community whose agreeable red wine was in the past referred to simply as 'Crozes'. Tain serves as the unofficial centre of the *appellation* and is ringed by Crozes-Hermitage, Serves, Erôme, Gervans and Larnage to the north; by Mercurol and Chanos-Curson to the east; and by Beaumont-Monteux, Pont-de-l'Isère and Roche-de-Glun to the south.

The villages all lie within easy distance of the main Paris to Nice highways, the A7 and N7, but somehow contrive a strangely timeless existence. The central café is likely to have its shutters firmly closed; the main square looks almost derelict. Horse and cart go clopping serenely around narrow streets that end abruptly in uneven clumps of vines; old women in black watch with listless eyes from behind closed windows, their eternal vigil only rarely interrupted by the movement of a passing vehicle. There is no one in the streets, not even the traditionally observed group of old *pétanque* players. Away in the vines the heavy silence is fleetingly broken by guttural cries that urge a stubborn mule to greater endeavour. Here the land is man's master, and its dominance is reflected in the lifeless, detached villages all around.

The Crozes-Hermitage *appellation* is much larger than Hermitage and covers about 1,150 hectares. It is an expanding area, too, for most of the vines are planted on gentle slopes and flat ground away from the east bank of the Rhône. This is the one area in the northern Rhône where mechanical harvesting takes place, and with the incentive of being able largely to work their vineyards with machines, the *vignerons* are encouraged to extend their planting. The only other place in this part of the Valley where such growth has occurred is at St-Joseph, where the extensions were triggered by changes in the geographical zone of *appellation*.

Historically, the wine of the region is obscure. Very little is recorded about it until the eighteenth century when, it appears, wine from the village of Larnage was sold on a fairly regular basis to England; this was called, not *vin de Larnage*, but *vin de Mure*, after Larnage's leading family, and it was always sent across to Bordeaux before being shipped north. This was not the first local wine to go abroad, however, for the white wine of nearby Mercurol was sent to England around 1309, according to village archives. To whom it went is not known.

Today the best red wines come from a small place called Les Chassis, which lies south of Tain on the way to La Roche-de-Glun, and from Gervans; while the best white is undoubtedly from around Mercurol. It is no coincidence that the vineyards of Gervans are on steep, well-exposed slopes overlooking the Rhône, and indeed the village possesses a situation nearly identical to that of Hermitage, with its southward-facing hillsides and granite topsoil. The vine-yards at Les Chassis stand on the plain among dry stones and some clay–limestone. They give a good, well-balanced wine that has greater flesh and earlier appeal than the wine from the more granite-based vineyards near Tain. Local *propriétaires* such as Jaboulet, Graillot, Chapoutier and the team of Tardy and Ange like to use Les Chassis as a principal constituent when they are making up their red wine *cuvées* from their holdings in different parts of the *appellation*. The only drawback with this site is the soil's inability to retain water, which makes it drought-prone in certain years – 1989 was an example. Meanwhile at Mercurol the vineyards are mostly on hillsides, and the predominantly sandy soil seems ideally suited to the cultivation of the Marsanne and Roussanne grapes.

Red Crozes-Hermitage is usually made entirely from the Syrah grape, although the inclusion of up to 15 per cent of white grapes is permitted at the moment of fermentation. The Cave Co-opérative at Tain and one or two other growers would sometimes take advantage of this ruling but nowadays find it less necessary to do so because the white wine is selling well in its own right.

Vinification of the red wine follows the same basic method as that used for Hermitage, although in a somewhat abbreviated form. Some growers, like Chapoutier, still ferment in wooden vats after an initial treading down by foot and a destalking. They are nowadays the exception, however, as most producers now used closed vats, made of stainless steel, concrete or with enamel lining. Certainly there is now a lot more sophistication in the methods of the progressive growers than there was during the 1970s, and cellar care has taken giant strides forward.

There is no uniformity on destalking and destemming. Jaboulet destalk, Étienne Pochon destalks about half, and Philippe Desmeure most of his crop. In 1990 Tardy and Ange destalked in order to tidy up the harvest after it had been brought in by harvesting machines. 'Some big stalks can remain, and the process of destalking allows us to really clean up the harvest to make absolutely sure of a well-sorted introduction of grapes into the vats – any green flavours will also be prevented at source,' commented M. Bernard Ange. Meanwhile a grower like M. Alain Graillot says he is after fruit and extract above all, so all he does is to pump the whole grapes into his concrete and *beton* fermenting vats. 'Quite a lot remain whole this way,' he says, 'and I back this up with two to five days' cooling of the crop at 18°C, allowing a cold maceration before the primary fermentation which may itself run for fifteen to twenty days, but never passes over 30°C: hence maximum extraction of aromas', he states.

Shorter *cuvaisons* of ten to fourteen days are practised by producers like the enormous Cave Co-opérative and Tardy and Ange, while the presence of stainless steel vats in cellars is now much more widespread. Étienne Pochon at Château Curson uses *inox* for his extended maceration over three weeks; the Cave Co-opérative de Tain forgo the stockage of their red Crozes in wood, and use stainless steel for their roughly 30,000 hectolitres before about 5,500 hectolitres are bottled on the premises in January following the harvest – a very rapid process.

The *vin de presse* is sometimes added by a grower like Philippe Desmeure, and kept separate by people like Chapoutier and Étienne Pochon. When a vintage needs a bit of extra beef is when this wine is most commonly included. After the malolactic is completed, it is time to roll out the barrels. New oak fever has hit Crozes in the same way as in many French *appellations*. M. Pochon for his Château Curson uses young oak of 1 to 3 years in the form of Bordeaux *pièces*; Alain Graillot uses 225-litre *pièces* that are generally between their second and fifth year; Tardy and Ange rely on *demi-muids* (660 litres) or 65-hectolitre *foudres*, one-third of which are in their first or second year of work. Jaboulet have a movable policy on wood-ageing. For their top *cuvée*, the delicious Domaine de Thalabert, they left the 1988 for one year in a mixture of 28 per cent brand new *pièces* and 72 per cent one-year-old *pièces*. In 1989 the Thalabert spent ten to twelve months in a mixture of first-, second- and third-year *pièces*, while in 1990 35 per cent aged in first-year casks, over about twelve months. The youngest, first-year casks spend the previous season housing Hermitage La Chapelle, Côte-Rôtie Les Jumelles or Cornas. Chapoutier, meanwhile, use mainly *pièces* – French oak – with some *demi-muids* over a ten and twelve-month maturation for their La Petite Ruche and Les Meysonniers reds respectively.

The good name of Crozes is very much in the hands of these *vignerons* and some of their colleagues – those who are prepared to put in the money and the effort to upgrade the wines. Fifteen years ago or more, red Crozes fell into two categories: either it was a mass-production wine, utterly bland and almost soupy, with little Syrah *typicité* – a delight for a Burgundian *négociant* who could whack out large amounts to supermarkets. Or it was a rustically produced, hot country wine – a beefy, coarse peasant linked by name to the immaculate Hermitage. The one exception to this rule over the years, providing a thoroughbred class, has been Paul Jaboulet's Domaine de Thalabert, an excellent wine made from 38 hectares of the family's vineyard at Les Chassis.

In the early 1990s there are more clean, sophisticated wines – both red and white – and the future looks more exciting and challenging. Gone are the days of many *domaine* wines being left for too long – two or three years – in dirty old casks, while their fruit – much of the essence of red Crozes – gradually ebbed out of them. Growers like Graillot, Philippe Desmeure, Tardy and Ange, Étienne Pochon, Jean-Michel Borja, Jean-Louis Pradelle, the Fayolle brothers, Albert Belle, Alphonse Cornu and the principal *négociants* such as Jaboulet, Chapoutier and Delas are combining to give Crozes a better name and greater hope. But beware – there is still plenty of wine circulating which has been bottled by obscure names and *négociants* outside the Rhône area, all called Crozes, all nice and cheap in the supermarket or the local *bistrot* and nearly all lamentable in quality.

A prerequisite for good red Crozes is that there should be a lively, direct fruitiness on the bouquet. This wine can show off the early wild fruit aromas of the Syrah in a blistering way when it is well vinified and under around three years old. Indeed, there is great appeal in drinking some *cuvées* when they are running with surges of fruit on nose and palate. Tasting notes refer to raspberry and sometimes blackcurrant flavours, which are striking and vigorous and very clean on the palate, and supported by tannins that are rarely too raw and oppressive. For a person used to lighter, more modern wines, this version of 'fruitiness' will be exacting, since greater depth and thoroughness exist in the wine than would be found in a simple Gamay or short-vinification country wine.

Red Crozes curls up and withdraws for a little while after its explosive entrance, and typically some of the fruit-laden and delightful wines retreat around two and a half or three years after the harvest – 'go dumb', the growers say – as they settle into a more typical sit-down wine routine. Here the Syrah again shows its class, with the wines developing a complexity on the bouquet and more intricate flavours on the palate as their tannins round and the fruitiness mellows. In this stage one is nearer to considering minor Hermitage wines; in the first stage one is close to the simple style of good St-Joseph *rouge*. When comparing Crozes with its neighbour St-Joseph across the river, Jean-Louis Grippat and Michel Chapoutier agree that the main difference between these two wines comes from the frequently clay-limestone soil found at Crozes against the granite, more acid terrain of central St-Joseph locations. 'This gives the St-Josephs finer, less heavy tannins and a slightly paler colour', comments Michel Chapoutier.

Some *vignerons* seek out the more considered style of wine right from the start: Jaboulet's Thalabert, Desmeure's Cuvée Particulière, Graillot's La Guiraude and the Fayolle brothers' Les Voussères are examples. These *cuvées* generally receive greater wood-ageing, and exposure to young wood in the case of Graillot, Desmeure and Jaboulet. Such wines in years like 1990 and 1989 need three or four years to settle and to start to emerge from a solid structure. When they have great depth of extract and the sound tannic support of 1990, they step neatly in style between Hermitage, with its generous, profound and very long flavours, and Cornas, with its abrupt, stern Syrah blackness. In such years the wines are capable of showing well from around five years up to a dozen years, and odd well-cellared bottles will keep going even longer.

Evidence of the continuing trend towards the production of superior red and white wines comes from a small but significant statistic that emerges from interviews with the Tain Co-opérative over the years. In 1974 there were 710 subscribers, in 1982 550 and in 1990 there were 400 cultivating *appellation* vineyards – a very marked indication that these vineyard owners increasingly wish to strike out on their own, vinifying, bottling and selling their wine themselves. The Co-opérative still plays a very important part in local proceedings, since it is responsible for over half of all the wine made at Crozes; it supplies local *négociant* houses with some of their Crozes, as well of course as bottling wine under their own name – a massive 705,000 bottles a year – so any vinification improvements there are to be applauded.

While techniques have evolved in the making of white Crozes-Hermitage, this wine remains something of a standard middle-ranker, rather along the lines of ordinary Mâcon *blanc*. It rarely excites in the same way that a red Crozes can, and the best development over the past fifteen years has been a cleaning-up of its vinification, so that it is now fresher and cleaner-tasting. Somehow the Marsanne at Crozes does not produce wines of a remotely comparable stature and class to those produced off the granite and clay on the Hermitage hill. While Jaboulet seemed to have diminished the standing of their white Hermitage through a combination of making it from half Roussanne and pursuing the most modern low-temperature vinification methods, they have succeeded in raising the quality and interest of their white Crozes Mule Blanche through the very same methods.

The Jaboulet Mule Blanche comes from a single 7-hectare vineyard, and is made from 45 per cent Roussanne (planted in 1970)and 55 per cent Marsanne (about thirty-five years old). It is vinified in stainless steel, and since 1964 the malolactic has been blocked, through keeping the wine at about −7°C for two weeks after the alcoholic fermentation. Freshening the wine is the prime aim, one in which the family have been very successful. In some years there is a brief encounter with one-year-old wood – the 1989 received five weeks, the 1991 four months prior to an early bottling between February and April. In other years, like 1990, the wine is stocked only in stainless steel before bottling.

The result is a wine of greater liveliness and character than many white Crozes, whose drawback is frequently an overt flabbiness and lack of sharp definition on the palate. The 1989 Mule Blanche combined fresh aromas with some local depth on the bouquet, while the palate bore some nutty flavours on the attack which ran on to a very pleasant liveliness on the finish – a touch of *nervosité* undoubtedly triggered by the presence of the Roussanne. This was an elegant wine, an adjective rarely found attached to Crozes *blanc*, which on average represents between 8 and 10 per cent of the total Crozes production–around 4,200 hectolitres (1989–5,257 hectos, a record).

Around the *appellation* there is a concerted effort by the more enlightened growers to freshen up their white wine, but a personal view is that this area is not a natural *terroir* for good white wine – it is an uphill struggle, and white Crozes has never held the same fruity appeal and medium weight of good St-Joseph – a much underrated wine – across the river.

Of those who have made above average whites over the past fifteen years, Bernard Ange and Charles Tardy at the Domaine des Entrefaux are good examples of growers who have modified their work methods to try to master the challenge. They were about the first private *domaine* to perform a temperature-controlled fermentation, which nowadays takes place at around 15–17°C; and in 1988 they started to vinify and raise part of their white crop (15 per cent) in new oak *demi-muids* – a figure that rose to 28 per cent in 1989. They have a special *cave climatisée* for this, which gives an ambient temperature of 13–14°C. As a result the last cask finishes its fermentation as late as the end of November. Racking, fining and a return to wood then occur, prior to assembly with their vat wine in March or April, filtering and bottling – with the malolactic blocked, which has been done systematically from 1986. The result for them is white wines that need a year or so to settle down: at six months they carry a fresh, straight *bonbon* bouquet – very much a standard low-temperature smell with little or no local definition. On the palate there is a light nuttiness, but again definition is lacking. After about eighteen months, however, the wine has developed in excellent style: some citrus and nutty aromas, a striking flavour of almond on the palate, a very good weight – a discreet reminder that this is a southern wine – and a clean finish. This is a very good, modern style of white Crozes, helped in Bernard Ange's words by 'the wood bringing in some *gras* – almost some flesh'.

Tardy and Ange rely almost wholly on the Marsanne, as do a majority of leading growers – Borja at the Cave des Clairmonts, Philippe Desmeure at the Domaine des Remizières, the Pradelle brothers and the old-fashioned Raymond Roure at Gervans. Alain Graillot, a rising name, has 20 per cent Roussanne in his 2.5 hectares of white grapes, but that was something he inherited when he bought his *domaine* in the autumn of 1988. He made a very good white in 1988, 1989, and in 1990; curiously, the 1990, when tasted in January 1992, bore Chenin Blanc characteristics on the bouquet – a chalky, rich aroma – while the palate contained an interesting mix of freshness and depth. Apart from M. Graillot's good cellar work, this may suggest that the plains and short slopes of Crozes, as opposed to the Hermitage hill, are suited to a spot more Roussanne to make the white more interesting. In any event, only the curious should lay down their white Crozes, for these are emphatically wines that are best drunk within the first five or six years – two to four years being the real moment of excellence.

Two of the earliest *émigrés* from the Cave Co-opérative were Messieurs Tardy and Ange (not a music-hall duo, just brothers-in-law). They will now be known by Rhône enthusiasts overseas, since they have distributed their good red and white wines to a large extent in the United States and Britain, the names under which they sell being Domaine des Entrefaux, the Domaine des Pierrelles (mostly used in the US) and the Domaine de la Beaume, all labels rather than different wines.

They started to bottle part of their wine in 1980 and have built up their vineyards to the extent of having 11 hectares (8 Syrah, 3 Marsanne) around their cellars at Chanos-Curson and 13 hectares at Beaumont-Monteux (95 per cent Syrah). 'We're lucky,' comments Bernard Ange, who with his curly dark brown hair and pervasive enthusiasm, always seems younger than his years, 'because we have my nephew of twenty-five, François Tardy, coming in: this means we've got people in their twenties, thirties and – oh dear, just in their fifties – working as a team and keeping senior citizen Charles Tardy on his toes! He and I combined our vineyards when we left the Co-opérative, which is why they're split between Chanos and Monteux. The Chanos vines are more on the slope, and we find that the Syrah there produces a tougher, more backward wine, rather in the style of Gervans, than it does from the more typically plain vineyards of Beaumont, where we're working on stony, Alpine-deposit topsoil, just right for reds. So we blend the wine of the two places.'

Their cellars are a little north-west of Chanos-Curson, where both men were brought up, and the building's dry-stone exterior is set off in summer by a dazzling blue wistaria that dominates the whole courtyard. At the right time of the early summer there are also white and violet lilacs in full bloom, and an abundant rosé-coloured tamarisk giving the *domaine* an aspect of colourful fecundity.

The Tardy and Ange red wines are excellent middle-weights. They never have the fleshy liquorice tannins of a Thalabert or Graillot's Guiraude *cuvée*, nor the drier, upright tannic support of Desmeure's Cuvée Particulière, but they are notable for a good berried fruit extract on the palate. In years like 1988 and 1990, they made wines delightful to drink over the course of about eight years, but the balance is sufficient to make the odd forgotten bottle a nice surprise. For example, a 1985 tasted in 1990 was developing complexity, with the sort of *sous-bois* smells on the bouquet given off by maturing Syrah, and a solid but rich depth of flavour on the palate – a wine that could show well up to 1996 in extreme cases. They also do a more solid *cuvée* called Le Dessus des Entrefaux; this wine receives longer wood-ageing – a bit over the usual year – and a higher percentage of new oak than the normal one-third that sees first- and second-year barrels. It is a more forceful *cuvée*, more of a long-term, winter-drinking wine. It seems best produced in ripe, generous years like 1990 since there is a tendency for the additional wood tannins to compound some of the raw tannins that occurred in 1987 and 1989 as a result of those years' weather conditions.

Close neighbours of MM. Tardy and Ange are the Pradelle brothers, Jacques and Jean-Louis, whose father used to be in the Cave Co-opérative but who had latterly been selling his grapes to the Tain *négociant* house of Chapoutier. With both sons in their twenties and both eager to make wine themselves, their father agreed in 1978 that they should start to vinify and bottle all their own wine. They have 3.5 hectares of predominantly Marsanne vines and 17 hectares of Syrah, all at Mercurol, half of them on the zigzag of short slopes and half on the plain, which in their *quartier* contains quite an element of smooth, rounded stones which are evidence of the Rhône's old route past the east side of today's hill of Hermitage.

A bouncy man with a woolly bobble-hat perched on the top of his head, Jacques said that both he and his brother had studied at wine school at Beaune, which had been an invaluable training. 'We now know more about things like when to age our wine in *foudre* and when to age it in a smaller *pièce*, and a lot of little details that add up to helping you make a better wine. Demand for our wine has allowed us nearly to double the size of our vineyard in the last ten years. We age the Syrah for around a year, although our inclination would be to leave it a little longer. The other great thing that bottling our wine has brought is the new friends and people we have met. We have a completely new horizon now, since we sell half our wine to Germany, Switzerland, the Netherlands and Denmark, and it's very interesting and educative to hear foreign people discussing our wine.' Dark-coloured, the Pradelle red is made in the firm, orthodox style of an eight-year Crozes, one that needs about three years to settle, soften, and show lively aromas when it comes from vintages like 1985 and 1988. In lesser years like 1987 they also come up with creditable offerings – in this case a quietly fruited and scented wine that was very drinkable inside its first four years. The white Pradelle is less inspiring, but the red is good, reliable and shows the earthy, *terroir* side of the Syrah.

While the Tardy and Ange duo and the Pradelles represent the influx of the 1970s, the star turn of the 1980s was Alain Graillot, who before 1985 had never made a drop of wine in his life. He used to work on the export side of a Paris-based company selling agricultural treatment products to areas like Latin America. At the age of forty he decided to make the break, and in a memorable quote, when asked why he wanted to make wine, replied, 'I wanted to make a *Syrah* wine, which I couldn't do with a full-time job.' A native of Vienne, M. Graillot had been bitten by the Syrah bug through visits to and purchases from Guigal, Jean-Louis Grippat and Paul Jaboulet, but when he started, his precise wine-making knowledge was about the same as that of most people who draw up their car outside a *vigneron*'s cellar to fill it up with bottles for the return to their town apartment.

M. Graillot made his 1985 taking a month and a half off from his Paris job and using the harvest from a rented vineyard around the prime Les Chassis site. This was a very creditable effort, the red Crozes being a wine with a lot of raw fruit aromas when young, some very good fruit on the attack and a well-knit structure – a wine that was drinking very well in 1991. His red St-Joseph, bought in grape form off a grower on the slopes at Andance, where there is some good granitic soil, was also well made, being an initially rather tucked-up wine which was notable for its concentration of the fruit extract – one that will drink well until around 1993.

Having moved to Tain with his wife and two sons, M. Graillot stepped up a gear, and by 1992 his vineyard and cellar developments had moved ahead at speed. He bought the whole *domaine* – vineyards, cellars and all – in 1988. He has 18 hectares surrounding the cellars, mostly on stony soil, with a little sand present – 'sandy-siliceous' is how he describes it – plus just 0.12 hectare on Les Greffieux at Hermitage, from which a red 1989 was the first issue, and 0.5 hectare of Syrah from St-Jean-de-Muzols, near Raymond Trollat, which is added to the Andance purchase of grapes for his St-Joseph.

As a man whom the French describe as *dynamique*, M. Graillot has got to grips with the cellars and the commercial side as well: he works with large 100–150-hectolitre fermenting vats made of concrete and *beton*, and rotates his young oak *pièces* on a pretty regular basis – they are bought after they have held one harvest and are kept for three to four years. On average his red stays for around one year in cask. His top-name Crozes, La Guiraude, is selected after M. Graillot has tasted from every one of his 200-odd casks and is set aside as a *cuvée spéciale*, while his regular Crozes *rouge* is assembled from a mix of wood-aged and vat-stored wine. In a lighter year like 1987 this was 60 per cent *pièce* and 40 per cent *cuve*; in other years, like 1988, it is nearer 50–50. 'The *cuve* allows for more fruit, the cask allows for more structure,' comments M. Graillot.

M. Graillot's wines are indeed impressive, both the reds and the whites. Like many growers whose quest is to seek continuous improvements in their wine, M. Graillot is lending more attention to the vinification of the whites. 'I like ripe but also fresh whites if possible, so while I'm considering wood fermentation in future, the drawback of recent years has been the very ripe state of the harvest. I'm frightened of any loss of acidity – that's why I'd never do a *macération pelliculaire* and also why I block the *malo*.' His whites are fermented in enamel-lined vats at 15° (1991) or 18° (1989/90) and have a touch of wood exposure before bottling in April. They have greater depth of bouquet and flavour than the most overt examples of low-temperature fermentation – after two years both his 1990 and 1988 had developed some very appealing lasting fruit on the palate and are ideal to drink until around the age of four for optimum enjoyment.

The red Crozes standard *cuvée* is a fruit-laden wine when young, blessed with a vibrant purple Syrah hue and finished off with some moderate chewy tannins, giving it enormous appeal as a summer lunch or buffet wine, to drink surrounded by pretty girls or handsome men, whichever is your taste. This then develops a more serious side after about two-and-a-half years, and becomes more measured, the fruit changing its emphasis and the wine temporarily becoming a little dumb. But it is also good to drink, more as an indoor evening wine with a stew or red meat, when it is around four or five years old.

The Guiraude *cuvée* is exposed 100 per cent to cask before bottling, and is a more solid, rich wine with traces of tastes like raspberry and perhaps chocolate on the palate. It is more compact and restrained than the straight Crozes, and behind some solid but elegant flavours comes an appealing thread of final fruitiness. It was extremely successful in 1990, 1989 and 1988, needing four or five years before becoming capable of showing its true range of flavours.

M. Graillot's Guiraude is likely to live for eight to twelve years, while he is specially pleased to make just two *pièces*, or 600 bottles, of red Hermitage. Here straightaway one can taste the greater complexity of wine made off the mighty hillside, allied to a superior length of finish. The 1990 is a fifteen- to eighteen-year wine, carrying lovely fruit and overall dimension, while the 1989 is only a little behind, its flavours being a little drier than the 1990's – a ten-to sixteen-year wine. Unfortunately this stylish wine is not for general consumption.

A good, solid chap, M. Graillot looks quite at home in his perky flat hat and vineyard boots, a far cry from the lightweight suits sported on the Avenida Atlântica in Rio. His success in such a short time, starting from such little working knowledge, is quite amazing, and should give hope to anyone hitting forty and wondering what on earth they are doing with their lives – it can be done, folks, just run out and find some Graillot Crozes *rouge* and console yourselves!

Many of today's *domaines* in the area closest to Tain have been making wine since the early part of the nineteenth century at least; the Domaine la Négociale records show wine being made on the property just after the Revolution, while the Michelas family have been wine growers at Domaine St-Jemms near Mercurol since 1851, and Étienne Pochon's family worked 2 hectares of Marsanne vines on the slope above Curson before the phylloxera attack of the last century. The first two properties originally belonged to powerful local families – in the case of Domaine St-Jemms, the Counts of Revol back in the sixteenth century.

Robert Michelas is another ex-Co-opérateur who has spread his net wide beyond just the Crozes *appellation* – he now makes wine from Cornas, St-Joseph and Hermitage, as well as from his 13 hectares of Syrah and 3 hectares of mainly Marsanne. His Crozes holdings are spread between Mercurol and Pont-de-l'Isère, with some of his Syrah in the favoured Les Chassis *quartier* just south of his *domaine*. During the 1980s he pressed hard to increase the scale and workability of his operation – he was an early machine-harvester, for example. His red wines are of a reasonable quality; one might call them commercial rather than singular. M. Michelas has a penchant for presenting his wines at wine fairs – indeed he has something of a train spotter's enthusiasm for this – which in the experience of the author can often represent a contra-indicator as to the true quality of a *domaine*'s wine. Nevertheless, his daughter is now a qualified *sommelière*, which is cause for worthy satisfaction at this property.

While M. Michelas has increased the amount he bottles during the 1980s from about 18,000 bottles to over 55,000 bottles, a man who went from 0 to 50,000 bottles in 1988–90 was Étienne Pochon of Château Curson. He and his father Édouard were Co-opérateurs from 1965–1987, selling their harvest. Like all people they were on five-year contracts which are difficult and expensive to break if the *viticulteur* wants to leave. They started to vinify from 7 hectares in 1988 and by 1992 had reached 8.5 hectares of red and 1.5 hectares of white vines (90 per cent Marsanne, 10 per cent Roussanne).

An agricultural engineer, Étienne Pochon is a reserved, careful man whose attention to detail is reflected in very meticulously made wines. The top red *cuvée*, Château Curson, is very good. Like all M. Pochon's wines, its crop has been destalked, and after selection by tasting it receives nine months in casks of one to three years' age. The 1991 is a very attractive, finely chiselled wine and contains an elegant fruitiness; the 1990 is a clean, stylish wine with quiet authority. It will run for ten years or more since its constituents are very well balanced. The 1989 is a tougher wine, more upright and sturdy – this will drink well towards 1999.

In addition, the Domaine Pochon red wine, which is bottled in June after the harvest and receives no cask ageing, is a fruit-laden example of good, fresh Crozes – a wine to get on and drink within its first four or five years.

Like more and more growers, M. Pochon uses organic fertilizers. 'I'm glad we have vines on the slopes and the plain', he says. 'I get a decent maturity and some good acidity off the *coteau*, but on the plain the potassium levels have been diminished over the years through the use of chemical treatments, which gives less chance of a sound acidity. I like to vinify on a plot by plot basis – this means that each of my eight initial *cuves* are made up of grapes from vines of the same age, the same rootstock and so on.'

M. Pochon's whites receive a *macération pelliculaire*, and also, contrary to a grower like Graillot, are partly vinified, then transferred to wood before bottling in April. M. Pochon wants to bottle with the '*malo*' done in future to work towards a more complex wine. The Château-Curson *blanc* 1991 was a stylish, well structured wine of good length. It was more lively than the 1990, and both wines should drink well after two years or so.

Meanwhile one family continues to run its *domaine* in much the same way as it has over the past twenty years. Jules Fayolle was one of the few independent growers back in the early 1970s, and was therefore known to the first British wine importers seeking out a single-vineyard Crozes. The *domaine* is today run by his twin sons Jean-Paul and Jean-Claude, but the attachment to the old ways remains strong, with the red wines given one to two years in older casks, and just occasionally, almost eccentrically, as much as eight-and-a-half years. This was the case with a 1975 Crozes Les Voussères which Jules Fayolle bottled in March 1984 simply because he felt like it – this bottling tasted of wood and was considerably dried-out on the palate, a bit like munching into a plum skin, when tasted in June 1984.

To arrive at the Fayolles' farm, where they also grow apricots and cherries, it is necessary first to traverse the main Paris-Nice railway line, whose crossing near the centre of Gervans is always firmly placed in the down position. Shades of the France of old Jean Renoir films are recalled when a solemnly dressed and straightfaced *madame* emerges from a little house, waddles over with the utmost aplomb and slowly proceeds to wind up the level-crossing gate, no doubt swearing under her breath at the unwanted disturbance.

M. Jules Fayolle, a lean man with startling black eyebrows that seem about to take off from his face and fly away, has been making wine since he was a boy. His two sons took up the family business at the tender age of fourteen, so they have been well versed in traditional methods learned at first hand – quite the opposite of the wine school/outside *œnologue* adviser route taken by most of today's young *vignerons*.

The Fayolles have gently increased the size of their plantation, to include both Crozes and Hermitage itself. They have about 2 hectares at Hermitage, the red coming from 1.5 hectares on Les Diognières, the white being first made in 1988; at Crozes they have around 3 hectares of Marsanne and 7 of Syrah. Their Crozes vines are mainly on half-slopes, which are simpler in upkeep and give a larger yield than the full, steep slopes that run sharply down nearby from their neighbour M. Raymond Roure's *domaine*. They rarely have major worries about their grapes failing to ripen, since they are favoured by the same micro-climate as is enjoyed by Hermitage, with a mean temperature of about 13°C; it is remarkable to observe the pansies and mimosa in full bloom on the Gervans hill in January, for instance.

During the 1980s the Fayolle wine eased towards a greater consistency and elegance than previously. Until the mid-1970s, for instance, the white would always be left in cask for a year, giving it a heavy, often partly oxidized taste. Now the whites are more cleanly made, in a refined but traditional style where the emphasis is on plump rather than under-ripe fruit. There are three versions of the red: a standard, the Voussères (produced off granitic soil) and Les

Pontaix (produced off a more clayey soil). The Pontaix is the most full-bodied wine of the trio, and it takes four years or so to unravel the solid tannins in it. The Voussères contains an excellent fruit extract and is more stylish, with swirling Syrah aromas and sound length *en bouche* – a cracking example of sophisticated red Crozes when caught right, as in 1985 or 1988, and ideal to drink between five and seven years old, when much of its richness is still present. The red Hermitage Les Dionnières is a bit of a bridesmaid wine – it is generally sound enough, but never quite takes the drinker by the scruff of the neck as the wines of a single vineyard should.

Another property where the younger generation recently took over is the Domaine des Remizières at Mercurol. In 1990 M. Alphonse Desmeure ceded the reins to his son Philippe, who at thirty-four had already spent fifteen years working with his father. This is a first-rate *domaine*, where the wines have gained in quality and consistency over the past few years. Of their 17 hectares at Crozes, as many as 5 are planted with Marsanne; their vineyards are spread over mostly Mercurol, with some plots at Larnage and near Tain. At Hermitage they work 2.2 hectares of Syrah (Rocoules, L'Hermite) and 0.8 hectare of Marsanne on the Maison Blanche. The red Crozes is wood reared over the course of twelve months and the Hermitage red a little longer. Both wines show the benefits of care in the vineyard – sorting of the grapes from mid-July to mid-August to master the yield and make the final harvest more consistent is an example of the trouble taken. The Crozes has a good length and lively fruit – very successful in 1991 and 1990, while the Cuvée Particulière is one of the unsung heroes of the *appellation*: the bouquet emerges in a powerful, musky way after four or five years, and behind the wild Syrah fruit lies some upright support and surprising complexity. A year like 1990 will show very well around 1995–98, while the 1986 was one of the best Crozes of its year – showing richness and the room for further potential after six years.

The Desmeure Hermitage comes, like father Alphonse, with a reserved style. It is upright, a wine of pedigree and quite removed from the opulent, overtly fleshy wines favoured by some Hermitage houses. The 1991 has an excellent fruit extract and discreet tannins, the 1990 carries great depth and lots of tightly knit flavours – when tasted before bottling it suggested a measured evolution over fifteen years or so. Just a stroke behind the excellent 1990 are the quietly powerful 1989 (delightful to drink around 1995–8) and the more classic, firm 1988. The last-named bears a resemblance to the 1983, a wine that after nine years still bore some austerity alongside a lovely, long aftertaste.

In Alphonse's time the Domaine des Remizières name was most founded on its whites. These continue to rely on a traditional vinification involving oak that since 1985 has become younger – two to five years. The Crozes *blanc* is half reared in cask, half in stainless steel over twelve months, the Hermitage *blanc* receives eighteen months in wood. The Hermitage is a good representative of the *appellation*, with a year like 1989 showing a true Marsanne mix of warm flavours and strength. This will age and develop well. The ample 1990 is a genuine, full southern wine which will show especially well around 1995–7, while the attractive 1991 is similar in style to the 1987, which after five years had advanced to show a well scented, almost floral bouquet and discreet richness on the palate. The Remizières white Crozes is another authentic local offering, with traces of almond on the bouquet and sound, nutty flavours on the palate. Given a consistently high standard for both the reds and whites from Crozes and Hermitage over four or five vintages, Remizières is definitely one of the top names at Crozes to look out for, even if only 15 per cent of their wine is exported.

A *domaine* that has taken a different standpoint to most of the smaller *vignerons* is the Cave des Clairmonts, an unusual gathering of four families within one organization. Run by the energetic Jean-Michel Borja, their stance is to produce fruity, forward wines in both red and white form. The red is made from a little over 75 hectares, the white from about 8 hectares – which makes them a very large private concern. The reds are ideal to drink in their first two or three years – they are made to emphasize their fruit and accessibility, and have no pretension to developing a considered side later on in life. A major claim to fame was the adoption of one special *cuvée* of the 1989 to celebrate the tenth anniversary of Willis Wine Bar in Paris, the Rhône pioneer in the French capital; this was a wine drunk liberally and very successfully, bursting with pure Syrah fruit, in the last months of 1990.

For the future, other names to note or monitor in this *appellation* on the move are Albert Belle, a refugee from the Co-opérative with cellars at Larnage, the young triers Dard and Ribo at Mercurol, and the irregular but sometimes inspired Michel Ferraton from Tain – his top *cuvée* is called La Matinière.

From the past, names like Roure and Bégot continue with their old-fashioned approach; in the case of Bégot, the vineyard of 5 hectares has been gamely taken on by the late Albert's widow Marcelle, who stays loyal to organic vineyard and cellar methods started back in the early 1970s. Both these producers still incline to extensive cask-ageing, a damaging aspect in the past due to a tendency of their wines to oxidize prior to bottling.

As for the local *négociants* or those with vineyard holdings at Crozes, Paul Jaboulet set a shining example with their Thalabert red and Mule Blanche white – delicious, classy wines that give the *appellation* a good name and the consumer some of the best value for money in the Rhône of the early 1990s. Chapoutier, who cultivate just over 10 hectares at Crozes, tend to blow hot and cold with their two Crozes, called Les Meysonniers and La Petite Ruche. The former is made from forty-year vines, the latter from fifteen-year vines, both on the clay–limestone surface of Les Chassis. In some vintages, the Meysonniers is bursting with exuberant Syrah fruit when tasted *chez* Chapoutier, but this does not always carry through to the end wine in bottle. The Meysonniers receives twelve months' cask ageing, La Petite Ruche ten, and the style of these wines is easy, plenty of fruit and plump flavours making them what Michel Chapoutier memorably terms 'more disco than baroque' – while he is equally quick to assert, quite correctly, that his Hermitage wines are definitely more baroque than disco.

Louis de Vallouit from St-Vallier owns a total of 5 hectares between Crozes and Larnage, the majority being Syrah, the white being Marsanne. His style of vinification has remained traditional over the years, and as with his Côte-Rôties, his Crozes reds display a soft, easy fruitiness – more the finished fruit jam from the garden than the raw berry picked off the hedgerow. They represent a fair ratio between price and quality.

Delas have been investing large sums in transforming their vinification premises at St-Jean-de-Muzols, and now vinify 40 per cent of their Crozes themselves, buying in all from about twenty *domaines*. They produce about 1,000 hectolitres of red and 200 hectos of white; the reds are soft and good to drink early in a vintage like 1991, and more complete and interesting in years like 1990 and 1988, which will drink well over the course of about six years. Their white Crozes, bottled in March after the harvest, is more variable. Both the 1991 and the 1987 were uneven, but in compensatiton the 1986 was a well-worked wine, showing some ripe but elegant flavours on the palate.

Finally, the massive Cave Co-opérative at Tain is turning out slightly improved red and white Crozes from the old, very irregular days of the 1970s. The wines are more *soignés*, and therefore less prone to bottle-sickness and lack of balance. The 1989 *blanc* had fair richness on the palate and is several rungs higher on the quality ladder than it used to be, while the 1988 red, bottled in January 1989, possessed decent *mâche* or chew on the palate, and tasted much like a local *négociant*'s wine with a slightly hot finish. But again, that is an improvement over past offerings.

Crozes-Hermitage Vintages

The best years before the 1980s were 1979 (some reds like that of Tardy and Ange were twelve-year wines), 1978 (exceptional, especially the Thalabert) and 1976. Before that, 1973, 1971, 1969, 1967, 1966, 1964, 1961 and 1959 were all good or very good. Crozes can surprise in its old age – three examples: a 1959 Paul Jaboulet Aîné *blanc* drunk in 1974 initially showed a hint of oxidation on the bouquet, but the palate developed richly with about half an hour's airing and left a strong hazelnut flavour on the finish – an excellent wine. A 1964 half-bottle of red Crozes Paul Jaboulet Aîné (not Thalabert) kindly given to the author by Rhône enthusiast Robin Jones of the Croque en Bouche restaurant in Malvern, England, when tasted in 1987, still held lovely softened raspberry flavours and great roundness on the palate, the Syrah refusing to yield to the passage of time; the colour had rusted, but there was a vegetal and smoky aroma on the bouquet which with air turned drier, towards coffee-beans. And lastly, a half-bottle of 1969 Thalabert drunk in Tain to celebrate Derby day in June 1984: its colour held a middle band of red, topped by rust and underlaid by black, while the bouquet was showing a variety of vegetal, mulberry and coffee-bean aromas – all very deep and powerful. The palate had the taste of dried fruits and finished with spice and southern heat. The favourite for the Derby that year was a colt called El Gran Señor, which was the perfect description for this Thalabert.

Disappointing vintages for both whites and reds were 1975, 1977 and, to a lesser extent, 1980.

For details of the years before 1982, see Hermitage. The general style of wines in most years is similar, with a Crozes clearly possessing a much shorter longevity – not much past fifteen years for most reds, while the whites of the modern day are best consumed within four or five years of release.

1982　The hot summer and intense heat during vinification brought problems to Crozes. Many of the reds were short-lived, and somewhat unbalanced. Like the whites, most should have been drunk up by now. The whites suffered notably from lack of acidity. This was a turning-point vintage for the more switched-on growers, who realized the urgency of their need for sophisticated cellar equipment that could control temperature and bacteria efficiently.

1983　A very good vintage. Cooling was again needed during vinification, but the end wines held greater balance than the overripe 1982s. The tannins were austere, and are now at a stage of lending a dry feel underneath the wine's richness. Very striking, leathery and smoky aromas have come through, and these reds have the power to live for twelve to fifteen years. An excellent, very dense Thalabert and a very firm Tardy and Ange *rouge*. A big, strongly flavoured Mule Blanche *blanc* from Jaboulet.

1984　A difficult vintage of middling quality. The Syrah suffered from *coulure*, and there was late flowering for the whites. A vicious storm on 4 October cooled and slowed down the vinifications, allowing good extraction of perfumes on the whites. The reds were only fairly coloured, and several had rather mean bouquets. A bit short on the palate, they lacked the guts to develop to any extent.

1985　Very good indeed. The weather perked up to give a very fine late summer. The reds had solid colouring and most were packed with fruit and ripe, agreeable tannins. Warm and concentrated, many of these wines were delicious to drink in 1991–2, but they will keep going for a few years after that. Excellent Thalabert, Les Voussères from Fayolle and Tardy and Ange *rouge*, and a very good first red from Graillot. A fresh, clean red from Chapoutier. The Paul Jaboulet Aîné Mule Blanche *blanc* was powerful and rich.

1986　A variable vintage. A very dry year then produced rain at harvest time, which started early, around 17 September.

The reds are marked by some dry, aggressive tannins which override what fruit was extracted and make many of the wines lean. The best *cuvées* settled to produce some middle-weight wines after five years, and one hopes that their lack of generosity will ease in the bottle. The whites were better, showing fresh aromas and lively fruit, although some were short *en bouche*. For the reds, a successful La Guiraude from Graillot – still young, and a richly scented and flavoured Cuvée Particulière from Alphonse Desmeure. A discreet year for Thalabert – likely to be at its best around 1993–5, its aromas and flavours are less vibrant than usual.

1987 Some rot affected the harvest, which turned out better, fuller red wines than were first expected. The colours are plum rather than purple, and the best *cuvées* have a sound degree of extract on the palate, albeit with slightly hot finishes. They are discreetly scented and will provide sound drinking at reasonable prices towards 1993 or so, providing they do not dry out in the meantime. The whites are a little unbalanced, lacking the structure to provide further sustained drinking. A successful Thalabert from Jaboulet – well crafted.

1988 Very good indeed. A solid, classic vintage that produced red wines of full Syrah warmth and tannic support. They are darkly coloured, have bouquets packed with still latent aromas, and show a tightly knit structure on the palate. This will be a long-lived vintage from most growers – certainly nine to twelve years for the reds. The whites are delicious, full of firm flavours and excellent balance, which augurs well for their drinking until around 1993–4. All the principal producers have made good wines this year; it is worth noting that the Thalabert, once marked by new oak, had by 1992 settled down as a full, stylish wine.

1989 Generally a good vintage, though not as good as the publicists trumpeted early on. The summer was again very fine and too dry, and the effect was to invest some of the reds with lean, slightly green tannins – so selection should be carefully made. The best wines, from growers like Graillot with an excellent La Guiraude, contain concentrated fruit with strong tannic support. They are more *nerveux* in style than the robust, straightforward 1988s,

and may develop greater breadth and complexity after four
or five years. The whites have a pleasing weight, are nicely
scented and will drink well before around 1994.

1990　An excellent vintage for the reds, good for the whites. 'The
growers had it easy', stated Alain Graillot fairly. The
year was very dry, but rain fell at opportune moments,
particularly in August. The reds are all dark and carry
warm, enticing bouquets of great promise; their fruit is
ripe, almost overmature, they are richer than the 1988s
and their excellent balance will give them a lovely, orderly
development over twelve years or so. The special *cuvées*
and most selected wines will show well around 1995, the
early, fruit-packed *cuvées* are delicious already. Excellent
work from Graillot, Desmeure and Étienne Pochon at
Château Curson, while the outstanding Thalabert will run
over twenty very rich years or so.

The whites start life rather dumb, hiding some fat, chewy
flavours. They will develop in a quiet way, led by the rich
southern extract achieved by most growers. A slight lack
of acidity may mean that it will be difficult to know when
to expect them to show well.

Leading Growers at Crozes-Hermitage

The nucleus:

Belle, Albert	26600	Larnage
Borja, Jean-Michel		
Cave des Clairmonts	26600	Beaumont-Monteux
Chapoutier, M.	26600	Tain-l'Hermitage
Cornu, Alphonse		
Domaine du Pavillon	26600	Mercurol
Desmeure, Philippe		
Domaine des Remizières	26600	Mercurol
Delas Frères	07300	St-Jean-de-Muzols
Domaine Fayolle		
Les Gamets	26600	Gervans
Graillot, Alain	26600	Tain-l'Hermitage

Jaboulet Aîné, Paul	26600	La Roche-de-Glun
Pochon, Étienne		
Château-Curson		
Tardy, Charles, and Ange,		
Bernard	26600	Chanos-Curson
Domaine des Entrefaux		
Pradelle, Jean-Louis		
Domaine de Pradelle		
de Vallouit, Louis-Francis	26600	St-Vallier
Vidal-Fleury	69420	Ampuis

Other producers:

Arnavon, Luc	26600	Mercurol
Bégot, Marcelle	26600	Serves-sur-Rhône
Bied, Bernard	26600	Mercurol
Cave Co-opérative des Vins		
Fins	26600	Tain-l'Hermitage
Chave, Bernard	26600	Mercurol
Chomel, Maxime	26600	Gervans
Collonge, Gérard		
Domaine la Négociale	26600	Mercurol
Combier, Maurice	26600	Pont-de-l'Isère
Dard et Ribo	26600	Mercurol
Dumaine, Olivier	26600	Larnage
Ferraton, Michel	26600	Tain-l'Hermitage
Flandin, Robert	26600	Crozes-Hermitage
Fraisse, Raymond	07300	St-Jean-de-Muzols
Margier, Charles	26600	Mercurol
Marsanne, Jean, et Fils	07300	Mauves
Martin, Michel	26600	Crozes-Hermitage
Michelas, Robert		
Domaine St-Jemms	26600	Mercurol
Mussell, Cecile		
Peichon, Pierre	26600	Erôme
Roure, Raymond	26600	Gervans
Rousset, Robert	26600	Erôme

6

St-Joseph

St-Joseph has had two distinct phases in its relatively short life: June 1956 to June 1969, when it was a snug local *appellation* centred on a handful of communities on the west bank of the northern Rhône – total vineyard area in 1971, 97 hectares; and June 1969 to early 1992, when the area allowed for cultivation was vastly increased – total area under vine in 1992, 640 hectares, including 80 hectares of vines under three years old. Such a stampede of indiscriminate planting finally provoked action from the Syndicat des Vignerons de St-Joseph, and from the spring of 1992 new legislation was designed to cut back the total area potentially available for vineyards from 7,000 hectares to under 3,500 hectares, and over a thirty-year period to reduce the incidence of vines planted in unsuitable sites – mainly on flat ground at the foot of the slopes, and high ground above 300 metres.

'We had to act to ensure that St-Joseph came only from the best *terroirs*', commented Growers' President M. Amorique Cornu-Chauvin. 'Of the current 640 hectares, some will lose the right to make St-Joseph because their vines weren't old enough to produce St-Joseph by the 1991 harvest – it's clear that people hastened to plant when they heard of the proposed changes. There'll be others whose vines are poorly sited, while I can think of one place – Charnas, near Limony, where there are 50 hectares of good vineland that should have been allowed originally in the *appellation*. There may be about 200 hectares altogether out of the 640 that don't qualify under the new rules. Their growers will be allowed to continue to produce St-Joseph from them for thirty years, but will be encouraged to plant in special "shop window" zones of better exposure in the meantime.' Such redevelopment of special areas will be a slow process judging by the average cost, however – probably over £30,000

(US$54,000) per hectare over a three-year period.

So for some years to come this will remain an *appellation* whose red and white wines, as elsewhere in the north of the Valley based on Syrah and Marsanne with tiny amounts of Roussanne, need to be chosen from a nucleus of sound growers. The expansion has been fast and furious in the past ten to fifteen years, and there is a wide spectrum between the best and the worst wines here as a result.

The original *appellation* area in 1956 created a superior outlet for largely terrace-cultivated vines running from a point on the west bank of the Rhône about 8 kilometres north of St-Péray to a couple of communities about 6 kilometres north of Tournon. From top to toe the *appellation* ran over just 13 kilometres (8 miles) and comprised, from south to north, six communities – Glun, Mauves, Tournon, St-Jean-de-Muzols, Lemps and Vion. When looking for quality it is worth remembering these names – their vineyards and most of their *vignerons* were producing wine considered superior to ordinary Côtes du Rhône upwards of thirty years ago.

Today St-Joseph can be made all along the west bank of the Rhône, on plateau, plain and slope, all the way from Guilherand in the south – opposite Valence – up to Chavanay, 4 miles below Condrieu in the north. Instead of six communities within the *appellation* zone there are now twenty-five. From north to south the extra ones are Guilherand, Châteaubourg (some sound vineyards), Sécheras, Arras-sur-Rhône, Ozon, Sarras (opposite St-Vallier), Talencieux, Andance, St-Étienne-de-Valoux, St-Désirat (home of the go-ahead, quality-conscious Co-opérative), Champagne, Peyraud, Serrières, Félines, Charnas, Limony (some steep slopes here, also a *commune* producing Condrieu), St-Pierre-de-Bœuf (hillside vines, also Condrieu), Malleval (also Condrieu) and Chavanay (very much the centre of activity in the new area of St-Joseph and a source of very good St-Joseph as well as a Condrieu *commune*).

What the legislators did in the past with this *appellation* in many ways was to make large parts of it not much more than a northern division of the mass-produced Côtes du Rhône from the south of the valley. We are back to an old complaint – there is no point in having a hierarchy if every wine is at the top of it. There is a wry old joke about St-Joseph (vintage *c.* 1985): on the label, *pied de coteaux* equals the plain; *tête de coteaux* equals the plateau . . . and, oh yes, *coteau* may in some instances actually mean *coteau*.

The original name of St-Joseph comes from a hillside near Tournon, and not, as some fanciful *vignerons* would have one believe, from St-Joseph himself, who is supposed to be the patron of betrayed husbands. Exactly how long wine has been made in this region is not known. All talk of the Syrah's early cultivation refers to the eastern banks of the Rhône round Hermitage and, strangely enough, Tournon is not mentioned as a wine-producing area until the reign of Louis XII (1498–1515). Then, according to Élie Brault, in his *Anne et son époque*, the monarchy would only allow its very own wines to be served at the Court of France. There were at the time three royal vineyards, those of Beaune and Chenove in Burgundy and the much-esteemed Clos de Tournon.

The wine of Tournon remained in royal circles for some years more, for it is recorded locally that King Henry II (1519–59) always kept a personal reserve of several barrels. The style of the wine he so liked can be judged from a quotation of 1560 by the first head of the College of Tournon, now one of France's oldest secondary schools, who praised the 'delicate and dainty' wine of Tournon and Mauves, which was sold as far away as Rome and which the princes and king of France were prepared to acquire for themselves at no little cost.

Mauves is a little village just south of Tournon. Old history books have spoken of its wine as being the worthy rival of the mighty Hermitage – and not entirely without reason, for it is today the home of many of the leading wines of St-Joseph. The celebrated French writer Victor Hugo (1802–85) had evidently encountered, and enjoyed, the wine, for he mentioned it in *Les Misérables*. Describing a social gathering, Hugo wrote that, in addition to the ordinary table wine, there was served a bottle of 'this good wine of Mauves'. Hugo hastened to add that no more than one bottle was brought out because it was 'an expensive wine'.

Nowadays the wines of Mauves and Tournon remain as the quality centre of St-Joseph, supported by wines from the communities of St-Jean-de-Muzols and Chavanay. Outside these four places there are some *vignerons* doing good work – examples are Maurice Courbis at Châteaubourg, Louis Chèze near Limony, Pierre Gaillard above Malleval and Alain Paret at St-Pierre-de-Boeuf – but as the production figures below show, there are great amounts of very ordinary red St-Joseph sloshing around these days when compared with the past.

The average production of St-Joseph per annum over the following periods has been:

1966–9	1,873 hl
1970–4	3,073 hl
1975–9	4,980 hl
1980–4	11,807 hl
1985–9	17,838 hl

Now let us do a little sleuthing to see roughly how much of this is first-division quality wine. Premise number one: much of the best St-Joseph comes from Mauves, Tournon and St-Jean-de-Muzols, all included in the 1966–9 figure. Take the *whole* of that figure – 1,873 hectolitres; allow another 15 percent for *dérogation* and a doubling of this figure to take into account vineyard expansion in these prime areas; we arrive at 4,308 hectolitres. Premise number two: of the newer areas, Chavanay in the *département* of the Loire produces a leading quality of St-Joseph. In the years 1987–9, the Loire supplied an average of 3,846 hectolitres of *appellation* St-Joseph from its three communities St-Pierre-de-Bœuf, Malleval and Chavanay. Let us be generous and say that 40 per cent of this is wine similar in quality to that regularly made from Mauves, Tournon and St-Jean – 1,538 hectolitres. Add up the two figures for 'quality-sourced wine' and we have 5,846 hectolitres out of a recent average of 17,838 hectolitres, or just under one-third.

Readers can crimp and crab at these calculations, but they represent an attempt to show just how much the concept of quality can be undermined if *appellation* regulations are tampered with. In other words, politics – local or national – play their part in succeeding in bringing the name of a wine down to the lowest common denominator. The author may shout about the invigorating quality of St-Joseph as he has known it over more than two decades, but that may mean nothing to the poor consumer who has forked out £5 or US$9 'for the same wine' at a local store. On production figures alone there is double the chance of that consumer buying a St-Joseph that does not match the quality of the wine which originally created the *appellation*.

Looking back to the pre-*appellation* days of the early 1950s, the wine from this west side of the Rhône was sold mainly in bulk as Côtes du Rhône, at a purely nominal price. The vineyards were therefore tiny, since many local farmers found it more profitable to concentrate on growing fruit. There is a thriving fruit Co-opérative at Mauves, for instance, which has always been well patronized by the big jam manufacturers of Lyon.

Gradually, St-Joseph started to become known as a wine under its own name, and the trend away from the vines was halted by increased demand for it and therefore rising prices. In some places anciently abandoned vineyards were brought back to life. The large *négociant* companies began to take an active interest in it, especially as they found St-Joseph a conveniently cheap alternative to the more expensive Hermitage wines.

The vineyards at the heart of this now straggling *appellation* are not only most often on slopes above the Rhône, but contain vines of a considerable age. Growers like Bernard Gripa, Émile Florentin and Raymond Trollat have Syrah vines ranging from forty to ninety years old, which gives them a ready source of the most strongly extracted grape juice at harvest time – very much a factor in the quality of their wines. Many of these slope vineyards still have to be tended manually. The local word for the dry-stone terraces is *chalais*, and these are tended by vineyard workers carrying the reliable *hotte* (pannier). Until the mid- to late 1970s horses were still used in the vineyards, and nowadays Émile Florentin, the doctor of general medicine from Mauves, is one of the few cultivators to have one for his 4–hectare Clos de l'Arbalestrier, which he works with his son Dominique. This noble beast – name unknown – is useful for carrying grapes at harvest-time as well as tilling the doctor's plot, since no fertilizers or chemical products are used by Dr Florentin.

The Syrah accounts for about 93 per cent of the total plantation – the ratio of red to white wine at St-Joseph has been static over the past fifteen years – and is generally used on its own to make the red wine. Since 1979 a maximum of 10 per cent of white grapes, the Marsanne and the Roussanne, can also be put to the making of the red, provided that they are all fermented together at the same time. It is not quite clear why this change of ruling should have occurred; one suspects that it is a purely commercial decision, rather than one totally inspired by a desire to seek a softer quality of wine. The red St-Joseph is much better known and easier to sell than the white, so the inclusion of white grapes in it would mean that there was that much more to sell.

Although these 'west-bank' vines around Tournon and Mauves are grown on largely granite-based ground similar to that of Hermitage, they do not yield wines to rival the depth and fullness of their neighbour across the river: indeed, their calling-card is an exuberant fruitiness that shows itself off from the earliest days in cask, and makes many of the best wines a delight to drink vigorous and young, at under five years old. Why there should be such differences of style among Syrah wines is explained in two ways by some of the growers. First, the soil, notably at Mauves and St-Jean, is less firmly granitic and more gravelly and fine than at Hermitage – schistose, almost. And second, the St-Joseph vineyards do not benefit from quite the excellent exposure of the unshielded Hermitage hill, which is always open to sun and wind.

Soils obviously vary right along the length of this *appellation*, which is 64 kilometres (40 miles) from north to south, and which for some locals has an unofficial north St-Joseph-south St-Joseph divide, the break coming at Sarras. A cross-section are the chalky-silty vineyards of Maurice Courbis at Châteaubourg, while his Glun holding is on granite. A grower like Pierre Coursodon has his Syrah at Mauves growing on a largely granite-based, slightly decomposed soil, and his Marsanne vines on a rich, clayey soil on the *lieu-dit* of Le Paradis above the village. At the original *quartier* of St-Joseph, Chapoutier and Jean-Louis Grippat grow their Syrah on a poor, granitic soil, which is prone to subsidence after any serious rainfall; there is also some sandstone there. On the slopes above St-Jean-de-Muzols, Raymond Trollat's old Syrah vines grow in a very fine schist topsoil. Further north, Louis Chèze above Limony has his vineyards on granitic but stone-covered soil, while around Chavanay *vignerons* like André Perret and Didier Chol cultivate their vines on a mainly granitic surface.

The great merit of the best St-Joseph is that it shows off the excellence of the Syrah in a most appealing way. St-Joseph *rouge* is a wine of two phases. Most often its charm works as the lightest and fruitiest of the northern Côtes du Rhône reds, yet even when it is young there is still a tandem of a dark purple, almost black colour and a heady bouquet of blackcurrants and raspberries to surprise the drinker. And the best *cuvées* can evolve into serious, sit-down wines when taken from the top vintages – 1983, 1985, 1988, 1990, for example – and drunk aged about seven to twelve years old. Lacking the complexity of a Côte-Rôtie or an Hermitage, the full-bloodedness of a Cornas, and possessing finer tannins than most Crozes-Hermitage, St-Joseph *rouge* is a thoroughly appealing wine, one most often chosen for quiet enjoyment and regular drinking, that will prove to be a good friend rather than a respected acquaintance. In particularly fruity years like 1985, Jean-Louis Grippat puts it neatly when he calls his standard *cuvée* 'a wedding wine'.

Because of its easy, uncomplicated style, St-Joseph is not really a *vin de garde*. There are obviously exceptions – a 1967 Coursodon red drunk in 1986 still carried rounded fruit on the palate, and good length, while a 1971 Coursodon red drunk in 1991 had a still ripe, southern-sweet bouquet, with some delicate fruit and a tender, drying finish – but a well-looked-after wine from a top vintage should last for around twelve to fifteen years. Personal preference is the key factor: for those who thrive on fruit and the richness of youth, these are wines to drink between two and seven years old. Others will enjoy the animal musk, *sous-bois* smells and aged Syrah complexities that develop in the bottle – without much drying out – after more than seven years. The chosen style of the wine-maker should also be considered, as well as the particular *cuvée* he has packaged up. A *vigneron* like Pierre Coursodon now makes several *cuvées*, his principal Le Paradis St-Pierre being a wine that requires three or four years to soften. Likewise Bernard Gripa, whose Vieilles Vignes 1988 is a superb wine, and one that will be showing tremendously well around 1996–9: his standard *cuvée* by contrast is a perfect summer wine for early consumption, a feature very often of the Gérard Chave and Marsanne brothers' wines, which can be delightfully fruity when drunk before three years of age. Whatever the style, St-Joseph is always a good partner for veal, pork and simple poultry such as roast chicken or quail. The young, fruity *cuvées* are excellent companions for pasta dishes and charcuterie.

In 1990 the highest-ever amount of St-Joseph was made – just over 21,050 hectolitres of red and 1,750 hectolitres of white. These are a bit under half the totals made at Crozes across the river, and a long, long way ahead of the other big northern *appellations* – three times Côte-Rôtie and four times Hermitage, for instance. Both the red and the white are vinified in much the same way as Hermitage. The most traditional group of growers is centred in the old heart of the *appellation*, and in the cellars of Mauves, treading down for the *pigeage* is still practised in open wooden vats. It is now common, however, to have fermentations done in closed concrete, enamel-lined or stainless steel vats. Many growers like to introduce their grapes without destalking and destemming, and fermentation temperatures for the reds run in the high 20°sC to about 32°C.

Those who destalk are often under the guidance of an *œnologue*.

One such is Louis Chèze, who has destalked all his crop since 1987. 'You gain space in the vats, and the wine carries greater perfumes – less astringent or herbaceous smells', he says. Having destalked for a while, another young grower, Pierre Gaillard is not so sure, and comparative blind tasting of three casks of his 1991 red – one not destalked, one half destalked, one completely destalked – showed evidence that the destalking could make the wine flatter and more neutral tasting – less typical of its St-Joseph *terroir*. Of the big, well-known names, both Jaboulet and Chapoutier destalk. 'We do it to obtain finer tannins', says Louis Jaboulet.

After the malolactic the wines are racked, generally fined and placed in cask for a spell of perhaps six months to one year. Exceptions to this occur, with some producers disdaining the use of wood altogether – Paul Jaboulet's Grand Pompée, which is the issue of 60 per cent bought-in grapes and 40 per cent bought-in wine, never goes into wood, although their one-off Cuvée Personelle of 1986, a 3,500 bottle wine bought off several growers near Côte-Rôtie, received a long stay in wood – eighteen months. At the opposite extreme Émile Florentin keeps his red wines in cask for over two years before bottling them, with neither fining nor filtration: the Clos de l'Arbalestrier cannot be accused of showing off the fresh fruit of the Syrah – it is very much a dense, peppery, drier style of wine than one normally associates with St-Joseph. As elsewhere in the northern Rhône, there is a growing interest in the use of young oak, but while some of the barrels may be of Bordeaux origin, not all the modernist growers are plunging headlong into regular rotation of new casks each year.

Sylvain Bernard is just thirty, and represents a young man's view of new oak. For St-Joseph he takes a moderate line. 'While I only use *pièces* for my Domaine de Fauterie red, I'm not into changing my casks every three years or anything like that. Our wines have an agreeable amount of tannins already – I don't want vanilla, banana or wooden plank infusions in my wine – I don't think St-Joseph has the structure necessary to stand up to such treatment,' he comments.

Likewise, Jean-Louis Grippat has a down-to-earth policy – 'I'm not looking for an addition to my St-Joseph,' he says, 'so in a small year like 1984 or 1987, some of it will not go into any wood, old or new. I use mostly the larger *demi-muid* size, and even in strong years my ratio is only about one new cask for seven old ones.' More keen on young oak is Louis Chèze, who for his top wine, the Cuvée Classique, in 1988 used 30 per cent new oak and in 1989 15 per cent over a total of ten months. The difference is explained by the 1988 being a stronger wine more capable of handling the oak.

Of the large producers of St-Joseph, the Cave Co-opérative de St-Désirat, which accounts for around one-fifth of all the wine, ages its special *cuvées* like the 1986 Cuvée du Bicentenaire in new oak for around six months, and its standard *cuvées* for about one month, while the Tain Co-opérative, which represents over 10 per cent of all wine, leaves their top *cuvée* one-third in new cask, one-third in three- to five-year casks, and one-third in stainless steel for nine months, before assembling.

In the past, both St-Désirat and Jaboulet have produced red wines made by the *macération carbonique* method, and although their wines made in this way have been fruity, they have lacked the thorough aromas and ripe, tangy fruit flavours of classically made St-Joseph.

The white wine vinification has evolved over the past decade, and white St-Joseph is often one of the secret 'good buys' in French white wine. Few growers bother with the Roussanne – the offbeat Émile Florentin at Mauves is one of its few supporters – and the Marsanne crop is generally vinified in enamel-lined or stainless steel vats, although Raymond Trollat at St-Jean-de-Muzols still uses old casks for the fermentation, and Bernard Gripa at Mauves and Louis Chèze at Limony ferment partly in new oak. Barrel-fermentation is gently coming back into fashion at some *domaines*, which is little surprise, since this has been the essence of working with the Marsanne for many generations – with good results to show for it.

As fermentation temperatures for the whites have been controlled, often between 15–20°C, and the wines now spend less than their former six to nine months in cask, so their style has changed. One of the curiosities of St-Joseph *blanc* made during the 1960s and the 1970s was its durability, for even after showing a well-scented and roundedly fruity side when young, bottles put to one side would still show supremely well after a dozen or sometimes twenty years. In contrast to the Marsanne wines of Crozes-Hermitage, white St-Josephs have much greater class, appeal and staying-power. Whether modern vinification will affect this remains to be seen.

When soundly made, white St-Joseph shows more exotic aromas and more marked fruit than white Hermitage – peaches and apricots, and sometimes greengage, seem to be present on the bouquet. The palate is well weighted, with more richness and underlying depth than are found in most whites made in the Loire or Bordeaux, for example, and the fruity chewiness on the finish is particularly appealing. Elegant and attractive, these are whites that are under-estimated in much the same way that the whites of Lirac in the southern Rhône are discounted. But drink one in winter, for example, and luscious, balmy summer days are brought to mind – there is none of the angular green kick given by so many French regional whites vinified in the modern way. Good white St-Joseph shows extremely well after two or three years, and as it ages, so it acquires greater richness and fullness of flavour towards eight or ten years old.

To demonstrate the surprising longevity of white St-Joseph, two examples may be given. A 1964 made by Jean-Louis Grippat from old vines was drunk in the summer of 1986: very pale gold, the colour had held well. The bouquet held a very good combination of richness and aged aromas – acacia seemed to be present. On the attack there were some lovely *fresh* plum or greengage flavours, with age seeping in to supply a rather burnt edge to the finish. It was very long and had held on remarkably well. Jean-Louis Grippat's comment that since 1964 the Marsanne vine-stock had not changed in any way – no new clonal varieties – provided an interesting insight into the current quality of these white wines.

On a lesser scale, a 1976 Coursodon *blanc* tasted in the summer of 1986 also showed a colour that had held extremely well, with barely a trace of gold in it. There were floral and delicate aromas on the nose, and excellent balance on the palate, with a richness that grew with exposure to air. It was also long *en bouche*. Both these wines were charged in alcohol – the Grippat around 14° and the Coursodon 13° – which certainly provided much of their combustion to keep going.

The Coursodon family at Mauves are one of the original sources of very good red and white St-Joseph. Gustave Coursodon has retired in name but always seems to be on hand to help out his son Pierre with a piece of advice or a choice comment. He has been very active over the years in showing his wines at regional wine fairs and in spreading the St-Joseph name. With a beret frequently perched on the top of his head, and a lot of sidelong glances accompanying his comments, he looks very much the cheeky Frenchman.

The Coursodons live on the main square in Mauves, and their vineyards are dotted about on the slopes and the plateau above the village. Not since Pierre's grandfather's time had they cultivated parts of the vineyard, and the recent reclaiming of terraces that had been left abandoned for over twenty years necessitated the building of a road to gain access to the *parcelles*, quite apart from the arduous task of clearing and replanting. This vineyard had caused certain problems for his grandfather in his day, as Gustave explained. 'Since my father was both mayor of the village and owner of a fair-sized vineyard, the Germans had no hesitation in occupying our house early in November 1942. As we depended on our vines for our existence, like everyone else we had to carry on as usual in order to earn our living. The Germans certainly accounted for a lot of our wine, but over all I would say that the Occupation didn't directly hamper our daily working of the vines, except for the time when an aeroplane fell on them.'

Pierre Coursodon has almost tripled the size of his father's exploitation, so that he now owns 5 hectares and rents a further three. These are spread over about ten plots, with 1 hectare given to the Marsanne. During the 1980s the wines from this *domaine* became a little less intense and full-bodied than in the time of Gustave, which may have something to do with the introduction of young Syrah cultivated on the high plateau above Mauves, which is much less of a sun-trap than the south-facing slopes right by the village.

M. Coursodon works with a variety of wood in the raising of his reds – some of his *foudres* of about 25-hectolitre capacity are ex-white spirit barrels from Alsace and Germany, while he also has *demi-muids* and some young oak *pièces* in his modernized cellars. His vinification is still largely traditional, with a thorough crush, no destalking and an extended *cuvaison*. His most serious wine, the Paradis St-Pierre, receives around fifteen months in cask; this is a St-Joseph of the old school, with a darkly extracted colour, a firm berry fruit bouquet and plenty of substance and length on the palate. This is a wine that typically needs four or five years to settle and achieve a rounded harmony. M. Coursodon's standard red *cuvée* is really rather standard – a thinner version of the Paradis and of anything made by his father in his time. Meanwhile the whites remain very sound, possessing a gentle fruit extract. They have been modernized in their making, with fermentation in young oak, and are unlikely to live as long as bottles made before the 1980s.

The older growers like Gustave Coursodon can remember the first wave of prosperity that hit St-Joseph with the granting of *appellation contrôlée*, and a *vigneron* like Raymond Trollat, now in his early sixties, has seen two waves of prosperity occur in the *appellation*. A man whose looks bely his age and whose healthy outdoor complexion is a good advertisement for life on top of a well-exposed hillside, M. Trollat cultivates 2 hectares of Syrah and one of Marsanne on some finely decomposed schist. Commenting on the main differences *appellation contrôlée* had made to him, he said, 'Well, of course, our wine sells for more than before, which is very welcome, and we also now bottle most of it. I must say, though, that I really enjoy being out in the vines, and even vinifying the wine, but when it comes to bottling and sticking on labels one by one . . .' His Gallic shrug and sharp whistle of breath were sufficient to demonstrate his feelings about *that* particular aspect of progress!

M. Maurice Courbis (left) and M. Gustave Coursodon

The second wave occurred in the mid-1980s. Suddenly St-Joseph was fashionable. *Bistrots* in Lyon had their customers clamouring for 'St-Jo' – a wine that was seen to be simple and *sympa* – good, refreshing stuff. At the same time Rhône wines were moving into a limelight of much greater publicity from both the French and the international press. In 1984, an indifferent vintage on the whole, there occurred a price rise of just 5–10 per cent above the excellent 1983s, but come the 1985 vintage, there was a price rise that ranged from a minimum of 10 up to a full 30 per cent – whereupon the *bistrots* of Lyon adopted the wine. Aren't folk strange?

While *vignerons* like Jean-Louis Grippat, Pierre Coursodon and Bernard Gripa modernized or built new cellars, Raymond Trollat has remained steadfastly conservative. He is one of the unsung heroes of St-Joseph, since over a period of at least twenty-five years he has been turning out delicious, thoroughly intense reds and whites – as good a yardstick about the old-fashioned values of the *appellation* as one can find in the best years. They are vinified in a traditional way, the whites fermented in old barrels and the reds stored in a mix of old oak and chestnut for up to eighteen months before bottling.

M. Trollat's vineyard enjoys a superb exposure in the Aubert *quartier* at the top of a hill directly facing Hermitage. His reds are usually very expressive, with a dark fruit smell – a mix of berry and tar aromas, the latter perhaps from the cask. On the palate they are firmly structured with a straightforward, earthy style, and in vintages like 1990 and 1989 are ideal to drink around five to ten years old. His whites, which have a firm following in the United States, are good to drink young, when their rounded, peach-like flavours show to best effect.

In the early 1970s M. Trollat lived in complete isolation at the top of a winding road that leads up the hillside from near the old railway station of St-Jean-de-Muzols. Vines and apricot trees surrounded their farm, and there was not another house in sight. Now there are more than a dozen houses-cum-villas, and the road up to the top of the hill has become rather like one long driveway. *Vignerons* who were ageing and who didn't have sons to continue their work were easy prey for the developers – in the late 1970s M. Paul Réat and M. Jean Minodier both took the obvious decision. The distressing feature was the disappearance of the quality vineyards of St-Joseph – the terraced hillsides of places like St Jean-de-Muzols – while the plain running alongside the Lyon-Nîmes railway was being busily planted for replacement St-Joseph.

M. Minodier had himself found that bottling his own wine was a worthwhile development. Not only did he and his wife meet a wide selection of French visitors, including film stars from Paris, but he was also determined not to yield to the financially tempting offers made for his wine by the big *négociant* houses of the region. As he said, 'I want to keep my identity as a true *vigneron*.' Now one of the few *domaines* with young owners near M. Trollat is the Domaine de la Côte Ste-Épine, whose 3 hectares are worked by M. et Mme Michel Desestret: their red is an example of an intense St-Joseph, suitable for some bottle ageing before drinking as a sit-down accompaniment to winter food. Near them, Delas started to produce wine from a 1-hectare holding on the Coteau Ste-Épine from the 1992 vintage, so some signs of belief in the quality of this vineyard still persist.

Luckily, Tournon and Mauves still possess thriving vineyards and thriving *vignerons* . . . if some of the changed façades, new porches and upgraded motor cars are an indication. The leading grower at Tournon is Jean-Louis Grippat, who makes eminent wines from his 3.4 hectares of Syrah and 1.5 hectares of Marsanne. His locations are superb. He has 2.5 hectares of the available 12 hectares of the St-Joseph vineyard itself, which stands on the right of the road leaving Tournon for Mauves – all his Marsanne is here. He also rents the prime site of the Hospice from the Benevolent Hospital of Tournon, right on the very steep Tournon hillside, and this is the source for his solid and extremely rich Cuvée de l'Hospice, made from vines of over sixty years old. From 1994 there will be a further 1.5 hectares of Syrah in production from another choice site, Le Clos des Hospitaliers, also right above Tournon itself.

M. Jean-Louis Grippat

M. Grippat is enthusiastic about his wine-making and takes the visitor through the finest points of it as he wanders through his cellar, extinguished cigarette end in his hand much of the time and piece of chalk at the ready. This last is whipped out of recessed pockets in his working trousers and serves to illustrate details by graphic design on his cellar floor. M. Grippat is also distinguished by what comparatively few Rhône growers possess – a finely angled nose that is a definite advantage for tasting. 'My family have always been wine-makers, as far as I know, and used to live in St-Péray. In 1884 a branch of them moved to Mauves, choosing their wine country well, and later my branch came from there to Tournon. What this means is that I have access to a good selection of Rhône wines, since Bernard Gripa here at St-Joseph and Pierre Darona at St-Péray are both cousins.' M. Grippat's other source of distinction is that he is now helped in his work by his eldest daughter Sylvie who is keen to learn much of what her father knows and does intuitively.

Since 1988 M. Grippat has made his wine in a brand new cellar built across from his old one, so that his capacity is now much greater. In so doing some elements of his vinification have changed – he now works a pneumatic press instead of his old wooden back-breaker, and he has two stainless steel vats that he mainly uses for fining, racking and assembling his wines, plus a three-month storage after they have done their malolactic. In addition to his St-Joseph, M. Grippat produces white Hermitage from 1.2 hectares and red from just 0.3 hectare planted on the Murets section of the hillside.

M. Grippat's is a quality *domaine* – his pseudonym could be the mountain goat, for his vineyards are perched on narrow terracing, and his fortitude is compelling. One very cold February he was discussing his methods and outlook with the author in the excellent Restaurant Pic in Valence until after midnight. At seven the next morning he was seen from the safety of the author's hotel room in Tain out pruning his precipitous Tournon vineyards in a biting wind.

Very good whites have been made by M. Grippat over the years. He ferments his Marsanne in stainless steel or enamel, with one or two *pièces* of his Hermitage crop in new oak on the grounds that this may bring a little bit of extra length to that wine. There is then a storage in vats, except for three months in *pièces* before bottling, with the malolactic done, on the whole, around fifteen months after the harvest. An exception was his 1990, a year of low acidity; this was bottled after about six months with the '*malo*' partly blocked by filtration. In contrast to his 1991 St-Joseph *blanc*, which combined a good fruit attack with quite substantial length, the 1990 carried almost a dried raisin smell and great fatness on the palate. It will evolve through spells of being very closed or dumb and spells of lush richness – not a wine that is easy to catch on its best days because of a stop-go development.

His 1991 Hermitage *blanc* M. Grippat compares to a more delicate version of his 1986; this possesses a quiet richness and is the sort of wine that may take time to develop and prosper. It should drink well around six to ten years' old. The 1990 is more of a charmer, with a variety of attractive aromas, good length and depth. It is a big wine, however, and will drink well over more than eight to ten years. His 1989 and 1988 white St-Josephs were both refined wines, the 1989 having the edge with some delightful, firm peach aromas on the bouquet, a good balance and an elegant finish.

The 1989 Hermitage *blanc*, bottled around the same time as the St-Joseph, was also a powerful wine, with lively fruit on the attack and the promise of a prolonged development. The 1988 Hermitage *blanc* had an oily, very *typé* Marsanne bouquet, and agreeable richness on the palate that ran through to a chewy finish. This seems to be an eight- to ten-year wine, while the 1989 could live for around fifteen years. The St-Joseph whites, by and large, are wines that lend themselves to drinking around the ages of three to five in less full-bodied years like 1987, and around three to ten or a dozen years old in big vintages like 1989.

M. Grippat's red St-Joseph splits into two *cuvées*. The standard one is showing more consistent quality than a few years ago, and the 1988 was especially impressive – a dark plum-coloured wine, with a racy Syrah fruit bouquet and a steady Syrah backbone underneath some early fresh fruit: a wine to drink around 1993, but one with stamina for the future. The 1990 was also very good, with an intense berried fruit bouquet and the roundness and elegant tannins of this first-rate vintage. The 1989 is more delicate, with a higher overlay of fruit, and a commendable elegance. The top *cuvée*, the l'Hospice, receives more wood-ageing and in 1990 carried plenty of guts and quite noticeable tannins when young. Firmly concentrated, it will do well over twelve years or so. The 1991 is more gentle, with some cherry fruit all the way through – a wine to drink a little earlier. The 1989 was a really solid-quality wine – showing vibrant fruit aromas, a bold attack surging with firm fruit, and good length all the way through. The 1988 is a more closed number, with some extreme tannins in it, and will need some years – perhaps until 1995 – before loosening its tannic grip.

M. Grippat's red Hermitage is usually a refined wine which even in a very good year like 1990 has sufficient elegance to show well after about six years.

M. Grippat was also enterprising in making a *vin de paille* in 1985 and 1988. In 1985 he made just 150 litres from his Marsanne holdings at Hermitage – which took 600 kilograms of grapes, a tiny bit less pro-rata than Gérard Chave. M. Grippat harvested the crop with a normal maturity, but the autumn had been so dry and hot that the natural alcohol degree was high anyway. He then laid out the grapes in roughly half-bunches on a series of trays used for the dispatch of peaches – out of the sun in an open garage. A rigorous selection of the grapes followed, twice in six weeks, getting down to single grape selection and discard. Apparently the INAO encourage a two-month exposure for the grapes on *palettes*, but after six weeks M. Grippat found his sugar content rising towards a degree of over 20°! A whole day was spent pressing the grapes, and during fermentation M. Grippat made his unusual discovery: 'The malolactic was done inside the grapes, on an intracellular basis, while they were drying out – something I had not considered.'

The end wine came out at 15.5° alcohol, with 90 grams of residual sugar per litre. A literal pale straw colour, the bouquet on both the 1985 and the 1988 has been very generous and full, with an essence-like extract of oils – not quite like a late-harvested Gewürztraminer with its petrol smell, less pungent. The palate runs with honeyed flavours and rich fruit, ending with a very clean finish. Both wines were very successful, but remain a curiosity rather than a commercial reality.

Sometimes confused phonetically with Jean-Louis is his cousin Bernard Gripa, who lives a couple of miles south at Mauves, and who exchanges the use of cellar equipment and utensils with him. M. Gripa is an interesting man to talk to, very thoughtful and an articulate provider of perspective on local wine-making and issues thereof. A dark-haired, slightly cross-eyed man, he works about 5 hectares at St-Joseph (3.5 Syrah, 1.5 Marsanne) and 1 hectare at St-Péray (0.9 Marsanne, 0.1 Roussanne).

'I started about four years after Jean-Louis, in 1963–4,' he commented, 'and in those days a lot of the wine was sold to *bistrots*. My father had a very good client in Vienne, and the wine would be sent off to him in barrels. The client would fill his own bottles and sell it as *vin de Mauves* – that had as much drawing-power as St-Joseph, as the St-Jo name wasn't known then. This was a species of bar that has largely disappeared around here since then – a real *bistrot à vin*; they didn't sell beer, pastis or fruit juices,' he added, with a wry smile.

'We were typical of many *vigneron* families in that way. This arrangement continued until the *bistrot* closed in 1974, so we then switched to selling to local *négociants* like Vérilhac and Chapoutier. Since the second half of the 1970s, I've been bottling the wine here, and now it all sells to a wide audience – hotels and restaurants in the Ardèche and Paris, private buyers in France, and overseas to the United States, Switzerland, Belgium, the Netherlands and Japan.' The roll-call of export destinations marks a considerable expansion of horizons in around a dozen years, but this is typical for many of the good *vignerons* of St-Joseph.

In 1989 M. Gripa tried fermenting a little of his St-Jo *blanc* in new oak, but generally he controls the temperature at around 18°C and likes to have the malolactic done – 'despite the relative lack of acidity, I find the wines finish better with the *malo* done' is his comment. His vineyards are mostly around Tournon, on a granitic surface, and he makes a select *cuvée* which he calls Le Berceau (in French this means the cradle), so called because his holding is in the *quartier* St-Joseph, the *berceau* of the *appellation*. The white Berceau is made from fifty-year-old Marsanne and has a tremendous elegance on the bouquet, with a finer peach or greengage aroma than is encountered in most white St-Josephs. Its flavour is also stronger, with an oily extract in it which is very appealing. It ends with a dried fruit chewiness, and is a super wine.

M. Gripa's top red, his *cuvée* Vieilles Vignes, is another cracking effort. Again, it is a finer wine than many in the *appellation*. Deeply coloured, with black streaks apparent, it has a sustained berried bouquet and a firm tannic base driving it along in years like 1988, 1989 and 1990. In a softer vintage like 1985 it evolves towards a more ruby colour and some vegetal aromas more quickly – around six or seven years old – but like many of the solid-style St-Joseph reds it can pass through a rather dumb intermediate phase, failing to show much on the bouquet and tasting a bit taut on the palate, around four or five years old.

Two of M. Gripa's neighbours in Mauves work in the old way at both wine and fruit production, which round here means mainly apricots and cherries. Following the death in 1990 of eldest brother Jean, the Marsanne family is composed of two brothers, André and René, who with one of their sons cultivate 2 hectares of Syrah, spread out above Mauves, as well as 0.8 hectare of Syrah at Crozes. They are an example of old agricultural France at its best. When Jean was alive, the three brothers would each don a straw hat as they set off to graft new vine-stock on a sunny May day, no doubt regarded as a touch eccentric by the local neighbourhood. Being a trio helped for this labour-intensive task, though, since it takes time and trouble. Most growers nowadays buy their vine-stock already grafted from the local *pépiniériste*, but the Marsannes would use their time well: it is slow work, but a good man does 600–800 plants in a day, his speed accentuated by having a brother behind him to pile up the soil to keep the *greffe*, or cutting, from the sun and to stop it drying out. Within a year, the young plant's vegetation will have risen to the top of a 5-foot stake.

The Marsanne wine is aged in *demi-muids* for fifteen to eighteen months: no concessions to modernism have even been contemplated by the family. Their wine is always distinguished by ample fruit extraction, the intensity of which varies with the relative ripeness of the year's tannins. The 1983, for instance, was excellent, full of surging power when young, but possessing enough balance and tannic support to run for perhaps a total of twelve to fifteen years. The 1985, by contrast, was also strongly fruited in a wild Syrah way, but the tannins were much softer, making it a wine to drink before its tenth birthday or so.

As befits someone who is a protégé of Gérard Chave, Jean Maisonneuve makes a full-bodied, traditionally styled, red St-Joseph from his 1.3-hectare vineyard at Mauves. He laments the fact that most of his land is more suitable for fruit trees than for vines, for he would clearly rather be a *viticulteur* than a mixed *agriculteur*. He has been bottling his wine since 1977 and is pleased with the new range of people whom he has met through selling it from his home on the main square. Although his wine label is not very scenic, the wine inside the bottle is good and offers further testimony to the right of Mauves to be called the unofficial capital of the St-Joseph *appellation*.

To the south of Mauves there is one *domaine* which has made a firm impression, its hillside vineyards standing outside the original *appellation* zone. Maurice Courbis's family have been viticultural at Châteaubourg since 1587, so he says, for he has the ability to shoot a grand line which leaves one guessing about its ratio of truth to humour. His 10.5 hectares of vines are split between a prime site at Châteaubourg, on a hill called Les Royes, and Glun just to the north, and he also has 1.5 hectares at Cornas.

M. Courbis has a traditional, balanced view of life. He cannot understand why certain elements at Cornas should demand a sudden large increase in the permitted yield, since he can see the threat that poses to quality. He makes a very sound superior *cuvée* of Cornas called La Cotte, which is a solidly built wine made to last, while his top St-Joseph, Domaine des Royes, is also well extracted and has sufficient tannins to need four or five years to unwind. Both these wines are bottled after about twelve to fourteen months in cask. Although one-third of his St-Joseph is white, this is a relatively less impressive offering, containing reasonable fruit but sometimes lacking a sound balance.

Up in the newer northern zone, the core vineyards and the best wines come from Chavanay and its surrounds. There is a strong concentration of youth making wine in this area – Didier Chol, André Perret, Marc Rouvière, Philippe Faury, Pierre Gaillard at nearby Malleval and Louis Chèze above Limony. These are all names to look out for. Didier Chol (the de Boisseyt part of their title refers to a place, which they use as a brand, hence Domaine de Boisseyt) has planted on the granite slopes above Chavanay, and is making a very well-crafted red St-Joseph, a wine whose emphasis is for stylish length on the palate. Aged for almost two years in wood, his reds are ideal to drink after around four years (1987) or six years (1988).

Like the others in this group, André Perret made an excellent 1988 red St-Jo, but his burgeoning skill as a *viticulteur* is demonstrated through his successful 1987, which contained a surprising depth of colour and amount of end tannin for its year. Like his neighbours, Perret runs two red *cuvées*, his superior being called Les Grisières, which is made from thirty-year vines – called 'old' at St-Joseph . . . go tell *that* to a Cornas *vigneron*! This is bottled after about eighteen months, which can be spent stored part in stainless steel, part in wood, and carries an excellent nearly black colour, firm tannins, sound balance, and is likely to keep for up to ten or twelve years. First made in 1988, this has got off to a flying start with the 1988, 1989 and 1990 offerings.

One of the impressive new names in this northerly part of the *appellation* is Louis Chèze, who works a St-Joseph vineyard of around 7 hectares (6 hectares Syrah, 1-and-a-bit Marsanne) that is located in different places on terraces (manual work) and flat ground (machine cultivation) around the plateau above Limony, approached by a curling, twisting road. M. Chèze is also excited by his two hectares at Condrieu, which will start producing *appellation* wine with the 1992 vintage.

His outlook is modern – *macération pelliculaire*, 30 per cent of the crop raised in new oak for four months for the whites – and total destalking, plus exposure to brand new oak *barriques* over ten months for some of his best red *cuvées*.

His whites are well worked; neither 1990 nor 1991 was an easy year, but M. Chèze came up with a very good, fresh but nicely weighted 1991 and a gutsy 1990. His top red, the Cuvée Prestige de Caroline is very successful, with a thoroughly good trio of wines in 1988, 1989 and 1990: the 1988 – rich, peppery and well-scented – was a firmer wine than the plump, appealing 1989 whose ripe aromas and flavours indicate a shorter life of seven years or so. The 1990 just tops the other two, being deliciously rich and dense on the palate, the Syrah fruit and the young oak combining well. It will take until around 1994 to integrate its elements together but will then provide excellent drinking – perhaps to the age of ten.

M. Chèze's standard *cuvée*, the Classique, carries a wild fruit, sometimes tarry bouquet and in vintages like 1991 and 1990 is good to drink around two to three years old to catch its fruitiness.

Keeping up the momentum around Chavanay are a series of growers whose work, especially with their red wines, brings some welcome repute to the St-Joseph name. The wines of Marc Rouvière, Philippe Faury (including his solid white wines), Yves Cuilleron, Alain Paret, Pierre Bonnard, Pierre Gaillard (particularly the excellent Clos de Cuminaille), René Rostaing (better known for his Côte-Rôtie) and Daniel Vernay (better known for his family's Condrieu) are all worth seeking out. Elsewhere in the *appellation*, do not forget that fine *vignerons* like Gérard Chave, Bernard Faurie and Alain Graillot make a little St-Joseph *rouge* – Chave's is what he calls an amusement and is stacked with fresh Syrah fruit, a true delight to drink either at about two years old or later on, around five or six years old. Then the Houses of Chapoutier, with a fine holding at St-Joseph itself which makes a frequently enjoyable wine called Deschants, and Jaboulet with their Grand Pompée are also very sound sources of the wine, as, increasingly, are Delas from St-Jean-de-Muzols, who buy in grapes from around Chavanay.

In the southern part of the *appellation* another name to consider is Pierre Guillermain, a young grower making a well-reputed red at Lemps.

Lastly there is the Cave Co-opérative of St-Désirat, whose transformation from a sleepy local affair into one of the most go-ahead enterprises in the Rhône is in large part due to the work of M. Georges Chaléat, who has shaken up the 100 or so subscribers in this formerly fruit-conscious flatland between Serrières and Sarras – so that now they have planted Gamay on the high plateaux, Syrah on the hillsides and increasing amounts of fine white *cépages*, including the Viognier and the Marsanne.

Their installations are extremely modern, with plenty of stainless steel vats, and part of the reason for improved quality is the careful selection of the harvest after it has been picked: better vines and better selection are what more Co-opératives should practise.

The Co-opérative vinifies part of the red grape harvest without any crush, in *raisin entier* form, over a two week fermentation. They also destalk part of the crop, and give these grapes a 20-day *cuvaison*, adding relatively less of the *vin de presse* from this process into the final wine.

Some of their wine is very light, quaffing, supermarket produce with a very friendly price attached to it – dangerous, perhaps, for the good name of the St-Joseph *appellation* if it sets the standard in people's minds for St-Josephs. Perhaps the Co-opérative sees such purchasers as completely discrete from those who would buy higher-priced, more serious offerings of St-Joseph. Worth more attention are their special *cuvée* wines, which are slightly marked by new oak, and which are cleanly made and possess good weight on the palate. Wines like the Cuvée du Bicentenaire provide very good drinking in a measured, sit-down way with red meat or stews when they have emerged from a dumb phase after about five years. The new oak can oppress the regional and varietal stamp, but these top *cuvées* are nevertheless very good wines in their own right. The fact that they come from a Cave Co-opérative is all the more commendable.

St-Joseph Vintages

1961   Excellent. It would be a surprise if many bottles had managed to still hold together.

1962   Very good.

1963   Poor.

1964   Very good, but there are unlikely to be many bottles tasting as well as the Grippat *blanc* tried in May 1986.

1965   Poor.

1966   Very good.

1967   Excellent. Well-stored bottles of red could provide good examples of the old fruit/vegetal aromas and a lingering southern richness – a Coursodon red tried in May 1986 was still showing well.

1968   Poor.

1969   Very good. The red wines were robust and developed very well.

1970   Good. The large crop undermined the strength of the wines, but they held a sound balance which has sustained them for longer than expected. The reds are starting to tire.

1971   Excellent. A strongly flavoured vintage that matured very well. The colour of the reds is ruby to brick now and their warmth is gently slipping away. The very good whites have tended to become oxidized.

1972   Good, particularly for wines made in Mauves. The reds have passed their best, but still have a residual southern sweetness that is keeping some bottles interesting, especially on the bouquet. A good, fruity year for the whites, which are now over the top.

1973   Very good. Despite the very large crop, the red wines were dark and well scented; they have now become rather thin. The whites, attractively styled when young, are past their best.

1974   Mediocre. Better for the whites than the reds.

1975   A small crop of light wines similar to the 1974s. The fruity red wines were best drunk young, while many of the whites were acidic and unbalanced.

1976   Generally good. There was some rain just before the harvest, but growers managed to make quite a full red wine, with a sound colour and bouquet. The reds have developed well, but should be drunk soon. The whites were rich and powerfully flavoured and odd bottles may still show impressively, driven by an alcohol extract of about 13°.

1977   Disappointing. The summer was cold and rainy, and light, irregular red wines resulted. The white wines were also light, and neither should be kept.

1978   Excellent. A healthy harvest that permitted the growers to make strongly coloured and well-constructed red wines, which are notable for their excellent balance. The traditionally vinified reds from the leading villages will still be impressing with their Syrah richness around 1992–5. The whites were also very fine, but should be drunk up soon.

1979   A goodish vintage, which has progressed in the bottle. The reds did not have the extract and intensity of the 1978s, but in their quiet way have built up appealing complexity as they have aged. The emphasis is on a rich fruitiness, which has started to lose its vigour. Drink soon to enjoy them best. Sound white wines which should be drunk soon as well.

1980   Good. The reds were well coloured, and in ageing have not lost much of their depth. They display a rounded set of jam aromas on the nose, but the dustiness of age is creeping in. The alcohol and hot flavours are emerging on the palate, and the wines are now drinking at their peak. The whites were richly flavoured but are in need of drinking.

1981   Rain during the harvest hurt the colour of the reds. This was a fair vintage. The reds are thinning in colour and on the bouquet already show secondary, older aromas. Still quite vigorous and spicy on the palate, they may continue to be drinkable until around 1995 – for those who like their wines really old. A small crop of whites was not very successful – light and uneven in many cases.

1982   Variable – some well-modelled wines, others hit by high volatile acidity. The reds were often over-ripe, and in some instances lacked colour. They have evolved fairly quickly, and do not have the balance to live and develop for long, unless they are packed with alcohol. Drink up the reds and move on to a more all-round year like 1985. The whites from the best growers were worth the time of day, since their sheer richness pulled them along successfully. They, too, are going nowhere and should be dispatched.

1983   Very good indeed. A much larger crop than 1982, but the reds held better overall balance. It was a year for the old-fashioned wine-makers – the Syrah's tannins were very firm and there was a rich substance of colour and matter on the palate. These are big wines, and many are likely to live towards 1998 or so. The more standard, fruit-concentrated *cuvées* will be best enjoyed before 1993. The whites were elegant, their balance and discreet fruit being delicious in the first five years. Odd bottles will live past 1993.

1984   A variable vintage. Things got off to a late start with a cold bout of −10°C in February. Many of the reds were a bit lightly coloured, and unless selection of the harvest was carefully done, some green flavours resulted. The best *cuvées* had an enjoyable middle weight, some dark flavours, and were ideal to drink between 1987 and 1991. The whites were fresh, contained more acidity than most vintages, and their intrinsic richness has allowed them to have better ageing prospects than the reds.

1985   Very good. It was very hot and dry during the harvest, and there were some repetitions of the over-heated vinifications of 1982. Some reds lacked vigour and developed quickly. The best *cuvées* are ideal to drink before around 1994 – this was a year for the fruit extractors, not the tannin merchants, at St-Joseph. The whites were excellent, rich in alcohol and strength of flavour and very well balanced. Well-scented and long *en bouche*, some could run for ten years or more.

1986   Quite a good vintage, but some of the reds contain an austere green acidity which makes them taste hard. The best growers had to work hard to achieve a customary rich flavour in their reds, so several wines lack depth and balance. The best are emerging from a dumb passage, and will drink well in the traditional aged Syrah way between 1992 and 1997. The whites were more generally successful, with some rich bouquets and attractive length on the palate. They will drink well over the course of about eight years.

1987   Quite good – better than the popular perception, but one has to stick to the front-rank growers. The year was saved by a splendid, hot September. The best *cuvées* held a sound colour and were very good examples of middle-weight wines delightful to drink around four to six years old. A coming-of-age vintage for several young growers around Chavanay, whose meticulous cellar work proved their merit for future reference – growers like Chol and André Perret. The whites were very good, lighter than surrounding years, but agreeably scented and engaging on the palate, with a soft refinement. They are delicious to drink now, but could be kept for a different, aged style of white wine over the course of seven to nine years.

1988   Excellent. A cracking year for the reds which allowed the *vignerons* the chance to make four-square, solid Syrah wines that possessed excellent balance. More complete than the 1983s, and a touch less generous than the 1978s and 1990s, this is a keeping vintage. The wines are darkly coloured, show a depth of promise on the bouquets, and are long and chewy on the palate. Some lighter *cuvées* are for drinking around 1992–3; otherwise special *cuvées* and those made by the best growers from Tournon, Mauves, St-Jean-de-Muzols, Chavanay and Châteaubourg will show extremely well over the course of ten to fifteen years. The whites possessed a very thorough Marsanne fruit, sometimes oily extract. They also have great balance and their depth gives them good prospects during the 1990s.

1989   Very good, although the style of some of the reds was a little *nerveux* or delicate, with parts of the vineyard suffering more from the drought this year than in 1988. Many of the reds were darkly coloured despite the very large crop and their tannins are less secure and less dense than those in the 1988s. They showed racy fruit aromas when young and will be initially more imposing than the firmer 1988s. They can be long on the finish, and this again is another year in which to seek out the best *cuvées* from the best growers – to have good Syrah with ageing potential of up to eight to twelve years in the cellar. The whites also showed well early on; they have good fruit on the bouquet and are ripe-tasting on the palate. They will drink especially well around 1992–4.

1990   An excellent vintage, overall the superior of 1988. Harvesting around mid-September brought in a large, healthy crop. The fruit extract in the reds is particularly notable, but it is surrounded by wrap-around tannins that with the higher than usual alcohol extract give very gutsy, sustained flavours in the young wines. The reds are all soundly coloured and give every indication of developing ample, complex bouquets with time. The standard, more fruit-driven *cuvées* will be delicious around three to five years old; the prestige *cuvées* will drink really well if left for five years or so, and have a long life in prospect.

The whites were rich and fat, sometimes too opulent. Lack of acidity may be a problem, but the best have ripe aromas and great warmth on the palate – an old-fashioned southern power marks them.

Leading Growers at St-Joseph

The nucleus:

Bonnard, Pierre	42410 Chavanay
Chapoutier M.	26600 Tain-l'Hermitage
Chave, Jean-Louis	07300 Mauves
Chèze, Alain	07340 Limony
Chol, Didier	
Domaine de Boisseyt-Chol	42410 Chavanay
Courbis, Maurice, et Fils	
GAEC des Ravières	07130 Châteaubourg
Coursodon, Pierre	07300 Mauves
Cuilleron, Yves	42410 Chavanay
Cave Co-opérative de St-Désirat	07340 St-Désirat
Faurie, Bernard	07300 Tournon
Faury, Philippe	42410 Chavanay
Gaillard, Pierre	42860 Malleval
Graillot, Alain	26600 Tain-l'Hermitage
Gripa, Bernard	07300 Mauves
Grippat, Jean-Louis	07300 Tournon
Guillermain, Pierre	07300 Lemps
Jaboulet Aîné, Paul	26600 La Roche-de-Glun
Marsanne et Fils	07300 Mauves
Paret, Alain	
Chai-St-Pierre	42410 St-Pierre-de-Bœuf
Perret, André	42410 Chavanay
Rostaing, René	69402 Ampuis
Rouvière, Marc	42410 Chavanay
Domaine du Chêne	
Trollat, Raymond	07300 St-Jean-de-Muzols
de Vallouit, Louis-Francis	26240 St-Vallier
Vernay, Daniel	69420 Condrieu

Other producers:

Bernard, Sylvain	
Domaine de Fauterie	07130 St-Péray
Blachon, Roger	07300 Mauves
Boucher, Michel	42410 Chavanay
Boucher, Pierre	42860 Malleval
Bourrin, Dominique	42410 Pélussin
Cave Co-Opérative de Sarras	07370 Sarras
Cave Co-Opérative de Tain-l'Hermitage	26600 Tain-l'Hermitage
Chanal, Roger	
Château de Villars	42410 Pélussin
GAEC Collonge	26600 Mercurol
Delas Frères	
Desbos, Jean	
Desestret, Michel	07300 St-Jean-de-Muzols
Domaine de la Côte St-Épine	
Florentin, Emile	07300 Mauves
Fogier, Elisabeth	07300 St-Jean-de-Muzols
Gonon, Pierre	
Lantheaume, Guy	07300 Mauves
Lombard, Jean-Yves	
Maisonneuve, Jean	
Michelas, Robert	26600 Mercurol
Montez, Antoine	42410 Chavanay
Cave Co-Opérative du Péage-de-Roussillon	38550 Péage-de-Roussillon
Perrier, Pascal	07370 Sarras
Pichon, Philippe	42410 Chavanay
Ribo, François, et Dard, René-Jean	26600 Mercurol

7
Cornas

The sight of a mature Cornas tumbling into a broad-based wine glass is unforgettable. What richness, vigour and virility are portrayed in that startling dash of colour – and the heady scent of blackcurrant and raspberry that accompanies it is sufficient to surprise the most cosmopolitan of wine tasters. For here is one of the hidden treasures of the French wine world, one that sailed through the 1980s without making so much as a passing concession to the 'time is money' mentality so firmly revered during that decade. As far back as 1763 the village priest, a M. Molin, had been moved to record much the same sort of comment: 'The mountain of this village is most entirely planted with vines which produce a very good *black* wine. This wine is much sought after by the merchants and is very heady.'

Cornas lies to the south of the main area of the St-Joseph *appellation*, on the same west side of the Rhône, and with St-Péray marks the end of the northern Côtes du Rhône. It is a small village which has undergone some superficial changes brought on by proximity to busy, industrial Valence just across the river. New housing has sprung up in the past fifteen years – the view from the vineyards now includes groups of bold orange-coloured roofs, intruders into the previous soft pastels of light brown Ardèche tiles. And there is more activity in the village than in the 1970s – more people, more bustle.

But *vieille France* is a stubborn creature. The arrival of the mobile *boucher-charcutier* in the Place de l'Église stirs up a commotion. It provides the perfect backdrop for some impassive watching of the visiting stranger. Indeed, suspicion about a new face generates the question – undoubtedly impost-related – 'Are you from the Water Authority?' The *épicier* has hung up a sign 'Order your fish for Thursday' outside his shop, the gossipers continue their social speculation, and an old man with a stick walks slowly along the rue

Pied la Vigne and into the Place du Pressoir.

Towering over the village is its church. Its lank spire is visible for miles around and the patch of ground around its front door is the village centre. Inside the church is a memorial plaque to those fallen in the two world wars. Many of the names are from old wine-growing families that still work the slopes above Cornas.

The village's wine tradition goes back some thousand years. A Latin document of AD 885, from the canonry of Viviers, records that wine was at that time being made by an unnamed religious order. This is the first definite mention of the wine of Cornas, although it is said locally to have been appreciated by the Emperor Charlemagne as he passed through the village in 840. A good legend is virtually obligatory for any self-respecting wine community, and it is much more than probable that there was wine being made at Cornas in 840, when Charlemagne happened to be in the area!

Further evidence of Cornas's 'holy' origins comes in the register books of the St-Chaffre-de-Monastier Abbey, also in the diocese of Viviers. Here it is stated that 'a nobleman named Léotard gave to the Abbey of St-Chaffre a field measuring four *manses* and a vineyard, on the condition that the brother responsible for the order would offer his colleagues a fine annual dinner that included lampreys and big fish.' This agreement ran between the years 993 and 1014, but unfortunately it is difficult to be precise about Léotard's generosity, for the ancient measure of a *manse* has long since disappeared from use.

It does seem probable, though, that the religious orders were cultivating only small vineyards at this time; the local church documents take great care to point out with precision all boundaries and geographical situations, and the description 'a vine' occurs frequently in the old, often Latin, writings. By the time of M. Molin's enthusiasm in 1763 the scale of cultivation had evidently greatly increased, for the mountain was almost completely covered with vines.

Today the *appellation* vineyards extend over 70 hectares on the hillsides behind the village. In the second half of the 1980s there was a mild increase in planting, since growing public repute and a string of good vintages succeeded in raising the asking price for the wine, and growers can now sense more economic rationale in cultivating these arduous slopes. Some 10 hectares were newly planted in that time, vines that will be on stream by 1992–3.

This is a tiny area compared with the past. As long ago as 1927, at a time when vineyards were being abandoned because of the shortage of men to look after them following the First World War, a local document describes the annual village wine production as around 5,900 hectolitres: in the 1970s the most abundant harvest, the 1973, yielded little more than one-third of this figure, 2,029 hectos. The average for the decade was 1,458 hectolitres.

But the 1980s brought a trend that was both disturbing and short-sighted. While the area under vine has moved within close limits – 1971: 53.4 hectares; 1982: 66.8 hectares; 1989: 70 hectares – the volumes of production have increased dramatically. The most abundant harvest of the 1980s, the 1989, yielded 3,082 hectolitres (over 50 per cent more than 1973), and the average for the decade was 2,179 hectos (just under 50 per cent up on the 1970s). And yet the vineyard has risen in size by only just over 30 per cent.

So the drive for increased intensiveness of production has hit Cornas. The debate on this in the early 1990s was becoming acrimonious among the local community. In 1989 a group amongst whom the controversial newcomer *œnologue-vigneron* Jean-Luc Colombo was evident was pushing for an allowance of 50 hectolitres per hectare plus right of *dérogation* for another 7.5 hectos, totalling 57.5 hectolitres per hectare. That this request should be put to Paris in the name of the Syndicat des Vignerons does Cornas a disservice: in the early 1980s a total including *dérogation* of 38.5 hectolitres was allowed. Quality takes another beating in this case from extensive use of more closely planted Syrah clones, ones that are disease-resistant and high-producing, plus the surge of extra wine made from young vines as opposed to the densely concentrated grape-juice of old vines. Older growers like Auguste Clape and Maurice Courbis are appalled at this short-sightedness that will end up threatening the good name of their *appellation*, and who can blame them?

The vineyards are spread to the west of the village and run in three principal divisions. The most southerly *quartier* is Les Renards, which runs over the top of the hill visible from the village, and has an excellent exposure. As with the other hill flanks at Cornas, the highest vines here go up to 300 metres or so, the *coteau* starting at around 125 metres. The soil here is granite-based with some clay topsoil, and the odd patch of limestone covering. The clay content helps to preserve the water reserves, which is a vital asset in drought years like 1989 and 1990.

At a level opposite the church, and in full view of the community, is what the locals call La Côte, the Coteau de Tezier. The soil here is again granite-based, with a covering of decomposed stone. This makes the vines sited here more drought-prone.

To the north, following the broad line of the road to St-Romain-de-Lerps, stands the Chaillot *quartier*, and just below it the *quartier* of Les Mazards. Chaillot is actually out of sight of the village on a more north-westerly flank of these Ardèche outhills, and it is here that recent planting activity has concentrated. The soil here is granite-based with some limestone and a decomposed topsoil. Auguste Clape admits that it would be 'a lovely place to make white wine if we were allowed'. There are also pockets of clay here, especially at the *lieu-dit* of Les Arlettes, right on the northern edge of the *appellation*: Jean Lionnet cultivates over 3 hectares here.

The Mazards vineyards grow on granite that is topped with clay, and in some places sand. Through being lower down the slope the vines here are more drought-resistant than those higher up, and also have the clay to help them. Auguste Clape commented that in 1989 a mere 2–3 mm (0.08–0.12 inches) of rain fell at Cornas between April and the harvest in September. The average weight of a bunch of Syrah taken off the high slopes was 250 grams; bunches picked at the bottom of the slopes weighed 410 grams – a very clear indication of the impact of the drought in certain places.

Cornas is a thumping big red wine, the like of which rarely exists these days; one of the reasons for this is that it has traditionally been made from old vine plants. This fact is a direct result of the handing down within families of properties that have to be worked personally, by hand and by foot, even in the 1990s. The old local saying runs that the *vigneron* must have '*bon dos, bon pied et bon œil*' (a good back, a good foot and a good eye), and so *domaines* have remained small, with any hired labour having to compete with higher-paid jobs over in Valence or easier branches of agriculture such as fruit-growing. Methods have therefore generally remained conservative, and some of today's older growers are cropping vines planted by their grandfathers. René Balthazar still works some nineteenth-century plants, while Auguste Clape's 'older vines' average sixty years. For him, young vines are twelve-year plants. In most other *appellations* growers refer to thirty-year vines as old and five-year vines as young.

The Second World War brought problems for Cornas as the growers went off to fight. There was also a bad frost in 1939 which meant that a *vigneron* like Roger Catalon only made 375 bottles from his 1-hectare plot. 'My vineyard was, like many others, abandoned after I was made a prisoner of war near Trier. But I managed to escape in February 1941, and came straight back to my *boulot*,' he recalls. A man of eighty who has been making wine since he passed his education certificate at thirteen, M. Catalon loves what he does: 'There are those who like to play *boules* – I like to go into my vines.' He remembers the 1940s as being downbeat years for Cornas. 'The *cafetiers* of Valence and Vienne would take our wine as *vin de Cornas*, but they really only wanted a wine of no more than 11° to get their customers to drink more – we were selling a wine passed up and down the zinc counters in those days.'

By the 1950s the local *négociant* houses were starting to take the wine and spread it around the region. Vérilhac, Delas and then Paul Jaboulet Aîné worked with Cornas, and that is why the rare bottles of Cornas dating from the 1950s that one used to find in cities like Marseille, Avignon or Aix-en-Provence were from houses like Vérilhac – the *vignerons* were hardly doing any of their own bottling.

The first person to bottle his Cornas had been a man who worked on the SNCF, the French railways, and who owned a choice part of the Renards vineyard, a holding now split between Auguste Clape and the Michel family. M. Bessénay started this practice in 1952–3, which was quite a departure for the time. 'Well, the market was part *pichets* in Lyon, part *négociants* for later bottling', comments M. Clape. 'Either way we didn't need to bottle – the *négociants* would bring their 660-litre *demi-muids* to the cellars and take the wine away in them. That's one of the reasons there are no splendid cellars at Cornas – everything is on a very modest scale. The only bottling that would take place was for weddings and family events. Otherwise the wine would go away in *pièce* to private buyers eighteen months after the harvest, and they would bottle it themselves with a *mise en bouteille par l'acheteur* label. The wine would sell out very early on', he recalls. 'In 1957 it was all sold by November, and with a tiny crop, prices soon doubled. That's why I started to bottle some of my wine between 1958 and 1960 onwards.'

In the late 1960s fortunes started to look up a little. The year 1968 had been a disastrous vintage nearly everywhere in France, and Burgundy was going through a rocky period, with expensive, irregular-quality wines. Buyers began to look further afield and around 1969/70 some export orders trickled through. By the early 1980s, under twenty of the sixty vine-growers actually bottled their wine, although increased fame and prices during the 1980s raised that figure to around thirty, as well as bringing in some of the first new blood to work the Cornas hillsides for many years.

The task of making such difficult terrain pay is a perpetual problem for growers at Cornas. In the 1970s there were attempts to maximize production by cultivating the more accessible land between the village and the hillside where tractors could be driven. But this resulted in weak and unrepresentative wines showing up in local or national tastings, and during the 1980s the trend reverted towards scrubbing out the high hillsides, clearing them of stubborn oak trees and thick brush, to plant vines in better locations. One concession to modernism that saves much labour is helicopter spraying, which was introduced in 1990.

While the granite-based soil plays a strong role in drawing out the full power of the Syrah, Cornas is also favoured by its local climate. The village is situated at a point where the Rhône Valley is very broad and the vineyards are set well back against the Valley's western flank. They are thus quite thoroughly sheltered from the *mistral*, whose cooling force is widely dispersed across the corridor of the valley. As a result, the level of heat in the vineyards is often greater than elsewhere in the northern Côtes du Rhône, and this in turn aids the natural development of the grape harvest. 'I don't actually treat against rot,' comments Guy de Barjac. 'For me, the two main problems are *cicadelles* (locusts) and *ver de la grappe* (grape-worm), and these can be attended to by lighter treatments.' Such naturally well-ripened grapes, many of them taken from old vine plants, contribute directly to the wine's unvarying intensity of colour and fullness of flavour.

In a hot, dry summer like 1989, harvest-time is declared on 10 September, and the holdings are sufficiently restricted for most growers to have their crops into the cellars within three to eight days of intensive work by family, friends and some temporary labour. The 10 hectares that Jean Lionnet works – 4 his own, 6 rented – take a little longer to clear. Opinion is divided over destalking and destemming. The modernists like to do it, the traditionalists don't. So Jean Lionnet destalks totally, Guy de Barjac destalks 80–100 per cent according to the vintage, and Alain Voge destalks half or more of his crop. Marcel Juge, Auguste Clape and René Balthazar, on the other hand, do not destalk.

Alcoholic fermentation takes place in closed concrete vats or old open wood containers. Jean Lionnet is unusual with his six upright stainless steel vats – concrete rather than wood is now the most commonly found receptacle. The length of the primary fermentation is nowadays around ten to fourteen days; Auguste Clape's *cuvaison* in 1989, for instance, lasted for ten to eleven days, two days less than usual, since he did not want to extract tannins that were too hard; while Guy de Barjac has for some years returned to a twelve-day fermentation after experimenting with a reduced time to see whether he could obtain a lighter wine of more immediate appeal. M. de Barjac explained the reasoning behind his earlier policy, and its failure is encouraging for those keen that Cornas should retain its individuality: 'I used not to ferment my grapes for more than six days, as my biggest concern was to make a wine that showed finesse. One of the great problems of Cornas is that, when young, it tends to be very coarse, and it is regrettable that pressure of demand deems that it be bottled and sold when still in its infancy. I was trying to produce a wine that could be readily appreciated at the time of its purchase, but it was the 1977 vintage that changed my mind. This wine was fine and light, but I considered that it resembled more a lesser Burgundy than a Cornas, and the last thing I wanted to do was to lose the Cornas style in my wines.'

M. de Barjac continued: 'I therefore started by increasing the length of fermentation to eight days, which was what the 1978 vintage received. That was such a big year that I have advised friends and customers to keep some of the wine for the year 2000. I like my wines to have ageing prospects – let's say at least a dozen years, and I realize that the six-day-fermentation wine didn't have enough tannin or quite enough body to support such ageing.'

The young wine then generally receives one or two rackings before being set to age in wood, and here again the ranks divide between modernists and traditionalists. The most extreme modernist is Jean Lionnet, whose whole vinification process differs from that of the majority and who is inextricably bound up in the concept of new oak, while others who use new oak to some extent include Alain Voge and Guy de Barjac – the latter uses Burgundian *pièces*, one in eight of which are brand new. The traditionalists – Noël Verset, Auguste Clape, Marcel Juge, René Balthazar, for instance – use aged oak whose size can range from 10–20-hectolitre *foudres* (Clape, Courbis) to 600-litre *demi-muids* (Balthazar), to 225-litre *pièces*

(Clape, Verset, Juge, Robert Michel).

The stay in wood runs up to two years, although most growers now perform their last bottling run between eighteen months and two years after the harvest. Auguste Clape bottles in the spring and the summer, the latter run being one of the latest of any given vintage, while Jean Lionnet, Marcel Juge, Guy de Barjac and Alain Voge all bottle in the spring, eighteen months after the harvest. The wine receives less cask-ageing than in previous times, because of both steady demand and cash flow – two whole years in cask used to be the norm until the mid-1970s.

For Guy de Barjac, 'Ageing in wood is not a question of fifteen to eighteen months – it's more a question of the wine having two winters to deposit itself well. That's why I have never fined nor filtered.' From 1990, de Barjac cut down on his activities, so that part of his crop is now made by Sylvain Bernard, and part by Jean-Luc Colombo. He receives a little of the crop from the two tenants to keep his eye in on the vinification. While some of the growers like Clape fine with egg white, very few filter their wine, and one of the joys of aged Cornas is the sight of a black-backed bottle waiting to be uncorked to reveal all its dense, dark flavours.

As a young wine, Cornas is a shocker – the sort of wine to make the nervous laugh, the windy cry. At a couple of years old it is a savage, black-tanned wine that leaves the eye impressed and the palate and teeth darkened. There are rasps of tannin all over it – the bouquet has a fiery berry fruitiness, the flavours are crushed and intense. There is promise, but the first, overwhelming impact is power.

One might expect a wine of this nature to be strongly alcoholic, but this is not the case. It is very rare for a Cornas to exceed 13° alcohol strength, whereas a Châteauneuf-du-Pape, for instance, will often contain 14° or even a little more. Why the wine should be so dense and concentrated when compared with a Syrah-based Côte-Rôtie or a St-Joseph made nearby is one of the only semi-solvable riddles of the wine world. There is no doubt that the main factors are the local granite – a perfect match with the Syrah, which at Hermitage produces a wine of still greater richness and generosity – plus the *micro-climat*, the age of the vines and the outlook of most of the *vignerons*. But one couldn't write an exam paper and give THE answer – the variables shift too much for that.

As the initial coarseness wears off, Cornas develops a more

harmonious side. The austerity of the Syrah settles, and plum and dried fruit flavours emerge on the palate, while the bouquet gains in depth and complexity. But the heat – noticeable on the bouquet and on the aftertaste – never really departs; the mastiff never becomes a poodle. The strongest vintages such as 1976, 1978, 1983, 1988 or 1990 will have a life-span of easily twenty years, while the wine from very good harvests like 1989 and 1985 will run for fifteen years *sans problème*. The same goes for more difficult vintages like 1980 which, because they were well crafted by the growers, are indicating continued life and good drinking until at least 1997.

Most Cornas is not ready to drink until it is six to eight years old, whatever the vintage; before that, its broad range of nuances and aromas is but barely developed, and to the imbiber the sensation can be akin to that of attempting to drink a heavy black syrup. Cornas is an unpretentious wine, but like good Hermitage it does cry out for, and repay, long keeping. As its structure loosens past its tenth birthday, so it reveals greater complexity, and later on in life there appear the damp, roasted aromas of old Syrah, with a pleasing southern warmth. Whereas Hermitage can hold this Syrah sweetness at very advanced ages – forty or fifty years – Cornas, the more modest country wine, retreats towards dryness on the finish with great age.

Cornas's best-known grower and the one who makes the best, quite exceptional wine, is M. Auguste Clape, who since 1989 has been joined in his work by his forty-year-old son Pierre-Marie. As with many small family holdings at Cornas, the problem of the succession of the Clape estate has vexed his supporters over the years, and with Pierre-Marie having left his job in Valence as a teacher of mechanical engineering, this *domaine* has received a strong lift for the future.

The Clapes own 4.5 hectares and rent one more. Two hectares are on the Coteau de Tezier, 1.5 hectares on Les Renards, and 2 hectares are split between the *quartiers* of Chaillot and Les Mazards. The *domaine* wine is assembled from all four sources a month before bottling, and the process of tasting the different constituents in M. Clape's intimate, musty *cave* – with just the right amount of mushroom growth on the walls of the innermost cellar to keep him happy – is a fascinating exercise.

As an example, his 1988 was made up of four wines, tasted in cask in April 1990.

M. Auguste Clape

1988   Les Mazards (*pièce*), dark colour, nose very closed. Austere on palate, dry flavours, end-tannins give it good length.

1988   Twelve-year 'young' vines (*pièce*), purple, bright; palate is firm, dark and strong tannins on it, forceful.

1988   Tezier thirty-five-year vines (*foudre*), more substance on bouquet, more open. Good weight on palate, very good crushed fruit, nice tannic follow-through.

1988   Renards eighty-plus-year vines (*foudre*), firm colour; good depth and warmth on bouquet, aromatic. Elegant start on palate, has substance and a tannic finish. Good structure.

1988   *assemblage* of the four sources (*foudre*). Dark purple. Bouquet warm, not very open, but shows promise. Good weight on palate, very good balance on the attack, runs on to a crushed fruit and nicely tannic ending. Should develop well, will probably be showing well after ten years, though should keep well.

By February, 1991, when tasted in bottle in England, this wine had come together very well:

Dark, young Syrah purple. Bouquet aromatic already, but depth and balance there. Excellent balance which underscores the true power of the wine. Superb extraction of fruit and very lasting length. Will show earlier than some hard tannin years, will be great around eight to twelve years old.

Like the other northern Rhône champions, MM. Chave and Guigal, Auguste Clape possesses the rare talent of being able to make good wine every year, whether the grape harvest has been good or bad. Over the last twenty years he has acquired a very loyal nucleus of followers around the world, especially in Britain and the United States, but he is such an unpretentious man that his life-style and habits have shown no outward change. The arrival of his son in the family business prompted him to extend his cellar in 1989, but there is little material accolade for the man whose good wine and good name have helped to raise Cornas from the ranks of a curious country wine and put its name on the world wine map.

A quiet man, M. Clape nevertheless displays a firm, discreet sense of humour and his softly spoken asides are well worth waiting for. He often wears the sort of rough wool sweater favoured by English university professors; with his glasses and grey hair, it is only to be expected that here is a man of knowledge. Indeed he is, always ready to explain his latest experiments in the cellar and find out reactions to them, which he does with a phlegmatic, almost scholarly air. He would never make a fuss about it, but he holds firm views that the quality and the singularity of Cornas should not be subverted by a helter-skelter dash for increased business margins – manifestations of which he sees in the drive to increase the *appellation* zone and in the desire to raise the production of wine per hectare by as much as 50 per cent.

M. Clape was not actually born into a wine family, only arriving at Cornas after his marriage – which makes his consistent success with his vintages all the more remarkable. Perhaps it is no coincidence, therefore, that his approach to wine-making is remarkably unbridled: his attention to detail is intense, and he is ready to vary fine points within his methods according to circumstances. Like MM. Chave and Guigal, he is not an early harvester. In 1989, for instance, he waited for eight days after the *ban des vendanges* before harvesting, saying that he prefers an over-maturity to too marked an acidity in his wines.

In his fifties, M. Clape even went back to school to study the theory of viticulture at the Beaune wine school in Burgundy, probably Europe's foremost institute of its kind. There he survived the new-oak philosophy, for he is a traditionalist on this subject. He explains: 'I was happy fermenting in open wood vats during most of the 1970s, but there was no *tonnelier* around here to repair them and maintain them, so I turned to concrete. As for ageing-casks, here you need neutral wood with no tannin in it. The Syrah must breathe – it needs the wood to allow it to loosen up – and eighteen months in older casks does the job nicely.'

As part of the Ardèche *département*, Cornas's natural source of wood in the past has been chestnut from the hills to the west. But an involuntary experiment of ageing his 1973 in oak and chestnut proved to M. Clape that chestnut was not the right medium for his wine's stockage. He mistook the identity of one of his barrels and so had one lot of chestnut-aged wine on his hands. The difference between the 'oak wine' and the 'chestnut wine' was marked; both bore a similar bouquet, but on the palate the 'chestnut wine' was dominated by the tannin emanating from the wood of the barrel. By contrast, the youthful fruit and grapiness of the 'oak wine' were much in evidence, and this barrel appeared to have the greater future. M. Clape found that in the general way wines matured in chestnut came round after about two years but were unlikely to attain the smoothness and suppleness of flavour of wines matured in oak. It is interesting to think that the very traditional Ardèchois family of Chapoutier at Hermitage until the late 1980s depended almost entirely on chestnut for the raising of its wines.

Of his recent vintages, M. Clape is most pleased with his 1990, 1988 and his 1983. The 1983 he regards as a very closed, tannic wine – less generous and complete than his exceptional 1978 – but one that will develop over more than twenty years. The 1988 he likes because of its direct, firmly worked style – the sort of thorough wine that gives Cornas its good name. The 1989 he considers will be a 'quieter' wine, with a higher level of acidity and slightly less depth of rounded extract: by 1992 this was showing a pleasant fruitiness, but lacked the usual intensity of M. Clape's wines – more suited to summer luncheons than winter dinners. But it is the mark of the man only to laud two or three vintages in ten. He then pulls out a nine-year-old bottle of his 1981 – not a revered vintage – and one finds a wine showing an attractive, pepper-inspired bouquet and some good berry fruit on the palate. The wine is very approachable, its weight is pleasant and it will still drink well in around 1995. Alongside the heavy artillery of the tannic and ripe years, this is a perfect complement.

An illustration of the village's long-established tradition is shown by the fact that two of its families, the Michels and the Lionnets, have been making wine there for over 400 years. Robert Michel took over from his father Joseph in the late 1970s, and at the time – aged about thirty-one – was one of the only young family *vignerons* at Cornas, a problem that still exists to an extent today. Growers like Clape, Juge, de Barjac, Marc Maurice and Balthazar are all in their sixties, while the two Verset brothers and Roger Catalon are all over seventy. The next wave of *vignerons* really depends on people like the forty-five-year-old Jean Lionnet and the now forty-two-year old Robert Michel, although Sylvain Bernard, Jacques Leménicier, Thiérry Allemand and Jean-Luc Colombo appeared on the scene in the late 1980s and early 1990s to provide extra impetus. As Robert says, 'It's not as if we can be compared with St-Joseph where expansion is shooting ahead on the easily manageable flat ground. This is all hard work here, up the hillside in hot sun and on your feet all day, and young people aren't prepared to do it.'

Robert Michel now produces three separate wines in bottle, which seems to be an unnecessary division of his spoils, acting to drag down the overall calibre of his *domaine*. There is a *pied de coteaux*, from his vines at the foot of the hill, whose style is light and fruity and approachable within four years. There is an intermediary Cuvée de Coteaux from the Renards vineyard which is more darkly coloured, richer and more tannic on the palate, and finally, an excellent La Geynale, a specially selected *cuvée* made from fifty-plus-year vines, which has the true Cornas backbone and depth, with a massive fruit underlay in a year like 1988 – a solid, intense, keeping wine.

More than half the Michel 5–hectare vineyard is planted on the full slopes above the village, while the rest stands at the foot of the hills. As the family have always said that they believe their full-slope wine to be decidedly superior to anything produced lower down the hillside, it is perplexing that they have chosen to isolate the good and the less good wines rather than assemble a well-crafted single-*domaine* wine. On the world stage – represented for most buyers by the selection held by their local wine merchant – Cornas is an insignificant wine, and one would have thought that the circulation of widely different versions from the same *domaine* would only act to confuse people trying to get to know it.

Like Auguste Clape, Robert Michel is not an amateur of new oak, and vinification at his *domaine* is traditional. The family gather *en masse* for the *vendange* towards the middle of September, and the grape harvest is crushed lightly before fermentation in closed vats over the course of ten to fifteen days. Around Easter every year they hold their own little wine fête, when all their regular customers come to collect the wine ordered the previous year and to taste the wine that has just been barrelled. The general scale of operations at Cornas is indicated by the fact that the average order placed is for only about thirty bottles.

The Michels find their way of life both varied and stimulating. As the father said: 'I wouldn't change my profession for anything. It is a good feeling to see your own wine, finished and bottled up, and then to see to whom it is going and whether it is likely to be appreciated. I used to sell almost completely to the trade, but more and more of my clients urged me to bottle it myself and sell it direct to them. What I really enjoy is having the people come to me: then I meet all sorts and nationalities. We even had a visit from a man who had read your book in Cairo, so life is full of surprises!'

While Robert Michel has retained most of the techniques practised by his forebears, Jean Lionnet took radical steps to change his vinification and outlook during the late 1980s, and is now providing the *appellation* with a healthy degree of fireworks. This is a name to note – make no mistake. An energetic man with a deep, gravelly voice, brilliant clear blue eyes and a mat of grey hair that makes him resemble Derek Jacobi playing the Roman emperor Claudius, he is the third wine generation of his branch of the Lionnets. The other, older branch is now represented by Pierre Lionnet, who has taken over after the retirement of his father, Michel.

Jean Lionnet works a total of 10 hectares at Cornas – 4 his own and 6 rented – which now makes him one of the big hitters of the *appellation*: he was cultivating 6 hectares in the mid-1980s. Half his vines are thirty to eighty years old and half six to twenty years. He is gradually increasing his holding, having cleared a previously uncultivated area of 0.75 hectare in 1990, and his epicentre is in the northern part of the *appellation*, around the Chaillot *quartier* where his holding has some clay topsoil over the granite.

Forty per cent of the wine – made from the young vines – is sold to *négociants*, and 60 per cent is now bottled. M. Lionnet only started to bottle a tiny amount of his wine in 1976, and it wasn't until the 1985 harvest that he extended the process. His wine is therefore a relative newcomer to most Rhône enthusiasts.

The turning point for him came in 1987 when he built a new cellar, concentrating heavily on stainless steel and completely changing his vinification. The process is interesting, the results impressive, and his most signal achievement is to have successfully bridged modern techniques and thinking with the production of a classy but thoroughly intense Cornas: extra polish has been brought without sacrificing local authenticity in a way that has been rarely accomplished by modern crusaders elsewhere in the Rhône.

To make his Cornas, M. Lionnet destalks the whole crop and places the grapes to macerate in the stainless steel vats for twenty-six days at 30°C (the 1989 process). After the initial five days, he does a *remontage*, or pumping over of the *chapeau*, three times a day until finally once every three days. 'I like a long maceration,' he comments, proudly displaying his shiny battery of vats, 'and with the *remontage* system I keep the *chapeau* moist, so we get a supple effect in the wine – none of the unwanted hardness. During this time about 50 centimetres' worth of carbonic gas builds up at the top of the vat for natural protection.'

The *jus de presse* and the core *jus de goutte* are kept separate, the wine is racked and then kept at 20°C to obtain the malolactic. Once this is done – normally rapidly – M. Lionnet takes the wine off its lees, leaves it for four to six weeks to rest, and then moves 60 to 70 per cent of it into his new oak *pièces*, where it stays for twelve to fourteen months. He has a strict rotation of 20 per cent new casks each year, so in fact the wine is exposed to wood one to five years old. The remainder of the vintage is stored in enamel, fibre-glass or stainless steel vats to preserve above all the fruit and freshness in it.

After an egg-white fining and light filtration to take out any big particles, the wine is bottled in February or March, about eighteen months after the harvest. None of the finished wine is brought together from the different vats and *pièces* until a month or so before bottling.

Investment capital has obviously played a part in this success story, since Cornas as a whole is clearly an undercapitalized *appellation*. Over the years growers have been very cautious, and any improvements in equipment or expansion in the vineyards have clearly been financed out of hard-earned cash flow. So M. Lionnet has taken the bull by the horns in his working of his *domaine*'s finances. But he has also made a commendable shift in philosophy in an old-fashioned community, which takes courage of conviction and a strong determination that will ride out any of the tongue-wagging that such moves generate from inevitable local sceptics.

'I had to take a deep breath and get rid of my family's nearly 100-year-old casks, for instance', he comments. 'All my casks are Bordelais; most of the wood comes from the Allier and Vosges, but I find it's a continuous learning process about which wood from which supplier: I use Moreau, Bernard and Radoux, but no house can 100 per cent guarantee a wood, and finding good wood remains probably the hardest problem. I think the new barrels bring colour, and the cask wine also has a higher volatile acidity than the vat wine, which is why I like to use both sources.'

Tastings of M. Lionnet's Cornas reveal that he is making a success of using new methods with traditional raw materials. His 1989 pre-assembly, tasted in April 1990 from a mixture of fibre-glass, enamel and wood, showed every sign of being made from a number of promising sources:

1989 Cornas (Fibreglass), very dark, some black; sleek, berried fruit nose. Middle-weight attack, the tannin is well knit. Fair length.

1989 Cornas (Enamel), very dark; crunchy fruit bouquet, good depth; very sound weight and nice fruit on palate, good chewy finish, good balance. Made from his oldest vines.

1989 Cornas (Fifth-year cask), good chocolatey nose, very sustained; very good extracts on palate, burnt flavours, fruit hidden. Good depth, very solid but not aggressive.

1989 Cornas (Third-year cask), firm colour; quite closed nose;

| | very closed flavours on palate, lean. Tannins are drier on the finish. |
| 1989 Cornas | (Second-year cask), more open nose, starting to show some roundness. Palate has nice chewy, berry fruit flavours. Good length. |

Just as revealing are tastings of M. Lionnet's wine made before he changed his cellar and vinification, and of the wine made afterwards. The dark 1988 possessed the firm, impenetrable aromas of young Cornas, and although solid and quite stern on the palate, there was a pleasant final chewiness – a greater presence of fruit from the mid- to end-palate than one would normally find in young Cornas. This is a wine that needs to be put away until at least 1996, and which will live for over fifteen years.

The 1987, from that difficult vintage, is very good. It bears a dark plum colour, and on the bouquet its attractive aromas have started to develop a Cornas *typicité* or authenticity. On the palate there is a lot of blackcurrant fruit on the attack and plenty of substance that is sustained right through to the end. It is an elegant wine, but also very rich and well extracted – probably the best 1987 made at Cornas – and ideal to drink around 1992–5.

The 1986 was made in the old style, fermented in open wood and destalked to only 50 per cent. 1986 was a more diluted year at Cornas, and several of the wines are marked by severe, rather astringent tannins. The Lionnet offering shows the colour toning down towards a matt pale purple, the bouquet evolving towards slightly vegetal secondary aromas, and the palate loosening with a quite sweet attack and a lack of length: a wine whose evolution is likely to be rapid, and which should be drunk before around 1994.

The 1985 was actually destalked 100 per cent, and 20 per cent was placed in new oak. At five years' age this showed a well-sustained dark colour, and a notably rich, ripe bouquet, attractive blackberry fruit on the palate, and a good chocolatey finish. The aftertaste showed very good, rich end-fruit, and this is a wine that has ways to go – certainly it will still be showing well around 2000–2002.

M. Lionnet's wines depart from many at Cornas with their greater richness and generosity. They are a triumph for succulent flavours and extract over austerity and are well worth seeking out. An active policy towards exportation is pursued, led by sales to the United States, Britain and Belgium, as well as to good local restaurants. M.

Lionnet's prices are higher than most in the *appellation*, but the quality is there.

A *vigneron* who has always held an open mind about his vinification methods, and who makes an extremely stylish and pleasing Cornas, is M. Guy de Barjac, who looks like a French version of Robert Taylor. His lugubrious smile precedes a perfectly natural display of Gallic charm. He has an unusual background for a *vigneron* in that he speaks three languages and has a university degree. M. de Barjac explained how he had become a wine grower. 'My family have owned vines at Cornas for many generations, and when it came to finding a job after university my thoughts led me here. I must admit that there was the possibility of the army, but when I stopped to think, well, it's either military college or Cornas, I knew very well where I would end up.'

M. de Barjac is sixty-four years old, and has tired of working alone. His 2-hectare exploitation is the maximum size that he feels he can hope to maintain properly on his own, and since 1990 he has worked a *métayage* system under which part of his crop is taken by the promising Sylvain Bernard of Domaine de Fauterie, who also makes St-Péray and St-Joseph, and the other part by the resident *œnologue* at Cornas, Jean-Luc Colombo, whose Cornas wine sells under the name of Les Ruchets in a Bordeaux-shaped bottle, at some 40 per cent above the going rate for Cornas – a silly attempt to impose Italian designer-wine values on this *appellation*. M. de Barjac still retains a little of his crop to make his perennially stylish Cornas himself.

M. de Barjac's vines are in just two plots, the one nearest the village being at the foot of the slopes on a site called Le Barjass (so named after his family's holding there since the fifteenth century), the other being in the Chaillot *quartier* away to the north-west. Many of the Barjass vines are eighty years old, while his younger vines are twelve years old. For vinification and harvesting purposes, M. de Barjac brings in two deliveries of grapes to his cellars in the village, the *vendange* being worked according to the age of his vines. The two loads are vinified apart and assembled straight after their exit from the vat following completion of the malolactic.

While he uses only *pièces* from Burgundy for his ageing, M. de Barjac is faithful to old utensils for some parts of his work. His press is an old vertical one with an enormous spoked wooden top wheel, and his bottling process is done by hand, a very gummy activity indeed. He neither filters nor fines his wine and on average in the 1980s produced 10,000–12,000 bottles a year, three-quarters of which was exported – mainly to Britain, Switzerland and the United States. 'One day there came to Cornas an extraordinary visitation that you more likely see outside Notre-Dame,' he recalls when discussing exports. 'A bus of Japanese tourists – forty of them from the city of Nagoya – pulled up. Well, you can imagine this caused a commotion in Cornas – all those people, their cameras, the bus blocking the road . . . they had come to see me, having read about me in a book, and they all came down into my cellar.' He pauses at the thought. 'They eventually ordered sixty cases of my wine.'

The Japanese have very good taste, for M. de Barjac's wine is consistently good. If anything, it reached new standards of excellence during the 1980s after once or twice losing its way during the vintages of the 1970s. His 1989 is well structured, immaculately clean *en bouche*, and has a firm elegance about it – it seems likely to show very well from about 1995 onwards. His 1988 is a sterner wine, with more backbone and sturdiness and potential lying quietly on the bouquet. This is more of a ten- to fifteen-year wine. And his 1987 is showing some developed aromas on the nose, with a clean, fruity finish backing up agreeable roundness on the attack – this is a wine to enjoy around 1993–5. His 1986 is a success from an awkward year – he destalked 50 per cent of the crop, and obtained some good raspberry flavours on the palate. It has acidity to drive it along, and is quite a big wine in its way, one that should age correctly over seven to twelve years.

M. de Barjac is one of several growers of a generation who cannot be sure who will take over from them. M. de Barjac's son is not interested in wine-making – hence his arrangements with the *métayage* – and similar doubts hang over on the future of the Marcel Juge, Verset brothers – Noël and Louis – and René Balthazar *domaines*. The thin, wiry and directly spoken Marcel Juge makes one of the best, most authentic Syrahs at Cornas which, when he hits the target, proves to be one of the leading wines of the year – as in 1985 and 1986. His wines are marked by consistently good colour, but there is generally a delicious fruit extract which gives some of his *cuvées* great elegance and length. M. Juge is something of a maverick, and is perfectly happy to call his different wines by different names or codes. From his 3 hectares he comes up with a *pied de coteaux* wine (more fruit, elegance) and a Cuvée C (Coteaux) which in 1988 was rich, closed on the bouquet and long on the finish; then, just to confuse completely he makes in 1985 and 1986 a Cuvée SC (Super Cuvée) – two excellent wines, very well balanced, with a deep extract and very good tannic support. The division centres on the age of his vines – some are twelve years, the oldest over eighty – and on their relative location on the hillside, but at times one feels that drinkers of Cornas need a degree in sleuthing and a diploma in the geography of the Ardèche.

Like M. de Barjac who has used old Syrah cuttings of his own to continue with the true local, Petite Syrah, M. Juge is wary of what he calls the recent clonal variety – 'recent' meaning that it was introduced around the late 1960s and early 1970s. 'The Petite Syrah that we have here is still the old, small one. The new clonal variety produces larger grapes which are less affected by *coulure*, and have longer stems and branches. Their wines have less degree and colour – look what has happened on the plateau at Côte-Rôtie where it has been widely planted. As it's so naturally productive the new version doesn't need to be pruned in the Guyot way to encourage it – it can be pruned *au Gobelet*,' he observes.

A stiffer style of Cornas, very much the black strap wine of yore, is made by Noël Verset and by René Balthazar – but the sad question to ask about them and about Noël's brother Louis, whose wine is a little lighter, is who will take over, if anyone? Noël is now into his seventies and Louis has just hit seventy. Noël's wine is better known: his 2.5 hectare holding is made up of very old vines which produce a dark, raw, tannic Cornas which in a vintage like 1988 is full-blooded and direct, in need of ageing for at least nine or ten years before becoming approachable. In 1989 the wine held notable richness with its tannins well enveloped in a dense extract. Only some end heat gave the clue to the underlying power of the wine, which will run for fifteen or more years. In 1987 his wine was well worked, having sufficient density to develop well over eight years or so, while in 1986 there was a slight lack of depth with some rather rasping tannins in his wine. But this is a serious producer, and it can only be hoped that, like their late father, he and Louis live to 100.

Like the Versets, René Balthazar represents the current end of the line of a wine dynasty. He is sixty-six, and has a little under 1.5 hectares which his father tended before him. His son works in a factory and it is not certain that he will follow his father into the vineyard. M. Balthazar only began bottling part of his production in the mid-1970s, and now sells around half in this way – about 3,000 bottles – which comes from his high *coteau* vines, whose age ranges from over thirty years (a plantation of 1959) to under 100 years. Extremely self-effacing, M. Balthazar has the sort of postage-stamp cellar that makes wine tasting and conversation an intimate business at Cornas. He stores his wine in *demi-muid* – 'they keep the wine's perfumes better than the *pièces*' – for eighteen months to two years. His wines have a solid structure and develop an interesting complexity as they age. His 1988 had a warm bouquet, good balance and end-tannins that worked well with the fruit extract – perhaps a twelve-year wine. His 1987 could surprise with a decent fullness on the palate, and it, too, is marked by a bouquet that has more soft spice or pepper aromas than many at Cornas. The acidity in this wine could allow it to blossom by the mid-1990s, and it may well keep longer than his 1986.

While M. Balthazar is very quiet and retiring about his work, Alain Voge is altogether a more worldly, chatty man, from a younger generation, which with the likes of Jean Lionnet and Jacques Leménic-ier, who used to work with Alain Voge, is seeking out improvements in the wine-making process. Like M. Clape and M. Lionnet, M. Voge also owns 3 hectares at St-Péray, which with his 6 hectares at Cornas give him plenty to do. In his late forties, M. Voge has a bright face and darting eyes that shine with enthusiasm for his life as a *vigneron*. He has never been afraid to experiment with different methods over the last twenty years, and has gradually increased the size of his exploitation by about 1 hectare every ten years. With his holdings spread over a dozen plots, he has a lot of running around to do, and his mother is drafted in to help tie the vines to their stakes in the vineyards and to contribute to the bottling effort in his cellars.

M. Voge used to age his Cornas only in wood during the 1970s, but he then altered the process to combine a first year in concrete or enamel with a few months – perhaps six to eight – in cask. In so doing he was seeking to extract more fruit for his wines, and as his vineyards have aged past the thirty-year mark, the concentration and richness of his wine have been intensifying. Like many of the growers, he now does a straight Cornas and a Vieilles Vignes *cuvée*, and the latter particularly catches the eye, with very good offerings in 1986 and 1988 – the former one of the best wines of a variable vintage, with greater depth and roundness than most.

When asked how he likes to drink his wine M. Voge is representative of the culinary tastes of several of his colleagues: 'Roast meats, game or strong cheese such as Roquefort, Bresse Bleu or nicely matured goat's cheese . . . and if you follow my advice,' he adds with a beaming smile, 'I'm sure you'll never have been healthier!'

In the 1950s it was the local *négociants* who were most active in commercializing Cornas, and it is interesting that today those who present this wine among their *gamme*, or line-up, of wines, succeed in selling one of the most authentic wines on their lists. The many small cultivators who combine apricot- and mixed fruit-growing with cropping a few old Syrah vines remain true to their instincts, and the *négociants* like Paul Jaboulet Aîné, Delas and Vidal-Fleury are delivered either very wholesome, ripe grapes or young wine dripping with much of the *vrai* Cornas blackness. At tastings of Jaboulet's wines during the 1980s, one of the wines that regularly stood out as an example of 'pure', old-fashioned wine-making was their Cornas, a rumbustious giant in some vintages alongside a number of rather well-groomed wines of medium stature. The Jaboulet 1983 and 1986, for example, were excellent – both very long *en bouche* and filled with rich flavours. The former was a truly black wine. After one or two less impressive years, the Jaboulet Cornas was back on form in 1990. Like recent vintages, one quarter of the wine was exposed to first-year oak. Carrying a very solid, dark colour, this was very thick wine, with firm flavours and plenty of quite soft tannins. It will evolve well over fourteen years or more. Typically, Jaboulet have to go to great lengths to get their Cornas together – for just 190 hectolitres they may have to buy from as many as fifteen to twenty-one different proprietors before the wine is assembled in December following the harvest and bottled between one year (lighter vintages like 1984) and eighteen months (a stern year like 1983) after the harvest.

Delas actually owned 1 hectare of vines at Cornas until the early 1980s, and as one of the Cornas pioneers, their Cuvée Chante-Perdrix is also highly reliable and sometimes very good, the 1983, 1985 and 1988 showing a degree of concentration that makes them likely to live for around twelve years or so. But Delas have never found Cornas an easy wine to sell, and by the early 1990s had reduced their annual intake of grapes and wine from 300 hectolitres to 120 hectolitres. Meanwhile, from other indirect sources, both Vidal-Fleury and the Cave Co-opérative of Tain-l'Hermitage are ageing some of their annual production of Cornas in new oak – a sign, perhaps, that this wine is meriting serious attention as a third 'big *appellation*' behind the region's Hermitage and Côte-Rôtie.

Cornas Vintages

1955   Good. The wines were rather light, but had an agreeable harmony.

1956   Good. Soft, well balanced wines.

1957   A very good year. The wines were robust and fairly tannic, but have now dried out.

1958   Mediocre. Light wines.

1959   A good vintage of well balanced, strongly scented and very ripe-tasting wines. They are now past their best.

1960   Good. Sound wines that lacked a little elegance, but which are now finished.

1961   An excellent year. Big, full wines that held a good balance between their fruit and tannin. They have stood the test of time well, but any remaining bottles will only possess the last threads of their former richness; they now serve more for curiosity than for good drinking.

1962   Another excellent vintage, only a little less powerful and attractive than 1961. The wines should have been drunk by now as their powers have faded.

1963   Very poor. Extremely light wines.

1964   Very good. Sound, well balanced wines that aged extremely well and showed great finesse in so doing. They need drinking up. A very good de Barjac.

1965   Mediocre. Light, acid wines.

1966   A very good year. Strongly coloured wines that with age obtained a soft, full flavour. They should be drunk without delay.

1967   Excellent. Big, heavy wines of immense colour that were full of tannin when young. They developed very well on the bouquet and showed great length, but have now started to dry out. Drink up.

1968   Poor. Very light wines.

1969   Very good. Darkly coloured and well-extracted wines, some of which have remained in the grip of some rustic tannins for longer than expected (Clape, for example). Several *cuvées* were rich on the palate and need to have been drunk for best results. Others, like A. Clape, will still provide good drinking towards 1995.

1970 Good. The crop was large, so the wines tended to lack the strength of the very best years. They have started to lose their fruit and depth in most cases.

1971 Excellent. A magnificent vintage almost on a par with 1961. The wines were very full-bodied and heavily coloured, and had enough acidity to assure them an extended lifespan. They have progressed very well, and are right at the stage of showing the multi-layered aromas and complex flavours of good, old Syrah. They can live on for a few years more. Notable wines from Auguste Clape and Joseph Michel.

1972 A very good vintage of richly coloured, strongly scented and flavoured wines – they showed exuberant fruit and life early on, and have developed well. They are starting to show their age. Drink soon.

1973 Very good. Cornas started to catch the eye of buyers after the fifth consecutive good vintage, and prices ex-cellars doubled to 12 francs a bottle (all taxes included). This year there was a large crop of well coloured, well balanced wines. Not a full-bodied vintage, these wines now have little room for improvement.

1974 A medium vintage, with wines lacking in colour and flavour. The foremost growers like Clape and Joseph Michel made some good bottles, but even these are now in decline.

1975 An average year of well-scented wines whose early trump card was an accessible fruitiness. They developed in a pleasing way over their first ten years, but are now losing their grip, and tiring. Their style is similar to 1981.

1976 Generally very good. A healthy harvest gave well coloured and attractively scented wines which have an equilibrium that is guiding them along a long road. They are still intense on the palate and show signs of retaining much of their strength until at least 1996.

1977 A mediocre vintage, but one that gave major craftsmen like Auguste Clape the chance to display their skill. The harvest was rot-affected, and many of the wines were palely coloured and high in acidity: their lack of a robust Cornas depth was damaging. But the best *cuvées* have held up a plum colour very well and show a slightly cooked fruit aroma on the nose and a discreet southern depth on the palate. These can drink until around 1995.

1978 A magnificent vintage that has gained in eminence as it has aged. The wines were fairly dark, but most impressed with the sheer tannic and berried fruit extract on bouquet and palate. Undoubtedly hard to start with, age has unravelled some of their tannic grip, and there is a ripe, but still quietly austere flavour developing. They should be set aside for drinking around 1993 at the earliest, and will live towards 2005 without problem. Notable wines from Clape and Jaboulet.

1979 Quite a good vintage. The wines were short on acidity and their first years were marked by the emergence of some soft fruit ahead of some middling tannin. The bouquet has opened up and a degree of finesse is now being shown on the palate. These discreet wines are likely to drink at their best until around 1993–4.

1980 Very good. Brightly coloured wines of good intensity of fruit and tannin. They have kept together well with age, and are now showing more depth and variety of aroma on the bouquet, albeit with a hint of reserve. The wines are still fully charged on the palate and show the capability of providing successful drinking until 1995–9. Note the *cuvées* of Clape, de Barjac and Juge.

1981 Good. The wines were fairly coloured, but an indifferent summer meant that the growers had to work hard to extract any concentrated matter from the grapes. The colour is just slipping a little, but the palate shows a good combination of fruit and heat, with a touch of final spice. These wines are drinking well now, and can continue for another five or six years. Note the wine of de Barjac, Juge, Michel and Clape.

1982 A good vintage, but one that was extremely difficult to vinify, given intense heat day and night in September. The wines are less dark than usual, and because of their lack of acidity have started to evolve quite fast. They are not steeped in tannin; for Cornas this vintage at its best can be called sensuous, for there is a generosity and headiness on palate and bouquet that in the best examples is compelling.

To enjoy their concentrated flavours, drink before 1993; otherwise these wines may pull through to around 1997, but beware the lack of acidity. Notable wines from de Barjac, Noël Verset and Clape – all drinking well now.

1983   Very good. The wines were very dark and chock-full of quite severe tannins. Less all-round and complete than the 1978, this is nevertheless a promising vintage, with its combination of early fruit and tannic length. The wines will take their time to come round, and will certainly run past the year 2000. It is to be hoped that the wines will loosen up with age – there is some risk of their remaining closed and a bit hard. Very good *cuvées* from Clape, Voge, Balthazar, de Barjac and Jaboulet.

1984   A fair vintage. Late ripening and rain at harvest-time followed on outbreaks of *coulure* (Michel lost one-third of his crop). There are some meagre wines this year, and some that show exemplary discreet richness, so careful selection is needed. Bottles from the same grower are also evolving at different speeds. The very best carry a plum colour, a pleasant stewed fruit aroma on the bouquet and sound fruit on the attack. Some wines can finish short, and this is a vintage similar to 1979 – drink around 1992–5 to get the best out of it. One of the best 'off-vintage' wines ever made by Auguste Clape – some bottles are a sheer delight. Well-crafted wines also from de Barjac and Delas, the former requiring earlier drinking than the latter.

1985   A very good year on the whole. Some caution is needed due to a modest level of acidity in the wines, which may age more quickly than expected. The wines were well coloured, notable for excellent aromas on the bouquet and packed with higher alcohol levels than usual – 13–13.5°. There is discreet tannic extract, but the wines are stylish above all. Excellent offerings from Clape, Juge, Jean Lionnet, de Barjac, Noël Verset and Jaboulet.

1986   A fair vintage with some bright points. Much-needed rain arrived too late at the end of September, and a large crop was brought in. There are some soundly coloured wines whose main problem is a variability of depth. Some wines show well-extracted fruit on the attack, but other *cuvées* are disconcertingly hard, with raw tannins present. Select carefully. Good wines from de Barjac, Marcel Juge (a delightful, fine Super Cuvée) and Jaboulet. A vintage to put by until perhaps 1995–7 in the hope that the green tannins will settle down.

1987　A fair vintage, where the growers had to play poker with the weather. The cut-off day was 2 October, when it rained heavily and continued to do so for some days after. Those who harvested after that date made much diluted wines; those who picked earlier have wines with a sound dark cherry colour and bouquets that are beginning to open and show some evolution already. Attractively fruited on the palate, they run through to a clean, elegant finish, and are wines to enjoy from now until around 1995. Good work from Jean Lionnet and Guy de Barjac.

1988　A very good vintage. There was a helpful rainfall in the spring that allowed the vines to build up reserves, and a touch of mildew in midsummer. The wines are solid in every respect: darkly coloured, while strongly extracted fruit and tannins run on the palate. They finish with a delightful chewiness and are likely to age in a straight-forward way over twenty years or so. Good wines from Auguste Clape, Jean Lionnet, Alain Voge, Noël Verset, Guy de Barjac and René Balthazar.

1989　A very good vintage that may prove to be delicious and multi-flavoured when it has aged for eight years or so. It is more rounded, more opulent than 1988. The summer was drought-affected, a very large crop was brought in, and there is greater acidity than in the 1988s. The wines are darkly coloured and show a good fruit extract that is well integrated with some middle-weight tannins. The best *cuvées* are very long *en bouche*. This is the sort of year that will present itself easily in older age, since it doesn't have as much usual Cornas austerity in it. Very good offerings from Noël Verset, Chapoutier, Lionnet, de Barjac and most front-rank growers. The wines will drink well from six to ten years old onwards, and may keep going for fifteen years.

1990　An excellent vintage, with greater depth and balance than 1988 and 1989. While very dry, the summer was less hot than the previous year, and about 20 mm (·8 inch) of rain at the end of August redressed the situation. Growers had to take care to combat some oïdium. The harvest was wonderfully ripe and gave wines of good degree, excellent colour and plenty of well sustained flavours on the palate. They are powerful, but well balanced; their richness and depth are greater than most years of the 1980s and they will live and show splendidly over twenty years or so.

Leading Growers at Cornas

The nucleus:

Clape, Auguste	
Balthazar, René	07130 Cornas
de Barjac, Guy	
Jaboulet Aîné, Paul	26600 La Roche-de-Glun
Juge, Marcel	
Lionnet, Jean	
Michel, Robert	07130 Cornas
Verset, Noël	
Voge, Alain	

Other producers:

Allemand, Thiérry	07130 Cornas
Bancel, Élie	
Bernard, Sylvain	07130 St-Péray
Boissy and Delaygue	07130 Cornas
Catalon, Roger	
Chapoutier, M.	26600 Tain-l'Hermitage
Colombo, Jean-Luc	07130 Cornas
Courbis, Maurice and Dominique,	07130 Châteaubourg
Delas Frères	07300 St-Jean-de-Muzols
Dumien-Serrette	
Fumat, André	
Gilles, Louis	
Leménicier, Jacques	07130 Cornas
Lionnet, Pierre	
Maurice, Marc	
Michelas, Robert	26600 Mercurol

Sozet, Louis	07130 Cornas
Teysseire, Jean,	07130 St-Péray
Thiers, Jean-Louis	07130 Toulaud
de Vallouit, Louis-Francis	26240 St-Vallier
Verset, Louis	07130 Cornas
Vidal-Fleury	69420 Ampuis
Cave Co-opérative de Tain-l'Hermitage	26600 Tain-l'Hermitage

8

St-Péray

St-Péray, the last of the northern Rhône vineyards, has a curiously confused identity, not at all akin to that of a quiet wine community. Behind the village, characterized by the soft-coloured local Ardèchois stone of some of its houses and flattered by its large market place that is shaded by irregularly spaced plane trees, the vine-covered slopes reach out and up towards the hilly loneliness of the Ardèche. Within five minutes of driving towards St-Romain-de-Lerps, Lamastre or even Touland to the south, the meandering road has taken the visitor into a secluded world of quiet hills, sweeping valleys and an occasional farmhouse. Sounds carry with remarkable clarity, be they the tinkling of a goat bell or the cry of a sheep separated from its flock. It is hard to imagine that on the other side of St-Péray, on the short plain that runs east of the village the vines spread nearly into the urban confusion of Valence. They are halted by the Rhône, an impassive witness to the uneasy liaison being formed between town and country.

Such is the incongruous setting for the Rhône's most incongruous wine which, along with the fortified Grenache wine of Rasteau in the south, is something of an anachronism these days. To call St-Péray the Rhône's best sparkling wine is factually correct, but in the sweep of internationally available sparklers it is but a tiny player, with a silent walk-on part somewhere at the back of the stage. The still white wine is really this tiny, obscure *appellation*'s only hope, and in the late 1980s some encouraging signs of progress emerged on this. There are only around 65 hectares under vine at St-Péray, producing an annual average of only 2,315 hectolitres during the decade of the 1980s, so to make an impact on the world or even French stage there is just one option – outstanding quality and cleanly made wines; otherwise it will remain a regional curiosity, or what America's great

Rhône enthusiast Robert Parker feels compelled to describe as 'the Rhône Valley's viticultural dinosaur'.[1]

Strangely enough, these minute vineyards carry both lengthy historical and popular traditions. The still white wine attracted attention from two Roman writers: Pliny, in his *Natural History* Book XIV, Chapters 1 and 2, and Plutarch, in Book V of his *Table Talk*.

Little is then heard of the wine until the nineteenth century, when its popularity seems to have been widespread. The young Napoleon Bonaparte was stationed as a cadet at the garrison of Valence and in later years spoke of St-Péray as his first wine discovery. Lamartine, Alphonse Daudet and Guy de Maupassant are all said to have referred to the wine in their writings, and a vaudeville entertainer called Marc-Antoine Desaugiers (1772–1827) even wrote a song entitled 'Le Voyageur de St-Péray', which went as follows:

> *A vous, je m'adresse, mesdames,*
> *C'est pour vanter le Saint-Péray.*
> *Il est surnommé Vin des Femmes,*
> *C'est vous dire qu'il est parfait.*
> *La violette qu'il exhale*
> *En rend le goût délicieux*
> *Et l'on peut dire qu'il égale*
> *Le nectar que buvait les Dieux.*[1]

The most famous story about St-Péray concerns the German composer Richard Wagner. In a letter from Bayreuth dated 2 December 1877, he wrote as follows to a leading *négociant* house: 'Will you please send me as soon as possible those 100 bottles of St-Péray wine which you offered me.' Wagner was then busy composing *Parsifal*, and it is popularly presumed by local *vignerons* that passages from this opera must have originated at the bottom of a glass of their wine.

Today the vineyards of St-Péray and Cornas border one another

---

[1] To you I address myself, ladies,
It is to praise St-Peray.
It is nicknamed the Wine of Women,
Which means that it is perfect.
The violets that it exhales
Give it a flavour of delight
And one can say it matches
The nectar that the gods would drink.

in the Hongrie *quartier*, which is positioned towards St Romain-de-Lerps, and it would need a discerning eye to know where the Syrah stops and the mainly Marsanne vines start. With over 90 per cent of the plantation, the Marsanne is the traditional majority grape at St-Péray, but in the last few years growers like Jean-François Chaboud, Sylvain Bernard, Jean Lionnet and Bernard Gripa have all launched more Roussanne. In the case of Sylvain Bernard a full 30 per cent of his 2.8 hectares are occupied by Roussanne. But just to confuse the issue, the laws decree that St-Péray can be made from *three* grapes – the Marsanne and the Roussanne, plus the Roussette. The trouble is, that while the *vignerons* talk locally of the Roussette, the identity of this vine has never officially been made clear.

When discussing the problem of the Roussette, some *vignerons* are apt to declare that the word 'Roussette' is merely a local term for the Roussanne vine. Others bravely suggest a difference, without being able to specify it, and say that in the past the 'Roussette' has caused great consternation to the French fraud inspectors. These gentlemen would like to see the Roussette excluded, since they claim that St-Péray should be made solely from the Marsanne and the Roussanne; the difference between the Roussanne and the Roussette is so minimal that much good time is wasted trying to find it!

One man who is able to shed light on the exact nature of the Roussanne vine is Jean-François Chaboud, who makes one of the best sparkling St-Pérays. In 1972 he received some Roussanne cuttings from the late Dr Philippe Dufays, the viticultural expert who owned Domaine de Nalys at Châteauneuf-du-Pape, and has since been able to observe this plant's characteristics as compared with Marsanne and the Roussanne grown at Hermitage; the latter, he avers, is distinct from the Roussanne that he is growing.

'My Roussanne is distinguished by a series of jagged edges on the leaves, which also have a lot more veins on them than the Marsanne leaves. The Roussanne grape is also more pointed than the Marsanne, and while a bunch of Marsanne will weigh a little over 1 kilo, the Roussanne gives only about half as much fruit per bunch. This Roussanne, even in a normal year, gives less juice than most other local vines and also has a lot more pips in the grapes. I find that it is extremely susceptible to attacks of oïdium and the grape juice easily risks becoming oxidized at the precise moment of harvesting. I therefore make sure that its grapes enter the press completely intact. I have one and a bit hectares of Roussanne and in 1981 made nearly

2,500 litres of wine from them, at a degree of around 13° Gay Lussac. I sell this as still wine, but it doesn't really live much more than a couple of years, which convinces me further that this Roussanne is not the same as the one planted on Hermitage Hill. As to finding out the truth about the two vines,' he added with a laugh, 'well, I think that's a story that I shall leave to someone else, for the moment anyway.'

For his part, the skilled and thoughtful Bernard Gripa, whose cellars are north of Cornas at Mauves, considers that the Roussanne in about one-tenth of his hectare of St-Péray is a vine that comes 'from the exterior – perhaps it's Savoyard by origin. I planted it myself, but find that it doesn't compare necessarily with the few *ceps* that you find at St-Péray,' he comments.

The vineyards of this tiny *appellation* are spread out over a wide area, with the result that the vines grow in a variety of soils, exposures and heights. The most southerly location is the *coteaux* at Toulaud, where the main vineyard is called the Côte du Pin. Jean-Louis Thiers and Bernard Gripa have holdings here, on a largely granite-based soil, with patches of flint, and right at the top, at a height of over 300 metres, Sylvain Bernard planted his vineyards on abandoned vine holdings in 1983–4. This *terroir* is thought to bring roundness to the wine.

Just below the village of St-Péray is Crussol, marked by its ruined castle where the young Napoleon climbed to prove himself. In this area there is more limestone and broken stone, producing the lightest wine of the *appellation*, most of which goes to the St-Péray Co-opérative.

Nearer Cornas the soil becomes more clayey, with some sand and loose stones. Little of the chalk that makes Champagne so famous is therefore detectable at St-Péray – one determinant as to its different style, before grape varieties and reasons of outright quality are considered.

In all sparkling wines a certain tartness is welcome, and the growers will harvest around mid-September in years of high heat and drought like 1989, in an attempt to bring in grapes which still contain some interesting acidity. For the still whites the *vignerons* like to wait longer: Jean Lionnet, for instance, harvests his holdings of Marsanne (80 per cent) and Roussanne (20 per cent) as late as possible in order to obtain maximum richness in his wine.

After pressing and a brief decantation, the grape juice is fermented in concrete, enamel-lined or stainless steel vats, with the Marsanne and Roussanne kept apart. The taste is less for wood fermentation than in the past. As Jean-Louis Thiers commented: 'I want to steer away from the old cask taste of St-Péray of past times – I'm seeking a fresher wine with greater finesse, so that's why I use enamel or steel.' As he is one of the few local *vignerons* to have attended wine school recently – at Beaune – one can understand his quest for improvements. However, an opposite view to this is taken by Jean Lionnet who has been satisfied with his fermentations in wood.

Most growers aim to control temperature during fermentation at 18–20°C or so. Jean Lionnet at Cornas, who now makes one of the best modern-style St-Pérays, a still white that is both invigorating and nicely weighted, goes even lower to 13–15°C. 'I do a skin maceration or *macération pelliculaire*,' he comments. 'I destem the grapes, and leave them at 10°C in stainless steel for twenty-four hours, with a light sulphur treatment to stop them starting to move off. I press them, take the first juice – 90 per cent of the total press – add yeast, drop the juice into stainless steel and then have a one-month maceration, nice and steady, at 13–15°C. After transfer, half spends about four months in new oak, the other half is put into vats, and bottling occurs in early May. I block the "malo", since I reckon my wines can handle their 13° alcohol with a nice underlying acidity.'

The blocking of the malolactic is more modernist than most traditional growers at St-Péray are prepared to countenance, but there are signs of a gradual realization of the need to smarten up the vinification methods for what can be a very bland wine. The gradual use of wood during the brief ageing process is another interesting development in the making of the still white wine. Sylvain Bernard of Domaine de Fauterie used young wood for five or six months in the 1985, 1986 and 1987 vintages, and for a briefer time in 1988. But as a young grower short on ready capital, he was constrained by lack of space in his cellar from using wood in 1989 and 1990; he intends to return to its use in due course.

St-Péray must by law be made exactly as champagne, with even the yeasts used in the wine coming from that famous wine region: these are sent down in liquid form in glass jugs, or *bonbonnes*, by express train from Champagne. But it is a community that holds its own viticultural traditions very close and it is interesting that few, if any, of the growers have ever trained in Champagne or, indeed, have ever seen the inside of a *champenoise* cellar. The art of wine-making has instead been handed down from father to son over many generations and is consequently seen as a highly personalized affair. Whether M. Dupont down the road makes his wine in this or that style is not of interest to the *vigneron*; he has his own particular way of making his wine, which is therefore the right way.

Around April or May after the harvest – 'before the big heat of summer,' say the growers – the wine is bottled; it has a clear, almost transparent colour and no bubbles.

The leading *mousseux vignerons* like Pierre Darona and Jean-Louis Thiers do not give their wine a vintage, so at this stage M. Thiers, for example, adds in a little of the previous year's wine to balance it out. In the case of his fruity 1989 wine, a little of the firmer 1988 was added. This he does every year, with the final wine sold non-vintage.

At the moment of bottling, a blend of sugar and yeasts, known as *liqueur de tirage*, is put into the wine to encourage a further fermentation; the liquid content of this mixture can be around 4 centilitres per litre, although the growers are careful not to make the wine too sweet in years when very ripe grapes have been harvested: for example, 1985 was less topped up than the under-ripe 1984. The yeasts serve to reactivate the wine, and its renewed fermentation converts the sugar into alcohol, producing amounts of carbon dioxide as a result. The carbon dioxide gas generated has, quite literally, nowhere to run – except to the bottom of the bottle. As it slowly dissipates through the length of the bottle, bubbles appear on every side, and the wine becomes effervescent. The pressure of the imprisoned carbon dioxide is very great, and occasionally a dud or weak bottle explodes under the strain.

The bottles are then stacked in long, closely packed rows in the cellar. About a year later, with the secondary fermentation well finished, they are transferred nose-down, to wooden holders known as *pupitres*. The *pupitre* is made up of two pieces of wood, each containing sixty holes, which stand leaning in on one another like an inverted cone. The bottles are placed neck-first into these holders, in an almost horizontal position.

The *pupitre* is a *champenois* implement and has become more standard at St-Péray than the old local *tréteau de remuage*. This is a trestle table with four trays on top of each other, a large affair 1.5 metres high, with holes for 120 bottles on each level. Only very occasionally does one see a *tréteau de remuage* in a St-Péray cellar nowadays, since the operation of turning the bottles can generally be done only very carefully, with one hand at a time, because of the wearing away of the holes over the years.

When the bottles are put in their wooden *pupitres* or *tréteaux* the wine in them is far from clear, for the secondary fermentation has brought with it a large amount of dead yeast cells and sediment. For a month the bottles in the *pupitres* are turned in pairs by a deft flick of the wrists: every day they draw nearer to the vertical, and the sediment inside them starts sliding slowly down towards the neck.

'Turning' is one of the most skilled, and least pleasant, tasks in the whole elaboration of a sparkling wine. The amateur goes into the cellar and happily turns a couple of bottles, only to see the sediment dance about in a burst of crazy merriment. The experienced *caviste* in Champagne turns as many as 25,000 bottles a day – and promptly wishes he hadn't, for turning encourages an inflammation of the wrist joints that brings on arthritis at an early age. Perhaps the end product is suitably comforting.

By the time the bottles are in a near-vertical position, the sediment is well lodged in their necks. The next operation is disgorging and corking. The bottles are placed one by one, with their necks frozen, on a rotating disgorging machine, which whips off the tightly sealed cap. The upper liquid slowly starts to run out, and with it the sediment, and the bottle is immediately topped or 'dosed' with a mixture of cane sugar and St-Péray, half a centilitre per bottle. It is then passed straight on to the corking machine, as the grower naturally does not want to lose all his good hard work and fine bubbles. Should he so desire, the grower can at this point make a *demi-sec*, or sweeter wine, through the simple addition of more cane sugar to the solution; this comes to 2 centilitres of *liqueur* per bottle. During the 1980s the taste for this *demi-sec* has revived to a certain extent, and more growers now offer both a *brut* and *demi-sec*.

Jean-François Chaboud is the only leading grower selling vintaged *méthode champenoise*, something he has done since the 1970s. He reasons that the wine of even allegedly indifferent vintages such as 1977 or 1987 will come round in time, and that it is much more interesting for the consumer to chart the wine's progress if it carries a year and a definable character of its own. It is also easier these days to market a product with a vintage – superior status seems to be purveyed.

St-Péray *méthode champenoise* is a country-style wine, very regional in its way. After a little time in bottle to settle down and lose an early raw, sometimes green aspect, the wine becomes rounded, and in the best examples can follow through with a sound, clean finish. Characterized by a firm, sometimes light straw colour, which is darker than most modern white wines, the sparkling carries a certain fragrance of apples in the more modern vinifications and a scent of straw and a discreet 'earthiness' in the old-fashioned vinifications. Again, on the palate there are two styles of wine – the ancient and the modern. The old-style vinifications produce a wine with a strong, grapy taste and a depth typical of the Côtes du Rhône – if well handled this makes the wine agreeably full; if not, distressingly heavy. The modern vinifications produce a *méthode champenoise* that continues on the palate with an appley flavour and a tartness and liveliness that are welcome, especially within the clean finish. But beware – St-Péray sparkling is not a wine that should be specially cellared to obtain greater roundness and complexity like non-vintage champagne from good houses: it tends to tire and become flabby after six or seven years. While it has been known to take the sting out of bad hangovers, St-Péray is best served well chilled as an apéritif.

While St-Péray could just about defend itself on the wider world stage fifteen years ago, today the sad fact is that it has been overtaken by a series of snappily made sparkling wines, produced on a larger scale, competitively priced and well marketed. It's not just a case of good Saumur upstaging St-Péray, one can think of lively Spanish sparklers and very good offerings from the New World. Judging it in the 1990s is therefore a different exercise to the early 1970s – and much of this obscure *appellation*'s sparkling wine cannot in all honesty now be deemed to be very interesting.

By the early 1990s, indeed, there were very few growers making the *mousseux* in their own cellars – principally Darona, Chaboud, Teysseire and Thiers. Of larger entities, the Cave Co-opérative de Tain-l'Hermitage and the Cave des Vignerons de St-Péray vinify on their own premises. Given that the full 65-hectare vineyard is worked by only sixteen or seventeen *viticulteurs*, such a limited spread of vinification is not surprising.

Confidence in the *appellation* has also been eroded by the gradual demise of its *négociant* concerns, which in the 1930s to 1950s were the visible and active standard-bearers for St-Péray. These have progressively disappeared – one of the reasons given was the loss of *négociant* family members during the Second World War – so that today there are only two such suppliers, Gilles Père et Fils and Cotte-Vergne: but alongside the other major northern Rhône enterprises like Jaboulet, Vidal-Fleury and so on, they are minnows.

Jean-François Chaboud has made efforts through taking over the Malleford brand name and reviving it, but he is very realistic about the threat the *appellation* faces from land sales to people wanting a second or retirement home. This has been a constant theme over the past twenty years, and as Valence has grown and spread, so the pressure to buy, and therefore to cash in the chips and sell, has grown. The best route for the *appellation* definitely lies in markedly increasing the proportion of still wine made here – and if it is in the hands of go-ahead vinifiers like Sylvain Bernard and Jean Lionnet, so much the better.

For a long time the most active *vigneron* on behalf of St-Péray has been Jean-François Chaboud. He is an enthusiastic man in his late forties, just losing a little of his hair, but not through worry, for he makes and sells without difficulty one of the best wines of the *appellation*. His sparkling St-Péray is very stylized, with a robust, full flavour to it, but equally a long and attractive finish that sets it apart from many of the other wines. He has always bottled his wine earlier than most – around the end of January – so that he can achieve a finer *mousse* than would otherwise be possible.

In front of a blazing log fire in the sitting-room of his neat house, which stands next to the cellars, he explained that his experiments with using the Roussanne grape in the sparkling wine had not been successful. 'You can see that I make a still wine from 100 per cent Roussanne, but that is the only way I can do anything with this generally difficult grape. I once tried making a sparkling wine composed half-and-half of Marsanne and Roussanne, but it simply didn't work; the wine was unbalanced, lacked acidity and simply wasn't *vif* [lively] as I would have hoped. All my *mousseux* is now made only from the Marsanne.'

He went on: 'Pierre Darona, with 11 hectares for him and his son, and I are the largest growers here now. I have about 10 hectares spread between the Hongrie *quartier* above the village and in the Crozette *quartier* on the way to Le Pin, just to the west into the hills. The soil at Hongrie is white clay, and I find that the wine from it is fuller than the wine coming from nearer the Cornas road down on the plain. There the wines are drier and a little more acid. Since the 1970s I have worked out a way of building up terrace walls on my hillside so that I can cultivate the flat ledges mechanically; this has saved me a lot of time, as before I did all my vineyard work with horses, which are, of course, a lot slower.'

While Jean-François Chaboud lives right in the village of St-Péray, Pierre Darona's farm and cellars are tucked away on a hillside in a beautiful rolling valley that leads south-west towards Toulaud. M. Darona's family have been making *méthode champenoise* wine for at least fifty years and part-own, part-rent their 11 hectares of vines in the *quartier* known as Les Faures, near their home. Like M. Chaboud, M. Darona is only able to look after a vineyard of this size because he has attached three-quarters of his vines along rows of wire – which, once they are successfully trained, saves him time in their pruning and upkeep – and because he too is able to drive a tractor along the slopes and half-slopes of his vineyard.

Mme Darona explained that they were fortunate to have an alternative source of income if the grape harvest was poor, and pointed from the cellar door to their clumps of apricot trees. 'As St-Péray *mousseux* must by law be left nine months after its bottling, and we leave it for twelve months, it's a great help to the family funds to have a more rapid income each year from the apricots.' The Daronas make about 70 per cent of their wine in the *mousseux* way, and it has a fine style, without perhaps showing a wholly definable local character. While M. Chaboud's wine can be drunk with certain first courses such as raw or cured ham or cold *quiche lorraine*, M. Darona's is better as a straightforward, chilled apéritif.

The other leading grower at St-Péray is Jean-Louis Thiers, whose father André has always made a little wine, but who would class himself as more of an *agriculteur*, a well-known face at six in the morning at the Mauves fruit market, selling his cherries and apricots. Jean-Louis attended wine school at Beaune for two years, and naturally wanted to emphasize that side of the family farm, which also does dairy and beef. He has therefore moved to bottling the whole production from their 5 hectares spread between Toulaud above their cellars and rented vineyards on slopes at St-Péray. 'We used to sell everything to Cotte-Vergne, but in 1980 I felt that rising prices gave us the chance to do it ourselves.'

M. Thiers has invested in stainless steel to control the temperature and the cleanliness of his vinification, and he makes a sound *méthode champenoise*, one of the more attacking, less heavy new-style wines. His still white is also made in the fresh style, with a bracing, crisp finish. This is stored in enamel or stainless steel vats before bottling one year after the harvest. He relies over 90 per cent on the Marsanne for both wines.

The other *domaine* of some size belongs to the Milliand family, who have 6 hectares under vines. The observant traveller will pick out the large and faded wall advertisement of 'Léon Milliand et Cie' on the way to Valence, and this is one of the traditional families of wine-makers at St-Péray. The brothers René and Michel have always been very keen on their shooting and like to go out after birds and game, something they have in common with a large proportion of the French population. A Sunday walk in the French countryside is a perilous business, with a mass of trigger-happy *chasseurs* combing the fields ready to fire off at anything that moves. Indeed, birds are few and far between, since anything with the remotest semblance of flavour is shot at, which lets out practically only magpies and sparrows! Michel bottles a part of his harvest but brother René sends all his grapes to the Tain Co-opérative.

There is a handful of *vignerons* from Cornas who double up with a little wine from St-Péray, and most notable among these are Auguste Clape and Alain Voge, who both belong to the Cave des Vignerons de St-Péray, which makes their sparkling wine in the village centre, under what used to be the Hôtel des Bains and is now a retirement home. Then there are growers like Jean Lionnet, Bernard Gripa and Sylvain Bernard who only produce still St-Péray, which the locals term the *tranquille*; their work shows that an effective wine can be made from these vineyards. In style the best St-Péray *nature* has a little more blatant weight than a St-Joseph *blanc*. On the bouquet there is a hint of *terroir*, a southern depth, and the palate shows richness and chewiness. In style, a good, typical St-Péray like a 1989 from Sylvain Bernard's Domaine de Fauterie is nearer a Crozes-Hermitage than a St-Joseph *blanc*: a little heavier, a little more chewy and fuller on the finish. The wine of a grower like Lionnet is marked by its exposure to new oak, but these are wines that drink well over two to six years and which can provide good value for money over that time.

One of the only new boys at St-Péray in the 1980s was Sylvain Bernard, a slight, fresh-faced man in his early thirties. His Domaine de Fauterie is a charming farmhouse and cellars surrounded by gaping drops off hills on the way to Le Puy, west of St-Péray and a little outside the main track of the *appellation*.

He makes three wines – St-Péray *tranquille*, St-Joseph red and Cornas. His St-Péray was very successful in 1989 and 1991; these are capable of showing well over about six years. The St-Joseph is more inconsistent, with the challenge or difficulty of achieving full ripeness in grapes growing at a height of 350 metres at Glun apparent in a drought year like 1991, when the onset of October rains obliged M. Bernard to harvest earlier than he would have liked – severe crop sorting was needed as a result. The 1990 was a spicy, well scented wine, and the 1987 was well worked. Most successful of his reds is the Cornas, made since 1990 from 1.4 hecteres on the old de Barjac vineyard at the *lieu-dit* Le Cayret. Here some of the Syrah vines are 90 years old. M. Bernard pays rent to M. de Barjac in the form of part of the crop – the rest he vinifies; the 1990 and 1991 were very good, full wines, both likely to run for a dozen years or so.

The *négociant* scene is less stimulating. The house of Eugène Vérilhac, which in the 1960s and 1970s also sold some very interesting well-matured bottles of Hermitage and Cornas, has disappeared off the scene. Gilles Père et Fils own around 1 hectare of vines, the mainstay of their *vin blanc nature* being a wine called Le Clos du Prieuré. Like several of the producers, they have increased the proportion of still wine over the past ten years, and it now stands at around 40 per cent of their total. Their wines are not exceptional, while the brightest spot on the producer-*négociant* front is provided by the house of Cotte-Vergne, who work from modern cellars beside Crussol, and who have wisely made the *vin nature* 60 per cent of their production.

Until 1981 there was another *négociant* in the village, the agreeable Amedée Dubourg, whose speciality was cheaper Ardèche wines, such as the Côtes du Vivarais. He retired in that year, and as none of his seven daughters was anxious to take over the business, his cellars are now being used by the Tain-l'Hermitage Cave Co-opérative for the vinification of their sparkling St-Péray, whose annual production comes to something over 50,000 bottles.

Until the post-war years St-Péray used to be a barrel-making centre for the northern Côtes du Rhône, with a prosperous community of four *tonneliers*. Sadly, 1973 saw the retirement of the last of them, M. Vinard, who at sixty-five decided that he had worked hard enough and long enough all by himself.

A grey-haired, slight man who belied his years, M. Vinard explained that he took over from his father. Methods had not changed in his time, and 90 per cent of a *tonnelier*'s work today remains entirely manual. Over the years the wood used has undergone changes. Years ago it was entirely oak, but in the 1950s and 1960s there was a trend to much more chestnut, taken from the Ardèche and the Isère. But now there is a fashion for oak again, with the difference that much of it is no longer imported from Austria and Russia; instead, nearly all of it now comes from the rest of France.

A *tonnelier*'s time is divided between carrying out repairs and making new barrels. Much the hardest and most skilled work is the repairs, and it is the lack of experienced hands for this that *vignerons* most regret. To repair the area around the stopper or underneath the metal bands of a 585-litre oak barrel is a difficult operation. 'Some of the barrels I used to be sent were as much as a 100 years old', said M. Vinard. 'It is very precise and delicate work to graft on to the grain of such old wood.'

M. Vinard found no one prepared to take over his work, and at a time when it was not fashionable to use new oak, his business closed down. Nowadays in the northern Rhône wine houses there are *tonneliers* with Paul Jaboulet (a father-to-son tradition), Chapoutier and the Tain Cave Co-opérative. The *avant-garde* growers have the habit of rotating their stocks of new oak within five or six years, so there isn't the demand for careful restorations on old barrels that existed in the more thrifty and traditional days of M. Vinard.

St-Péray Vintages

The white wines of St-Péray are not intended for very long keeping. As a general rule, the sparkling wine should be drunk within five or six years. The still wines can hold together a little longer, but are often most enjoyable when two to five years old, while their freshness combines easily with their natural middling weight.

1964	Excellent.
1965	Poor.
1966	Good.
1967	Excellent.
1968	Mediocre.

1969   Excellent. Fruity and aromatic wines.

1970   Mediocre. The crop was very large, and the wines somewhat unbalanced.

1971   Excellent. Attractive, harmonious wines.

1972   Very good. Quite high in acid content, the wines also
possessed good fruitiness and general refinement.

1973   Good. A plentiful harvest gave wines that were fruity, but
sometimes a little unbalanced. Better for the sparkling
wines than the still wines.

1974   Medium. A vintage that varied from grower to grower.
Some of the wines were rather 'flabby' and lacking in
charm, while others possessed good bouquet and richness.

1975   Medium. A small harvest yielded grapes that were best
suited for a sparkling wine vinification. The still wines were
light and fruity.

1976   Very good. Both the sparkling and the still wines were
fruity and full of good substance.

1977   An irregular vintage. Quite a large crop gave wines tending
to be over-acidic. They were light on the palate.

1978   A small harvest of well-ripened grapes gave correspondingly well-balanced and attractive wines, with good roundness to them.

1979   A good vintage. The sparkling wines possessed plenty of
fruit. The still wines were a little short on liveliness.

1980   A large crop, with fruit and a medium weight in the wines.

1981   Another large crop gave wines tending to lack balance.
They were lightly fruited. Better for the sparkling than the
still wines.

1982   The hot summer gave a very ripe harvest that resulted in
blowzy still wines and rather flabby sparklers.

1983   A good vintage. The wines were well rounded, and had
solid extract on the palate. Much better balance than the
1982s.

1984   Some rot on the harvest made life difficult. A light vintage
for the still wines. The sparklers were a little better, with
some taut early fruit.

1985   A good vintage, especially for the still wines that contained
reasonable early fruit and showed some length on the
palate. Rather uneven quality for the sparklers.

1986   A large crop whose wines were generally sound, if a trifle short on acidity. The still wines were well scented, but need drinking.

1987　The largest crop on record – over 3,150 hectolitres. The relative under-maturity of the grapes meant more sparkling wine than usual, and this was successful if vinified in the modern way, with growers able to capitalize on a lively fruit on the attack. Drink up now. The still whites lack balance.

1988　A good vintage. The wines were well rounded on the palate, and held sound balance. They are now showing decent length and should be drunk while their bouquets show up well.

1989　A very good vintage. The year was extremely dry, and the wines held a firmer constitution than in most vintages. The still wines have good *gras* and depth on the bouquet, and on the palate have achieved a well flavoured roundness. They will drink well until around 1994–5. The sparkling wines have also been correct, and are a shade superior to the 1988s.

1990　A vintage where the still wines need selection. The best – Clape, Lionnet – are quite richly scented and hold decent depth on the palate. They should be drunk in their youth. Other wines reflect a lack of acidity and their fruit is rather sticky. A sound year for the sparkling wines.

Earlier Exceptional Vintages　1962, 1961, 1957, 1955

Leading Growers at St-Péray

The nucleus:

Bernard, Sylvain	07130 St-Péray
Chaboud, Jean-François	07130 St-Péray
Clape, Auguste	07130 Cornas
Darona, Pierre, et Fils	07130 St-Péray
Gripa, Bernard	07300 Mauves
Lionnet, Jean	07130 Cornas
Teysseire, Jean et Fils	07130 St-Péray
Thiers, Jean-Louis	07130 Toulaud
Voge, Alain	07130 Cornas

Other producers:

Balthazar, René	07130 Cornas
Cave les Vignerons de St-Péray	07130 St-Péray
Cave de Tain-l'Hermitage	26600 Tain-l'Hermitage
Maison Cotte-Vergne	
Fraisse, Marcel	
Fraisse, Robert	} 07130 St-Péray
Gilles Père et Fils	
Juge, Marcel	07130 Cornas
Mme *veuve* Mathon	07130 St-Péray
Maurice, Marc	07130 Cornas
Milliand Frères	07130 St-Péray

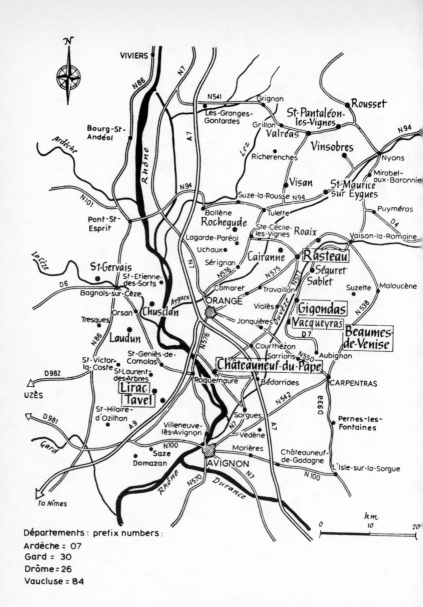

Southern Rhône

9

Rasteau

Rasteau's Grenache-based *vin doux naturel* is the least-known *appellation* wine in the Côtes du Rhône, and in many ways this is not surprising. Made on similar lines to port with a fermentation arrested by the addition of alcohol, it is a truly heady wine with a blatant grapiness and coarseness that is not to everyone's taste. In the South of France there are several of these Grenache-based country wines, and their market is the bars and *épiceries* of the region. Banyuls, the Rivesaltes of Cazes Frères and the extraordinary Grenache Noir Tuilé of José Puig in Claira are the best known of them and, with Rasteau, are some of the very few to be allowed full *appellation contrôlée*: to foreign eyes that often represents no great distinction, however.

The village of Rasteau is situated about 20 kilometres north-east of Orange and has a typical Provençal character; a small, disordered collection of brown roofs cluster around one another near the top of a hillock, while below them the narrow streets and alleyways guard a stillness that only the occasional footfall or distant exclamation can disturb. The two social centres of the community are, for the men, the main square and, for the women, the communal *lavoir* or wash-house. In the evenings, and all day on Sundays, the beret-wearing, cigarette-smoking locals play their endless games of *pétanque*, while the housewives come out to the *lavoir* and scrub clean their family linen, standing in carefully numbered stalls like racehorses at the starting-gate. In summer they are surrounded by a green spread of vines that presses right up to the village limits; in winter the little hills and plains have turned a light brown, discreetly matching the tiles on the Provençal rooftops.

It is difficult to estimate for how long Rasteau has been a wine community, for the village is notably lacking in documentation and local records. The first written mention of vines to have been found dates from the year 1005, when Bishop Humbert II of nearby Vaison started to rent out his episcopal vineyard to some private growers at Rasteau. Under the terms of the agreement, payment was to be given in kind, to the tune of half a hogshead of wine every year. By 1009 it is recorded that Humbert's successor, Bishop Pierre II of Mirabel, was even giving away some of the choice vines from the well exposed hill of St-Martin near the village. It is not known when the Church finally relinquished ownership of its vineyards at Rasteau.

Until 1932 only red, rosé and white wines were made, under the title 'Côtes du Rhône'. In that year some growers started making a *vin doux naturel* from their Grenache vines, and this received its own *appellation contrôlée* in 1944. The late Baron Le Roy, tireless campaigner for Rhône wines and France's premier wine diplomat of this century, was a fervent admirer of the Grenache *vin doux*, and once said of it, 'We used to be lacking a pearl in the Côtes du Rhône, but Rasteau has given us one with its *vin doux naturel*.'

One may well ask why it is the Grenache, certainly not the most refined of grapes, that forms at least 90 per cent of any bottle of Rasteau *vin doux naturel*. What about the other southern Rhône vines, like the Cinsault, or the now popular Syrah? Perhaps the answer to this lies in the two main properties of the Grenache grape: its wines tend to be heavily alcoholized and also age rapidly. Although a *vin doux naturel* has alcohol spirit added to it, it is obviously in the grower's interest to minimize the amount of his alcohol addition, and to maximize his natural sugar content. Another aspect of the fortified Grenache wines is that they are thought to be better the more they are aged, even to the point where they acquire a curious semi-maderized taste. This taste is called *rancio*, a word of Spanish derivation, and a *rancio* wine is considered the undoubted superior of a younger *vin doux*.

Ten per cent of the wine can be made from grape varieties other than the Grenache Noir, Blanc or Gris. In the case of the red Rasteau *vin doux naturel*, there is more support for an 'improver' *cépage* like the Syrah than in the past, when a journeyman vine like the Carignan would have been used to fill out the remaining 10 per cent. Not only are some of the private producers and the Cave Co-opérative of Rasteau becoming more conscientious about their *vin doux naturel*, they are also trying to make it more interesting and more complex – and, ultimately, better. The Syrah seems to add to the bouquet and depth of flavour on the palate, whereas the Carignan, unless its plants are very old, is one-dimensional and rather hard, while the Cinsault is overridden by the strength of the Grenache without serving to soften it.

Rasteau remains very much a typical example of an old-fashioned *vin du coin* – one that appeals to local palates and local custom but is extremely difficult to transport outside its immediate ambience. Indeed, it was dealt something of a body blow in the mid-1980s by the legislation that substantially increased the yields permitted for the local vineyards. The growers are now allowed to make 42 hectolitres per hectare, up from 35 hectos per hectare, for their more expensive Côtès du Rhône Villages wines, and 52 hectolitres, up from 50 hectos, for their standard Côtes du Rhône.

This has had a dramatic effect on the Rasteau *vin doux naturel*. The average production in the period 1975–9 was 2,672 hectolitres per annum; the average production in the years 1980–5 was 3,564 hectos; and the highest recorded year ever was 1979 with 5,087 hectos. But the declared *vin doux naturel* for 1986 was 896 hectolitres, for 1987, 886 hectos and for 1988, 949 hectos – average 910 hectolitres. Producers clearly feel they have better uses for their Grenache and their time.

Planted around the village, of course, are the usual Côtes du Rhône Villages vines: besides the Grenache these are notably the Cinsault, the Mourvèdre and the Syrah. Generally, the *vignerons* depend on their older Grenache vines for the *vin doux*, since they yield the most concentrated, sugary grape-juice. In years of bad weather, production of the *vin doux* is evidently much restricted, as by law the Grenache grapes must contain the sugar equivalent of 15° when harvested.

Most of the vines grow on what are known as *garrigues*; *garrigue* is a local term indicating a large mass of stony, infertile soil that will support vines, lavender and trees, but almost nothing else. Some of the best Grenache plots spill over into neighbouring Cairanne and Sablet and are on gentle slopes composed of heavy clay: with their good exposure these vines invariably yield well-matured grapes.

Rasteau is one of the sixteen full Côtes du Rhône Villages; and the harvest for these wines starts in mid to end September. The Grenache *vin doux* vines are left for a further two weeks in order to achieve maximum maturity. This extra time has a significant effect on the grapes, which, under the influence of the southern Rhône Valley's warmth and wind, contract into hard, sugary masses. Even in

December it is possible to see on the vines healthy-looking bunches of Grenache grapes inadvertently missed during the *vendanges*. Although their skin is by then slightly shrivelled, the grapes are very sugary to the taste.

Over 90 per cent of the *vin doux naturel* is 'white', that is, a wine vinified along orthodox white wine methods. Thus the grapes are pressed on arrival at the cellar and are then fermented away from the skins until the density of the must reaches the desired level: this is around the equivalent of at least 15° alcohol by volume. The *mutage*, or addition of pure alcohol, is then performed, which stops the fermentation, retains the wine's sweetness, and increases the total alcohol degree to 21.5. Thereafter, some growers, like the Meyer family at the Domaine des Nymphes and Thierry Masson at the Domaine Bressy-Masson, place the wine in cask for a year or so in order to soften and round it a little and to add to the oxidation effect that is considered highly desirable. Other growers store the wine in vat for several months before bottling.

To give some idea of the condition of the grapes when they enter the cellar, M. Thiérry Masson, the leading private grower at Rasteau, estimated that for his *vin doux naturel* he needed 1.5 kilograms of grapes to make a bottle of wine; for his Côtes du Rhône Villages red wine (also based on Grenache) only 1.1 kilograms. The Bressy-Masson family have for a long time been the only makers of the unusually named Rasteau *Rancio* wine, although the Domaine des Nymphes has made a little. The *Rancio* gains its title from being matured for considerably longer than the usual *vin doux*. In the old days of M. Émile Bressy, who died in 1976, the *domaine* would age their wine in cask for anything between seven and ten years, during which time a curious literally 'old' flavour, reminiscent of a table wine past its best, would be taken on. This is the esteemed *Rancio* taste, and the wine will have both a dark golden, almost crushed caramel, colour and a welcome roundness that is not evident in the less matured version. Nowadays M. Bressy's daughter, Marie-France, and her husband, Thiérry Masson, prefer to age the *Rancio* for about five years before bottling, and the wine is still very successful.

Most of the Rasteau *vin doux* is made like white wine for one major reason: the resulting colour. As M. Andrieu, the President of the Cave Co-opérative freely admitted: 'We used to be the only people to make a little red *vin doux* – it forms under 10 per cent of our total VDN production – because although we feel it to be the equal of the white, it is very hard to market owing to its somewhat cloudy red colour. The difference in its vinification has two sources: either we do the *mutage* with red juice, which is the modern way, or in the past we have left the skins in the fermenting vats for three or four days at the very beginning. I think that this makes the red VDN a slightly coarser, grapier wine than the white, but at the same time, it definitely tastes less sugary – which some would consider an advantage.'

Other makers of the red *vin doux* are André Roméro at the Domaine la Soumade, Robert Charavin and the Meyer family at the Domaine des Nymphes, but only tiny amounts of this are now being made – just 78 hectolitres, for instance, in 1987, against 469 hectos in 1982.

'White' is a misnomer for the majority of the *vin doux*, for its colour is very dark gold, or almost caramel. Its bouquet, and indeed its flavour, are both sugared and full of vinosity and can resemble burnt brown sugar or even marzipan: it is difficult to situate the exact sensation they give, for the fortification of the wine suppresses in large part the traditional Grenache red wine aromas and seems to leave it instead with a blend of raw grapes and alcohol that can be overbearing to sensitive palates. In the South of France Rasteau has traditionally been drunk as an aperitif, but is now more and more served either at the end of a meal as a dessert wine, for which it is usually chilled, or as the filler for the local melon.

Having formed a little under one-third of all the wine at Rasteau in the 1970s, the *vin doux naturel* plays a much less prominent role these days. The rest of the wines made in the neighbouring *domaines* are either Côtes du Rhône Villages red, white or rosé, or Côtes du Rhône *générique* red, white or rosé. Always full-bodied, these wines are becoming more stylized as a wave of *vignerons* who set up in the late 1970s or early 1980s exert their skills. The wines have greater roundness and less sheer heat than fifteen years ago, and their progress is very much along the lines of that made by the leading producers at nearby Cairanne, whose wines the Rasteaus closely resemble.

Leading exponents among the private growers include Paul Joyet at the Domaine des Girasols, who has been making Rasteau Villages since 1983. His vines are over forty years old, and some of his wines are placed in cask – they are well scented and stylish. Thierry Masson at Domaine Bressy-Masson makes a fully flavoured, ripe red Rasteau which is given extra support by the presence of around 10 per cent Mourvèdre. Jean-Pierre Meffre at the Gigondas-based Domaine St-Gayan also enhances his red Rasteau with the use of Mourvèdre, and again this is a successful wine. The Domaine des Nymphes goes for a lighter style, derived from the use of grapes that have been semi-macerated for high fruit extraction, and the result is an appealing fruitiness. André Roméro, whose father was an *ancien* Co-opérateur, actually produces a Cabernet Sauvignon *vin de pays*, while as a Rhône his red Villages pursues a more elegant style, made from Grenache, Mourvèdre and Syrah, and possesses a bit more body than the Nymphes wine. The excellent Cairanne-based Domaine Rabasse-Charavin, in the hands of Corinne Couturier, makes a well-balanced, full-tasting red from 7.5 hectares of Rasteau vineyards. These private growers are supported by the very good work of the Cave Co-opérative, whose red Rasteau is always very soundly made and capable of showing a true, warm Grenache pepperiness; on average it contains 65 per cent Grenache, supported by 20 per cent Syrah and 10 per cent each of Carignan and Mourvèdre. These wines are ideal for drinking between two and six years old as a rule, and are just right for strong-tasting winter dishes such as stews and casseroles. Meanwhile, the white and the rosé are less impressive, although work is afoot to improve the white through the planting of superior *cépages*. At present, the production of both is limited.

The *vin doux naturel* occupies a curious position at Rasteau, therefore, for it brings the village fame rather than fortune. The *vignerons* rely much more upon their Côtes du Rhône table wines to earn themselves a living, and realize that demand for the *vin doux* is very restricted. As M. Maurice Charavin, a member of one of the oldest wine families, observed, 'It's the VDN that I export in medium quantities – to Switzerland, Denmark and Belgium – and I find that its greatest benefit for me is its prestige. I make and sell much more Côtes du Rhône wine, on which I depend completely for my living.'

M. Charavin owns 13 hectares of vines and, in addition to his *vin doux*, makes red, rosé and white Côtes du Rhône and Villages, the white from the Grenache Blanc and Clairette grapes. He admits that he is hindered by the problem of the *rentabilité*, or viability, of his *vin doux naturel*, for he says: 'I leave it three or four years in cask, and it needs at least this long to take on a sort of old, partly maderized taste. If I didn't have to keep the money rolling in, I would ideally age it for twice that time, since Rasteau gains much more smoothness at a much faster rate in wood than it does in bottle. Still I drank a twenty-five-year-old bottle not long ago, and it was in great shape, with the just right amount of senility!'

This taste of old age is much revered in the region, and is the key to the very individual Rasteau *Rancio* of the Bressy-Masson *domaine*. The late M. Émile Bressy's father was one of the first growers to make a Rasteau *vin doux* in 1932 and, before the Second World War, decided with Émile to try ageing his Rasteau longer than usual. Every year a little of the *vin doux naturel* was put aside, and after six or seven years the Bressys discovered that their technique was a great success, for it endowed the wine with a smoothness on the palate that had not previously been evident; something vaguely akin to the difference in flavour between a ruby and a tawny port, perhaps.

M. Bressy was a cautious man, who needed gentle persuasion and prompting if he was to talk about his unique wine. His pride was apparent when he would state categorically: 'You'll not find another bottle with the label Rasteau *Rancio* on it; it was I and my father who started it off, and this is the only *domaine* making it now.' This is no longer true in the 1990s, but the *Rancio* remains an item of curiosity rather than commercial validity.

The small cellar at what is now the Domaine Bressy-Masson is full of *Rancio* barrels, some of which lurk, semi-forgotten, in hidden corners. All are well stoppered up and have the word '*Rancio*' written in faded chalk on their front. Around them the Côtes du Rhône barrels are easily visible, with their shininess and new chalk letters, which make them look like eager young schoolboys mixing with their sagacious elders.

In the 1990s there is no doubt that Rasteau will be one of the front-line names of the Côtes du Rhône Villages seeking to gain promotion to its own full *appellation* status – for its red wine. In a strange way, the *vin doux naturel* is almost an echo from the past, and not a specially welcome one, except for a few fiercely regional zealots.

Rasteau Vintages

The Rasteau *vin doux naturel* is not usually given a vintage, since it is more often than not a blended wine. Since the 1970s, however, the custom for the Cave Co-opérative has been to offer its *vin doux naturel* with a vintage attached. The difference between vintages is slight, given the necessity to obtain a natural alcohol extraction of at least 15° from those grapes selected for the *vin doux naturel*.

Leading Growers at Rasteau (*vin doux naturel* and Côtes du Rhône Villages)

Bressy-Masson	
Domaine Bressy-Masson	
Charavin, Maurice	84110 Rasteau
Domaine de Char-à-vin	
Cave des Vignerons	
Chamfort, Bernard	
Domaine de Verquière	84110 Sablet
Charavin, Didier	
Domaine des Papillons	
Charavin, Émile	
Domaine Wilfried	84110 Rasteau
Charavin, Robert, et Fils	
Colombet, Philippe	
Coulon, Daniel	
Domaine de Beaurenard	84230 Châteauneuf-du-Pape
Couturier, Corinne	
Domaine Rabasse-Charavin	84290 Cairanne
Girard, Louis	
Domaine de la Girardière	84110 Rasteau
Gleize, André	84150 Violès
Joyet, Paul	
Domaine des Girasols	84110 Rasteau
Liautaud, Jean	
Domaine du Sommier	84110 Séguret
Martin, Yves	84150 Travaillan
Meffre, Jean-Pierre	
Domaine St-Gayan	84190 Gigondas
Meyer et Fils	
Domaine des Nymphes	84110 Rasteau
Nicolet-Leyraud	
Richaud, Marcel	84290 Cairanne
Roméro, André	
Domaine La Soumade	84110 Rasteau
Saurel, S.	
Domaine de la Combe Dieu	84 La Baumette
Vache, Francis	84110 Rasteau

10

Beaumes-de-Venise

Running around the southerly end of the Dentelles de Montmirail mountains, and appearing to possess a natural fusion with its olive- and vine-covered hillside, is the village of Beaumes-de-Venise. This is the home of the Muscat de Beaumes-de-Venise, often regarded as the best of the South of France's several *vins doux naturels*, or fortified sweet wines. As the translation implies, *vin doux naturel* is a bit of a misnomer, for the Muscat de Beaumes-de-Venise and its brother wines from nearer the Mediterranean all have a little pure alcohol added to them.

Of these *vins doux naturels* – other prominent examples include the Muscat de Frontignan, Rivesaltes and Banyuls – Beaumes-de-Venise has achieved the highest profile outside France, with a popularity that grew sharply in the late 1970s. Britain took to the wine in a big way at that time, and the United States has also proved a strong export market. By the early 1990s suppliers like Paul Jaboulet Aîné were exporting regular amounts to Hong Kong, the Far East and Australia, and the prosperity of this *appellation* is now set on a much firmer footing.

Twenty years ago, this was an unhappy area. Future prospects seemed dim, there was a dwindling band of *vignerons* who bothered to cultivate the Muscat, and many *viticulteurs* preferred the easy life of growing high-degree red grapes for sale to the local Co-opérative to produce red wines. The production figures of 1966–9 inclusive show this very starkly. The average yearly amount of Muscat de Beaumes made over those four years was 2,790 hectolitres. The average yearly amount made over the four years 1985–8 inclusive was 10,115 hectolitres. From under 115 hectares of Muscat planted in the mid-1960s, the vineyard rose to around 230 hectares by the early 1980s, then to over 330 hectares by the early 1990s.

Beaumes-de-Venise itself is an old village that dates back to the early years of the Roman Empire. Taking advantage of the sulphur spring at Montmirail, the Romans established Beaumes as a small spa centre, and all sorts of their relics have since been found, such as swimming-pool walls and lengths of water piping. Also found, on the St-Hilaire hillside overlooking the village, has been a large bas-relief depicting a *vendange* scene and the treading down of the harvest. The locals are naturally convinced that the grapes being trodden are Muscat, but whatever their identity, it is certain that wine has been made at Beaumes since the Roman era.

Away to the west, towards Vacqueyras, is one of the village landmarks, the church of Notre-Dame d'Aubune, which looks down on the Cave Co-opérative. It is on the approximate site of a decisive eighth-century Gallic victory over the Saracens; after the battle the Saracens were forced to take to the local hills and for months hid out in the grottoes and caves that abound above and around Beaumes. ('Beaumes' comes from a Provençal word, *baumo*, meaning grotto, 'Venise' from the French *Venaissin*. In feudal times the village formed part of the Comtat de Venaissin, a papal fiefdom.) Every year on 8 September there is a pilgrimage to the church in celebration of this ancient victory.

By the Middle Ages Beaumes-de-Venise's wine had achieved local fame, in that the papal court in Avignon was drinking it regularly. In 1348 Pope Clement VI went as far as buying a vineyard near the village in order to secure himself a permanent supply of the wine; the property was to remain in papal hands until 1797, just after the French Revolution.

The sweet Muscat is thought by most of the growers themselves to date from no earlier than the beginning of the nineteenth century, and the small amount then made enjoyed a strong, strictly regional popularity. In 1859 the Provençal poet Frédéric Mistral referred to it in his classic work, *Mireio* (Mireille), the story of a rich girl's frustrated love for a lowly peasant. Writing in Provençal, Mistral said:

Lou bon Muscat de Baumo
E lou Ferigoulet
Alor se chourlo a la gargato.[1]

[1] *Le bon Muscat de Beaumes*   The good Muscat of Beaumes

By the 1860s, much of the village's prosperity derived from the cultivation of table grapes – the Chasselas – from olives and from walnuts, with expanding fruit plantations thanks to new access to the water of the River Durance. Indeed, the Vaucluse's first apricot trees are said to have been planted at Beaumes in 1882.[1] All this meant that viticulture, knocked out by phylloxera in 1870, took a back seat. Table grapes yielded better revenues than grapes destined for wine, and there was no producers' grouping to exercise any economic clout with buyers and markets.

The first step up came with the granting of *appellation contrôlée* for the Muscat de Beaumes-de-Venise, thanks largely to the hard work of the late Louis Castaud of Domaine des Bernardins, in October 1943. But this served to focus minds rather than immediately to create action. By the early 1950s things were close to rock bottom; there were only about 40 hectares of Muscat vines, split between a few *domaines*, and in 1951 bad weather wiped out the whole crop: not a drop of Muscat was made in that year.

Fortunately for all concerned, a Cave Co-opérative was formed at Beaumes in 1956, which, with its spreading of costs, persuaded many of the local farmers to resume growing the Muscat wine grape, the Muscat *à petits grains*, in addition to the normal southern Rhône red wine varieties such as Grenache, Cinsault and Mourvèdre. In that first year the Co-opérative's total production ran to a proud 100 hectolitres of Muscat.

The Muscat is a vine of Greek origin, dating back to several centuries BC, and is now widely planted around the Mediterranean, as well as in Alsace, where it makes a dry white wine. There are many variations of it, however, and at Beaumes-de-Venise the Muscat *à petits grains* is the same variety that is used in combination with the Muscat d'Alexandrie to make the fortified Muscat de Frontignan of the French Mediterranean. Outside France, it is the vine that gives the very good liqueur Muscats of the state of Victoria in Australia.

True to form, though, the Muscat at Beaumes has two sub-varieties, the *grain blanc* and the *grain noir*. Since the late 1970s the inevitable hand of officialdom has extended to a formal recom-

---

Et le Ferigoulet   And the Thyme
Se boivent à la régalade.   Should be swilled back.

[1] A. Allègre, *Monographie de Beaumes-de-Venise* (Léonce Laget, 1981).

mendation that the Muscat *à grains blancs* should be the only variety henceforth planted. Talking to the growers, however, one discovers that this edict may not have been applied with what should have been due diligence over the attainment of an optimum quality.

Yves Nativelle of Domaine de Coyeux has this to say about the two varieties: 'The *noir* is excellent in small quantities. It has a thicker skin, and if you want juice, it's the white that supplies it. What the *noir* brings is a certain *charpente*, some very agreeable body to the wine, while the white contributes finesse. But you won't find the *grains noirs* these days down at the *pépiniériste* – the INAO have struck them off.'

Let Guy Rey of Domaine St-Sauveur at Aubignan explain his point of view: 'Historically my 6 hectares of Muscat have been about 65 per cent *blanc* and 35 per cent *noir*. The *blanc* gives a pure white wine, the *noir* gives one with a certain golden tint in it; the *noir* has several favourable factors – it is more rot-resistant, a more regular producer, and for example in 1983 it avoided the rot, while the *blanc* suffered. You tell them apart, by the way, through the colour of the leaf – the *noir* has an olive-coloured leaf, darker than the *blanc*'s.'

The *grain noir* by itself is therefore considered to make a wine that is too dark in colour, and what colour the wine has is taken on during the eight to nine months' ageing, with the insertion of a light caramel mixture to ensure even levels through a vintage. Surely it would be easier and more natural to rely on a dark-skinned grape for this?

The two Muscat types are grown in a surprising number of different soils all about the village, ranging between pure sand in the south, sand and stones in the east and heavy clay in the valley behind the line of hills north of the village. The effect of these combined differences on the wine is ultimately very hard to judge, for there are now so few small growers that one of the problems is that of forming a yardstick with which to evaluate the *appellation*. In addition, the Cave Co-opérative – responsible for more than nine-tenths of the Muscat – always makes a blended wine from holdings throughout the *appellation*. As a consequence, no one sector holds a specially esteemed reputation, and the wine is sold as straightforward Muscat de Beaumes-de-Venise, accompanied by a *domaine* name where applicable.

Beaumes-de-Venise is the only place in the Côtes du Rhône where Muscat wine grapes are planted, and the vine's liability to several different diseases has always hindered its wider cultivation. Its main complaint is oïdium, which, having taken hold of the vine, paves the way for additional attacks of grey rot; money and time must therefore be spent spraying the plants with sulphur treatments – all of which adds to the *vigneron*'s overheads. While the Grenache, Mourvèdre and other customary red and rosé vines remain largely trouble-free, the Muscat also attracts a bug called the *araignée rouge*, or red spider, which can shear the vine of all its foliage if it is not sprayed with insecticides.

M. Yves Nativelle

Of the private growers, M. Yves Nativelle of Domaine de Coyeux was the first to plant a majority of Muscat when he bought the *domaine* in the late 1970s. Generally the *vignerons* have been cautious in their exposure to a vine that they feel can be difficult to cultivate and a low producer. Bernard Leydier of the very good Domaine de Durban now has 14 hectares of his total 30-hectare vineyard under Muscat, while Yves Nativelle's Muscat holding is now around 60 hectares out of a total estate surface of 130 hectares: around 30 hectares are planted with Villages vines, led by the Grenache, with support from the Cinsault, Mourvèdre and Syrah.

The Villages wines come in red form, and Beaumes-de-Venise has a quietly growing reputation for these through the efforts of growers like M. Nativelle, M. Étienne de Menthon at the Château Redortier, and the Croset family at the Domaine du Cassan, hidden away at the hamlet of Lafare. All these growers also make substantial red Gigondas, as well as red and rosé Côtes du Rhône *générique*, so they have various different commercial strings to their bows.

The Villages grapes, which in recent years have been upgraded with replacement of the Carignan by notably the Syrah and the Mourvèdre, are harvested ahead of the Muscat. In hot years like 1988 and 1989 this is between 10 and 20 September. The Muscat is a quick-maturing grape, but the growers are at pains not to leave it so long that *pourriture noble* or noble rot develops: as Guy Rey says, 'That would mean too much loss of juice.' Accordingly an early harvest for the Muscat would be 19 September 1983, a late harvest 18 October 1984. The idea is to catch the Muscat just as it is beginning to wrinkle and harden. Its sugar content is then well concentrated and should give the equivalent of about 15° alcohol by volume.

The fermentation of the Muscat broadly follows the lines of white wine-making, but greater than normal care is taken with the selection of yeasts. Philippe Batigne, the director of the Cave Co-opérative until the early 1990s, explained: 'We're looking to keep the fermentation temperature between 7°C, when it just about starts, and 13°C for around twenty days. So we press the grapes on arrival, leave them in an enamel-lined cool chamber at 0°C for a decantation of forty-eight to seventy-two hours, raise the temperature up to 7°C and then let them ferment for about two weeks at up to 13°C. The third stage of the process is to accelerate the fermentation for a final week between 13°C and 20°C. We never pass 20°C and this will leave about 120 grams of residual sugar per litre. Combined with 15.5° naturally, this transforms into 22.4°, which fits between the 21.5° and the 23.5° required by legislation.'

The Co-opérative and Yves Nativelle perform a low-temperature vinification, which contrasts with past methods at Beaumes, where cooling the wine was to keep the must to around 25°C. Bernard Leydier of Domaine Durban recalled that his first low-temperature fermentation (between 14°C and 18°C) was in 1984, while the

Domaine Castaud-Maurin has remained faithful for longer to a fermentation in the low to mid-20°sC. Guy Rey of Domaine St-Sauveur reduced his fermentation in 1982 from an average temperature of around 31°C to about 26°C. He found this helped him cool the Muscat must better as he went along.

The big problem facing the growers each year is the *mutage*, or addition of alcohol. They watch the specific gravity of their vats descend as the sugar is converted into alcohol, and have to be ready and on hand to add the alcohol in the right amount. The alcohol comes from a single source, a distillery at Jonquières nearby, and is about 96 per cent. The more sugar in the wine, the less alcohol is put in. Most growers apply the alcohol all at once, not gradually, and then pump the vats around to mix everything together well. The Cave Co-opérative will then sometimes rack the wine three times in the space of forty-eight hours, to make sure that the fermentation has halted. By and large the addition of the alcohol ensures that the fermentation will not run for more than another twelve hours at most.

The addition of the alcohol serves to kill many of the yeast cells driving the fermentation, the last sugar remains unconverted, and the wine's degree is strengthened to about 21.5°. The small growers then like to leave the wine to its own devices as much as is feasible, so that it can clear on its own if possible – fining is not liked because it is detrimental to the wine's aromas.

Consequently the wine is stored in stainless steel – as for the Co-opérative – or concrete or enamel-lined vats until around March when bottling occurs. In the past, bottling took place a few months later. One last twist in the tale that sets Beaumes apart from the other Rhône *appellations* is that at this stage they don't know whether their wine will actually qualify for VDN *appellation* status. Only the INAO controllers from Perpignan, who check their local Frontignan first, can decide, and they usually breeze into Beaumes between March and May. For the Co-opérative a final task is to expose the wine to the cold, at −4°C for two weeks, to precipitate the tartrates, then to filter and bottle the wine. They assemble all their different *cuvées* into one wine at the moment of cooling for the tartrates, in order to emerge with a uniform wine under their own name. Because they handle such large quantities of Muscat, they keep bottling from March until near the end of the year. Philippe Batigne made an interesting point about the use of stainless steel during that time when he commented: 'It's not good to use the stainless steel any earlier in the process since it doesn't allow so much intra cellular circulation which will encourage the development of the aromas. We found the same with our rosé.'

Once INAO approval has been given, the *vignerons* are free to put their Muscat on sale. The wine therefore receives very little ageing before it is bottled. For the handful of private growers, with the exception of the more recent arrival Yves Nativelle, this is a departure from the practice of the past, when the *vin de l'année* would not necessarily go on sale until later. In the early 1970s some were accustomed to leaving the Muscat in its concrete vats for an extra year, or occasionally even an extra three years, according to the style of wine they were seeking. Wood has never been used in the ageing of Muscat because it is believed to suppress some of the wine's tremendous bouquet and fine, translucent colour. Freshness and grapiness are above all the most desired characteristics in the Muscat, and although the very best examples of it, such as the Domaines Coyeux and Durban and the Paul Jaboulet Muscat, possess great roundness on the palate, their trump card is undoubtedly the aromatic and all-pervasive Muscat sensation, something that few other grapes possess with such potency.

During the 1980s, developments in the vinification process, such as monitored temperature control, directly improved the quality of the wine. There is nowadays a greater elegance and finesse about the Muscats of Beaumes, a purer fruitiness and a more delicate aftertaste. The wine has much going for it – one can see how it became the fashionable drink among the middle classes of southern England about ten years ago, since a hostess was certain of waking up her guests and provoking conversation from them when serving the highly scented Muscat. The headiness of its bouquet is inescapable; the orange-gold colour is alluring, and the ample flavours and length on the palate declare themselves much more opulently than in any sweet wines from Bordeaux, unless they are very old and venerable. So at that time wine merchants were besieged with requests for Rhône wine – not the Châteauneuf, not Hermitage, not Côte-Rôtie; the one Rhône known by many non-specialists was Beaumes.

Formerly drunk principally as a dessert wine, the Muscat de Beaumes is now very popular as an aperitif, and is a great café favourite in the southern Rhône Valley. To show how tastes can differ, Mme Leydier of Domaine Durban drinks it as a dessert wine, her son Bernard as an aperitif; and Bernard even mentioned a local habit of mixing Beaumes-de-Venise with champagne as an aperitif . . . to help the wines served later on show better! As an accompaniment to food, Muscat is also popular with the local Cavaillon melons, and with cheese such as Chaume. Like most *vins doux naturel*s, it is generally served chilled, but too much cold can destroy its flowery bouquet. The wine's elevated alcohol degree – which can often be forgotten when drinking it, a costly mistake – ensures that its orange-tinted colour retains its depth for some years, but the Muscat cannot be regarded as a keeping wine; after five or six years it starts to lose the full piquancy of its strong, grapy aromas.

The style of today's Muscat de Beaumes is in fact an evolution of an old sweet wine that used to be made until the Second World War. This was sold by a *domaine* like Louis Castaud's as *vin Muscat*, with wax capsules, wax for the neck, and the vintage showing. The wine was nearly extinct, however, with only a tiny number of *vignerons* persevering with it. One such grower at the time was the late M. Jacques Leydier, father of Bernard Leydier of Domaine Durban, which makes a very good Muscat these days.

M. Leydier, who died in 1981, was a phlegmatic, pipe-smoking man, always ready to discuss aspects of his wine-making. His explanation of the old-style wine was as follows: 'It was a more natural wine, in that little or no *mutage* was carried out. We were not more than half a dozen making it, and what we would do would be to pick the grapes fairly late, probably after the middle of October. They were already well concentrated in sugar, but to intensify this we would lay them in bunches to dry out on straw or cane mats known as *claies*. A month or so later we would press the dried-out grapes and proceed with a normal white wine vinification. Our aim was to have as naturally sweet a wine as possible, but if the summer had been bad and the grapes had come in in bad shape, this was obviously hard to achieve. When the *appellation contrôlée* was granted in 1943, the regulations decreed that a fortified wine of not less than 21.5° be made; that was the beginning of the Muscat de Beaumes-de-Venise as we know it today.'

With the Dentelles de Montmirail on one side of it and the massive Mont Ventoux away on the other, the Domaine Durban stands well concealed, high up (at 500 metres) in some of the most forbidding countryside in the Côtes du Rhône. Rows of apricot and cherry trees add colour in the spring, while the light brown *domaine* is given some protection from the sweeping *mistral* wind by a little batch of pine trees that stand around it. From Roman times onwards there used to be a community called Urban roughly on the site of the *domaine* and, like Montmirail, it became famed for its copious sulphur spring. When interest in this waned, however, the community declined and eventually disappeared. It was M. Jacques Leydier who bought the property in the late 1960s and who restored both it and its wine to their former eminence.

Today M. Leydier's son Bernard is running the property with his brother Jean-Pierre and with the capable help of his wife Nicole, who seems firmly in control of the commercial side of things. Bernard explained more about the *domaine*: 'We also have vineyards at Gigondas, as well as Côtes du Rhône Villages vines here, but my family has always been most proud of its Muscat, which is certainly the hardest wine to vinify well. We have 14 hectares of Muscat altogether, and find that it is a vine that needs a lot of care, and one that up here does not live very long, never much more than thirty-five years. With the highest permitted yield fixed at not more than about 30 hectolitres per hectare, versus 45 hectos or more for the red wines, you can see that a lot of work and worry never yields more than a little wine, especially as the grapes have to be so perfectly ripe, and without blemish, when they are harvested. My father, funnily enough, used to consider that the Muscat could age well, and spoke of a thirty-year-old bottle that he had drunk in 1973, which, despite bearing a slight taste of *rancio*, or light maderization, had been very fine and smooth, with only a small loss of bouquet and colour.

'Times have changed a lot since my father's day. Fashions come and go, but it's astounding to think that there was no interest at all in the Muscat after the war. Now if you come to visit me in January, for instance, you will find I have no Muscat to sell until I have been allowed to release the recently vinified wine, which means that I am a wine-maker with no wine to sell for three or four months of the year if I don't plan ahead very carefully. I would like to age the wine for longer, but as you can see, there is absolutely no possibility of this.'

One of M. Jacques Leydier's colleagues in the uneasy times before the Muscat gained its own *appellation* was M. Pierre Castaud, who comes from the oldest wine family at Beaumes-de-Venise and who, as a young man, learned to make the old-style wine with his father Louis. M. Castaud, a soft-spoken, grey-haired man in his seventies, retired in 1976, leaving the running of the Domaine des Bernardins to his brother-in-law, M. Jean Maurin. He spoke about the old days: 'The pre-war wine was a less heady drink than today's Muscat, but because so much depended on the state of the grapes, we could never be sure how much, if any, we would be able to make every year. My father worked hard for the right of *appellation*, as he saw that it would encourage a great expansion in the making of Muscat here. Once the *appellation* was granted in 1943, we had, of course, to change our vinification methods and start adding alcohol spirit to the wine. That complicated things! We were accustomed to leaving the wine to ferment itself out, but the new laws demanded much greater vigilance over the state of each vat. When I was making the wine here I used barely to sleep for two weeks, as it is such a delicate task to know when exactly to add the alcohol. Any mistake with the *mutage* risked spoiling the whole year's crop, so at night I used to get up every two hours or so to check on how the density of the must was changing.'

The Domaine des Bernardins (now called Domaine Castaud-Maurin) has 10 hectares of Muscat which are split into two holdings. They have 7 hectares on sandy soil at Les Bernardins, on the side of the hill on the way to Lafare, and some younger vines on broken stones at a place called St-Véran, the soil of which yields a much lower crop. The Bernardins' vines are fifty-five to eighty-five years old.

The Domaine des Bernardins Muscat under M. Castaud was the best in the *appellation*. He differed from his fellow growers in that he would press his grapes very hard before fermentation, and although this would provoke a large lees with the inclusion of odd skins in the vats, the wine gained enormously in depth of colour and bouquet. It was a really thorough but well-balanced wine.

M. Maurin, who is now helped by his British son-in-law Mr Hall, uses a modern Vaslin press, but only presses the grapes relatively lightly. The wine ferments on its lees for a month at a temperature in the low 20°sC, and after the mutage it is stored until bottling around March or April. While the trend in the *appellation* has been towards a finer style of wine, the Castaud-Maurin wine is rather heavy, with a sweetness predominating on the bouquet that hides some of the fresh Muscat aromas. There is a nuttiness on the palate that is appealing, however. The *domaine* also makes a fairly tannic red Beaumes-de-Venise and a straight red Côtes du Rhône.

The third private grower of Muscat, whose family started with the sweet wine in 1964, is Guy Rey, a man who clearly likes the outdoor life, if his agility with his tractors is any guide. He is a true farmer by disposition, working with a common-sense practicality more than the thoughtful *viticulteur*'s approach of Bernard Leydier or the sophisticated commercial approach of Yves Nativelle of Domaine de Coyeux.

Guy Rey's father first planted Muscat in 1959. Before then, the family had made some Côtes du Rhône red and *vin de table*, and had also cultivated vegetables and fruits like tomatoes and melons. In 1975 they switched wholly to wine, and now grow 52 hectares, of which six are Muscat, the rest Rhône and Ventoux varieties.

M. Rey *père* would age the Muscat in 225–litre *pièces* for two or three years, but this required a lot of upkeep. As the taste moved away from the more darkly coloured wine to a fruitier, fresher one, so the Reys altered their vinification, and this *domaine* now makes a very good Muscat. Pale gold in most vintages, its colour is bright and attractive. There are ripe, soft aromas on the bouquet – apricots, almost – and the attack on the palate impresses with its dry, soft fruit that extends to an interesting dried grape finish. A clean finish and sound balance round the wine off nicely. The St-Sauveur wine is exported to Britain, the United States, Belgium and Germany, but its small quantity makes it less easy to find than the Domaine Durban, for example; the latter even runs to the sale of a few bottles at a time at the local filling station in Beaumes!

The individual who qualifies best for the title of mover and shaker at Beaumes-de-Venise is Yves Nativelle of Domaine de Coyeux. In a region where few, if any, newcomers tend to think big, M. Nativelle is the man for large-scale thought and action. His Domaine de Coyeux was hewn and chivvied out of unfriendly terrain high above Beaumes. It covers 130 hectares altogether, and when M. Nativelle moved here in the late 1970s, there were already 29 hectares of Muscat whose wine the previous owner would sell off in bulk. There are now over 60 hectares of Muscat, most of which grow right in the lee of the Dentelles de Montmirail on a strong red soil covered in jagged, pale gold stones.

A stocky, well made man, whose style is Parisian, M. Nativelle avers that he is or was a 'technocrat'; his past was spent at Rhône-Poulenc, in market research and marketing, and he must be one of the only Rhône growers to have spent a year at Europe's top business school of INSEAD at Fontainebleau. His international air is rounded off when he mentions that both his father and grandfather were Masters of the Cadre Noir Horse at the Equitation School of Saumur, and a Snaffles print on the wall of his office confirms his upbringing among horses.

M. Nativelle says that he wants to make a Beaumes that is finer and drier than most have been in the past, and his vinification is run at low controlled temperatures in his large, modern cellars. He performs the *mutage* between ten and fifteen days after the harvest, and places great emphasis on the need to work with grapes that are 'extraordinarily rich in sugar', to allow a natural fermentation of alcohol that is as high as possible before the *mutage*.

The Coyeux Muscat is indeed a very good wine; it is assembled from its different vats with a sorting of the juice beforehand to ensure a well-balanced mix between the *grains blancs* and *grains noirs*, the latter providing wine that opens up later than the former. Orange-yellow in colour, it develops its aromas after two years, the early bouquet at the time of release implying under-ripe fruit. The time in bottle allows greater richness to emerge, and an exceptional length on the palate that rounds off with a clean, tangy finish.

M. Nativelle also makes a red Beaumes-de-Venise and a Gigondas. The harvest for both is destalked, and fermented at temperatures around the 25°C mark. The Mourvèdre receives a little new oak. Well-balanced and stylish, these wines nevertheless have sufficient body to drink well between three and seven years old.

M. Nativelle typically is not a straight-down-the-line thinker on what should be eaten with Muscat de Beaumes. 'Drink it with *foie gras*,' he says expansively, 'that's what a lot of people do in the United States and Belgium, and with sorbet – Georges Blanc at Vonnas does a sorbet with a Muscat base. And in Brussels once I was served a dish of wild boar with Muscat in the sauce, and very good it was.' When asked whether the wine would match cheese well, he accepts that this would be perfectly possible, even though he has never tried it. There are now around 1,500 hectolitres of Domaine de Coyeux Muscat each year, which makes it potentially the most distributed private wine: Paul Jaboulet Aîné's well-known and excellent Muscat sells about half as much as Coyeux, just over 100,000 bottles, in any given year.

Jaboulet, like nearly all *négociants* serving a Muscat, rely on the large Cave Co-opérative for their *vin de Muscat*. Those also marketing

Muscat these days include Pascal, Pierre Perrin (the Beaucastel family from Châteauneuf), Vidal-Fleury, Les Grandes Serres (a Châteauneuf-du-Pape *négociant*) and Métairie (a Burgundy house).

Meeting the able Director of the Cave Co-opérative, Philippe Batigne, who in 1991 moved to the good *négociant* house of Pascal, one has been aware of the progress made by this previously very provincial grouping. A touching landmark was the Co-opérative's proud dispatch of twenty-five cases to New York in the summer of 1974, as well as an even smaller shipment in 1972 to the Rhône pioneers in Britain, Yapp Brothers. Now the world map behind M. Batigne's desk is covered with blue pins, the big names like New York and Tokyo alongside many exotic ones – Anchorage, Bangkok, Bora Bora, Abidjan and Martinique.

This is a big operation. The Co-opérative's Muscat accounts for around 1 million bottles a year, alongside around 3 million bottles of red, white and rosé wines. The subscribers owning Muscat vines number around 150, and the largest part of the plantation centres around the foot of the Dentelles mountains on clay–chalk soil. There are a further 180 subscribers who grow the traditional southern Rhône *cépages*, like the Grenache. Giving an idea of how the vineyards are spread between the Co-opérateurs, M. Batigne said that just two own 35-hectare plantations, some hold 15–20 hectares, but that the vast majority cultivate just half or 1 hectare of vines. Since the mid-1970s the training of the vines has moved increasingly to the use of wires rather than the old Gobelet method, bringing greater aeration and hence ripeness for the grapes. With greater technology applied to the vinification, standards in both vineyards and cellars have been raised, which is very much to the credit of management at the Co-opérative.

M. Batigne said he 'wants the aromas in the bottle when the consumer opens it', and his low-temperature fermentation aims specifically at maximizing the aromas in the wine. It is bottled from January onwards, and has gained in finesse over the past ten years. Not only is it reliable, but it is also fresh and long on the palate, and has a pleasant weight, just a bit lighter than in the old days. Muscat in gin fizz was M. Batigne's offbeat suggestion for the wine – one measure of gin, with lemon and Beaumes-de-Venise.

Other Beaumes Muscats that come from Vidal-Fleury or Jaboulet are vinified in a different way, according to M. Batigne. For example, in the case of Jaboulet, who have sold a Beaumes-de-Venise for nearly twenty years, Jacques Jaboulet goes south to the Co-opérative to make the wine according to his specifications, which can vary the strength of the pressing, the temperature of fermentation, the density at which the *mutage* is applied, and so alter the final style and weight of the wine. The Jaboulet style is for a lively Muscat with a clean, nutty finish, and is a very successful offering, as is the Vidal-Fleury Muscat. The last-named carries a firmer, pale gold colour, is opulently scented and mixes soft fruit with delicate flavours on the palate.

Apart from Yves Nativelle, who is a native of the Aveyron, another outsider who came south – 'in search of hot weather!' – and started to vinify his crop in 1981 was Étienne de Menthon of the Château Redortier. The difference is that he does not make any Muscat; his 30 hectares are planted in rugged country dotted with clumps of colourful yellow broom at a height of 350–450 metres. This Savoyard from Annecy arrived in 1956 at Suzette and gradually built a Provençal *bastide*, or farmhouse, and cellars to go with it. Until 1981 he was a Co-opérateur, and his first grape mix was 60 per cent Grenache, 20 per cent Syrah, and 20 per cent Cinsault. The amount of Syrah has been increased in the absence of the Mourvèdre. As M. de Menthon explained: 'It's too high here for the Mourvèdre. It's hard to even reach 10° ripeness with it by 20 October. With the Syrah I have to destalk because there is a slightly woody side to it right here if I don't. Having the vines at this height means that I harvest later than most – in some years I'll still be doing it in early November – but remember that our nights are fresh, and I prefer to use nature to cool the vats during fermentation than anything more violent in the cellars. Being up here we avoid the morning mists that they get down on the plain – it's the same for Yves Nativelle at Coyeux.'

M. de Menthon makes red and rosé Beaumes-de-Venise Villages and red Gigondas from 4 hectares of vines near Amadieu's Romane Machotte holding – these are further high-altitude plantations, at 350–400 metres. He stores all his red wine in concrete vats for between one and two years before bottling. Having tried wood in 1981, he found that its smell impinged on the wine. His reds are excellent: they hold an appealing dark cherry colour, are well scented and firm enough on the palate to be called measured rather than lively. Typically, in a good vintage with strong tannins like 1989 or 1983 the Beaumes red drinks well after about three or four years. In fruitier, softer-tannin years like 1985, 1988 and 1990, the wine shows well a little earlier. The rosé is made by the *saignée* method, is bottled early in the New Year, and is clean and fresh.

M. de Menthon has a relaxed, cool-as-you-like manner as he talks about his *domaine* and his work; this is no surprise since his only disturbances are birds singing from the pine and oak trees, insects humming in the sun, and once a day the poor postman grinding the engine of his Citroën as it crawls up the steep gradients. The tracks that run in the lee of the Dentelles are some of the great hidden corners of the southern Rhône Valley.

Down the tracks from the Château Redortier is an altogether more rustic affair, the Ferme St-Martin, which is owned by Guy Jullien. Their 18 hectares are planted with Grenache (70 per cent), with the difference made up of Syrah, Cinsault and Carignan. To age their red Côtes du Rhône *générique* and their Beaumes Villages red they use wood – old *demi-muids* – and some of the Beaumes is made by *macération carbonique*. The colour is a bright red rather than anything darker, and these are honest, local wines that just lack a bit of guts and depth.

Perhaps the most hidden of these several hard-to-find *domaines* is the Domaine de Cassan, owned by the Croset family and located near the hamlet of Lafare. They make firm-tasting reds that receive about eighteen months' ageing in cask; both the red Beaumes-de-Venise and the Gigondas are impressive to drink after four years or so.

Beaumes-de-Venise Vintages

It is more fashionable now for houses like Jaboulet and Vidal-Fleury to join the ex-Domaine des Bernardins, now Castaud-Maurin, in giving their wine a vintage. Domaine Durban also now do this. There are only marginal differences between one year and the next once the neutral alcohol has been incorporated, and the best guide is to select a favourite producer and roll with his chosen style of wine as the years go by.

As for how long to keep the wine once it has been opened, the Co-opérative gave up using corks in their Muscat bottles in 1970, and now their wine is distinguishable by its gold-coloured screw-cap. Not only has this proved cheaper, but it also allows for consumption over an extended period of time. The Co-opérative's estimate that a Muscat will remain in good order for a month after opening is somewhat optimistic, but there is no doubt that the wine will lose little of its bouquet and flavour until ten days after opening. For real *aficionados* of the Muscat de Beaumes this problem should never arise, but in exceptional circumstances it will prove beneficial to keep the bottle chilled once it has been opened.

Leading Growers at Beaumes-de-Venise

Domaine Castaud-Maurin	84190 Beaumes-de-Venise
Co-opérative Intercommunale des	
Vins et Muscats	84190 Beaumes-de-Venise
Croset, Paul	
Domaine de Cassan (no VDN)	84190 Lafare
Jullien, Guy (no VDN)	84190 Suzette
Leydier, Bernard	
Domain Durban	84190 Beaumes-de-Venise
de Menthon, Étienne	
Château Redortier (no VDN)	84190 Suzette
Nativelle, Yves	
Domaine de Coyeux	84190 Beaumes-de-Venise
Rey, Guy	
Domaine St-Sauveur	84190 Aubignan

11

Gigondas

─────────

Close to Mont Ventoux, and blending into the low hills underneath the startling, spiky Dentelles mountains, is Gigondas, the home of one of the southern Rhône's best, deepest red wines. A straggling village that forms a cul-de-sac with its little winding approach road, Gigondas rarely shows any signs of life; many of the houses that huddle underneath the ruined château are abandoned and decaying, while for much of the time the only sound in the tiny *place* is the slow trickle of water from the wall fountain; even the shop, the café, the *caveau de dégustation* look as if they are all installed for a film set rather than for real use. Wine communities in the Côtes du Rhône tend to be drowsy places, but Gigondas achieves a positive state of repose.

Although the vineyards extend all around the village, most of the wine cellars are on the strip of land between it and the River Ouvèze, 3 kilometres or so away to the west. Gigondas houses around thirty-five private *domaines* that bottle their own wine, as well as two large *négociant* companies (also vineyard owners at Gigondas) and a small but quality-conscious Cave Co-opérative. Its wines are also actively sold by northern Rhône organizations like Paul Jaboulet Aîne and Guigal, who buy direct from *viticulteurs*. Several of the *domaines* are built on the approximate sites of Roman villas, for in the first century AD a community of country residences was established at Gigondas by the veteran centurions of the Roman Second Legion, then head-quartered in Orange. Relics, like earthenware amphorae and an excellently preserved Bacchus head, have been found between the village and the river and indicate that the centurions were by no means teetotal. After all, the word 'Gigondas' stems from the Latin *jocunditas*, so 'merry city' obviously gained its name from the benevolent impact of its wine.

It is not known how widespread the Roman vineyards were, nor whether wine-growing continued uninterrupted into the ninth century, when the next historical records are found. By that time the vineyard pattern that had evolved was one common to most of France, with the Church in possession of many of the leading *domaines* and properties and busily seeing to their untrammelled cultivation. Thus, at Gigondas the nuns of the abbey of St-André, beside the River Ouvèze, grew mainly vines and olives for their living. With the arrival of the popes in Avignon in the fourteenth century, the superseded Bishops of Orange took to spending much of their time at St-André, where they could console themselves with the deep, heavy wine that is still made from the vines of the adjoining plateau. At the same time the Prince of Orange, in his guise as *seigneur* of Gigondas, was a substantial local vineyard owner, being credited with possessing at least sixty vineyard plots. So much did he own that he used to let out one of his foremost vineyards, the 'du Prince'. Consequently the vineyards were generally in few, but powerful, hands.

Records dating back to 1592 show that there was a small amount of well-esteemed white Gigondas then being made, but the red wine had more commercial value, and most of it was regularly sold outside the community – to the chagrin of the local inhabitants. During the seventeenth century quite frequent trading was conducted with the monks of the Montmajour abbey near Arles; surrounded as they were by the Camargue water-flats, the good monks found themselves in possession of plenty of rice but with no wine for their religious services. Since they held traditional ties with the abbey of St-André, there was no hesitation in selecting Gigondas as their *vin de messe*. Indeed, so well must they have appreciated the remnants of their Mass wine that by the eighteenth century the abbey of Montmajour is recorded as a vineyard proprietor at Gigondas; like the abbey of Aiguebelle, near Montélimar, this holding was forfeited during the French Revolution.

The château of Gigondas is thought to have been built in the early part of the seventeenth century, for it was around then that the Princes of Orange used it as one of their hunting lodges. The ruins visible today represent perhaps insufficient evidence, but one can well envisage the stately rooms harbouring rollicking banquets composed of steaming game dishes, all washed down by draughts of sturdy Gigondas.

Wine-making continued steadily, if unspectacularly, into the nineteenth century, when welcome momentum was injected into the thinking and outlook of the *vignerons* by Eugène Raspail, a member of a prominent French political family who owned an estate at Gigondas. Experimenting with sulphur treatments against the growing disease of oïdium, and performing massive replanting with superior vine strains, Raspail went a long way towards placing Gigondas further up the French wine hierarchy, as well as ensuring that it was exported to a number of overseas countries. Suitably encouraged, a few growers turned to bottling a part of their wine, and the family of Hilarion Roux of Domaine Les Pallières succeeded in winning a Gold Medal at the 1894 Paris Agricultural Fair.

Despite such progress, the general practice remained that of bulk-selling both grapes and wine. There are still *vignerons* who recall how, before the First World War, horse-drawn carts laden with grapes would leave the village for some of the stately private houses of Avignon. The grapes would be vinified in private cellars under the streets of Avignon and the wine kept for personal consumption.

Until the Second World War Gigondas was often employed as a booster wine, or *vin de médecine*. Just as Hermitage used to bolster Bordeaux in times gone by, so the shippers of Burgundy would come down to Gigondas shortly after the harvest and purchase individual vats according to their likely powers of propagation. In weak burgundy years the demand was obviously significant. Little advance in the wine community's fortunes was apparent, therefore, until the 1930s, when both Gigondas's main *négociant* companies, Amadieu and Meffre, were formed. Their presence naturally brought extra attention to the village and, significantly, helped to keep much of the local wine actually at Gigondas; formerly this wine would be sold as 'Côtes du Rhône' to merchants in Châteauneuf-du-Pape, Orange and Avignon, who showed little concern about acknowledging on their labels whether or not the wine was from Gigondas.

The only regular on-site bottlers of wine by the early 1950s were the House of Amadieu and the two private *domaines* of Edmond Chauvet of Domaine Le Péage and the Roux brothers at Domaine Les Pallières. Continuity at Le Péage is sadly not guaranteed into the 1990s, since M. Chauvet is well into his eighties and his son was tragically killed in a pot-holing accident in 1985.

With an admirably united front, the *vignerons* of Gigondas took measures to ensure that, once and for all, their wine received its due recognition. Thus all cultivation of the mass-producing, slightly harsh-tasting Carignan grape was forbidden in the search for a high-grade and well constituted red wine, and growers were made to exercise more vigilance in discarding unripe, unhealthy grapes at harvest-time. Patience and hard work were finally rewarded in 1971, when Gigondas received its own *appellation contrôlée*, and today it stands alongside Châteauneuf-du-Pape, Lirac and the recently promoted Vacqueyras as one of the southern Côtes du Rhône's four fully fledged red wine *appellations*.

As the above narrative illustrates, Gigondas is a wine that has won its colours the hard way, by dint of prolonged effort, and the growers themselves take great relish in recounting the history of the wine's promotion. One unhappy consequence of the wine's progress, however, has been the spoliation of some of the wild countryside that surrounds Gigondas. Growers have sought to maximize their advance and have bulldozed and reshaped parts of the terrain so that it is capable of, but not necessarily suitable for, the bearing of vines. This is particularly noticeable on some of the once tree-clad foothills around the Dentelles mountains, but in their quest for higher production, and consequently higher income, one or two *vignerons* seem to have thrown aside all the fundamental rules of wine-making. Cold, shaded vines can be seen clustered in the lee of the Dentelles, receiving at best about four hours' sunshine a day. Such grapes that will eventually make a bottle of Gigondas will do nothing to enhance the *appellation*'s good name.

One of Gigondas's main characteristics is its overt, very winy headiness, an element which derives in part from the preponderance of Grenache in it, and in part from the siting of the vines, which grow mainly on slopes whose gradients vary sharply. The steepest hillsides are tucked against the Dentelles, and vines are cultivated very high up them – as high as 565 metres – on rich, yellowish clay. This soil is perhaps a little lush for the Grenache vine, which traditionally likes very spartan ground, but defenders of the high-level planting point to the total absence of rot (*pourriture*) on their vines. If it snows in winter, for example, these high vines are the ones that are affected; their eventual blossoming is retarded, and they remain behind the other vines right up until the *vendanges*. This is no bad thing, say the growers, because their lower sugar content helps to balance out the high alcoholic content of the wine – one of the criticisms sometimes levelled against Gigondas.

Lower down, at about 300 metres, the medium slopes are probably the most suitable for the vines. On a less clayey, stonier ground, which retains all moisture very well, the Grenache is in its element, along with the other permitted vines: the Syrah, the Cinsault, the Mourvèdre and the Clairette.

Since the mid-1970s the *vignerons* have twice changed the permitted percentages in their attempts to foster the good name of Gigondas, and just before the 1986 harvest the traditionalists' view re-established itself. By this ruling the maximum Grenache Noir permitted was raised back from 65 per cent to 80 per cent; the Syrah and the Mourvèdre together or separately can constitute 15 per cent minimum, and the other grapes – the Cinsault and the Clairette – are allowed to the tune of 5 per cent maximum. 'Above all, we wanted to reduce the Cinsault, which produces a lot of wine with little degree and which therefore added little to the true Gigondas style. This style revolves around the Grenache, which we therefore all agreed to increase to its former level,' stated M. Roger Meffre. Growers were given three years to reduce their Cinsault, and in the replanting, most opted for the Syrah, which is less disease-prone than the Mourvèdre and which in these parts gives more fruit after the age of about thirty than the Mourvèdre.

It is from the middle slope areas that Gigondas is said to draw its finesse and guiding middle structure, while the partly sandy, partly stony plain around the River Ouvèze is supposed to supply the wine's typical robustness and earthiness. There are, however, no specially named growths or *climats*, and the wine is always sold simply as 'Gigondas', followed by the name of the grower's *domaine*.

Any variations in the style of wine from one *domaine* to the next most often occur through differing cellar treatment or from the fact that a *domaine* has all its vineyards grouped on the plain or middle slopes, for example. Come harvest-time at the start of October, the village wakes fitfully from its habitual somnolence, as temporary *vendangeurs* crowd into the only bar and walk about the tiny streets and alleys. Some of them are students; many are North Africans, who cross the Mediterranean to join their friends working full-time in France.

In the vineyards the growers brief their *vendangeurs* to carry out a sorting, or *triage*, of the grapes as they go along. This is absolutely paramount in difficult years like 1987 and 1991 when the weather has been rainy at many of the wrong moments and rot is fairly widespread in the vineyards. Anything rotten – generally between 3 and 5 per cent of the crop, but rising to at least 10 per cent if the year is bad and the grower conscientious – is to be discarded: such grapes are either used to make a very ordinary table wine known as *rapé* or are left on the vines for the benefit of the local bird population. *Triages* are effective only if the grower himself is on hand to supervise; otherwise the back-weary harvesters are not inclined to stop and scrutinize what is going into their buckets.

As the area under vines has more than tripled in the last fifty years – to the present 1,180 hectares, with a further 120 hectares holding vines for future production – harvesting lasts over the course of an extended three weeks. Again, it is noticeable that attitudes towards the treatment of the grapes before fermentation have changed since the early 1970s, and more *domaines* are now only lightly crushing their grapes, if at all. The excellent Domaine St-Gayan, for instance, used deliberately to put half their grapes uncrushed into the fermenting vats, seeking, as M. Roger Meffre would say, 'to bring softness and aromas to our wine'. The Meffres now have an automated pump rather than a purely manual system, but it is set to allow a very light crush on half the crop, with 40–50 per cent still entering untouched. The Cave Co-opérative fills its vats half with uncrushed grapes that haven't been destalked and half with extremely lightly touched grapes that have been destalked. They, too, are able to control the crush pressure on the harvest more accurately than in the past due to updating their pumping machine. Overall, only a few *domaines* like Raspail-Ay undertake destalking.

Some growers, like the Cave Co-opérative, then mix their different grape varieties in the crushing pump before filling the fermenting vats; others, mindful of the fact that the Grenache and Mourvèdre grapes reach maturity at different times, ferment the different grape varieties in separate vats and assemble them only the following spring. The difference between the two types of wine is very hard to discern.

Gigondas has such a long viticultural history that not all the fermenting vats are made of the usual concrete or enamel. Some of the older *domaines* have stone vats built into the rock walls, and the Domaine de St-Cosme is still using some seventeenth-century vats that were burrowed into the rock below ground-level.

After the grapes have fermented for one or two weeks, the wine is racked off and left to develop its malolactic fermentation. The following spring it is generally put to mature in cask; the *vignerons* adhere to a local saying that when the first flowers appear on the vines, it is time to transfer the wine to the barrel. In the past, ageing in cask has lasted for about two years, or even longer in the case of the most traditionally minded *vignerons*, but a reassessment of technique has occurred since the mid-1970s, so that several *domaines* are now ageing for only a matter of months in cask, and some by-pass wood altogether, seeking a fresher style. Among those who have reduced their ageing in cask figure some of the very best *domaines* in the *appellation* – notably St-Gayan and Les Goubert: St-Gayan age for ten to fourteen months and Les Goubert for six months, part in new oak, part in older oak and part in concrete. The wines of both *domaines* carry greater elegance than the really rumbustious old-style Gigondas.

New oak has made a limited entrance at Gigondas, and while not especially favoured by a grower like Roger Meffre, it is used in some special *cuvées* by very good producers like Gilbert Peysson and his daughter Véronique at the Domaine de Font-Sane, by Jean-Pierre Cartier (Cuvée Florence), Daniel Brusset, Edmond Gras at Domaine Santa-Duc and the Cave Co-opérative, for example. There is a more cautious attitude towards its use than at Châteauneuf-du-Pape, with some growers concerned about its influence in drying out their wines.

Meanwhile, traditionalists like Raymond and Guy Boutière of the Domaine du Pesquier and the Domaine Les Pallières continue with an extended ageing in old casks, the former over twelve to eighteen months and the latter ranging from two to two and a half years in their large *foudres*. Occasionally Pierre Roux will bottle a backward vintage like the 1981 over four years after the harvest, three years of which have been spent in cask. Although the Pallières wine lightened and softened a little in character during the 1980s, Pierre Roux remains a leading exponent of front-rank gutsy Gigondas, one that expresses the power and appeal of the Grenache.

Once bottled, Gigondas needs a further two or three years to develop a true harmony between its bouquet and its strong flavour. Always a wine of great depth of colour, it can startle the uninitiated with its near-black inkiness and its surging bouquet. The aromas of the bouquet are hard to define, for there goes with the raspberry or blackberry fruitiness a certain elusive, earthy scent not unlike fresh black truffles; perhaps the smell of a forest after an autumnal rainstorm would be a pleasantly poetic way of putting it.

The French call this sensation a *goût de terroir*, and its force on the bouquet continues on to the palate, sometimes bringing with it, in addition, a little intriguing spiciness. A typical Gigondas has great profundity of flavour but not always the well-formed richness to make it a balanced wine; perhaps this rather discordant aggression is one of its main charms, for refinement and sophistication would appear to be uneasy parties to most bottles of Gigondas. All in all, it is often one of France's biggest wines, never to be idly quaffed, and one that demands conscious effort on the part of the drinker. Bright summer days are not for Gigondas; its required companions are the fireside of winter and the glow of a hot dish of game.

As if in recognition of this, the late 1980s saw the emergence of some very well made, more elegant styles of Gigondas. These are wines which contain less Grenache than the typical offerings, and which seek to project a clean but well founded fruitiness on the palate. It is noticeable that this is the style favoured by merchants like Guigal and Paul Jaboulet Aîné, for whom Gigondas is one of a number of red wines offered from the southern Rhône. These are more rounded, more succulent and hold smoother tannins, and can be drunk earlier than the typical, initially more rasping Gigondas reds. As cellar techniques and vineyard care continue to tighten up, more of these fresher, sleeker and very successful wines will emerge from the younger growers. It is to be hoped that the pursuit of greater sophistication and 'breeding' will not result in a severe diminution of local character for these more modern wines.

Inevitably, during the health-and-fitness-obsessed 1980s, some producers went to extremes and attempted to make a lighter, innocuous Gigondas ready for early drinking. The Cave Co-opérative's Cuvée du Président – a robust, hearty wine in 1983 – became made 100 per cent by the *macération carbonique* process, which is also used in the making of the Château du Trignon red. The latter wine especially is clean and very correctly made, but one feels that the *vignerons*' undoubted talents would have been more properly exercised in attempting to make a more complex, multi-faceted wine typical of its *appellation*. In this context the decision of the growers as a whole to increase the permitted level of Grenache Noir in the wine from 65 per cent up to 80 per cent is welcome: it is a conscious measure to preserve the central character of Gigondas and to prevent it from slipping towards becoming just another banal southern wine.

Gigondas is not a *vin de garde* in the style of the northern Côtes du Rhône Syrah wines – the heavy percentage of Grenache precludes that – but the best vintages should live for between twelve and fifteen years. Older vintages drunk at a retrospective round-up in 1986, for example, included a 1976 Grappillon d'Or from Bernard Chauvet – brick-red and drying out fast – a 1975 Pesquier from Boutière that was well softened, still nicely ruby-coloured and only a tiny bit dry on the finish, a 1974 Romane Machotte from Amadieu that was burnt and dried-out, a 1974 St-Gayan from Roger Meffre – attractive prune bouquet, middle-weight wine but drying acids on the finish – and the wine that proves the rule, a 1973 Pallières from Hilarion Roux that, despite a brick-orange colour, bore a lovely delicate flavour on the palate that had softened but not lost its southern roundness. A 1967 Pallières was markedly old, and struggling to ward off the advance of the dried flavours of prune, toast, resin and tea that signalled its loss of grip.

The ideal ages to drink Gigondas are generally between five and twelve years, when the wine will be mellow but certainly not tame. It is often compared with its southern neighbour, Châteauneuf-du-Pape, but does not attain the other wine's complexity, particularly on the bouquet, or its comparative finesse: Gigondas carries more of a kick and often betrays its alcohol more.

Around 4 per cent of the harvest is made into rosé, which also carries full *appellation* status. A tiny amount of white wine appears, although since 1971 it has not had the right to its own full-fledged Gigondas *appellation* status, and is sold as 'Côtes du Rhône'. As elsewhere in the region, the white *cépages* are led by the Grenache Blanc, the Bourboulenc and the Clairette.Quality control has been exercised by forbidding more than 5–10 per cent of Ugni Blanc, while the Picpoul and the northern *cépages* of Marsanne, Roussanne and Viognier are also permitted. Only four or five growers make the white, led by Amadieu, Roger Meffre and the Cave Co-opérative.

Historically the white has held a marked tendency to oxidize after about three years, and it has also been very heady, with a pronounced high alcohol content. Amadieu are making attempts to upgrade the quality of the wine by conducting a low-temperature fermentation at around 18°C; this is bottled in the spring following the harvest, and is described by Jean-Pierre Amadieu as 'quite a fragile wine, one to drink before its second birthday'. White wine made at Gigondas really remains a novelty.

The rosé holds full Gigondas *appellation* status, but is rarely found far beyond the region. Like the red, it can contain a maximum 80 per cent Grenache, and 15 per cent of one or other or both of the Syrah and the Mourvèdre, but as it is intended to be a lighter, fresher wine, there is a maximum of 15 per cent Cinsault allowed. Despite these measures the rosé is still a potent wine, too potent really, with a degree of alcohol that can go towards 14°. Not all the *domaines* make a rosé, and there is no doubt that Gigondas is best appreciated when it is red.

The village's largest vineyard-owning family is that of the late Gabriel Meffre. His three children, Jacques, Christian and Sylvette, each own one-third of their late father's 900 hectares of vines spread around the southern Rhône, which had made them the largest owners of *appellation contrôlée* vines in France. Gabriel Meffre was one of the pioneers of furthering the prosperity of Gigondas and putting the name on a more international map. Pierre Amadieu, whose family business has just entered its third generation with the entry of grandson Pierre, and Gabriel Meffre owned the largest businesses at Gigondas during the 1950s onwards. Indeed, Gabriel Meffre's story is one of the great viticultural tales. Today Jacques and Christian have sold their one-third shares of his business, but it is worth recalling how this vast enterprise was built up.

M. Gabriel Meffre himself was a native of Séguret, the neighbouring village, while his wife was born in Gigondas. The son of a modest viticultural family, he shrewdly recognized the southern Côtes du Rhône as a region that, although little-known, was full of potential for the grower who was prepared to expand. In 1930 he bought the Gigondas Domaine de Daysse, and 20 hectares of vines, and by 1936 had become a *négociant* in his desire to market as much wine as possible. M. Meffre then found his progress slowing down, but the stagnation of the war years soon disappeared, and in 1946 southern France suddenly found itself encumbered with masses of surplus army material, mostly American, for which the resale market was, not surprisingly, very small. Seizing his opportunity, M. Meffre stepped in and bought up a whole fleet of bulldozers, earth-shovellers and heavy-duty vehicles, with the idea of using them to carry out vast new vineyard plantations. His capital outlay was, of course, small, and in the same year he transformed the Domaine St-Jean vineyards, near Travaillan. Situated on the huge, windswept Plan de Dieu flatland that extends away west from Gigondas, this *domaine* had been abandoned after the German occupation, and its nearly

40-hectare vineyard had fallen into a wretched condition. Meffre set to work with his machinery to such effect that today the house is more a veritable château and there are nearly 200 hectares of long rows of well-kept vines. Since 1982 training of the vines along wires started to replace the old Gobelet method; now less than 80 per cent of the vineyard is made up of the traditional Grenache, under 5 per cent is split between Cinsault and Carignan, and around 10 per cent is composed of more recently planted Syrah. The benefit of the wire training is that it is considered to produce better aeration and exposure and hence ripeness of fruit. Four hectares of Bourboulenc and 1 hectare of Clairette planted in 1986 were also destined to produce an aromatic white fermented at low temperature.

Meffre's ex-army machinery was largely the reason for his rapid success: whenever he bought *domaines* that had mostly slope vines, he was able to enlarge them by bulldozing any obstructive hills into a favourable south-facing position, and where *domaines* were on flat ground, it was again no problem to bulldoze away the scrub and few trees capable of co-existing with the vine on such poor terrain. Expansion therefore knew no bounds, particularly on the already mentioned Plan de Dieu, where between them the family own six *domaines* and around 500 hectares of vines.

During the 1980s the Meffre company tried to raise the quality of their business, cutting down on the bulk or *vrac* side of their trade. However, sales of wine in bottle from the Meffre vineyards – around 2.5 million bottles or half capacity – are still only one-eighth of their total wine sales around the world. Meffre remain easily the largest distributors of Côtes du Rhône wines, and many people's first experience of them will have come in the form of a correct, middle-range product with no particular defects, but with no particular star qualities or sharply defined character either. Most notable in their higher range are generally the Gigondas Domaines des Bosquets and La Chapelle, and until the late 1980s, the Châteauneuf-du-Pape, Château de Vaudieu; this is now run separately by M. Meffre's daughter Sylvette Brechet, and its quality has continued to rise. The company also makes the widely marketed Gigondas Baumanière from their vineyards at the Château Raspail in Gigondas: this is a concession granted by the famous three-star restaurant at Les Baux.

Opposite Meffre is the village's other *négociant* company, Pierre Amadieu, which is smaller and older. M. Amadieu was the first grower to follow the example of Hilarion Roux and bottle a good part of his wine. Since the firm's foundation in the 1920s he has thus been able to build up a strong network of sales to restaurants all over France, and this is one of the main sides of his business.

The Amadieu family own two *domaines* at Gigondas, La Machotte and Le Romane, whose 80-hectare vineyards are advantageously sited on the slopes of the narrow valley that runs between Sablet and Gigondas.

M. Amadieu's son, Jean-Pierre, an enthusiastic man who specializes in the vinification of their wines, explained that their vineyards are among the more highly placed at Gigondas, varying between 300 and 500 metres and situated in generally clay–limestone soil. To get the vineyard going when it was replanted in the early 1970s, the Amadieus used a flock of about 1,000 sheep which would be brought down from the mountains to Gigondas in the summertime. 'Their droppings were excellent for the vines and also seemed to help thwart bad attacks of rot. We did have to corral them in, however, as otherwise they would wander far away and we used to have trouble finding their offerings!' commented M. Amadieu.

M. Amadieu also makes a respectable Côtes du Rhône and Côtes du Ventoux, the latter from his nearly 60-hectare vineyard near Mazan and beside Crestet. The most special treatment is reserved for his very good, robustly styled Gigondas. This is aged for between one and two years in old oak *foudres* of 32-hectolitre capacity, and each vintage is bottled in two to three lots. M. Amadieu is not likely to leap into new-oak experiments with his wine: he feels that such a process could harden it more than is desirable. Indeed, one of the few growers systematically ageing Gigondas in new-oak Burgundy casks over about six months is the talented M. Daniel Brusset from Cairanne, who exploits a 14-hectare holding at Gigondas.

The Meffres and the Amadieu family are Gigondas's largest landowners; generally, the *appellation*'s other *domaines* are much smaller and much older. One of the most interesting is the Domaine St-Cosme. Its present owner, M. Henri Barruol, is a small energetic and entertaining character, who stumbled into being a *vigneron* through marriage – and has no regrets at all in either department: 'I used to be a full-time wood carver,' he explained, 'and after marrying and moving to Gigondas, I learned a lot about wine from an old schoolfriend who is a local oenologist. That was nearly thirty years ago, and now, with the benefit of hindsight, I'm really glad I kept up wine-making at St-Cosme.' Having bottled his wine at St-Cosme during the 1970s, M. Barruol then preferred to sell it when young to a merchant in Châteauneuf-du-Pape. His son entered the family business in the early 1990s and is keen to revert to *domaine* bottling and a sharpening-up of quality.

It is just possible that M. Barruol has in his possession some of the oldest fermenting vats in France. When he was enlarging his cellar thirty years ago he unearthed some small vats of some 1,000- and 4,500-litre capacity that had been carefully built into the soft stone walls of the cellar. These had been put one on top of the other in staircase fashion, on four levels, with a top-to-bottom height difference of 5 metres. The system operated with great logic, and racking of the wine would be performed by simply letting it run down little communal channels to the next lowest vat. About 1 metre up the walls of each vat the stone wall is inset to accommodate the wooden planks which would be used to prevent the must from overflowing during the primary fermentation. With this restraining barrier over the vats, all *remontage*, which today is carried out with pumps, would be encouraged quite naturally. The fermenting wine would push upwards, unsuccessfully, and so churn itself over.

Unfortunately, M. Barruol is unable to indicate the precise age of these vats: 'I have had experts here, and they are all undecided – or unprepared to commit themselves. The vats definitely date from at least the eleventh century, but since the *domaine* is on the site of an old Gallo-Roman villa, it is very possible that they are much older still. After all, the Romans made plenty of wine here at Gigondas.'

Another *domaine* whose cellars are close under the village is the Domaine de Longue-Toque, run by Serge Chapalain. For readers of Tintin, M. Chapalain is similar in appearance to the Professor, but before the libel writs are issued, it must be emphasized that he is a lot more practical and a lot more active than the Professor.

M. Chapalain took over the *domaine* from his father in the early 1980s. M. Roger Chapalain, who died in 1986, used to be the Mayor of Gigondas; he was one of those people whose late arrival into wine-making gives them precious extra objectivity and resource with which to approach the problems.

As a full-time army officer until 1962, M. Chapalain *père* had encountered some singular wines while travelling the world. A jovial, jolly man, he used to cite the wine made in the Central African republic of Chad by the missionaries for their church services: 'I don't know whether it was due to divine inspiration or what, but they somehow managed to come up with two crops of grapes every year!'

The *domaine*'s vineyard covers 23 hectares, planted with 65 per cent Grenache, 20 per cent Cinsault, 10 per cent Syrah and 5 per cent mixed between Mourvèdre and Clairette. Serge has cut back on the proportion of the crop entering the fermenting vats uncrushed, from around two-thirds to one-quarter. Sometimes a vat is mixed, with uncrushed harvest underneath a top half which has been crushed. Having tried in his father's day to produce a wine that was less hard and more supple than customary Gigondas, Serge is now gently trying to put a little more weight back into the Longue-Toque wine.

He uses his ageing casks discreetly, not wanting the wine to be over-exposed to this external source; after a stay of just under a year on average for a part of his total crop, he bottles the red wine and it joins a stock that during the 1980s he consciously tried to develop. The intention is to have three or four vintages on sale at any one time.

The Longue-Toque wine is never fined or filtered when sold in France, although it is filtered for export. It is capable of being among the best at Gigondas, but there are some vintages when it rather loses its way: the 1984, for instance, was a bland, accessible and drinkable wine with no real stamp of character on it, while the 1981 was a dull wine lacking in the splendour and depth shown vividly by the 1980. In 1983 a small crop and a lack of Grenache resulted in a solid, brightly coloured and concentrated wine. But the 1985 and 1986 came in the form of sound, 'safe' wines which lacked the Gigondas concentration and firmness of stamp. The style sought here is elegant, so do not expect the firepower that is this *appellation*'s hallmark.

One of the leading and most typical of the traditional wines of Gigondas comes from the 25-hectare Domaine Les Pallières, owned by the family of Hilarion Roux and run on his own by Pierre Roux. The *domaine* is tucked away in the north of the *appellation*, on the way towards Sablet, and on a hot summer's day is enveloped in a stillness and a mantle of sweet Provençal aromas that make the visitor feel he is entering an enchanted garden. Warm briar scents drift and hang in the air, the vine-leaves stir with torpid ripples, and much the busiest members of the community are the cicadas with their vital chirping.

It is not difficult to understand why Pierre and his late brother Christian have over the years been almost as retiring as their vines hidden away here at over 200 metres. Pierre will come down to the plain for an important local wine fair, but he is not happy in the public eye and retains a quiet diffidence despite his *domaine*'s well-travelled reputation.

He is convinced that Pallières should remain faithful to its custom of presenting well-aged, ruby-coloured wines which, by the time they are released for sale, have completed a considerable part of their evolution. The last of the four bottlings of the 1981 vintage was done in March 1986, for instance, while the dense 1978 was not generally released until the spring of 1982.

Three-quarters of the *domaine*'s wine is bottled, but as with the 1985 harvest, when there was a slight lack of acidity, it may remain a year in concrete vats before entering the wood. The style is well marked by the Grenache, which forms 65 per cent of the *cuvée*, providing it is not knocked by poor fruit setting, as occurred in 1983: in that year the Grenache content was reduced to 50 per cent, with Mourvèdre 15 per cent, Cinsault 5 per cent and Syrah up from its usual 15 per cent to 25 per cent.

The colour of many of the Pallières wines is therefore plum rather than cherry, matt rather than lustrous. When the wine is five or six years old it starts to reveal a beguiling spicy fruitiness. Memories of peeping into Father's box of Havana cigars come back when considering the bouquet, and the wine's overall strength of flavour and persistence of plum-like or prune aftertaste make it the ideal accompaniment for roasted red meat, powerful cheese like Roquefort or Stilton, and all kinds of game, notably the local speciality, *marcassin* (young wild boar), or hare. Pallières wines made after the 1980 vintage have lightened up a little, and are unlikely to blossom and run much past their twelfth or fifteenth year. But the depth of extract in an awkward vintage like 1986 is still greater than many other southern Grenache wines.

Accompanying the Domaines of Pallières, Raspail-Ay and Les Goubert in the top four at Gigondas is Roger Meffre's consistently excellent Domaine St-Gayan. In 1991 M. Meffre *père* took something of a retirement, his son, the capable Jean-Pierre running the *domaine*, with his father on hand if needs be: it is hard to keep down an enthusiast! Their 14—hectare Gigondas vineyard stands on the plain of clayey soil topped with broken chalkstone on the way to Sablet. The *mistral* wind regularly comes flying down the plain to pummel their vines, among which those that are Syrah can be identified by their training along lengths of wire, as is stipulated in the *appellation* rules at both Gigondas and Châteauneuf-du-Pape. This method is called 'Royat', being an ordinary Gobelet pruning with the wire led through the sturdy vine shoots, and helps to channel the extra abundant vegetation that the Syrah always carries.

Although they follow the *appellation* rules about how much Grenache and Syrah should be used in making their red and rosé Gigondas, the Meffres do not seem entirely convinced that the southern Rhône is the optimum home for the Syrah. As Jean-Pierre, a lanky, friendly young man in his early thirties, commented: 'There is a certain controversy going on about the suitability of the Syrah down here in the Vaucluse *département*, because the Syrah isn't all that easy to vinify well. If fermentation isn't just right, the wine can acquire a nasty taste that we call – no disrespect to your country – a *goût de pommes anglaises*. Why we should call it English apples, I don't know, but it is rather the same taste that you find if you leave the wine too long on its lees, and is especially noticeable on the bouquet.'

The Meffre family has been at this property since 1400, and Roger recalled that the style of wine made by his father was tougher and longer-lived than the wine he is now making. 'Equally, twenty-five years ago there was no Syrah on the *domaine*, and now the proportion is up to nearly 20 per cent.' At this point Jean-Pierre added that the problem with the Mourvèdre was that it was more prone to illness than the Syrah – oïdium, for example – which was why they had planted it more at their Rasteau Côtes du Rhône Villages vineyard, where it could upgrade that wine with greater impact than their Gigondas. 'The Mourvèdre also suffers from something called *l'esca*, a fungus that instals itself inside the vine wood and eats it away inside; the vine's circulation is prevented and the plant dies within two to three years.'

To raise their wines, MM. Meffre *père* and *fils* are not supporters of new oak. They choose to give them between eight and fourteen months, varying with the vintage, in *demi-muids* of about 600 litres which have been in their possession for several years. During its *élevage*, the wine spends around two years in concrete vats, so that at least three years have passed before bottling. The Meffres make one of the finest, classiest Gigondas reds, since they successfully fuse a well-rounded power with a balance and discretion of flavour that make it quietly very impressive. In boxing parlance, this is the sort of wine competing in the higher weights, but holding the skilled footwork and strength of a young Muhammed Ali. There is always a lot of depth in the wine – even in tricky years like 1986 and 1987, the Meffres provided wines with substance and a thoroughness of taste; their discipline in discarding unwanted fruit is severe, and this transfers straight away into the quality of their wines.

The St-Gayan red carries with it an interesting complexity of tannin, acidity and strong fruit flavours. Roger Meffre finds the scent of truffles in his wine, while to others it is blackcurrants, with, before the wine is six or seven years old, a deep tannin firmly locked in. The family were very pleased with their 1986, which holds appealing ripeness and richness that are slowly showing themselves after five years. There are a succulence and depth in the wine, greater complexity than the 1985, and it will drink very well around 1992–8 or later. Given the late rot that attacked the grape harvest, this wine is very much a personal triumph for Jean-Pierre, who likens it to their excellent 1979 which itself was only slightly behind the superb 1978.

The skill of Roger and Jean-Pierre Meffre is indicated by their work in lesser years. Even in 1984 and 1987 they produced wines that were profound, given the conditions. The 1987 holds spice flavours and tannins on the palate, even though the colour is pale; this is typically a finer form of Gigondas, suitable for a lamb dish, for example, and one that will provide enjoyment towards 1994 or 1995: it won't be worth hanging on to, since its greatest appeal will come while it is still holding tightly together. Top vintages from this *domaine*, which also include a firm, upright 1988 and a ripe, densely fruited and very thorough 1989, as well as very successful and stylish 1983 and 1985, can easily live for twelve or fourteen years. The St-Gayan wines are neither fined nor filtered.

One of the other leading *domaines* at Gigondas is very small, with only 7.5 hectares of Gigondas vineyards, although the Cartier family also own a similarly sized vineyard running over the Sablet and Beaumes-de-Venise *appellations*. The property is run by Jean-Pierre Cartier – not surprisingly, since the smiling-eyed M. Cartier *père* admits to something over eighty. 'We had about 99 per cent Grenache until 1973,' stated Jean-Pierre Cartier, who in a short time has imposed his stamp on the *appellation* as an innovator and restless spirit. 'Of the traditional vines round here, I think excessive prejudice worked against some of them. Take the Aramon, which along with the Alicante and Carignan was regarded pretty poorly. Well, we had some Aramon high up the hillside whose yield was only around 30 hectos; but it gave very good wine, with a strong colour and ageing possibilities.'

The Goubert vineyard now contains around 65 per cent Grenache, with 25 per cent Syrah and around 5 per cent mixed between Cinsault and Mourvèdre. M. Cartier started to bottle his wine with the 1973 crop, it having been sold to *négociants* before then. M. Cartier also makes a firmly flavoured red Beaumes-de-Venise and a dark spicy red Sablet, both Côtes du Rhône Villages, primarily from Grenache and Syrah in the proportion of two-thirds to one-third, as well as an interesting Côtes du Rhône *blanc* from the three northern varieties, Roussanne, Marsanne and Viognier, which are fermented at 18–20°C.

M. Cartier has a lively sense of humour – he describes a *cuvée* of red which is being tasted as 99 per cent Grenache, the 1 per cent missing being because they may not have rinsed the vat to perfection. His wines are all well made and well worked – he likes to explore possibilities, but has the skill to extract dense and authentic wine, whatever challenge he sets himself. Before 1985 the family's red Gigondas received a brief ageing in old oak *demi-muids*, and the Cuvée Spéciale spent a mere six months more in wood. Now he works with a limited amount of new oak, notably in his Cuvée Florence; this runs with tannin and solid flavours that merge well with the distinctive new-oak imposition. M. Cartier is opposed to fining and filtering, and it is worth looking out for wines like his 1990, 1989, 1985, 1983 and 1981, which contain a firm but polished extract of rich flavours, a definite Gigondas style with a little extra finesse in them.

The very smallest landowners at Gigondas are represented by the Cave Co-opérative, which after some years of uneven quality and consistency is once again making wines that rank among the best from any Rhône Co-opérative. It has an average yearly production of 15,000 hectolitres of all wine, of which 8,000 hectolitres are Gigondas. One hundred and ten members contribute their harvests, an increase on the numbers in the late 1970s.

The reception of the grapes has developed from the normal pump crusher to a pallet crusher, which is gentler with the harvest and allows most of the grapes to enter the fermenting vats almost unbroken. About half the crop is destalked, with the different grape varieties mixed prior to fermentation. The Co-opérative, run now by the enthusiastic M. Jean-Pierre Palon, also produces a 100 per cent *macération carbonique* wine, the Cuvée du Président, as well as a heady, robust Gigondas rosé, which forms 6 per cent of the Gigondas production.

The 1983 vintage was less successful than the quality of the harvest deserved, and it was from the 1985 harvest onwards that the Co-opérative started once more to show some form. The Tête de Cuvée receives fifteen to eighteen months in wood, some of which is new and some of which is in the form of 600-litre casks, and, as a wine founded on 80 per cent Grenache, is punchy and substantial when young. This is certainly more interesting than the *macération carbonique* wine, which is highly one-dimensional in taste: clean enough grape fruit, but obtainable at half the price elsewhere in France. The Co-opérative also makes a respectable white Côtes du Rhône from the Clairette and Grenache Blanc grapes: these are vinified at low temperature, the wine is bottled young and should be drunk before its third birthday. Standards are generally on the rise again here, which is good news. Respectable Gigondas red is now also made by the neighbouring Caves Co-opératives of Sablet and Vacqueyras.

OTHER LEADING DOMAINES

CHÂTEAU DE MONTMIRAIL

This 30-hectare *domaine* is run by Maurice Archimbaud, the Mayor of Vacqueyras, and his son-in-law Jacques Bouteiller. The vineyards are in one grouping, at an altitude of 170–230 metres around the Château de Montmirail, which lies to the east of the village of Vacqueyras.

The vineyard is made up of 65 per cent Grenache, 15 per cent Syrah, and 10 per cent mixed between Mourvèdre and Cinsault, the proportion of the latter having been decreased to conform to the maximum 5 per cent legislation. The vines grow in the clay–limestone soil typical of the Dentelles de Montmirail. The area is criss-crossed by small streams, and the rich clay subsoil generally therefore retains its humidity in even the driest summers.

Up until the First World War Montmirail was a big thermal station, and the wines are now vinified in the old spa establishments where once water would be bottled. A maximum of 15 per cent of the harvest is destalked, and fermentation occurs in concrete vats for around ten days. The wine is then passed into enamel-lined vats of around 50- or 100-hectolitre capacity for a year, and the preparation is topped up with a brief six-month stay in cask.

The first bottling of Montmirail Gigondas in a lighter year like 1984 or 1987 received no cask-ageing; the second bottling received six months. M. Bouteiller is thereby consciously launching his wine at different palates so as to satisfy both those who like the effect of wood and those who prefer a more purely fruity wine.

The Montmirail wines are very consistent, demonstrating the ability of the family *vignerons*. The style is often an accurate reflection of the year: for instance, the 1984 was a supple wine, with a middling colour but a good, spicy bouquet and agreeable fruit on the palate. The 1985 and 1989 held good fruit – the latter a richer wine – while the 1988, 1986 and 1983 are firmer wines, possessing a stern, plum-flavoured fruitiness when young, and a chewiness at the end of the palate typical of *domaines* making solid but elegant wines. The Montmirail Cuvée de Beauchamp drinks well from the age of three in light vintages and from the age of five in the stronger years. They are not wines for long keeping. The *domaine* also makes a good red Vacqueyras from its 20-hectare vineyard nearby.

Archimbaud, Maurice et
   Bouteiller, Jacques
   Château de Montmirail   84190 Gigondas

DOMAINE DE FONT-SANE

A 14-hectare vineyard with a growing reputation, Domaine de Font-Sane is run by Gilbert Peysson and his daughter Véronique. They make a firm style of Gigondas, with a regular depth of tannin in it that suggests a life of over ten years. The 1986 was a well-worked vintage, with some finesse on the palate but enough final heat to keep it running into the mid-1990s. The 1988 held a deep colour, and showed spicy aromas on the bouquet at an early stage. Although it finishes a little toughly, it has good length and promise for the future. The 1989 was a plumper wine with great appeal – darkly coloured, it has a richness and intensity of flavour that suggest very good drinking after six years or so.

Peysson, Gilbert et Fille
    Domaine de Font-Sane   84190 Gigondas

DOMAINE DU GOUR DE CHAULE

An enterprising *domaine* run by Mme Beaumet and Mme Bonfils, the latter the daughter of an *agriculteur* who left her work at a temporary employment agency in Carpentras in 1985 to return to the land. The mother-and-daughter combination make their wine with the help of an *œnologue* from Gigondas.

The 10-hectare property is planted with 80 per cent Grenache, 10 per cent Syrah and 10 per cent mixed between Cinsault and Mourvèdre; the soil is predominantly clay–limestone. The ladies have a cooling machine which in the early 1980s helped their fermentations to avoid the blatant jamminess that affected some wines in the southern Rhône. The wine receives fourteen to eighteen months' ageing in old oak prior to bottling.

The wine is middle-weight, with a generally sound colour that has just a touch of black in it; the strong presence of the Grenache is noticeable, marked by some hot, spicy flavours on the palate. In the strong vintages like 1981, 1983, 1985 and 1989 these wines need at least six or seven years to soften and develop more expansive aromas and flavours than are shown in their guarded youth.

Mesdames Beaumet-Bonfils
    Domaine du Gour de Chaule   84190 Gigondas

DOMAINE DU GRAPPILLON D'OR

Bernard Chauvet and his son Paul cultivate fifteen different plots on the middle plain below the village. Their 15 hectares are planted with 80 per cent Grenache, 15 per cent Syrah and 5 per cent mixed between Cinsault and Mourvèdre. The traditional predominance of the Grenache did not occur in 1983 when *coulure* hit the Grenache and the fruit failed to develop. Accordingly the wine in this vintage and in 1984 was firmer in style than usual, carrying a darker colour. The harvest is never destalked and the wines receive one year in cask, with storage in enamel vats for another eighteen months before bottling. In vintages like 1986 and 1988, they are generally direct and full-blooded in the time-honoured way – suitable companions for robust winter stews or cuts of roast meat when the chill winds blow. They represent the middle-ground at Gigondas – straight-forward wines with a nice southern kick in them.

Chauvet, Bernard et Paul
   Domaine du Grappillon d'Or   84190 Gigondas

DOMAINE DU PESQUIER

Raymond and Guy Boutière's 15-hectare Gigondas vineyard is composed of 75 per cent Grenache, 15 per cent Syrah and 10 per cent mixed between Mourvèdre and Cinsault. In 1991 Raymond withdrew to a more backseat role, leaving his son Guy, a lean man with a brief mat of blond hair who has worked hard on the commercial side, to make a good, traditionally styled Gigondas that has above-average keeping powers.

The wine is fermented in concrete and aged in old wood for eighteen months to two years. It develops excellent rounded flavours and aromas of fruit and cedar if left for eight years or more: the 1983, 1985 and 1989 were very well balanced, and contained some solid tannins that have held the wine's evolution in check. They will both show well around 1992–5. Meanwhile, even in less notable vintages like 1984, 1982 and 1975, very supple and drinkable wines emerged after about six years.

More than 60 per cent of the Gigondas is bottled, and since the mid-1980s the *domaine* has exported mainly to Britain, Belgium and Germany. The Boutières also own 12 hectares of Côtes du Rhône vineyards, some of which are at Sablet. This is a sound *domaine* making good wines without any fuss or seeking-out of notoriety.

Boutière, Guy
   Domaine du Pesquier   84190 Gigondas

DOMAINE DE PIAUGIER

The 25-hectare Domaine de Piaugier is run by the Autran family, with the father, Marc, looking after their vineyards at Sablet and Gigondas and the son, Jean-Marc, running the vinification of their Côtes du Rhône red, their Sablet reds and their Gigondas red. The son is keen on marketing ruses, and puts his top-line Gigondas in a brown-coloured Piedmontese bottle. Made mainly from about 80 per cent Grenache and 15 per cent Mourvèdre, the Gigondas 1985, of which there were precisely 5,765 bottles and 50 magnums, was a more solid wine than many that year. Very darkly coloured, the bouquet was reticent when young, but the promise for an interesting evolution was apparent on the palate. Very deeply extracted, the Piaugier wines achieved an intensity in 1988 and 1989 that makes them worth investigation as representatives of the modern school of winemaking at Gigondas.

Autran, Marc et Fils
   Domaine de Piaugier   84110 Sablet

DOMAINE DU POURRA

Jean-Claude Chassagne has taken over the running of this *domaine*, which has 16 hectares of vines at Gigondas on slopes in the Pourra *quartier*. The Gigondas is made from 75 per cent Grenache, 15 per cent Mourvèdre and 5 per cent each of Syrah and Cinsault. Allowed about eighteen months in old wood, this is a robust wine with decent ageing potential in the firm vintages. The 1981 was very successful, carrying a typical peppery intensity on the bouquet and displaying rounded flavours on the palate after nine years. The 1982 was light and much less successful. This is certainly a *domaine* to consider in good years like 1989 and 1990, but one senses that too much is being offered: the family also have 8 hectares at Sablet, 6.5 hectares at Séguret and 4 hectares at Violès, making a Sablet Villages called Les Abeilles, a Séguret Villages called La Combe and a straight Côtes du Rhône from Violès. Just to top up, M. Chassagne makes a little *vin doux naturel*, aged in cask, from his holding at Rasteau.

Chassagne, Jean-Claude
   Domaine du Pourra   84110 Sablet

DOMAINE DE RASPAIL-AY

This very good 17.5-hectare *domaine* has been run since 1982 by Dominique Ay, an ex-helicopter pilot whose chunky physique confirms his practical, no-nonsense attitude to his wine-making. His late father François used to be the President of the Syndicat des

Vignerons, and it is in the grounds of the Domaine Raspail-Ay, right beside the main D7 road, that most of the Gallo-Roman treasures and relics of Gigondas have been found.

The old estate used to be much larger, but sadly, in accordance with the French law of equal right of inheritance, it was split into four parts. In the working of his vineyard, M. Ay *père* discovered all sorts of glass and earthenware relics, including completely intact second-century tumblers and long-stemmed glasses that were presumably used for wine drinking.

François Ay was very well read and much interested in history, and related a story of how the family vineyard had almost fallen into abandonment during the nineteenth century: 'After phylloxera the Raspail family found themselves hard pressed to finance the replanting of the entire vineyard, which had not then been split into four. However, they did own one valuable asset, a marble statue called the Diadumenos of Vaison-la-Romaine. This they had acquired for virtually nothing, and they determined to try to sell it to save the vineyard. The Louvre in Paris hemmed and hawed but wouldn't buy it, and just as the Raspails thought all was lost, the British Museum stepped in and brought the Diadumenos. That was in 1869, and with the British money the Raspail family were able to restore their vineyard. The statue is still in the British Museum, but I have never seen it.'

The Raspail-Ay vines stand all around their cellars a little below the village, and are made up of 65 per cent Grenache, 15 per cent Syrah, 7.5 per cent Cinsault, 6.5 per cent Mourvèdre and 6 per cent Clairette. As the first variety to ripen, the Syrah is vinified on its own, while Dominique Ay also chooses to vinify the fruit from his oldest vines, forty-five-year Grenache, first. 'They have the highest degree so I don't want them to overripen', comments M. Ay. 'These older vines are also pruned in the Gobelet fashion, whereas the young vines are trained along a single wire. The Gobelet vines are more covered by foliage, so in essence they are less aerated and receive less exposure to the sun.'

The Raspail-Ay crop is entirely destalked and after a traditional crushing undergoes a twelve- to eighteen-day fermentation; the wine is then racked into oak barrels ranging in capacity from 47 to 130 hectolitres. It remains in these for around two years, with a final three- to six-month burst in smaller *demi-muids* of 660 litres immediately before bottling. M. Ay does not want his casks to impart a lot of tannin to his wine – some of the barrels are thirty to forty years old. Like many *domaines* that do not possess large stockage space, he also bottles a vintage in several takes, generally of 3,000 bottles at a time. This means that a start-to-finish span of nine months in the bottling of a single vintage can lead to different styles of wine circulating under the same vintage's label.

The Raspail-Ay wines are always well structured and are amongst the classiest of all Gigondas, with good combinations of fruit, richness and tannins. In the better vintages like 1983, 1985 and 1988 the colour is intense and the wines are suitable for drinking between six and ten years of age. They are neither fined nor filtered, and develop agreeably spicy and complex aromas after five or six years in bottle. A third of this front-rank *domaine*'s wine is sold off to *négociants* and another third is exported, mostly to the United States, Austria, Belgium, Switzerland and Britain. A very small amount of rosé is made by the *saignée* method: correct wine but of little significance beside the very good red.

Ay, Dominique
   Domaine de Raspail-Ay   84190 Gigondas

DOMAINE DU TERME

An 11-hectare *domaine*, whose red wine is made from 80 per cent Grenache, 15 per cent Syrah and 5 per cent Mourvèdre. The Syrah plantation has been increased, replacing excess Cinsault that was forbidden by the 1986 change of rules. The style of Rolland Gaudin's wines is firm, with decent extraction of tannin working well with steady levels of rounded fruit. They are wines that need five to seven years to settle down in the stronger vintages like 1978, 1981, 1986 and 1989 – these will retain their grip for a full ten to twelve years. By contrast, the 1983 was a lighter, more overtly fruity and spicy wine that should be drunk up now.

M. Gaudin also works a vineyard at Sablet, producing a sound Côtes du Rhône Villages *rouge*. The commercial side of his vineyards is looked after by his daughter Anne-Marie, while he bears the responsibility of being President of the Syndicat des Vignerons, in which capacity he must keep the peace over issues such as new vineyard exploitation and the consequent change in the face of the countryside.

Gaudin, Rolland
    Domaine du Terme   84190 Gigondas

DOMAINE LES TOURELLES

Roger Cuillerat tends his 8-hectare vineyard on his own. He has been bottling a part of his crop since 1970, and like many small growers has his plots spread about, with the largest being a 2.4-hectare patch on the slopes just below the Hôtel des Florets. His wine is made from 80 per cent Grenache and 10 per cent each of Cinsault and Syrah. After a light crushing and a traditional two-week fermentation in concrete vats, he leaves the red Gigondas, for a strong vintage like 1988 or 1983, first in old wood *foudres* of 22 and 37 hectolitres for eighteen months and then in 600-litre *demi-muids* for four or five months. A softer year like 1985 receives fifteen months. 'I want the wine to start its ageing gently, which is why it goes into the larger barrels first. It then begins to round out properly in the smaller container,' comments M. Cuillerat.

The Tourelles red is a promising wine, which carries greater elegance than many at Gigondas. M. Cuillerat is not going for the full-blown style, and the emphasis is on balance, good colour and early fruit on the palate. The wines generally bear good length and are suitable to drink between five and nine years old.

Cuillerat, Roger
    Domaine Les Tourelles   84190 Gigondas

Gigondas Vintages

1959   Very good. A sensational vintage at Domaine Les Pallières, considered by Pierre Roux to be his best ever.
1960   Mediocre
1961   Very good.
1962   Very good. Wines of notably good balance.
1963   Poor.
1964   Excellent. Very full-bodied wines.
1965   Poor.
1966   Good. The wines were sound, but a little lacking in charm and finesse. They are now very old.
1967   Excellent. A powerful vintage with the wines possessing

good balance and bouquet. A little of their richness remains in some bottles, like Les Pallières, as they gently fade away.

1968 Poor.

1969 Excellent. The wines were rich and harmonious, and their general elegance made them very good for drinking in their first twelve years. They are now some way past their best.

1970 Very good. An enormously strong vintage, high in alcohol and tannin. Some of the wines were rather harsh, but the best of them, from *domaines* such as Les Pallières, St-Gayan and the Château de Montmirail, were quite outstanding. They are drying out with age, and should have been drunk by now.

1971 Excellent. Well-coloured, full-bodied wines with a better overall balance than many of the 1970s. They are past their best, but presented good examples of Grenache-based wines that stood up well to the test of time.

1972 Very good. Wines with a deep colour and agreeable strength, whose good acidity level helped them to age very well. They are now tired and should have been drunk.

1973 A generally disappointing year. A very large crop gave lightly coloured wines whose quality varied considerably around the *appellation*. The wines from *domaines* that rigorously sorted their harvest, like Les Pallières, aged very well and developed a wholesome harmony on the palate. They should be drunk soon.

1974 Generally a mediocre vintage. Some full and fiery *cuvées* were made – fiery because after the passage of over ten years there was a definite unmasking of the alcohol. Many of the wines lacked richness and degree, however. They should have been drunk by now.

1975 For many growers a poor year, although some of the wines emerged creditably as they aged into the late 1980s. A small harvest gave often light-bodied wines short on colour and bouquet. While the colour is orange or brick now, a wine like the Domaine du Pesquier is well rounded, with soft fruit and likeable spice flavours on the middle- and end-palate. A vintage to drink up soon.

1976 Very good. A dry summer gave wines that developed great charm. Ruby-coloured, they gained expansive, opulent bouquets and a well-founded harmony as they aged. They never held much tannin, and have started to lose their structure, shorten on the finish and dry out. They should be drunk without delay.

1977   Quite a good year, although there were some unbalanced wines from the smaller *domaines*. The better wines, such as those from Les Pallières, Les Goubert and L'Oustaou Fauquet, have seen their pale colours turn to tile, but became very agreeable and supple with attractive length. Their bouquets have started to lose the great depth of aromas that they developed after about ten years, and these wines should have been drunk by now.

1978   Excellent. A sunny October brought great heat and a surge of late ripeness for the vines after a fine summer. The wines possess sound dark colours that have turned to ruby and tremendous spice, cigar-box and stewed fruit aromas developed on the bouquet. They have retained their richness and fullness on the palate, and their overall punch will ensure that they live comfortably into the 1990s.

1979   Very good. Well-coloured wines that are only marginally less full than those of the 1978 harvest. Good, complex bouquets and well-ripened fruitiness emerged ahead of the residual tannins; while the wines are now in their older, final phase of maturity, well-kept bottles could still provide interesting drinking. Note the wines of the Domaines de Longue-Toque and St-Gayan.

1980   A very large crop of good wines that have opened up and are now at their peak. The colours range from sound to dark, with the ruby of age entering. A little short on tannin, these wines had sufficient acidity to keep them together longer than expected. They are not noticeably full-bodied, and the best *cuvées*, such as that from the Domaine de St-Gayan, are drinking very well now.

1981   A reasonable vintage at the outset, much better ten years later. Many of the wines developed from indifferent beginnings into tasting very well and showing great quality. A very dry autumn unbalanced the grapes' ripening; some growers produced early-maturing wines that were a little low in acidity. Others came up with some robust, backward and initially hard *cuvées* that arranged themselves with age: the spicy secondary aromas and strong stewed flavours have emerged, followed by a firm, chewy finish. Wines from the Domaines Les Pallières, Les Goubert, L'Oustaou Fauquet, du Pourra and St-Gayan are all recommended: they will provide good drinking until around 1995.

1982   A difficult year for vinifiers gave wines that merit the term 'average'. The unseasonal heat during harvest-time meant that *cuves* were prone to overheating, with runaway fermentations risking turning the wine volatile. The majority of the growers did not possess cellar cooling equipment and many wines are therefore uneven, marked by a jammy flavour and lack of clear fruit on the palate. The colour of the wines is generally pale and already 'bricking': they should be drunk up, since their alcohol has started to stand out. A good *cuvée* was made by the Domaine du Pesquier, who have used cooling equipment in their cellars since the mid-1970s, while the Les Goubert will show at its best up to 1993.

1983   Good. Sizeable *coulure* on the Grenache vines altered the natural structure of the wines, pushing the Mourvèdre and the Syrah into greater than usual prominence. The colours were firm, sometimes dense with plenty of black streaks in them, and the bouquets with age have developed an intriguing, dried aroma complexity. It is on the palate that these wines excel, with the fruit merging well with generous tannins and some gutsy alcohol. Domaines Les Tourelles and du Terme are good examples of wines that were made in the softer style, and will drink well before 1993. The Domaines du Pesquier, Raspail–Ay, St-Gayan and Les Goubert are fuller, well-knitted wines that will need longer to round themselves out. The Raspail–Ay is particularly elegant, and the St-Gayan extremely concentrated.

1984   Mediocre. The summer lacked sun, there was cold weather during flowering, and again some of the Grenache was affected by *coulure*. The vintage is middle- to lightweight, with some wines bearing rather unripe fruit and higher than usual levels of acidity. The best *cuvées* show some lively fruit, decent spicy bouquets and pale colours. Wines from the top *domaines* like Raspail–Ay show a firm colour, and despite early evident acidity on the palate, had sufficient structure to settle down by the early 1990s. Lighter and more immediately drinkable are the wines of the Domaine Santa Duc of Edmond Gras, the Château de Montmirail – notably the Cuvée de Beauchamp – and a very fruity, likeable Domaine Les Pallières.

1985 Very good. The wines are well-coloured and full of fruit, and their tannins were notably rounded and well ripened, as opposed to the tougher tannins of the 1983s. With six years' age they settled down to show opulent aromas on the bouquet and great equilibrium on the palate. Their fruit is now very apparent, and some *cuvées* like the Domaine du Grand Montmirail will be best appreciated before around 1993 to capture the fruit. Other wines, like Raspail–Ay, Les Goubert, Les Pallières and St-Gayan, have held together more tightly and will provide excellent drinking towards 1996. All in all, a vintage of very great charm and appeal.

1986 The harvest was affected by rot late on, and any conscientious grower was forced to sort the grapes very carefully. The wines were decried early on and quality can be variable. Some very good ones emerged by the early 1990s, shrugging off some raw flavours and rasping tannins that threatened to dominate them. It will take some time for the bouquets to open and show their full worth, but there is an underlying richness supporting them on the palate which suggests some very good drinking from the best *cuvées* between 1992 and 1998. They are more difficult than the easier-styled, more approachable 1985s. Note the wines of the Domaines de Font-Sane, Les Pallières, de Boissan (Christian Bonfils at Sablet) and St-Gayan.

1987 Heavy rains in September and October brought on rot and an inevitable dilution of the wines. Some growers likened conditions to those of the disastrous 1963 vintage. But once again, those *vignerons* prepared radically to sort their harvest were able to supply soft, pale wines with a fine tannic content. The wines of Domaine Raspail–Ay and St-Gayan were both very well worked, and will drink very pleasantly over about six or seven years. The best advice is to taste these wines before buying.

1988 A good vintage, but not an outstanding one as was rumoured early on. The summer was very hot and dry, and in style some of the wines approach the 1985s. Their tannins are rounded, but the fruit is not quite as intense as that of the 1985s. Some growers like Dominique Ay of Raspail-Ay and Roger Meffre of St-Gayan have made very concentrated, tight wines that will need five or six years to loosen up – they are very compact with a strong tannic backing – while the Gour du Chaule, Domaine Daniel Brusset and Guigal wines are more immediately fruity and approachable. Most of these wines will drink well around six to twelve years old.

1989   A very good year, but not an easy one for the growers, who again had to contend with drought. This meant that the vines on the poor soil of the *garrigues* suffered, as did the short-rooted young vines. A storm in early September helped the older vines, but the fruit on the younger ones had stopped evolving by then. The later harvesters came out best, producing extremely dense, well-extracted wines with a good colour and prolonged richness *en bouche*. Early harvesters actually had to chaptalize, and their wines are much paler and less intense. For selection, stick to a reliable grower or to a reliable *négociant*. The better *cuvées*, from producers like Les Goubert, St-Gayan and Font-Sane, have a warm power on the palate, and will start to round out and drink well from about 1995 onwards.

1990   The year was also very dry, but rain at convenient moments helped to provide wines with great depth and power and perhaps a little more substance and staying power than the 1989s. Bits of rain in March/April started the vines off, and a storm at the end of August was also well-timed. This is another very good vintage, and the wines are well coloured, with an early potency of alcohol that will keep them evolving quietly over a dozen or more years. They will need several years to settle down and knit together their strong elements on the palate.

Earlier Exceptional Vintages   1955, 1949, 1947

Leading Growers at Gigondas

The nucleus:

Amadieu, Pierre	
Archimaud, Maurice et Bouteiller Jacques	84190 Gigondas
Château de Montmirail	
Autran, Marc, et Fils	
Domaine de Piaugier	84110 Sablet
Ay, Dominique	
Domaine de Raspail-Ay	
Beaumet-Bonfils, Mesdames	84190 Gigondas
Domaine du Gour de Chaule	
Boutière, Raymond et Guy	
Domaine du Pesquier	
Brusset, Daniel	
Domaine des Travers	84290 Cairanne
Cartier, Jean-Pierre	
Domaine Les Goubert	
Cave des Vignerons de Gigondas	84190 Gigondas
Chapalain, Serge	
Domaine du Longue-Toque	
Chassagne, Jean-Claude	
Domaine du Pourra	84110 Sablet
Cheron, Yves	
Domaine du Grand Montmirail	
Combe, Roger, et Fille	84190 Gigondas
L'Oustaou Fauquet	
Cuillerat, Roger	
Domaine Les Tourelles	
Domaine de Cassan	84190 Lafare
Faraud, Michel	
Domaine du Cayron	
Gaudin, Roland	
Domaine du Terme	84190 Gigondas
Gras, Edmond, et Yves	
Domaine Santa Duc	
Meffre, Roger et Jean-Pierre	
Domaine St-Gayan	

Peysson, Gabriel, et Fille
 Domaine de Font-Sane
Roux, Charles, et ses Fils   } 84190 Gigondas
 Château du Trignon
Roux, Hilarion, Les Fils de
 Les Pallières

Other producers:

Alexandre, E. et F.
 Domaine Les Teyssonnières   } 84190 Gigondas
Bézert, Pierre
 Domaine de la Tuilière
Bonfils, Christian
 Domaine de Boissan   84110 Sablet
Burle, Ed
 Les Palliéroudas   84190 Gigondas
Chastan, André, et Fils   84110 Orange
Chastan, Fernand
 Clos du Joncuas   } 84190 Gigondas
Chauvet, Bernard et Paul
 Le Grappillon d'Or
Crozet, Paul
 Domaine de Cassan   84190 Lafare
Faraud, Jean-Pierre   } 84190 Gigondas
Faravel, Antonin
Fauque, Jean-Claude
 Domaine St-Pierre   84150 Violès
Gorecki, J.
 Le Mas des Collines
Gras, André
 Domaine St François-Xavier
Lambert, Pierre
 Domaine de la Mavette
Meffre, Gabriel   } 84190 Gigondas
 Domaine des Bosquets
Meunier, Laurent
 La Gardette
Quiot, Pierre
 Domaine des Pradets

Richard, Georges
  Domaine La Tourade
Roux, Georges et Jean
  Domaine Les Chênes Blancs   } 84190 Gigondas
Veyrat, Veuve
  Château St-André

12

Vacqueyras

Vacqueyras duly received its promotion to sole *appellation* status in 1990. This was regarded by certain observers as having been in the tea-leaves for some time previously, but it nevertheless remains a little surprising to one foreign observer that Cairanne did not put in an application at the same time. Perhaps the fact that there is greater strength in numbers of private *domaines* making and bottling their wine – about thirty – and the fact that there was perfect agreement on policy between them and the well-run Co-opérative of Vacqueyras contributed to ensure a ruling in their sole favour.

Vacqueyras's red wines are full-blooded affairs; a sort of rough-house Gigondas comes from an *appellation* area of around 1,450 hectares. These are wines with great power and sometimes a coarse tannin that is very definitely southern in style. They are wines for sit-down drinking, are not for the faint-hearted, and if their promotion to full *appellation* status puts them close in price to Gigondas, then they will have become over-priced.

The village of Vacqueyras lies on the main D7 road between Gigondas and Beaumes-de-Venise. With many of its vineyards bordering directly upon Gigondas, there is a certain affinity of style between the two wines, but Gigondas has much greater breeding and balance. Wine-making has a long history here, since records show that as far back as 1414 there was an 'extensive' vineyard in the immediate neighbourhood. Little else has ever been recorded about the local wine, except that in the late sixteenth century a municipal decree had to be passed authorizing the full-scale protection of the vineyards from attacks by itinerant goats. Curiously, these animals were more partial to the ripening grapes than were the village children, and the legislation against them was suitably severe.

The village has had a quiet past, and when reminiscing, the

vignerons invariably turn to the story of Vacqueyras's most illustrious citizen, the Provençal troubadour Raimbaud. Born in 1180, the son of the village idiot, Raimbaud possessed great musical talent and charmed many a noble lady to his bedside with his deeply entrancing madrigals: indeed, these were of sufficient quality to secure him a royal appointment as Governor of Salonica. Alas, Raimbaud's success was brief, for he was killed in 1207 when fighting the Turks. The village is very proud of this rags-to-riches story, and in honour of it the Cave Co-opérative was named 'Le Troubadour' upon its foundation in 1957.

Within its former Côtes du Rhône Villages category, Vacqueyras was the top wine along with Cairanne. Most of the private *domaines* stick to traditional vinification methods, although in the past the Cave Co-opérative – the Cave du Troubadour – and the Domaine des Lambertins of Lambert Frères have used *macération carbonique* for part of their wine.

Over the past fifteen years considerable improvement in the vineyard plantations has occurred, with greater amounts of Syrah and more recently of Mourvèdre included. The Carignan has been largely replaced and much less Cinsault is present as growers concentrate on making a fuller, finer red wine. Very little white is made at Vacqueyras, with the Château des Roques, one of the few *domaines* offering one, relying on a mix of Bourboulenc and Roussanne.

One of the additional reasons why Vacqueyras is such a powerful wine is that many of the *viticulteurs* have remained loyal to their old Grenache plantings. This allows the Cave Co-opérative the option of producing a special selection of fruit from vines of more than forty-five years old, provided by many of their 132 members.

Among the different styles evident at Vacqueyras, the more elegant end of the spectrum comes from the Domaine des Lambertins and the Domaine La Fourmone, while the full, intense and firmly concentrated wine, with markings of Syrah and Mourvèdre, comes from producers like the Domaine du Château de Montmirail with their excellent Cuvée de L'Ermite, the Clos des Cazaux with their excellent Cuvée des Templiers, the Domaine le Sang des Cailloux – a descriptive name indeed – and the Domaine de Montvac of Jean Duserre-Audibert. The most robust, darkly coloured and potent style – wines that need ageing over several years and very often opening some time ahead of consumption – come well made from *domaines* like Le Couroulu of the Ricard family, from the Château des Roques, the Domaine le Pont-du-Rieu of Jean-Pierre Faraud, the Domaine La Garrigue of Albert Bernard, the Domaine des Amouriers of the Polish Jocelyn Chudzikiewicz, and Pascal Frères, whose Vacqueyras has always been a top-class example of firm, ripe Grenache. Another consistently good Vacqueyras is supplied by Paul Jaboulet Aîné, who buy around 60 hectolitres from two or three growers every year and age it for about six months in cask before release.

One of the characters of the *appellation* is Roger Combe of Domaine La Fourmone. He is an exceptional man, for he speaks Provençal fluently and also writes poetry in the local dialect. This he learned from his family, at a time when there were no organized classes in the village schools, and he is proud enough of his region and origins to put Provençal phrases on his labels; thus his Vacqueyras label carries the words '*Raco Racejo*', which means that the race perpetuates, or that the father and son resemble each other. In this respect he is fortunate to have both his son and his daughter helping to make and sell the family wine, made from 18 hectares at Vacqueyras and 9 hectares at Gigondas. Although he vinifies in a classical manner, his light crushing of the grapes plays up his intention of achieving an elegant style of wine. He is also uncommon among Vaucluse growers in his decision not to fine or filter following a six-to twelve-month ageing in cask. M. Combe makes a little rosé and white Côtes du Rhône but justifiably concentrates his efforts on his very good red, which he considers should be drunk by the time it is six or seven years old in the case of Gigondas (L'Oustaou Fauquet) and four or five years old in the case of Vacqueyras.

During the 1990s some quite marked differences of style will appear, rather similar to the tiering at Châteauneuf-du-Pape. This will mean that some of the wines will be great to drink when around three or four years old, while others will need a full six years or so to round themselves and reduce the potency and edge of their tannins. Those growers who are seeking an intense fruit extraction in the wines – people like Monique and Jacques Bouteiller at the Château de Montmirail, with their Grenache–Syrah mix, and the Vache family at the Domaine de la Monardière, who work on a Grenache–Mourvèdre–Syrah axis – are producing well-coloured wines whose bouquets and flavours are more lush than the traditional versions of Vacqueyras. Buyers should be on their guard for such developments, since it is a pity to miss out on these wines when they are relatively young.

Similarly, the 1990s are likely to bring an increase in attention to and investment in the white wines of Vacqueyras, which in the past have proved rather unreliable, due to the usual litany of faults of southern whites of the post-war years. More extensive planting of varieties like the Marsanne, the Roussanne and the Bourboulenc is occurring, and providing growers feel that they can charge a price that covers extra labour and cellar equipment, more will be seen of the white.

Vacqueyras rosé is made by a few of the *domaines*, but, as at Gigondas, this is often heady and of secondary interest.

Selected Growers at Vacqueyras

Archimbaud-Bouteiller,
  Domaine du Château de
  Montmirail
Archimbaud-Vache,
  Clos des Cazaux
Arnoux et Fils
  Le Vieux Clocher   84190 Vacqueyras
Bernard, Albert et Lucien
  Domaine de la Garrigue
Bungener, Georges
  Domaine du Clos de Caveau
Cave des Vignerons
  'Le Troubadour'

Chastan, A., et Fils
  Domaine de la Jaufrette   84100 Orange
Chudzikiewicz, Jocelyn
  Domaine des Amouriers   84260 Sarrians
Combe, Roger, et Fille
  Domaine La Fourmone   84190 Vacqueyras
Dusser-Beraud, Édouard
  Château des Roques   84260 Sarrians

Dusserre-Audibert, Jean
  Domaine de Montvac
Faraud, Jean-Pierre
  Domaine du Pont-du-Rieu
GAEC Le Parc Alazard Père et Fils   84190 Vacqueyras
  Domaine de la Colline St-Jean
Lambert Frères
  Domaine des Lambertins

Marseille, Pierre
  Domaine de Chantegut   84260 Sarrians

Mayre, Rémy
  Le Mousquetaire
Mourre, Gilbert
  Domaine Le Colombier   84190 Vacqueyras
Pascal Frères
Reynaud Emmanuel
  Chat des Tours

Ricard, Jean, et Férigoule, Serge
  Domaine le Sang des Cailloux   84260 Sarrians

Ricard, Pierre et Fils
  Domaine Le Couroulu   84190 Vacqueyras
Vache
  Domaine de la Monardière

Vacqueyras Vintages

The vintages for Vacqueyras closely resemble those of next-door village Gigondas. The wines differ in quality, but their (fortunes) from one year to the next are usually very similar. See Gigondas, Chapter 11.

13
Châteauneuf-du-Pape

Known the world over, Châteauneuf-du-Pape is a worthy centrepiece for the Côtes du Rhône. The old papal village that straddles a hillock 16 kilometres from Avignon possesses a certain and memorable aura, for not only does the name fire the imagination but the ruined castle tower too, with its broken walls recalling a splendour and magnificence long since departed. It was to this small village that the first of the Avignon popes, Clément V, would make his way in the early fourteenth century, humbly seated on his mule and ever anxious to inspect his vineyard: in the words of the Provençal poet Félix Gras, in his 'Cansoun dou Papo Clément V':

> Lou Papo Clément cinq, d'assetoun sus sa miolo,
> S'envai veire sa vigno, amount a Casteu-Nou;
> Porto dins sa saqueto, em' uno bono fiolo,
> Un taioun de jamboun, de pan e quauquis iou![1]

Clément had been installed as Pope in 1309. With relations badly strained between the King of France and the Papacy of Rome, and with Italy battle-torn by religious strife, he had no hesitation in choosing to remain in his native France. Besides, he was from Bordeaux, was fond of his wine and had already planted his own vineyard there, now known as Château Pape-Clément, in the Graves

[1] Le Pape Clément cinq, assis sur sa mule,
S'en va voir sa vigne, là-haut à Châteauneuf;
Il porte dans son sac, avec une bonne fiole,
Un morceau de jambon, du pain et quelques oeufs!

Pope Clement the Fifth, seated on his mule,
Goes off to see his vines, up there at Châteauneuf;
He carries in his bag, along with a good flask,
A piece of ham, some bread and eggs!

region. History relates that Clément had a few vines planted 'near Avignon', and it was in Châteauneuf that he spent his last night, in 1314, before dying across the river at Roquemaure. His return to his homeland was never completed. It was really his successor, Pope John XXII, who was responsible for the development of Châteauneuf-du-Pape's fortunes.

John was clearly a financially minded pope, and by setting in order the papal treasury was able to enlarge the modest official residence in Avignon. But he was a romantic too and longed to retire from the oppressive summer heat of busy Avignon to the tranquility of the surrounding countryside. A formal country residence was sought, and his choice fell upon Châteauneuf, which already contained the foundations of a large castle ruined in 1248. Between 1318 and 1333 the 'new château' was built. It was a monster construction, even by the affluent standards of the time, and Pope John was only able to move into it one year before his death. His new castle, or Châteauneuf, usefully performed a dual purpose; not only was it intended as a summer residence, but it also formed part of a protective line of castles around Avignon. The villages of Bédarrides, Sorgues, Noves and Barbentane completed the circle.

Pope John used the 10 hectares that went with the château for growing vines and olives, both of which were already exploited by the local inhabitants. He found the range of fruit that could be grown was restricted by the lack of a regular water supply to his new *domaine*, and it was the vines and olive trees that best adapted themselves to the partially arid terrain.

John's vineyards became the best-known in the village, but the community had been growing vines for at least 150 years before his arrival, as is witnessed by a document revealing that in 1157 Gaufredus, the unlikely-named Bishop of Avignon, congratulated one Frédéric Barberousse on the lands and vines that made up Châteauneuf. However, the first mention of the wine itself comes in the year 1320, when a regular traffic of full barrels of wine from Châteauneuf to the Palace of Avignon was reported, and of empty barrels on the way back, a journey which in those days would have lasted about four hours. By the 1360s both white and red wine are written up as coming from Châteauneuf to be drunk by Pope Innocent VI.

The Châteauneuf vineyard, although quoted as numbering 3.3 million vine plants in 1334 (today this would represent a surface area

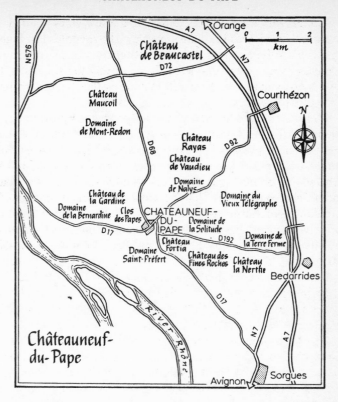

Châteauneuf-du-Pape

of some 1,090 hectares), belonged to a mass of small owners, and so John was unable to furnish all the wine needed for the papal feastings held in Avignon. Recourse was made to the nearby village of Bédarrides, today part of the Châteauneuf-du-Pape *appellation* area, for an annual delivery of 1,550 litres. Even this was still inadequate for the papal palace, if a menu of the year 1324 is anything to go by. A gargantuan feast was then held to celebrate the marriage of the great-niece of Pope John and comprised, *inter alia*, 55 sheep, 690 chickens, 580 partridges, 270 rabbits, 8 pigs, 4 wild boar, 40 plovers, 37 ducks, 50 pigeons and many other diverse delicacies.

The official papal stay at Avignon lasted from 1309 to 1378. It was a time of tremendous prosperity for the previously humble city, but not all the Popes maintained a firm interest in the château and vineyard at Châteauneuf. Bands of marauders were a deterrent on the road from Avignon, and of all Pope John's successors, only Innocent VI (1352–62) and Benoît XIII (1394–1423) really took trouble over the upkeep of the château and vineyard. Benoît exiled himself to become Anti-Pope in 1403, and the differences with Rome were not healed until 1410.

Thereafter, one assumes, the vineyard lapsed into local obscurity, without perhaps producing a quality of wine capable of attracting the attention of kings and nobles, for no further documentation on the wine of Châteauneuf-du-Pape exists before the eighteenth century, evidence of the inevitable decline in the village's fortunes after the return of the papacy to its seat in Rome. In 1562 the château had been badly damaged by the marauding Huguenot Baron des Adrets, but its dungeon and one tower had remained intact – until a fateful day in August 1944, when the retreating German forces contrived to blow it in half as they abandoned their encampment there.

The wine that we now know as Châteauneuf-du-Pape has not long held that name. Even into the early nineteenth century it was known within France as 'Châteauneuf-Calcernier', indicating the limestone deposits that were once exploited close to the village. The wine sold abroad during the eighteenth century went for the most part under the name of *vin d'Avignon;* it was taken up the Rhône by barge in 265-litre barrels and dispatched from Lyon to all destinations, including England and the United States. The leading wine to be exported at that time was that of the Château de la Nerte, which was sold under its own name. In 1750 this estate made sixteen and a half *tonneaux*, or barrels, representing about 45 hectolitres of wine from its 50-hectare land holding: the area under vines was therefore only a part of its activity.

In 1776 the Cassini map of the vineyard area showed the land under vines as just over 600 hectares. The high plateau in the north of today's *appellation*, beyond Château Rayas, was less planted because of the preponderance of large stones. The area around Domaine du Vieux Télégraphe and Domaine de la Solitude was preferred, for its covering of smaller stones made vineyard cultivation more straightforward.

The wine of La Nerte was the first Châteauneuf to be bottled, an enterprising practice that started in 1785. The owners, the de Tulle family, were bold with their commercialization, for by 1768 they are recorded as having overseas representatives in England and the

United States, selling their wine whose shorthand name was the Vin des Papes – shrewd marketing![1]

Shortly after the Battle of Waterloo in 1815, the Domaine de la Solitude was also bottling a little of its wine, and these two estates directly helped the growing reputation of the local wine. By 1822 the wine of La Nerte was considered the best of 'Châteauneuf-Calcernier' by the wine writer Dr A. Jullien, but it was not quite the same style of wine that we know today. Dr Jullien wrote: 'Well-coloured, the wines of La Nerte have a softness and agreeableness: the best moment to drink them is at the height of their maturity, after three or four years.' He also mentioned the wines of La Fortiasse (Château Fortia) and Clos St-Patrice, but it was La Nerte which undoubtedly led the field. While just one principal quality of wine seems to have been made from the different grapes being cultivated in the area, it is evident that such famous names as La Nerte and Fortia formed only a tiny part of the whole vineyard. In 1800 the Châteauneuf-du-Pape area was said to hold 668 hectares of vines, and in 1817, 820 hectares. The 1847 holding at La Nerte and Fortia together was reported as 22 hectares, which evidently made them a tiny part of a very large plantation, for these figures do not include the villages of Courthézon and Bédarrides – today part of the overall Châteauneuf-du-Pape *appellation* area. If these two villages and part of Orange are included in the vineyard returns for 1817, then the approximate equivalent of today's available *appellation* area comes to no less than 1,940 hectares.

By 1860 the wine of La Nerte was the most expensive of all Châteauneuf-du-Papes due to the heavy demand for it both in France and abroad. In a work of 1868, Dr Guyot cited La Nerte as a leading *cru*, along with Condorcet, Vaudieu and Coteau-Brûlé. Vaudieu had been built from 1767, and took its name from Val de Dieu, so-named because of its fertile location. But Coteau-Brûlé – at nearby Sorgues – cannot be reconciled with any of today's properties.

The year 1873 marked a watershed in Châteauneuf's fortunes with the arrival of phylloxera. Desperate *vignerons* tried flooding the flat ground and spraying novel chemical mixtures on to the vines, but to no avail.

Not surprisingly, many growers abandoned hope and turned to

---

[1]*Documents pour servir à l'Histoire de Châteauneuf-du-Pape*, Baron P. Le Roy de Boiseaumarié (Avignon, 1932).

the full-time cultivation of cherries, almonds, apricots and olives. The village, as a result, had two large olive mills up until the First World War, and its cherries found a confirmed market in England, where they were held in great esteem. Reconstruction of the vineyards was cautiously started in 1878; by 1890, 600 hectares were under vine, and by 1913, 860 hectares. This figure dipped during the Great War, but by 1920 planting had recommenced, arriving at 980 hectares out of a total possible of 1,300 by 1932.

At this time eight leading estates were quoted in the late Baron Le Roy's historical work on Châteauneuf-du-Pape. In alphabetical order, they were:

Cabrières-lès-Silex
    Owner: M. Henri Latour
    Vines: Grenache, Clairette, Mourvèdre (then called Tinto)
    Production: 140 *pièces* (225 litres each)

Château des Fines Roches
    Owner: Société des Grandes Caves de Lyon
    Vines: Grenache, Clairette, Mourvèdre, Syrah
    Production: 200 *pièces*

Château Fortia
    Owner: Baron Le Roy
    Vines: All old Châteauneuf varieties
    Production: 175 *pièces*

Château de la Nerthe (*sic*)
    Owner: M. Charles Bortoli
    Vines: All old Châteauneuf varieties
    Production: 180 *pièces*

Château Rayas
    Owner: M. Louis Reynaud
    Vines: Grenache, Clairette, Mourvèdre
    Production: red: 90 *pièces*; white: 30 *pièces*

Château de Vaudieu
    Owner: M. Pierre Quiot

Vines: Grenache, Clairette, Mourvèdre
Production: 150 *pièces*

Clos des Papes
Owner: M. Paul Avril
Vines: Grenache, Clairette
Production: 40 *pièces*, all sold in bottle

Domaine de Nalys
Owner: Mme Éloi Establet
Vines: All old Châteauneuf varieties
Production: 275 *pièces*

Some interesting observations from the early 1930s were that at that time Château Rayas was one of the rare *domaines* making white wine at Châteauneuf. Second, the average vineyard holding was very small, 80 per cent of the members of the Syndicat des Vignerons possessing under 5 hectares of vines. And lastly, yields seem to have been minute compared with today, making one speculate as to just how heady and concentrated the wine must have been. Baron Le Roy lists the harvest returns for a 4.75-hectare vineyard of a *petit vigneron*. Over the course of twenty-five years, the average yield shows an increase, but only to a figure of about half today's permitted level. In five-year groups, the annual yield averaged as follows:

1907–11	8.2 hl per hectare
1912–16	9.2 hl per hectare
1917–21	10.1 hl per hectare
1922–6	14.2 hl per hectare
1927–31	21.2 hl per hectare

In those years the main weather problems came from four years of hail, two years of mildew and one year of cochylis moth. One can only presume that the steady increase in yields was due to a variety of improvements in the techniques of working the vineyards. For this chosen small grower, a tractor would not have been an option, but Baron Le Roy was at the time gaining a small increase in the density of his own plantation through using one – his vines were planted in rows of 2.25 × 1.25 metres, as opposed to the usual 1.75 metres square. But this small cultivator would have gained from the introduction of steam-powered drills for planting: these allowed growers to go to a depth of 0.6–0.8 metre, instead of the previous 0.3–0.4. The benefit of these machines, which were introduced in 1893, was that the vine roots could reach further down for water reserves, since drought or very dry summers were very much a fact of life even in those far-off days.

Another factor that would have served to diminish yields when comparing them with modern times was that the vinestocks of the time were intended to combat phylloxera, rather than encourage greater production, as they are now. Growers would also not have possessed any cooling equipment, however rudimentary, to have efficiently saved vinifications from overheating, while most were involved in several different activities – raising animals, fruit and vegetable cultivation and so on – so that wine-making was not their top or sole priority.

The years after phylloxera were a period of reconstruction, but also offered the broad-minded an opportunity to experiment. Some *domaines*, notably Château La Gardine, planted Pinot Noir and Pinot Blanc, but these vines were subsequently abandoned as failing to adapt to the climate and the soil.

Châteauneuf-du-Pape occupies a notable niche in the history of modern viticulture, for it was there in 1923 that the first regulating laws were devised for table wines. These are now known as the laws of the *appellation contrôlée* in France and have since been copied by German, Italian and Spanish wine growers. The aim of the Châteauneuf-du-Pape *vignerons*, led by the late Baron Le Roy of Château Fortia, was to safeguard their wine from trafficking and general abuse, and to this end they drew up a charter containing six stipulations. These ran as follows:

1. A completely natural delimitation of the area to be planted with vines was proposed; only land capable of bearing lavender and thyme was to be cultivated, these two plants preferring an equally poor soil to the vine.
2. Only specifically named grape varieties would be allowed to be planted.
3. The training and pruning of the vines was to be regulated.
4. The wine was to contain a minimum alcohol degree of 12.5°. (This is still the highest minimum level in all France.)
5. At harvest-time there was to be a *triage*, or sorting of the grapes. At least 5 per cent of the crop to be discarded, this to

ensure the inclusion of only healthy, well-ripened grapes.
6. No rosé wine was to made, and wine that failed to pass a
    tasting panel would not be sold as Châteauneuf-du-Pape.

For their time these laws were monumental. Their efficiency is well
judged from their almost unchanged existence about seventy years
later, and they now form the basis of the national laws of *appellation
d'origine*, themselves only adopted in 1936.

Such exemplary vigilance over their wine was repeated by the
vignerons in a municipal decree in 1954. Flying saucers had just come
to people's attention, and the village decree firmly stated:

Article 1. The flying overhead, landing and taking off of aeronautical machines called 'flying saucers' or 'flying cigars', of whatever
nationality they may be, is strictly forbidden on the territory of
the commune of Châteauneuf-du-Pape.

Article 2. Any aeronautical machine – 'flying saucer' or 'flying
cigar' – that lands on the territory of the commune will be
immediately taken off to the pound.

As a small footnote in the welter of viticultural history, Randall
Grahm, the owner of the highly rated Californian estate Bonny Doon,
who is an enthusiast for Rhône *cépages* and wines, called a Grenache-
Syrah-Mourvèdre wine of his 'Le Cigare Volant' after reading the
above words. This is a somewhat lean wine (empathy with the cigar
shape?) perhaps due to the youth of the vines.

In the early 1990s, the vineyards at Châteauneuf-du-Pape are
pretty much full up: the area under vines is about 3,300 hectares,
and there is little scope for further grubbing out of unwanted
scrubland.

In the village itself, there are not many more than 3,000 inhabitants.
Being the home of such a well-known wine, as well as the unofficial
capital of the Côtes du Rhône, it bustles with activity for a large part
of the year. Tourists drawn by the magic and renown of its name
wander through the sloping, confined streets, sometimes pausing to
ring the doorbell of a *vigneron* who has a sign announcing the sale
of wine outside his house. Side by side, beret-wearing Frenchmen
and robed Arabs linger around the tiny village square and fountain
beside the main road through the village. Arabs from North Africa
now form a large proportion of the vineyard personnel and are
housed in simple quarters on the large *domaines* or in little houses

in the village when they work for smaller *propriétaires*.

The Pope's Castle

The Pope's castle used to stand just at the top of the village, and its solitary corner tower now makes an easily recognizable local landmark. From the tower the view is immense: vines on all sides, set into a spartan ground full of large cream and rust-tinted stones. Clusters of trees denote the old-established wine *domaines*. Across to the south-west the Rhône curls away in a beckoning sweep. Meanwhile, the village below continues on its daily path, just occasionally giving an indication of its wealth and importance when a smart local car dashes past a lumbering vineyard machine.

The variety of good vines at Châteauneuf-du-Pape is greater than in any other French vineyard, and altogether thirteen different grapes are allowed to go into the wine. Few *domaines* now actually possess the complete range but 'the famous thirteen' risk becoming a delusion foisted on drinkers by freewheeling marketing advisers.

The Château de Beaucastel, under the meticulous François Perrin, is one with the full range of thirteen, which he vinifies separately from one another. Traditionally, Châteauneuf has been a Grenache Noir *appellation*. A fascinating tasting was held in April 1989 to herald the opening of the village's official tasting-room: there were twenty reds altogether, from fifteen different *domaines*, covering 1970 (two wines), 1969, 1967 (two wines), 1966 (four wines), 1964, 1962, 1961, 1957 (two wines), 1953, 1952, 1949 (two wines), 1947 and 1939.

The overriding impression of this superb glance into Châteauneuf's past was that it was above all a Grenache tasting – an examination of this grape more than of the *appellation* itself over thirty-one years of production. This was because the wines were so marked by the Grenache, a personal estimate being that many contained upwards of 80 per cent of this foundation grape. Nowadays the red Châteauneufs are drawn up with greater emphasis on two strong support *cépages* – the Syrah and the Mourvèdre – that firmly mark the wine; this would mean that such a tasting held in the year 2010 would hold less of a theme – there would be a considerably greater divergence in the styles and evolutions of the wines due to the use of a greater variety of grapes and more widely differing vinifications.

Those *vignerons* with all thirteen vines have tracked down some of the lesser plants only with difficulty. After the phylloxera attack, some of the vines, like the Picardan and the Muscardin, all but disappeared, and it was a revived interest in seeing how the wine would turn out when made with all thirteen that brought them out of total obscurity.

The full list of vine varieties contains most of the Côtes du Rhône 'regulars'. It is: Grenache, Syrah, Mourvèdre, Cinsault, Counoise, Vaccarèse, Terret Noir and Muscardin (all red grapes), and Clairette, Bourboulenc, Roussanne, Picpoul and Picardan (all white grapes). (The Grenache Blanc and the Terret Blanc are also planted). The first four vines are the most widely planted, while the Muscardin and the Counoise in particular are rarely found anywhere else, the former seemingly being unique to Châteauneuf-du-Pape. Its origin is obscure, but one of the village's most prominent theorists, the late Dr Philippe Dufays, was always adamant that it bears no resemblance to the Muscat or Muscadet family.

Recently the Château de la Gardine has introduced Muscardin to its vineyard, while the present Baron Le Roy of Château Fortia is also a firm supporter of this grape variety, as he explained in the following terms: 'You know, we'd be better off here if we replaced the Cinsault with the Muscardin. The Muscardin doesn't produce a lot, makes a wine of low degree and spreads out over the soil, preventing tractors from passing freely between the vines, all of which combine to put people off it. But I believe that it gives a freshness on the palate and helps the wine to achieve elegance.' Like Baron Le Roy, François Perrin of Château de Beaucastel is not in favour of the Cinsault, for he invariably finds that it gives a rather mean-tasting, thin wine.

The Cinsault has been fading in popularity since the mid-1980s, but much of its plantation during the 1960s took place because of what are now seen as misguided directives from the Ministry of Agriculture. At that time the local Institut National des Appellations d'Origine (INAO), guided by two supposed Rhône legends, the late Philippe Dufays and Pierre Charnay, circulated advice to the growers recommending that they should seek to 'cool the ardour' of the Grenache by planting the Cinsault; further advice – also intended in theory to strip the wine of its overt, obviously feisty regionality – was that vinifications should be lightened up by the use of *macération carbonique*.

By the 1990s many are the *vignerons* who complain about the low acidity of the Cinsault, its high pH, its fast-maturing wines and its enormous production if not severely controlled. Jean Abeille of Château Mont-Redon commented: 'Between 1960 and 1970, we planted seven of our roughly 90 hectares with Cinsault, as recommended by the authorities – those that a lot of people call the *blouses blanches* – the men in white coats. But I've now had to set a team of five to go through that plantation grafting Syrah on to the old Cinsault wood because the Cinsault has been giving too much wine that is also too light.'

So for many of the *vignerons*, the Cinsault is now a tiresome sideshow. Of course, it takes someone with the offbeat skill and patience of Jacques Reynaud from Château Rayas to show what can be done with the Cinsault: from his Château de Fonsalette property in the Vaucluse Côtes du Rhône, he crops just 25 hectolitres per hectare with this vine, that grows in light, clay–limestone soil. His Cinsault when young has a bright, dark red colour, a vigorously peppered bouquet, and good weight on the palate, with the pepperiness livened up by some agreeable acidity. For him the Cinsault is a contributor to the Grenache, but for many it is a detractor.

When comparing Muscardin and Cinsault at the same age – say, just over two years – both wines have a marked strain of orange tint in their red colour, but the Muscardin possesses attractive aromas and a welcome crispness within its light fruit – something that many of the mainstream growers cannot or cannot be bothered to achieve with the Cinsault.

The equally little-known Counoise, like the Grenache, comes from Spain. Pope Urban V (1362–70) was presented with some cuttings of it by a Spanish vice-legate called Conejo, and the French subsequently altered the vine's name to 'Counoise'. Only a very few *domaines* now cultivate it, but it has strong support from Baron Le Roy, who considers it one of the best grapes at Châteauneuf-du-Pape. François Perrin has it planted at Château de Beaucastel and believes that a *cuvée* of Vaccarèse and Counoise together can form the good, firm backbone for a classically styled Châteauneuf. Individually, they do not display this firmness. Again, Château Mont-Redon have been experimenting with single vats of less-known grapes, and a two-year-old Counoise showed a red to light purple colour, with a peppery bouquet that is said to be typical of the grape, and a fruit somewhat reminiscent of loganberries on the palate. If the *vignerons* as a whole ever adopt Baron Le Roy's enthusiasm for the Counoise, they will find that it is a hardy plant, very resistant to rot, and one that is harvested at the end of the *vendanges*, just before the Mourvèdre.

According to an external source, Jancis Robinson in her *Vines, Grapes and Wines*, the Counoise is merely a grape whose alias is Aubun, a sort of sub-Carignan, which finds favour around Provence and parts of the Rhône Valley. This is excessively disparaging – perhaps there is a case of mistaken identity with the Aubun?

Along with the Muscardin, the colour of the Counoise juice is generally the lightest at Châteauneuf. According to Baron Le Roy, laboratory tests conducted at the Montpellier wine school produced average colour rankings for red wine *cépages* on the following scale – the higher the figure, the darker the wine:

Syrah	2.5–3.7
Mourvèdre	1.6–2.4 (the latter in small crops)
Grenache Noir	1.3–2.0 (the latter from old vines)
Cinsault	1 (the axis of the scale)
Picpoul	1
Vaccarèse	0.8
Terret Noir	0.7–1.0

Counoise   0.7–1.2 (the latter in a small, overripe crop)

Muscardin   0.7

Of other well-known varietals, Cabernet Sauvignon achieved a 2.5–3.8 reading, and Gamay 1.6–1.9.

In the last century a lengthy study on the likely all-round contribution of each grape was carried out by Commandant Ducos, a member of a leading Marseille family who owned the *domaines* of Condorcet and La Nerte, and who died in 1914. It is still interesting to read his findings, even though there will never be any consensus among the growers as to what proportion and blend of grapes makes an ideal vat of Châteauneuf-du-Pape. Ducos destalked one-third of his crop, and vinified all the grape varieties together, ensuring that each vat held a balanced proportion of the different varieties.

Ducos recommended that for him, the ideal vat should contain grapes in the following proportions: 20 per cent Grenache and Cinsault, to provide the wine with 'warmth, liqueur-like sweetness and mellowness'; 40 per cent Mourvèdre, Syrah, Muscardin and Vaccarèse, to give it 'solidity, durability and colour, accompanied by a straightforward, almost thirst-quenching flavour'; 30 per cent Counoise and Picpoul, to supply 'vinosity, charm, freshness and accentuation of bouquet'; finally, 10 per cent mixed Clairette and Bourboulenc, to bring 'finesse, fire and sparkle' to the wine.

Commandant Ducos's flowery recommendations – which do not include all thirteen varieties – have been eroded this century for one main reason. Just as with Gigondas, Châteauneuf-du-Pape was for many years sold to Burgundian merchants as a 'booster' wine, to provide the northern wines with body and alcohol in weak years. The wine would be sold by the vat shortly after the harvest and would be shipped straight up to Burgundy to perform its medicinal transformation. Seeing such an assured market before them, growers at Châteauneuf were encouraged to plant much more Grenache, a plant that gives a high-degree wine.

Paul Avril of Clos des Papes remembers being told about this by his grandfather: 'He used to say that in the 1920s, he would receive 100 francs for a cask of Grenache at 14.5° alcohol from Burgundian merchants, but only 50 francs for a cask of 12.8° Syrah/Mourvèdre – so that obviously made everyone plant a lot more Grenache.'

Despite several fashionable, high-profile *domaines* changing their vine allocation away from being too Grenache-led, there is still a massive leaning towards the Grenache on the part of the many small producers at Châteauneuf. A survey conducted by the Growers' Federation in June 1991 showed that within the *appellation* there were 369 different *viticulteurs*, whose vineyards were on average 79.25 per cent Grenache Noir, 5.6 per cent Syrah, 4.7 per cent Mourvèdre, 3.3 per cent Cinsault, 2.3 per cent Clairette and 2 per cent Grenache Blanc – the remaining nearly 3 per cent composed of the other seven varietals.

While the smallholders remain often fiercely devoted to the Grenache – one can think immediately of men like Henri Bonneau, Paul Féraud, Pierre André, Lucien Barrot and, in his quieter way, Jacques Reynaud – there is a solid grouping of what one could term 'dissidents', who are working to express Châteauneuf's local characteristics with a different slant. Prominent among this group are the Château de Beaucastel, Château La Nerthe, Château Mont-Redon, Domaine du Vieux Télégraphe, Domaine de Font-de-Michelle and Domaine de la Solitude. Through a combination of restructuring their vineyard plantations and revising their vinification processes through new equipment and new methods, they are now issuing red Châteauneufs that are often excellent, but delicious in a different way from those of the old school.

After the spread of the Cinsault in the 1960s, much of it under official guidance, the 1970s was more the decade of the Syrah. This had been very successfully planted – according to the history books – at the Domaine de Condorcet in 1878. But the modern reference point for it was, tellingly, not its local success, but its triumph on the granite slopes of the northern Rhône, where Hermitage and Côte-Rôtie were gaining world renown. Planting of the Syrah therefore increased during the 1970s, but as Paul Avril of Clos des Papes says, hitting the nail precisely on the head, 'Remember one thing . . . you can restyle your vinification every year . . . you can't do that with a vineyard.'

Hence it is not until the vines are maybe fifteen years old that their success can be gauged. Vieux Télégraphe, for instance, stepped up their Syrah exposure considerably in the 1970s – to around 15 per cent – and there is no doubt that it helped to provide their wines with firm purple to black colours that are always very shiny. Another leading estate like Château de la Gardine also runs to nearly 15 per cent Syrah.

A personal view is that the Syrah has been less successful in the southern Rhône than might have been expected: at the time of its upsurge in popularity, it seemed to be *the* solution to making more refined wines, with very little equivocation about adaptability to the southern Rhône landscapes. Tasting of single-*cuve* Syrahs in the south over nearly twenty years raises some doubts: the fruit doesn't always appear to have the sharp definition shown by the northern Rhônes: indeed the nearest that the best – certainly the Château de Fonsalette Syrah, mostly planted in 1960 with some additions in the mid-1980s, is perhaps the prime example – get to the northern hierarchy is to resemble a good St-Joseph red from the central village of Mauves. Many fall below this.

Over the years some growers have spoken of a certain jamminess, something of a taste of *pommes anglaises* – it's tough being an Englishman – which represents a rather muddling extract from the grapes, and a lack of weight of fruit and tannic support that are so central and vital to the northern reds. The lack of granite down south may certainly have something to do with this.

Robert Mayberry, a North American who has spent years studying and tasting the grape varieties of the southern Rhône, gives some clues when he writes: 'Agreement seems to be growing that Syrah, a northern *cépage*, retains its character best in cooler and more northerly parts of the southern Rhône, as it also does, many growers observe, on sandy soil, siliceous like the granite of the north.'[1]

The fashionable grape of the 1980s was the Mourvèdre, and here one feels decidedly happy with results. In the 1970s it was never very enthusiastically spoken about by the growers, many of whom considered it to be too hard and four-square, especially when young. But its qualities are now widely recognized – those of bringing depth, quality tannins and backbone to the wine, as well as what the Bordelais call 'breeding'.

The Clos des Papes with around 20 per cent Mourvèdre has been one of the largest proportional planters of this vine; its wines are elegant and distinctively chewy, with plenty of liquorice on the aftertaste. Château de Beaucastel under the late Jacques Perrin was also an early Mourvèdre supporter, and their outstanding 1981 – one of the best wines made in the Rhône in the last twenty years

---

[1]Robert W. Mayberry, *Wines of the Rhône Valley: A Guide to Origins*, (New Jersey:Rowman and Littlefield, 1987).

– was actually composed of 25 per cent Mourvèdre, which has contributed much of the wine's staying-power and still tight reserve over ten years later. The Beaucastel reds of the early 1990s are now regularly made from 30 per cent Mourvèdre and their 1989 Cuvée Hommage Jacques Perrin contained 60 per cent Mourvèdre. Leading *domaines* very typically hold around 10 per cent Mourvèdre now – Font-de-Michelle, Mont-Redon and Fortia have been increasing to near or above this figure, for instance – while Vieux Télégraphe and the newly revitalized Château La Nerthe (see page 394) both work with 15 per cent.

Meanwhile, the amount of Grenache planted runs with an exceptional low of 30 per cent at Beaucastel, between around 50 per cent and just over 80 per cent of any vineyard. At the low end of the scale comes Château La Nerthe, which since its purchase by David et Foillard in the mid-1980s has had an enormous investment pumped into it. The new director, M. Alain Dugas, has restricted the Grenache in the revised plantations to just 62 per cent, while another low-key holding is La Fagotière of Pierry Chastan with 60 per cent. Similarly, the Domaine de Nalys has 55 per cent, Domaine de la Solitude 60 per cent and Font-de-Michelle and La Gardine have 65 and 70 per cent respectively. More smaller properties are likely to go this way during the 1990s, and one cannot help but have a suspicion that the anti-Grenache league (probably encouraged by legislators in Brussels anxious to cut back on alcohol levels in red table wines) will become too zealous. Take away that Grenache central support, and you have stripped Châteauneuf of much of its heart and *typicité*. In the case of Beaucastel, François Perrin explains their small 30 per cent Grenache holding by saying: 'The best use of the Grenache is taking a small quantity from old vines – those of over fifty years. My father didn't plant any Grenache in his last six years here, and I haven't, so from around 1971 the share of Grenache statistically has fallen. If you work the Grenache and the Mourvèdre together, you have a greater chance of a finish that is *vif* and more acid – facets the Grenache on its own can't provide.'

What François Perrin is also very concerned about – a view shared by the most conscientious *viticulteurs* like Pierre André – is the quality of the modern Grenache root-stock, with its various clonal influences. The first selection introduced some years after phylloxera was the Rupestris du Lot: this came from American origins, was vigorous, drought-resistant due to deep roots that could seek out water and was thought perfectly suited to the local *terroir*. Today this still forms 65 per cent of the vineyard, and until the mid-1970s it was the most frequent new planting at Châteauneuf.

However, by the 1990s, there is a new king or favourite – the 110 Richter (please excuse the names). This is in part a cross from the Rupestris du Lot, and confers a bit less vigour on the grafted plant, with the aim of calming down the productive tendencies of the vine; its roots go deep as well, and by 1991 17 per cent of the vineyard was planted with this root-stock. However, local specialists estimate that it will be another fifty years before these two – the Rupestris and the Richter – are in what they would call a balance.

In the meantime there is another contender growing in popularity: this is the 140 Ruggeri (here we go again). This presents a new orientation, one nearer to the Rupestris du Lot, and is *the* strain for chalky or limestone soil, such as in the south of the *appellation* or for some of the sandier areas towards Courthézon in the north-east. This is vigorous and, like both the others, drought-resistant, and now forms 6 per cent of the plantation.

Other root-stocks that have been popular, but which are fading in the 1990s, are the SO4, the 44–53 Malegue and the Paulsen 1103. The SO4 (now 2 per cent) was used for the Syrah. Its problem is that it thrives on humid soil, and because of its small base, its stability could not be guaranteed without its being trained along wires. The 44–53 Malegue (2 per cent) was perhaps the most widely planted strain in the 1970s; it is now known to assimilate poorly any magnesium in the soil – and the Grenache vine needs lots of magnesium. Exit the Malegue. The Paulsen 1103 (2 per cent) is a cousin of the 140 Ruggeri, but doesn't have its compatibility with chalky soil – so it, too, is out of favour.

This topic may seem like an unwelcome diversion, but it is of vital importance for the 1990s and beyond. The subject we are intrinsically dealing with here on a greater scale than in past decades is water – the lack of it or the suddenness of it. All the above root-stocks are drought-resistant: with just 50 mm of water between May and July 1991 – now a typical occurrence – and a dowsing 230 mm (9 inches) dropping out of the sky in just four hours on 29 July 1991, quickly to be washed away, the shortage of water is an issue for which only a few growers have yet prepared themselves mentally.

Jean-Pierre Perrin of Château de Beaucastel has no doubts. 'The water shortage is going to be a dramatic problem for those growers who over the years have used herbicides. They've sprayed them on their vines, and the roots have therefore a tendency to turn to the surface of the soil to seek the moisture there. If you weed the vines and turn the soil, the vines will seek below the surface for resources. If you don't turn the soil, and leave all the work to the herbicides, the roots stay near the top soil and miss any reserves of water lower down. Equally, if you stop tilling the soil, when it rains, the water stays on the surface and doesn't filter through as it should.'

Jean-Pierre Perrin feels that the drought years from 1988 onwards may speed up people's awareness of the adverse effect that herbicides are having on their supposedly cherished vines. He also finds it strange that some large *domaines* have introduced water drip systems to nourish the vines – great lengths of piping that run alongside each row of vines, especially the young ones. 'This is expensive and time-consuming; it would be much easier just to hoe the vineyards to get the maximum benefit of any rainfall, with no wastage at all.'

At Châteauneuf, a mature vine's roots will go down to around 2.5 metres, against 4 or 5 metres in many vineyards. It may take ten years to reach the 2.5-metre mark, but, like many respecters of nature's ways, Jean-Pierre Perrin believes that the vine must suffer a bit to produce good wine: 'I can't imagine irrigating to make a good wine,' he states flatly.

One of the most interesting single vineyards that demonstrates the benefit of careful and natural handling is Pierre André's hectare or so at La Côte Ronde, east of the village towards Courthézon. This is just one of his thirty-one plots, and the vines there are 100 years old. Their health and vigour in midsummer is a revelation. Pierre André, now sixty-five, is tigerish in his view that nature should be allowed to take its course, without the intrusion of chemicals. Hard work there is a-plenty, but one look at his flourishing Grenache Noir vines of such colossal age is enough to convert even the most caustic of doubters. M. André hops around the vineyard, delighting in pointing out the stout members of his little troupe – some of them 8 feet high, with their vegetation sprouting lushly from seven branches. He then shows just how random planting was at the turn of the century by indicating a sole, fat, healthy Cinsault, and two rows away a single Clairette of the same age and vigour.

To stand with Pierre André looking over the old vines that he and two generations before him have treated so carefully, when at eight in the evening of a July day the sun is still reluctant to shed its fire, the crickets continue busy with their work, the jasmine plants banked on odd ledges above the vineyard still exhale their scents and there is a swooping view across to a mist-shrouded Mont Ventoux, one completely, humbly, understands his passionate defence of the *terroir*.

M. André is a determined Grenache supporter – his 16 hectares comprise 80 per cent Grenache – and along with him comes a body of well-known names, often with small to medium-sized holdings, like Bosquet des Papes, Lucien Barrot, Chante-Perdrix, Clos du Mont-Olivet, Paul Féraud of Domaine du Pegaü, Chante-Cigale and Domaine du Grand Tinel. The last-named differs in that its vineyard is large – 75 hectares.

There are also two more reclusive *vignerons* in the Grenache camp, whose talents are as extraordinary as their shyness. Both are utterly devoted to the Grenache, but in the way that partners are devoted to one another after forty or fifty years of marriage – nothing showy, almost taken for granted, but the view runs deep indeed. Henri Bonneau uses about 80 per cent Grenache in his Réserve des Célestins, while Jacques Reynaud uses mostly Grenache in most of his Château Rayas bottlings. M. Bonneau's wines, like his 1955, retain their depth and richness even after thirty years, as do the wines of the late Louis Reynaud at Château Rayas – his 100 per cent Grenache Château Rayas of 1962 is still moving along very richly.

Another band of *viticulteurs* with a very high proportion of Grenache in their vineyards are the mixed-culture vine growers; these men will sometimes have almost entirely Grenache-filled vineyards growing next to their cherry and olive trees. This group generally sell their grapes to *négociants*.

The *appellation* area is not confined to Châteauneuf-du-Pape but runs out from the village towards the neighbouring communities of Orange, Courthézon, Bédarrides and Sorgues. Nearly everywhere is to be seen its most characteristic feature, the large, smooth stones that always make a vivid impression on the visitor. These red and cream-coloured stones, varying in size from the equivalent of a Provençal tomato to that of a very well-grown melon, are not alluvial deposits from the Rhône, as is the popular belief, but are the deposits left by very ancient Alpine glaciers that descended across France until halted by the Rhône to the west of the village.

The stoniest land of all is to the north and north-west of Château-neuf-du-Pape; the vines of Château Mont-Redon, Château de Cabrières and Château Maucoil appear engulfed in a sea of stones, leaving the clay soil underneath barely visible. As a general rule, it is true to say that the more stones there are, the higher the maturity of the grapes will be, for the stones act to absorb the heat rays of the sun and reflect them back on to the vines. In midsummer, for instance, the stones remain warm to the touch until long after sundown, and in the late 1980s and early 1990s the extreme intensity of the sun still apparent as late as seven in the evening has become rather alarming.

While the stones help the vines to ripen, they also directly hinder the working of the vineyards. Before the introduction of machinery around 1950, all wooden implements like ploughs had to be metal-reinforced, and today wear and tear on even the most robust modern machines is no less considerable. New vine plantation, in particular, is a slow, painstaking process. Most of the young vines are trained against wooden stakes to save them from being buffeted by the southern *mistral* wind, and the drilling of two holes for the plant and the stake is very slow work on such unyielding ground.

Not all the *appellation* is so profusely covered in stones, though. In the southern part, near the Domaines St-Préfert and Condorcet, the land is more gravelly and so produces lighter, slightly less alcoholic wines. Then to the east and north-east, in the direction of Bédarrides and Courthézon, the land becomes alternatively more sandy and more clayey but still retains many of the stones. Well-sited *domaines* here are those of Beaucastel, Solitude and Vieux Télégraphe.

With three quite distinct soil types inside their vineyard area, many of the smaller growers are happy to have their vines spread out in different plots, or *parcelles*: this gives them ample opportunity to blend into a single vat grapes that differ in sugar content and maturity. Such blending was traditionally much valued by the popes, according to M. Paul Avril, of the Clos des Papes, whose 32 hectares are themselves spread into eighteen *parcelles*: 'The popes used to receive their taxes in kind from the local *vignerons*, and so installed one giant *cuve* into which went all the different wines. They were always delighted to find that the assembled wine from this *cuve* was of a consistently high standard,' he concluded.

Apart from the Syrah, which grows along wires, all the vines are trained in the usual Gobelet style, with a broad spacing of 2 metres between each plant to permit the passage of vineyard machinery.

By 1992, legislation is in hand to allow wire training of the white *cépages*. But because the *appellation* laws decree an obligatory sorting of the grapes, or *triage*, before vinification, no mechanical harvesting is done at Châteauneuf-du-Pape. This is certainly one of the more curious features when looking at the changing methods in France these days: the laws of 1923 are still holding up strongly in the pursuit for quality.

For the most part, the vines are disease-free, helped by the combination of sun and wind that is typical of the southern Rhône climate. The principal problems are *coulure*, or malformation of the fruit after flowering; *pourriture*, or rotting of the grapes, the *ver de la grappe*, or grape worm, that can cause rot; and oïdium, or powdery mildew. The Grenache, and particularly its younger vines, is susceptible to *coulure*, and the style of the 1983s, for instance, was markedly changed by the lower than usual amounts of Grenache in the wines. There are also occasional bouts of oïdium attacking several vine varieties, with the Picpoul, Counoise and Grenache most prone. The other growing problem, although it is one that Châteauneuf has experienced over the centuries, is drought, and the areas that contain less clay subsoil under the alluvial stones are more prone to this – around La Gardine, with its chalk subsoil, for example, and on the east side of the *appellation*, towards Courthézon, where there is a sandier subsoil.

Until 1869 Châteauneuf-du-Pape, like many French wine villages, respected a *ban des vendanges*, which regulates the opening date of the harvest to greatest common benefit. In olden days it used to be decided either by a committee of growers or, more often, by a local landlord or *grand seigneur*, since the custom dates back to the fifteenth century. In the days when many taxes and rents were paid in wine, the feudal landlords had no interest in receiving unripe grapes from their tenants on the land and so instituted the *ban* or public proclamation permitting the start of harvesting. By the eighteenth century the intention was more to give all growers an equal chance of making and selling their wine under similar conditions, and anyone who harvested before time was fined five *livres*, although his crop was not confiscated, as was decreed at nearby Cairanne. The official day of harvesting, according to local records, was most commonly a Monday, Sunday being excluded on the grounds that it should be consecrated to rest and what is obscurely termed *offices*.

In 1962, at the instigation of M. Pierre Lançon of Domaine de la Solitude, the *ban des vendanges* made a comeback at Châteauneuf-du-Pape. The ceremony now takes place in the cellars of the village château, and with great pomp a cross-section of the grapes is tasted. If they are judged to be ripe, a public declaration is cried out, allowing the start of harvesting two days later. The dates for this vary according to the vintage. In 1989 the harvest was called around 2 September, in 1984 it was nearer 20 September. Dates supplied by the Fédération des Vignerons for the period 1966–90 inclusive show an earliest average date of harvest over this time of 10 September – in 1990 – and a latest average date of 27 September – in 1971. Such dates encompass the totality of *domaines* at Châteauneuf.

Growers do not have to start harvesting immediately after the *ban*. A *vigneron* like François Perrin of Beaucastel takes each year strictly as it comes, so in 1987 waited until around 20 September; in 1988 15 September; and in 1989, like 1986 and 1969, started as early as about 3–4 September. Generally the first red grapes to be picked are the Cinsault and the Syrah; the Mourvèdre comes last.

When the *vendange* starts, the streets of the village swarm with activity, and a barely concealed feeling of excitement pervades the atmosphere. For three or four weeks Châteauneuf-du-Pape looks like a wine village – and smells like one. Open doors reveal newly washed barrels, lengths of rubber piping and churning presses. From even the quietest alleyways drifts a smell of fermenting must. Outside one or two cellars mounds of grapes are laid out on large tables, and are slowly sifted through by stooping workers. This is the *triage*, or rejection of at least 5 per cent of the grapes, initiated in 1923 and done either at the time of picking or sometimes at the cellars, where greater control can be exercised. In bad years over one-quarter of the crop is set aside by the most conscientious growers. In 1987, for instance, *domaines* such as Vieux Télégraphe had their harvesting interrupted by bad weather, which brought on rot. Their pickers therefore had to go through the vineyards twice subsequently, while Château Mont-Redon recall sending their pickers through the vineyards three times in 1975 in an attempt to harvest each grape variety strictly according to its maturity.

The inferior grapes taken out go towards ordinary table wine. The *triage* is most often performed in the vineyards, although close supervision is necessary since not every picker is able to perceive the difference between a good and a bad grape. To help, they are sometimes provided with two containers (often green and red to denote the difference) for the healthy grapes and the discard, or *rapé*.

When the *vigneron* finally receives the harvest at his cellars, he knows that the weeks ahead will be full of worry and preoccupation. With wines based on a single grape, the grower can happily watch over the progress and development of one 'child'; at Châteauneuf he must administer care and attention to widely differing 'children' – some vats filled with high-degree Grenache juice, others filled with softer white-grape juice and still others containing dark, highly scented Syrah juice. The grower must use his native wizardry to know when and in what proportions to assemble the vats and, above all, must ensure that his final wine is well balanced.

Nowadays such a thing as a 'typical' Châteauneuf-du-Pape is hard to find. This is because the vineyard is in a near-constant state of flux, with growers experimenting with alternating combinations of the thirteen grape varieties and with differing methods of vinifying them. The traditional Châteauneuf-du-Pape that would be fermented for a month or more and then aged for five years is now virtually a ghost from the past; growers simply cannot afford to keep their wine off the market for so long. This is partly why more white wine is being made: the 2–3 per cent of the crop made into white of 1981–3 became 5–6 per cent in 1987–9.

With so many variables at work, it is possible to come across four or more different types of Châteauneuf red that will please strictly according to the drinker's taste. During the 1970s the prime consideration for those *domaines* leaving the general herd was to lighten the wine. They may have wrapped up their actions in words such as 'seeking greater fruitiness', but there was no doubt that they were concerned about the future marketability of the classically heavy-laden style of wine. Early names in this lighter vein were Pierre Lançon's Domaine de la Solitude, Paul Coulon at the Domaine de Beaurenard and Philippe Dufays at Domaine de Nalys. The chosen method was to vinify the grapes by the *macération earbonique* system, or to adapt this, so that there were fewer intense tannins in the wine, a lighter colour due to a shortened *cuvaison* and contact with the skins, and an extraction of fruit that occurred more within the grape than without, and so was lighter and fresher. This epoch – the one of centrally recommended Cinsault plantation and *macération carbonique* to make Châteauneuf respectable for ignorant urban mass consumers – was not a famous one for the *appellation*.

The 1980s saw a continued drive for greater elegance. This was not quite gobbledegook for lightening the wines, but a serious attempt at putting leading wines alongside the best from Bordeaux; interestingly, given the past commercial liaisons between Château-neuf and Burgundy – with the southern wine being shipped north to boost the Burgundians in weak years – the point of reference for the growers is not Burgundy but Bordeaux. The word 'structure' became popular; elegance and length on the palate became more revered than density and alcoholic power, and finer tannic support was sought. The continued spread of the Mourvèdre helped this, along with refinements such as the way the grapes were handled prior to fermentation – to crush lightly or introduce whole grapes was very much a matter of debate – and the inevitable question of handling the wines in wood – the size of container (traditionally larger *foudres* have been used very commonly), the length of stay and the age and origin of the oak. A *domaine* whose wines represent the various twists and turns in this debate is Vieux Télégraphe: it has changed its style with different thought patterns prevailing in its making on several occasions since the second half of the 1970s, and in so doing has sacrificed some of the regionality that used to be present. The gain? In successful years, a delicious deep fruitiness, elegance and approachability; but in years where the politics of the wine-making served to impede rather than enhance the wine, a somewhat bland, overly commercial wine, without much local pedigree, has resulted.

While there are *domaines* seeking lighter wines easier to drink young – in this group come Domaine de Beaurenard, Domaine du Vieux Lazaret, Domaine de Nalys, Domaine Trintignant and most of the *cuvées* of Domaine de la Solitude and Château de Cabrières until a revision of policy at both estates in the late 1980s – there is still very much a hard core who lean towards the methods taught to them by their fathers and grandfathers. These are *domaines* like the Clos du Mont-Olivet, Bosquet des Papes, Les Clefs d'Or, the Domaine de Montpertuis, Domaine Lucien Barrot et Fils, Domaine du Pegaü, Le Vieux Donjon, Domaine Pierre André, and Henri Bonneau, plus of course many others who lead with a strong Grenache presence and a conservative outlook. In these cases a general custom is to light-crush the grapes – without destalking – and let the must ferment for two to three weeks. In most *domaines* closed concrete vats are used for the alcoholic *cuvaison*. By the spring, after the malolactic, all the wine will have been transferred to wooden ageing containers.

After a stay of twelve months to two years – usually in older wood and *foudres* rather than smaller *pièces* – the wine is prepared for bottling. Most of these *domaines* prefer to fine and filter their wine before releasing it for sale, so that the client is presented with an entirely clear bottle.

Obviously, variations exist. Some *domaines* like to destalk and destem before vinification – Château La Nerthe does this for the whole crop, and Château Mont-Redon for half the crop, whatever the conditions. 'We're after the softer tannins from the skins rather than the more astringent ones in the stalks and stems,' explains M. Jean Abeille of Mont-Redon. Equally, if a rich, long-lived and strongly coloured wine is sought, some or all of the juice from the second pressing will be added: Château de Beaucastel round off their wine in some vintages in this way, while Château Rayas, an exceedingly traditional, good and quirky *domaine*, have always added all the second-pressing juice.

Another variation of practice is the way in which the grapes are handled before they are fermented. In front-line properties like Vieux Télégraphe, there has been a retreat from a stance taken up in the late 1970s of crushing the grapes only very lightly, if at all.

Domaine du Vieux Télégraphe used to leave 30 per cent of their grapes intact, crushing the rest only lightly. In the mid-1980s they gently crushed all the crop; in the early 1990s they crush about half the crop, so they are still searching for an ideal. 'The gentle crush – whatever its exact percentage – serves to give our type of wine, one that is agreeable when young but which can age well', explains Henri Brunier *père*.

Château de Beaucastel actually leave as much as 80 per cent of their grapes intact but then follow their own *vinification à chaud* method, whereby the outside of the grapes is immediately heated to 80°C for about two minutes to extract the colour and the aromas inside the skin, as well as to take out enzymes which make the wine age and oxidize quickly. They destalk most of the crop, which has been unusual for Châteauneuf, and in 1987 François Perrin actually experimented with two open wood fermenting vats, the grapes being crushed by foot. 'They held 140 hectolitres each, one vat was Grenache, the other was Syrah, and we did a *pigeage* on the *chapeau* at regular intervals. My friend Gérard Chave at Hermitage is so keen on this method that I thought I would try it on a small scale. I'll keep a few bottles for myself to see, but most of the wine will go into the mainstream vats and casks,' commented François Perrin. After the *vinification à chaud*, things return more to normal at Beaucastel, with a cooling to 20–25°C, at which temperature a steady two- or three-week fermentation takes place.

Meanwhile considerable variations have started to occur in the producers' stance on the use of wood. There are some who are willing to pass up the use of wood in certain vintages – André Brunel at Les Cailloux and Jérôme Quiot at Domaine du Vieux Lazaret forewent its use in 1987 – 'the 1987 was too light – it simply didn't have enough structure', commented M. Brunel – while the Vieux Lazaret policy until 1987 was to expose their wines to no wood. This changed with the 1988 vintage, when they started to put a part of their wine through 225-litre *pièces* for two to five months. 'We think this brings a bit more complexity to our wine,' stated Vera Böker, a German lady who looks after the Vieux Lazaret marketing. 'We are going to stay with new wood, but its use will vary according to the style of the vintage. 1989, with its greater structure than 1988, received longer in wood than the year before.'

André Brunel first did some experiments with new oak in 1985, and makes no secret of the fact that he was prompted by the American taste for new oak, so that these wines were reserved for the American market. 'The Americans are keener than others on new wood, so I did it this way, with between two and nine months in cask. In 1988 I tried half brand new wood, half one-year wood, and we'll see how it goes,' he says.

François Perrin of Château de Beaucastel remains faithful to casks he has worked with over several harvests. 'I don't seek new oak for my reds,' he comments. 'I replace the casks when they are tired – that means at twenty to twenty-five years old; my wines receive between six and fourteen months in cask, but the time varies very much according to the vintage: 1987 had just six months; 1986 had over twelve months. The only grape variety that may lend itself to new oak in my opinion is the Syrah, on which I am doing some *essais*.'

The acquisition of Château La Nerthe (the 'h' has been restored as part of the rebuilding of the image) by the originally Beaujolais-based *négociant* group of David et Foillard and Éts Richard of Paris, and the insertion of large amounts of capital into its facilities have brought on stream the *appellation*'s leading battery of new oak casks. Now they work with *barriques* of one to three years of age, which combine in equal proportions with the old 50-hectolitre château *foudres* and the enamel-lined vats to store the wine over about a year before its bottling. Likewise, Château de la Gardine work with a total of around 200 young oak casks, which have a one year in three rotation. At four years old, these casks are usually sold off to local Côtes du Rhône *domaines*.

Another famous *domaine* that uses new or young oak for ageing a part of its red wines is Château Mont-Redon, but all these properties are exercising great self-control in case they overpower their wines. In many ways, ageing in young casks seems to serve three purposes at Châteauneuf; the first is the fermentation and short stay of white, higher-acidity grapes like the Roussanne – growers ranging from Alain Jaume's Grand Veneur to Beaucastel and La Gardine do this. The second is the addition of a little depth to red wines that are by nature rather light and soft: accordingly, about 10 per cent of the Domaine du Vieux Lazaret red spends about three months in one- to three-year casks, while about 15 per cent of the Domaine de la Solitude red is exposed to first-year Limousin oak barrels from the Côte d'Or, ageing for about a year prior to *assemblage* with wines kept either for six months in older *foudres* or in stainless steel. In both cases, the young oak brings greater structure to wines that are fruity and easy and not otherwise especially challenging.

Third and last are the properties like La Gardine and La Nerthe that have very successfully introduced the discreet use of young wood into their already firmly flavoured red wines. La Gardine 1990 is a wine that might tire after about eight years were it not for the support and spine brought from 20 per cent of the wine ageing for nine months in casks of one to four years old. The La Nerthe process described earlier was strikingly successful in 1990, when a superb wine, oozing intense fruit and great richness was made – a classic, with the 1989 red only a little behind it, the latter marked by more rounded tannins. The great achievement by M. Dugas and his team at La Nerthe was that the 1990's pure regionality came through, even with the use of some young oak. At La Nerthe, Nevers oak is preferred for the whites, as it is by several modernist growers, and Allier for the reds.

On one issue, most growers seem to hold a uniform attitude – the achievement of great balance in their wines without overweighting them with the extracts of heavily crushed stalks, stems and pips, or with the insertion of stale aromas and flavours from using worn-out casks. In the second half of the 1980s another development has come through the working of the *chapeau* of the must during fermentation, something which has preoccupied Marcel Guigal at Côte-Rôtie to a considerable extent. Mastery of this process brings the reward of greater aroma and a more concentrated, almost core fruitiness, since the top must is never allowed to even start to dry out. Château de la Gardine and Château La Nerthe both adopted automatic *pigeage* vats in the mid-1980s, whereby metal plates are moved down the vats for a few minutes at timed intervals. 'For us, the *pigeage* serves to extract the aromatic potential of the Syrah, also its colour and best quality,' comments Patrick Brunel of La Gardine. 'I don't think we could get this from a traditional vat: don't forget that in the past much of the action of the *pigeage* was done by the chaps treading and punching the open fermentation vat as the grape juice slowly converted itself.' It is also felt that this process helps to restrict any tendencies towards oxidation that a largely Grenache-based vat may suffer. Another way round this is for the growers to place the Grenache, lightly crushed, in the bottom of the vat and the Syrah, for example, on top of it – unbroken.

There is little doubt that the *pigeage* has played a role in contributing greater balance and finesse to these wines at their preparation stage. The Domaine de Beaurenard is another devotee of the automatic *pigeage*.

Macération carbonique has been a subject of much discussion and debate at Châteauneuf since the first tests at Narbonne were announced as successful in the 1950s. Two well-known *domaines* have mostly led the way in using adapted *macération carbonique* vinifications – Nalys and Beaurenard. Both start the process by using some totally uncrushed grapes – *raisins entiers* – with Nalys introducing an untouched harvest and Beaurenard a half-untouched crop. Nalys use carbon dioxide in their vinification, whereas M. Paul Coulon, whose new cellars were first used for the 1988 harvest, runs an extended fifteen- to twenty-one-day *cuvaison* in his automatic *pigeage inox* vats at a temperature of 32°C. But both like to accelerate the old procedures after fermentation. The Beaurenard wine receives six to nine months in cask, so that generally most of it is bottled within the year following the harvest. It is immediately striking for its racy fruit and accessibility, unusual in a red Châteauneuf, but it also possesses some discreet underlying tannin that gives it welcome backbone. Nalys, too, release their wine early, often within fifteen months of the harvest, and their results approach those of Beaurenard, although their reds do not have as great a substance on the palate.

The vinification by maceration with the help of carbonic gas is done by both Domaine de Nalys and now to a lesser extent by the Domaine de la Solitude. By this method, the grapes are piled directly from the vineyard into their vats, where the sheer force of weight breaks up the bottom layers and heats them up through the natural compression arising from the presence of so many grapes in a confined space. The vats are filled with carbonic gas, and in these circumstances, as fermentation gets under way, a maximum of fruit is extracted as opposed to a more normally balanced equation of fruit, tannin and acidity. This wine comes out much lighter in style than usual, and although it may not be 'typical' of Châteauneuf-du-Pape, it is both marketable and readily drinkable within a year or two, no doubt to the satisfaction of these growers' bank managers.

The main exponent of this *macération carbonique* style of vinification was since as early as 1954 M. Pierre Lançon of Domaine de la Solitude. In talking about his method, he made the following observations: 'What I want above all from my wine is bouquet and finesse. I attach less importance to colour and body, which you could say were the most typical characteristics of a red Châteauneuf-du-Pape. I use an adapted *macération carbonique* formula, whereby I leave the uncrushed grapes to ferment slowly in vats filled with carbonic gas. Under the action of the carbonic gas the grapes start to ferment within their skins, but to avoid giving the wine a purely *macération carbonique* taste – a simple fruitiness like that found in the wines of the Beaujolais – I then run off the juice and let the grapes ferment in the normal way. This permits the wine to regain its own Châteauneuf-du-Pape character. At the end of the fermentation, I run the wine off and press the left-over pulp three or four times. I generally add the juice of the first three pressings to give the wine slightly greater richness and then leave it to complete its malolactic fermentation. By before the New Year it is normally in the maturing casks, where I leave it to age for a little over six months.'

By the early 1990s, with Pierre Lançon in his late sixties, his sons Jean and Michel reduced the *macération carbonique* exposure of their wine to about one-quarter of the total crop. They favour this process for the Syrah and the Grenache, but not for the Mourvèdre, which is destalked and given a traditional twenty-five-day *cuvaison*. Cask-ageing, in a mixture of brand new wood and older *foudres*, has also extended a little, indicating that with a new generation this *domaine* is having second thoughts about its methods of the last three or more decades.

La Solitude was certainly a *domaine* whose wines spent some years in the wilderness. Until the mid-1970s the wine of La Solitude was always good and reliable, with some truly memorable wines like the 1964 and 1971 standing out, but a dull patch ensued. Said by some to have been the result of overcropping from the vineyards, some years like 1979 and 1981 were little better than glorified rosés. They had none of the richness that earlier vintages could aspire to after about five or six years. The 1985 and 1989 red Solitudes were more dense and much better wines, so one can only hope that matters are on the mend at this estate.

Old-timers would gruffly and correctly say that these hastened-along wines were not the real Châteauneuf, but while the 'real' Châteauneuf can be blandly talked about, it is an unfortunate fact of life that it is a wine unknown to many. When found outside the immediate vicinity of the production area the wine is often false, mixed or diluted. Perhaps it is the innate charm of the name, easily pronounceable, but a lot more 'Châteauneuf-du-Pape' is drunk than is ever made.

To their credit, the *vignerons* of Châteauneuf have held together in seeking to defend their name. The Syndicat des Vignerons is active in promoting the good name, not through superficial press advertisements but through extensive tastings, both of old wines and of the wines of young vintages. A visiting wine journalist, even one not well known to the growers, will have a tasting of over forty reds from the vintage laid on; of the top names, probably only the reclusive Jacques Reynaud of Château Rayas will not send a young wine (why should he, if he can eventually produce fine goods?). There is a smart tasting *salon*, built in 1989, in the centre of the village. The laws of 1923 have not been amended to encompass the spectacle of harvesting machines here – the discard of unsatisfactory grapes takes precedence; and there is still a great and stimulating network of private people trying to make their own individual wine under their own name.

The local *négoce* has been gradually raising its game, as well. In the 1950s and 1960s, local merchants were tiny beside the likes of Cruse from Bordeaux and Jadot and Latour from Burgundy. It was the big fish from elsewhere in France who secured the rich pickings, the best *cuvées*, from the mass of growers who did no bottling.

Nowadays things have changed. A new bottle has been produced – very similar to the estate-bottled one with its coat of arms, but with the words 'Châteauneuf-du-Pape Appellation Contrôlée' on it. This cannot be used by *négociants* outside the region. The company of Berger Pastis has revitalized three businesses by grouping them together and modernizing their working practices – now Ogier, Bessac and Malbec are all one unit. Père Anselme have expanded their access to single-*domaine* wines, guiding their vinification as well as looking after their selling, while the Caves St-Pierre are also improving both their wines and the presentation of them.

The trend is very much for Châteauneuf to be bottled within the *appellation* zone. M. Paul Avril, ex-President of the Syndicat des Vignerons, states that since the late 1970s the percentage of wine bottled on the spot has risen from a tiny 25 to around 60 per cent. The rest is sold in bulk, in order of volume, first to local *négociants*, second to Burgundian *négociants* and lastly to the *négoce* of Bordeaux. 'In the medium term it would obviously be desirable to enforce compulsory bottling within the *appellation* confines, as has been done in Alsace,' he said. 'But it's worth remembering that 80 per cent of all Alsatian wine was bottled in their region prior to their ruling. Our task is much harder, but that doesn't lessen our determination. It's been shocking to taste some of the bottles of Châteauneuf-du-Pape brought back from abroad by visiting *vignerons*, and we're fed up with seeing the wine and its name blatantly trafficked.'

At its best, Châteauneuf-du-Pape is indeed a majestic wine. Its alluring colour is reminiscent of rubies, while its powerful bouquet seems to nurture the many herbs and wild flowers that grow scattered about the hills and plains around Avignon. The bouquet remains intriguingly complex, however; its warmth certainly never deserts it, but the nuances within it can vary subtly during the course of drinking a bottle. The late owner of one of the best *domaines*, M. Jacques Perrin of Château de Beaucastel, used to put it like this: 'I can tell you that some of Châteauneuf-du-Pape's characteristic aromas resemble irises, violets and roasted almonds, for instance, but then we could turn to another bottle from another vat or another vintage and find that the predominating sensations were perhaps truffles, laurel and local herbs. In addition, these may alter the longer the wine is exposed to the air, so you can't really talk in black-and-white terms about what a Châteauneuf-du-Pape should specifically resemble – all of which, of course, adds to the wine's enticement!'

On the palate, traditionally made Châteauneuf-du-Pape is whole-hearted and enveloping, the sort of wine that staves off the cold on wintry nights. Generally rather tannic until its fifth or sixth birthday, the traditional style of wine thereafter 'straightens out', until its commanding elements of fruit, alcohol and richness are well fused.

This power and harmony will be retained in outstanding vintages such as the majestic 1961 and 1978 for thirty years or more, while the 1981 and perhaps the 1988, some 1989 and 1990 will run for twenty years or so, but Châteauneuf cannot be considered a 'stayer wine' like Hermitage with its Syrah tannic support. What the Grenache does perform at Châteauneuf is the task of giving its wines guts, chewiness and an alcoholic motor that will keep the wine ticking over for years after its demise has been presumed to have occurred. As examples of this longevity, a quick glance at some old wines tasted in 1989:

Clos du Mont-Olivet 1957 (bottle)
Exuberant ruby; very rich, gamey nose; palate is rich – very sustained peppery and toasted flavours. Not that complex. Good length, bouquet ageing with air. High predominance of Grenache in this.

Les Clefs d'Or 1953 (magnum)
Brightly hued, attractive; southern richness on nose – hot, cooked fruits and berries. Palate a little musty, but has excellent richness, balance is sound, and runs on to a quiet finish. Very good.

Domaine de Mont-Redon 1952 (bottle)
Clear, plum ruby colour; warm, coffee-bean aromas, tertiary smells (at the age of thirty-seven). Palate starts quite full but then thins; tiring on the finish. Its southern richness is pulling it along.

Château de la Gardine 1949 (bottle)
Pale brick colour, thinning; extreme coffee-bean nose, hint of dryness – more advanced than the Clefs d'Or 1949. Palate by contrast has a firm attack – its rich flavours are slipping, though. Alcohol coming through – the attack is the best moment.

Les Cailloux 1947 (bottle)
Thorough ruby, still has last vestiges of plum colouring. Bouquet is round, full – farmyard smells rather than coffee-beans, cigar

box or cedar. Delicious palate – power and firm flavours all together still. Balance very good. Runs through to some heat on the finish.

Caves St-Pierre 1939 Henri Bouachon (bottle, Sorgues bottling) Very pale, amontillado sherry almost. Nose very gentle, but still has rich tones; with air evolves quickly towards coffee beans, toast. Palate also rich, hangs in there at the start, but dries a little at the end, with heat in it. Delicate wine – its structure has sustained it. A very fine old gent.

None of these wines had ever left Châteauneuf-du-Pape, a strong point in their favour. But the tasting did go to show that, while the Grenache Noir may lose its colour at quite a young stage, and its wines may show a tendency to oxidize through a steady erosion of tannic support, the sheer guts that it imparts to its wines keeps them from the grave for a very long time. What is now going to be fascinating in Châteauneuf-du-Pape reds of the period 1978 onwards is to see what effect on their longevity the increased proportions of both Syrah and Mourvèdre in some *domaines* will have. There will be a stiffer backbone, provided notably by the Mourvèdre, there will be a stronger purple colour, courtesy mainly of the Syrah, but there will be reduced engine capacity thanks to the lower levels of Grenache in some of the best-known wines. The question has to be asked – will such richness as was apparent in those wines from the 1939–57 period still be on the premises of the wines of the 1970s and 1980s when they have reached the same age?

If a general rule has to be given, the reds are ideally drunk between six and twenty years old. The lower figure refers to wines that open up earlier or are made by growers with fast-maturing styles of wine: years like 1976, 1982, 1987 and 1991 apply here. A middle figure applies in years like 1979, 1980 and 1985. A little longer might be needed for vintages like 1983, 1986, 1988 and 1990 – plenty of tannins, plenty of alcohol and extract, the tannins sometimes quite hard. And the longest-lived years of the past two decades will be 1978 – magnificent, opulent, astoundingly rich and heady wines stuck together by super-glue as it were – and 1981, more austere, but a vintage whose depth and classic qualities are just slowly edging out into the open, very much a wine for lovers of Pauillac and stand-offish clarets. Somewhere in between comes the 1989, which has tremendous *puissance*, with ripe, thick flavours but such succulence that the wines might round out earlier than expected. These are all vintages where the best wines will still do themselves justice after at least thirty years.

Turning to the producers, those who generally make the longest-lived wines comprise the Château de Beaucastel, Le Bosquet des Papes, Clos du Mont-Olivet, Château Rayas and Château La Nerthe. In the case of the last-named, it remains to be seen how their updated vinification and use of a different spread of vines of different maturities will affect the ageing – in the past, alcohol and tannin were the twin motors for many of the wines, whereas now greater elegance is being sought. With Château Rayas, the wines have become more fleshy, more rounded and what the French term '*sphérique*' since Jacques Reynaud succeeded his father in 1980. The older wines like the 1978, 1967 and 1962 will live for twenty-five to thirty years more easily than the years like 1981, 1983, 1985 and 1989; some of the last group are deliciously silky, but do not contain the power of the earlier wines. The 1988 may be one of the longest-lived Rayas reds of recent times.

Wines from the Domaine du Vieux-Télégraphe dated 1978 or earlier will also keep well, as will many of the then Domaine de Mont-Redon reds dating from 1975 or earlier. Both these properties lightened their wines in the second half of the 1970s, chasing a fruitier, more accessible style, whose general effect was to make their wines less interesting and complex. The Château de Mont-Redon (as it is now called) produced a sterner 1985, however, and subsequent vintages show a partial return to the fuller sort of wine. Another property whose wines in the past held great longevity is the Clos de l'Oratoire des Papes, but since 1976 their wines have lost much of their depth.

With very few exceptions – Château Rayas (plain burgundy bottle), Château de la Gardine (brown, misshapen bottle) and Jean Marchand of Clos des Pontifes (special colour and design) – these properties use a special bottle to represent their *appellation*. The bottle is the classic burgundy shape but has embossed below its neck the old papal coat of arms, surrounded by the words 'Châteauneuf-du-Pape Contrôlé'. Only owners of vineyards who have bottled their wine at their *domaines* are permitted to use this attractive bottle, so all wine from the *négociant* trade outside Châteauneuf comes in the usual plain one with the local *négoce* now also carrying an embossed bottle. As a reliable yardstick for buying a good, genuinely made wine from

Châteauneuf, this embossed bottle serves an admirable purpose for the consumer.

With such a powerful, full-bodied wine as Châteauneuf-du-Pape, it is best to serve strongly flavoured food that will enhance and complement it. Thus any game, red-meat dishes or a good wintry stew are ideal. Cheese, too, is a good companion for the red wine, notably the stronger varieties such as Camembert, Roquefort and Stilton, or any goat's cheese or garlic-based cheese such as Gaperon or Boursin.

Increasingly found outside France, and listed in the cellars of top restaurants, white Châteauneuf-du-Pape has existed for a long time. Old archive documents show it was being made in the fourteenth century (source: Baron Le Roy), but it never really caught on. Even in 1932 the previous Baron Le Roy wrote that Château Rayas was one of the 'rare' *domaines* making a white wine. In the first edition of this book, written in 1974, the white wine was described as 'really no more than a novelty' outside a handful of producers who were named as Domaine de Nalys, La Terre Ferme, Château de Beaucastel, Les Clefs d'Or and Château Rayas. Since then the attitude towards it has radically changed, and instead of around 2 per cent of the crop being made into white wine, 5–6 per cent is now white – around 5,750 hectolitres. It is also always more expensive than the red wine: the 1985 was selling for 6,000–6,500 francs per *pièce*, with the red at 5,000 francs per *pièce*, while the average cost per bottle *départ cave* for the 1988 was 35–40 francs for the white and 28–33 francs for the red. By 1991, with French inflation restrained at around 3 per cent, these prices had advanced to around 55–65 francs for the 1990 white and 45–55 francs for the red from average *domaines*.

Unfortunately a trend is growing for multi-tier pricing at Châteauneuf, with special *cuvées*, Vieilles Vignes wines (often the growers' arithmetic could be called into question with these), and special packaging all seemingly providing a licence to lever up prices. The speculative fires that are also caused by certain publicity-conscious reporting systems – exaggerated prose, points out of 100, lots of fanfare – also do not augur well for a steadiness of pricing and commercial progress unless care and restraint are exercised.

Paradoxically, many of the best, most thoughtful *vignerons* admit that making good white wine in the southern Rhône is their greatest personal challenge. Attention has turned markedly towards the mastery of this subject, and accordingly methods have evolved.

Before the 1970s, the white grapes were usually harvested late on. Many of the white grape vines had been planted higgledy-piggledy in the middle of red grape vineyards. No exact science was made of planting by variety, the main criteria being to replace old Grenache Noir stock with the occasional white variety like Grenache Blanc (good for alcohol degree), Bourboulenc (helping the red wine's bouquet) or Clairette (softening the red wine). No special attention was paid to the white varieties, which many growers could not be bothered to harvest or vinify apart from the red crop, especially as the vinification of the whites was a delicate and time-consuming process of its own.

Those growers making a little white wine were therefore working with what today would generally be regarded as overripe fruit. Such a condition was turned to his advantage by the ingenious Louis Reynaud of Château Rayas, who until the 1950s made a sweet white from Clairette (with some noble rot) and Grenache Blanc (no rot, but very ripe). Most of the olden-day whites were also fermented without temperature control, and were as a result full, blowzy and prone to oxidation. The malolactic fermentation was never usually blocked, and southern Rhône whites in those days resembled their even more southerly Spanish and Italian counterparts, many of which were straw gold in colour and *rancio*-tasting before the age of three.

A *domaine* like Font-de-Michelle, owned by the Gonnet brothers, who are cousins of the Bruniers of Vieux Télégraphe fame, is typical of the ones that set out steadfastly to overcome these problems. Earlier harvesting is a cornerstone of its process. White wine makes up around 10 per cent of its production, and is vinified from 50 per cent Grenache Blanc, 25 per cent Clairette, 20 per cent Bourboulenc and an increasing 5 per cent Roussanne. The Gonnets follow closely the ripening of their Grenache Blanc, and when they judge it to be ready they pick all four grape varieties.

'We'll obviously achieve a decent alcohol level with the Grenache ripe,' says Jean Gonnet, 'but at the same time the Clairette will have a better acidity, as will the Bourboulenc and Roussanne to a certain extent. Doing it this way allows the Bourboulenc in particular to exert a fresh, aromatic influence on the wine, making it more interesting than the old style. We find that the date of harvesting for the whites is exceedingly delicate, and that being one or two days late for instance can upset the applecart.' The Gonnets may express worry, but in a vintage like 1986 their *blanc* was exceptional.

During the 1980s the fashionable white grape vine became the Roussanne, which started to sprout up in any self-respecting and go-ahead vineyard. It has been present at Châteauneuf for many years, permitted as one of the thirteen to enter either the red or the white. The Château de Beaucastel has 5.5 hectares of Roussanne, of which 2 hectares were planted all in one group, on stone-covered clay and chalk soil, in the late 1930s. The rest were planted around 1965–70. The fruit from these older vines now makes perhaps the most serious, stylish white Châteauneuf, which François Perrin sells as Roussanne Vieille Vigne, a separate *cuvée* since the 1986 vintage. Meanwhile other front-line *domaines* have increased their exposure to this grape known for its delicacy and lightly styled fruit extract: the Clos des Papes has 20 per cent (along with over 15 per cent Picpoul, a high amount for the latter), the Domaine du Vieux Télégraphe has used 15 per cent Roussanne in its white wine since the 1985 crop, and the Château La Nerthe now work with 25 per cent Roussanne. La Nerthe is one of the *domaines* that has largely reversed the usual *cépage* formulas in its 1980s replanting programme, and its white is now made from 30 per cent Bourboulenc, 25 per cent both Clairette and Roussanne and only 20 per cent Grenache Blanc. In a similar vein, the Brunier brothers planted 3 hectares at La Roquette in 1987 with exactly one-quarter each Roussanne, Bourboulenc, Clairette and Grenache Blanc – maybe a model white *domaine* in the budding?

Commitment to the white wine has its price, for the earlier harvesting of these grapes has two side-effects. First, extra fermenting vats have to be found, so that there is capacity for the reds when they are brought in, and second, it means that harvesting personnel have to be hired over a longer period of time. Château Mont-Redon has partially solved this problem of its vines maturing at different times by adapting the date of pruning. The early-ripening Syrah is now pruned last, around 15 February to 15 March, while the late-ripening Mourvèdre is pruned between the end of December and January. The result is that the time between the first and last pickings on their large estate has decreased from between twelve and fifteen days to now eight days. MM Abeille and Fabre of Mont-Redon are also happy to vinify all the grape varieties together in the same vat, an action which implements this new, compact harvesting policy.

After a *débourbage*, or separation of the pressed juice from the dirty matter brought in at harvest time, of twenty-four to thirty-six hours in stainless steel or enamel vats, the growers continue their quest for a fresher, fruitier wine, with some of them performing a fining using a bentonite mixture. Selected yeasts may then be added to bring on the alcoholic fermentation. For much of the 1980s, this was conducted at between 14° and 19°C, but growers have edged up as a group to 17–20°C, seeking riper and fuller aromas. Fermentation may last actively for ten to twenty days. While many properties now house stainless steel, automatic-control vats for this, some *vignerons* like to work with wood at the fermentation stage. François Perrin is one; he explains:

'I ferment half my Beaucastel Vieille Vigne crop in casks of one to four years – at natural temperatures of 25°C or 26°C – and half in enamel-lined vats. I'm delighted with the casks, but to get them to be just right, I buy them and wait for a year – nothing goes in them in the meantime. The Roussanne is the only *cépage* that handles the cask fermentation – the Grenache Blanc and the Clairette don't, and I also find I can round out the Roussanne more simply with wood, which is where it most easily does its "malo".' Just to serve up a quiet surprise he then offers a 1988 Roussanne for tasting . . . fermented in acacia wood from the Drôme *département* near Valence. This is pale, has honey and tropical fruit smells on the bouquet, with the inevitable splash of vanilla, and on the palate has great chewy length, almost like liquorice on the finish.

When the white moves towards its malolactic, a majority of growers like to take steps to block this off. 'I don't want the malolactic to occur because the wines tend otherwise to be flabby and low in acidity,' comments M. Jean-Pierre Boisson, the keen and go-ahead son of the owner of Domaine du Père Caboche. He uses a very high amount of Bourboulenc (increased to 40 per cent during the 1980s), along with Clairette and Grenache Blanc (25 per cent each) and 10 per cent Roussanne. He has stopped using a little Picpoul.

'I ferment at 16°C and after I have blocked the *malo*, I stabilize the wine by leaving it at −5°C for two weeks, which precipitates the tartrates to the bottom. After filtration, it is bottled a little after the middle of November. A wine like this, very fresh and immediately aromatic, should be drunk young, certainly within two years.' Also bottling their whites before Christmas are leading *domaines* such as Mont-Redon, Nalys, Vieux Télégraphe, and Font-de-Michelle. Les Clefs d'Or and Clos des Papes bottle between January and the spring following the harvest, while Beaucastel, with generally 80 per cent Roussanne and 15 per cent Grenache in their straight white *cuvée*, leave bottling until around the following September with a little of the end wine seeing casks for eight months.

The best white Châteauneuf-du-Pape is nowadays a wine of much greater standing than in the past. Unlike many of the temperature-controlled whites made around France today, it has more to offer than an initial burst of under-ripe fruit and a racy, tart freshness. This is why M. Boisson's advice about drinking the wine within two years is not applicable to all *domaines*. There are now really three styles of white Châteauneuf-du-Pape. There are the vinifiers who use young oak: Beaucastel, La Gardine, Grand Veneur, Mont-Redon (just starting), Vieux Télégraphe are examples; they work mostly with the Roussanne grape in this way.

Then there are the classic low-temperature, fast-bottling practitioners – no wood here as yet: Domaine de Font-de-Michelle and Clos des Papes are two examples, where a relatively early picking plays an important part. Then there are the traditionalists who are happy to pick very ripe fruit, ferment it with only very minor temperature vigilation and bottle the wine a year or so after the harvest: Château Rayas and Domaine du Pegaü are examples of this school, where the wines carry extraordinary depth of richness after six years or so.

Wines from the more modern school – the majority nowadays – are certainly a vast improvement on the white Châteauneufs of the late 1960s and early 1970s. They are much less prone to a fast oxidation, for one, but quality is still pretty uneven across the *appellation*, and there are some very boring bottles of white Châteauneuf on shop shelves around the world.

The best of these modern whites commence with a deadly pale colour and only fleeting hints of yellow, while the bouquets run with lively garden fruit aromas like apricots, peaches, apples and occasionally, more exotically, pineapples. The exotic aromas appear to be linked to the lowness of the temperature for the fermentation. Domaine Font-de-Michelle's Michel Gonnet admitted that they had raised their temperature from around 13°C in the early days to about 17°C or 18°C in the 1990s: 'At 13°C, we extracted exotic banana-type smells, but we realized that for a greater all-round keeping wine, we should be fermenting at the higher level.'

On the palate the wines start with a liveliness of fruit and sometimes tangy freshness, but there emerge a discreet weight and roundness to support the dried fruit and partially nutty secondary flavours that continue on to a lengthy, ripe fruit finish. There is an interesting chewiness and length even when young, and it is the delightful combination of fresh summer fruit flavours with a lurking substance behind them that renders the wine more lingering on the palate, more memorable in the mind. But one note of caution: as the habit of white wine-making spreads at Châteauneuf, so the gulf between the best and the worst widens. Recent tastings of young whites have shown a massive gulf in standards between the wine of the top estate, Château de Beaucastel, and that made by smaller *vignerons* less used to mastering the challenge of white wine vinification. Choose your *domaine* carefully with white Châteauneuf.

Leaders in the field of white Châteauneuf are the Domaine de Nalys, Domaine Font-de-Michelle, Domaine du Père Caboche, Domaine du Vieux Télégraphe, the Château Mont-Redon and Paul Avril's Clos des Papes. Good offerings also come from Les Clefs d'Or, Château de la Gardine, La Reviscoulado, Domaine de la Terre Ferme and the improving Château La Nerthe. All these wines come in the modern, fresh, aromatic style. The Domaine du Pegaü white, vinified in the traditional way, is also very good.

However, the best, most sophisticated white Châteauneuf-du-Pape comes from the Château de Beaucastel, which since the mid-1980s has stepped up its drive to perfect a technically sound vinification, giving a complex *grand vin* in the manner perhaps of a leading white Graves. Along with some of the Château Rayas *blanc*, the two Beaucastel white *cuvées* (one pure Roussanne, the other 80/20 Roussanne/Grenache Blanc) have the substance and the depth of structure to be able to age extremely well, although François Perrin of Beaucastel pointed out a phenomenon observable in his white wines that is also sometimes apparent with the best white wines at Hermitage from growers such as Gérard Chave: 'You can taste my white wines when a year or two old, and you'll see that they have a balanced acidity and that their aromas and general weight indicate a long life ahead. But suddenly I give you a three- or four-year-old bottle, and you say, "What is this resin taste in the wine? And the bouquet's aromas, as opposed to flourishing, are very suppressed." Your analysis is correct – the wine has a form of oxidation passing through it, carrying it from its youth into a state of honourable old age. This often occurs with my whites when they are between three and seven years old, and yet they are wines that will age perfectly well.' And to prove the point he pulls out a bottle eleven years old, followed by one that is dated 1956. The first wine, packed with rich straw-gold colours and an intense concentration of almost flower-like aromas on bouquet and palate, improves with about twenty minutes' aeration and is notable for its lovely clean aftertaste. The 1956, all gold, its flavours reminiscent of old burgundy, at twenty-six still possesses remarkable richness but begins to dry out towards a Château-Chalon style of wine after twenty minutes. In those days the Beaucastel *blanc* was made from 75 per cent Grenache Blanc, with the remaining 25 per cent split between Roussanne and Bourboulenc.

The results of Beaucastel's handling of their white wine in part new wood (30 per cent of the Roussanne in the classic *cuvée*, and half of the Vieille Vigne) and stainless steel before bottling are very impressive. François Perrin has succeeded in introducing some finesse into an intrinsically solid wine, and it has great width of fruitiness on the palate, a lovely weight and balance and a very sustained, chewy finish. Still greater finesse comes through with the pure Roussanne Vieille Vigne *cuvée*. This wine is more reticent when young, and is more marked by the new wood – 50 per cent, with 50 per cent exposed to *inox* – but it is very long *en bouche*. There is some southern depth on the bouquet, with hints of nuttiness, and the wine promises an extended period of development. When tasted at eighteen months old, the 1987 was a little hidden, but it held good structure and seemed like a wine that would evolve ahead of the 1988 (as indeed had come to pass by late 1991). 'It's asleep,' was François Perrin's comment, adding that he expected it to show more around the summer of 1991 onwards. Both the 1989 and the 1990 maintained the standard of initially firm, slowly evolving wines.

The Rayas white comes from the Grenache Blanc and the Clairette, with, in past vintages ending in the 1960s, occasionally some Sauvignon and Chardonnay. It is not as reliable as it used to be, however, but in good vintages like 1990 and 1985 it represents a solid and full-tasting example of the traditional white Châteauneuf.

Unlike the main regions of Burgundy and Bordeaux, Châteauneuf-du-Pape has never received an official ranking of its vineyards. About a dozen *domaines* lead in size of vineyard and quality of wine, however, and these are supported by a massive grouping of over 100 smaller growers who look after their own bottling and selling. In the past dozen years many small *vignerons* have taken up bottling at source, as is demonstrated by the more than doubling of wine bottled within the *appellation* to 60 per cent of the total. There is therefore every likelihood nowadays of finding a sound, honestly made bottle from just such a small grower in a liquor shop in London, New York, Sydney or Tokyo.

The largest *domaines* remain the standard bearers for the *appellation*, though; in size, the leaders are Château Mont-Redon, Domaine du Vieux Lazaret, Château de Vaudieu, Château de Beaucastel, Domaine du Grand Tinel, Château La Nerthe and Domaine du Vieux Télégraphe. They run between 95 and 60 hectares, and apart from Château de la Gardine and Domaine de Nalys, who both have 50-plus hectares, this is a breakaway group by size. There are some properties which have 30–40 hectares – Château Fortia, Clos des Papes, Clos du Calvaire, Château des Fines Roches, to name a few – but there are many, many growers who work 5–20 hectares. And a common thread links nearly all these producers. The running of the *domaines* is extremely rarely delegated, as is often the case in Bordeaux. Each owner is therefore totally responsible for his or her wine. Furthermore, the *vignerons* are determined to maintain the status quo. The vineyards are rigorously protected against development; only local *viticulteurs* are permitted to build within the *appellation* limits, and even their projects are closely scrutinized by all the councillors, from the Mayor (generally a *vigneron* himself) downwards. The story is told of a hapless foreigner who came to Châteauneuf to develop a small vineyard; after experiencing enormous difficulty in obtaining a regular water supply for his house and other similar impediments, he decided to give up and leave. The status quo survived.

LEADING DOMAINES

HENRI BONNEAU

Henri Bonneau, who lives in the middle of the village, is the sort of man with whom one could spend a very long time picking up quotable one-liners and flashes of insight into the art of working with the Grenache. During the 1980s his cover was blown by American and French journalists (but not Robert Mayberry) who obviously did not respect his wishes for anonymity, and the world is now more aware of the extraordinary wines made by this offbeat soul.

'We've been twelve generations here at Châteauneuf', he states, with the exact date on the tip of his tongue. 'A lady on my mother's side married Guillaume Rebollin on 4 September 1667. He was a *viticulteur* and *épicier*, and the family remained *épiciers* until 1938. So you're talking to a traditionalist – I'm against the Syrah, and rely about 80 per cent on the Grenache. In fact the other grapes like Mourvèdre, Counoise, Vaccarèse, the odd bit of Syrah plus the Clairette and the Cinsault, are all just a bit like the salt and pepper in the soup – it all boils down to the Grenache – and don't ask me to be precise about how much there is of the others.'

M. Bonneau has 5.25 hectares (he can be precise when it suits) close to the village of Châteauneuf, and 0.75 hectare on not such stone-covered ground that he likes less towards Courthézon. His thirteen plots are spread about, and his preference is to stay with old vines of fifty years or so, since he distrusts clonally selected Grenache, Mourvèdre and Syrah.

His family have worked in the same maze of interconnected cellars under Châteauneuf-du-Pape since the time of Napoleon III, and there are some wonderful winding nooks and crannies that M. Bonneau knows well as he moves around the rough earth-strewn surface, muttering obscenities about Napoleon Bonaparte. Any tasting in the company of a Briton is interrupted with a rapid, Provençal-infested verbal swipe about the wrong person being burnt at the stake – Joan of Arc and not Bonaparte – before he wanders off to another dull, grimy cask, full of marvellous young red wine.

M. Bonneau only destalks in years of extreme poor quality of harvest, while he favours a regular crush, which for most modernists would be extreme, one suspects. For the 1991 harvest he replaced his grandfather's old crusher, which unsettled his nerves probably more than the wine itself. The grape varieties are fermented together over fifteen to twenty days, although in 1987 this lasted just eight days. M. Bonneau adds the first press wine, and his wood-ageing runs for about two years in some *pièces* and two *foudres*, one of which is an ex-beer cask from Burgundy. Half a dozen egg whites per *pièce* serve to fine the wine, which is bottled unfiltered.

M. Bonneau does his own thing and likes to cock a snook at the world at large. Food and drink that he has procured himself, hearty flavours, good companionship and simple lack of pretence in people are what he likes; one can see that his eighteen-year-old son Marcel, named in the Provençal tradition after his grandfather, will continue this simple, direct and sometimes spiky approach to people who wander into his underground den. If he ran a restaurant, he wouldn't figure in the Guide Michelin, but would score 19 out of 20 in the Guide Gault-Millau: too talented and irregular for the old lady Michelin and her stays. So one listens and sort of believes when he says that his average yield is around 30 hectolitres per hectare, but that he doesn't bottle even half his wine in any year, and in 1982, for example, bottled no wine at all. During the 1980s he introduced a new *cuvée*, the Marie Beurrier, named after an aunt of his wife from Charolles, home of all good beef; this, he says, is a bit lighter than his main Réserve des Célestins.

M. Bonneau's wines are always very good and sometimes quite simply excellent. They bear the depth, richness and touch of eccentricity of Jacques Reynaud's Château Rayas, and both men amply show the quality of the Grenache in its ripest, plumpest and most seductive form. The 1981 was a very concentrated wine, full of raw extract and a lovely lingering length on the palate. The 1983 was also well coloured, and the bouquet showed some deep, black fruit aromas. On the palate it was delicious, with a lot of prune and dark fruit running on to a very chewy finish. The 1984 was a softer wine with a stimulating peppered finish; this is now drinking near its best. The 1985 was an elegant wine, with some ripe fruit supported by a series of rounded tannins. This will be drinking very well around 1992–5. The 1986 had an especially sustained colour for its vintage, a ripe, damson fruit bouquet and tremendous thoroughness of flavour on the palate, with an explosion of richness and heat on the finish. It is by some way one of the best 1986s, and will continue to show well deep into the 1990s.

Of recent vintages, the 1990 Célestins tasted out of the trusty 20-hectolitre *foudre* weighed in at over 15°. Very bright purple, the bouquet was restrained, but promised to reveal depth and complexity. Above all, the palate was concentrated but fine, with excellent length. The 1989 Célestins, tasted from *pièce*, bore more evident fruitiness, with a lovely dark, rich texture and a wild, almost leathery bouquet: this is more discreet than the 1990, a little more '*sphérique*', as the French so aptly put it. The 1988 Célestins, also tasted from *pièce*, and like the 1989 a wine of nearly a degree less than the 1990, was very solid, with robust elements wrapped in firm tannins: it is as intense as the other wines, but hewn from a different cast in terms of its style. This trio of wines fully represent what the Grenache can do and how it can express itself in three glorious, exuberant vintages.

The Marie Beurrier wine comes from vineyards nearer Courthézon; the 1988, the first year it was made, showed very ripe Grenache aromas on the nose and a growing richness on the palate which ended in a satisfactory tannic chewiness. Like the 1989, this was tasted from *pièce*; the 1989 possesses fair fruit, but is a little stern on the palate, and its balance is a touch questionable.

M. Bonneau's wines are not easy to find, since he sells mostly to private clients and friends; should a bottle of the Célestins ever show up on a wine-list or in a small local store . . . do not hesitate!

Bonneau, Henri
    Réserve des Célestins   84230 Châteauneuf-du-Pape

LE BOSQUET DES PAPES

This is an excellent 29-hectare *domaine* that makes one of the most solid, traditional, firm red wines at Châteauneuf-du-Pape. The Boirons own or rent their vineyards, which are split into as many as thirty-seven plots around the *appellation*. 'Our holdings have a 10-mile north–south spread, and a 4-mile east–west spread,' comments Mme Jo Boiron, who is closely involved in the running of the *domaine*. 'Most of our holdings are in the north of the *appellation* in fact, near the Gardiole, while we have other plots near Château Rayas and towards Sorgues, where the ground is quite gravelly.'

The 27.5 hectares of red vine vineyards are Grenache (75 to 80 per cent), Mourvèdre (9 per cent), Syrah (7 per cent), Cinsault (2 per cent), Vaccarèse (2 per cent) and just a little Counoise. 'In the 1950s, for example, we had more Counoise and Grenache and less Syrah, but we're now returning a little to the Counoise,' states Mme Boiron.

M. Boiron's cellars are just past the Clos des Papes vineyard, with a commanding view of the Châteauneuf vines and Mont Ventoux; his terrace is generally used by his fierce boxer dog to summon a reply from all the village dogs, especially when a visiting foreigner arrives.

Seventy per cent of the crop is crushed, and no destalking takes place. The harvest at a property of this sort lasts for two to three weeks, and the reception is helped by the fact that the house and cellars are on a slight slope; this gets round the need to pump the grapes into the fermenting vats. 'I want a true, bold Châteauneuf-du-Pape,' affirms M. Boiron, a comment that is to be expected from an ex-rugby player who took up basketball when his wife stopped him playing rugby because of his age. 'With the exception of the Syrah, I ferment the red grapes all together in concrete vats moving quickly to 28–30°C, and by the end of the fermentation we might have got to 32–34°C according to the density. I leave the wine for between one and two years in wood – not new wood, which may rob the wine of character – and in a size of *foudre* of around 30 hectolitres. I've tried ageing a little wine in two-year-old Allier oak casks of 600 litres, but I'm not keen – the wine comes out with less definition, even after a stay only of three months or so. Our bottling takes place at a variety of times according to the style of the vintage and the space in the cellar for storage.'

As a member of the Prestige et Tradition group, M. Boiron bottles his wine in runs of 12 hectolitres as many as twenty-five to thirty times a year at the Prestige facilities in the middle of the village. His first bottling was in 1964, a departure from his father's practice of selling the wine off in bulk.

The Bosquet reds are a must for anyone who likes the sturdy style of well-made regional wine in the authentic, traditional style. These are not early flirts, they are serious sit-down wines that need to be cellared patiently and drunk with strongly flavoured food. The 1990, before bottling, had an almost black colour, a succulent, ripe fruit bouquet and great power and earthiness on the palate that will keep driving it along as it ages. The 1989 is a full degree less – around 13.8° – and is excellent: a pretty strong colour is complemented by ripe aromas that suggest future breadth and complexity, while there is great structure and balance on the palate: there is real promise for a long evolution with this wine. The 1988 is more upright; there is plenty of tannin on the aftertaste, while the bouquet is a little dry and peppery. This is something of a bad boy who may redeem himself and soften out with time, and here there is greater potential delicacy than could be found in the 1989 or 1990.

In 1987, a year of diminished yields, M. Boiron made a wine of latent promise. A very typical Grenache wine, its aromas were a bit green, but there was enough extract on the palate to indicate a softening around 1994–6. The 1986 was very good indeed – something of a slugger of a wine. By the early 1990s it had developed well, with some exotic dried fruit aromas coming through on the bouquet and plenty of reserve left on the palate. It has greater persistence *en bouche* than many of its year, and seems set to show well out towards the year 2000. The 1985 is softer and more straightforward than many Bosquet wines, its pleasant roundness likely to hold towards 1996 or so. The 1984 is very good for the year, has held its colour, and while showing markedly ripe aromas, will defend itself well until around 1994. The 1983 started life as a 'leather and whips' type of wine – lots of austere tannins and rasp – but its robustness is loosening, and while there is a lack of fruit and *gras*, its intrinsic chewiness will keep it running and slowly ceding its grip towards 1996 at least. The 1982 is now tasting loose, with the bouquet rather stewed, but the 1981 will run towards 1994; it has some quiet richness and good length, but the signs of peaking are apparent on the damp smells of the bouquet. The 1979 is still showing well, driven by a harmony of elements that was present from the outset, while the 1978, last tasted in 1991, has a rampant richness on it, both on the bouquet, with sweet, almost fungal smells, and on the palate, which still provides an early surge of ripe fruit. Tremendous length of finish rounds it off in a glorious way.

To demonstrate just how long some of his wines can live, M. Boiron reaches for a twenty-three-year-old Bosquet des Papes 1966. This still had a sheen on its pretty ruby colour, and a sensational bouquet running with masses of cedar and spice aromas. Very rich on the attack, with lots of different flavours and fruit extracts, the wine was sustained by what seemed like tobacco flavours on the finish. It was a shade short, but held a delicate construction and lovely finesse. In those days there was only a very little Mourvèdre in the wine, as opposed to the current 9 per cent.

Since 1983, the Boirons have made 3,000 bottles of white each year from 40 per cent Grenache Blanc and 30 per cent each of Clairette and Bourboulenc, with a tiny plot of 0.25 hectare of vines of more than sixty-five years old for the Clairette and the Grenache Blanc. M. Boiron is thinking of introducing some Roussanne, and is keen on his holding of Bourboulenc: 'It matures very late, so doesn't get in the way; it doesn't rot, which is a big advantage, and above all it brings acidity. So you have the option of harvesting it earlier if you want more liveliness in the wine,' he explains. M. Boiron normally blocks the malolactic on this. In a vintage like 1990 it is a full and genuine wine, but as yet is less regular than the excellent red from this traditional *domaine* that could serve as a yardstick for old-fashioned, well-made and gutsy Châteauneuf-du-Pape.

Boiron, M. et Mme Maurice
  Le Bosquet des Papes   84230 Châteauneuf-du-Pape

LES CAILLOUX

A good wine of the modern, approachable style is made by André Brunel, whose octogenarian father Lucien now takes a back seat at this 20-hectare property. Thoroughly knowledgeable, and a man who carefully considers his options in making his wine, M. Brunel has changed some of the procedures due to his desire to make a 'practical wine' – a somewhat ominous statement for the purist, and one that means a wine that will keep for ten years, while being drinkable soon after purchase off the shelf.

The search for greater fruit has led M. Brunel to vinify between one-third and one-half uncrushed grapes, which are mixed into the middle of vats of crushed grapes. During the first part of the 1980s he also abandoned the use of wood in search of 'freshness', but since 1985 he has made some experiments with new oak, to the extent that there are now thirty *pièces* in his cellars. M. Brunel was led this way by taste in the American market, and so with his 1988 red he tried half brand new and half one-year wood, trying to improve the structure of the wine. His 1987, by contrast, did not go into wood, due to its lighter style. 'I found in the period when my wine wasn't going into cask that it lacked something – a potential for development,' comments M. Brunel.

The red is made up of 70 per cent Grenache, with 10 per cent Syrah and Mourvèdre also present, and increasing. The 1982 and 1984 reds started to show well after two to three years, but the old-fashioned 1981 was solid enough to live until around 1995. The 1985 was quite a smoky-tasting wine, with an appealing roundness on the palate. The 1988 was firmer, with more of a dried fruit content; the 1989 has a good, dark colour, and sound weight and concentration on the palate. The *cuvée* for the French market is certainly an eight- to ten-year wine.

However, commerce is commerce, and there has been a trend at this *domaine* over the past few years away from the chewy, thickly flavoured style to a more innocent, quieter sort of wine. Different *cuvées* appear in different markets, and for example the wine sold to an English supermarket group is a real high-street wine, with the emphasis on easy fruit and no hint of unwelcome tannin that may upset the buyers. Therein lies the trap: M. Brunel knows that buyers of wine in supermarkets are not those laying down the wine for a prized and rewarding ageing – the bottles will generally be drunk within a couple of weeks at most. Therefore the *domaine* has got itself into a position of trying to follow market dictates rather than sticking to convictions and making the sort of wine that the owner in his heart of hearts knows is best. M. Brunel is not alone at Châteauneuf in this respect – it is a dilemma facing many of the less well-known growers trying to break into overseas markets. Remembering the excellent, sustained Cailloux wines of the 1950s and 1960s made by his father and sold through the Les Reflets growers' association, this is a pity.

A very little white is also made, from the Clairette, Roussanne and Bourboulenc, and this has become a prominent example of good white Châteauneuf: it possesses succulent flavours and good depth of aroma on the bouquet. The 1989 and 1990 were both very successful.

Brunel, André
    Les Cailloux   84230 Châteauneuf-du-Pape

CAVES BESSAC

The Caves Auguste Bessac, based inside rampart-style walls near the centre of Châteauneuf-du-Pape, deal in the wines of both the northern and southern Rhône. The quality and selection of the wines improved in the late 1980s, and a smartening of the labelling has helped the general impression that this is now a firm whose wines can be taken more seriously than in the past.

At harvest-time the company buys grapes and newly made wine and matures them in extensive underground cellars. The wines have more regional character than in the past, and the southern Grenache-based *cuvées* remain their best offerings. Among the 1988s, the Gigondas Château St-André, Marquis de Valicourt showed discreet promise on the bouquet, and sound length with a warm and genuine southern flavour on the palate, while the red Châteauneuf-du-Pape, despite an evolution towards ruby and secondary aromas, bore a genuine ripeness and a satisfying chewy finish on the palate – a wine to drink towards 1996. The Côtes du Rhône Carte Or red can be a little obvious and sweet, but its extract in a good vintage like 1989 means it will provide correct drinking over four years or so.

Caves Bessac   84230 Châteauneuf-du-Pape

CAVES ST-PIERRE

Founded in 1898 by Henry Bouachon, this *négociant* company became the Caves St-Pierre in 1950. It is a very big local concern, working in the commercialization of 175,000 hectolitres of wines from the Rhône, Provence and Languedoc. It buys in wines selected through tasting at the *domaines* and rears them at cellars in Sorgues built in 1986. It also operates a mobile bottling unit that goes to growers' *domaines*.

In the past some of its most notable wines have been the Château-neuf Domaine des Pontifs and until 1986 the Domaine de Condorcet (q.v.). In the late 1980s the company launched a good, improved line called the Clefs des Prélats. This is presented in the new local *négociant* bottle, which bears a coat of arms and the words 'Châteauneuf-du-Pape Appellation Contrôlée', and marks out the wines from those bottled by *négociants* in Bordeaux, Burgundy or many miles away. On first showing, the white and the red are well-worked wines. The white 1990 held a fresh bouquet, but an appealing substance bolstered the wine and gave it a well rounded finish. The 1989 red Clefs des Prélats held a well-ripened fruit bouquet, fair weight on the palate and tannins that, while round and easy, ensured a good showing over five years or so.

Meanwhile, one of the most curious old Châteauneufs ever encountered was a 1939 red Caves St-Pierre, bottled in Sorgues by Henri Bouachon, and tasted in 1989. The colour was pale, almost amontillado, but the bouquet surprised with some early richness that quickly turned to dried coffee beans. There was a thin thread of richness on the palate, and there was no doubt that the wine's balanced structure had held it together for so long – it was truly a very fine old gentleman.

In the Côtes du Rhône, the Château de Bastet and notably the Château d'Aigueville normally provide solidly flavoured, respectable wines, while the house Tavel is usually sound. It will be interesting to see if the improvement at the top end of this range of wines filters through to the individual *appellations* lower down the order. Certainly developments here indicate a greater urgency and care being taken by local Rhône *négociants* to invest their wines with more pronounced local character.

Caves St-Pierre   84230 Châteauneuf-du-Pape

LE CELLIER DES PRINCES

This is Châteauneuf's only Cave Co-opérative. Founded at Cour-thézon in 1924, it vinifies the crop of ninety-seven different vineyard holdings from throughout the *appellation*. There are 545 Co-opérat-ive members who contribute grapes of all calibres from the surround-ing area. Attempts have been made to reduce the traditionally very high Grenache content in its wine, and a '*vigneron* bonus scheme' has operated to encourage the planting of different vines like the Syrah and the Cinsault – a practice that is hard to condone unless the Grenache is being well looked after and vinified in the first place.

Around 5,000 hectolitres of Châteauneuf red are made each year. This is never very inspiring, but has improved a little during the 1980s. It is not long-lived, and the 1989, for instance, will drink well by 1993.

The white Cellier des Princes Châteauneuf lacks clear definition, and can be dull.

Le Cellier des Princes   84350 Courthézon

CHÂTEAU DE BEAUCASTEL

Moving quietly along on the inside rails, with no frills, or fuss, the Château de Beaucastel has become the leading estate at Châteauneuf-du-Pape, and is now in a class of its own with a style of its own that lies outside the mainstream. Its red wines are not only the longest-lived, but more importantly, they consistently have a complexity, a range of flavours and an integration that are only sometimes matched by their neighbours, properties such as Château Rayas and Château La Nerthe. Beaucastrel red is a wine that exudes class, and deserves to be compared to the great wines of France these days.

Owned by the Perrin family, the château is run by the sons of the late Jacques Perrin, François and Jean-Pierre. Its 70-hectare vineyard is situated on the eastern side of the *appellation*, near Courthézon, and since 1988 the red Beaucastel has been made from 30 per cent each Grenache Noir and Mourvèdre, 10 per cent Syrah, 5 per cent Cinsault, with the remaining 25 per cent split between the other permitted varieties, headed by the Counoise. The Grenache and Syrah proportions have been allowed to decline consistently over the past ten to fifteen years, as a matter of policy.

Named after a Huguenot, Pierre de Beaucastel, the property has grown vines since at least 1832, and the successful transfer of it to M. Perrin's sons, following his death in 1978, shows that *domaines* can continue, and at the very least thrive, if the next generation is properly shown what to do.

M. François Perrin

François Perrin looks like the British actor Tom Courtenay. As he approaches forty, he is still fresh-faced, but he has a good strong jaw-line which suggests that his inclination to learn and interpret new ways is backed up by the intention to get on and do the business. A firm gaze accompanies his reflections on his *métier*: 'The key is to have very healthy raw materials – they allow one to work towards a *grand vin*. Much of my concentration now is on the cultivation of the vineyard – I want grapes that don't just look good to the eye, but are good inside as well. My father was well ahead of his time in suppressing the use of herbicides and pesticides here, and the danger drinkers face in my view comes from the advance of technological wines with their large advertising budgets – the *vigneron must* remain an artisan.'

In talking about the state of vine-stock at Châteauneuf, François makes some interesting points: 'At a certain moment we tried some clones here, but soon reversed that in order to take the cuttings from our own vineyard. I think clonal selection has been a great disservice to our *appellation*. Remember that the early intention behind cloning was to counter phylloxera at the turn of the century – not to push the vines for more production.'

François's elder brother Jean-Pierre joins in on a subject that is clearly fundamental to their thinking: 'In the 1960s, the Institut National des Recherches Agronomiques (INRA), which was basically a scientific organization, was looking into clones that would increase the production of all sorts of different organisms – there were ones for cereal, sugar cane, also cattle, where crossings would provide higher milk yielders. Wine merely followed this process, so you had these technocrats from the Ministry of Agriculture dealing with the vineyards as they did with cattle, and forgetting the *terroir*, and how it tires easily. The first three criteria being preached during that clonal advance were quantity of volume, quantity of degree and quantity of acidity – all very nice and cosy and simple, but there are many, many other elements involved in nature's balance and in working the soil on a regular basis.'

Back to François: 'People were looking for a magic formula – longer-lasting vine plants with much larger crops from them. Nowadays there are yields at Châteauneuf in certain places from young Grenache vines of 80–100 hectolitres a hectare, whose bunches are often made up of lots and lots of very small grapes.' His comments tally exactly with those of Baron Le Roy of Château Fortia – himself aghast at some of the high modern yields of clonally selected Grenache Noir – and with the ever-increasing amount of cutting back of the vineyards' vegetation and growth in midsummer, an activity that used to be much less intensive at Châteauneuf in the past.

The Perrins identify their main vineyard problem as the *ver de la grappe*, or grape-worm. They do not use herbicides and artificial pesticides against the grape-worm; they use a plant, *pyrèthre*, or pyrethrum, in powdered form. The *ver* turns up in three generations during the ripening cycle: first in June, then in July, and third in August. The Perrins never intervene on the first generation because at that time, just after flowering, the grapes are not yet formed. What they are working to avoid is the ability of the worm to pierce the grape-skin and cause rot, so treatment comes in July when the grapes are larger. In August, only one month from the harvest, they are reluctant to treat the vines at such a late stage. While they constantly monitor the state of the vines, the Perrins can be helped naturally by very hot temperatures that destroy the worms' eggs on their own.

However, such finesse in the treatment of the *ver de la grappe* is not applied across all *domaines* by any means: advice is circulated in basic written form from a part of the Chamber of Agriculture, the Protection des Végétaux, meaning that it is derived from functionaries who deal with a wide range of agricultural issues, have little time to discuss specifics and are not necessarily people who understand or specialize in wine-making and the soil. As Jean-Pierre Perrin encapsulates it, 'One must not be a sheep, one must have intelligence.'

François Perrin looks after Beaucastel and their Côtes du Rhône Coudoulet *domaine* on a day-to-day basis, while living at a 30-hectare Côtes du Rhône property, the Domaine du Grand Prébois that was bought in 1990 from the Mayor of Jonquières, Louis Biscarat, as he moved on to a larger political arena. Jean-Pierre is busiest with their Vieille Ferme operation – part own vineyards, part *négoce* – with a white Côtes du Lubéron, a red Côtes du Ventoux, a 100 per cent Bourboulenc white Côtes du Rhône, and a red Côtes du Rhône made from 20 hectares of Grenache, Syrah, Mourvèdre and Cinsault. Jean-Pierre also looks after their Pierre Perrin *négociant* affair. This sells an elegant red Côtes du Rhône *biologique*, which shows Mourvèdre influences in its tannins and length, a Cinsault-based Tavel, a fair Muscat de Beaumes-de-Venise, and two wood-aged wines, a firm but elegant Gigondas and a robust, quite hearty red Vacqueyras.

In any year the final proportion of grape varieties depends on tasting. All the varieties – and Beaucastel truly does possess the full thirteen – are vinified apart, and François Perrin has continued a special process started by his late father Jacques, known as *vinification à chaud*. François, always dressed in understated, well-cut casual clothes, looks intently through his thin wire-rimmed glasses as he precisely describes the details that allowed his father to make talented, good wine in moderate vintages, such as in 1968. 'My great-grandfather was more a scientist than an agriculturalist, and he did studies on the process in Burgundy. Growers used to heat the grapes via wood fires, but now it's steam that we use. While the temperature reaches 80°C outside on the skin, inside it's only 25°C: the outside temperature is only held for a minute and a half or two before we cool down to around 20°C. Fermentation will then start in the next twelve-odd hours,' explains M. Perrin. 'The main benefits of this process are colour extraction, and a destruction of bacteria so that no sulphur need be added. We find we don't need to add extra yeasts for getting fermentation going – the grapes' own yeast is sufficient. We also take out the enzymes that would otherwise encourage the wine's lightening of colour.'

Since 1987 Beaucastel have introduced *pigeage* or pumping down of the fermenting cap in their vats of Syrah to obtain greater concentration. The estate does not favour such treatment for the Mourvèdre, since François Perrin feels that it makes that vine's juice too hard, while in principle at least he considers the *pigeage* suitable for the Cinsault, since it is similar in structure to the Syrah, with comparable thickness of grapes.

Otherwise the vinification process has changed little in past years; the *assemblage* takes place in the spring after the harvest and the red is thereafter aged in around fifty family *foudres* of about 55-hectolitre capacity. These are meticulously kept, with smart red edges and gleaming varnish on the outside, and are replaced about every twenty to twenty-five years – eight of the fifty were brought in new from Burgundy in 1990, for instance. 'What we have here,' comments François Perrin, 'is old wood which won't bring tannin, but which will bring an oxidation necessary for softening the tannins.' The stay in wood varies with the vintage, circulating around the one-year mark: eight months in 1987, fourteen months in 1988 and twelve months in 1989 and 1990, when the tannins were firm but not severe.

Beaucastel then causes local farmers a problem by suddenly approaching them for 400–500 eggs when it is time to fine the wine with egg whites. No filtering takes place with their Châteauneuf, gravity being used to dispatch unwanted particles. François Perrin is very concerned about the effect that filtration can have on his wine, and in this respect is closer to many overseas growers than to many Châteauneuf-du-Pape *vignerons*. 'It's so much up to the customer. If he will bear with us and accept that a wine with a deposit is likely to have greater depth of flavour and a wider range of aromas, then I can send out unfiltered wine.'

Meticulous right through the vinification process, M. Perrin is at pains to store all bottled wine for at least one year. He reasons that bottle-sickness may last several months before wearing out, and he wants to present his clients with as near-perfect a product as possible. The bottle stock at Beaucastel runs to 600,000 bottles covering five vintages, and is housed in a recently built extension to the main cellars.

Beaucastel red is always a wine of supreme character. If one were to seek a yardstick to show the quality of which the warm southern half of France is capable, a sort of champion of the region, then this is it. Admittedly it is not the most traditional of Châteauneufs; by holding only around 30 per cent Grenache, Beaucastel is in a dissident camp, but on the other hand the Perrin family have developed the application of purely local vine varieties to form a delicious, striking fusion in their wine. For years there was an underground thread of disbelief in the area that the Mourvèdre could perform much further north than its coastal habitat around Bandol on the Mediterranean. It was also thought that vines like the Muscardin and the Counoise formed part of folklore rather then being serious contributors to the poise and class of the finished wine. But here we have a wine with a regional nature, containing much local *terroir* and warmth, that carries an undoubted international standing and sophistication – judged by the standards and tastes of this era or any previous one. It is frequently amusing to observe members of the wine press and trade discounting the full merit of Beaucastel's wine, since it often does not show prominently in tastings – when young. But the promise is there, and the wine needs several years to come out of itself.

The word 'dumb' is often used against it, as the aromas remain tight and the fruit has not emerged from behind a mask of tannin. Its colour runs from a middle to dark red in an awkward year like 1982 to a sleek purple–black in the excellent 1981, which is one of the best single Châteauneufs made in the past twelve years. The bouquet when young produces brooding raspberry or hedgerow fruit smells, which can become pungent and even 'gamey' in middle age. On the palate there is a sensation of cherry or blackcurrant-inspired fruit, which starts to assert itself, along with a rich, intense bouquet, only after about seven years. This is particularly true of the excellent 1964, 1970, 1971, 1978, 1979, 1981 and 1983 vintages, all of which can live for twenty to thirty years with a fabulous evolution of different smells and flavours during that time.

The 1964, when tasted in late 1991, carried masses of typical Châteauneuf richness and still displayed delicious dark fruit flavours – a supreme wine, showing on top form. At the same tasting of several vintages, the 1971 had softened into an impressive roundness with a persistent length on the finish. It, too, had more living to do.

The 1974 was a more upright wine, marked by a bouquet of almost pure autumnal scents – very successful given the year. The 1976 was a little uneven, with the first signs of dryness and slippage on the bouquet's warmth, offset partly by a thread of southern richness.

The 1978 – François Perrin's first vintage – was, like the 1979, dark plum-coloured, and its deep bouquet still had more to offer. The palate's early richness just tails off a little on the finish, but this will drink well towards 2001 or so. The 1979, with an enchantingly rich bouquet, held robust and challenging flavours: it is more 'violent' than the 1978 and was just loosening on the finish. 'The 1979 shows animal, gamey aromas now,' commented François Perrin, 'but I think it could revert to a fruit-inspired bouquet. In big vintages, the animal smell in our wine is strong, but in small years – like 1987, 1984 or 1972 – you never have this animal or farmyard bouquet.'

The 1980 proves that geese can turn into swans. Discordant and rather hard, almost mean, in its first six years, by 1991 it had gained width on the bouquet and much greater warmth. While still bearing some firm tannin on the palate, a fruit core was emerging to make the wine more approachable.

The 1981 combines austerity and roundness in François Perrin's view. A dark plum colour at its centre, it has since around 1988 carried an extraordinarily pungent bouquet – very gamey and musky and typical of ageing Mourvèdre. This bouquet can withdraw for certain periods during the wine's evolution, but at the age of eleven it was flamboyant. The palate's early richness is supported by a firm structure and the depth of extract in the wine is memorable. It will show very well during the 1990s.

The 1983 is something of a dark horse, for the vintage has not generally worked out nearly as well as the 1981 at Châteauneuf. This is a particular favourite of Jean-Pierre Perrin, and one can easily see why: there was *coulure* in the Grenache that year, giving a yield of only 17 hectolitres per hectare and the wine comes in at only just 13°. After eight years, its colour was still dark and clear, and the bouquet was rich, interesting and just a shade vegetal, indicating a cautious advance. The flavours were well moulded, there was very agreeable length, and a sustained finish. Its tannins were still firm, and the Mourvèdre's provision of liquorice chew at the end rounded it off in a firm, almost mineral but promising way. While several of the 1983s have started to fall apart a little as their tannins dry and expose a lack of flesh underneath, this wine is set fair for a sustained, long development. By comparison with the 1981, the latter carries greater ripeness and has a marvellously seductive roundness on the palate, but both qualify for the notebook abbreviation of TGV (Très Grand Vin).

The 1985, with its deep colour holding well, carries exuberant potential on the bouquet and tremendous depth of extract on the palate; after six years it had opened enough to be very appealing, with a final finesse and delicacy not apparent in the big vintages. It is about to enter a second stage of its evolution when the ripe fruit will take a back seat to some drier flavours.

1986 is a curious year all over Châteauneuf. When tasted in July and December 1991, the Beaucastel red veered towards the lean, with a medium weight of flavour and some damp aromas on the bouquet that lacked a certain depth. It has always been a 'sleeper' wine, with a zigzag of development that makes its future that much harder to predict. A personal view is that it will run in an awkward and sometimes agreeable way towards 1996/97; Jean-Pierre Perrin thinks it will stabilize and keep towards past the year 2000. *On verra*.

Of the two lesser vintages 1984 and 1987, the former is more tannic and less rich – this was a wine made with 50 per cent of the crop discarded for use as Château de Beaucastel. 1987 was a year of misfortune throughout – it was foggy and rainy in March and April and it rained during the harvest – but the Beaucastel is a well-crafted wine in a straightforward way. The colour is a matt plum and the nose has moved towards a second phase; while there is a slight lack of follow-through on the palate, there is a fair amount of chewy extract to make the wine very presentable for a luncheon or a white meat dish out towards 1993/4. Only 800 hectolitres of Beaucastel were made in 1987 – equivalent in the red grapes to a yield of under 13 hectolitres per hectare – which is a typical mark of this estate's professionalism.

The 1988 is rather an austere, military wine at present. The colour has a sound dark hue, but the bouquet is slow to open and the flavours are full of tannin and a sort of liquorice support. Jean-Pierre Perrin feels that their 1988 reveals symptoms of the drought that year and that perhaps their vines hadn't got used to the lack of water as they had by 1989 and 1990. The wine will take four or five years to start to open up, but one hopes that it will soften in due course and not remain too firm.

The 1989 Beaucastel, and the 1989 special *cuvée* Hommage

Jacques Perrin, are both exceptional wines. The Beaucastel holds a very intense cherry colour and a very promising blackcurrant fruit-inspired bouquet. There is excellent depth and extract on the palate, with a lovely surge of clean fruit on the attack. The whole wine is well knit and the tannins – round but firm – help support it towards a promising future. It is slightly finer than the 1990, but has masses of class about it.

The Perrins confess that they have waited patiently for good materials before bringing out a *cuvée* in memory of their father who died in 1978. The *cuvée* Hommage is composed of 60 per cent Mourvèdre, 20 per cent Grenache, and 10 per cent each Syrah and Counoise, and when first tasted in July 1991 was still residing in its 50.1–hectolitre *foudre*. This carries a very big colour with great intensity and a massive core fruit bouquet: one risks superlatives, but the fruit on the palate is tremendously clear and substantial; on second tasting in December 1991 the persistence of the crushed fruit flavours was the most striking aspect of the wine. Lovely length, a generous finish and great all-round harmony complete the picture of this wine of great depth – a star in a star year. A total of 45 hectolitres was bottled as Cuvée Hommage at the end of 1991, one-third in bottle, one-third in magnum and one-third in jeroboam. Jean-Pierre feels that the presence of the Counoise brings some liquorice flavours as well as a gamey side to the wine and that the Mourvèdre is the supplier of very ripe red fruit sensations; the mix of these two grapes permits an agreeable sweetness on the finish. Seeing François Perrin scrambling up a wobbly ladder with his *pipette* in search of this wine, balancing on one leg for the taking of photographs and then discussing it forcefully with his brother as he swirls it around his glass, one realizes that here, with this *cuvée*, the Perrins have released their natural restraint a notch and gone all out for a wine with an immediate, resounding impact – a fitting tribute to their skilled and independent-minded father.

The 1990 Beaucastel, tasted from *foudre*, held a dark black colour, and extreme depth of crushed fruit on the nose; after one year there was a hint of the smell of skin extract, as if the grapes had brought the drought into the wine's aromas. The attack on the palate has a very typical surge of fruit which is then held up by some chewy length on the finish. This wine again has great extraction of flavour, and great class. Bottled in midsummer 1992, it is likely to show very well over the course of at least fifteen years, but the fruit extract will be vibrant around the age of ten. At 13.3° alcohol, it is one of the 'quieter' wines of its year.

The Perrins are very enthusiastic over their work with white wine. In 1980 they first fermented some Roussanne in oak, and by 1986 a regular part of their Roussanne fruit was receiving cask fermentation at natural temperatures – around 25°C, against the controlled 20–21°C of the stainless steel or enamel-lined vats containing the Grenache Blanc and other white grapes.

The brothers produce two *cuvées*, a traditional one that contains 80 per cent Roussanne, supported, according to the year by 15 per cent Grenache Blanc and 5 per cent split between Bourboulenc, Clairette and Picardin. Thirty per cent of this Roussanne is cask-fermented and then resides in cask until bottling around June or July. All the wood is between one and four years old.

The Perrins never block the malolactic, so in a slow year, some part of the final wine in bottle may be pre-*malo*. The traditional *cuvée*, like the special all-Roussanne Vieille Vigne wine, carries greater complexity and ageing potential than most white Châteauneufs. As an example, the 1962 *blanc*, made from a very ripe harvest and in those days containing 60 per cent Grenache Blanc and 30 per cent Roussanne, still held some brief, clean ripe flavours when tasted in 1991; its alcohol emerged pointedly after an hour's air, but it was round and nicely balanced. A 1980 *blanc* (40 per cent Grenache Blanc, 55 per cent Roussanne) was most impressive when tasted at the same time. The bouquet was complex and refined, and excellent balance and finesse on the palate preceded a very long, clean finish.

Of recent vintages, the 1990 mixes well the power and guts of the Grenache Blanc with the dried fruits' finesse and length of the Roussanne, and the wine seems likely to remain firm for a while, with a gradual easing and development over ten years or more. After two years the more refined 1989 was still a little austere, but it held excellent fruit extract and great finesse. The balance is very good, and while the bouquet shows signs of evolution the wine will show very well around 1994. The 1988 is perhaps more solid, with a more restrained bouquet, excellent fruit and a sustained finish, while the 1987 is gentler, nicely weighted and offers great drinking over the course of five to eight years. Like the 1988 and its successors, it is well balanced.

The Vieille Vigne, from a 4-hectare plot of fifty-year-old Roussanne which provides just 15 hectolitres a hectare, is a great wine – another act of defiance by the Perrins to those who mentally write off the area south of Lyon or Valence as being incapable of supplying top-class wines by any world standard. Here we are getting into the realms of quality of top white burgundy or top white Graves – more perhaps the latter due to the stylistic changes and improvements that occurred there during the 1980s. This wine was started in 1986, and has all the trimmings – a justifiably high price for one, but also a wooden outer case and an exceptional quality. The 1986 was massively perfumed, with great rich aromas running around the bouquet. It needed about four years or so to settle, to integrate the young wood and try to curb some end heat at the back of the palate. The 1987 was a little darker – more yellow to the eye – and was very fine: overall, a lighter, more elegant wine that will present very rounded drinking over eight or nine years. The 1988 is progressing slowly, having passed through a dumb phase after around two years; the bouquet is definitely slow to emerge, but gives hints of future breadth, while the palate is marked by excellent depth and elegance. The flavours are good and strong, but there is a most appealing fragility within the wine that lends it its class. This is a wine whose ageing potential is certainly over ten years. Both the 1989 and the 1990 Vieille Vigne possess this great breeding, which starts with a sound, firm colour and an early showing on the bouquet of aromas like toasted almonds and citrus fruits. The palate's dried fruit flavours – apricots, for example – are substantial, and the wines have great length and quality. Their slowness to kick into life and show themselves sets them apart from nearly all other white Châteauneufs, and gives the lucky owner the prospect of great future pleasure.

Like many of the go-ahead *vignerons* of the Vaucluse and the Gard *départements*, the Perrins are involved in experimentation with the rare Viognier vine. In 1987 they planted 1.5 hectares, taking cuttings from Château-Grillet in the northern Rhône. These are near their Vieille Ferme property to the east of the Châteauneuf *appellation*, and were planted facing north on a dip under the top of a plateau; while the ground is covered in stones, it is sandy soil underneath. From 1992 this wine sold as a white Côtes du Rhône Coudoulet de Beaucastel. Yields are as yet very small – only 12 hectolitres in 1990, for instance; early tastings of the wine reveal a steely rather than floral side to the fruit on the bouquet, as found with most southern Rhône Viogniers. There is a fleshy, oily texture on the palate when the wine is tasted from stainless steel, and a firmer, more tropical fruit effect on the wine tasted from two-year-old cask. When blended 70/30 vat over cask, the result is an upright bouquet rather than the floral rusticity that so marks and typifies the northern Viognier, and which is its major calling card. The extract of fruit is sound and discreet, and it will be very interesting to see if Beaucastel can bring out a very good Viognier during the 1990s – already some markers have been put down by the Château St-Estève of M. Marc Français-Monier at Uchaux and, to a lesser extent, by Guy Steinmaier across the river in the Gard.

Outside their Châteauneuf activities, the Perrins also run an excellent, quality-conscious Côtes du Rhône *domaine*, whose wine is called Coudoulet de Beaucastel (ex-Cru de Coudoulet). This is made from a reduced proportion of Grenache for a normal Côtes du Rhône – 30 per cent, along with 30 per cent Mourvèdre, and 20 per cent each of Cinsault and Syrah. The property lies across the N7 road from the Château, and comprises 30 hectares. This is on a par with Guigal's Côtes du Rhône *rouge*: both are distinguished by their relative elegance and balance: they are both cleanly produced wines, with greater sophistication than most country-style Rhônes. The 1985 tasted splendidly at the age of six, with very appealing rounded fruit flavours. The 1986 is a leaner, more angular wine, while the 1988 is a mid-weight wine, ideal to drink around 1992/3. The 1989 is very classy, with great elegance and thoroughness: it will drink well towards 1994 or later.

Perrin, Jean-Pierre et François
   Château de Beaucastel   84350 Courthézon

CHÂTEAU CABRIÈRES

Château Cabrières – its official title changed in the late 1980s from Domaine de Cabrières Lès Silex – is an old, prestigious estate whose vineyards are in some of the prime sites at Châteauneuf. Its owners, the Arnaud and Jacumin families, have been involved with wine or with barrel-making at Châteauneuf for several generations.

The vineyards cover 36 hectares spread over 24 plots, and the red wine contains one of the lower proportions of Grenache – just half, with the rest made up of Syrah (15 per cent), Mourvèdre and Cinsault (10 per cent each) and a mix of Counoise, Picpoul, Muscardin and Terret Noir. The various sites are on some of the most exposed, stony clay–limestone subsoil parts of the plateau leading to Château Mont-Redon north of the village. There is also a prime location right beside the village château ruins, planted with Syrah.

The red vinification was modernized during the 1980s; there is a partial destalking of the crop and after fermentation (kept down to 28°C), the red wine spends six months in young oak casks, followed by nine months in *foudres*. Filtration and bottling are then carried out.

The Cabrières red has traditionally been a 'steady operator', with the occasional ability to hit the heights. The 1967 was an excellent, renowned wine which showed great vigour and depth for many years. When last tasted in 1989, it was tiring on both its *robe* and its bouquet. The palate held some richness and was more obviously Grenache-driven than the wines from the 1980s.

The 1976 Cabrières red was also more distinguished than many of its year, and the 1979 was very sound. During the 1980s the owners appear to have sought an easier, less robust and alcoholic style of wine. The 1989 was forward on the bouquet after only two years, inspired by an early fruitiness. There was fair weight of extract on the palate, indicating that it should drink well around 1994–6 – quite an early wine.

Around 5 per cent of the production is white; this is made from 30 per cent each of Grenache Blanc, Bourboulenc and Clairette, plus 10 per cent Roussanne. Efforts are being made to upgrade this, through new plantation. The vinification is cool-fermented (18°C), but the wine lacks a little character. The 1990 *blanc* held decent length, but represents the rather mainstream cool fermentation group in quality. The 1989 held sharper, clearer fruit and aromas.

Within the Château Cabrières grouping are two other family vineyards, the 20-hectare Domaine de Fusat and the 9-hectare Domaine de Jacumin.

SCEA Louis Arnaud et ses Enfants
   Château Cabrières   84230 Châteauneuf-du-Pape

CHÂTEAU DES FINES ROCHES

One of the old leading names at Châteauneuf-du-Pape, the Fines Roches estate totals 55 hectares of vines that grow around the rather Hollywood Gothic-style château that dates from the late nineteenth century. Part of the house is now a hotel-restaurant, catering for rich foreign tourists if the mark-ups on the exclusively Châteauneuf-du-Pape wine list are any yardstick.

Some of the wine is made by an adapted *macération carbonique* vinification, which produces a correct but uninteresting wine. The *cuvées* made in the traditional way improved during the 1980s, bringing back the standards that used to prevail here in the 1960s. Successful vintages were the 1979, 1983, and 1985, all of which possessed greater depth and authenticity of flavour than previous years. The 1989s from Fines Roches itself and from the Domaine Fabrice Mousset showed decent dark plum colours and a fair intensity on the bouquet; the Fines Roches red lacked some of the extreme depth of fruit of the best of the year, and should be drunk from around 1995 onwards. The Domaine du la Font du Roi, which is sold with Jacques Mousset as the owner on the label, was less impressive, while the Clos St-Michel (Guy Mousset) showed promise on the palate to settle and develop from around 1995 onwards – it is still chewy and backward.

The Mousset/Fines Roches stable of properties and wines goes back several decades; in the mid-1950s a magazine advertisement lists the Château du Bois de la Garde, the Château du Prieuré St-Joseph and the Domaine de la Courançonne as being under the Fines Roches umbrella. These days at Châteauneuf there are the Domaine Fabrice Mousset (Jacques Mousset's son), the Domaine de la Font du Roi, the Domaine de Clos du Roi and the Clos St-Michel. The owners' names attached to these are all family members.

There has been greater concentration in the late 1980s on white wine-making here, and the 1990 Fabrice Mousset *blanc* was a good *cuvée*, carrying an attractive freshness on the bouquet and good depth of flavour on the palate. The fruit was ripe and delicious, and the wine held together very well. The Fines Roches white 1990 was thinner and less well defined.

SCEA Château des Fines Roches
  et Château du Bois de la Garde   84230 Châteauneuf-du-Pape

CHÂTEAU DE LA FONT DU LOUP

Set snugly against a brief hillside, the Château de la Font du Loup is tucked away in vineyards bordering those of Domaine du Vieux

Télégraphe. A curiously styled house with its orange tiled roof and small thin turret to one side of the façade, it enjoys a fabulously sweeping view across to Mont Ventoux. Its 16-hectare vineyard is grouped all around the château and is assiduously worked by Charles Mélia, who took over when his grandfather retired from running the property in 1976.

'My grandfather was eighty-five when he retired,' commented M. Mélia, 'having fled from Morocco in 1942 and started here shortly afterwards. He designed the *cuverie* himself, having it cut into the hillside to permit crushing by gravity and attending to details like having an Italian designer put some yellow and green tiles on the outside of the vats – just to add a little bit of style.'

The red grapes number principally four in the composition of the red wine: Grenache, around 80 per cent, followed by Mourvèdre, Syrah and a decreasing amount of Cinsault, although there are odd clutches of Counoise, Muscardin and Terret. The oldest plot is a 1.5-hectare *parcelle* called La Comtesse, where there are eighty-year-old Grenache vines. They grow in two types of terrain – half are on sandy ground, which gives light, fine, aromatic wine, and half are on stony ground, which provides more robust, full-bodied wine.

Like many of the younger growers, Charles Mélia has become more conscious of priming the vineyards to a greater degree of precision than during the 1980s, when his attention was perhaps more fixed on the vinification and the improvement of his cellars. 'With the current bugs that vineyards are prey to, such as grape-worm or *ver de la grappe*, you have to be more vigilant. I've now taken to producing 400 tons of compost a year to help the vineyards; I mix it – half from *marc* and half from lambs' droppings – then ensure it is well fermented through the winter and spread it in March; I've been doing this since 1985 and feel it is definitely beneficial.'

Charles Mélia has a legal training, and it is no surprise to hear that he nearly became a teacher, since he reflects carefully before responding to questions in a precise, orderly way. 'I faced any young man's problem when taking on the estate, namely the problem of finance. That meant that I had to initially vinify in a younger style to get cash flow going. Now that I've come through the early years I'm in a position to move towards a more backward style of wine. I now crush the harvest, and have a three-week maceration, keeping the temperature at around 30–32°C, with two *remontages* a day. I'm not fussed by extremes of heat since I have spring water at 14°C here – the Font du Loup is the spring.'

The most robust *cuvées* are chosen for twelve to eighteen months' cask-ageing – often this is the wine from the more stony soil, while the wine from the sandier plots is kept in glass-lined vats until filtration and bottling around two years after the harvest.

M. Mélia's first bottling was in 1979 and the most substantial vintage he made in his early days was the 1981, a wine with a respectable dark colour and a more typical Châteauneuf style than his previous wines. His 1983 bore traces of *macération carbonique* fruit and was not long lived. The 1985 showed the progress of this *domaine*, for by the early 1990s it is one of the 1985s that has best held together. The Font du Loup style is anyway rather gravelly, finesse rather than guts being the order of the day, and the 1985 shows a very decent extract of fruit and tannin which runs into a long, satisfying finish: it is a wine likely to keep well towards 1999.

Of recent vintages, the 1988 is another example of the interesting style from this *quartier*: the wine is not fleshy, but has good persistence on the palate, somewhat like comparing a Graves with a St-Estèphe when one puts Font du Loup alongside Grenache-inspired wines that come from elsewhere in the *appellation*, like Clos du Mont-Olivet. There is a certain severity in the wine, which may yield with age. The 1989 has more substance; its aromas are very discreet, and its tannins are more prominent than many of the year. Again the emphasis is on elegance, on complexity and gradual development rather than on exuberant and showy flavours. The 1990 red is also closed, indeed a much more cautious offering than most 1990s, but there is sufficient weight and discreet richness on the palate to ensure steady progress over a dozen years.

The white vines are generally around ten years old; these are led by the Grenache Blanc (50 per cent), plus equal amounts of Clairette, Roussanne and Bourboulenc (about 16 per cent). This one hectare contributes around 4,000 bottles a year; since M. Mélia's purchase of a new *pressoir* with a very fine press setting, there has been no need for a *débourbage*. The fermentation can last for up to six weeks at around 18–20°C, with bottling in March the following year.

From the 1991 vintage, a second red wine has been made here, the Domaine du Puy Rolland, a 4–hectare property which borders the Font du Loup.

Font du Loup is an interesting *domaine*; the wines are not easy or *facile* on tasting, and take some getting to know. They have a *nervosité* and a fineness that point much to the terrain from which they come, and in this respect they are reminiscent of the reds of Château de la Gardine – very good wines, whose territory does not deliver corpulence and which are therefore often misunderstood by drinkers unaware of the variety of styles present at Châteauneuf-du-Pape.

Mélia, Charles
    Château de la Font du Loup   84350 Courthézon

CHÂTEAU FORTIA

This château and the 28.5-hectare vineyard surrounding it are the property of Baron Le Roy de Boiseaumarié, the son of the man responsible for the initiation of the vineyard laws in 1923. The château is very close to the village but nestles behind a protective group of trees on a tiny hillock at the head of the vineyards. Baron Le Roy has a welcome streak of eccentricity: while delivering a gush of words about the unfairness of the fiscal measures levied on wines held in stock – which is causing growers to make lighter wines and sell them early – he is dressed in a typical student's black Wrangler corduroy jacket with orange-coloured work boots on his feet. Darting glances over his narrow-rimmed glasses, emitting sharp whistles of breath, he moves zealously on to subjects ranging from the geology of Châteauneuf to the phenomenon of *coulure* hitting the Grenache two years running and the problem he faces with a new crusher with the screws set too far apart. He is not a man to be taken lightly – he has a profound store of knowledge on the *appellation*, its wines, soil and climate. In the family tradition his son has written a detailed survey of the geological make-up of the area.

In 1984 the Baron's Grenache vines produced fruit in a rarely encountered way. 'After two successive years of *coulure* the plant's vigour was under-used, and with very few grapes to nourish, it started to yield fruit from the base of the vine on the old wood below the current year's cuttings. There weren't a lot of grapes, but they were good bunches, nourished by the reserves of the plant. They appeared two weeks after the main fruit, and in the first half of October caught up to produce a degree of 13.8°. The old wood would never normally nourish grapes, but these ones to a large extent saved the day.'

One of the Baron's experiments has been to lay out newly picked bunches of Grenache crop on *claiettes* – a form of pallet – in front of the château, in a well-exposed position half a metre above the ground; to his satisfaction the evaporation of the liquid in the grapes resulted in a gain of 1.3° in only a couple of days. This technique brings extra richness to the wine, but also a somewhat raisiny taste.

The first record that vines were being cultivated around the old house dates back to 1763, and when the residence was enlarged into a château around 1815, a splendid vaulted cellar with walls nearly 2.5 metres thick was added. Nowadays the vines grown at Fortia are Grenache (72 per cent), Syrah (14 per cent), Mourvèdre (8 per cent) and a mixture of other varieties, including about 2 per cent of Counoise. The Baron is tired of some of the Grenache's caprices: 'We're back to *coulure* with it in 1991, especially in the older plants, which acts against quality,' he remarks tartly. 'Then, if you're working with clones, the grape bunches become so tightly packed together that they need discarding. This should be done in August, but the personnel are away then, so it has to be done in July, which is not to my satisfaction.' A menacing stare ends this mini-tirade. As for the whites, he has about 2 hectares, split between Clairette (60 per cent), Grenache Blanc (20 per cent) and Roussanne (20 per cent); as the Grenache is the highest yielder, its percentage in the final white wine is a bit higher.

Since the 1979 vintage Baron Le Roy admits that his wines haven't always been quite as full-bodied as he would have liked. In part he tried to make a 1983 that bore a newer style – 'a five- to eight-year wine' in his own words; in part he has had difficulty obtaining the colour and tannin extraction he would like, through using a modern crushing machine on which the setting of the screws has been wider apart than ideal. 'In the old days the harvest would often be rammed through when it got stuck in the crusher, and this had the effect of extracting lots of tannin, making the wine harsh initially but giving it great keeping powers. That was the crusher we used from 1924, and now I find I'm having to lessen the distance between the screws to regain this extraction.'

There is also some destalking each year, and an extended *cuvaison* in concrete vats in search of more *gras* – a fullness and richness in the red wine. Cask-ageing runs from between eighteen months to two years in 50-hectolitre *foudres* of Russian oak, larger and thicker containers than in the time of his father. 'My late father aged the wine in 225-litre *barriques*, but they drink 1.5 litres of wine a month and also dry out the wine. I make no bones about it – I detest new oak – it's too strong. You have to be a very great connoisseur of wood to get it just right, and it's very expensive. For growers doing short vinifications and macerations, young wood can help.'

Fining, filtering and bottling occur in all years except those written off by the press. 'I couldn't sell any 1987 overseas, so I sold it all off in bulk.' In all honesty, the Fortia wines at present resemble the unsettled state of mind of their owner. Their style varies beyond the raw elements provided by the harvest. The 1989 tasted out of barrel pre-assembly showed promise in the rather taut Fortia way – a firm colour, some spice on the bouquet and a good, straight-line persistence on the palate: not much generosity, but that is the traditional house style, which one encountered on a regular basis with vintages like the excellent 1976 and 1978 and very good 1979. The 1978 when drunk in 1991, for instance, was still a trifle hard and austere, holding back its future rounded flavours rather stiffly – a Bordeaux discipline rather than a Rhône warmth.

The 1988 was a straight, firm wine which will gently unfold during the 1990s, its longevity similar to the 1989 which is likely to be delicious around 1996–8. The 1986 is admitted to be not a great year by its maker; it holds some stern tannins, and its fruit is not that clearly defined – the overall balance is dubious. Both the 1984 and 1985 were full and ripe wines, with more plump appeal than usual from Fortia, but the 1981 and 1983 tend towards a lack of depth and dimension.

The white wine is fermented in stainless steel or enamel-lined vats at around 20°C for three to four weeks, and is bottled, with the malolactic blocked, in December or early January. Baron Le Roy does not regard his whites as keepers, and a 1983 drunk in 1991 had turned towards a flatness of taste on the palate, with the Grenache Blanc and the Clairette unable to pull the wine along. The Roussanne has been increased since then, and in a fat year like 1990, the wine drinks well early on, with an authentic richness and a clean, traditional style. Like many southern whites, this is liable to pass through a dumb phase after about eighteen months or two years, and drinking horizons should extend to about five or six years, no more.

A pressing question affecting this famous property is that of the succession, with the Baron's son currently working on his mother-in-law's *domaine* at Limoux in the south-west. One senses that the Baron is a tired man, and a slightly sad one behind all the bold and feisty talk, and one hopes that future years will not be turbulent here.

Baron Le Roy
    Château Fortia   84230 Châteauneuf-du-Pape

CHÂTEAU DE LA GARDINE

The Château de la Gardine and its 56-hectare vineyard are situated to the west of Châteauneuf-du-Pape, the château standing at the edge of the plateau that runs north towards the Mont-Redon vineyards, one of the more isolated spots in the *appellation*. La Gardine has always been one of the leading exporting *domaines*, with its wine well known in the United States, Canada and even Spain for at least thirty years. During the 1980s, there was a steady tightening-up in the quality of the wines here, with greater cellar investment and a more attacking approach to vinification contributing extra quality and dimension.

When bought by the late Gaston Brunel immediately after the Second World War, the estate's 8-hectare vineyard was in a state of near-abandonment. He developed it to its current size with a clearing policy – *défrichage* – and with purchases of plots that now total thirty. These are all gathered together on this west side of the village. Greater emphasis has been placed on white varieties, which were doubled during the 1980s to 6 hectares, made up of Grenache Blanc (40 per cent), Roussanne (30 per cent), Bourboulenc (20 per cent) and Clairette (10 per cent). The Roussanne is partly twenty-five years old, and hopes are that the extra Roussanne will raise the quality and freshness of the white. The 50 hectares of red are composed of Grenache (70 per cent), Syrah (12 to 15 per cent), Mourvèdre (5 per cent), and 10 per cent split between Cinsault and Muscardin.

There is a firm inclination towards all things technological at La Gardine; of the two brothers, Maxime runs the vineyard and Patrick the cellars, and great progress and investment occurred within the cellars during the 1980s. However, there is an interesting aspect to La Gardine's vineyards, for they serve to show how Châteauneuf can vary in style due to factors other than the usually quoted ones of different grape amalgams and different vinification processes. Certainly during the 1960s and early 1970s, the La Gardine red could sometimes be light in colour and body, and a personal view is that this was partly due to a fixed factor – the thin, possibly unpropitious soil of parts of the vineyard, particularly the area nearest the Rhône, where the top layer is only ever between 20 and 40 centimetres deep; the Domaine de St-Préfert of Camille Serre has plots in similar locations and its wines are fine, but fragile, almost pebbly on the palate. Such vineyards are susceptible to drought in long, dry summers, and while irrigation is an option until mid-August, it is an exercise which, unless very skilfully handled, can upset the ripening rhythm of the fruit. A second factor applicable to La Gardine during the 1960s was the youth of a section of the vineyard.

The estate is an early harvester – 7 September 1990, 3 September 1989 and 15 September 1988. The vinification reception varies by vintage – anything from no crushing, to some destalking, to total destalking and a full crush. Patrick Brunel's pride and joy are the ten stainless steel *pigeage* vats with a capacity of 1,870 hectolitres, which have operated since 1989. These immerse the cap of the fermenting mass for two or three minutes in the morning and evening, and Patrick Brunel is in no doubt about the merits of this system, which is also used at La Nerthe and Beaurenard: 'We destalk all grapes intended for *pigeage*, and I consider the process serves to extract the aromatic potential, plus colour and general quality of the Syrah that we couldn't obtain in a normal *cuve*. If you think about it, the *pigeage* was done in the past by foot in open fermentation tuns, so we're coming back to that process in a more organized way. I also think we have a much more flexible attitude towards our vinification than in the past: we now may crush the Grenache, but not the Syrah – in which case the Grenache is pumped into the bottom of the vat, with its skins broken, and the Syrah placed quietly on top.'

In pursuit of the extraction of greater aromas, the *cuvaison* has also shortened from between eighteen and twenty-five days to between twelve and eighteen days. The attitude to wood-ageing has also changed since 1980; the average stay is nine months, but the 140-hectolitre barrels are used less than before, most often on stubborn vintages like 1988. The main focus now is on young oak in smaller casks, of which there are around 200 at any given time, with a one-new-year-in-three rotation. In the final wine there will be about 15–20 per cent which has been exposed to young oak, while the rest has stayed in vats of stainless steel or glass lining, or in *foudres*.

Patrick Brunel defends himself discreetly when asked as to how and why he chooses his young wood. 'I don't want the wood to mark the wine. Remember that there were six *tonneliers* at Châteauneuf in 1932, so there was a consistent supply of new wood in those days as casks wore out and were replaced all the time. We take our wood from Demptos in Bordeaux; it's mostly Nevers wood with a medium smoking, and we put the wine at its youngest stage in the older casks, working back through two rackings to the brand new oak.' He does not feel that this process over the space of nine months unduly disturbs the wine. Fining occurs before the wine enters the casks, and bottling comes, preferably without filtration, about two years after the harvest. Storage in bottle at the château ensures that a vintage like the 1988 was not put on sale until March 1992.

Tastings of La Gardine from 1990 backwards reveal the discreet spine provided by the use of the young oak; wine that has not had any wood exposure reveals greater Grenache *typicité*, with peppery, solid, warm flavours, while that exposed to oak is more modern, less Châteauneuf, holding firm cherry fruit flavours – not typical associations for Châteauneuf. But the blend of the two is indeed a good fit, with extra life and dimension discreetly provided by the cask treatment, without the all-important loss of local stamp.

The 1989 red is notably round and ripely flavoured, with tannins and liquorice chewiness emerging quietly on the finish. This elegant, classy wine may live in good form for ten to twelve years, a little less than the 1990. The 1988 is an interesting wine, with more rigid structure than the 1989 and the promise of a superb bouquet developing around 1996–8; in some ways it is more complex than the full, quite obvious 1989. Less prominent years like 1986 and 1980 have been well worked, while the earlier vintages of 1981, 1979 and 1978 were all very successful; the 1979 in particular was one of the best of its year, with a very profound bouquet and great length on the palate to complement its elegant style.

Since the mid-1980s, the Brunels have produced a special red, the *cuvée* Génération, which in some vintages can have been exposed entirely to new oak for its ageing. The 1985 captures the Gardine style in a nutshell: it has a peppery, quite powerful bouquet, and plum fruit flavours that are slightly reminiscent of good red Graves, with a length and finesse that indicate excellent drinking around 1994–5.

The estate is also pressing ahead with a revitalized white wine. The Brunels recognized that their white vines were not old enough to produce fruit that bore great *gras*, so they consciously elected to aim for aroma extraction. The varieties are vinified apart, with the Roussanne and the Bourboulenc fermented in new oak. 'The Roussanne expresses itself well in the wood,' states Patrick Brunel, reflecting a now commonly accepted wisdom at Châteauneuf, 'and the Bourboulenc brings welcome acidity, since it is a poor ripener. We're frightened of oxidation on the Grenache Blanc, so we vinify that and the Clairette in normal vats at around 20°C.'

The varieties are assembled in mid-December and bottled soon after. The special white *cuvée* Vieilles Vignes differs in that all the *cépages* are fermented together in new oak and spend eight to twelve months in cask before bottling. Both whites are sound, well-weighted wines, with depth of flavour taking precedence over freshness on the palate. When young, the Vieilles Vignes is overpowered by the standard vanilla flavours of the new oak; at two years of age, an integration slowly starts, with a hint of marzipan on the bouquet, and a welcome vigour and depth on the palate; the wood resurfaces right on the finish. By the age of four, the Vieilles Vignes has refined itself further, and both the bouquet and the palate declare soft aromas and fruits, with just some final chew provided by the cask treatment. The 1989 and 1987 are both wines that can live for seven to ten years.

The Château wine comes in a special bottle; this is brown and misshapen, and has embossed below its long, slender neck the words: 'Château de la Gardine Mise du Château'. This design is used on both the normal 75-cl bottle and the more recent 50-cl bottle. Always keen on their innovations, the Brunels have also made a Côtes du Rhône *primeur* for some years. Of greater interest is their Côtes du Rhône Villages red, a sound wine to drink when three to four years old, which comes from their 50-hectare property at Rasteau and Roaix.

The final oddity about this progressive *domaine* is their public telephone box, which stands by the house in the shade of a laurel tree. It was installed after a chance meeting between Patrick Brunel and the Minister of Telecommunications at the Agricultural Fair in Paris; there had been a delay in putting one in for the people of this part of Châteauneuf, and when the Minister heard, he ordered its immediate installation in a privileged place beside the Château. Needless to say it has never been vandalized.

Brunel, Maxime et Patrick
    Château de la Gardine   84230 Châteauneuf-du-Pape

CHÂTEAU MAUCOIL

Adjoining the Château Mont-Redon is the 22-hectare Château Maucoil, a property that once served a useful purpose for the Prince of Orange. He appropriated it in 1571 and then sold it off ten years later. The estate was actively supervised until he was in his eighties by the late M. Pierre Quiot, who with his wife also owned another Châteauneuf-du-Pape *domaine*, the Quiot St-Pierre, as well as the Gigondas Domaine des Pradets and the Côtes du Rhône Clos des Patriciens.

The major part of the plantation is taken up by the Grenache Noir, with support from the Cinsault, Mourvèdre, Counoise and Clairette. Under the guidance of M. Jacques Ravel, M. Quiot's son-in-law, it is to be hoped that steps are taken to beef up the wine of Maucoil. It is the best of the family's wines, but tends to be light and lacking in the wholehearted character expected of a *domaine*-reared and bottled Châteauneuf-du-Pape.

Domaine Quiot SCV
  Château Maucoil   84100 Orange

CHÂTEAU MONT-REDON

The largest estate at Châteauneuf-du-Pape, and historically the best-known abroad, is the Château Mont-Redon, which has a 95-hectare vineyard. This has belonged to the Plantin family since 1921, and when they bought it there were no more than 2 hectares under vines. Large tracts of land were cleared away and replanted with a majority of Grenache, but some stock of each of the thirteen *cépages* was planted, including as much as 4 hectares of Syrah in 1926. By the 1950s and 1960s, the red wine was mainly composed of around 80 per cent Grenache and 10 per cent each of Cinsault and Syrah. In the early 1990s, there is less Grenache, less Cinsault, and more Mourvèdre. The figures are roughly 65 per cent Grenache, 15 per cent Syrah, 8 per cent Cinsault, 7 per cent Mourvèdre and 5 per cent diverse varieties.

The *domaine* is run by first cousins MM. Didier Fabre and Jean Abeille, who are grandsons of M. Plantin. It is one of the showpieces of Châteauneuf-du-Pape, with healthy, carefully tended vineyards and a spotless efficiency inside the cellars. Between them they have five sons, which, under the French laws of equal inheritance, could well cause problems over the succession in years to come – one hopes not.

Mont-Redon lies in isolated country in the north-western corner of the *appellation*. Up here there are few windbreaks in what is in winter an austere, chilly landscape; a few small poplars, one or two tool huts, the pale blue smudge of their doors sidling out of a light brown, stone-filled landscape. The scene seems suitable for a Gustave Courbet labourer, brought south from the plough to the pointed hoe, chipping away among the massed rows of rounded stones. Close to the *domaine* there is just a small, round hill, which gives the property its name.

This is one of the oldest wine *quartiers* of the region. A document of 1344 speaks of the wines of Mourredon, Les Cabrières – the adjoining vineyard – and Bois Renard, now the Domaine de Beaurenard. Unlike Château Rayas, for example, with its fine, siliceous soil, all these properties, which are on the higher plateau of Châteauneuf-du-Pape, are distinguished by their typical local terrain made up of literally thousands and thousands of rounded stones – which make excellent doorstops or garden edgings if the visitor is feeling light-fingered!

Didier Fabre is a bearded man, with a measured, almost learned air; in discussing the vineyard he is very phlegmatic and methodical. His dark-haired, lively brother-in-law Jean Abeille is the self-confessed 'Latin side of the duo'. M. Abeille recounted that since 1981 they had planted about one-quarter of a hectare with all thirteen permitted grape varieties. 'Having them all together like this allows us to monitor each variety and to better judge whether we should increase the plantation of any *cépage*. I think that all the lesser varieties at Châteauneuf originally disappeared because they were the most awkward ones to cultivate; there was also the fact that after phylloxera more alcoholic wines were sought, which meant growers turned to the Grenache.'

The Mont-Redon plantation of Syrah is now at a stable 15–20 per cent, but the Mourvèdre notably is being increased at the expense of the Cinsault, from 5 per cent, aiming for nearer 12 per cent. M. Abeille explained: 'The Mourvèdre gives spice and a green pepper flavour to the wine and adds even more structure and solidity than the Syrah, whose aromas I consider to be more floral, more violet. The problem with the Cinsault is that after imparting some early fruit it dries out quickly. The case of the Cinsault here is funny because around 1964 the INAO recommended the planting of the Cinsault to calm down the Grenache – to break the fire of the alcohol of the wine. We went ahead and planted 7 hectares of Cinsault between 1960 and 1970, and now – in 1991 – I have a team of five grafters out in the vineyards systematically grafting Syrah on to the base of the older Cinsault vines. The Cinsault hasn't worked out.' So much for directives from the centre – especially those designed to strip the wine of its local authenticity, as occurred with several measures introduced from government office sources in the 1960s – including *macération carbonique* vinification.

MM. Fabre and Abeille have for some years been very keen to set Mont-Redon apart from the old-fashioned, heavy wines that used to typify Chateauneuf-du-Pape *rouge* and explain their attitude in simple terms: 'We don't want our wine to have more than about 13.7° of alcohol, since we are trying to make wine that people can enjoy and, above all, drink rather than look at. Our 1977 would be a case in point: the vintage was not particularly good, but our wine was very harmonious and was nice to drink even five years later – *un vin sympathique.*' As a result, half the harvest is now destalked every year, whatever the conditions.

This general policy served to provide some attenuated wines in the late 1970s and in one or two years of the early 1980s: an absence of the strength and concentration of Mont-Redons of the 1950s and 1960s was apparent, with wines that lacked the extract to impress drinkers seeking the challenge of the south in their glass. Some *macération carbonique* wines even started to be released, and very few of these – in years like 1979, 1982 and 1983 – held much ageing potential past around eight years.

The greatest changes during the 1980s at the level of vinification came from the experimentation with young oak from 1983–4 onwards. The owners felt that their old large *foudres* were drying out the wine too much, so they turned to the use of Burgundian casks of Allier oak for about 30 per cent of the wine of any given vintage; meanwhile the rest of the wine spends between eight and fourteen months in the regular *foudres*. There is also a tremendous selection of grape cocktails residing in cask before any final *assemblage* is even considered – out of a *foudre* might come a wine of 70 per cent Grenache, 15 per cent Cinsault, 5 per cent Syrah and 10 per cent Vaccarèse, Counoise and Muscardin; out of a small, brand new cask might come a wine of 70 per cent Grenache, 20 per cent Syrah and 10 per cent Mourvèdre; and out of a three-year-old cask might come 80 per cent Grenache and 20 per cent Syrah. All these will be put together, based on tasting and testing, into the final Château Mont-Redon.

The effect has been to stylize the wines more than before – these are definitely sharp operators now; one expects them in a human form to wear Hugo Boss suits and dark glasses, but not to take that over the top – just the right amount of cool and cred. The 1990 red, tasted pre-assembly, showed the promise of a dark colour, a strongly formed blackcurrant bouquet and a definite tannic underlay; it is likely to come together after six or seven years, and providing the new wood presence isn't overstated, will bear a definable Châteauneuf character.

The 1989, assembled as the final wine in July 1991 and bottled in October 1991, has a cherry, purple colour, and is also a stylish wine, with sleek fruit and an unobtrusive middle weight to it; it needs time to settle – towards 1995 – but is a very good wine and has the potential to run for twelve-plus years.

The 1988 is a well balanced wine, with dried fruit flavours on the palate – not as round and plump as the 1989, and its bouquet needs time to develop. The 1987 needs to be drunk before about 1993 since it is showing signs of drying out, but none the less is an agreeable, medium-weight wine. The 1986 is a problem: like many of its year it shows signs of decline; the colour is very ruby, and there is a drying out on the finish. But in the words of Jean Abeille, 'It reminds me of the 1964, which plunged down very quickly, but then didn't move and stabilized after that.' *On verra*, Jean. The 1985 is one of the better of the year, since it has retained great fruit and roundness in an appealing way; the fruit is likely to show especially well towards 1993, but the wine should live past that date.

Notable among earlier vintages are 1978 and 1981. The 1978, when tasted in 1991, was still extraordinarily tight-knit, with a lovely harmony of flavours on the palate, tremendous width and still plenty of opening-up to do to add to an already impressive amount of richness. The 1981 when tasted in 1991, was a very satisfying wine, with great elegance and a tight composition; this has gained in richness with age, and the bouquet is a classic Châteauneuf example, with plenty of cedary and leathery aromas apparent.

Auction-room attenders are well advised to look out for older vintages of Mont-Redon; the wine has always been very well distributed around the English-speaking world, and old wines like the 1971, 1967, 1961 or 1957 are well worth tracking down – they are likely still to be in good, voluptuous form if well cellared, something that the new chic wines will not be able to match in twenty years' time. It is worth noting that in 1988 the word 'Domaine' was dropped from the title, so these wines are now found either as Château Mont-Redon or as Vignoble Abeille.

The white Mont-Redon is generally very good. The estate is the largest vinifier of white at Châteauneuf, producing over 60,000 bottles annually. This is made from 40 per cent Grenache Blanc, 20 per cent Bourboulenc and Clairette, 10 per cent Picpoul and Terret Blanc and Gris and the difference, which is increasing, of Roussanne; the last-named vines were planted in 1983/4. Fermented mostly in stainless steel at the low temperature of 16°C, the white is bottled from December onwards, with the malolactic blocked. It is always a fresh, crisp-tasting wine that shows well early on, but then goes quiet just before its second birthday. Of recent years the 1989 has greater all-round balance and keeping possibilities than the 1990.

The domaine is also proud of its *eau-de-vie*, or alcohol spirit made from the distilled grape *marc*. A certain amount of spirit is always taken by the state as a form of tax (it is particularly used in hospital surgery), but the *domaine* keeps the best of what remains and ages it in small 670-litre oak casks. Two thousand bottles of this 'Marc de Châteauneuf-du-Pape' are made every year and go out to a small, regular clientele. The *eau-de-vie* is strong stuff, having an alcohol content of 42 per cent, and is best drunk as a *digestif* at the end of a meal.

Mont-Redon has an export system of different labels for different importers in any given country. As a consequence, the wine – the same, whatever the label – can be found as Château Mont-Redon, Vignoble Abeille, Vignoble Fabre or Les Busquières. In the United States, traditionally only the Mont-Redon has been sold. The estate also sells a good white Côtes du Rhône (70 per cent Grenache Blanc, 20 per cent Bourboulenc, 10 per cent Roussanne) and a fruity, well-made red (70 per cent Grenache, 20 per cent Cinsault, 10 per cent Syrah) from their 20-hectare *domaine* near Roquemaure in the Gard.

Fabre, Didier, et Abeille, Jean
    Château Mont-Redon   84230 Châteauneuf-du-Pape

CHÂTEAU LA NERTHE

Formerly the best-known, most widely vaunted château of Château-neuf-du-Pape, the Château La Nerthe (the 'de' has been dropped and the 'h' reintroduced by its new owners David et Foillard and Éts Richard) has had large amounts of money and new expertise put into it, and by the 1990s shows signs of regaining its former glorious reputation. Indeed, some of the very best Châteauneuf red from the 1990 vintage came from La Nerthe – a considerable triumph, given the vicissitudes that the estate experienced during the 1980s.

The château dates back to 1599, and has undergone a series of ups and downs during its long history as a wine estate. It was first brought to eminence by its early owners, the de Tulle family from Piedmont; always eager to commercialize their wine as widely as possible, the de Tulles had by 1750 started exporting it to Germany. By 1785 they had gone a step further and were selling their wine in bottles to European countries and in barrels to the United States, notably to the city of Boston. This represented a considerable advance in the fortunes of the vineyard, for documents of the time point to the great difficulties experienced by the de Tulle family in selling their wines in the early part of the century.

La Nerte gained in stature throughout the nineteenth century, partly, no doubt, thanks to the antics of its old dashing owner, the Marquis de Villefranche. He moved freely in the high society of Paris and, when questioned on his activities, invariably claimed that his wine infinitely prolonged man's capacity for enjoyment. His sales technique was, of course, impeccable, and the wine of La Nerte came to grace many an important table.

But then fortunes changed dramatically. Phylloxera destroyed the vineyard and temporarily the *domaine*'s reputation was lost. A new owner from Marseille let the replanted vines decline into near abandonment, and by the outbreak of the Second World War the wine of La Nerte had virtually ceased to exist.

In 1941 a new family, the Mottes, bought the estate at public auction. They worked in textiles in the north of France, and installed a manager to run it. M. René Derreumaux and his son, also René, were in charge of the estate until 1985, when it was sold yet again, this time to a Burgundy wine firm with a presence in David et Foillard, and a *négociant*, Richard, from Paris.

M. Derreumaux *père* faced considerable problems when attempting to start restoration work on the château in 1941: 'No sooner had the Motte family turned their thoughts seriously to rebuilding the vineyard than the German Luftwaffe arrived to take over the château as their local operations centre. The château and its outbuildings were occupied until August 1944, when the British Air Force relieved us in a really pinpoint raid: I shall never forget their accuracy in dropping twenty-two bombs on the outbuildings and leaving the château untouched.'

During the 1960s and 1970s, Château de la Nerte emerged as a property with a very well-defined style of wine – a massive red, inky-coloured and potent, and running with firm tannins and great berried fruit extract. However, after the initial burst of spending and upgrading on both vineyard and cellars that had taken place after the Liberation, the estate was allowed to run gently downhill. The château became hidden among dense clusters of surrounding undergrowth; the interior, with the Motte family absent most of the year, was not properly maintained; and until 1982 no ordered replanting of the vineyards occurred. While local *domaines* like Vieux Télégraphe were investing in smart, modern cellars, the Nerte installations remained antiquated.

This was very sad, since the estate lies in one of the most renowned parts of Châteauneuf-du-Pape: the châteaux of Fortia and Fines Roches and the Domaine de la Solitude are the bordering vineyards. The area under vines and its composition were two of the early targets for the new management. The 65 hectares were reshuffled straight away; the 7 hectares near the property's entrance, at the Étang de Cort-Noué, were forty-year-old Grenache. Seeking a modern style of wine, they were replaced by Mourvèdre, on a different planting pattern – 2.25 x 1 metres instead of the old 1.75 x 1.5 metres between rows. Wooded areas were cleared, notably the Clos de Beauvenir, a walled zone near the château, whose rich, stone-covered soil had been allowed to become overgrown; here the 3 hectares were filled with Bourboulenc, Roussanne and Grenache Blanc. In other wooded areas, Syrah and Mourvèdre were popped in, relentlessly drawing down the Grenache presence overall to around 57 per cent.

In 1991 a major step was taken – the acquisition of the 25-hectare Domaine de Terre Ferme (q.v.), from Pierre Bérard. This vineyard lies between La Nerthe and Vieux Télégraphe on the plateau de la Crau, and its soil is similar to that of La Nerthe, which splits into three styles – clay–sand, clay–limestone and powdered brown limestone, the latter providing the finest wine. As befitted a traditional *domaine*, Terre Ferme brought greater Grenache with it – in fact it was composed of 65 per cent Grenache, 20 per cent Syrah, 10 per cent Mourvèdre and 5 per cent mixed, and overall its soil was more *galet* stone-covered than much of La Nerthe. Terre Ferme is being slotted straight into the La Nerthe empire, so that by 1991 the line-up of vines was, for 81 hectares, Grenache 62 per cent, Syrah 9 per cent, Mourvèdre 15 per cent, Cinsault 5 per cent and a final 9 per cent of diverse red varieties; for the 9 hectares of white, the split was 30 per cent Bourboulenc, 25 per cent each of Clairette and Roussanne, and 20 per cent Grenache Blanc.

The developments span the vineyards and the cellars. An imposing new stone portal has been put up at the entrance off the Sorgues road; the area in front of the château has been cleared of wild undergrowth, the façade has been replastered, and some lime-coloured shutters have brought a new air of sober smartness to the place. The enterprising new technical director, Alain Dugas, also cracks a stern whip when it comes to harvest-time.

'It has to be a precise operation,' he says, betraying just a hint of his old accountancy observances. 'Getting the maturity just right is the key. We now have just a twelve-day spread between picking the first ripe grape – Syrah – and the last – Mourvèdre. There are ninety people in the vineyards for those twelve days. We start the harvesting of the whites at five in the morning; we do the sorting or *triage* at the cellars because it's more efficient and controllable. The only grape I'd consider leaving for longer is the Mourvèdre, to see if that would bring greater fatness or *gras* to the wine.'

La Nerthe is around the early harvest brigade now, since it is very conscious of its high natural degree – around 14° is aimed for, so the 1990 start was 8 September. Upon reception, modern and therefore different thinking to the norm comes into play: systematic destalking, a breaking of all the grapes, and the use of automatic *pigeage* vats for some of the wine in some vintages: in 1987, a year of considerable rot, there was almost no *pigeage*, but in 1989, with a healthy crop, there was one per day. M. Dugas aims to extract the glycerol of the wine before the fermentation proper starts, which can run for up to twenty-four days.

Like all the 'dissident' wine *domaines* at Châteauneuf – those outside the Grenache mainstream – La Nerthe uses a combination of receptacles to raise its wine – one-third *barriques* of one to three years, one-third old 50-hectolitre *foudres*, and one-third enamel-lined vats. The *élévage* of the wine lasts for around a year, varying by vintage and by grape variety: a Grenache/Mourvèdre *cuvée* may spend twelve months in young oak; a Grenache/Syrah duo only six to eight months, while the Cinsault stays in vat throughout. Fining and filtration precede bottling.

La Nerthe has always been a serious, top-flight *domaine*, so judgement of its wines takes a relative air when one describes some of them as disappointing. However, under the old 'knock 'em out in the aisles' regime of M. Derreumaux there were disappointments. The last really successful wine of the *ancien régime* was the 1981; bottled in 1984, it was black and unyielding, with latent *cassis* aromas on the nose, and firm, chewy liquorice and tannic flavours on the palate. The 1983 La Nerthe was a ten-year wine, with reasonable depth, and the finely structured 1984 was actually capable of living about fifteen years, despite a lesser vintage. The special Cadettes *cuvée* was classic in 1977, and successful in 1978 and 1979. The straight Nerthe of 1977 is drinking very well now, with plenty of stamina left, and its depth is more suggestive of a 1979.

The new regime went to work with 1985 in the old cellars, and 1986 in the entirely restructured cellars, and by 1989 and 1990 had really started to find its feet, taking the red wines into a different, higher league than anything before – outstanding wines that walk the tightrope between 'interference' through modern methods and 'authenticity' and expression of the region. The 1990 La Nerthe carries a dark plum-purple colour, a rich, well-extracted bouquet with a touch of youthful austerity, and a striking, sappy fruit flavour on the palate wrapped in a depth and core fruitiness that are utterly delightful. This is classic wine, well-balanced and long on the finish, one that holds tight its regionality but also displays finesse and elegance. The 1989 La Nerthe also captured an extravagant richness and fruitiness, and its tannins are a shade more rounded than those in the 1990. Both these wines can run for ten to fifteen years without mishap.

The 1988 La Nerthe is less well balanced, and the elements of heat and tannin and fruit are a little out of synchronization. It is a bit dry at the finish, and may remain austere for much of its life. The 1987 is a crafty wine; the *triage* gave a yield of just 25 hectolitres per hectare, and there is – for La Nerthe today – plenty of Grenache – 70 per cent. The bouquet has developed some fragile peppery aromas, and there are genuine extract and weight on the palate that exceed those encountered in most 1987s. A very brief *élevage* before bottling helped to arrange this wine well. The 1986 is also superior to many 1986s, but is ageing and drying to suggest drinking before about 1994: this was three-quarters Grenache, and its ruby colour and rich, damp smells on the nose are true to type. The 1985 was notably softer than preceding vintages, and this now needs drinking up.

The top-of-the-line red is called the Cuvée des Cadettes, with which the estate is continuing. The tone has been dropped a notch or two since the cannonball days of 1978 and 1979, when the Cadettes was a *vin noir*, massively heavy in extract with alcohol turning around 15°, but at least saved by an intense blackcurrant and cedarwood appeal.

The Cadettes *parcelle* of about 5 hectares was planted by the Commandant Ducos; it is made up of mostly Grenache, with plenty of Mourvèdre and a little Syrah in support; the vines are around sixty years old. This receives a little longer in new or one-year cask than the regular La Nerthe; the 1990, for example, was transferred from wood to vat in November 1991, and bottled in June 1992. This carried an intense blackcurrant-style extraction, a chewiness imparted to an extent by the young wood, a dark colour and all sorts of intense, rounded aromas: an excellent wine, but one with less pure regionality than the La Nerthe 1990.

The Cadettes 1989, a year of greater roundness and softer tannins, was bottled in June 1990. This, too, is highly successful: the colour was dark plum to purple, the bouquet intense and showing early signs of expression, and the flavours expansive with some excellent final support from the cask influence. The 1988 Cadettes is more dominated by its tannins and a firmness that halts the finish a little early; the 1986 is very good for its year, with a sound structure and tannic support, and enough acidity to keep driving it along; its richness is showing through well now, and it will drink vigorously through until around 1996. This vintage of Cadettes was launched straight into the brand new cask system, with as much as 83 per cent of the wine in first-year wood, the rest in vat. At that stage the La Nerthe *cuvée* received no more than 22 per cent new oak.

Like many modern wineries, La Nerthe now has a second red wine, the Clos de la Granière, and a keen interest in white wine-making. The Cuvée des Cadettes' 10,000 bottles a year are a lot beside the 3,000 bottles of special white, the Clos de Beauvenir. The white *cépages* of Bourboulenc and Grenache Blanc are vinified together, the Clairette and Roussanne apart, the latter in *barriques* that are new or first-year. As with several local *domaines*, the fermentation temperature has been raised since 1988 from around 15°C to 18–20°C; this is considered to give a better extraction that in turn will encourage longer and more complex ageing. With the malolactic blocked, bottling of the classic La Nerthe white is done from the stainless steel vats around March, while the Beauvenir, made from cask-fermented Roussanne and vat-fermented Clairette, is held in cask prior to bottling around June.

For the white wines, M. Dugas prefers to use Nevers oak. 'It is more subtle than the Allier oak,' he reasons, 'but I'm not impressed with it for the reds; for those we use a mix of quite strong and medium smoked Allier, preferring the strong smoking to cut down on the vanilla influence in the wine.'

The La Nerthe whites are still finding their way; on a general level they are very sound, but the consistency is not there yet. The La Nerthe 1990 seemed to fall prey to some of the over-fatness and excess power of the vintage for the whites; the 1989 contained soft, squeezy fruit, a lushness in it indicating a life of six years-plus: some might consider it a shade *flatteur*, a little too obvious. The 1988 *blanc* had more grip, with firmer fruit flavours and reasonable length – a wine to drink around 1993–4, but a little hot at the end. The 1987, the first year the Roussanne and Bourboulenc were introduced, has evolved successfully, and carries a discreet richness that continues long on to the finish. The 1986, just Clairette and Grenache Blanc, shows why the greater acidity of Roussanne and Bourboulenc has helped; by 1991 it was succulent and fleshy, but not that thorough, and liable to dip away abruptly.

The first vintage of Beauvenir *blanc* was the 1989; this received ten months' cask, which is its predominant feature; by the time the wood has calmed down, 'Where will the wine be?' is a valid question about it. The 1990 – eight months' wood – needs time to around 1993 or later to form itself; the fruits and aromas are detectable on their own, and this has greater balance, elegance and therefore promise about it.

Apart from their flagship property here, David et Foillard also own the Côtes du Rhône Domaine de Renjarde at Sérignan du Comtat in the Vaucluse; this is where M. Dugas cut his teeth in 1970, having left his accountancy responsibilities way behind in Paris. Its red wine is made from Grenache (60 per cent), Syrah (25 per cent) plus Cinsault, Mourvèdre and Carignan (all 5 per cent). Bottled in June after the harvest, its 300,000 bottles are all exported.

Château La Nerthe   84230 Châteauneuf-du-Pape

CHÂTEAU RAYAS

This is the most extraordinary domaine at Châteauneuf-du-Pape, and probably in the whole Rhône Valley. A veritable dynasty of eccentrics seems likely to end with the unmarried Jacques Reynaud, an inscrutable, smiling man in his sixties who has long foxed visitors and locals alike with excellent wine derived from unorthodox behaviour.

The Rayas vineyard is 'about 13 hectares', according to Jacques Reynaud, 15 hectares according to officialdom. It stands past the Château de Vaudieu; the Pignan plateau between the two estates gives amazing long views across to Orange, with just odd clumps of cypresses breaking up the pale brown panorama. The house and cellars are well hidden, much as their proprietors have been over the years; the cellars especially are nondescript, a faded yellow outside, with a damaged wood cover on runners protecting a dowdy little glass-topped door that opens on to some chaotic bottling and vinification facilities.

The Reynaud family used to be notaries in the Provençal mountain town of Apt, and their connection with Châteauneuf-du-Pape started in 1894, when Jacques's grandfather decided to retire there. In the process he bought the château and the largely wooded land that went with it. There were a few vines, but phylloxera was still a recent memory. Accordingly M. Reynaud *grandpère* was content simply to potter about among his cornfields, olive groves, apricot trees and cherry orchards.

His son Louis, on the other hand, was greatly attracted by the idea of having his own vineyard and accordingly went off to agricultural school in Angers to learn his trade. On his return he planted the vineyard in a way that today seems unreasonable, but which is cogently justified by his son Jacques: 'There are fifteen *parcelles* covering 13 hectares, it's true, so the very small average size certainly contributes to our extremely limited yield per hectare. I think the largest plot I have at Châteauneuf is the 2 hectares of Pignan near

M. Jacques Reynaud

Courthézon. When he was planting, you must take into account some of the factors that guided my father to set out the vineyard in this way. First, all the trees and dense brush that surround our plots: in the 1920s we had no bulldozers, so we couldn't at all easily knock down these barriers. The series of plots also diminishes the effect of summer storms, and my father was certainly mindful of the tidal wave that passed through the vineyards in January 1924: it's commemorated on the Roman Wall in Orange. Lastly, the larger the open expanse of ground, the more prone you will be to erosion.'

This is where Jacques Reynaud really starts to come into his element, looking out across his vineyards, cheeks puffed out and habitually hidden eyes widened under a smart tweed flat hat. 'Once the soil is balanced, you shouldn't have to treat it too much. You don't want to believe all the "remedies" the official authorities propose – the soil's ability to produce fruit goes in step with its reserves of water.' M. Louis Reynaud passed on to his son Jacques a deep mistrust of *appellation* rules and regulations, and there are often simmering campaigns being fought on this property's labelling, such as calling itself *premier grand cru* or Clos Pignan when there is no identifiable Clos. What is unshakeable, however, is a belief in quality, which means getting the best wine into the bottle whatever happens. Even in his late seventies, Louis Reynaud's kindly exterior, twinkling eyes and soft voice did not conceal this challenging belief: he ran a tight, disciplined ship, and son Jacques was not taught his trade in any methodical way, generally being invisible to vineyard visitors when there were exchanges of views and tastings. Consequently the supreme consistency of excellence of Louis Reynaud's wines wobbled when Louis died in 1980. The estate still produces incredibly tiny amounts of wine per hectare – down to 7 hectolitres per hectare with the *coulure* problem in 1984 – but the glorious regularity of superb wines is now sometimes fulfilled, sometimes a little missed.

Jacques's tour of his vineyards, hauling a battered station wagon along behind his prancing black dog, provides high entertainment as little by little this modest, private man reveals his thoughts.

'I don't want to exceed 20 hectos a hectare in yield, and while the division of the vineyard into so many small, enclosed plots is one reason for the restriction of the crop, another important one is the lack of humidity in the soil. Much of the Grenache was planted in 1945, but we've replanted at intervals, perhaps a bit every five years. The vineyards in front of the cellars are twenty-three-year-old Grenache, but they're in light, pretty sandy soil and look less stout than the fifteen-year-old vines right next to the cellar where it's less sandy. Much of the soil is chalk–limestone, very fine, and I have been working to reduce its alkaline content. We also only cultivate four or five branches on the vines as another quality control, while the grape harvest is thinned at the end of July, when if I want more colour in the wine, for example, I take out the inner grapes on the bunches. I don't like grapes getting too fat and diluted.'

By now the dog in front has taken six consecutive wrong turns as the car rolls along. He is a large, black poodle whose long entwined dreadlocks make him look Rastafarian. When asked his name, M.

Reynaud sucks his teeth, gives a barely perceptible shrug and with a pause says, 'Well, "Chien". But when I *really* have to get him to obey, I call him "Noir".'

In the cellar further evidence that M. Reynaud is plain different comes forth. He gives his answers after a great delay, as if thinking up a new reply to the same question according to the identity of the questioner. On the barrels in the disorderly cellars are chalked Greek letters followed by a number: they apparently make no sense. M. Reynaud explains: 'The Greek P refers to Rayas, then I reverse the vintage, so that 58 is 85. With white Rayas, my father used 'S' for *sec*, so that double *pièce* over there marked P°S is Rayas White 1990. With Fonsalette, I use the Greek π (pi) because in the Revolution it was owned by the Piellat family, a word that has now become Pialade – hence the pi. I invented the Greek markings', he adds proudly.

For the wine made from the Rayas, Fonsalette and Pignan vineyards, there are nearly 200 barrels with Greek lettering chalked on them. Most are double *pièces* of 450 litres, with a sprinkling of 600-litre *demi-muids* and standard *pièces*. They look very downbeat, dull brown with black streaks on them, in contrast to the shiny new wood so fashionable and prevalent in many cellars. But then M. Reynard is not a fashionable man. 'In my grandfather's time we had a little of the other permitted grapes – Muscardin, a little Picpoul. I've never seen the Mourvèdre,' he asserts a shade wickedly. 'At Rayas we rely on the Grenache for the red, the Grenache Blanc and Clairette in equal measure for the white. The oldest Clairette dates back to 1948. In my father's time, odd amounts of Cinsault and Syrah were included, or Chardonnay and Sauvignon. I like the Cinsault because it diminishes the ardour of the Grenache – it civilizes it, while the danger with the Grenache is that it sometimes lacks true depth.'

M. Reynaud vinifies all his wines centrally at Rayas; Pignan Châteauneuf comes from that 2-hectare vineyard and also a selection of wines that M. Reynaud considers inferior to Rayas, while his Pialade is a second-string Fonsalette. It is at Rayas that one can taste a superb single cask of Cinsault taken from his Fonsalette property. The 1990 Cinsault sits quietly in a post-war double *pièce*, and shows the benefits of cropping back to secure a yield of only around 25 hectolitres per hectare. The colour is bright and not very dark, but the bouquet has an exuberant peppery smell – very vibrant indeed; the palate has good weight and freshness, the liveliness bringing a good top edge to the pleasant depth. This is an excellent example of what can be achieved with this now rather out-of-favour grape when meticulous care and trouble are taken over it, and as such it serves a very useful purpose in providing the red wines with finesse.

The white Rayas is fermented in enamel-lined vats, at 'atmospheric temperatures', until after the tumultuous fermentation, when the wine is transferred into barrel for about nine months. There it stays while its malolactic takes place naturally, unless it has not occurred by the first spring after the harvest. In this case, M. Reynaud filters the wine to take out the bacteria and stop any malolactic breaking out. He thinks his 1987, for instance, was bottled possibly 'without the *malo* done'. He then bottles the wine in November or December, which since the late 1980s is about five months earlier than usual.

The whites from the Reynaud properties are less consistent than in the time of Louis. Oxidation can rapidly set in, and selecting a Rayas *blanc* can be something of a hit-or-miss affair. Most recently the 1985 had a sound weight, was full on the palate and finished long and clean – good wine – while the 1989 and 1990 have been successful as well: of the two, the 1990 needs longer to settle – perhaps to 1993/4 – but this is pretty well worked in an awkward year for whites. The bouquet is big and fat, but there is finesse on the palate and very lasting flavours. The 1989 has a quieter style, and greater early balance: it is ripe-tasting, and will show well over its first half-dozen years. Of M. Reynaud's whites, it is often the Fonsalette *blanc*, composed of half Grenache *blanc* and one-quarter each Clairette and Chardonnay, that outperforms the Rayas.

The red Rayas is fermented from grapes that are invariably harvested among the last at Châteauneuf – frequently at the very end of October and sometimes in All Saints week in November. In 1990, for instance, when growers found a two-degree gain in their red crop in a roughly ten-day spell after the first week of September, M. Reynaud harvested his Grenache as usual around the end of September or early October – and as a result has some *cuvées* weighing in at 15°C or more. When asked specifically about this, he shrugs diffidently, and says, 'One has one's habits – and anyway, I was busy with the white wines.' What is certain is that he wants a full maturity in his grapes before vinifying them. The harvest team is boosted by a Polish family of five, known to his sister, who drive down from Warsaw and stay for three or four weeks in total.

Fermentation takes place in concrete vats, some of which received enamel lining in 1990. Both the Rayas and the Fonsalette reds are put into cask in the spring and left for about just one year, without any racking, before filtration and bottling the following spring. No fining is done.

The wood-ageing process has been radically shortened at Rayas since the days of Louis Reynaud, and even during Jacques' period of command. Louis would leave the red for four or five years; until the mid-1980s Jacques would let the wine spend between one and a half and two-and-a-half years in cask, but he now turns the wine out on to the market with much greater rapidity, including skipping the two-year spell in bottle that Louis systematically applied before release. Cash flow rather than just philosophy is clearly a consideration here. What was once a proud stock of 100,000 bottles in 1974 has now been massacred by buyers who are often foreign and who arrive bearing fat cheque-books and greedy looks. When Jacques wants to find an 'old' bottle to taste, a veritable voyage of discovery occurs. Shamble down this nearly empty bottle corridor, turn right, grope around to plug in the naked light-bulb, avoid a couple of old tennis racquets, shift some empty crates, and presto – a couple of bearded, grimy bottles lying in the bottom of an old box. They have no labels, so Jacques holds them up against the light-bulb, peering at their necks to see which carries the lighter colour: this exercise is designed to tell whether he has Fonsalette or a Rayas in either of his hands, but of course takes no account of the vintage, on which he is non-committal anyway. One suspects that his real satisfaction is in getting the visitor to enjoy the wine, with just a spot of work attached to guessing what on earth he is drinking.

The Rayas red is an absolute must to track down in certain vintages nowadays, but greater selectivity is needed than used to be the case, especially as the wine is always expensive. In an average year, there are now about 20,000 bottles of Rayas, 8,000 bottles of Pignan. The 1978 Rayas is excellent – a ripe, rounded wine with delicious lingering flavours – and likely to show well past the year 2000. Very much a hallmark of the best Rayas is the plump extract that the Reynaud family have always achieved from their Grenache; the flavours are like prune or old cooked fruits and have an absolutely delicious ripeness and roundness to them.

The 1979 Rayas is in some instances an exceptional wine – supremely elegant, rich and wonderfully long, with a tremendous depth of fruit and pepper on the bouquet. But other tastings have shown a dull wine, lacking flair and marked by a lack of balance through excess acidity. Some of the wine spent two years in wood, while some was bottled about a year later, in January 1983 – and the last bottling provided an inferior wine. Jacques Reynaud, despite hand stick-on labelling for much of the time, now tries to bottle all the Rayas in the spring eighteen months after the harvest in just one extended run.

In 1980, M. Reynaud says that he made too much wine, and that his Pignan 1980 contained Rayas. This was a wild-tasting wine, a strong, peppery and alcoholic bouquet preceding some raw fruit on the palate. The colour was a reasonable purple, but the wine was not greatly balanced, and certainly not a leading example of this year that has improved markedly in many cases with bottle age.

The 1981 Rayas was made from mostly Grenache and bottled in April 1984. After initially tasting almost a shade volatile, but showing some promise, it has developed into a supremely elegant, exciting wine with a superb bouquet that shows a bit of dry evolution in its peppers and dustiness. It is tremendously rich on the palate, and has a concentration of taste that is so much a feature of top Rayas. Enormous roundness and balance complete the excellence of this work of inspiration. Like many of the Rayas successes, its ageing possibilities are long, since the Grenache motor will continue to tick quietly over, even though the ruby tint and certain drier flavours indicate a closer horizon.

In 1982, as in 1980, M. Reynaud produced no Château Rayas, since he felt the quality of the vintage was deficient. In 1987, when Rayas was hit by hail, he managed just 25 hectolitres of wine from the vineyard, so there was no Rayas that year. A vintage of Pignan received a helping hand.

The 1983 harvest was affected by *coulure* on the Grenache, but M. Reynaud came up with a silky, very appealing wine. Its damson fruits combined well with gentle amounts of tannin – there were much softer tannins in his wine than in many others that year. The bouquet was almost floral and the length impressive. Not a heavy-weight wine, it is now drinking very well.

1984 was an even smaller crop than 1983, and maturity was not easy to obtain. This wine can vary from tasting to tasting, and can even show entirely differently according to atmospheric conditions. Early in its life, the bouquet was peppery and hot, with a certain greenness of flavour on the palate that was typical of the year. However, two tastings in 1991 of the same bottle three days apart revealed two quite different wines. On the first occasion, a very hot summer's day of humid, unsettled weather with a *mistral* wind, the bouquet was a bit firm, the palate rather green and stark, and there was a wine lacking thoroughness. This was also thought to be the case by an experienced French fellow taster. Yet, on return three days later, the same wine displayed ripe aromas, fair depth and some dense, mature prune-style fruit on the palate. Some gentle end tannins were still in evidence, as had been the case in previous tastings. When on form, the 1984 is a finely styled wine, which seems likely to continue to show well some way into the 1990s.

The 1985 Rayas was a similarly weighted wine, but held greater ripeness and richness of flavour. The bouquet has opened well and it is an immediately likeable, charming wine, already drinking very well.

The 1986 possesses a middling colour that has started to turn towards ruby; the bouquet carries mature, quite dusty aromas and shows signs of a certain wear and tear. The palate is quite full, but again there is a dryness and a lack of generosity present similar to many wines of the vintage. The wine does finish with decent length, however, and has a shade more warmth left in it that many other offerings: it is just that one is used to the full richness of the Rayas wines, and it is not surprising to hear Jacques Reynaud's quiet comment *'petit, ce vin'*, when considering his 1986.

The 1988 Rayas is excellent. An attractive, sound colour starts it off, while there is great breadth and ripeness of smell on the bouquet. On the palate there is a beguiling richness and finesse, with a very persistent depth of well extracted flavour; this is *grand vin* – it has the velvety texture of the best Rayas and promises to live a long time – upwards of fifteen years.

The 1989 started life with a bright, purply colour – a very pleasing aspect. The aromas are a little cooked, but show promise to develop with age. The richness and width on the attack are followed by some chewy tannin, and the wine needs until around 1997 to settle down – this is one of the less accessible Rayas reds of recent years, but is very good none the less.

One *cuve* of 1990 Rayas, tasted out of an old 33-hectolitre *foudre* in mid-summer 1991, revealed a bright, dark colour and masses of glycerine; the bouquet was round, sweet and a little cooked, while there was a controlled vigour on the palate – some good work from M. Reynaud, considering the alcohol level of 15.6°. The wine held a really delicious chewy finish, and most surprising of all was just how fine it was, despite all the massive, ripe elements present in it.

As a side comment, perhaps after his vinification experiences of 1990, M. Reynaud observed that with the 1991 vintage he was going to cool the fermentation of his red Rayas if necessary, something that he did not do on either of his Rayas *cuves* in 1990. The above tasting comments apply to what he terms 'Rayas I'; by midsummer 1991, 'Rayas II' had not finished itself, and was an even stronger wine, around the 16° mark.

Tasting out of a broken glass in the shabby little bottling room of Rayas, where curled-up wine magazines from the mid-1950s vie for space with little bundles of the famous Rayas label, all about to be applied by hand, where 'Chien' or 'Noir' wanders around licking up patches of wine on the floor, and where the cellar tools are strewn around in a haphazard way, it is hard to believe that in some vintages this *domaine* produces one of the finest Châteauneufs and one of the finest red wines from France, let alone from the region south of Lyon. The world would be a much less intriguing and provocative place without the mysterious and eccentric Reynaud dynasty.

Reynaud, Jacques
   Château Rayas   84230 Châteauneuf-du-Pape

CHÂTEAU SIMIAN

The château itself is at Piolenc, 15 miles north of Châteauneuf, and the Serguier family of Yves and his son Jean-Pierre cultivate about 4 hectares of very dispersed vineyards around Châteauneuf. The red vines are mostly on the plateau de la Crau, near the Château de Cabrières, and are headed by 80 per cent Grenache, and 10 per cent Syrah and Cinsault. The tiny amount of white is pure Clairette, planted in the 1980s.

The red Châteauneuf receives around eight to twelve months' ageing in old family barrels; it is vinified in the traditional way, with a crushing preceding a three-week *cuvaison*. Bottling is between eighteen months and two years after the harvest.

The red, as in 1989, holds a good fruit extract, and the aromas show themselves earlier than the most backward *domaines*. The tannins tend to discreetly hold the wine together, making this a wine suitable to drink around six to ten years old. It is not a flashy style of wine, but is serious and well made.

The white is fermented at 18–20°C, and bottled, with the malolactic blocked, around February. This is very representative of modern-style white Châteauneuf, and has enough weight and length on the palate to be interesting. Typically, this is a wine to drink straight after bottling or when eighteen months old – like many southern whites, it can traverse a dumb patch around nine months old.

The property is proud of its abandonment of the use of herbicides since 1988 after a spell of fifteen years with them. There is also a Côtes du Rhône vineyard making red and white wine close to Piolenc.

Serguier, Yves et Jean-Pierre
   Château Simian   84420 Piolenc

CHÂTEAU DE VAUDIEU

Built between 1767 and 1777, the Château de Vaudieu is a striking edifice, perhaps the one that most evokes the *belle époque* of pre-Revolutionary times at Châteauneuf. It stands away from the road in a tall circle of trees on the way to Courthézon, and now that it is occupied by the late Gabriel Meffre's daughter Sylvette Brechet, steps have been taken to revive it from the near-dereliction that threatened when the Meffres arrived in 1955. The cellars were rebuilt in 1976, to allow the stockage of three crops at any one time, while more wine is being bottled on the spot than previously. Mme Brechet is now restoring the living quarters, and more generous times beckon this property.

Only 24 hectares were under vine in 1955, and over the next ten years Gabriel Meffre reclaimed abandoned vineyards and cleared heavily wooded land around the house. At present the Grenache is the principal vine (75–80 per cent), backed by the Syrah (10–15 per cent), the Cinsault and Mourvèdre (10 per cent between them). The vineyards are all around the château, the treeless landscape being marked by masses of Alpine stones that largely hide the clay–limestone soil.

Vaudieu used to be one of the few estates to systematically destalk the harvest. Their length of *cuvaison* is ten to fourteen days and cask-ageing is conducted for at least one year in ex-Italian distillery barrels of 30 hectolitres and up. Before 1976 the wine was rarely wood-aged.

A conscious effort is being made to thicken up some of the Vaudieu *cuvées*, with welcome results, since for most of the 1970s the wines seemed lightened and short on colour. The 1978 was a manly wine, however, with deep aromas, ripe flavours and a complexity on the palate that spread into a long aftertaste. Although less intense, the 1981, 1985 and 1989 were marked by a quietly imposing fruitiness that was supported by a solid depth; of the last few vintages, the 1978, 1981 and 1983 will be best drunk between eight and fourteen years old; the 1985 and 1989 are more six- to ten-year wines, with the 1988 in between the two groups.

250 hectolitres or 10 per cent of the average production is made into white wine. Its constituents are Grenache Blanc (75 per cent), Clairette, Bourboulenc and Roussanne, which are harvested by the third week of September or earlier in search of higher acidity. Vinified at around 21°C in stainless steel, the wine is bottled in April. This is a good wine which during the 1980s gained in refinement. It has a persistent dried fruit finish, and shows well after a couple of years. The 1990 was very successful.

Brechet, Sylvette
   Château de Vaudieu   84230 Châteauneuf-du-Pape

LES CLEFS D'OR

Pierre Deydier, a cheerful and good-looking man in his mid-forties, runs this very good, consistent family vineyard, having taken over from his octogenarian father Jean, one of the veterans of wine-making at Châteauneuf. The vineyard was first planted by Jean's father Maurice, who ran a barrel-making business at the turn of the century. In those days *tonneliers* often doubled as wine advisers or *œnologues* when commenting on matters such as the correct racking from one cask to another. Gradually Maurice turned to growing vines and making his own wine.

The Clefs d'Or red has a very typical Grenache-inspired character, showing a good complexity of flavour and impressive, strong aromas. It is very representative of the school of wine-makers who seek a thorough extraction, as in the 1986, which has greater depth and stamina than many of that year. It is made from 75 per cent Grenache Noir, with the remaining quarter mostly composed of Mourvèdre (12 per cent), plus Muscardin, Counoise and Vaccarèse. The different varieties are vinified together 'on the *bouillabaisse* principle'; destalking only occurs in years like 1991 when the Grenache has suffered from *coulure*, while the crush is slighter than in the past – perhaps 40 per cent of the grapes enter the fermenting vats whole.

The red receives cask-ageing – no new wood is used – that can vary between one and two years, although the light 1987 stayed just eight months in cask; the first bottling of a strong but ripe vintage like the 1989 took place twenty-two months after the harvest, but several bottlings are run each year. Reds made up until the late 1960s could live for twenty years or more – a magnum of 1953 drunk in 1989 was still in exceptional form – but nowadays it is safer to drink the Clefs d'Or red before it is fifteen to eighteen years old. The 1990 is well extracted and just a little firmer than the 1989, whose tannins are more rounded. Both are very good wines, with the 1989 likely to drink well anywhere between eight and fourteen years old. The 1988 is more austere, an upright wine with good persistence of flavour and an interesting future in prospect; it may have started to open up around 1997, and promises to reveal complex aromas and flavours. It is similar in style to the very good 1981 Clefs d'Or. The 1985 has advanced and is now drinking well, while the 1986 is opening and showing dried fruit flavours, certainly a lean rather than fleshy wine.

Around 60 hectolitres of good white are made each year, from one-third each of Grenache Blanc, Clairette and Bourboulenc; these are all vinified together in enamel-lined vats at 20°C. This is bottled in January or February and combines the freshness of a controlled-temperature vinification with a satisfying underlying depth that is taut enough to hold the wine together for three to five years.

The Deydiers also own a 12-hectare Côtes du Rhône vineyard called the Domaine de Beaumefort at Mondragon, where the red is made from Grenache (60 per cent), Cinsault (25 per cent) and Mourvèdre (15 per cent).

Deydier, Jean et Pierre
   Les Clefs d'Or   84230 Châteauneuf-du-Pape

CLOS DU MONT-OLIVET

M. Joseph Sabon's three sons Jean-Claude, Pierre and Bernard make an excellent, traditionally styled Châteauneuf from their 25 hectares of vines that are spread throughout the *appellation*. The Sabon family is steeped in wine-making, since Joseph's brothers are Roger of Domaine des Terres Blanches and Noël of Domaine Chante-Cigale. The French laws of inheritance mean that the plots are well dispersed, varying from the *quartier* of Mont-Olivet north of Château Fortia (clay-limestone soil with few stones) to the Pied de Baud near Château Mont-Redon (very stony) to the *quartier* Les Gallimardes south of the village near the Nicolets' Chante-Perdrix (clay with a gravel subsoil, arid ground).

As befits a classic father-to-son *domaine*, the Grenache accounts for 75 per cent of the vineyard, the difference made up with Mourvèdre, Syrah and very little Muscardin and Cinsault. Vinification takes place in their cellars in the lee of the remaining Castle wall, and equipment includes the old family crusher, now electrically powered but still doing a good, controlled job. An extended three-week fermentation in concrete vats is followed by considerable cask-ageing, in a mixture of 30- to 50-hectolitre *foudres* or 225-litre *pièces*.

'Our ageing in wood varies from one or two to six years,' explained Jean-Claude Sabon, a droll, relaxed individual given to dry one-liners, 'since the style of the vintage must decide the duration. That's why our 1980 spent only a bit over two years in cask, while the very tannic, full-bodied 1978, 1979 and 1988 will all have spent around five years.' The attitude is a mixture of policy and *laissez-faire*, for in 1991 there was still some 1984 in cask – 'because it's been slow to sell, having been written off from the start by the media'. The Sabon *foudres* date from the grandfather's time, and there is positively little question of new-wood experiments being carried out at such a no-nonsense *domaine*.

There is a light filtration before bottling, but no fining. Over the years Mont-Olivet has provided excellent, consistent wines that express much of the depth of character and regional style of Châteauneuf. They are strong, uncompromising and very satisfying if given ample bottle-ageing. The 1990 red before bottling was extremely sustained on the palate, with a large proportion of sixty- to 100-year-old Grenache vine fruit in it; the bouquet will take time to emerge, but it is an excellent, dense wine whose alcohol of 14.5° is well integrated. The 1989, with a Grenache content similarly high at around 85 per cent, is a shade more rounded on the palate, with ripe, almost sweet aromas and a strong, crushed fruit presence; this contains a little more Mourvèdre than the 1990.

The 1988, from a bottling of March 1991, showed a more direct approach, both on the bouquet and on the palate, and plenty of liquorice and dried fruit that ran on well to a long finish. Typically of its year, this is a wine that comes more from the leather locker than the fruit garden, the latter being the mark of both 1989 and 1990; an interesting complexity will develop with time, and it is reminiscent of a quite forward 1981. The *domaine* was successful with its 1987, which needs until around 1993 to settle and deliver its best potential, since there is greater richness in it than in many of that year. The 1986, from a *cuvée* bottled in 1990, showed signs of drying out with a noted lack of substance, but this is a vintage whose evolution is zigzagging along. The 1985 is a sweet, round and well-softened wine that will hold until perhaps 1996.

Of earlier vintages, both the difficult 1982 and 1984 were well worked, the former one of the best of an unsatisfactory, sticky year and the latter showing well in the early 1990s. The 1981 was one of the best wines of its year, marked by impressive elegance and excellent balance following three years' cask-ageing. The 1979 is an imposing, manly wine with a slight final dryness apparent, perhaps the result of a stay of five years in cask. The 1978 is still a delicious, fully flavoured wine, with all the heat and aromatic power of that outstanding vintage. This, like the best Mont-Olivets, will show well for twenty years or more: for example, a magnum of 1959 drunk in 1989 showed a lovely cedary and spicy bouquet and a richness of flavour that held and even improved with air, while a 1957 bottle tasted also in 1989 provided great richness on the palate, with a hint of wilting on the nose, which, despite a raw power, had become very fungal and gamey. A magnum of 1966 tasted at the same time was still in fine, lingering form with a firmness of taste that promised well for some time to come. Since the *domaine* still relies largely on the Grenache, since the vines are old and well tended, and since the vinification has not been falsely modernized, the Mont-Olivet reds remain some of the best candidates at Châteauneuf for long cellarage and great shared pleasure with friends at later dates.

Alongside around 700 hectolitres of red, there are around 50 hectos of white each year, made from older Clairette and Bourboulenc (40 per cent each) and 15 per cent Grenache Blanc and 5 per cent Roussanne, both younger plantations. Vinified in stainless steel at around 16°C after a direct press, this has its malolactic blocked and is stored in enamel-lined vats until bottling in midsummer. The style is for a ripe, expressive wine with a fair degree of weight in it. It is correct but not startling.

The Sabon brothers' real love is undoubtedly their red, and this ties in with one of their relaxations – a spot of rough shooting which helps to exercise the dogs, but also occasionally helps to provide something to go with the 1978 or 1979.

Sabon, Les Fils de Joseph
  GAEC du Clos du Mont-Olivet   84230 Châteauneuf-du-Pape

CLOS DE L'ORATOIRE DES PAPES

The property of the Amouroux family, this 40–hectare vineyard is grouped to the north-west of Châteauneuf-du-Pape. It is an all-female affair, run by the *Veuve* Amouroux and her daughters. The wine has always been classically made, with an ageing of at least two years in cask, and used to be one of the best to be found: richly flavoured and long-lived, it was in the past a fine example of the 'traditional' Châteauneuf-du-Pape. Quite outstanding bottles from the 1940s (an excellent, long-lived 1947), the 1950s (a top-notch 1959) and the 1960s (a very good 1967) are but distant memories when one reviews the wine since the late 1970s. Made in a lightened style and rushed into bottle, these later wines have in no way matched the former high standards here. Perhaps attention has been diverted towards a growing *négociant* business. There is also a rather nondescript white Châteauneuf.

Amouroux, Mme, et Filles
  Clos de l'Oratoire des Papes   84230 Châteauneuf-du-Pape

CLOS DES PAPES

One of the top-flight domaines at Châteauneuf, the Clos des Papes provides excellent, stylish and thoroughly well-made wines on a most consistent basis. The 32-hectare *domaine*, split into eighteen *parcelles*, is owned by M. Paul Avril, an energetic man in his fifties whose neatly cut grey hair used to be a perfect match for his recently deceased African grey parrot, the guardian of the cellar entrance. M. Avril works with his bright, enterprising son Vincent, who has spent time studying wine in Burgundy, but has also had productive stints at Château Mouton-Rothschild, commercial school in Zurich and in Australia. Mental horizons at this *domaine* are therefore refreshingly high and wide.

The Avrils were Châteauneuf's first consuls and treasurers, from 1756 until 1790, and the highlight of their various vineyard holdings is the 4 hectares within the Clos des Papes site directly behind the village château: this area is easily distinguishable by the Burgundian-style wrought-iron gate that stands at its entrance.

M. Avril is a great supporter of the Mourvèdre, and since the 1960s has gradually reduced his holding of Grenache to around 70 per cent through the medium of successive plantings of Mourvèdre (over 15 per cent) and Syrah (5 per cent). Vaccarèse, Muscardin and recent plantings of Counoise make up the balance: the last-named is felt to bring some finesse and a certain bold spiciness similar in part to that of the Mourvèdre, while the Muscardin is thought to add aroma.

'With plots spread around, ripening obviously occurs at different rhythms,' states M. Avril. 'In our more stone-covered *quartiers* the stones serve to limit the evaporation of the water residing in the clay underneath, while on some of our finer, sandier soil – a bit like that at Château Rayas – the grapes bring wine of greater strength. In very dry years, the northern areas of the *appellation* may lead the south by eight to ten days in ripening, unless we have a good mid-August rainfall – around 30 mm, for example.

'Vineyard control has become more and more important now that clones are being used. I aim for an average of 30 hectolitres a hectare, so I have to take steps when pruning – cutting back to four or five branches – debudding, and ensuring that only five or six bunches per plant remain at the time of the *véraison*, when the grapes are turning colour, around July. There would be twelve or thirteen bunches if the plants were left alone, especially if you are using the anti-mildew strain of Grenache.'

In discussing the construction of his wine, M. Avril *père* has clear views. 'You shouldn't fall below 60 per cent Grenache – you need it to bring the *gras* to your wine. Mourvèdre up to 20 per cent and Syrah between 10 and 15 per cent are fine. Remember what divergence of degree you're dealing with here: my wine's average final degree is 13.5° to 13.8°, but that's composed of Mourvèdre (maximum 13–13.2°), Syrah (12.8° to 12.9°) and the Grenache, which can be over 14°. So you will always find different styles of wine at Châteauneuf if based on nothing else than alcohol degree or power.

These are important issues, since people tend to forget that while they can redo or restyle their vinification each year, that is not something you can do with a vineyard. So it's not until fifteen years later, after the first planting, that you really can judge the influence of a vine – and see that the Syrah may bring a *goût de réduction* to the wine, for instance, as well as colour and some tannins. I personally find the Syrah here less fresh and fine than in the northern Rhône.'

Since the 1981 crop, M. Avril has been vinifying in a radically modernized cellar, constructed on broadly similar lines to that of Domaine du Vieux Télégraphe. The harvest is introduced into the vats from above, there being only a light crushing just to burst the grapes. Destalking only occurs in less ripe years like 1987 or 1984, or when there is *coulure* on the Grenache as in 1991. The *cépages* are generally vinified in pairs, with the Grenache never less than 50 per cent of a vat, and a *remontage* of the fermenting vats is carried out for ten minutes at the start and end of each of the twelve to fifteen days, with the temperature held at 30–32°C.

There are around twenty *barriques* of first- or second-year oak in the Avril cellars, but Paul Avril is at pains to stress that they are not devotees of new oak. 'We have enough natural tannin here, and when you find tannin and liquorice at the end of the wine – that's the Mourvèdre doing its bit!' The final wine is only assembled after the various grape varieties have spent around twelve months in mainly 50-hectolitre barrels. The longest the wine spends in wood is eighteen months, a reduction of about six months over M. Avril's early wine-making days. 'Strangely, one of the reasons for this is the *mistral* wind, which robs the atmosphere here of humidity and so leads the wines to dry out more rapidly. We keep a humidifier here running at around 70 per cent humidity as a constant measure.'

The red wine is bottled somewhere around two years after the harvest, and while there is some fining with egg whites before the cask-ageing stage, the Avrils now hardly do any filtration on their wine, finding it curious that the American market formerly demanded filtration, but now renounces it.

M. Avril claims that the greatest advantage provided by his new cellars is the temperature control that allows him to finish the sugars and malolactic fermentation efficiently. Whatever the inner secret, it is striking that his wine leapt forward to a top-notch quality in the late 1970s and early 1980s. The 1979 and the 1981, both tasted in mid-1991, are exceptional wines; the 1979 can run until around

1998–2000; there is some ruby turn in the colour; the bouquet has gone through a vegetal, truffly phase; but there is still fine tannin and liquorice at the finish. Paul Avril compares this vintage to his 1989. The 1981 has started to evolve and open, but is absolutely delicious now, still retaining a southern fire at the end, which is well set within flavours of great balance and weight – this wine can run until the turn of the century.

Of recent vintages of the red, the 1990 has a dark, almost black cherry colour, a very solid and promising bouquet, and a firm attack on the palate that is wrapped up in plenty of tannins and *gras*: tasted before bottling, this is a big but fine wine – a definite success. The 1989 has a delightful sheen in its dark colour, a similar cherry fruit bouquet just starting to emerge and a surge of deep fruit running along the palate. A rich wine, it should be put away for four or five years, and will certainly last for around eighteen years.

The 1988 has a less opulent bouquet than the 1989 and 1990, but there is very good extraction of fruit on the palate, with a restraint in the power: it is made of 70 per cent Grenache, 20 per cent Mourvèdre and 10 per cent Syrah and is likely to develop well and quietly over the course of about fifteen years.

The 1987 was a fine, well-worked wine; the 1986 held very good fruit early on, but is evolving into a second, drier phase and should live well for ten years-plus. The 1985, bottled in April 1987, has turned in colour, but still has good length of fragile fruit and is now showing very well – not a wine to set aside for long. The 1984 was something of a 'sleeper' vintage, one that most pointed to M. Avril's consummate skill as a wine-maker. It was a difficult year, but the wine held great finesse and enough quiet substance to give it the legs to run until around 1994 in excellent style. M. Avril's 1983 was another excellent wine, although in much larger scale: it held supreme balance and structure, possessing a lovely integration of fine fruit flavours like blackcurrent and raspberry with a firm tannic background.

Of the annual total of around 120,000 bottles, M. Avril makes about 10 per cent white from a mixture of Clairette (25 per cent), Roussanne, Bourboulenc, Grenache Blanc (20 per cent each) and Picpoul (15 per cent). He is one of the few growers deliberately to harvest his white grapes behind the red: in 1990 he started the reds around 12 September, and the whites on 22 September, in pursuit of a maturity that would bring with it ripe fruit or dried apricot flavours.

After pressing, there is a decanting at 8°C or 9°C for about a day, and the juice is then left after racking to mount slowly to 17°C or 18°C, with the fermentation lasting three to four weeks. 'A long fermentation is the sign of having a well-structured wine, one full of *gras*, in my opinion,' says M. Avril. 'My grandfather used to do about one cask of white, but we started more properly with it in 1955, when we planted 2 hectares of Clairette, Picpoul and Grenache Blanc. Roussanne and Bourboulenc weren't so popular in those days.'

The wine is bottled in March or April, with the malolactic blocked, and is very good for drinking over several years. The 1990 weighs in at around 14°, and has a compelling nose of peaches, apricots, even a little marzipan. A chunky wine, it will soften and flesh out around 1996. The 1989 was a shade finer, but still carried excellent mature flavours and a good fruity grip that sets it into a league well above the standard low-temperature category of white Châteauneuf, and which shows what a little extra thought and planning can bring to the process. A 1982 *blanc* tasted in 1991, which by the textbook should have long since blown out on a tide of flabby, low-acidity oppression, was in fact delightfully persistent, complex and full of citrus and dried fruit on the palate. This was a wine ready to show good things for at least another six to eight years, and it is no surprise that the Clos des Papes *blanc* is very popular with M. Avril's band of 3-star restaurant customers.

Avril, Paul, et Fils
  Clos des Papes   84230 Châteauneuf-du-Pape

LA CUVÉE DU VATICAN

This 17-hectare vineyard is owned by M. Félicien Diffonty, the Mayor, an alert man who has always enjoyed being involved in the village's affairs and projects. One of his more memorable actions as Mayor was to have white wine instead of *pastis* served at receptions. His family have been wine growers for several generations, and his brother Rémy owns the Domaine du Haut des Terres Blanches. The Cuvée du Vatican red is a good example of a 75 per cent Grenache-based Châteauneuf, which during the 1980s has quietly modified its style to seek less sheer power and greater support from the Syrah. Very sound 1986 and 1988 – this is a *domaine* that should turn out good value for money wines with laudable regional authenticity during the 1990s.

Diffonty, Félicien
  La Cuvée du Vatican   84230 Châteauneuf-du-Pape

DOMAINE PIERRE ANDRÉ

This is a very traditional family *domaine* of 16 hectares around Courthézon in the north-east of the *appellation*, one where the future has been guaranteed by the entry of the daughter of the house into the affair. Pierre André, a small, neat man who looks markedly younger than sixty-five, is the third generation of his family to be growing vines, which he has gradually grouped so that some of the thirty-one plots now actually run side by side. As a result, the soil varies from clay in the Gardiole *quartier* to broken rock in the L'Étang area; overall there is a clay–limestone thread running through M. André's vineyards.

The varieties are headed by Grenache (70 per cent or more), Syrah (15 per cent), Mourvèdre (10 per cent) and a mixture of Picpoul, Counoise, Cinsault and Muscardin.

M. André refuses to use herbicides or pesticides on his vines after trying herbicides in the mid-1960s on 2 hectares of his vineyard. 'I was very dissatisfied with the effect they had, especially on the vines growing in the sandy soil, where a lot of young shoots appeared above the line of the graft, telling me that the vine was adapting to nourish itself from the surface rather than further down in the soil.'

Taking such a stand means more work. After the harvest, around November, there is the spreading of compost, be it of horse or mushroom, followed by the hoeing-in of grass under the soil. Then, in the spring – around March and April – there is the *décavaillonnage*, where the soil is dug away from the foot of the vine so that any roots that have sprung during the winter can be cut away. After a month the soil is replaced, to a lower level than the protective couch built around the base of the vine for the winter months. Most of this work of cutting and tidying up has to be done by hand. Subsequently there is another task of hoeing if rain has encouraged the grass to grow. In May, about the time of flowering, there is cutting of the tips of vine shoots to tidy up to let tractors pass, and that is about the last trimming done by M. André. This is in contrast with those growers who proudly talk about their midsummer cutting back of vegetation, something which M. André considers should not even arise if one avoids clonally selected vines and cultivation without artificial aids.

M. André likes to harvest quite late, in conscious pursuit of a certain evaporation in the grapes that results in a higher degree and greater depth in the final wine. In 1988 the combination of a harvest produced with his vineyard methods and waiting brought a wine of around 14.5°, whereas many other growers struggled to reach 13°. Harvesting is done by all the family with some temporary help, and lasts three weeks. M. André's daughter Jacqueline, who joined him in 1984, reflects a younger point of view by wishing to do the whole harvest in ten days, starting later and finishing earlier, for more secure control over the crop.

The grapes are pumped into concrete vats, duly crushed; for the 1986–90 harvests, M. André used a lighter crusher which did not please him. Fermentation can run towards 32°C, and M. André admits that it is harder to finish the wine without cooling facilities – 'But that's like the old days – my 1988 took a year to finish.' The first press wine is added, courtesy of an old hydraulic *pressoir*, and while there is no filtration at any stage, there is fining with egg whites before bottling.

'I'm very particular about where I get my eggs from, and I have a free-range farm in the Drôme *département* that supplies me with about 500 eggs at a time. Clearly, I can't use 500 egg yolks, so I rang up my friend Guy Jullien of Restaurant Beaugravière at Mondragon, and he took the yolks to make ice-cream. He was so pleased with their quality that he now buys all his chickens from the same farm!'

The *domaine* is flexible about length of wood-ageing. This can range from six months to three years or more. The 1988 harvest, with some firm tannins, received eight months in the family's 40-hectolitre barrels; 1986 received two years; 1981 over two years; and 1978 four years in wood. Whatever the stay in wood, the wine is never bottled under two years after the harvest.

M. André's reds are an excellent expression of typical Châteauneuf made by careful, traditional methods. Both his 1989 and 1988 have been very good; the former has a heady, dried fruit, rich bouquet which will develop well with age, while the palate is very tightly knit, with length and balance promising long life. The 1988 is a great expression of the Grenache (about 75 per cent of the wine), and has more complexity than the 1989; its elements are still more discordant, it is less obvious and less fleshy than the 1989, but it promises greatly over a dozen years or so. The 1990 is very heady, a strong wine with plenty of chewiness and clear Grenache expression in it; it may lack a little of the roundness of the 1989. M. André skipped the 1987 vintage for bottling purposes, and of his earlier vintages, the 1980, 1981 and 1985 have been notably successful. The 1985 has more stamina and depth than many of its vintage, the 1981 is very dense but a little hard, while the 1980 is an exemplary wine, a ruby colour showing and some excellent softness within a tight structure holding the wine together well. It is drinking extremely well now, and will continue in good shape until at least 1995.

M. André makes a little white, from a mixture of Clairette (pink and white vines, very old), plus some younger Bourboulenc and Roussanne (planted in 1985) and Grenache Blanc. This is solid, direct wine, cleanly made and ideal to drink within five years.

Domaine Pierre André   84350 Courthézon

DOMAINE PAUL AUTARD

This 12-hectare *domaine*'s vineyards stand mainly between Courthézon in the north-east of the *appellation* and the village of Châteauneuf-du-Pape. The plantation for the red wine is made up of 50 per cent Grenache, with the rest made up of mostly Syrah, Mourvèdre, Cinsault and Muscardin. The soil varies from some purely stone-covered areas to sandy, finer soil around La Côte Ronde near the road to Courthézon.

Jean-Paul Autard likes to destalk the whole crop, and is looking to make a wine marked more by finesse than by power. The 1989 red is a seven- to nine-year wine, but will show well after only four or five years, for instance. It is a middle-weight wine that just lacks the potential to reveal the core extract of full Châteauneuf when it has aged. In style this would appeal more to French palates than Anglophone ones.

The white is made from one-third each Grenache Blanc, Clairette and Roussanne. This was more successful in 1989, when there was greater grip in the wine and a balanced finish, than in 1990. The 1990 is a little too fat – a feature of several of the whites of that year.

The Autards also own a 12-hectare Côtes du Rhône property.

Autard, Jean-Paul
   GAEC Hoirie Paul Autard   84350 Courthézon

DOMAINE LUCIEN BARROT

As part of a wine-growing family installed at Châteauneuf since the mid-eighteenth century, Lucien Barrot reflects a thoroughly conservative approach handed down from one generation to the next. He wanders around his cellars, faded yellow Gitane *maïs* drooping from a corner of his mouth, coins jingling in his pocket, and with the help of his impressive dark eyebrows explains in ringing Provençal tones that his only adaptation from a strictly old-fashioned technique has been 'first, the fact that I press the *marc* more lightly, and second, that I keep the fermentation temperature within a band of 26–30°C, whereas in the past my ancestors would have reached 32–34°C in a hot autumn.'

Eighty per cent of the vineyard is planted with Grenache Noir, supported by Cinsault, Syrah and Mourvèdre. Fermentation lasts a full three weeks and cask ageing can run for five years, since M. Barrot bottles over an extended period. His 1979, for instance, was first bottled in the spring of 1982, and the last *foudres* were bottled in the spring of 1985.

M. Barrot's wines win by knock-out rather than on points: his 1979 had dark, stern flavours with rasping tannic undertones, while the 1981 was marked by dense flavours, an impenetrable colour and a chewy, liquorice aftertaste: both were pretty massive wines, similar to the well-balanced but equally tannic 1983. The 1985 was packed with firm fruit flavours and a heat on the palate that made it a wine to set aside until around 1993, while the 1986 is full of guts and more obvious tannins. This should not be approached much before 1995.

M. Barrot is now working with his son Régis, and it may be the presence of a younger pair of hands that has contributed to a slightly greater channelling of the energies of the 1988 and 1989 vintages here. While both wines still carry great heat and power, they are a shade less wild than in the past. The 1989 is particularly impressive, with masses of extract and tannins at the finish, but the promise of a superb bouquet opening up after eight to eleven years.

M. Barrot's 20 hectares of vines are spread around the *appellation* in many different *parcelles* – hence the absence of the name of a *lieu-dit* or specific site for this property. In typical Provençal fashion, there was a lawsuit taken out against the colourful M. Barrot by the Confrérie des Chevaliers du Tastevin of Clos Vougeot in Burgundy over his use of the Cuvée du Tastevin title for his wine; since the 1980s this wine has been known therefore as simple Domaine Lucien Barrot et Fils.

GAEC Barrot, Lucien, et Fils   84230 Châteauneuf-du-Pape

DOMAINE DE BEAURENARD

A seventh-generation wine *domaine* owned by M. Paul Coulon, who is helped by his enthusiastic, trail bike-riding son Daniel, in the running of their 29-hectare vineyard situated north of the village. Four grape varieties form the nucleus of the wine – Grenache (70 per cent), with Mourvèdre and Syrah both 10 per cent, Cinsault 8 per cent and a handful of other *cépages* making up the difference. Some plots of Grenache contain eighty-year-old vines. Half the harvest is lightly crushed, with the crusher rollers deliberately set well apart, while the rest enters the vats untouched.

In the late 1980s the Beaurenard cellars were completely revamped, to allow more press-button temperature control and such refinements as automatic *pigeage* or punching-down of the fermenting vats. The aim has been to extract greater fruit from the harvest.

M. Coulon *père*, a good-looking, urbane man, explains his cellar policy: 'At each arrival of the tractor loaded with the 30-kilogram harvest boxes, I fill the vats alternately with a box-worth amount of partly crushed grapes and then the equivalent of uncrushed crop, and so on alternately. This releases carbon dioxide which is absorbed by the whole grapes, causing an intra-cellular fermentation. Since there isn't a lot of juice produced straight away, fermentation is slow, and will gradually continue for two to three weeks. I also include the first two pressings, which means another week before the sugars are finished.' M. Coulon adds that in his grandfather's time the method was to leave the wine to stew almost until Christmas, when the malolactic fermentation would occur without anyone fully realizing it. Of course, there was tremendous extraction of colour and tannin, which was topped up by at least three years' ageing in wood. Now Paul and Daniel Coulon leave their red Châteauneuf for only nine to twelve months in their 30- to 50-hectolitre *foudres*, or in a few new oak *pièces* whose effect they are cautiously testing: in the 1989 red, for instance, Daniel estimated the presence of new wood wine to be no more than 2.5 per cent.

The Beaurenard red Châteauneuf is invariably a charming wine, marked by pleasant soft fruit flavours that have agreeable support from gentle tannins. The wines were a little off-form in 1981 and 1983, lacking some of the depth and longevity found in years like 1978 and 1979. But the second half of the 1980s saw a move towards a greater extraction with a resounding, succulent fruitiness apparent in wines like the 1989, which is one to drink between four and seven years old. The 1987 was well crafted, and for its year will show longer than some – to around 1994. The 1988 has a little more evident tannin in it.

Overall, the Beaurenard style is very much to make medium-weight wines which are pleasant to drink inside five or six years, while still carrying Châteauneuf nuances. The *domaine* also makes a middle of the road white Châteauneuf from 60 per cent Clairette, some of which are very old, 30 per cent Grenache and 10 per cent Bourboulenc; this is fermented at around 18°C and bottled in the early part of the New Year.

The Coulons also own a 45–hectare Côtes du Rhône domaine near Rasteau, further east in the Vaucluse, and this produces a very respectable Grenache-based red as well as a rosé. The family encourages visits to their cellars in Châteauneuf to see their collection of *vignerons*' working tools, in their Musée du Vigneron.

Coulon, Paul et Daniel
    Domaine de Beaurenard   84230 Châteauneuf-du-Pape

DOMAINES MICHEL BERNARD

This is a group that is not a pure, orthodox *négociant* organization. Founded in 1981, it is a collection of around forty southern Rhône *domaines*, a dozen of which are at Châteauneuf-du-Pape. Its link man and president is Michel Bernard, a stout, bearded and ambitious personality who is the selector of the wines. A student of law and politics at Aix-en-Provence University, M. Bernard was called to the family vineyard near Orange in 1971 after the death of his father. He realizes that at Châteauneuf there is sufficient volume of wine to support an intensive marketing and packaging campaign around the world – unlike many of the other top Rhône wines whose vineyards are too small for such ambitions.

'Most of these properties were owned by good *vignerons* who were not used to selling off their wine in bottle; quite a few of them were getting on in years and didn't have the urge to do their own bottling and marketing,' comments M. Bernard. 'The grouping guides the growers on their vinification, and the wines' ageing is under my control. At Châteauneuf, we make around 480,000 bottles of red and 20,000 of white each year; the red is led by Grenache with a presence of around 80 per cent; these are typically traditional *domaines* which in total cover around 120 hectares. They range from backward styles, with long wood-ageing, at the Domaine de la Guérine, to more midstream seven- to nine-year wine like that from the Domaine de la Vialle or the Domaine des Trois Plantiers, at 30 hectares the largest in the grouping.'

M. Bernard himself concentrates most on the white Châteauneuf; Grenache Blanc (40 per cent), Clairette (30 per cent) and Bourboulenc (30 per cent) with a few sundry varieties are the constituents, and this he sells as Domaine de la Serrière and Château Beauchêne, the latter a property he bought in 1988 and which is set to become the group's flagship. This is a clean, middle-range white Châteauneuf very much marked by the low-temperature fermentation process.

The group's largest volume of wine is in Côtes du Rhône red, which is sourced in the Vaucluse; quite a lot of the wine for this and the Villages comes from around Cairanne. M. Bernard offers the interesting observation that for someone working from around Orange, sourcing wines from the Drôme further north is not easy, since most of the villages there are really satellites of the powerful Cellier des Dauphins organization.

M. Bernard is clearly pleased with the results of his work. 'We sell about 4 per cent of all Rhône wine to the United Kingdom. This includes wines from the northern part of the Valley – Crozes, St-Joseph, Côte-Rôtie and Hermitage.' Thirty per cent of the group's wine is exported, with the major emphasis on Europe, since 'selling Rhône wines to the Americans has been a very hard task', according to M. Bernard. One last curiosity about this group is that M. Bernard publishes many press releases and cuttings, but nowhere is there a list of the *domaines* and their owners within his grouping. Perhaps this is considered likely to interfere with the central Michel Bernard name, but the *domaines* at Châteauneuf remain something of a mystery.

Domaines Michel Bernard   84100 Orange

DOMAINE DES CHANSSAUD

A traditionally run 15-hectare *domaine*, Chanssaud possesses some of the oldest Grenache vines in the *appellation*. Situated north-west of the village past Mont-Redon, the property has plots of ninety- and one hundred-year-old Grenache; indeed the average age of the vines is thought to be over fifty years, which explains why this *domaine* rarely has yields in excess of 30 hectolitres per hectare.

Roger Jaume and his son Patrick now have 80 per cent Grenache planted, a typical proportion for a *père-en-fils* vineyard, plus 8 per cent each of Syrah and Mourvèdre and 4 per cent Cinsault. Roger Jaume recalls that in his father's day, the family had some Mourvèdre in the vineyard, but it was very much dotted about at random among the Grenache, while there was then almost no Syrah planted.

The wines are given a fifteen-day *cuvaison* followed by a maximum sojourn of eighteen months in cask. Vintages like the forceful 1978, 1979, 1981, 1983, 1986 and 1989 received the full eighteen months; the lighter 1982 and 1987 were bottled and on sale after sixteen months. The style of the Chanssaud wines is straightforward and old-fashioned. Elegance is not a part of their make-up, there is more a robustness derived from the Grenache which generally needs five or six years to settle down. Successful years were the 1979 – typically firm and spicy on the palate – and the 1980 – nervous and closed initially, but which settled down into an excellent stew or hot-pot accompaniment after five years. The 1983, 1985, 1987 and 1989 have also been well made, the last-named showing special promise. Patrick Jaume also makes an old-style, rich and full white Châteauneuf (Clairette with a little Grenache Blanc) and a very respectable Côtes du Rhône red from their 15–hectare vineyard outside the Châteauneuf boundary.

Jaume, Patrick
    Domaine des Chanssaud   84100 Orange

DOMAINE CHANTE-CIGALE

This is a 40-hectare *domaine* run by M. Christian Favier, who took over from his father-in-law, M. Nöel Sabon. The vineyard is split up into about thirty plots and is dominated by the Grenache (80 per cent), with the difference made up of Syrah (10 per cent), Mourvèdre (5 per cent) and Cinsault (5 per cent). It was the grandparents of M. Favier who gave the *domaine* its 'singing grasshopper' name; no actual site at Châteauneuf carries this name. Under M. Favier only small concessions have been made to modern wine-making – new fermenting vats, for instance. Otherwise the wine is made in a traditional way, with an extended three-week fermentation following the crushing of 70 per cent of the grapes. Emphasis is placed on ageing in cask, with a minimum of eighteen months normally, which can rise to near four years in the case of vintages like the 1976.

The red is sound, satisfactory Châteauneuf – generally a fair representative of a Grenache-driven wine, without the height of character offered by the best *domaines*. Recently the 1986 and 1989 have been successful, with classic Châteauneuf aromas in evidence and good 'flesh' on the palate. These are eight- to ten-year wines. Off-vintages like the 1987 can be a little thin.

A very little white has been made since 1984, mostly from the Clairette and Grenache Blanc, with a little Roussanne. This leans towards a rich style rather than carrying a pure young fruity zest, and in a fat vintage like 1990 should be drunk within three or four years.

Sabon–Favier
Domaine Chante-Cigale   84230 Châteauneuf-du-Pape

DOMAINE CHANTE-PERDRIX

The 18 hectares of the Domaine Chante-Perdrix are in the southern part of the *appellation* not far from the Rhône. The vineyards are grouped around the Nicolet brothers' house, and are typical of their *quartier*, with a stony and gravel soil which does not retain a lot of moisture. They are therefore allowed two regulated irrigations in the event of drought, between 1 July and 15 August.

Guy and Rémy run this normally front-line *domaine*, while Guy's son Frédéric has set up the Cave Perges on his own. It has a traditional plantation of nearly 80 per cent Grenache Noir, some of which are fifty years old, while Mourvèdre, Syrah and Muscardin are the other prominent varieties. The Syrah and the Muscardin were more widely planted in the 1980s in place of old Grenache: the objective with the Muscardin is to soften the Grenache and bring extra aroma to the wine.

The Nicolets vinify their red Châteauneuf traditionally – a middling crushing followed by ten days' to two weeks' *cuvaison* and a stay in cask that varies between a year and thirty months according to the weight of the vintage. The 1981 and the 1986 received the full length of ageing, for instance; the 1982 and the 1987 were bottled after little more than a year.

When the Reflets association was founded in 1955, the Nicolets started having their wine bottled there, and have continued with this system ever since. Apart from the unusual Château Rayas, theirs is one of the lowest average yields in the *appellation*, around 25 hectolitres per hectare over 1975–85. The reason for this appears to be the poverty of their soil, which is always prey to drought.

Until 1984 the Chante-Perdrix red was generally one of the deepest, most hard-hitting wines at Châteauneuf. But a shorter *cuvaison* and stay in wood, coupled with the effect of dry summers, have made some of the 1980s wines less full-bodied and impressive than usual. The 1985, the product of a large crop, was peppery and spicy on the palate, but is tending to dry out, while the 1986 was unusually pale and light. Better years have been the older wines, like the 1978, 1979, 1980, 1981 and 1983, or the most recent wines like the 1989. These are marked by masses of tannin, solid prune and plum-like fruit and a density that makes one wonder when exactly they will open up. The Chante-Perdrix reds are not wines that will live as long as some, since their tannins are often rather dried-out: in big, strong vintages, these wines are superb to drink when they are nine to fourteen years old.

While the reds can be very distinguished, the white is less compelling, even though a small amount has been made each year since 1960. It is composed of 60 per cent Grenache Blanc and 40 per cent Clairette. Vinified in the traditional way, it should be drunk young while there is still freshness present. Otherwise it can lean towards excess fatness, as in 1990.

Nicolet Frères, et Fils
  SCEA Chante-Perdrix   84230 Châteauneuf-du-Pape

DOMAINE DE CONDORCET

One of the famous names at Châteauneuf in the past century, partly because it belonged with the Château La Nerte to Commandant Ducos, Condorcet is now undergoing a minor revival. The 14-hectare property belongs to the *Veuve* Simone Bouche, whose grandparents bought it in 1919 for 32,000 francs, payable in pieces of gold.

Although Syrah has grown on the estate since 1878, its current proportion is very small, with Grenache and Cinsault predominating. The vinification is traditional, and a vigorous, sturdy wine results. Until 1986 it was bottled by the Caves St-Pierre, but with Mme Bouche's son having completed agricultural college, the family are now vinifying and bottling themselves.

No white is made, but a Côtes du Rhône red comes from their 6-hectare vineyard near Sorgues.

Bouche, Simone
    Domaine de Condorcet   84230 Châteauneuf-du-Pape

DOMAINE DE CRISTIA

Alain Grangeon's Domaine de Cristia is a good example of the quality that during the 1980s started to emerge in the middle ranks of vineyard owners at Châteauneuf. His holding of a little over 11 hectares is a typical middle-rank size, as is the red vine mix of 70 per cent Grenache, 10 per cent Syrah, 8 per cent each Cinsault and Mourvèdre, and 4 per cent Muscardin. The vineyard's plots are situated mainly in the north-east of the *appellation*, near Courthézon.

The red is vinified in an entirely traditional way, with an extended *cuvaison* of two to three weeks and two years' ageing in *foudres*. In 1989 the red showed the benefit of such treatment – an intense colour and rich wild fruit aromas on the bouquet. An attacking fruity start on the palate was rounded off with some firm support tannin and the wine will drink well over the course of eight to ten years.

The white is vinified in a modern way, with the use of 20 per cent new oak since 1988, and bottling a year after the harvest. Made from 41 per cent Clairette, 28 per cent Grenache Blanc, 21 per cent Bourboulenc and 10 per cent Roussanne, it is a rounded, rich wine, whose ample flavours would be livened up by a little more acidity from a stronger Roussanne presence. Very well vinified, it is just the sort of wine to select in a less sunny vintage when the natural acidity levels are higher.

The Domaine de Cristia is a promising estate to keep an eye on.

Grangeon, Alain
  Domaine de Cristia   84350 Courthézon

DOMAINE DURIEU

A large man, with a black beard streaked with grey and a rumbling, resonant voice, Paul Durieu has a commanding presence. A relative newcomer to wine-making, he inherited his 21 hectares of vines at Châteauneuf from his mother and his 28 hectares of Côtes du Rhône near Camaret from his father.

His Châteauneuf vineyard is near Château Mont-Redon and the red is composed of Grenache, Syrah, Mourvèdre, Cinsault and Counoise. Curiously, he found that the *domaine* used not to have enough Grenache to be fully balanced, so that when he took over the property he planted 5 hectares with the staple grape.

M. Durieu is still searching for a fixed style of wine: his early vintages like the 1978 and 1980 were wines of good balance, colour and considerable richness, while the 1981, which combines agreeable dried fruit flavours with a marked liquorice edge on the palate, containing sufficient southern warmth to keep going quietly until 1998–2000. But his 1982, 1983 and 1988 were lighter, almost like a good Lirac from across the Rhône. The 1989 is a seductive wine with early round flavours supported by some discreet tannins – a six- to eight-year wine with some better Châteauneuf definition.

M. Durieu performs a light crushing, finding that the transportation of the grapes on the 3 kilometres from the vineyard to the vinification cellar does part of this work, which is completed by the must-pump taking the grapes into his enamel-lined vats. M. Durieu is cutting down on the wood-ageing of his wine to well under two years, so that it spends a little time in concrete vats before bottling. His objective is to sell 'something ready to drink'.

M. Durieu is bottling only about half of his production, since he has been spending his spare money on putting the vineyard in order. He is helped on administration and bookkeeping by his wife Hélène, a typical task for a Châteauneuvoise. Taking over a *domaine* at Châteauneuf-du-Pape is an arduous and capital-intensive task, and if M. Durieu's wine can regain some of its former concentration of flavour and extract, then it will lodge among the good middle-ranking Châteauneuf reds.

Since the late 1980s, a white Châteauneuf has been made. Typical on the bouquet of a low-temperature-fermentation wine, it has a discreet charm and length on the palate that show through well after about a year or so.

Durieu, Paul
    Domaine Durieu   84230 Châteauneuf-du-Pape

DOMAINE FONT-DE-MICHELLE

Jean and Michel Gonnet run this progressive *domaine*, and make very good red and white wines in a modern style, combining finesse with a certain amount of local vigour in their *cuvées*. They are the sons of the late Étienne Gonnet and nephews of Mme Henri Brunier of Domaine du Vieux Télégraphe. Their great-grandfather, Jean-Étienne Gonnet, cultivated barley, olives and about 3 hectares of vines around the year 1890, and the family's activities continued in much the same way until 1950, when Étienne Gonnet enlarged the vineyard from 10 to 24 hectares over the space of fourteen years. This involved buying and clearing wooded scrubland around the *domaine* on the *lieu-dit* Font de Michelle. He cleverly grouped most of the small holdings, so that most of the 30 hectares are now mainly integrated side by side on the gentle slopes that descend from Châteauneuf towards Bédarrides, with a 6-hectare plot on the Vieux Télégraphe plateau. The soil is largely clay–limestone, covered by masses of *galet* stones, with gravelly patches.

The Gonnet brothers have a justified reputation for producing one of the best white Châteauneufs, and it is interesting to hear Jean Gonnet's comments on the wine that makes up 10 per cent of their production.

'Making white wine here needs research, since there are new techniques that can be applied, providing they balance one another. Let's take the date of harvesting. I work with 50 per cent Grenache Blanc, 25 per cent Clairette, 20 per cent Bourboulenc and 5 per cent Roussanne; the Roussanne dates only from the mid-1980s. At all costs I have to avoid overripeness in order to preserve freshness in the white, so I follow the Grenache Blanc's maturity. When that's ready, I pick all the white grape varieties, so that the Grenache's alcohol is offset by the Clairette's acidity and the Bourboulenc's young aromas. It's a very precise operation that in recent years has started very early indeed because a one- or two-day error of judgement can upset the applecart.' M. Gonnet is getting used to cutting short his August holidays – he started the white harvesting in 1990 on 4 September and in 1989 on 3 September; the record was the long, hot summer of 1976: 2 September. The red harvest starts about a week later.

In making the white, the Gonnets declare their *triage* to be almost the act of maniacs; four men are on the tractor vigilating and discarding from the boxes as they are gathered. After the pressing, there is a twenty-four- to thirty-six-hour decanting at 10°C, and the addition of a bentonite fining solution and the temperature of fermentation is eventually held at 17°C. In the early days of controlled temperatures, the Gonnets worked at 13°C, and came up with exotic fruit or banana style smells; for a wine of longer keeping potential they prefer to work at 17°–18°C – this brings a wine that they consider can flourish over six years or more. After a two-week fermentation, the wine is racked and stored in stainless steel, passed through the cold and filtered and bottled all at once in mid-December, with the malolactic obviously blocked.

For a wine whose early emphasis is on young, clean fruit, the white Font-de-Michelle evolves very well; the under-ripe apricot style fruit transforms after three or four years into a rounded peachiness with unusual cooked, almost caramel hints on the palate. It is very good when young, very good but a bit unusual when older – take your choice.

The red is made from 65 per cent Grenache with principal support from the Syrah, Cinsault and Mourvèdre. The Mourvèdre has been drafted in to help ageing possibilities.

As befits a *domaine* of modern temperament, the Gonnets destalk the crop a little each year – perhaps 10 per cent, or more in the case of *coulure*. Only about 25 per cent of the grapes receive a light crushing and the juice ferments for around twenty days in 150-hectolitre stainless steel vats, with a daily *remontage* to help extract fruit and aromas. The different *cépages* are only added together after the malolactic in the early New Year, and ageing in old 80-hectolitre *foudres* then lasts for six to twelve months according to the style of the year. Since the late 1980s, a tiny proportion of the wine that goes into their special Cuvée Étienne Gonnet is passed into new *barriques* – twenty of them, ranging from new to two years old. The selection of the wood – Allier and Limousin are preferred – is done by tasting from different casks and by following the Rhône Interprofessional Committee's guidebook to cask-ageing.

During the stay in wood, there will be two rackings, a light filtration and then bottling in about five runs from fourteen months after the harvest up to twenty-one months after the harvest: the later bottled wine is stored in stainless steel after its passage through the wood.

Of recent vintages, the white 1990 has great elegance and authority – it is very aromatic, but is firm and capable of good development over five years or so. Its fullness is slightly greater than the 1989. The red 1990 has a firm fruit intensity swelling up on the palate, and enough guts and acidity to promise a balanced roundness by the mid-1990s; it contains more Grenache than the 1989, which is another stylish wine, with a resounding fruitiness present within it and elegant length on the finish: this is a wine that will drink well around 1995–7.

The 1986 has advanced, with a matt ruby colour and the bouquet turning a bit gamey and sweet; it lacks a little density, and should be drunk by around 1994 or so. The 1985 is less persistent on the palate than the 1986, and has become fragile with age, while the 1983, with its firm tannins at the start, has evolved to display mature dried fruits and a little dryness on the finish, indicating the need to drink it up. As a demonstration of the power of the 1989 and 1990 vintages, all these earlier wines weigh in at around 13.8° or 13.9°, while the other two are 14.2° and 14.4° respectively. The special *Cuvée* Étienne Gonnet 1988 is a little different; bottled in September 1990, 30 per cent of this received new-cask ageing. It has a dark, pepper/spice bouquet with greater depth than the usual *cuvées*, and the wood serves to give the wine more tannic support on the mid-palate. This is a well integrated wine; its elements are firm but show the promise of good fusion given time.

The red Font-de-Michelles have edged up the ladder of quality at Châteauneuf, and now show a more serious intent – that of being wines capable of improvement and greater complexity if allowed around five to eight years to do so. They come from the modern, stylish school, but display local characteristics, and during the 1990s there is every chance that these wines will continue their progress. Whether Michel Gonnet will continue his advance up the mountain-sides that he likes to tackle is another question; in the last five years he has climbed the Himalayas – with a close shave due to failure of oxygen at extreme altitude – and broken his leg on Mont Ventoux. Perhaps he will have to content himself with patrolling the vineyard on the local plateau.

In some overseas markets, a second-wine label from this good *domaine* appears under the title Source aux Nymphes.

Les Fils d'Étienne Gonnet
   Domaine Font-de-Michelle   84370 Bédarrides

DOMAINE LOU FRÉJAU

The Chastan family name is synonymous with the northern area of the *appellation*, near Orange. The Domaine Lou Fréjau is run by Serge Chastan, and takes its title from a local word, *fréjau* being the patois for the rounded stones that cover the generally clay–limestone soil.

The red wine is made from 70 per cent Grenache and 20 per cent Mourvèdre, with 10 per cent mixed varieties. Vinified traditionally, it spends fifteen to eighteen months in *foudre* and is a classic representative of its zone. The northern area of the vineyard produces wines that are middle-weight and quite complex – unlike the big, robust wines found nearer the village. The Lou Fréjau 1989 red, for instance, held a dark plum colour and almost overripe, seasoned aromas on the bouquet. The palate was marked by well-advanced plum flavours that were dry in style rather than fresh and exuberant. With ageing of five or six years, a very satisfying, good length and complex wine will emerge.

The white, vinified at low temperature, is made from 40 per cent Bourboulenc and Clairette with support from 20 per cent Grenache Blanc. In 1990, it was a wine of latent promise, needing a couple of years to emerge from a quite discreet start. The style is delicate, and the vinification very well conducted.

M. Chastan also makes sound Côtes du Rhône Villages red, and this is a *domaine* whose wines present good value for money.

Chastan, Serge
   Domaine Lou Fréjau   84100 Orange

DOMAINE DU GRAND TINEL

One of the larger properties at Châteauneuf, with a 75-hectare vineyard, the Domaine du Grand Tinel was built up by Élie Jeune's father Gabriel who conveniently married a girl with vines in her dowry. These were at the Domaine de la Petite Gardiole and combined with M. Jeune's own vineyard to form such a large holding. The Grenache accounts for around 80 per cent of the red vines, there is 5 per cent Syrah, and the remaining 15 per cent is split between the Mourvèdre, Muscardin, Counoise and Cinsault. The vineyard plots are spread all around the *appellation* area, and both harvesting and *cuvaison* are conducted by *quartier*.

The vinification of the red is traditional: a moderate crush, with no destalking or destemming, a fifteen- to eighteen-day *cuvaison* in concrete or more recently acquired stainless steel vats, the addition of the *vin de presse*, a light filtration and storage in *foudres* of around 50 hectolitres for six to twelve months according to the vintage's style. Since 1989 M. Jeune has done some tentative experiments with young oak casks, but he finds that they bring quite hard tannins, and their use is restricted to no more than 2 per cent of the overall wine. Bottling comes some months after the stay in wood – some of the 1988, for instance, was bottled as late as 1991.

This is a fast-improving *domaine*. The first bottling was in on a limited scale around 1969, but the wine remained essentially a *négociant*'s purchase – to Burgundy or Switzerland or local merchants – until a real stepping up in the mid-1970s. Even so, only around half the production or about 150,000 bottles appear each year now, although the aim is to go higher.

Élie Jeune is a man of few words, but his manner loosens very gradually over the course of a few years' acquaintance. He has a very down-to-earth approach; although trained at Beaune, he employs a *caviste* for oenological details, has a sizeable permanent staff and takes his relaxation in the snow or the sun. The property is efficiently run and he comes across as a very sensible businessman-farmer.

Rather like the man himself, the red wines opened up and showed greater depth of character throughout the 1980s. They are representative of the strong-extraction, full-bodied school of Châteauneuf, very thorough and satisfying with a touch of class apparent in the 1989 that puts it close to the big league of top wines. The 1990 is also extremely well made, since the depth of flavours conceals the fact

435

that the wine carries 14.8° alcohol; there is a sheen in the colour, a lively, striking bouquet and a good surge of fruit on the palate – and underneath there is a tannic residue that is not intrusive: very carefully made wine. The 1989 is another full but sleek wine, with nothing discordant in it; just sustained flavours and an intense crushed fruit bouquet. This is a full degree less than the 1990.

The 1988 is a more 'square' wine, just lacking some of the flair of the two later vintages; both it and the very sound 1986 lack a little intensity and are good, mainstream wines. The 1988 needs to be left until around 1994 to settle and open, while the 1986 should show greater variety of flavour and secondary aromas after a quiet phase in 1991.

Of older vintages, both the 1981 and 1978 are sterling wines. The 1978 Grand Tinel is a Grand Vin, without doubt. It is splendid, its harmony and great fruitiness are supported by lovely depth and weight, and it is indeed a cockle-warming wine that still has lots of life in it. The 1981 is one of the leading offerings of its year, still tight as a drum with a firm, upright style and excellent depth on the bouquet. Its flavours are the dried, starker ones rather than the more generous, plumper tastes of the 1978. The 1979 was also very successful, and along with the 1983 will be good to drink out towards 1995.

While the top vintages are definitely wines that can live for approaching twenty years – and Grand Tinel is certainly one of the top ten *domaines* in the best vintages – the lesser years like 1980, 1984 and 1987 are wines to drink within around eight years. The *domaine*'s next real challenge is to produce excellent wines of a slightly softer style in lesser years, because with 1989 and 1990 it has shown what it can now do with first-class raw materials at harvest-time.

The first white wine was made in 1978; this comes from one-third each of Grenache Blanc, Clairette and Bourboulenc. After pressing, it is left to decant at a natural temperature for as long as four to five days before the alcoholic fermentation takes place over the course of eighteen to twenty days, at a temperature of 17–18°C, in stainless steel. This is bottled around February or March. The style is ripe rather than just fresh; there is good roundness, with pleasant dried fruit richness on the palate, and M. Jeune admitted that in 1990 they had to work hard to control the alcohol (it ended at 13.6°); the result is a very good wine.

M. Jeune is seeking to edge the quality of this *domaine* ever higher; he is adamant that over-production in the vineyard will never occur; the Grenache vines average over fifty years old and he is by nature conservative in his approach to their cultivation. Since the mid-1970s, Grand Tinel has been actively marketed outside France, so that now over half the bottled production goes to countries like Japan (since 1978), the United States and Britain. The best compliment to pay this *domaine* is that it is very dependable, and in top vintages very impressive.

Jeune, Élie
    Domaine du Grand Tinel   84230 Châteauneuf-du-Pape

DOMAINE GRAND VENEUR

This is a very sound 12-hectare *domaine* situated in the north of the *appellation* and run by the hard-working, meticulous M. Alain Jaume, a man whose neat appearance and polite manner are reflected in his carefully made red and white wines.

The 10 hectares of red Châteauneuf are planted 70 per cent Grenache, 10 per cent each of Syrah and Mourvèdre, and 10 per cent split between various *cépages*. The soil in the northern zone is very stony, and the style of the red wines slightly finer than the more robust *cuvées* that come from nearer the village. M. Jaume favours destalking and a regular crush, and after an eighteen- to twenty-day *cuvaison*, the wine is raised in *pièces*, of which one-fifth are new oak.

The red is always cleanly made at Grand Veneur, and takes the style of its *vigneron* – who is open to try new methods and who seeks finesse as well as substance in his wine: the results are very successful. In a ripe year like 1989, the wine is likely to carry a complex, interesting bouquet and good, rounded depth on the palate after about six to seven years' age. The 1988 is a finer wine, a little less tight-knit on the palate and suitable for drinking around 1994. But these are wines that can be drunk happily earlier since they do not carry the weight of tannin and guts of many traditional *domaines*.

M. Jaume is also forward-looking in his white wine vinification. From his 2 hectares (Clairette 45 per cent, Grenache Blanc 45 per cent, and Roussanne 10 per cent), he makes two *cuvées*; one is pure Roussanne, La Fontaine, which is vinified and raised in new Nevers oak. Bottled six months after the harvest, this carries a firmer than usual yellow colour, and a bouquet that is slow to emerge initially; there is some fatness of flavour, but the wine needs time to settle away from its new oak imprint. It is made from vines that are only fifteen years old, and will gain greater breeding when the vines have grown up a little more. The traditional white is a sound wine with some fat fruit flavours on the palate – in less sunny years it comes into its own because of the high proportion of Grenache Blanc and Clairette.

The Jaumes also make a red Côtes du Rhône Villages from their 5 hectares just outside Châteauneuf, and a red and rosé Côtes du Rhône.

Jaume, Alain
    Domaine Grand Veneur   84100 Orange

DOMAINE DU HAUT DES TERRES BLANCHES

This is a 53-hectare estate which has been turning out mainstream Grenache-inspired wines in a pretty consistent way for many years. Rémy Diffonty and his son Joël have their plots well dispersed around the *appellation*, the predominance being in the northern area. They describe their soils in broad terms as being a mix of very stony clay and lighter, sandier ground.

The grape mix is 75 per cent Grenache, 10 per cent Syrah, 8 per cent Mourvèdre and 7 per cent Cinsault. The vinification tended during the early 1980s to a lighter, more *macération* style, but by the 1990s attempts had been made to extract greater density. The reds now receive a traditional vinification and ageing of at least one year in oak.

The 1989 red held sound richness on the bouquet, and its ripe, plump style on the palate indicated a life of under ten years. It was a good yardstick wine for the vintage – very correct, with some personality of its own.

The Diffontys are one of the few families who offer old vintages of Châteauneuf – in some cases, they have wines of over fifteen years old for sale.

Diffonty, Rémy et Joël
    Domaine du Haut des Terres
    Blanches   84230 Châteauneuf-du-Pape

DOMAINE DE MARCOUX

The Domaine de Marcoux is known at Châteauneuf as one that produced very good, long-keeping red wines in the 1960s and 1970s under the late Élie Armenier, who died in 1980. It is now run in a different way by Châteauneuf's tallest *vigneron*, Philippe Armenier, a man in his mid-thirties who measures 1.98 metres (6′ 5″), and who works with his sister Sophie in the *domaine*.

The vineyard covers 24 hectares, composed of Grenache (70 per cent), followed by Mourvèdre, then Cinsault, then Syrah. The vines are on average fifty years old, with the largest grouping being a holding of 12 hectares near the Château Mont-Redon estate. The soil is mostly covered with white alluvial stones.

What sets M. Armenier apart from most other *vignerons* is his adherence to bio-dynamic methods of cultivation and cellar care. Homoeopathy is at the root of this belief, as are the works of Rudolph Steiner. The central belief is that the key forces in viniculture come from the sky and not the soil: the soil is just there to act as a corridor in the process. This belief translates into M. Armenier receiving a wooden box from his viniculture contact or guru in the Loire Valley; this is filled with little containers of dark soil and mixtures whose origins are flowers like dandelion and camomile. These are used to compost the vineyards – spiritually rather than in reality since one is talking about 4 grams (a tumblerful or so) per hectare for some treatments and only up to 180 grams per hectare for others. All the while M. Armenier is guided by a pre-ordained calendar, which tells him what actions he must take in the vineyard or in the cellar according to the alignment of the planets and stars.

This is a big subject, as they say, and one that singles M. Armenier out from the majority of his fellow *vignerons*. In terms of his vinification, he works with 70 per cent of the crop crushed, the rest left alone. The *cuvaison* lasts for twelve to twenty-four days, the Syrah having a shorter run than the Grenache, and ageing in wood is quite short, up to only eight months as long as space in the cellar permits. Old *foudres*, some of which were beer barrels around the time of the First World War, are used for this, and the finished wine is bottled around eighteen months after the harvest. A light filtration is done.

Only small amounts of Domaine de Marcoux were bottled before the end of the 1970s, so the wine from the 1960s is hard to find.

However, it is a long-lived wine, well marked by the Grenache and representative of carefully made Châteauneuf of its time. It is difficult to say where the Marcoux wines will go in style during the 1990s; the straight Châteauneuf carries a sustained plum colour and is markedly round in style, a wine that conveys a harmonious rather than a punchy taste, and one to drink around six to eight years old. The 1989 for example, runs wild with very plump fruitiness and round aromas and will provide excellent drinking in its first six years.

The Vieilles Vignes *cuvée* is altogether a bigger wine, made of 80 per cent Grenache, with support from the Terret Noir, Counoise, Mourvèdre and Bourboulenc. This comes from vines of over sixty years of age, and carries a strong, dark colour, an intense bouquet with blackcurrant and damson fruit smells, and a tremendously deep fruitiness and concentration on the palate. The 1989 is the sort of wine whose longevity is hard to predict since its elements are very strong but very well integrated, and it could run for anything between twelve and twenty years.

This property also makes about 10 per cent of its production as white wine, from roughly 40 per cent each of Clairette and Bourboulenc and 20 per cent Grenache Blanc, with the Roussanne on stream since 1991. These generally grow in thinner soil; the Clairette, for example, is in more sandy soil at La Charbonnière near the noted white wine Domaine de Nalys. This is fermented in enamel-lined vats at 17–18° over about twenty days, the malolactic is blocked and bottling takes place at the end of the year or in January. This is sound mainstream wine that is pretty fine in style, and the white range has been sharpened since 1989 by a Vieilles Vignes (ninety-year vines) which has good depth of richness and *gras* on the palate – a wine capable of showing well over eight to ten years, anyway. No Vieilles Vignes white was made in 1990 for lack of volume.

Philippe Armenier sums up his new philosophy in the following way: 'The four elements of the vine that count are the fruit, flower, leaf and root. Bio-dynamic culture has allowed me to rediscover my role as a *vigneron*, away from the past and the way that education now leads you towards the cellar mainly. I'm more interested in the vineyard and its cycles now, and more aware of it.'

Whether this is a way of working that will make the wine better is open to debate, but there is little doubt that in the 1990s more growers will spend more time mastering the skills and tasks needed to keep their vines in sound, natural order. The 1980s in the Rhône and elsewhere were the decade of technology and 'indoors' in wine-making, and the 1990s promise to be a decade of the 'outdoors'.

GAEC Armenier, Élie et Philippe
    Domaine de Marcoux   84230 Châteauneuf-du-Pape

DOMAINE DE MONTPERTUIS

A typically scattered local family *domaine*, the very good, traditional Domaine de Montpertuis comprises 25 hectares of fully owned or rented vineyards under the care of Gabriel Jeune and his son Paul. Since the mid-1970s the Jeunes have replanted one-third of the vineyard, gradually lowering the Grenache Noir proportion to 75 per cent. It has been replaced in the first instance by the Syrah, although the Jeunes think that too much Syrah can be unbalancing, and there is support from the Mourvèdre, Cinsault and Counoise.

Fermentation takes place in enamel-lined and concrete vats, and a stay of over a year in cask rounds off the wine. In strong vintages like the 1978, 1981 and 1988 the Montpertuis red is full of dark tannic flavours which end in a chewy, full-bodied aftertaste. In such years, there are few pretensions to elegance or sleekness of style – it is a good, old-fashioned Grenache wine. The 1989 was a big voluptuous wine likely to last for eight to eleven years, and its fruit was particularly charming.

The Jeunes make a good, clean white Châteauneuf with fine, soft fruit in it. It is made principally from the Clairette, with Bourboulenc, a little Grenache Blanc and the fruit of a few veteran Picpoul vines. In a sunny year like 1990 or 1989, it has substantial dried fruit flavours that suggest a broadening of its complexity over three or four years.

This is a core *domaine* at Châteauneuf – highly reliable, with wines that truly reflect their *terroir*.

Jeune, Gabriel et Paul
    Domaine de Montpertuis   84230 Châteauneuf-du-Pape

DOMAINE DE NALYS

Following the death of Dr Philippe Dufays in 1978, this *domaine* has been split up a little and now covers 50 hectares instead of its former 80 hectares. Dr Dufays, until 1955 a practising doctor, was an intelligent man deeply interested in all aspects of viticulture and was renowned for his studies on the Châteauneuf-du-Pape grape varieties and for his wit in talking about them. The full range of thirteen grapes is grown at the *domaine*, with the red wine dominated by the Grenache (55 per cent of the total plantation) and by the Syrah (18 per cent). The wine is made in the accelerated manner, with only uncrushed grapes loaded into the fermenting vats. After a short stay in wood, the wine is bottled over a period ranging from six to fifteen months following the harvest. On the bouquet it shows its overtly fruity, maceration origins, but there is also a softness, with just a little tannin, holding the wine together at the very end. In more solid, well-rounded vintages like 1989 this makes it a wine capable of an interesting second phase of development after about five years; in a plump, fat year like 1985 there is so much early fruit that the wine becomes more one-dimensional – a good drink over the first five years, but definitely light for a Châteauneuf.

M. Pierre Pélissier, the *œnologue*, admits that he is aiming to make rounded, easily accessible red wines, and believes that in the firmest vintages they should have been drunk by the time they are eight years old.

Nalys also makes a very successful and well-reputed white wine from primarily the Grenache Blanc, Bourboulenc and Clairette, with some support from the Roussanne. It is said to possess more natural acidity due to the high incidence of clay in the vineyards. Marked by a crisp, tangy fruitiness when young, it has fair weight and a sort of salty bite which settles after about three years. In a year like 1990 it carries considerable richness, and outscores many of the other cool-fermentation whites. It is always very clean on the finish and over the years has been one of the most consistent of the front-rank white Châteauneufs. It is well worth seeking out in the restaurants surrounding Avignon, since Nalys only exports small quantities of its total 40,000 bottles of white and 160,000 bottles of red each year.

SCI Domaine de Nalys   84230 Châteauneuf-du-Pape

DOMAINE DU PEGAÜ

This is one of the big-hitting, old-fashioned *domaines* whose wines are concentrated, thorough and make no concessions to modern sanitized palates. Paul Féraud tells his stories with a sharp eye for observation and countryman's relish for old expressions. He works with his daughter Laurence, whose entry into the family concern prompted him to turn to larger scale bottling in the late 1980s.

The vineyard covers 12 hectares, spread out over ten plots, with the largest holding of 5 hectares towards Bédarrides in the east at a *quartier* called La Font des Papes. The soil is often clay, but there is chalk as well, and overall about half M. Féraud's vineyards are stone-covered. The vines are 80 per cent Grenache, with the difference made up of Syrah, Mourvèdre and bits and pieces of Cinsault, Counoise and Vaccarèse. M. Féraud admits to preferring the soil to the cellar. After trying some herbicides, he gave them up and now works his vineyards in a natural way, despite the extra cost involved. 'You either like working the soil or not,' he states. 'You don't come to Châteauneuf if you're frightened of a bit of sweat. It's not my vinification that brings the *goût de terroir* to my wine – that comes from what's in the grape when it is brought in – that's where the secret lies.'

As a stout defender of well-tried methods, M. Féraud is not an early harvester, favouring a certain over-maturity to help the *typicité* of the wine. The *triage* is done in the vineyards, the crop is lightly crushed without destalking and then vinified in concrete vats for ten to fifteen days. The *vin de presse* is added if extra tannin is required, and the young red wine spends at least two years in 40- to 50-hectolitre barrels, although in the case of a 1979 or 1981 this can rise to five or six years. No fining or filtration occurs before bottling.

The results are impressive. This is one of the richest, biggest old-style Châteauneufs, a true expression in a vintage like 1990 of the Grenache's powers. M. Féraud also makes a Vieilles Vignes *cuvée*, from vines of sixty to eighty years, and this is another extreme, ripe expression of the Grenache – dark purple when young, ripe fruit hiding within a reticent bouquet that needs six to eight years to loosen up, and a surge of dark flavours and tannins on the palate. In hot vintages, some of the Pegaü wines weigh in at around 15° alcohol, but the elements are so strongly flavoured that the result is wines of great roundness and intensity. This is particularly true of the extraordinary 1989 – a wine that will show splendidly after eight or ten years. The firm 1988 has good length and needs time to settle, the 1987 promises to gain spiciness and will drink well around 1993, and the very good 1986 is another intense, chewy wine, with tremendous length, which will start to open up around 1995 onwards. Of M. Féraud's older vintages, the 1981 has gained the damp, animal aromas of age on the bouquet, and shows the pepper and spice flavours of maturing Grenache on the palate – it will still be good for drinking towards the year 2000.

M. Féraud also makes a very interesting white Châteauneuf, one that reflects the desire to produce authentic wine driven by the *terroir* rather than by the hand of the maker. It is made of Grenache Blanc (60 per cent), Clairette (20 per cent) and 10 per cent each of Roussanne and Bourboulenc. This has existed since the early 1980s, with M. Féraud seeking non-stony soil for the plantation. He vinifies by leaving the grapes to macerate initially for two to four days, followed by an alcoholic fermentation of six to eight days at higher temperatures than normally now popular – around 18–22°C. He usually blocks the malolactic fermentation and bottles about six months after the harvest.

His whites are very good indeed; they carry a little more colour – pale straw – than many, and their aromas are ripe and lush, almost with a hint of late harvesting in them. Their style on the palate is truly southern – there is great depth and persistence and they have extreme quality – a lovely depth of flavour abounds. In style they are reminiscent of the Château de Fonsalette whites of Jacques Reynaud, excellent wines which have enough extract to keep them going and showing well for at least ten years. The 1986, 1989 and 1990 are well worth seeking out.

Féraud, Paul et Laurence
   Domaine du Pegaü   84230 Châteauneuf-du-Pape

DOMAINE DU PÈRE CABOCHE

This 32-hectare vineyard is owned by Théophile Boisson and is actively run by his son, Jean-Pierre, a very enthusiastic and open-minded young man. The name of the property, derived in an amusing way, dates back to the alliance of the Boisson and the Chambellan families in 1772, when Jean-Louis Boisson from Jonquières married a Chambellan daughter. The Chambellans, like many families at the time, had two occupations: they were both *vignerons* and the village blacksmiths. The occupation of blacksmith merited them the nickname of *Caboche*, which is a horse's plated shoe, and thus the name of the *domaine* was created.

Their vineyards are mostly grouped together, the largest plot being their 17 hectares on the plateau de la Crau, between Vieux Télégraphe and Nalys. The predominant vine is the Grenache (70 per cent), followed by the Syrah (15 per cent) and Mourvèdre (7 per cent), while the Boissons' interest in making white wine is illustrated by the 15 per cent of the vineyard that is accounted for by Bourboulenc (40 per cent – high at Châteauneuf), 25 per cent each of Clairette and Grenache Blanc, and 10 per cent Roussanne. The family pick their harvest in especially shallow buckets, so that as far as possible the grapes arrive intact at the cellars, located in the village. Thereafter all the grapes except the Syrah are lightly crushed, M. Boisson considering that the Syrah contributes better fruit when vinified whole to start with; fermentation takes place in stainless steel vats that have been installed since 1973. Following an active fermentation of ten to twelve days, the wine is left on its big lees for two more days to obtain some tannin extracts and is then transferred to concrete vats to help start the malolactic fermentation. After a filtration comes ageing in barrels for ten to eighteen months, the length of time varying according to the style of the vintage and the *cuvée* being made.

The standard red Père Caboche is a correct wine, one that stiffened in fibre in the late 1980s. More gutsy is the Elisabeth Chambellan *cuvée*, which has better depth on the palate and which is good to drink before it is eight years old. The reds are generally upstaged by the very good, fresh white wine. This usually has a pale colour, and the bouquet becomes rounded and less *nerveux* by the summer following vinification; clean fruit flavours are apparent on the palate and typically this is a wine to drink either fresh and right off the bat in its first year, or when it is three or four years old, and showing more ripeness. The 1989 *blanc* was particularly stylish.

Boisson, Jean-Pierre
   Domaine du Père Caboche   84230 Châteauneuf-du-Pape

DOMAINE RICHÉ

This is a good 12-hectare estate whose red and white wines of the late 1980s showed steady and consistent quality.

Nadyne Riché's grandfather was a Châteauneuf *vigneron* in the 1920s, and is said to have been bottling and dispatching his Châteauneuf to the royal family of Romania at that time: this must rank high in the 'most obscure' records of the *appellation*.

The vineyard is composed of the Domaine de Baban, and the 2 hectares of the Domaine Riché near Orange. The 11 hectares of red vines are planted with 70 per cent Grenache and 10 per cent each of Mourvèdre, Cinsault and Syrah. The predominant soil is a typical red clay–limestone with coverings of stones.

After a traditional vinification, the red receives 12–18 months in cask and a stay in vat before bottling. The 1989 red was a wine of character; the colour was an attractive purple, and the bouquet bore the cooked dark aromas of old-style Châteauneuf. On the palate, there was sufficient acidity to give the wine a lively feel alongside some good depth of flavour and a chewy aftertaste. This will show very well around 1994 or so.

The white is made from 45 per cent Grenache Blanc, 40 per cent Clairette and 15 per cent Bourboulenc. This was well worked in the quite difficult white wine year of 1990, with the Richés bringing out a freshness and an elegance that underpinned the firm flavours. The 1990 Domaine Riché white should be drunk before it is about four years old.

Riché, Claude et Jean
   Domaine Riché   84230 Châteauneuf-du-Pape

DOMAINE DE LA ROQUETTE

This *domaine* changed hands in September 1986, when René Laugier reached sixty-five years with no children, and decided to sell to the Brunier family of Vieux Télégraphe fame. Its 30 hectares are composed of twenty-seven red, three white vine plantations, and its location is first class. Forty per cent of the vineyard is on the plateau de Piélong, which is a middle plateau running from west to east across the north end of the *appellation*; Mont-Redon is on one side, Le Crau on the other, and here is some of the stoniest terrain of all.

Five other plots in different locations complete the red grape line-up: these are nearer the middle or southern zones. Three hectares of Syrah lie along the route to Roquemaure, due west of the village; some Grenache is planted on the drier ground near the route to Sorgues, 3 hectares of Mourvèdre grow in the Quartier de Pignan near Château Rayas and a final area of Syrah is placed on the very southern edge of the *appellation* limit. Such diversity of plantation is of course commonplace at Châteauneuf, but it leaves the Bruniers with more variables in deciding the style of the Roquette wine than they have been used to with their Vieux Télégraphe property.

Overall, the red vines come in at 70 per cent Grenache, 20 per cent Syrah and 10 per cent Mourvèdre, while the white vines, all planted by the Bruniers when they moved in, are one-quarter each of Clairette, Grenache Blanc, Bourboulenc and Roussanne. The Bruniers chose the light, sandy soil near Château Rayas for them, and while the vines are still young, great hopes are entertained for Roquette as a white wine *domaine* in the future.

The red wine vinification is similar to that of Vieux Télégraphe, with only a very gentle crush, and fermentation since the 1987 harvest in stainless steel; this is followed by a year's storage in concrete vats and six to eight months in large *foudres* that are about twenty years old. The white is all stainless steel-fermented, although barrel fermentation is set to commence. Bottling of the white occurs in April, fitting in after the major white wine activity at Vieux Télégraphe has finished.

There are, and will remain, distinct comparisons between the style of wines from the very well-known Vieux Télégraphe and the less well-known La Roquette. The Brunier policy is to seek wines that are not troublesome or over-weighty. The Roquette tannins appear softer and more rounded by nature than those of the brother *domaine*, so that in a vintage like 1990, different *cuvées* of the wine before final assembly showed very good, fine structure on the palate. When there was a Mourvèdre presence in the vat, extra length and greater reserve accompanied the wine; by the time it has all been put together, a final emphasis on open fruit is likely to come forward after around five or six years. The 1989 red is an extremely attractive wine in the modern style: it exudes a juicy, succulent fruitiness, and has enough flesh to indicate greater dimension on the palate around 1994 – the sort of wine that is ideal to serve in a restaurant. The 1988 has started to show some evolution on colour and nose, with a pebbly, spicy

Grenache character emerging after three years; it is less concentrated than the 1990, and is a wine to be drinking over the next two or three years.

The white, called Clos La Roquette, is still, as they say, 'starting out'. Different tastings of the 1990 indicate what one would expect from the product of such a young vineyard – a decent liveliness on the bouquet, but a lack of true depth on the palate; calling it 'simple' would be extreme, but it is clearly a wine that will develop greater width and complexity over future vintages.

Frédéric Brunier lives with his wife and young family at the Domaine de la Roquette itself in the middle of the village, and describes Roquette as 'having a different structure to Vieux Télégraphe; Daniel and I can make wines of similar aromas, but here there is less tannin, less alcohol and less general power – that's the nature of the *domaine*.' Half the Roquette production has always been sold to private clients in France, and half is now being exported to the United States, Britain and the countries of Benelux.

Brunier Frères
  SCEA La Roquette   84230 Châteauneuf-du-Pape

DOMAINE ST-BENOÎT

This is a *domaine* that has set out to improve the concentration and depth of its wine since the 1990 vintage. It is a grouping of three vineyards formed in late 1989 from the holdings of Pierre Jacumin, Marc Cellier and Paul Courtil, and runs to 26 hectares. Grenache dominates with over 70 per cent of the total plantation, supported notably by the Mourvèdre (12 per cent) and the Syrah (5 per cent).

Gérard Jacumin is working closely with Marc Cellier in the preparation of the wines, and steps have been taken to extract greater ripeness from the harvest. Previous to 1990 the wines were on the light side, with the colour of the 1987, 1988 and 1989 turning to brick early on and a lack of substance hampering their development. Three *cuvées* are made, headed by the Vieilles Vignes, from Grenache of sixty years, with a second *cuvée* of Grande Garde containing over 20 per cent Mourvèdre. Both these wines in 1990 showed a sound colour and good grip on the palate, indicating that progress is being made at the *domaine*.

A little white is made, from 45 per cent Clairette, 25 per cent

Grenache Blanc, 20 per cent Roussanne and 10 per cent Bourboulenc.

Jacumin, Pierre, Cellier, Marc,
  et Courtil, Paul
  Domaine St-Benoît   84230 Châteauneuf-du-Pape

DOMAINE DES SÉNÉCHAUX

This 30-hectare domaine is owned by the Raynaud family, whose roots at Châteauneuf go back to the mid-fourteenth century. After the Second World War the vineyards were increased to their present size by the late Pierre Raynaud, and until the late 1980s it was his son-in-law M. Roland Bensamoll who ran the property.

The *domaine* takes its name from a place 500 metres as the crow flies from the village which used to be called the Bois de Sénéscaud, now Sénéchaux. This is one of the two core vineyards, 12 hectares in total of stone-covered terrain opposite the Château de Vaudieu; it is complemented by a further 12-hectare holding, also stone covered with slightly thicker soil, next to Château La Nerthe. Before 1950 the Raynaud family would also grow cherries among these vineyards, with grandmother Raynaud selling them at the now defunct Châteauneuf-du-Pape cherry market, which ceased in the late 1970s.

The predominant vine is the Grenache Noir (70 per cent), followed by the Cinsault (10 per cent), Syrah and Mourvèdre (5 per cent each) and the remaining permitted grape varieties. They are vinified by an intriguing mixture of old and new equipment. The 1930s crusher and 1965 cooling machine stand alongside the stainless steel iso-thermal vat that is used to control temperatures. The approach is traditional, with a three-week *cuvaison* kept near 28°C in the concrete fermenting vats; after assembling the *vin de goutte* – free-run wine – with selected amounts of the *vin de presse*, the final wine remains in oak for at least eighteen months.

The Sénéchaux reds have in the past been marked by a raw heartiness of flavour, with spice elements emerging after five or six years of bottle age. The family policy was stated to be that of making wines to keep, so that even in middling years like 1980 the red was best left for seven or eight years. The wines made before the mid-1980s – notably the 1979, 1981 and 1985 – have been or are all good to drink around the ten-year mark, while the lesser vintages of 1982 and 1984 were correct, but candidates for early drinking.

Recent evidence is that the *domaine* is going through an unsettled patch, with the 1989 red lacking the depth of many of the wines of this first-rate vintage. There is also a white wine, made mainly from Grenache Blanc with support from the Roussanne, Bourboulenc and Clairette; it is not a leading example of its *genre*, but efforts are being made to improve it.

Raynaud, Annie
 Domaine des Sénéchaux 84230 Châteauneuf-du-Pape

DOMAINE DE LA SERRIÈRE

This is the Châteauneuf family *domaine* of Michel Bernard, head of Domaines Michel Bernard (q.v.), a quasi-*négociant* grouping dealing in wines of both the northern and southern Rhône. It covers 5 hectares, and was supplemented in 1988 by M. Bernard's purchase of the Château de Beauchêne, north-east of Orange. The red is largely composed of Grenache, while the white is mostly Grenache Blanc, Clairette and Bourboulenc, from vines in fairly stony terrain west of the Château de Beaucastel. With the reds, M. Bernard is seeking a certain suppleness of style, and perhaps one-quarter of the harvest enters the vats uncrushed. The 1990 white Château Beauchêne, Vignobles de la Serrière, was a plump, quite powerful wine, already rounded after a year; the 1989 red of the same name held a bright plum colour, a bouquet of evident pepperiness and a decent density on the palate: sound wine, but just missing a beat of dimension.

Bernard, Michel
 Domaine de la Serrière 84320 Châteauneuf-du-Pape

DOMAINE DE LA SOLITUDE

The over 400-year-old Domaine de la Solitude, in the ownership of M. Pierre Lançon, has for more than twenty years been a practitioner of modernism at Châteauneuf-du-Pape. Hence the vinification of the reds has been exposed to forms of *macération carbonique* since the late 1960s, and the period of the mid-1970s to mid-1980s was a particularly depressing one, as a series of watery-coloured wines were turned out which bore little resemblance to the noble name of their *appellation*. M. Lançon's sons Jean and Michel now deal more actively with the viticulture and the commercial side of the business, however, while their father resides at the family vineyard in the Gard *département*, the Château de Vallonnières, and there are signs that more authentic and enjoyable Châteauneuf-du-Pape will emerge during the 1990s from this previously good estate.

The elements for making good wine are certainly in place. The estate is in one single plot, 45 hectares in all, the 40.5 hectares of red vines made up of Grenache at 60 per cent, Syrah 15 per cent, Mourvèdre 15 per cent and increasing, with 10 per cent split between the Cinsault and diverse varieties. The Mourvèdre has been doubled since the mid-1980s, which will give the wine greater backbone, and the Cinsault is slowly being cut back. Jean Lançon mentioned that, if left to its own devices, the Cinsault is well capable of producing double the authorized amount – around 70 hectolitres per hectare.

The 4.5 hectares of white vines are also being sorted out, with the *cépage mode* here being the Roussanne, the only new white vine planted since the mid-1980s, and now standing at about 10 per cent of the white; the rest is composed of 30 per cent each of Clairette, Bourboulenc and Grenache Blanc. These vines are deliberately planted on north-facing slopes to gain greater freshness, but the Lançons prefer to place the Grenache Blanc in poor soil and the Bourboulenc in richer soil, without which it is hard to obtain full ripeness.

The estate sells two Châteauneufs – Solitude and La Jacquinotte – out of the 80 per cent it bottles. The Jacquinotte soil has less clay in it than the Solitude, but both vineyards are in some of the stoniest of all ground in the *appellation* – on a *lieu-dit* called La Côte d'Or, a plateau that stands at 70 metres.

The red vinification has been cut back from a widespread use of *macération carbonique* to about 20 per cent of the total now, which is a welcome relief. Destalking occurs if there is a lot of stalk and stem by rapport with the grapes, so that in 1991 – a *coulure*-affected year – there was destalking. Likewise, the Syrah and the Mourvèdre are destalked because they have a longer *cuvaison* than the Grenache; the Mourvèdre receives a totally traditional vinification that may last for twenty-five days, whereas the *macération carbonique* is exercised on the Grenache and the Syrah. It is noticeable that after the application of *macération carbonique*, the press wine has quite a lot of sugar in it, so caution has to be taken in assembling it with the *jus de goutte*.

Since the 1985 vintage, the *domaine* has brought in new *pièces* of Limousin oak from Marsannay. As a result there are now three containers for ageing: either the fifty new-oak casks, where around 15 per cent of the wine spends one year; or the old family *foudres*, where the wine spends six months – Jean Lançon is frightened of the taste of old wood – or stainless steel six months or so. A single wine is assembled around two years after the harvest, and bottling occurs after filtration and some fining.

Jean Lançon's view of new oak is uncluttered: 'I'm increasing its use gradually,' he says. 'It adds tannins, burnt aromas, vanilla, and helps the aromas to develop more. There is also a more sustained colour with new oak.' A stairway to heaven for him, perhaps?

The red Solitude has taken a turn for the better, providing its local character can wriggle out from under the new oak mantle that is being flung down upon it. The 1990 is a sleek wine, with decent depth on the palate and some lurking cherry-style fruitiness – it is likely to need three or four years to integrate and will become a sound, modern Châteauneuf around 1996. The 1989 is well balanced, and although the Grenache is a little hidden, it shows the promise to open up around 1994 with safe fruits that are not too wild or markedly local in flavour and texture. It is a marked improvement on some past wines, however. Of earlier vintages, the 1985 red has held its colour well, and is a complete, soft wine now, with signs of complexity creeping in as it ages. Previous to this there are the quite glorious wines of years like 1964, 1967, 1969 and 1971 to track down, although they will be tired if they have not been well stored.

The white Solitude is fermented at around 20°C, and bottled early in the New Year, with the malolactic treated according to the style of the vintage. Thus in 1989 and 1990 – hot, ripe years – it was blocked, while in the cooler year of 1987 the malolactic was allowed to do itself. The white production is being aimed to increase towards 15 per cent of the total, and the wine is fresh and sound in the modern way, although the fruit sometimes lacks a little definition and can be a bit 'fuzzy'.

Like some of their neighbours in the Gard *département* across the Rhône, the Lançons are showing great interest in white wine-making, and at their Château de Vallonnières have planted Viognier and Roussanne to accompany the Clairette and Grenache Blanc. For the Viognier they chose the poorest possible ground – large stones on a plateau near Sabran, while for the Roussanne the site selected was particularly well aerated to avoid any potential problems of rot.

Domaine de la Solitude was one of the first estates at Châteauneuf to bottle part of its wine, and it is good to see efforts now being made to re-galvanize it somewhat. The first record of bottling goes back to 1815, when the then owner Paul Clair Martin returned from the Battle of Waterloo with the highly prized Croix de la Légion d'Honneur. He proceeded to work full-time on his vineyard and in 1827 despatched five 265-litre barrels to Greenwood and Butler of England. Although the *domaine* was then making both white and red wines, the English preferred the red and would receive what was termed '*Vin Rouge de la Solitude*', a name that had already appeared on the first bottle labels.

GAEC Lançon Père et Fils
   Domaine de la Solitude   84230 Châteauneuf-du-Pape

DOMAINE DE TERRE FERME

The 25-hectare property of this name, formerly owned by the Bérard family of Bédarrides, was bought by the Château La Nerthe in 1991; the vineyard lies between La Nerthe and the Domaine du Vieux Télégraphe, and much of its soil is clay–limestone covered in large *galet* stones. The La Nerthe purchase involved only red vines – Grenache, Syrah, Mourvèdre principally, and the wine from here will henceforth be sold as Château La Nerthe, forming part of the overall Nerthe vineyard and production.

In the mid-1980s the *négociant* side was sold to M. Robert Dahm, and the white vine content was included in this deal. The 1990 Domaine de Terre Ferme, containing as usual a strong percentage of Grenache Blanc, upheld the tradition of this property supplying one of the better white Châteauneufs, a full wine with ample flavours that will drink well in its first two or three years. The red Terre Ferme 1989 is also full and well coloured, but its fruit lacks clarity; the wine is just a little stewed, and should drink well around 1993.

Pierre Bérard died in the early 1990s, and Jacques, his son, is now in his sixties, with no one to take over the succession – hence the sale to La Nerthe. In his time Jacques has provided much entertainment as well as considerable tasting expertise in front of his fellow *vignerons*, and was a supporter of the use of *macération carbonique* on the Syrah and Mourvèdre, but not on the Grenache. Under the new arrangements, red Terre Ferme will disappear, but the white will continue.

Domaine de Terre Ferme   84370 Bédarrides

DOMAINE DE LA VIEILLE JULIENNE

This 10-hectare *domaine*'s vineyards are concentrated in the northern end of the *appellation*, in the well-known *quartier* of Le Grès, on the way to Orange. Seven of the hectares lie around the domaine itself.

The soil is generally dense, with a predominance of red clay and the large *galet* stones.

The average age of the vineyards is fifty-five years, with some turn-of-the-century Grenache dotted around the *domaine*. The vine mix for the red is 70 per cent Grenache, 10 per cent each Syrah and Mourvèdre, 5 per cent Cinsault, and 5 per cent split between Counoise, Clairette, Bourboulenc and Picpoul.

Maxime Daumen only makes red wine; he likes to vinify the Syrah, Mourvèdre and Cinsault apart, and after about a ten-day *cuvaison* in the *domaine's* enamel-lined vats, the wine is assembled and aged in 50 hectolitre *foudres* for twelve to eighteen months, according to the style of the vintage.

The Vieille Julienne red is a consistent wine over the vintages, and a good representative of the Grenache-inspired school of Châteauneuf. The 1989 was very good, for example, with a firm, spicy bouquet and notably well-ripened flavours on the palate. It held a long finish, and promises to be an eight- to eleven-year wine. The *domaine* also makes red and white Côtes du Rhône.

GAEC Daumen Père et Fils
   Domaine de la Vieille Julienne 84100 Orange

DOMAINE DU VIEUX LAZARET

This is a very large estate, its 82 hectares spread across thirty-five *parcelles*, while another 4 hectares will come into production by 1994. This new area is on the plateau des Combes, towards Roquemaure in the Gard, on chalky soil, and used to be one of the old locations for the owner Jérôme Quiot's *chasse*, which for a Provençal is something of a dilemma – wine or game.

The red wine is made from Grenache (75 per cent), Syrah (15 per cent), and Mourvèdre and Cinsault (5 per cent each). The *domaine* takes the *triage* or discard very seriously; it is first done in the vineyards with the harvesters guided beside the tractors as to what should stay and what should go. And then there is a further discard once the wine has been made, bringing the total *triage* in some years past 20 per cent.

The approach at Vieux Lazaret is modern and commercial. Destalking is practised on the Syrah more than on the Grenache, and the aim is to provide an easy-to-drink wine rather than anything backward and testing. The wine of individual *cépages* is assembled at the end of the year, is filtered and then spends a little time in wood. Before 1987 there was no wood-ageing, but now about 10 per cent of the final wine spends two to five months in new casks from Burgundy. This is encouraging, and much needed, since some of these wines have leaned heavily towards a light fruitiness without much underlying depth and regional stamp.

The 1987 red, for instance, should be drunk around 1992 – a middle-weight wine, it will be pleasant but never startling. The 1988, bottled like all the reds one year after the harvest, is a soft, rounded wine with decent balance but not much impact. It has some length on the palate, and is likely to show at its best around 1993–5. The 1989 spent longer in wood and has a better structure, more depth and greater promise for development over ten years or so: its fruitiness is particularly exuberant. The 1990 holds a middling colour and a bouquet with some potential and a cherry-type fruitiness on the palate supported by some gentle tannins: this is a typical Vieux Lazaret wine, very rounded in style, and will drink well around its fourth birthday.

Since 1989 the estate has also made, bottled and marketed the red wine of Domaine Duclaux, a 12-hectare property owned by a close friend of the Quiot family. This is composed of 73 per cent Grenache supported principally by Mourvèdre (11 per cent), Cinsault (8 per cent) and Syrah (6 per cent). The 1989 and 1990 both have a bit more backbone than the Vieux Lazaret wines, and the 1990 in particular is ample *en bouche*, with a certain generosity on the bouquet and on the finish that lends character. This wine is not as yet exposed to cask-ageing.

Vieux Lazaret's white Châteauneuf forms about 10 per cent of the production, and is made from 30 per cent each of Bourboulenc,

Clairette and Grenache Blanc, with a final 10 per cent of younger Roussanne vines. In 1990 a part of the Roussanne crop was vinified in cask before being integrated into the end wine, a trend that will continue. With the malolactic blocked, it is bottled in various reprises from mid-December through to May. It is an arch exponent of the fresh, low-temperature school, with a hint of subtle weight on the palate: a wine to drink in its first two years only.

Mme Quiot's family also own a 42-hectare *domaine* in Provence near Puyloubier, and their best wine is a very drinkable Domaine de Hilaire Houchart rosé, composed of 60 per cent Cinsault.

Apart from the Domaine du Vieux Lazaret, two brands circulate for this estate's Châteauneuf: Les Couversets goes to one supermarket chain in Britain, and Les Arnevels goes to another.

Famille J. R. Quiot
   Domaine du Vieux Lazaret   84230 Châteauneuf-du-Pape

DOMAINE DU VIEUX TÉLÉGRAPHE

The 60-hectare Domaine du Vieux Télégraphe has risen to the front rank in Châteauneuf since the early 1970s and consistently turns out elegant, clean and well-vinified wines: in some years the red is top-class, although during the 1980s there was a conscious policy of producing a ripe, succulent style of wine, rather than anything too upright and backward. Since the 1983 vintage, the white has developed into one of the best in the *appellation*. The Bruniers also own the Domaine de la Roquette (q.v.), which is run by Henri's son Frédéric.

The estate name is taken from a site on the plateau near Bédarrides where in 1793 Claude Chappe, the inventor of the optical telegraph system, built a tower to help with his experiments. Wine-making here was started by Henri Brunier's grandfather Hippolyte in 1900; soon afterwards he was bottling his own wine and taking it to fairs in Germany, Belgium and Switzerland. The family are proud of their winning of a gold medal at the first National Culinary and Gastronomic Exhibition held in Paris in 1927. But then family politics intervened, and Henri Brunier's father and uncle fell out with one another.

Henri Brunier tells this intimate family story with the air of a seasoned pro, a man who even well before he entered his sixties was able to cope with the comings and goings of people and their whims and prejudices. He has now eased into a back seat behind his two sons in their early thirties, but is still around enough to ensure that nothing goes wrong, and gently to reveal some of the fortunes that have befallen him earlier in life.

The vineyards of the Domaine du Vieux Télégraphe

'My uncle went off with the Vieux Télégraphe name and about 4 hectares and then did a deal with Louis Reynaud of Château Rayas to have him use the name and look after the vines. I was about fifteen at the time, and knew that my uncle liked to go to Avignon to promenade and admire the pretty girls; I wanted to sort this matter out, so went off to Avignon and made sure that my uncle bumped into me as I walked along the main avenue. We agreed on a rendezvous to discuss family matters, which resulted in my uncle arranging the transfer of the Vieux Télégraphe name and the vineyard back to me from M. Reynaud. This was about 1940, and I think the arrangement with Rayas had lasted for about ten years. The curious thing is that until we told Jacques Reynaud this story after his father's death, he knew absolutely nothing about this previous connection between our two properties.'

It is little surprise that a teenager of such resolve and initiative made a success of the Vieux Télégraphe he reclaimed. M. Brunier extended the vineyard and reshuffled its line-up of *cépages*. In the early 1990s, this stood at 70 per cent Grenache, and 15 per cent each of Syrah and Mourvèdre. In the last five years, the Mourvèdre has been increased, to the detriment of the Cinsault. Daniel Brunier commented that this process started in 1987: 'We took out roughly fifty-year-old Cinsault since we found it only gave concentrated juice about one year in five. While it can bring finesse and good balance, it is a natural overproducer – which dilutes its juice – and it also suffers from the *ver de la grappe*, grape-worm.' The now enlarged Brunier vineyards are on the windswept plateau of Crau covered by some of the densest gatherings of typical Châteauneuf stones – heaps and heaps of purple-tinted *galets* are strewn all over the site.

Since 1979, the Bruniers have worked with a cellar that, in its earliest days, represented a radical modernization for Châteauneuf. Their harvest receiving holders run along rails between two lines of stainless steel fermenting vats, so grapes from the same load can be emptied into different vats if desired. This also gives the option of introducing uncrushed harvest into the vats by gravity rather than by a more violent pumping. The degree of crushing of the harvest has varied over the years at Vieux Télégraphe, and seems to be an important factor in determining the final style of wine. In the early 1980s – when the 1982, 1983 and 1984 vintages resulted in lighter wines than usual – Henri Brunier was one of the early practitioners of the *raisin entier* system of leaving up to 30 per cent of his crop uncrushed. But during the mid 1980s, the *domaine* reverted to a steady crush for the whole crop with the stated aim of seeking a wine with greater depth. By the early 1990s, the crop is 'about half crushed, with no destalking', according to Daniel Brunier.

Fermentation takes place in the stainless steel vats for around two weeks and the young wine is then transferred to concrete vats for about a year; the *vin de presse* is always added to the *vin de goutte*, the first wine, to bring a bit of structure and tannin. But the days of using a Vaslin press are over – the system has been pneumatic and much gentler throughout the 1980s.

The stay in wood has been cut back in a big way here. 'In the late 1970s, I would leave the wine for about two years', says Henri

Brunier, his sometimes distracted air leading him to break off during a tasting to sweep clean part of the cellar, whistling rustically as he busies himself about, 'but we have cut back to around ten months and now, in 1991, to six to eight months. I judge that extra time in the past to have brought in more oxidation than positive elements.'

Neither father nor sons are in favour of new oak; their ageing *foudres* are 'probably ten to forty years old'. But they are well aware of the need to rotate and renew these barrels, so there is a quiet replacement policy to avoid any dryness inserted into the wine by exposure to excessively old *foudre* wood.

M. Henri Brunier

In any given year, about 85 per cent of the Vieux Télégraphe wine is bottled; the rest is sold in cask to *négociants*. There is no pre-bottling filtration; this has occurred before the stay in wood. The total process therefore takes about eighteen to twenty months; the 1987 spent just six months in cask and was bottled earlier then the fuller 1989, for instance; the latter spent eight months in cask.

When striving to judge the Vieux Télégraphe wines and summarize their style, one is dealing with something of a moving target. A 1978 red drunk in 1991 bore a classically complex Châteauneuf bouquet – aromas of cedar, prune present – and the palate held round, firm flavours and an intensity that indicated further development with time. A 1981 drunk in 1991 was also holding itself together well on the palate, with rich, ripe flavours and a solid structure. Both wines had a hint of ruby in the colour. But policy has consciously changed since those days. Daniel Brunier explains: 'In the past, our tannins were more severe; we had longer macerations, and never destemmed. We think our wines have more aroma and balance now, and want them to show well after six to nine years. We fully recognize that this marks a change of style here over the past fifteen years.'

In the second half of the 1980s, the *domaine* tightened its grip over those wines made in the 1982–5 era. But the fact is that this property is now supplying fruity, ripe and rich wines that have a plump appeal, and an ease and accessibility about them, which for some drinkers makes them less interesting, less multi-dimensional if you like. The emphasis is on a luscious fruitiness, and the style fits somewhere between a Beaucastel and a Rayas at one extreme and a Domaine de Nalys or a Vieux Lazaret at the other: they are softer and less complex than the first two, and more solid and thorough than the last two.

Looking back over other years, the 1979 was a chewy, tannic wine that is now drinking very well, and could soldier on for a few years more. The 1980 was finely balanced, with much wild blackcurrant fruit – extremely elegant and a great success in a difficult year; it now should be drunk up. The 1982 was one of the better wines of this tricky vintage, suitable for early drinking, while the 1983 and 1984 were both mid-weight wines, more fruity than substantial and a little disappointing for that, with quite rapid evolution.

The 1985 had greater depth, but the emphasis once more was on a flattering early fruitiness – a very up-front sort of wine with not much mystery about it. The taste of concentrated black fruits held early appeal, but the wine should not be specially cellared, since it lacks potential to become more complex and more interesting. The 1986 was endowed with greater tannic content, even though the style of tannin was lean rather than round, which was much a product of the vintage. This is slowly settling down and losing some of its raw flavours and will drink well around 1992–7. The 1987 was, like many of its vintage, a delicate wine but has enough extraction to show well around 1991–3.

The 1988 held greater structure and backbone than these earlier wines. After three years, there was a certain evolution on the bouquet, but there is a long finish on the palate and enough quiet tannins to ensure that it will not only drink well immediately, but will show well towards 1995 or so. The 1989 was bigger and fuller than the 1985, and has a sweet, rounded texture; the fruit is very ripe and it is likely to be what the French call '*sphérique*' around 1995: a delicious, easy wine, but one lacking a little self-expression.

The 1990 has sterner support than the 1989; it carries more alcohol (perhaps 14.3°C against 14°), and is darkly scented on the bouquet. Overall it is an elegant offering – the emphasis is on style in the modern way, where there is plenty of round fruit with some tannic support. It should drink well around 1997 or so.

Henri Brunier remembers his father making 500 or 600 bottles of white each year, mainly for the family, and in 1980 he decided to take the white more seriously. There are now 3.5 hectares out of the sixty devoted to white *cépages*, with another 2 hectares due for plantation in the spring of 1993, after the clearing of some untilled land. The oldest and most prolific vine is the Clairette (40 per cent), with some sixty-year-old plants; this is followed by the Grenache Blanc (30 per cent) and the Bourboulenc and Roussanne with 15 per cent each. The area chosen for the white vines contains more limestone in the soil, and more sand, and a gradual transfer of the white vines away from the stoniest areas of the clay plateau will occur over the coming years.

A recent development has been the vinification of the 15 per cent Roussanne in casks of three to four years' age. The Bruniers contend that this gives the wine just a bit more complexity and *noblesse*, but they do not like to expose the Clairette and Grenache Blanc to wood, since, like many other local *vignerons*, they fear a fast oxidation from such treatment.

The other Brunier tactic is, as with their cousins at Font-de-Michelle, an early harvesting of the white crop. Their plateau of Crau near Bédarrides in the east is high enough to encourage a faster ripening than elsewhere in the *appellation*. Since the early 1990s they have also raised the fermentation temperature from about 16–18°C to 20°C to obtain more interesting scents. The cask-fermented wine is introduced into the mainstream stainless steel-fermented lot in November, and the final wine is bottled in January, with the malolactic blocked for freshness.

The Vieux Télégraphe whites have progressed outstandingly during the 1980s. Take the lighter years of 1984 and 1987, which serve to display the wine-making skills of the Bruniers to the full (ask any switched-on grower what he sees as his greatest challenge and many say 'mastering the making of white wine down here'): the 1984 developed stunning secondary flavours like dried apricot and nuts after eighteen months, and its gradual and steady flourishing in the bottle revealed continued ripe fruitiness with just a hint of fragility on the finish when tasted in the autumn of 1991; similarly the 1987 has done well with age, and certainly both wines were helped by higher acidity levels in those years. The 1986 after four years gained tremendous fullness on the bouquet, an opulence that would have been hard to envisage when tasting it young. Full, but well balanced on the palate, it finishes cleanly. The 1988 is a firmer wine, with its flavours more tightly knit, but it shows the promise of greater aromas and softness if given four to six years. The 1989 was very well balanced, with its fruit extract indicating well the ripe nature of the flavours derived from a very healthy harvest: this is a wine that will develop consistently over the course of perhaps five to eight years, and possesses a bit more balance than the 1990; while the latter carries lovely, complex dried fruit aromas like apricots on the bouquet even when young, its power and length on the palate do not appear to hold great permanence. The lack of acidity shown by several of the 1990 whites may yet haunt it.

Vieux Télégraphe is one of the best-travelled Châteauneufs; 85 per cent of it is exported, principally to the United States, Britain, Switzerland, Canada and the Benelux countries. As such, the red acts as something of a yardstick for many drinkers of Châteauneuf. What needs to be emphasized, however, is that it is a yardstick for the modern, sleek version of the wine, one that is some way removed from the robust, powerful, Grenache-dominated offerings coming from the many traditional medium and smallholder *vignerons*. It's well worth trying both styles with different foods and perhaps different friends.

Brunier, Henri, et Fils
   Domaine du Vieux Télégraphe   84370 Bédarrides

PÈRE ANSELME

This is an influential company in the affairs of Châteauneuf-du-Pape, and it is fair to say that the better its work in the vinification and raising of wines from Châteauneuf and the southern Rhône, the better the general image of the area will be in far-flung parts of the world. Since the second half of the 1980s, a revitalization has occurred, through greater identification with individual *domaines* and their wines, as well as the development of *cuvées* that are unusual and challenging within the southern Rhône, such as one of the white Viognier grape, with around 3,000 cases of this sold as Vin de Pays d'Oc.

The company works under two brand names – Brotte (Laurent

Charles) and Père Anselme. The firm was set up by Charles Brotte in 1931, and is now run by the tanned, debonair Jean-Pierre and his son Laurent, a very likeable young man who is evidently keen to move the company along. The Brotte brand name has in the past been aimed especially at the hotel and restaurant trade inside France. The company sells 2 million bottles of all Rhône wines each year, and its proportion of Châteauneuf exceeds 15 per cent of the total production.

Greater identification with single *domaines* – a very sound commercial move if the company wanted to edge its profile and status higher – first occurred via an old agreement dating back to the mid-1970s with the Domaine de la Petite Bastide of M. Diffonty for part distribution of his wine. In 1985, an arrangement to guide the vinification and run the export of the wines of the Domaine François Laget started, and in 1989 a similar system started with the 7-hectare Clos Bimard, a 90 per cent Grenache *domaine* standing to the west of the village. Finally, since 1988 there has been a single selected *cuvée* bought in, called the Cuvée Prestige, which is a top-of-the-line wine.

Recent tastings show that this *domaine*-led policy is helping to raise the quality of the wines much nearer to the sound, individual style of the private *domaine* owners who form the basis of Châteauneuf. The Clos Bimard 1989, for instance, held a dark plum colour, a sustained, well-ripened fruitiness on the bouquet, and a good mix of fruit and stuffing on the palate that ended in a satisfactory liquorice-inspired finish. This is an eight- to ten-year wine. The Cuvée Prestige of 1989 was also good – perhaps a shade superior, with a clearer fruitiness, good harmony on the palate and the prospect of drinking very enjoyably around five to eight years old. Meanwhile the other Châteauneuf *cuvées* receive around two years' ageing in 40- to 50-hectolitre *foudres* before release.

The company also works with as many as ten Côtes du Rhône Villages, headed by their Séguret, where they have an exclusivity in the production of the Château de la Font du Jonquier. In 1991, the Laudun domaine of Château Le Bord in the Gard was bought, bringing 8 hectares of vines whose wine is softer in style than many of those from the Vaucluse. 'Reds from places like Vacqueyras and Rasteau have a very marked, firm southern Rhône style,' comments Jean-Pierre Brotte. 'Séguret is approachable, and in their soft way so are St-Gervais and Laudun from the Gard.'

Underneath the Villages hierarchy come wines such as those from the Côtes du Rhône Domaine de la Grivelière, a 25-hectare property near St Géniès-de-Comolas in the Gard where the principal varieties are Grenache, Mourvèdre and Cinsault: the red here receives six months in cask. Alone with the ambitious plans to launch the Viognier from the Gard *département* to a wider audience, Père Anselme seems to be gearing itself up to become a very serious player in the high quality–high quantity Rhône stakes during the 1990s.

Two final distinguishing features exist at this company: one is their own special bottle, the 'Fiole du Pape', created in 1956 with a distorted shape and a covering of artificial dust that simulates great age – tasteful for some. There is also a Museum of Wine-makers' Utensils, featuring old presses, ploughs and tools, which is open seven days a week, at the company's premises in the village.

Père Anselme   84230 Châteauneuf-du-Pape

PRESTIGE ET TRADITION

Prestige et Tradition is an association of eleven growers who share bottling and storing premises. Their vineyard holdings are not generally large, averaging between eight and twelve hectares, and for this reason it has proved all the more economical for them to divide the overhead costs necessary for bottling and holding stock. These are traditional smaller growers' vineyards, with heavy emphasis placed on the Grenache, and the style of wine made is mostly time-honoured – backward, robust and tannic when young, with a dense matt red colour. In the best vintages such as 1981 and 1989, these wines need five or six years before starting to show their true worth, and should generally be drunk before they are twelve years old. The practitioners of this approach are MM. Barrot, Jean and his nephew Lucien (q.v.), Boiron (q.v.), Jouffron and Michel (q.v.). Three of the last-named *domaines* – the Lucien Barrot, the Bosquet des Papes and the Vieux Donjon – are generally the best of the grouping, with the Bosquet des Papes being one of the longest-lived red Châteauneufs. A lighter but authentic local style is sought by MM. Jeune, Jouffron, Laget, Mestre and Pécoul, while the very modern approach is undertaken by MM. Lançon and Revoltier. The Lançon wines since 1985 have shown greater depth, however.

Barrot, Jean
  Cuvée du Hurlevent
Barrot, Lucien
  Domaine Lucien Barrot
Boiron, Maurice
  Le Bosquet des Papes
Jeune, Jean
  Clos de la Cerise
Jouffron, René, et Fils
  Réserve des Cardinaux
Laget, Marie
  Domaine de l'Arnesque   84230 Châteauneuf-du-Pape
Lançon, Pierre, et Fils
  Domaine de la Solitude
Mestre, Jacques
  La Cuvée des Sommeliers
Michel, Louis
  Le Vieux Donjon
Pécoul Frères
  La Cuvée des Bosquets
Revoltier, Joseph et Fils
  Domaine de Farguerol

LES REFLETS

This is an association of growers founded in 1954 to bottle, condition and store the wine of each grower under the same roof. Since its inception Les Reflets has done much to further the name of Châteauneuf-du-Pape, led by the three *domaines* Les Cailloux, Chante-Perdrix and Clos du Mont-Olivet (q.v.). The Les Cailloux is the lightest, most stylish and approachable wine of the three, its strength of flavour having lessened under André Brunel. The Chante-Perdrix and Mont-Olivet are both discussed elsewhere. The remaining wines are generally well made and typical of traditional, Grenache-inspired Châteauneuf. The Domaine de la Solitude may be returning towards a weightier style capable of living for eight-plus years, but its wines were in the wilderness from 1975 to 1985. The Domaine Perges makes good Grenache-inspired wine which in firm vintages like 1983 and 1988 is good to drink around eight to ten years old. The 1989 is a wine which combines density and good style, and will show very well around 1996.

The members of Les Reflets are:

Brunel, Lucien
  Les Cailloux
Descarrega, Charles
  Les Cabanes
Girard, Robert
  Cuvée du Belvédère Le Boucou
Lançon, Pierre, et Fils
  Domaine de la Solitude   } 84230 Châteauneuf-du-Pape
Nicolet Frères, et Fils
  Domaine Chante-Perdrix
Nicolet, Lucette et Fréderic
  Domaine Perges
Sabon, Les Fils de Joseph
  Clos du Mont-Olivet

LE VIEUX DONJON

This is a very traditional 13-hectare *père-en-fils domaine* that is part of the Prestige et Tradition grouping. Lucien Michel relies on the Grenache for 85 per cent of his red, with support from the Syrah and Cinsault. Mourvèdre has been planted, and his holdings spread over eight *parcelles*.

Part of the vineyard comes from Lucien Michel's wife's family, and at forty-six, M. Michel has harvesters picking his grapes who have come every year for forty years and knew him as a baby. M. Michel is not in favour of applying artificial treatments to his vines, nor does he filter his wines, which are aged for around fifteen months in wood.

The Vieux Donjon wines have always been stout and stalwart examples of traditional Châteauneuf. In the 1960s this *domaine* was making very robust *cuvées*, and the tradition has been continued with a slight tilt towards elegance by Lucien Michel. The 1986 red is a full wine, but needs until about 1993 to settle and soften some of its raw power. The 1987 is a correct wine, light and pleasant for drinking over six to eight years. The 1988 is middle-weight, just lacking a shade of thoroughness on the palate, while the 1989 is a big, dark wine, with excellent fruitiness on the bouquet and plenty of richness in it. It combines good depth with an elegant finish, and has a life of twelve years or more in prospect.

Michel, Lucien
  Le Vieux Donjon   84230 Châteauneuf-du-Pape

Châteauneuf-du-Pape Vintages

The vintage chart that follows is intended as a broad guide to the whole of Châteauneuf-du-Pape. It is very difficult to be exact for the whole *appellation*, since its large size means that vintages can differ substantially from one area to the next. Results vary too according to which grape varieties are grown, the method of vinification and the time for ageing in the wood as practised by different *domaines*. As an extra guideline, therefore, specific *domaines* have occasionally been quoted.

1955   A very good vintage. The wines were both richly flavoured and well balanced. They are now generally over the top.

1956   Generally a very mediocre vintage. Disappointing, light wines.

1957   A very good but tannic year that took a long time to come round. Many of the wines are now past their best, with the fading of their colour and flavours bringing an unmasking of the alcohol. There was a famous Domaine de Mont-Redon, which when last drunk in 1989 was well advanced, with a precarious richness still apparent among a host of coffee and toasted aromas – this contained 80 per cent Grenache, like the 1961, as opposed to the nearer 65 per cent level of the early 1990s. The Clos du Mont-Olivet still has some richness in it, and very satisfying gamey or fungal aromas on the bouquet.

1958   A very poor vintage.

1959   A very good year, although lighter and less complete than 1955 or 1957. The wines failed to match the very high standards of the northern Côtes du Rhône, but certain vineyards – notably Château Rayas and Clos du Mont-Olivet – produced excellent red and white wine. The reds softened out very well with ageing but should now be drunk without delay.

1960   A very ordinary year. The wines were considered undistinguished by many growers, and only the very best were ever bottled. The Château Fortia was a well-crafted wine.

1961   A superb vintage, the best since 1945, and only possibly rivalled by the 1978 since. The wines fulfilled many *vignerons'* highest expectations: rich in colour and flavour, they had tremendous balance and grace, and the most traditionally made, such as Beaucastel, Rayas, Clos de l'Oratoire des Papes and Mont-Redon, are still showing well. Most striking are the subtle prune and coffee aromas on the nose, and the splendid wave of rich, spiced flavours that presents itself on the attack shortly after opening. There is very great length in these exceptional wines, and while a certain drying-out is starting, they can still drink well past 1996.

1962   A very good year that was inevitably overshadowed by 1961: the crop was large and very healthy – Henri Brunier of Vieux Télégraphe harvested grapes with the equivalent alcohol of 14°5 on 3 September, but recalls that he could have started on 28 August – a record. The wines were powerful and well balanced. They should be drunk up soon. A notable year at Vieux Télégraphe and at Château Rayas – the white Vieux Télégraphe (80 per cent Grenache Blanc, 20 per cent Clairette, cask-fermented) has gone through the thirty year barrier in fine style.

1963   Extremely poor.

1964   An excellent vintage of limited quantity. The wines were very full and well coloured, but have now softened out and are starting to lose their grip. There is some residual richness on the aftertaste, but for many of the wines, the game is up. An outstanding year at the Domaine de la Solitude, while the Château de Beaucastel red was rich and still sustained itself well in 1991.

1965   A weak, disappointing vintage.

1966   Very good. Sound and quite full-bodied wines, although they lacked a little of the all-round charm of the 1964s and 1967s. They are now waning, although the biggest wines, such as those from Clos du Mont-Olivet, Clos des Papes and Beaucastel, are showing the gentle, rich and still sustained flavours of well-aged Châteauneuf. Consider drinking soon.

1967   An excellent vintage; with 1978, 1981 and 1989, the best since 1961. Very tannic and full of dark promise in their youth, the wines developed a many-sided fullness and harmony. Their length is most impressive, but time is catching up with them, and they are likely to be best drunk before around 1995. Those that stand out as still showing well are Château Rayas, Jaboulet's Les Cèdres, Lucien Brunel's Les Cailloux, Domaine Élie, Armenier, Mont-Redon and Clos du Mont-Olivet.

1968   Mediocre. Generally light wines, although the red Beaucastel was carefully selected and resulted in a light but well-knit wine – certainly a leader in the vintage.

1969   A good and, in places, very good year. The quality of the wines varied according to which *quartier* they were from, but some of the best, such as Château Fortia, Les Clefs d'Or and Château de la Gardine, developed intriguing, complex bouquets. With time the alcohol has emerged, while the palates are soft and at times tenuous. These wines need drinking forthwith. The excellent Château Rayas is still in fine form, marked by wonderfully softened flavours and great length of finish.

1970   A very good vintage, although not quite up to the standard of 1967. Strongly scented and rich in flavour, the wines have now advanced to show some of the damp, truffly flavours of age. The most typical Grenache-dominated wines are still motoring along if well cellared, only slowly ceding some of their power. Recent tastings of the very good Clos des Papes and Domaine Élie Armenier (now Marcoux) indicate that the best wines should run towards the mid-1990s.

1971   Generally a very good vintage. The classically made wines developed very well, but have started to lose their vigour and fruit, and show signs of slipping. The best still have a residual southern warmth, however. Wines made in the brand new, lighter style, like those from the Domaines of Beaurenard, Nalys and La Solitude, were particularly successful.

1972   Good. The wines were well perfumed and charming. They should be drunk soon.

1973   A large crop inevitably tended to reduce quality and the result was wines that were only 'medium to good'. The wines were often short on colour and bouquet, and only occasional bottles will still be in good order.

1974 Good. The wines were fine – discreetly scented and well endowed with fruit and tannin in their early days. They were very good to drink in their first ten to twelve years. The most successful wines from *domaines* like Beaucastel and Rayas are now showing at or near their peak.

1975 Generally a poor vintage. Certain parts of the *appellation*, such as the Domaine de Beaucastel, were affected by hail, while those growers who were able to harvest normally found their wines deficient in colour and body. By contrast, wines made in the modern style, such as those from the *domaines* of La Solitude and Nalys, proved very good for early drinking.

1976 A good vintage, although quality varied. The harvest looked like being excellent until the advent of rains in September. Some *cuvées* were therefore light, while others lacked acidity. The vintage has not worked out as well as hoped, and the best wines, such as those from Château Fortia, Domaine de Beaucastel and Domaine de Mont-Redon, should be drunk.

1977 Mediocre. The wines improved with age, however. Although light on colour and extract, some attractive, aromatic *cuvées* emerged. Drink up. Château de la Nerte provided a well-extracted red.

1978 Excellent. The best vintage at Châteauneuf in the last twenty years, fuller and more complex than harvests since. The nearest vintage in style is the 1989. The wines have an intense black-cherry colour that has held well. There is an attractive lustre on the *robe*, while the bouquets are massive and opulent. Very well balanced, there is so much depth of rich flavour and concentration that these enormous wines will live into the next century. The fullest *cuvées* are marked by great fruit, warm spicy flavours and amounts of still-brooding tannin that prop them up. Notable wines came from Vieux Télégraphe (much denser than their current style), Fortia, Beaucastel (both enormous, power-packed wines with excellent ageing prospects), de la Nerte, Les Cailloux, Clos du Mont-Olivet, Les Clefs d'Or, Vaudieu, Domaine de la Tour St-Michel, Le Bosquet des Papes, Montpertuis, Grand Tinel and Château Mont-Redon.

1979 A sound vintage where a large harvest produced medium-weight wines that are now in full evolution. They are generally very well scented, and although some *domaines* came up with unbalanced *cuvées*, the best wines, such as those from Domaine de Nalys, Clos des Papes, Beaucastel, Beaurenard, Montpertuis, Rayas, Fortia, la Gardine, Mont-Olivet and Château des Fines Roches, show great charm and elegance through their simple fusion of fruit and tannin and the openness of their flavours. They are now mostly drinking at or near their best, with great length on the palate, but should continue to retain their lovely, spicy warmth for another few years yet.

1980 This has become a generally very good, underrated vintage. Flowering was late, the summer for the most part undistinguished. But a very fine autumn saved the day, and despite the large harvest, the growers brought in a crop that gave darkly coloured wines. Many of these remained tough and uncompromising in their first years, with stern dark fruit hiding within a tannic surround and bouquets slow to reveal spicy aromas. It is as if this vintage never really had a youth, since it has now emerged into a creditable, softer and more integrated middle age, with the best wines showing well – notably those from the Domaine du Vieux Télégraphe, Beaurenard, the exceptional Château de la Gardine, Domaine Pierre André, Domaine Durieu, the Cuvée du Tastevin, a transformed Domaine de Beaucastel and Les Cailloux. Very complete, well-balanced whites were made by the Domaine de Nalys, Domaine de Mont-Redon and Domaine de Beaucastel.

1981 A very good, often excellent vintage that has emerged from the shadows as the wines have developed in taking style. The summer months were too dry for a balanced ripening of the fruit and a smallish crop needed some selection by the growers. The wines were soundly coloured when the best *cuvées* emerged, but several of them seemed dogged by a lack of balance, relatively high acidity and very firm tannins. After ten years they had started to come together extremely well, showing that it never pays to write off a vintage completely. They now reveal good, firm structures and underlying richness, as well as the prospect of a long life and splendid development. Wines to note in this year of firm flavours and drier tannins are Chante-Perdrix, Domaine Durieu (twenty years), Les Cailloux (a twelve-year wine), an already quite well-evolved Château Rayas, Grand Tinel (twenty years possible), an excellent Clos des Papes, the Domaine du Pegaü (sixteen years-plus), Château de Vaudieu, a backward Château La Nerthe, Le Bosquet des Papes, Château Mont-Redon, Vieux Télégraphe and the quite outstanding Beaucastel, the last-named one of the best single Châteauneufs made in the past dozen years: a wine of quite exceptional structure, density and class, one with an outstanding future running into the next century.

1982   A very large crop, the product of a fine flowering and a very warm summer, produced only average wines. One of the major pitfalls was the heat at harvest-time, which meant that vats lacking access to cooling equipment fermented at dizzy temperatures. The result was a stewed fruit aspect or jamminess in many of the wines, a lack of clean fruit and varietal definition. The wines have a fragile balance, mid-red colours and should be drunk without delay on the whole, since there is a lack of body to support what in some wines is a heady alcohol degree of 14° or more. Good red *cuvées* in the circumstances were made by Clos du Mont-Olivet and Les Clefs d'Or. Paul Avril is rightly proud of his white, which by 1991 held strong almond and citrus aromas on the bouquet and great depth and complexity of flavour, culminating in a long, persistent finish – something of a one-off white that will live towards the end of the 1990s.

1983   A small harvest, affected by *coulure* on the Grenache, produced some very good wines, but also some only average *cuvées* from certain growers. Fearful of repeating the heavy alcohol content of 1982, some growers picked too early, and harvesting was further complicated by rain and poor weather. This led to unevenness in the quality of the wines, some of which started to lose their grip after nine years' ageing. The best wines are notable for a still-balanced structure, and a quietening of the tannins that has loosened them up earlier than expected. Colours have often turned ruby, and the bouquets are tending to open up into a second phase of evolution. Wines to look out for are a first-rate Clos des Papes, an exceptional Réserve des Célestins from Henri Bonneau, an elegant, delightfully flavoured Château Rayas which will drink very well by 1993, as well as meaty, backward *cuvées* from Bosquet des Papes, Domaine Lucien Barrot, Grand Tinel, Clos du Mont-Olivet and Beaucastel – the last-named is one of the quiet, slowly developing stars of the vintage. Domaine de Nalys and Domaine de Font-de-Michelle provided easy, refined reds that should be drunk up without delay, while in a slightly similar vein Château Fortia departed from tradition with a wine to be drunk by around 1993.

An excellent, rich and well-balanced white was made at the Domaine de Beaucastel, and this will live for many years.

1984   An average vintage, although some respectable *cuvées* could emerge with time. A lack of heat and fine weather left the grapes struggling to ripen, and some growers waited until the second half of October before picking. Acidity levels were higher than normal, and the colour is sometimes pale. The wines are not noticeably fruity, nor do they have great length. Those with decent structure and some tannic support include Les Clefs d'Or, Beaucastel and a very good Clos des Papes: after ten years, they will be tiring. Two longer-lived wines of quality came from Château de la Nerthe and Le Bosquet des Papes. The Vieux Télégraphe is a mid-weight wine holding some sweet, spicy flavours – a little *flatteur*, perhaps. Very little Rayas was made – 90 hectolitres from the 13 hectares due to the Grenache *coulure* – and from different tastings the wine can hold a dark plum, very ripe bouquet with similarly delicious prune and plum flavours on the palate – but bottles do vary.

It was a good year for the whites, which showed a delicate blend of weight and freshness. Notable were the Vieux Télégraphe, Mont-Redon and Clefs d'Or. They have developed a secondary phase of greater richness and complexity and are still very interesting.

1985   Another hot year, in the mould of 1982, was saved by some rain in the late summer. A healthy crop was brought in, and the wines are often very good, although by 1992 they had evolved at great speed, with a short life often in prospect. There was a good extraction of colour and the bouquets are very broad and open now – definitely past the first flush of fruitiness. The fruit on the palate is plump, but often has started to recede with age. The best wines carry elegance and style, helped in many cases by the Syrah. The special Cuvée Génération from Château de la Gardine was notable, as were the Clos du Mont-Olivet and two stylish offerings from the Clos des Papes and the Château de la Font du Loup. Along with Les Cailloux and Domaine Marcoux, they will drink well out towards 1993–6. The Beaucastel is lovely now, but will run towards 1997; like the very good Domaine Pierre André, it was one of the biggest red wines of the vintage. The Rayas is another mid-weight wine, while a good, short-term offering came from Mont-Redon (drink by 1993).

Notable whites were made by La Reviscoulado, Château Fortia and especially Château Rayas, the latter providing its best white for some years – a full, clean wine with good weight and appealing dried fruit and nut flavours. Other whites were often too rich and rather flabby.

1986   The midsummer was very hot, but by September the weather had broken with a vengeance. Some harvesting took place in the rain, and the best growers exercised a severe *triage* or discard on their crop. The resultant red wines are uneven in quality, the most striking aspect about them often being their rather stern, green tannins that can lend them an unwelcome astringency. Matters are further complicated by the reds evolving at markedly different speeds. Some have turned ruby already – after six years – and seem to have lost their grip on the palate, with a fall-off in depth of flavour. Others are opening and rounding out more slowly and evenly, so selection is of great import-ance with this vintage. Front-rank offerings came from Henri Bonneau with his Réserve des Célestins – plump and lusciously dense flavours – and from Paul Féraud at the Domaine du Pegaü, showing that for the Grenache flag-wavers at least, top quality was possible: both these wines will show very well around 1995–7. Other wines to note from this year were Lucien Michel's Vieux Donjon, the Cuvée des Cadettes from Château La Nerthe, Le Bosquet des Papes and sound Grand Tinel and Château de Beaucastel.

The whites were more strongly scented than the 1985s, a little less heady, and have prospered better with time. They have gained breadth and interest of flavour and after five to seven years are likely to provide excellent drinking if chosen from good *domaines*, such as Vieux Télégraphe, a flourishing Domaine du Pegaü or Château de Beaucastel. They may live even longer if well cellared.

1987   Rain in the spring, rain and fog at harvest-time and a small crop, averaging only 28 hectolitres: a variable vintage of light, unsteady reds with some exceptions where a high percentage of the crop was cast aside. Many of the wines are short on colour and depth on the palate – 'not wines that ask a lot of questions', in the words of François Perrin of Beaucastel. Honourable *cuvées* were made by Clos du Mont-Olivet (drink towards 1993), La Nerthe (more weight than most), and Domaine du Pegaü (drink towards 1997). The wines from Domaine de Beaurenard (drink towards 1994), Château de Mont-Redon (towards 1993) and Beaucastel (towards 1993) were well worked – Beaucastel produced under half its normal quantity, for instance. The whites were much more successful; they were similar in style to the 1984s, with better than normal levels of acidity and a good fruit texture on the palate. They are developing well, revealing discreet aromas on the bouquet and growing length and grip on the palate. The Château de la Gardine Vieilles Vignes was successful (will run towards 1995), as were the Château La Nerthe (finely weighted, drinking well now) and the Beaucastel (opening up, will develop towards the mid-1990s).

1988   A very good vintage, one where the Grenache was able to assert its best qualities, which means that it is less obviously attractive than either 1989 or 1990. This was the first of a run of drought years, and several of the wines contain more acidity than usual; by 1989 the vines are thought to have better adapted to the dry conditions, which helped ripening in that year. Harvesting was complicated by some rain, but the crop was generally abundant. The red wines are initially firm; their colour is solid, while on the bouquet they carry dried fruit aromas that have a certain reserve – this is just the sort of vintage that with age produces wines of stunning complexity and appeal on the bouquet, as opposed to the years that, like 1989, start out with ripe, flagrant aromas. There is good density on the palate on many of the reds, strong but not severe tannins and a discreet fruit. The reds promise to evolve in a stop-go way, at times closing up and traversing dumb periods, but are likely to provide very good drinking after around seven years if traditionally made. Notable front-rank wines from Château Rayas, Domaine Pierre André, Henri Bonneau's Réserve des Célestins, Les Clefs d'Or, Domaine du Pegaü, Clos du Mont-Olivet, Château de Beaucastel and Domaine du Vieux Télégraphe. Also worthy of note are the Domaine du Caillou, Le Bosquet des Papes, Château Mont-Redon, Château de la Gardine, Bessac's Carte d'Or, Clos des Papes, Henri Bonneau's Marie Beurrier *cuvée*, the Font-de-Michelle Cuvée Étienne Gonnet and the Château La Nerthe Cuvée des Cadettes.

The white wines were generally successful in a firm way; initially quiet on the bouquet, they have started to open up and have good, quite solid fruit flavours with considerable length on the finish. Of the early runners, Domaine de Nalys, Domaine du Père Caboche, and Domaine de Font-de-Michelle showed well, while the Beaucastel whites were excellent and likely to develop great complexity over a long life.

1989   An excellent, luscious vintage of big, rounded red wines with great depth and appeal; very well-balanced, early developing whites completed a very satisfactory picture for the growers. Another drought summer brought no rain after May; the old vines defended themselves, but the young ones suffered. The lead-up to the harvest was completed in hot, sunny weather, and some growers were picking by the first week of September, one of the earliest dates since the Second World War. The colour levels in the reds are very good, and most of the wines possess great balance. The bouquets are likely to open and show well within the first five or six years, while on the palate there is generally strong fruit extract and sound but rounded tannic support. This vintage fits between the very fruity but less full 1985s and the full-blown, expansive and very generous 1978s. Top-rank reds came from Château de Beaucastel (both the regular *cuvée* and the Cuvée Homm-age Jacques Perrin were exceptional), the excellent Domaine du Pegaü and Chapoutier's Barbe-Rac, Château La Nerthe Cuvée des Cadettes, Clos des Papes, Clos du Mont-Olivet, Domaine de St-Siffrein, Domaine du Grand Tinel, Château La Nerthe, Domaine de Marcoux Vieilles Vignes, Domaine Pierre André, Henri Bonneau's Réserve des Célestins, Lucien Barrot et Fils, Le Bosquet des Papes, Château Rayas, Jaboulet's Les Cèdres, Les Cailloux, Le Vieux Donjon, Domaine de la Roquette, Château Mont-Redon, Domaines Grand Veneur la Janasse and Roger Perrin. The longevity of some of these wines is questionable, and it is possible that they will advance at a faster rate than first thought – perhaps a life of between eight and twelve years awaits several of the mainly Grenache-based wines.

The whites were generally strongly flavoured, and those exposed to some new oak are likely to take longer to form themselves than the rest. There is a pleasant richness in many of them, with the probability of excellent drinking after three to five years. The Vieilles Vignes from La Gardine, the Beaucastel whites – all very well made – are likely to live longer, while among the gentler offerings of note figure Domaine du Vieux Télégraphe, Château Mont-Redon, Domaine du Père Caboche and Domaine de Nalys.

1990 A very good, powerful vintage. The wines were more extreme than the 1989s, both the reds and the whites, with more violent flavours and at times very heady levels of alcohol. The year was marked by another very dry summer, and the harvest was slow to ripen. In about a ten-day patch at the start of September, the sugar levels of the Grenache leapt by about 2°, frequently to above the 14° mark. Harvesting for many started around 10–15 September. The reds are uniformly well coloured, and those *domaines* that concentrate on the Grenache made really dense, potent and expressive wines; indeed, the *vigneron*'s main task was often to tame the wines, and to achieve a measured balance from the assembly of some 'wild' *cuvées*. This is a vintage which is likely to live for many years thanks to the sheer weight of extract in the wines, but it is less uniformly successful than the better balanced and more stylish 1989. Excellent promise from the reds of Beaucastel, La Nerthe, Clos du Mont-Olivet and the Nerthe Cuvée des Cadettes. Also very good are the Clos des Papes, Domaine du Grand Tinel, Domaine du Pegaü (both standard *cuvée* and Vieilles Vignes), Les Clefs d'Or, Château Rayas, Domaine de Font-de-Michelle, Bonneau's Réserve des Célestins and Domaine du Vieux Télégraphe. These are wines that should be drunk from between six years old in the lighter styles (Vieux Télégraphe) and eight years old up in the more robust styles.

The whites were also very opulent, sometimes too much so for their own good. While carrying heady, fat aromas, their flavours gush forth on the palate and they can be a bit overblown. Good, early wines were made by Domaine de Terre Ferme, Domaine Riché, Domaine du Vieux Télégraphe and Les Cailloux. Wines of greater authority and long-term potential came from Font-de-Michelle, the Château La Nerthe Clos de Beauvenir, Beaucastel – a more lush, 'southern' Vieille Vigne than usual – and Domaine de Montpertuis.

Earlier Exceptional Vintages 1954, 1952, 1949, 1947, 1945, 1944, 1942, 1937, 1934, 1929. With bottles of this age much depends first, on who made them and, secondly, on where and how each bottle has been kept. Some of the wines of the Châteaux Beaucastel and Rayas, for instance, are still in tremendous order, whereas old wines from the *négociant* houses will often have passed their best. Moreover, if the wines have been stored from an early date in the colder, more northerly climate of Britain, they are likely to have aged more slowly than those that have remained near the scene of their production.

Leading Growers at Châteauneuf-du-Pape

The nucleus:

84370 BÉDARRIDES
Brunier, Henri et Fils, Domaine du Vieux Télégraphe

84230 CHÂTEAUNEUF-DU-PAPE
Abeille-Fabre, Château Mont-Redon
Avril, Paul et Vincent, Le Clos des Papes
Boiron, Maurice, Le Bosquet des Papes
Brunel, André, Les Cailloux
Bonneau, Henri
Brunel, Maxime et Patrick, Château de la Gardine
Deydier, Jean, et Fils, Les Clefs d'Or
Féraud, Paul et Laurence, Domaine du Pegaü
Jeune, Élie, Domaine du Grand Tinel
Jeune, Paul, Domaine de Montpertuis
Le Roy, Baron, Château Fortia
Nerthe, Château La
Reynaud, Jacques, Château Rayas
Sabon, Les Fils de Joseph, Clos du Mont-Olivet

84350 COURTHÉZON
André, Pierre et Fille, Domaine Pierre André
Perrin, Jean-Pierre et François, Château de Beaucastel

Other producers:

84370 BÉDARRIDES
Bérard, Père et Fils, Domaine de Terre Ferme
Gonnet, Jean et Michel, Domaine Font-de-Michelle

84230 CHÂTEAUNEUF-DU-PAPE
Armenier, Philippe, Domaine de Marcoux
Amouroux, Andrée, Clos de l'Oratoire des Papes
Arnaud, Louis et Enfants, Château Cabrières
Avril, Juliette
Avril, Maurice, Domaine Le Père Caler
Avril, *Veuve* Geneviève, Le Font du Pape

Barnaud, Paul, Cuvée du Conclave des Cardinaux
Barrot, Jean, L'Hurlevent
Barrot, Lucien et Régis, Domaine Lucien Barrot et Fils
Bessac, Caves
Boiron, Henri, Domaine des Relagnes
Boisson, Jean-Pierre, Domaine du Père Caboche
Bouche, Simone, Domaine de Condorcet
Brechet, Sylvette, Château de Vaudieu
Brunel, Max, Domaine Le Soulida
Brunier Frères, Domaine de la Roquette
Carré, Ghislaine, SCEA du Chantadu
Caves Saint-Pierre
Chapoutier, M., Domaine de la Bernardine
Château des Fines Roches
Chausse, G., et Fils, Les Combes
Chausse, Henri, Réserve des Diacres
Comte de Lauze, Jean
Coulon, Georges, Domaine de la Pinède
Coulon, Paul et Daniel, Domaine de Beaurenard
Courtil Thibaut, Claude, Clos des Brusquières
Descarrega, Charles, Les Cabanes
Deville, P., et Fils, Clos St-André
Diffonty, Félicien, et Fils, La Cuvée du Vatican
Diffonty, Rémy, et Fils, Domaine du Haut des Terres Blanches (also
    vinifies and bottles Domaine de la Glacière)
Durieu, Paul, Domaine Durieu
Fabre, Henri, Domaine de la Tour St-Michel
Geniest, les Successeurs de Louis, Mas St-Louis
Girard André, Lou Patacaiau
Giraud, Paul, Domaine Les Gallimardes
Giraud, Pierre, et Fils
Giraud, Robert, Cuvée du Belvedère Le Boucou
Gradassi, Paulette, Domaine des Saints Pères
Grangeon, Étienne, Domaine de Cristia
Jacumin, Cellier, Courtil, Domaine St-Benoît
Jacumin, Pierre, Cuvée de Bois Dauphin
Jean, Comte de Lauze
Jean, Philippe, La Réviscoulado
Jeune, Jean, Clos de la Cérise
Jouffron, René, et Fils, Réserve des Cardinaux

Laget, Marie, Domaine de L'Arnesque
SCEA Laget-Royer, François
Lançon, Pierre et Fils, Domaine de la Solitude
Maffret, Serge et Jacqueline, Domaine des Plagnes
Magni, André et Fils
Marchand, Jean, Domaine de Bois Dauphin, Clos des Pontifes
Maret, Michel, Domaine de la Charbonnière
Mathieu, Charles, Jacqueline, André, Domaine Mathieu
Maurel, Mme Guy et Fils, Clos St-Jean
Mayard, Jean-Luc, Domaine du Galet des Papes
Mestre, Jacques, Cuvée des Sommeliers
Mestre, Jean-Claude, Domaine de la Côte de l'Ange
Mestre, Charles, Le Chêne-Vert
Michel, Lucien, et Fils, Le Vieux Donjon
Moulin, André, Domaine Moulin-Tacussel
Mousset, Louis, Château des Fines Roches
Nalys, Domaine de
Nicolet Frères et Fils, Domaine Chante-Perdix
Nicolet, Lucette et Frédéric, Domaine Perges
Millet, Paulette, Domaine de Nalys
Palazzi, Jacky, Domaine les Mascaronnes
Pécoul Frères, La Cuvée des Bosquets
Père Anselme
Père Pape, Domaine du Clos du Calvaire
Puget, Pierre, et Fils, Domaine la Crau des Papes
Quiot, Famille J. R., Les Arnevels
Quiot, Jérôme, Domaine du Vieux Lazaret
Raynaud, Annie, Domaine des Sénéchaux
Revoltier, Joseph, et Fils, Domaine de Farguerol
Riché, Claude et Jean, Domaine Riché
Royer, Jean-Marie, Clos des Marquis
Sabon, Roger, et Fils, 'Les Olivets'
SCEA Domaine Rogne, Le Père Papité
St-Pierre, Caves
Sabon-Favier, Domaine Chante-Cigale
Serre, Camille, Mme Vve, Domaine de St-Préfert
Trintignant, Jean, La Reviscoulado
Usseglio, Jean-Pierre
Usseglio, Pierre
Usseglio, Raymond

Versino, Jean et Jean-Paul, Domaine Bois de Boursan

84350 COURTHÉZON
Autard, Jean-Paul, Domaine Paul Autard
Berthet-Rayne, Christain, Domaine Berthet-Rayne
Bonnett, G et M-C, La Bastide St-Dominique
Co-opérative Vinicole 'Le Cellier des Princes'
Du Peloux et Cie
Grangeon, Alain, Domaine de Cristia
Granget, Bernard, Domaine de Husson
Jamet, Jean-Paul, La Vallée du Mistral
Mélia, Charles et Françoise, Château de la Font du Loup
Pouizin, Claude, Domaine Clos de Caillou
Quiot, Domaine SCV, Château Mancoil
Raymond, Émile, Domaine des Cigalons
Sabon, Aimé, Domaine de la Janasse
Sinard, Robert et Fils, Domaine St-Laurent

84100 ORANGE
Arnoux, Antonia, Domaine de la Villeneuve
Bernard, Michel, Domaine de la Serrière
Daumen, Père et Fils, Domaine de la Vieille Julienne
Chastan, André et Thoumy, Martine, Domaine de Palestor
Chastan, Claude, Domaine de St-Siffrein
Chastan, Pierry, La Fagotière
Chastan, Serge, Domaine Lou Fréjau
Chaussy, Jacky, Mas de Boislauzon
Jaume, Alain, Domaine Grand Veneur
Jaume, Patrick, Domaine des Chaussaud
Perrin, Roger

84420 PIOLENC
Serguier, Yves et Jean-Pierre Château Simian

30126 TAVEL
Delorme, Christophe, Domaine de la Mordorée

14

Tavel

Tavel, historically considered to be the finest rosé area of France, stands on the west bank of the Rhône 16 kilometres north-west of Avignon and 40 kilometres north-east of Nîmes. It is in the *département* of the Gard, and the crossing of the river brings with it a marked change in the face of the countryside. The 'market garden' aspect of the Vaucluse *département* across the river – watered, productive green fields bordered by windbreaking rows of cypress trees – has abruptly disappeared. In its place the eye sees, above all, aridity: parched columns of vines and austere rocky hillocks with little but a dried-out brush capable of growing on them. West of Tavel the sparseness increases, and the land becomes a maze of small valleys and woods, with groupings of vines encircling the many semi-forgotten villages.

Tavel fits into the pattern of the countryside. It is a tiny place and has an admirably narrow main street running through it. Sleeping dogs increase the narrowness, but the passing traffic respectfully organizes itself to steer right around them. On either side of the road little houses lean jumbled together, their brief balconies adorned with picturesque climbing flowers. The air of a wine village seems to be lacking, though: most of the main growers live outside the village, and it is only at the end of a long, hot day, when thirsty tractor drivers roll in from the fields, that Tavel gives a clue as to its true identity. With the long rays of the last sun lancing down the main street, the busy swallows looping overhead and the vineyard workers idly chatting in little groups, Tavel at last comes alive.

When wine was first made at the village is not clear. Records are patchy, but it is known that King Philip le Bel (1268–1314) once passed through Tavel on one of his grand tours of the kingdom. Without dismounting from his horse, he lustily drained a goblet and

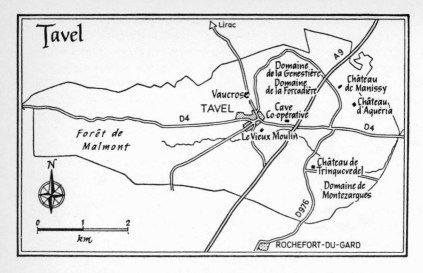

exclaimed, 'There is no good wine except for Tavel!' Later the poet Ronsard (1524–85) is said to have described the wine of Tavel as *sol in amphora*, but although *vignerons* are fond of this reference to their wine, they are unable to point out the work in which it figured.

Meanwhile, Tavel had graduated from early fame at the papal table in Avignon to regular appearances at the Versailles Court of the Sun King, Louis XIV (1638–1715). The custom was to ship the wine from the local port of Roquemaure, now the unofficial centre of the Lirac *appellation*. Considerable quantities were sent beyond the immediate territory, all passing under the name of 'Côtes du Rhône' rather than Tavel. Recognition of the wine's place of origin seems to have come only in the mid-eighteenth century: in a communication of 1765 a cardinal in Rome requested the Archbishop of Avignon to secure 'more of that wine of Tavel' for their annual rendezvous the following year.

One of the legends that grew up with the wine at this time was that it was extremely durable. No journey was considered too long for it, and the port of Roquemaure handled a large proportion of overseas shipments for Italy, England and even the Indies. The prevailing taste then was for drinking wines such as Tavel when they were quite old, which was just as well, for Tavel must have aged very quickly when taken on prolonged sea journeys in only very small casks.

Throughout the eighteenth century and later Tavel was strictly defended by its *vignerons*. Careful rules were drawn up, such as the prohibition of the entry of all outside grapes and wine, on the grounds that their presence in the community could not enhance, and would probably only harm, Tavel's reputation. A *ban des vendanges*, or official date of harvest, was also fixed rigorously every year. This became a useful ploy for the *seigneur* of Tavel, who always decreed himself a three days' start on his fellow *vignerons*. There was never, of course, any arguing with the mighty *seigneur*!

By 1828 Tavel was in full prosperity, and its vineyards covered nearly 730 hectares. Most of the plots were on the series of little hills south and west of the village, and their slope wine was some of the best that could be found in the locality. Alas, the phylloxera attack reduced the whole vineyard to almost nothing, and the harassed growers were forced to replant on all the chalk–sand flatlands immediately next to the village; these were nearer than the hillsides, and although the wine was less good, they could be worked more easily and more cheaply. The hillside area, covering some 250 hectares, went largely uncultivated until 1965, when concerted action by many of the villagers led to their using bulldozers to clear out the scrub on the slopes that had generally been regarded as infertile. The chalky soil that was revealed was covered in masses of white and crumbly flat stones, and this ground has since lived up to its old reputation as being one of the best areas of Tavel. The *parcelles* are much smaller than those on the Vallongue plateau, and many belong to members of the Cave Co-opérative, which is one of the most celebrated in France.

Inspiration for the total clearance of the hillsides had stemmed from a similarly successful action performed on the Vallongue, which lies north of the village, in 1957. At that time Tavel's name was well established in the United States, but with the vineyard totalling no more than 200 hectares, growers found they did not have enough wine to serve their other home and foreign markets properly. The Vallongue, a well-exposed raised plateau, seemed ideal for their purposes but was thickly wooded and established as a paradise of rabbits, hares, partridges – and, of course, French marksmen. It must have been a heart-rending decision for some of the *vignerons* who had grown used to their regular plates of game, but good sense prevailed and the ever-united wine community undertook to follow the example of Gabriel Meffre of Gigondas and bulldoze into shape nearly all the plateau. Now there are long rows of vines on the

Vallongue, which stretch away towards distant clutches of cypress windbreaks; with their uneven heights and shapes the far-off trees resemble a ragged band of part-time soldiers. Right away to their north-east the further side of the Rhône Valley is visible, with the Dentelles de Montmirail and Mont Ventoux shimmering blue-grey some 30 kilometres distant. The view from the Vallongue is one of the best of the southern Côtes du Rhône vineyards, and the feeling it gives early on a summer's day is almost ethereal.

As a result of all this activity, the vineyards now extend over about 950 hectares. Small parts of the *appellation* have been disturbed by the building of the motorway to Spain, along with access roads. Barring further construction projects, the vineyards are at virtually full capacity.

Altogether nine different grape varieties can be planted. These are headed by the Grenache, which by the rules cannot exceed 60 per cent of a *vigneron*'s plantation, and by the Cinsault, of which there must be at least 15 per cent.

In recent years there has been a slight trend away from the Grenache, which reflects a central dilemma facing the growers. Several are seeking to make a wine of reduced alcohol content – hence the reduction in Grenache – but the replacement grape varieties commonly considered as 'improvers' – the Syrah and the Mourvèdre, for instance – give full-bodied, robust wines high in extract and colour. With hot summers like 1982, 1983, 1985, 1988, 1989 and especially 1990 bringing crops of very ripe, concentrated grapes, Tavel risks becoming a heavyweight among rosés and even red wines, unless *vignerons* take specific steps to counter this in their vinifications. In 1990, some wines of between 14.5° and 15° were produced – which is far too powerful and very misleading for drinkers who expect rosé to be an agreeable, discreetly flavoured accompaniment to summer or Oriental foods, for instance.

This is a serious problem for an *appellation* restricted to making only rosé. Blush wine out of California, attractively bottled and fresh-tasting Italian rosés, elegant Loire rosés like Bourgueil or Sancerre – there are any number of pretenders and worthy alternatives to Tavel nowadays. The sort of wine that set the standard for rosé in the past – well coloured, with highish alcohol and firm flavours on the palate – may not now be so acceptable or palatable to drinkers who may, as one Lirac grower commented, seek a 'white wine style of rosé rather than a red wine style'.

This is not to suggest that Tavel should abandon its style or local character – its very essence is to carry a resounding, thorough flavour, but not one that is marked by an all-pervading sensation of heat and heady alcohol.

In the plantation mix, the Cinsault is regarded as the vine capable of 'smoothing out' part of this defect: its share of the total vineyard has consequently increased to 20 or 25 per cent. But the Cinsault is a pretty neutral grape, so while the growers may be toning down their wine, they are not adding positively to it in recompense.

So cellar techniques have fallen under increased scrutiny. At Tavel, having an *œnologue* to advise you seems as much *de rigueur* as having a psychoanalyst in California, and the current line of thought presented to many of the growers is that they should at all costs stop the secondary, malolactic fermentation in order to preserve levels of acidity in the wine. This will retain greater freshness and 'zip' on the palate, and will encourage wider and deeper aromas on the bouquet if the wine is fermented slowly at low temperature.

Wines fermented under controlled conditions with their malolactic blocked are therefore a new, important group at Tavel. They denote a departure from the style of rosé made here over the years, with fewer gentle, almost floral aromas apparent on the bouquet, and more grapey, almost yeasty aromas in their place. Earlier release on the market has also meant that these wines are more aggressive-tasting, less refined on the palate when first appearing on sale. It is therefore important to catch them at the right moment, after they have settled in the bottle and lost some of the standard one-dimensional aromas brought by low-temperature fermentation: the second half of their first summer is a good starting-point.

The Grenache and Cinsault are the natural bases of Tavel, although *coulure* on the Grenache, as occurred in 1983, 1984, and 1991, can knock the usual grape structure considerably. Properties like the Château d'Aquéria had only 25 per cent Grenache in their wine in 1984, for instance, against 45 per cent normally. The growers rarely make use of the full complement of nine varieties available to them. In rough order of importance, the other seven are: Clairette, Bourboulenc, Syrah, Mourvèdre, Picpoul, Carignan (not more than 10 per cent of this is permitted) and Calitor, which is slowly disappearing from use.

The Syrah and the Mourvèdre have been permitted only since 1969, and their presence in or absence from a Tavel rosé makes a lively subject for conversation among the wine-making fraternity. These grapes undoubtedly inject colour and a little extra body into the rosé, but therein lies the key dilemma now facing the *appellation*. The late M. Georges Bernard of Domaine de la Genestière used to consider that even a small percentage of either grape was sufficient to dominate the wine; the Allauzen family at the very good Prieuré de Montézargues have recently planted only a very small amount of Syrah, not wanting to produce a wine that is too firm. They have planted a little more Mourvèdre. On the other hand, Jacques Lafond, who also makes a very good Tavel at Domaine Corne-Loup, has 10 per cent Syrah in his vineyard, which contributes to the consistent, sound pink colours that his wines always bear. Along with the Cave Co-opérative and the Domaine Le Vieux Moulin of Gabriel Roudil et Fils, the Corne-Loup usually carries the most sustained dark pink colour in the *appellation*. For the consumer this question of colour and depth on the palate is clearly subjective, and personal preference should come from trying the various styles and hues.

Most of the vines are ideally suited to growing in Tavel's hot, dry and windy climate. Apart from the incidence of *coulure* on the Grenache, which rose during the 1980s, a minor irritant is the effect of the wind on the young Mourvèdre vines. Unlike the more densely covered Syrah, the Mourvèdre carries only light vegetation and is accordingly more prone to snapping in the wind.

Historically, the greatest vineyard menace has – surprisingly – come from the local rabbits. These raiders gladly ate up many neglected vines during the Second World War and in the post-war years turned their attentions to all the newly planted young vines – so much so that they virtually became Tavel's public enemy number one. Their assault was particularly severe at the Château de Manissy, which is run by a religious order. Perhaps it was specially invoked divine providence that brought on the myxomatosis attack of the 1950s, for the Château now has an eminently thriving vineyard! And in case of a return of this problem, the growers could always copy their counterparts at Châteauneuf-du-Pape, who have recently introduced trained ferrets to combat the rabbit menace.

At the time of the *vendanges*, which after a hot summer like 1990 can start as early as 3 September, it is the fast-maturing Cinsault grapes that are picked first, followed by the Grenache. The *vignerons* then proceed with their orthodox rosé vinification, which can be by the *saignée* method, with a maceration of the grapes for twelve to twenty-four hours, or by direct pressing of the harvest. Both methods achieve the extraction of colour, the *saignée* maceration producing greater intensity in the pink or pale red, as well as providing the wine-maker with more volume of wine for each entry of grapes from the vineyards. One of the few *domaines* to make its wine by direct pressing is the Seigneur de Vaucrose, but as M. Lévêque ages his wine for over a year and does not release it until it is around two years old, the effects of this initial treatment are difficult to track accurately.

Once the harvest has entered the cellars, therefore, the grapes are left to macerate for between twelve and twenty-four hours in enamel-lined or stainless steel vats. Piled up together, the grapes gradually crush each other, so lightly breaking their skins and freeing some of their juice. The vats are cooled during the maceration since the growers do not want fermentation to get properly under way. Colour extraction is their prime objective, but should they wish their wine to carry a bit more body they allow the maceration to continue for a few hours more.

The grapes are then removed for a light pressing that will provide more juice. In most cellars the temperature of the must never exceeds 22°C now, whereas in the past traditional vinification deemed the level to be around 25°C. Armand Maby, the ex-Mayor of Tavel and a man who likes to experiment with new techniques, explained why temperature control was so important: 'The grapes often come in from the vineyards at a temperature of around 27°C, so I have to cool them the moment they enter my cellars or else I'd end up with a red wine on my hands. Stainless steel tanks allow for far closer temperature control than the old concrete vats, and I can now drop them down to 15–18°C, and sustain that level.'

Like M. Maby, leading *domaines* like Montézargues, Corne-Loup, Vieux Moulin and Aquéria run their primary fermentation at controlled levels of 16–20°C. It can run for six to twelve days at this rate, bringing greater fruitiness in the eyes of some growers and greater perfumes and bouquet for others. The different grape varieties are most commonly vinified together: only *vignerons* who hold large single plots planted with just one *cépage* will vinify that *cépage* apart.

The stage is then set for the blocking of the malolactic fermentation, a process now done by most of the *appellation*. The degree of sophistication and efficiency differs according to the cellar instal-lations and space available to the grower. *Domaines* like the Château d'Aquéria, La Fermade and Vieux Moulin have been generally blocking the malolactic since the early 1980s. Their system is to fine the wine with a bentonite solution right at the end of the alcoholic fermentation; the wine is then racked and a dose of liquid sulphur dioxide is applied to deal with any remaining bacteria. Racking is thought to take out 70 per cent of the solid particles, while speed in applying the liquid sulphur dioxide is vital to catch the lactic acids; a delay means that they are sent to sleep, but not eliminated.

Very hot water can be used for sterilizing bottles, and the final bar to the malolactic thereafter is a filtration just before bottling, which for some growers now starts in January, for others in March. The wine in the meantime is stored in glass- or enamel-lined vats, and many of the *domaines* bottle a harvest in several runs over the course of a year.

Blocking the malolactic sounds like a major fuss, and a big event in the lives of the growers. So it is. Vincent de Bez of Château d'Aquéria commented: 'In 1982 our *malo* here was still only half-completed by August following the harvest. The wine wasn't settled, it risked breaking out while on the way to a customer, and with a very ripe crop that year, the wine could also become flabby very quickly. That's what decided us to start blocking the *malo* from 1983, and a good thing it was in that year. There we had wines running up to 13.5°, which needed to retain what freshness they could. Since blocking the *malo*, I've sent a cask of our wine to the Cameroons – there were no problems with it, which is the proof that this system works well.'

Quantifying the effect on the liveliness of the wine is difficult, but Jacques Lafond of Domaine Corne-Loup estimated that a wine whose residual acidity was 3 grams per litre after its primary fermentation, was reduced to 2 grams after the malolactic. In his view, the same wine with its *malo* blocked would only have fallen to between 2.8 and 2.7 grams after a year, indicating stronger freshness in the second type of wine.

Nearly all growers at Tavel now block the *malo*; the danger is that unless carried out with the utmost care, the process can ruin a wine and the reputation of its *domaine*. The use of a liquid sulphur solution is one that must be done with great delicacy and fineness of judgment. So often sweet wines are spoiled by overriding sulphur – a weakness that occurs even in good châteaux in Sauternes, for instance. So the *vignerons* of Tavel are running a risk in their search to produce a fresher style of wine.

One of the most agreeable aspects of a Tavel rosé is its clear-cut, dry flavour, which is achieved by fermenting nearly all the sugar out of the must. The next stage in producing a lively, summery wine after the blocking of the malolactic is early bottling – for most, but not all, the growers.

One fallacy that has for some reason always accompanied Tavel is that it is a keeping wine, a *vin de garde*. No rosé can pretend to be a *vin de garde*, and no rosé was ever designed to be. If a *vigneron* sought to make a *vin de garde*, he would make a red wine with tannin in it, not a pink wine without tannin. That said, there do exist quite sharply differing attitudes among the growers towards the question of maturing Tavel. At the Château de Manissy, for instance, the monks of the Sainte Famille leave their wine to age for a year or more in underground wooden barrels. At the Seigneur de Vaucrose the wine is only put on sale two years after the harvest. This sacrifices elegance and freshness in favour of riper, nuttier aromas and flavours, and some would say that this therefore represents the *clairet* wine of old – a singular wine that should not be compared like for like with today's international rosés. As usual, it is all down to taste, for there are those who love the Manissy *rancio*, dry taste, especially if it is in a bottle of twenty years' age or so!

The majority school favours early bottling, with the wine never nowadays put into wood. Until the 1985 harvest the Château d'Aquéria fermented its wine in large casks, but these wore out, and the eventual explosion of a couple of casks dictated a change to stainless steel in 1986. The Domaine Le Vieux Moulin also sometimes used to mature its wine in cask for two or three months, on the grounds of providing a little extra bouquet; this procedure was stopped in the late 1970s in order to keep the wine as fresh and lively as possible. The Domaine du Vieux Relais of Félix Roudil has also used oak for a few months on its wine.

Over the years one of the recurring problems facing rosé wines has been that of their image. They are commonly criticized as being a kind of half-caste: neither red nor white, they are too trivial and inconsequential for many wine drinkers, who, if they think about them at all, see them as the product of some illegitimate and probably clandestine union. Tavel certainly does not fall anywhere near this category; its wines are stamped with strongly definable character and an inescapable fullness. The best are refined, elegant, refreshing and very easy to drink. In short, they are among the best in the world.

But the grip of this southern Rhône *appellation* on the top of the rosé hierarchy certainly weakened during the 1980s.

At its best, Tavel holds an unaccustomed and very agreeable depth that goes beyond the light, forgettable airiness of many rosés. This depth is not easy to achieve: too much weight and the wine can become clumsy. In turn this is surrounded by a great, clean fruitiness and length of bouquet. Ostensibly a light wine, Tavel is nevertheless very complete. Underneath all the superficial fruit and charm there is a substantial, sometimes chewy finish, which with its clean length rounds off the pleasure of drinking the wine.

When young, much Tavel is a lustrous pink, entrancing the eye and the palate with its satisfying simplicity. But with modern vinification techniques prevailing, its true elegance does not emerge in the very first flush of youth. Only as it approaches one year old does this late 1980s–early 1990s version of Tavel start to assert its class and draw away from watery imitations.

Just under half of all Tavel is made at the Cave Co-opérative, whose foundation in 1937 did much to help the small cultivator, previously completely dependent on the *négociant* trade for selling his wine. There are now 140 members and the wine sets a fine example for Co-opératives everywhere. About half of the overall plantation under its members is in Grenache, with around 20 per cent Cinsault and 10 per cent Syrah. The presence of the last-named explains why the Co-opérative wines are usually firmly coloured, with tinges of British Post-Office red creeping into the pink.

The Co-opérative Tavel is consistently good, although it is sometimes heavier and more alcoholic than the wine of the best private *domaines*. Since 1986 it has blocked the malolactic fermentation. The wine retains its firm character and clean finish with some extra early zest.

Beside the well-run and prominent Co-opérative, the private *domaines* are few and small.

LEADING DOMAINES

CHÂTEAU D'AQUÉRIA

This is one of the largest single *domaines* at Tavel, with 49 hectares of vines north-east of the village. High wrought-iron gates stand with an air of fading majesty at the entrance to the vineyard, and the cellar buildings next to the splendid seventeenth-century house are softened by wisps of wistaria draped in a disorderly way over them.

The view from the château, which is completely surrounded by its own vines, has changed with the building of a new road. Nevertheless, the shaded garden and the broad stone stairways flanked by rosebeds and lavender make it into something approaching a dream residence, all the more so because there are well-stocked cellars to go with it.

Château d'Aquéria rosé was one of the first French wines to appear in the United States after the ending of Prohibition. Indeed, its speed in establishing a foothold in the US market was largely responsible for the early surge of popularity there for Tavel rosé, a popularity that has never deserted the wine. The man who achieved this was M. Jean Olivier, the long-standing owner of Château d'Aquéria who died in 1974. M. Olivier, who was a close friend and contemporary of another great local wine character, the late Louis Reynaud of Châteauneuf-du-Pape's Château Rayas, had several friends from New York and Boston who had tasted and enjoyed his wine on trips to Europe in the late 1920s. In 1932, after the lifting of Prohibition, he promptly arranged for a shipment of his wine to be sent off to them. The word was gradually spread around, and the wine grew so much in renown that Château d'Aquéria came to reserve the large part of its production for America alone.

Today the Château is run by M. Olivier's son-in-law, M. Paul de Bez and his son Vincent. Their plantation revolves around the Grenache, which forms 45 per cent of the vineyard, while other major contributors are the Cinsault, Clairette and Mourvèdre. In places some of these vines, which over the years have been planted all together, are sixty years old. There is no Syrah because it was found to clash with the Mourvèdre and to overrun the wine – hence its removal.

Aquéria rosé is in the front rank at Tavel. Before the blocking of the malolactic, the wine was more full-bodied than many. It has been made in the new style since 1983, and the 1985 was a very successful year – well balanced, with subtle flavours developing after a year in bottle. The 1986 was a firm wine, clean and correct, but like some of its year it lacked aromas and was low on charm. The 1988 (crisp, fresh) and 1989 (a fuller wine) were both well made. Very consistent, but just a beat off the very top, the rosé is accompanied by a very good red Lirac, made from a 7-hectare vineyard near Roquemaure on the eastern extremity of Tavel. Notable for the presence of 45 per cent Mourvèdre in it, it is excellent in its first three or four years, and well worth looking out for.

de Bez, Paul et Vincent
   Château d'Aquéria   30126 Tavel

CHÂTEAU DE MANISSY

Along the road from Aquéria stands an anonymous old Provençal *mas*, or farm, and it is here that live the monks of the Sainte Famille, a religious order for people of late vocation. Founded in Holland at the end of the nineteenth century, the order soon afterwards began to look out for overseas bases, and in France it came upon the Château de Manissy which was already a wine *domaine* noted for the quality of its soil and the fine exposure of its vines. This did not deter the monks from settling down at Manissy, since their late-conversion philosophy means that they group together men of a large variety of skills. Wine-making is, unfortunately, neither a common nor an easy occupation to learn, though, so the first monks had to endure all the trials and tribulations of learning from scratch an entirely new trade.

There are seven monks living full-time at the château, and they receive regular visits from foreign brother monks, who are often called upon to help in the 28-hectare vineyard. The chief *caviste*, or cellar master, is always a member of the order. The last one, for instance, Frère Roger, had spent over thirty years at Manissy gradually acquiring all the skills necessary to make their rosé. Never in the slightest bit complacent about his adopted *métier*, he would say: 'It's very hard work making the wine, but also extremely pleasing to be faced with the challenge. As the wine is very rounded from age-ing for a year in wood, I would advise it to be drunk no more than chilled in summer (about 10°C) and at room temperature in winter (the old room temperature, before central heating, of about 15°C).'

The Manissy Tavel is a wine apart: in no sense can it be compared with the fresh, pink wines that have discreet weight on the palate and which suit cold luncheons served out of doors on hot summer days. The nearest rosé wine it resembles, even though the Manissy is much drier and more overtly oxidized, is that of the very good Côte d'Azur family Ott, whose Château de Selle is a full-bodied, slightly orange-hued wine with great length and persistence on the finish. The Selle wine's great advantage, however, is the ripeness and richness which it possesses, as opposed to the much drier, waning texture of the Manissy. However, *chacun à son goût*.

The brothers of Manissy are calm, gentle people, well able to accept the vagaries of the world. Wine-making is often temporarily put aside when weatherbeaten old tramps wheel up on misshapen bicycles, seeking refuge and solace from the outside world. All are courteously attended to; never is a word of exasperation uttered. The tramps sometimes come complaining of the tremendous heat and their terrible thirst, clearly in the hope of a quick glass of Manissy Tavel. When satisfied, their rough faces are transformed into delighted smiles – surely a fine testimony to the restorative powers of the wine.

Château de Manissy   30126 Tavel

CHÂTEAU DE TRINQUEVEDEL

A viticultural *domaine* since before the French Revolution, this attractive soft stone château with its smart white shutters stands a little to the east of the village, on the way towards Rochefort-du-Gard. The property comprises about 30 hectares of vines; when bought by the Demoulin family in 1936, the vineyards were in very poor condition, being mostly planted with low-grade hybrid vines. In 1960 M. Demoulin started to bottle his wine, and it is now exported to Britain, the United States and several other countries.

The wine is made from all nine varieties allowed, led by the Grenache (45 per cent), Cinsault (20 per cent), Clairette (16 per cent) and the remainder made up in order of importance by the Carignan, Bourboulenc, Syrah, Mourvèdre and Calitor. The juice is fined before fermentation, which is done at cool temperature, with bottling in the spring.

The Trinquevedel Tavel is generally solidly structured, well rounded and marked by an extremely attractive pink. In the more complete vintages like 1983, 1985 and 1989 it has good length, an overall sound depth of flavour and a lingering, chewy finish. It is more interesting to drink when very young than the most modern-style Tavel like that of La Forcadière, and generally continues in good shape for three to five years.

Demoulin, F.
    Château de Trinquevedel   30126 Tavel

DOMAINE CORNE-LOUP

This is a very good 26-hectare *domaine* owned by Jacques Lafond, who, like his father, was a Co-opérateur until departing the Cave Co-opérative in 1966. He started to bottle his own wine from 1976 onwards, and now it is one of the best Tavels.

The vineyards are split into half a dozen plots on Campey and Torette, which are on the Route de Valiguières, north-west of Tavel. The plantation is led by 60 per cent Grenache, 15 per cent Cinsault, 12 per cent Syrah, with the remaining 13 per cent made up of Clairette, Mourvèdre and Carignan.

The Corne-Loup wine is vinified at around 17°C after a brief maceration, and the malolactic is blocked. The different *cuves* are assembled before bottling, which starts from January, since M. Lafond has some export clients seeking a very young style of wine. Overall, M. Lafond sells 70 per cent of his wine in bottle, and 30 per cent in bulk. Sixty per cent of his production of about 100,000 bottles is exported, mainly to West Germany and the rest of Europe, although orders from Japan are increasing: perhaps this new rosé export market is to be the saviour of Tavel, since the growers' applications to the authorities to be allowed to make red wine have in the past been refused.

The name Corne-Loup is derived from the name of an old *quartier* of Tavel that used to be visited by wolves: a watcher would be posted to look out for them, and the blowing of the horn by him would be the signal for everyone to seek refuge indoors.

The Corne-Loup wine is invariably soundly coloured, hints of pale red underlying the pink. It is a firmer wine, slightly less floral than it used to be, because of the push towards fresh flavours and early drinking. Well-vinified from year to year, it is one of the most consistent wines of Tavel, a good ambassador for the *appellation*.

Lafond, Jacques
    Domaine Corne-Loup   30126 Tavel

DOMAINE DE LA FORCADIÈRE

Owned by the ex-Mayor of Tavel, M. Armand Maby, the Forcadière vineyards at Tavel cover 44 hectares, which are spread over three locations – the Vestide and Campey sites, with their broken stone coverings, the Olivet *quartier*, where the slopes are sand-covered, and the Vallongue and Cravailleux areas where there are the rounded alluvial stones, or *galets*. The plantation is headed by the Grenache at 55 per cent, with support from the Cinsault at 15 per cent. The remaining *cépages* are the Mourvèdre, Syrah, Clairette, Picpoul, Carignan, and Bourboulenc.

M. Maby and his son Roger are very up-to-date wine-makers, and the style of their wines has evolved and continues to evolve as they seek improved techniques. They are not slaves to precedent, so in some vintages (the hotter years) they will block the malolactic in the rosé, while in others they won't. The Tavel, which gains its colour from a roughly two-day maceration, and is vinified with the use of stainless steel, is an excellent example of the fine style of wine here, a fact that was particularly relevant in the 1990 vintage, when the Forcadière Tavel was markedly more elegant and better than many wines of that year. A pale pink, its colour is lighter than Tavels of the past, although its underlying substance is betrayed by the lines of glycerine that run down the glass. The bouquet is softly scented, with a clear Grenache presence, and the palate is more refined than in wines of ten to fifteen years ago. There is a Provence rosé drinkability about the wine, which some would applaud, and others decry because of a loss of regionality. Well-balanced, and finishing clean and dry, the Maby Tavel benefits from being drunk in its second or third summer, since it takes about eighteen months to show and express itself more.

The *domaine* sells its Lirac with another registered mark-name, La Fermade. The red is co-led by the Mourvèdre and the Grenache (45 per cent each) – certainly an unusual policy for the region – with support from the Syrah and the Carignan. It is fermented at a controlled level of around 25°C, and receives a year in vat, followed by ageing in large barrels and in smaller, newer oak *pièces* – the latter receive around 20 per cent of the wine for just a few months. Bottled after two and a half to three years, it holds a sound red colour until into its sixth or seventh year – longer than in the Grenache-dominated days – and develops an opulent, fruity bouquet given time to evolve. Rich and broad on the palate, and topped up with a touch of end-tannin, this is a classier form of red Lirac, a step above many of the try-hard but workmanlike wines made there. In a strong vintage like 1986 or 1989, the Maby red Fermade can live for eight to ten years, but drinks very well when around five to six years old.

M. Maby has also made great efforts to develop a more sophisticated white wine at Lirac. His family's vineyard holding for the white covers 10 hectares against the red's 32 hectares, and the grape breakdown is Clairette 40 per cent, and Grenache Blanc and Picpoul 30 per cent each. Some of this is fermented in *inox*, and a part in new oak barrels, at 16–18°C. Bottled early in the new year, the wine shows all the aspects of low-temperature treatment, such as underripe apple smells on the bouquet, and a hint of sweets with some southern depth lying behind them. Very pale, the wine is suitably lively and zesty on the palate, but as with most of the wines made this way, the weight and roundness of the flavours do not emerge until the wine is about two years old.

M. Maby is a friend of some of the most thoughtful wine-makers in the Rhône, Gérard Chave at Hermitage and François Perrin of the Château de Beaucastel at Châteauneuf-du-Pape: the three meet to discuss ideas and innovations.

Maby, Armand, et Fils
    Domaine de la Forcadière   30126 Tavel

DOMAINE DE LA GENESTIÈRE

Historically, one of the best Tavels has come from a completely restored *domaine* just outside the village, the late M. Georges Bernard's Domaine de la Genestière. This property now sells its wine under the name of M. Bernard's widow Andrée, who lost her husband in 1983 after a prolonged illness which he bore stoically.

M. Bernard's wine was always outstanding, the very epitome of what a crisp, dry rosé should be. A beautifully pure pink in colour, it had a perfect balance of fruit and finesse that made it a joy to look at *and* to drink!

At the moment most of the high standards at this *domaine* have been maintained, although the wine has been less successful than previously in more difficult vintages like 1984. It is very much a traditional *domaine:* the Tavel is not bottled until the malolactic is completed, while the red Lirac receives cask-ageing for two or three years and the white Lirac is made at only mildly controlled temperatures.

The Domaine de la Genestière covers 35 hectares of vineyards at Tavel and 10 at Lirac. M. Bernard felt that the Syrah and the

Mourvèdre intruded in a rosé, so the *domaine* Tavel is made up of 50 per cent Grenache, 20 per cent Cinsault and the remainder from a mixture of Carignan, Clairette, Picpoul and Bourboulenc. With a brief maceration – a minimum of twelve and a maximum of twenty-four hours – the *domaine* is seeking a thoroughly well-balanced wine that is elegant, unfolds well in its first two years and is never too alcoholic; these wines rarely exceed 12°, in contrast with some of the lumbering lesser lights of the *appellation*. Bottling starts as soon as the malolactic has finished – in February or March generally – and the wine is put out on sale in the spring. Any one vintage is bottled bit by bit over the course of a year, and sells under two labels, the Domaine de la Genestière and the Domaine Longval.

M. Bernard used to lead a very private life, to the point of sometimes appearing to be on the fringe of the wine community. One of his joys was his faithfully restored *domaine*, complete with authentic eighteenth-century timberwork and a hall in pure Andalusian style. Like him, his daughter is a keen horsewoman; she has started an equestrian school next to the house and is renowned for her prowess in fighting bulls from horseback, as is the custom in Portugal and Mexico, in fights in which the bulls are not put to the sword. Here the greatest emphasis is placed on the speed and manoeuvrability of the horse, and the rider's skill in understanding and controlling the horse is paramount: all being well, Mlle Bernard will perform a season in Spain.

The Genestière wine used to stand up to travel far away in times gone by: in peaceful days it was imported to Cambodia, and was regarded as a successful companion right through a meal: when the wine is well made, as it was in 1985, 1986, 1988 and 1989, it has the class to partner both meat and fish.

Particularly good dishes to accompany Tavel are oysters and lamb or veal: the wine's dryness makes for an excellent combination, while it is also delightful with classic picnic dishes such as quiches and light pastry-covered onion or leek *tartes*.

Orientals have always held a soft spot for Tavel, and the main clients of this *domaine* are the Chinese restaurants in Paris. They buy the rosé rather than the white and red of Lirac: these last two are good but not startling wines, the white lacking a little character and freshness, while the red is firmly coloured and flavoured and a good companion for lamb or pork.

Bernard, Mme Andrée
   Domaine de la Genestière   30126 Tavel

DOMAINE MÉJAN-TAULIER

This is an approximately 32-hectare vineyard run by M. André Méjan, the son-in-law of the late M. Valéry Taulier. The *cépages* are led by 60 per cent Grenache, with support from 15 per cent Cinsault, 5 per cent Carignan and a recent introduction of Syrah, along with Picpoul, Clairette, Mourvèdre and Bourboulenc.

The aim is to make a light style of Tavel. Clean and fresh, the wine is released in the early summer, has its malolactic blocked, and is simple and satisfying to drink within three years.

Méjan, André
   Domaine Méjan-Taulier   30126 Tavel

PRIEURÉ DE MONTÉZARGUES

Further down the Rochefort road from Trinquevedel and hidden in a small gully that overlooks the plain running across to Villeneuve-lès-Avignon, is the Prieuré de Montézargues, one of the best but historically less well-known properties at Tavel. The 32-hectare vineyard is run by the children of the late Louis Allauzen; situated on the flank of a low hill, the vines are led by the Grenache (55 per cent) and Cinsault (15 per cent), the balance made up of Carignan, Picpoul, Clairette, Mourvèdre and a little Syrah. These grow in mainly sandy soil.

The Allauzens are young, keen and charming – relaxed folk who carry a late 1960s tranquility about with them. Wine-making used to be the occupation of their father on his own, and in his day most of the wine was sold to the *négociant* trade: now over 80 per cent of their average 1,200-hectolitre crop is bottled at the *domaine*.

Their harvest receives a one-night maceration in stainless steel tanks, and since 1984 it has been fermented at the controlled temperature of 18°C rather than the previous 25°C: their cooling machine and 360-hectolitre glass-lined vats are in underground cellars, where the coolness helps to keep the wine in stable, fresh conditions.

Until the mid-1980s the family did not have the requisite bottling facilities, so their wine was stored in the vats underground for up to eighteen months before being sold. Now they bottle from March onwards, having blocked the malolactic, and have thereby brought extra elegance and freshness to their wine.

There is clearly family pride behind this excellent Tavel: two sisters, one brother and one brother-in-law work on the property, with one full-time employee and extra help brought in for pruning and harvesting. The Allauzens produce full but very well-rounded, complete rosés. Always carrying an entrancing pink, the wine softens on its bouquet after a year, while a long finish follows the soft fruit that appears on the attack of the palate.

Small amounts of their wine are exported, including to Japan, and this is a *domaine* to look out for and enjoy in the years to come.

Allauzen
Prieuré de Montézargues   30126 Tavel

LE VIEUX MOULIN DE TAVEL

One of the few *domaines* to have its cellars right in the village itself is Le Vieux Moulin de Tavel, which makes very good wine. The owner, M. Gabriel Roudil, is grey-haired and slight but possesses a toughness and resilience that stem from over fifty years of hard outdoor work. He is now keeping a watchful eye on his three sons, who look after the daily cellar and vineyard work, and admits that this is a far cry from his grandfather's time, when the family employed fifteen full-time workers. The French laws of equal family inheritance have since reduced the property to 48.5 hectares at Tavel and 7 hectares in the Lirac *appellation*. Their Tavel holding is split into numerous plots, the smallest of which is under 1 hectare. These lie mainly on the plateau of Vallongue and on the *quartier* of Vestide.

M. Roudil is thorough and painstaking over his wine but concedes that luck can just occasionally help out a *vigneron*. In 1973, for instance, it was his small grandson who pointed out the need for an early harvest; near the middle of September M. Roudil had taken him out to show him the vines and by chance had given him a Cinsault grape to eat. 'I waited for his grimace at the grape's bitterness, but instead he just asked for another one. I knew then that I had to harvest straight away, mobilized everyone and everything I could find, and the next day the *vendange* had started,' said M. Roudil. His alacrity was well rewarded, for he managed to avoid the disastrous rains that helped to spoil many later-picked southern crops.

The Vieux Moulin rosé is one of the firmer Tavels available. Its colour is usually an intense dark pink, and the palate is often full and heavier than other local wines: cleanly made, it will often be a wine suited to sitting down and drinking with food.

Roudil, Gabriel, et Fils
  Le Vieux Moulin de Tavel   30126 Tavel

La Protectrice de Tavel

OTHER DOMAINES

Jean-Pierre and Pascal Lafond's 35-hectare Domaine de Roc-Épine is a good example of an easy, attractive style of Tavel: usually a pretty pink, it carries well-knit but open flavours which finish cleanly. Made from 60 per cent Grenache, 15 per cent Cinsault and 10 per cent each Syrah and Carignan, it is bottled with the malolactic blocked, is less heavyweight than some *cuvées*, and suitable for warm summer drinking with or without food.

The Domaine du Vieux Relais belongs to Félix Roudil, the brother of Gabriel of Vieux Moulin, and his children. Previously a member of the Co-opérative, M. Roudil makes a wine that when young is a bit stereotyped on the bouquet – full of grapey, almost yeasty aromas that need time to fade and calm down. It carries a delicate pink colour, and the palate shows firm, almost spicy flavours. It is best drunk within three years.

The 20-hectare Domaine de Tourtouil of M. Édouard Lefèvre is one of the few domaines that continues to make its Tavel by the direct press method – extracting the pink colour through the first pressing rather than relying on a short maceration of the grapes in contact with their skins. M. Lefèvre also bottles his Tavel with the malolactic blocked. The main grapes are Grenache (60 per cent), Cinsault (15 per cent) and Carignan (10 per cent). The wine is substantial enough to need food; solidly weighted and well coloured, it should be drunk within three years.

Tavel Vintages

Vintage lists are of secondary importance at Tavel, where the rosé should definitely be drunk young. Most of the *vignerons* are emphatic about this, and their wine supports their views. An interesting development, however, has come about with the advent of the modern, low-temperature fermentations that tuck up the wine pretty severely during its first year to eighteen months; whereas it could have been advisable for nearly all Tavels of the 1970s and early 1980s to be drunk before they were just two or three years old, the new style has in a way deferred the period for good drinking of these wines. The blocking of the malolactic fermentation, allowing the retention of greater acid in the wine, may also have a prolonging effect. So a valid life for enjoyable drinking is really towards four years now. The clear exceptions to this are the Château de Manissy and the 'Seigneur de Vaucrose'; the former is aged in wood, while the latter is stored for two years before release, so that if one's taste is for deep-orange, drier tasting wines, then these *domaines* are of interest. Recent vintages have been:

1962   Very good.
1963   Poor.

1964 Good.
1965 Very good.
1966 Very good.
1967 Very good.
1968 Mediocre.
1969 Mediocre.
1970 Good.
1971 Excellent.
1972 Good.
1973 Excellent.
1974 Good.
1975 Mediocre.
1976 Very good.
1977 Mediocre.
1978 Very good.
1979 Very good.
1980 Very good: great fruit and roundness.
1981 Good: light, fresh wines.
1982 Average: a large crop, wines varying widely between pale/ light and firm/solid.
1983 Good in parts. *Coulure* hit the Grenache, and a strongly ripened harvest produced wines that were robust and in some cases almost like light reds. The lack of finesse and elegance meant that these were wines to be drunk sitting down with food – a long way from being pleasant, quaffing summer wines.
1984 Mediocre. A difficult year in the vines, with severe *coulure* hitting the Grenache. The crop was not well ripened, and the wines lacked body. Chaptalization was allowed for the first time in forty years as the wines struggled to achieve passable degrees of alcohol. The wines were poorly structured and should have been drunk already.
1985 Very good. Well-rounded, fleshy wines with plenty of style and elegance and depth. The flavours on the palate softened well after two years, and were very long on the finish.
1986 Good. Solid wines with marginally less balance than the 1985s. Firm colour was extracted, and the bouquets were intense, occasionally a little hard. Weighty on the palate, they were best drunk within three years.
1987 Fair. The unsettled summer meant that the grapes were less

ripe than in recent years, and the *vignerons* had to select in order to extract wines with decent weight. The wines were pleasant to drink in their first three years – this was a vintage for those of modern taste who like their Tavel less full-bodied than in the past. There were some thin *cuvées*, however.

1988 Good. The wines were well coloured, their ripeness helped by some rain during the summer, and they held sound depth on the palate. The bouquets developed well after a couple of years, and the main problem with them was that some *cuvées* did not have very rounded fruit – the fruit was a bit hard. They should have been drunk by 1992.

1989 Very good. Attractively coloured wines, they are richer than the 1988s, more generous on the bouquet, and show pleasing balance and length on the palate. They will drink very well up to four years old or even a little older.

1990 Good in parts. The main problem was the tendency for some wines to be highly alcoholic – witness the Domaine de Tourtouil with 14.5°. The wines were generally well coloured and full bodied and should be drunk around 1992/93. Some *cuvées* may live for longer due to their alcoholic power. Note a very good, refined Forcadière.

Leading Growers at Tavel

The nucleus:

Allauzen
  Prieuré de Montézargues
Bernard, Mme Andrée
  Domaine de la Genestière
  Domaine de Longval
Cave Co-opérative des Grands
  Crus de Tavel
Demoulin, François
  Château de Trinquevedel
Lafond, Jacques   30126 Tavel
  Domaine Corne-Loup
Lafond, Jean-Pierre et Pascal
  Domaine de Roc-Épine

Maby, Armand et Roger
　Domaine de la Forcadière
Olivier, Société Jean
　Château d'Aquéria   } 30126 Tavel
Roudil, Gabriel, et Fils
　Le Vieux Moulin de Tavel

Other producers:

Amido, Christian
Charmasson–Plantevin
　Les Trois Logis
Delorme, Christophe
　Domaine de la Mordorée
de Lanzac, Norbert
Lefèvre, Édouard
　Domaine de Tourtouil
Leperchois, Christian
　Domaine des Carabiniers   } 30126 Tavel
Lévêque
　Seigneur de Vaucrose
Domaine de Manissy
Méjan-Taulier
　Clos Canto-Perdrix
Roudil, Félix, et ses Enfants
　Domaine du Vieux Relais
Roussel, Pierre
　Domaine des Jonciers

15
Lirac

═══════

The *appellation* of Lirac runs alongside Tavel, and many of the Tavel growers make some red and white Lirac to offer with their rosé. But this is an *appellation* that suffers from its neighbours' greater eminence: it is the 'nearly' *appellation* of the Rhône. If customers want southern Rhône red, they go to Gigondas or Châteauneuf; if they want rosé, they go to Tavel. And as the area is not considered a natural home for white wines, Lirac misses out on that front as well.

This image problem has existed for the last fifteen years, although Lirac has never hit the headlines since its inception in 1945. It is a sad state of affairs, for there are some talented wine growers who are making excellent reds, fruity rosés and very successful whites.

Curiously, it is the rosé that in the past has brought the *appellation* what little fame it has ever known. Generally under-appreciated, the Lirac rosés are consistently good and sometimes outstanding, and represent fine value for money.

But the rosé market is collapsing. Modern drinkers may be lured by pink champagne and its promise of good times and high living, but still rosé is not seen in the same racy light. It has a much more humdrum image, and anyway there are good, well-packaged rosés now being made in Burgundy, the Loire, southern France, Italy – to say nothing of California and Australia. Growers have seen the demand for their rosé fall away dramatically since about 1975, when it accounted for 50 per cent of all Lirac, so that now it forms no more than 20 per cent of all the wine made.

On the increase, justifiably, is the production of white wine. In the early 1980s, this formed under 3 per cent of all Lirac. By 1989 about 7 per cent had become white wine. Low-temperature fermentation and modern cellar care used on southern white grapes is a strong formula, and Lirac whites are the quiet heroes of this *appellation*.

Crisp and fruity when young, they always possess enough weight to be interesting shortly after bottling, or if allowed to age for a couple of years. The reds, meanwhile, continue discreetly along their way, rather lost in the line-up of southern French red wines, and forming over half the *appellation*'s total production.

The *appellation* takes its name from one of four small villages that lie in a ring near the Rhône about 16 kilometres north-west of Avignon. Lirac itself is an unmemorable place, with severe stone houses looking on to a spartan main square that lacks even the slightest motions of everyday life. The other villages are a little more *mouvementé*, notable Roquemaure, which stands right beside the Rhône 6 kilometres east of Lirac. Vines were grown here, and extensively in the neighbouring area, in the thirteenth century, but the first firm evidence of a wine transaction is not before 1357; then the papal Court, under Innocent VI, purchased twenty casks from a Roquemaure merchant called Guillelmi Malrepacis and also drew on stocks of wine available from St-Laurent-des-Arbres.

Roquemaure is first identified in literature in the texts of Livy ('The War with Hannibal'), since it is deduced that Hannibal sent his elephants across the Rhône on rafts at Roquemaure, although Livy makes no mention of the part of the Rhône that was crossed. Bernard Levin, in his *Hannibal's Footsteps*,[1] maintains that the crossing was near Fourques, just outside Arles. It was obviously a perilous operation, for the elephants' rafts had to be covered with earth as a ploy to overcome their alarm at not finding themselves on *terra firma*; then they had to be loaded on – females first, to persuade the males to put their best foot forward – and they had to face the hordes of noisy Gauls waiting on the eastern bank. Later, when his troops were contemplating the crossing of the Alps with some despondency, Hannibal harangued them in a famous speech that spoke of their exploit of 'taming the violence of the mighty Rhône'. Crossing the Alps and fording the Rhône were obviously the two most difficult physical feats that he accomplished on his journey from Spain to Italy.

Roquemaure's easy accessibility and convenient situation next to the Rhône attracted both farming and commercial interests, and the local wine-makers were active in the defence of the quality of their wine and in ensuring that their market was not upset by intrusions of wine from other regions. Thus in the early eighteenth century the

---

[1] Bernard Levin, *Hannibal's Footsteps* (London: Jonathan Cape, 1985).

panel, or consuls, of Roquemaure refused to allow Châteauneuf-du-Pape to pass for a local wine, saying that it was only very ordinary and that it also bore a prejudicial *goût de terroir* – bold words indeed!

The protection of the wine of Roquemaure, and of that of the surrounding Gard *département*, was formalized in 1737, when a royal decree for the first time named different wine-making areas under a grouped title, that of La Côte du Rhône. The decree specifically mentioned all the four villages that today make up the Lirac *appellation* – Roquemaure, Lirac, St-Laurent-des-Arbres and St-Geniès-de-Comolas – as well as Tavel, Orsan, Chusclan and Codolet. All these '*véritables bons crus*' were to have the letters 'CDR' burned on to their barrels, along with the vintage year of the wine, while no wine from outside this region was to be stored at Roquemaure, whose port was a busy shipping centre for the Gardois wines to Britain, Holland and Germany.

By 1774 Roquemaure was the principal wine-producing community of the Gard *département*, figures of that year showing that altogether 1,226 *muids* (barrels) of 675 litres each were made there, with the next most important village, Laudun, producing only 772 *muids*.

The other two villages in the *appellation*, St-Laurent-des-Arbres and St-Geniès-de-Comolas, lie north of Roquemaure, just off the Orange–Nîmes main road. St-Laurent is easily the most striking village of the four, with a well-preserved fortified church dating from the twelfth century: its tower and walls are a local landmark, visible for some distance all around. During the early part of the nineteenth century Pauline Malosse de Casal, the elaborately named owner of the Domaine du Sauvage, exported wine from St-Laurent through the Mediterranean port of Sète to destinations as far away as Britain, Holland and even the United States. This *domaine*, and its wine Vin du Camp d'Annibal, have since disappeared without trace.

St-Geniès is the most unfortunately sited village of the four, for it lies near a large, smoky steelworks and spends many of its days enveloped in a sort of unhealthy morning mist. The *mistral* wind blows the factory fumes south towards St-Geniès, and the effect of this semi-perpetual haze on the surrounding vineyards can only be harmful: it is noticeable that the grapes ripen less quickly with this smoky barrier between them and the sun.

Even though its wines have not been widely heard of, Lirac has one great claim to fame in the history of French viticulture. It is a dubious honour: phylloxera is said to have started there in about 1863. By all accounts the then owner of the Château de Clary, which has remained a wine *domaine* to this day, was a great experimenter and innovator and would take delight in making the most unlikely wines from his vineyard: these included ports and madeiras. One day he tried planting some Californian vine cuttings to see how they would fare at Lirac, but this time he had made a grave miscalculation. The American vines, being resistant to the phylloxera insect, carried plenty of the little creatures in their roots. The defenceless French vines were easy prey for them, and Clary's vineyard was promptly devoured by the phylloxera, which went on to ravage most of Europe's vines. Other tales may be told about the outbreak of phylloxera, but the Lirac growers strongly believe in the authenticity of this one.

Lirac was granted its own *appellation contrôlée* in 1945, but the vineyard was then less than a quarter of its present size (now about 730 hectares), and most of the wine would be sold in bulk to merchants. A notable exception was the Château de Ségriès, which in the summer 1963 list of the Professional and Businessmen's Wine Vaults in the City of London (Gerald Asher under another name) was one of the five red Rhônes, the 1959 vintage selling for 9s 6d (47p) a bottle. The Rauzan-Gassies 1955 was, at £1, just over double the price, the Château Margaux 1955, at £2.25, about four times the price. Was the Ségriès dear or the Margaux cheap?

Fame and fortune generally continued to elude Lirac, and it was not until the early 1960s that its popularity began to pick up from almost nothing. Then the arrival of several families from Algeria marked the turning-point. Expelled with nothing to their names, the ex-colonists were determined to retrieve their situation. Having bought *domaines* throughout the *appellation,* they set out to gain a better price for, and a wider distribution of, their wine by selling it bottled. Lirac stalls appeared at all the major French wine fairs, and little by little spread greater knowledge and appreciation of these agreeably uncomplicated wines.

Much of the land bought by the ex-Algerian settlers was wooded and uncultivated, and it was a major task to make it fit for vines. One of the best examples of their plantations is the plateau that runs west of Roquemaure; here the vines date from 1962, and their limestone–clay soil has a surface closely resembling that of Château-neuf-du-Pape, being covered with piles upon piles of smooth, rust-coloured stones. These range from the size of a potato to that of a water melon and, strewn all over the vineyard, perform well their function of radiating heat on to the vines. Elsewhere on this plateau there are patches of almost pure limestone and dense sand underneath the stony covering. The sudden open spaces of these young vineyards come as a surprise in the generally rather scrub-covered countryside; as one stands on this plateau on a clear day amid the intense light summoned by the driving *mistral* wind, the eye is dazzled, both by the pale shades of the soil and by the long, distant view across the Rhône Valley.

Apart from the Roquemaure plateau, most of the other *appellation* vineyards are on gentle slopes that run away from the respective village centres. Near St-Geniès the soil is strewn with paler, chipped chalk stones, on which red-grape vines are grown. Many of the white-grape vines are grown on the lighter, chalk or limestone soil.

Out of keeping with most of the Côtes du Rhône, Lirac has a large amount of Cinsault vines, most of which were planted in the rapid expansion of the early 1960s; these undoubtedly contribute towards the native softness noticeable in many of the red wines – along with differences in both the soil and level of moisture that prevail between the Gard and the east bank of the Rhône.

The Grenache at a minimum of 40 per cent remains the majority grape, while the Syrah – often around 15 per cent of a vineyard – is a more recent but well-planted vine. The Clairette similarly accounts for 10 per cent or so of the plantation.

Although the founding grapes at Lirac were the Mourvèdre, Cinsault and Grenache, it was only in the 1970s that the Mourvèdre started to move back towards favour, being taken up by growers like Maby at La Fermade and Lombardo at Domaine du Devoy. *Vignerons* say that it needs a deep soil with good retention of water – conditions which it receives at Bandol further south on the coast – and that it suffers in the driest years like 1982 and 1988. Its general effect is to inject a little more staying-power and depth into the red wines, along with a stronger colour, and it is now regarded as a core participant in most red Liracs, sometimes up to 45 per cent, as with the Château d' Aquéria and La Fermade.

Other grapes to be found within the *appellation* are the gradually disappearing Carignan, which anyway is not permitted to make up more than 10 per cent of the vineyard, the Ugni Blanc (the grape used in the making of Cognac, where it passes under the name of St-

Émilion), the Bourboulenc, the Marsanne, the Calitor, the Picpoul and the Maccabéo. This last grape is rarely found in the Côtes du Rhône, and, according to Jancis Robinson in *Vines, Grapes and Wines*,[1] is the Spanish Viura, the producer of light, fast-maturing whites that is also widely planted in the Côtes du Roussillon area of France. At Lirac the growers think it adds something special (never defined) to the wines.

In a hot, ripe year like 1990, where the crop was helped by some rain in late August, the *vendanges* can come in the first week of September. Back in the 1970s, the norm was to harvest towards the end of September, although there were some *vignerons* at that time who preferred an earlier date to capture extra fruitiness and tartness in their whites and rosés; the whites of Lirac have in the past been especially prone to early oxidation, but thankfully much of this problem has been solved through new cellar techniques and earlier vineyard operations.

The red wine is vinified along traditional lines, although some growers like Verda handle the harvest very tenderly, with light crushing resulting in perhaps 20 per cent of the crop remaining almost intact as fermentation starts.

The Verdas are owners of the leading *domaine*, Château St-Roch, and in order to extract sufficient tannin to allow their red wines to keep for eight years or so, they leave the grapes to macerate for a week before a final alcoholic fermentation of between four and eight days takes place. After racking, the wine is stored in enamel-lined vats for about a year to settle and clarify.

At this stage the *cuves* are still split on an individual grape variety basis, so that the Verdas for example, do not assemble the various varieties until a year after the harvest. The wine will then have a stay in cask whose length varies according to the depth of the vintage: the 1984 received three months' ageing, for instance, the 1985 and the 1989 nearer nine months. Ten per cent of the best red wine of St Roch from the best vintages receives over a year in cask, and comes out as their special *cuvée* Ancienne Viguerie: this is one of the most solid, well-structured wines of the *appellation*.

There are two marked schools of thought about wood-ageing for Lirac, however. Besides the Château St-Roch, there are *vignerons* like Christian Leperchois of Domaine des Carabiniers and Jean

[1] Jancis Robinson, *Vines, Grapes and Wines*, (London: Mitchell Beazley, 1986).

Duseigneur of Domaine Duseigneur who leave their red Liracs in cask, the former for eighteen months or more. But there is a solid body of producers who above all want a tightly knit but fresh wine. As M. Joseph Lombardo of the excellent Domaine du Devoy puts it, 'The tannins of Lirac have great finesse, derived from the soil here in the Gard, and they risk being overwhelmed by the coarser tannins that the wood would bring in.' M. Lombardo therefore crushes and destalks a part of his crop and operates a semi-*macération carbonique* vinification which culminates in a two-year stay in concrete vats for his red.

This emphasis on a fresh style is also practised by most of the ex-Algerian *pied noir* growers, as they are known in France, who arrived from North Africa – Assémat, Marie Pons-Mure and Rousseau, for instance. Their wines' fruit is always clean and firm, and in lesser vintages like 1984, 1987 and 1991, their reds drink well within eighteen months of the harvest. The bolder vintages like 1989, 1985 and 1983 should be drunk between three and seven years old.

Lirac is the best red wine in the Gard *département*, and it is most interesting to see how these west bank wines differ radically in style from the east bank wines of the Vaucluse *département*. The strong, sometimes harsh *goût de terroir* evident in wines such as Cairanne or Vacqueyras is noticeably absent at Lirac, where the reds are lightly styled, fruity and easy to swill back without too much thought. They are not the sorts of wine that will make a strong initial impression on a first-time Rhône drinker, being dwarfed by their neighbours, the Vaucluse or even the Drôme wines, into a sort of downbeat modesty. Certainly, the less good examples that one finds outside France lack any sort of backbone of flavour, and this is the risk that the wine runs if it is not well made.

The longest-lived wines by and large come from the best *domaines*, properties like Château St-Roch, Château de Ségriès, and La Fermade, with the Château de Bouchassy and Roger and Jean-Jacques Sabon at Domaine Sabon also making wines that show well from around their second year until they are seven to ten years old. The two densest wines come from Château St-Roch and Château de Ségriès: under François, the son of the Count, Ségriès's red is now invariably well coloured and in need of at least four years' bottle-age before its bouquet opens up and its palate softens. Meanwhile M. Armand Maby is experimenting with the use of some new oak in the ageing of his red Lirac, a process which has perhaps added to his wine's structure.

The main body of reds, as represented by the well-made Domaine du Devoy, are wines entirely suited for early and uncomplicated drinking. Their colour – a pale, orthodox red with no streaks of black or purple visible – beckons from their earliest days, and there are invariably an attractive harmony and light fruit – akin almost to a plum jam or ripe strawberries – in support.

These wines possess such an embracing softness on both bouquet and palate that they are delightful to drink all round the year, and, unlike some of their heavyweight neighbours, satisfy even in summer, when other more heady wines have been put aside until the arrival of the autumn breezes. To avoid an unseemly rush towards a *primeur*-styled Lirac, growers are sensibly forbidden from releasing the wine from their cellars until 1 May of the year after the harvest. So red Lirac remains the gentle red of the southern Rhône, its *cru* Beaujolais-style reminiscent of good Juliénas or Fleurie. Drunk at cellar temperature or slightly chilled, this main body of Lirac red can be delicious with cold meats, pâtés, pasta or white meat dishes.

Most of the Lirac rosé is made by the *saignée* method, with a maceration of several hours of the Grenache and Cinsault grapes to gain a little colour, and then about a week's fermentation. Growers like Assémat, Mme Pons-Mure, Lombardo and Verda control the fermentation temperature of their rosé vats, limiting them to 20–22°C, as opposed to around 28°C for the reds. The wine remains in stainless steel, glass or enamel-lined vats until its malolactic is completed, and is bottled in its first spring or early summer.

By macerating the grapes over a night or so, and occasionally adding in 5 per cent of Syrah, the growers are able to adjust the depth of colour in their rosé. Likewise, if the wine needs a little more guts, perhaps 5 per cent of Mourvèdre can be added; or should a lovely gulping wine be sought, the proportion of Cinsault can be increased. In this respect the growers of Lirac hold an advantage in flexibility of style over single-grape rosé-makers elsewhere, such as at Sancerre, and in other parts of the Loire or Burgundy.

Dazzling pink when young, a good Lirac rosé is often on a par with Tavel, and indeed in some vintages is lighter and fresher. Refined and delicately fruity, the wine is usually well balanced, crisp and clean-finishing, and not over-alcoholic – this last factor stemming in part from the abnormally high amount of Cinsault grapes that go into it: up to 80 per cent in certain *cuvées*.

It is also fortunate that at Lirac there exists none of the folklore of Tavel that endows rosés with legendary ageing powers. The growers suggest that their rosé should be drunk within three years of the harvest, although Jean-Jacques Verda considers that the St-Roch rosé will support up to five years' bottle age.

As the amount of rosé made has fallen steadily from the mid-1970s – it is now only 10 per cent of the production at the Domaine du Devoy and Château St-Roch, for instance – so the amount of white wine is increasing steadily. In the 1970s only 2–3 per cent of the harvest was white, but now it is nearer 7 per cent overall, and 10 per cent in the better, more progressive *domaines*. In 1986 a total of 831 hectolitres were vinified, and by 1989 this had risen to 1,221 hectolitres.

The grape varieties used for the white wine are generally the Grenache Blanc, Bourboulenc, Clairette, Picpoul and small amounts of Ugni Blanc and Marsanne. Proportions differ markedly throughout the *appellation*, with the three mainstays – the Grenache Blanc, Bourboulenc and Clairette – usually accounting for 30–40 per cent each when planted.

The Verda family made their first white wine in 1960, but in 1977 changed the combination of vines used and the method of fermentation. Their Grenache Blanc (30 per cent), Clairette and Bourboulenc (35 per cent each) grow in more meagre soil, dominated by limestone, than their red-grape vines, a policy that is also pursued by Joseph Lombardo of Domaine du Devoy who made his first white wine in 1986, and whose 2 hectares of white vines have a primarily northerly exposure.

In all instances the growers are seeking to achieve a freshness in their whites that is not conferred by traditional planting and vinification. The cellar treatment of the whites runs along modern lines. The crop is pressed and left to settle at around 6°C for about twenty-four hours. After this *débourbage*, fining takes place with the use of bentonite solutions; remaining particles are removed to secure a finer must before fermentation starts.

The juice then ferments, often now in stainless steel vats, at controlled temperatures from 14–19°C. After a twelve- to fifteen-day fermentation, the wine is taken off its lees, racked and filtered on a medium and fine setting. The filtrations complete the work of the settling and fining earlier; by taking out much of the bacteria they serve to help to block the malolactic fermentation, so that the wine is bottled with greater residual acid levels, around 4.2–4.5 grams rather than 3.5 grams or so.

Bottled between February and April, white Lirac is now the best-value white wine in the southern Rhône. When young it is very pale, only just off-white, and its bouquet is full of fresh fruit aromas: greengages, limes and even grapefruit spring to mind. The palate is most impressive, since underneath the young fruit there is a quietly imposing fullness and very good clean length. This southern weight is what saves white Lirac from being just another fresh and zesty low-temperature fermented white wine, one where the primary aromas of fermentation dominate and there is insufficient substance behind to guide the wine into a second, more complex phase of development.

After two years in bottle the colour has started to deepen towards a firmer yellow, while the bouquet has moved into a secondary phase where more nutty, dried apricot or peach aromas predominate. The palate – full, with dried fruit flavours, almondy nuttiness and hints of citrus – possesses strong length and a clean, chewy finish. After five years the wine is likely to become more markedly old, although well-balanced vintages like 1986 and 1989 will live on for nearer ten years.

Lirac as a whole produces good, eminently drinkable wines whose price has not been pulled up at the same fast rate as the northern *crus* such as St-Joseph; while its red wine is placed firmly in the middle of a band of lower image, easy quaffing wines, perhaps it will be through its white wine that this poorly known *appellation* will garner some fame and fortune.

One reason why Lirac may not today be better known is that the area has not continuously held vineyards in the last 100 years. There is therefore only a very patchy history and local wine tradition. The vineyards now set on the rocky *garrigues* around Roquemaure were first abandoned after the phylloxera attack but also, for a second time, between the two World Wars, when farmers preferred simple, low-outlay cultivation such as olives or minor forestation.

Between the establishment of *appellation contrôlée* in 1945 and the arrival of the ex-Algerian *vignerons* in the 1960s, there were only three private wine *domaines* at Lirac. They were the Château de Ségriès, the Château de Clary and M. Antoine Verda's very good Domaine du Château St-Roch: the first took up its own bottling only in the early 1970s, and even today Clary's wine is sent to a merchant nearby for both bottling and marketing, and as a result loses an unquestionably valuable 'château-bottled' identity, which can be extremely useful in promoting the name of an obscure *appellation*.

The owner of the Château de Ségriès is the Comte de Régis, Lirac's longest-serving *vigneron*. He has looked after the family property for over sixty years, although in the 1980s he handed over the day-to-day running of his wine estate to his son François. Now ninety years old, but young in spirit for his age, the Count lives in his fine pre-Revolution town house in Nîmes. Together he and his wife make a splendid *vieille France* couple – very polite, very charming and not at all taken aback by the eccentricities of the modern age. The Count explained how he had become a wine grower: 'Wine has not always been my family's main occupation, as the Château de Ségriès used to produce mainly corn. After phylloxera the vineyards were enlarged, but my father suddenly died when I was ten. What would you have done . . . ? I didn't really have much choice but to keep the vineyard going and to see that my five younger brothers and sisters were adequately cared for.'

The Ségriès vineyard covers over 20 hectares, with the plantation led by the Grenache Noir and the Syrah. The Count himself was President of the Growers' Association of Lirac for over thirty years and played a prominent role in seeing that the area obtained its own *appellation contrôlée* shortly after the Second World War. Now he is happy to lead a quieter life, mainly in Nîmes, but also keeping an occasional eye on his son's work at his Lirac and Bandol *domaines*, as well as checking up on his wife's property in the Mâconnais region, north of Lyon.

Since the second half of the 1970s the red wine of Château de Ségriès has firmly established itself in the front rank at Lirac, drawing away from a formerly over-light and straightforward style towards a more substantial and complex make-up. Eighty per cent of the estate's wine is red; vinified traditionally, a good vintage like the 1985 was held in concrete vats until bottling in the spring of 1988. The 1986 received a bit less ageing, but neither wine was filtered, having fallen limpid after an early fining and prolonged storage in vat. By contrast, the lighter 1987 red was sold off in bulk to a merchant, while the 1988 and 1989 both contain agreeable depth of flavour, the latter being preferable for its all-round quality.

On the bouquet, red Ségriès possesses aromas like gentle spices, and a steady backbone of tannin holds the wine together on the palate, making it one of the more long-lived samples in the *appellation*. The 1978, 1982, 1983, and 1985, 1988 and 1989 were all wines capable of keeping for eight to ten years, often opening up well after five years.

The château also makes a sound rosé, mainly by *saignée*, although in 1986 one-third was vinified by direct pressing to avoid the extraction of too dark a colour. 'In certain vintages the *saignée* method can produce rosés that are too close to small red wines; I prefer my rosé to be nearer a white in style and not to carry too dark a colour. Unfortunately a lot of the wine going to the merchant trade is well coloured, because that's thought to be what the public wants,' explained François de Régis.

Each year the *domaine* makes about 20 hectolitres of very respectable white wine from 50 per cent Clairette, 35 per cent Ugni Blanc and 15 per cent Bourboulenc. It is vinified at around 23°C, and is suitable for drinking in its first three years: clean and fruity, it represents the more traditional style of white.

The family of one of the other great veterans of Lirac still own and run the Château de Clary. This rambling *domaine* belongs to Mme *Veuve* Mayer, whose husband Marius died in the mid-1980s. Their daughter Nicole is now running the estate, which stands in secluded country beside the dense forest of Clary, north of Tavel: because second-century Roman relics, such as wine decanters, goblets and amphorae, have been found in its grounds, the Mayers are convinced that it is the oldest wine *domaine* in the region.

Certainly, the wine has been sold abroad for a long time; in the eighteenth century 600-litre barrels of Clary were regularly shipped from Roquemaure to Switzerland, Germany and Britain. The wine intended for France would also be shipped from Roquemaure, travelling by way of the country's many canals. This lively enterprise flourished for some decades but was abruptly halted when the château's owner, the Comte de St-Priest, was guillotined by the *révolutionnaires* in Montpellier.

The late M. Mayer bought the property in the 1930s and doubled the size of its vineyard to 55 hectares. He was very keen on drinking his wine with the game from the Forest of Clary: in days gone by this used to be wild boar and deer, but more recently hare, partridge and quail were most commonly found.

The arrival of the *pied noir* wine growers stirred Lirac from this easy tranquility and provided the area with badly needed momentum. They found vineyard cultivation and cellar techniques less evolved by several years than those practised on the large estates of North Africa, and their enthusiasm and uninhibited outlook greatly stimulated the worldwide marketing of the wines of Lirac. One of the first families to settle was that of M. Charles and Mme Marie Pons-Mure; like many others, this stalwart pair, now both well into their eighties, were forced to abandon their Algerian properties when independence was granted in 1961. Mme Pons-Mure had been running a wine *domaine* of over 345 hectares in the highly esteemed area of Oran: 'I had completely replanted the entire vineyard since the Second World War, so you can well imagine my feelings when we had to leave – with nothing in our pockets,' she said.

Her husband went on: 'I used to pilot myself about in a small plane in Algeria, so once we had arrived in France I decided to take a chance on hiring one and scouting out several likely wine areas. From the air I find it is much easier to spot and assess the potential of rural land, and this was what led me to Lirac, as I'd noticed the possibilities of the wooded plateau near Roquemaure. The land was bought cheaply because it was wooded and, once bulldozed flat, was planted with vines.'

Mme Pons-Mure resumed: 'Charles started making wine from 12 hectares of vines that I'd bought, and we decided to send some to the International Wine Fair at Mâcon in order to try and get our names on the map. The only problem was that we didn't have a *domaine* name by which we could be identified. At the time I was living in a tumbledown house that was slowly undergoing repairs, so I thought I would use the name "Castel Oualou" as a joke. [*Castel* is Provençal for 'castle' and *oualou* means 'there is no' in Arabic.] Well, that was all very well,' she continued, 'and the wine won medals at the 1962 Mâcon Fair, which meant that the name of "Castel Oualou" started to become known. One day, though, the official name inspectors came along and asked to see my castle. When I told them there wasn't one and that the castle pictured on my label came from *Snow White and the Seven Dwarfs*, they weren't at all amused. They made me print a cross through the Snow White castle, and the label has stayed that way ever since.'

Mme Pons-Mure's Domaine de Castel Oualou, whose cellars are side by side with those of Château St-Roch, is now run by Jean-Claude Assémat's son and covers 53 hectares; its wine comes in the light, quaffable style that is most typical of Lirac reds. In good vintages like 1983 and 1988, the wines are attractively deep cherry-coloured and delicately balanced, the fruitiness underpinned by steady Syrah support. In lighter vintages like 1984 the Syrah was used for up to 40 per cent of the *cuvée*, to give the wine extra punch and resilience; there is also a predominantly Syrah-based *cuvée* on its own, which provides good drinking over two to five years.

Castel Oualou's rosé and white wines are also correctly made, marked by light fruit and gentle aromas that make them good to drink young.

Charles Pons-Mure himself used to run his own *domaine* at Lirac, the Domaine de la Tour, but he sold this to a relation, Mme Andréo, in the early 1980s, and it has since changed hands once more. He is one of the larger-than-life characters of the Rhône Valley, however. His craggy face has soaked up miles of travel, and the air he carries of explorer-cum-intellectual reminds one of that intrepid Scot, Fitzroy Maclean. Indeed, it would be no surprise at all to bump into M. Pons-Mure in the Caucasus of Russia or on a Western Isle in Scotland, as he is a rare and memorable character; for ten years champion yachtsman of North Africa, he has also on more than one occasion won the four-day tour of Algeria, driving Peugeots and Panhards around the desert.

The Pons-Mures's frequent winning of medals at important wine fairs has done much for Lirac's reputation over the years. Another family related to them, the Rousseaus, also worked hard on projecting the *appellation* and injecting life into it.

M. Louis Rousseau has now handed over the running of his *domaine* to his son Alexis, but, keeping up the family spirit, he arrived at Lirac via far-flung places, notably Algeria and Uruguay. His explanation of how he arrived in Lirac is colourful: 'In Algeria my business was livestock breeding and cereal growing, but after the first Algerian rebellion of November 1954, I thought that things could only get worse. Consequently, I went off with some friends to South America to see what possibilities there were in that part of the world. We hired a taxi for a month and visited most of the interesting Uruguayan estates. The result was that I returned with my family in 1956, having sold everything in Algeria, and was once more breeding sheep and Hereford bulls. Around 1963, when Uruguay's economy had really started to crack up, I came back to France and bought vineyards at Laudun and then Lirac.'

Alexis Rousseau makes red and rosé wines from the two *appellations*. Light, well-balanced and fruity, they are easy quaffing wines that can be enjoyed without ado in their first three years.

Close family connections continue elsewhere in the *appellation*, for Mme Pons-Mure's son-in-law, the enterprising Jean-Claude Assémat, owns the 36-hectare vineyard Les Garrigues. M. Assémat also sells his wine under the Domaines des Causses and St-Eynes labels and varies his method of vinification between a customary short fermentation and the use of *macération carbonique* for certain *cuvées*. His ordinary Lirac is put on sale a little more than one year after the harvest and, like nearly all the 'light-style' wines, is quite refreshing, without being particularly spectacular. More interesting is his pure Syrah wine, which carries more substance, and his low-temperature-fermented white wine made from Picpoul, Bourboulenc and Clairette. This last is suitable for early drinking, and is a good representative for white Lirac.

The best *domaine* over the years at Lirac has been, and still is, the Domaine du Château St-Roch, owned by Antoine Verda and jointly run by his well-qualified sons Jean-Jacques, who looks after the cellars and vinification, and André, a roly-poly, cheerful man who runs the vineyards. Jean-Jacques, a dark, bespectacled man in his thirties, explained how the *domaine* was created: 'My father started his career as a merchant at Châteauneuf-du-Pape but considered that this side of the Rhône held more potential for someone wanting to own vineyards. Consequently, he set about buying lots of land on the *quartiers* that are named Lescarce, Le Devès and La Pesade, all set on the gentle hills around Roquemaure. By 1955, he had bought almost 40 hectares, of which only eight already bore vines, but these were themselves very run down. Our first wine was made in 1960 from just 2 hectares of young vines, and slowly we increased the replanting to cover all 40 hectares.

'We also now own the Cantegril vineyards near Roquemaure and the wine from those 20 hectares is vinified here in the same cellars and sold as Domaine Cantegril-Verda. Our grape mix is much as it is elsewhere at Lirac, with the Grenache complying with its minimum 40 per cent requirement, the Cinsault accounting for 23 per cent, the Syrah and the Mourvèdre 13 per cent each and the difference made up of white grapes. Our rosé is usually about half Grenache and half Cinsault, while the red is generally made up of just under half Grenache, 25 per cent Cinsault, 15 per cent Syrah and 15 per cent

Mourvèdre. Our special *cuvée* of red, Ancienne Viguerie, would contain less Cinsault and more Mourvèdre for ageing purposes.'

Darting enthusiastically around the well laid-out cellars of St-Roch, Jean-Jacques continued, 'Lirac is known as a fruity wine, but I feel that it needs a little more development than that, which is why we like to leave it for between three and six months in our 4,000–litre oak barrels here. This develops its bouquet and helps to give it a bit more solid texture. As a result, I would say that our best vintages over the last few years – 1978, 1983, 1985 and 1989 – can live for six to perhaps ten years. Lighter years like 1984, 1987 and 1991 are best drunk within three or four years, while the 1986 and the 1988 are six or seven-year wines.'

About three-quarters of the St-Roch wine is red, and it is a good standard-bearer for the *appellation*. A wine of tremendous harmony, it has more depth and complexity than most of the Lirac reds, which is essential if these wines are not to remain semi-forgotten and nondescript. The opening-up of other sources of light red wine, ranging from subsidized East European countries to Australia, South Africa, South America, and, of course, jug wine from the United States, means that wines like the great middle mass of red Lirac are under continued threat of remaining the 'nearly' wines of France: not an enviable position in an age when marketing devices, cachet and satisfying a niche clientele are all factors that count towards the commercial success of a wine. All a long way from just growing vines and making wine, it seems.

A little over 10 per cent of the St-Roch production is now in white wine. This heads a nucleus of whites of excellent quality, other notable examples being the Domaine du Devoy, La Fermade, Les Garrigues and Château de Bouchassy. The 35-hectare Domaine du Devoy is owned by M. Joseph Lombardo, an ex-wine-grower from Tunisia, whose 200-hectare property there was nationalized in 1964. The Devoy vineyard is grouped in one plot on the plateau between Roquemaure and St-Laurent-des-Arbres, although M. Lombardo has a 2-hectare white-vine holding near St-Laurent. The white is made mainly from Grenache Blanc and Clairette, with support from the Bourboulenc and, unusually for Lirac, the Marsanne. The Devoy wines are all very well made, the reds possessing interesting blackcurrant fruit and sound depth, and the rosés and whites running with fruit and clean flavours.

Other *domaines* of note at Lirac are the Domaine Sabon – well-made, firm red wines especially; the Château de Bouchassy, where Gérard Degoul makes a traditionally styled red and a good, fresh white; the Château d'Aquéria, whose 7-hectare vineyard produces an elegant, solid red, made from 45 per cent Grenache and Mourvèdre each, and 10 per cent Cinsault, aged for six months in cask; the Château de Boucarut, with sound, correctly made wines; the Les Queyrades *domaine* of André Méjan based at Tavel, notable for good, well-coloured and fruited reds; the progressive Domaine de la Mordorée (rich Lirac and Châteauneuf reds); and finally the revived Cave Co-opérative de Roquemaure, whose new director is moving and shaking up their production of red wine.

Lirac Vintages

Most of the red wine of Lirac is made in a light, overtly fruity style, and these wines are suitable for quite early drinking – at anything between two and five years old. The slightly weightier wines, such as the Châteaux St-Roch and de Ségriès, as well as some of Armand Maby's *cuvées*, can be kept for up to ten years or so, but do not improve much after eight years. The rosés are made to be drunk young, and when more than four years old often show signs of maderization. The whites are best drunk young, before their sixth birthday, although they can live for eight to ten years.

1955   Very good.
1956   Good.
1957   Good.
1958   Poor.
1959   Good, the wines were well balanced.
1960   Generally mediocre, although there was an outstanding red at Château de Ségriès.
1961   Excellent. Wines of tremendous balance and finesse.
1962   Good.
1963   Poor.
1964   Very good. Robust, long-lived red wines.
1965   Poor.
1966   Very good. Well-perfumed, 'complete' wines of great charm.
1967   Good, although the wines were surprisingly quite consider-

ably inferior to those from Châteauneuf-du-Pape across the river.

1968 Mediocre.

1969 A mediocre vintage. The wines were disappointingly light.

1970 Very good. Full-bodied and tannic red wines.

1971 An excellent year. The reds were very well balanced and charming.

1972 Good. The reds were quite well coloured and light and easy for early drinking.

1973 Generally good. The rosés were light and fruity, while the reds proved suitable for drinking in their first five years. An exceptional year for the white wine of Château de Ségriès.

1974 Good. The reds and rosés were both attractively coloured and soundly balanced.

1975 Mediocre. A small harvest containing some indifferent wines. The reds were marginally better than the rosés.

1976 Very good. The red wines held great bouquet and overall finesse, and their tannin support enabled the heavier wines to progress well. A very good Domaine du Château St-Roch. Very good, attractively fruity rosés that showed very well for a little over two years.

1977 Generally a poor vintage, characterized by light, rather dull wines. Too much rain meant that the grapes were ill-formed and consequently acidity was high in many *cuvées*. Nevertheless, the Château de Ségriès succeeded in making a very good red wine.

1978 A very good vintage indeed. The growers' prayers were answered, and perfect weather during ripening led to a fair-sized crop of healthy grapes. The reds held remarkable colour and balance, with excellent work from the Château St-Roch, whose wine was very long-lived. The rosés were also successful.

1979 Good. The wines were suitable for early consumption. The reds were well scented and bore an easy fruitiness, especially that of Domaine du Devoy and the Syrah wine of Castel Oualou. The rosés were light and reasonably attractive.

1980 Mediocre. The reds were light, often unbalanced, and carried high levels of acid. A few good *cuvées* developed this year, while the rosés had a higher standard.

1981   Fair. Selection was necessary, since sporadic rains affected the harvest and raised acid levels. The Château St-Roch red, as one of the more full-bodied wines, showed well for about six years. The rosés and the lively whites both drank well young.

1982   Average. A very dry summer and tremendous heat at harvest-time caused severe vinification problems. The reds were not strongly coloured and many bore a stewed taste as a result of overheated fermentation. Lack of freshness also hurt the rosés and the whites.

1983   Excellent for the reds, very good for the whites and average for the rosés. The reds were firmly coloured and well knit with some strong tannins. The deepest *cuvées* may still show some life in 1993. The whites were well balanced and firmly fruity, the rosés lacked freshness.

1984   Generally mediocre. The Grenache was knocked by *coulure*, and changeable weather in the late summer prompted careful crop selection. The best reds, like those from Assémat and the Château d'Aquéria, held steady red colours and expansive bouquets after three years. They should have been drunk up. Pleasant, fresh rosés and whites.

1985   Very good. The reds were well structured, bore firm colours and were rich and fleshy on the palate. A ripe, very appealing vintage, the reds should now be drunk up as their trump card – their fruit – is losing its value. The rosés were aromatic and supple. The whites were excellent, and a few odd bottles may spring a surprise in the early 1990s – their balance is keeping them going.

1986   Generally good, although the balance of the wines was less obvious than that of the 1985s. The reds were firmly coloured, and with age their bouquets developed splendidly. They are now showing well on the palate, with the early tannins softened and integrated. In the case of well-extracted wines like La Fermade and Domaine Duseigneur they are drinking well now with prospects to continue towards 1993. A robust rather than fragrant year for the rosés, while the whites were rounded, nicely weighted and should be drunk soon to enjoy their older flavours.

1987   Mediocre. The growers had trouble in extracting colour and body for their red wines, and selection of the crop was an essential prerequisite. The most carefully worked *cuvées*, like that from Château St-Roch, are delicate wines that should be drunk by around 1993 at the latest. A much better year for the rosés and the whites, both of which were nicely aromatic and fresh on the palate. The whites could show well over about six years.

1988   Good. The reds hold middling colours, but growers with young vines found it hard to cope with the long drought that broke only once or twice with localized storms. The reds lack a little depth and thoroughness of extraction, but are superior to the 1987s. They will drink around their best after five or six years. The rosés were pleasant for early drinking, with a fair amount of depth on the bouquet. The whites carried attractive fruitiness and will show well over about five years.

1989   Very good. The reds were richly coloured and held greater density than the 1988s. The tannins are also a little stronger and these wines have sufficient balance to develop well for between five and nine years. The rosés were firm in style, the whites held good depth on the palate and will open and evolve very well over the course of about four years.

1990   Good. Flowering was about a week early, and despite the very dry summer, quantity was high. Rain at the end of August was very beneficial. The reds were well coloured, full wines which should keep well over six to nine years. The whites were very successful and after delicious early drinking, have sufficient complexity and depth to develop well towards 1995. The rosés were firm wines, with plenty of extract.

Earlier Exceptional Vintages 1952, 1949, 1947, 1945, 1943

Leading Growers at Lirac

The nucleus:

Assémat Fils
  Domaine de Castel Oualou
Assémat, Jean-Claude
  Les Garrigues   30150 Roquemaure
Degoul, Gérard
  Château de Bouchassy

Lombardo, Joseph
    Domaine du Devoy   30126 St-Laurent-des-Arbres

Maby, Armand et Roger
    La Fermade
Méjan, André
    Les Queyrades   } 30126 Tavel
Olivier, Société Jean
    Château d'Aquéria

de Régis, François
    Château de Ségriès   30150 Lirac

Sabon, Jean-Jacques
    Domaine Sabon   84230 Châteauneuf-du-Pape

Verda, Antoine, et Fils
    Domaine du Château St-Roch
    Domaine Cantegril-Verda   30150 Roquemaure

Other producers:

Amido, Christian
Bernard, Mme Andrée   } 30126 Tavel
    Domaine de la Genestière

Cappeau, Y. et C.
    Domaine du Sablon
Cave Co-opérative de   } 30150 Roquemaure
    Roquemaure

Cave Co-opérative des Vins
    de Cru Lirac
Duseigneur, Jean   } 30126 St-Laurent-des-Arbres
    Domaine Duseigneur

Fuget, Robert
    Château de Boucarut
Granier, Achille
    Domaine de la Croze
Leperchois, Christian   } 30150 Roquemaure
    Les Carabiniers
Mayer, Mme *Veuve*
    Château de Clary

Nataf, Edmond
    Domaine de Maillac   30150 Roquemaure
Rousseau, Alexis
    Domaine Rousseau   30290 Laudun
Roussel, Pierre
    Domaine des Jonciers   30126 Tavel
Roudil, Gabriel, et Fils   30126 Tavel
Testut, Philippe   30150 Lirac

16

Côtes du Rhône Villages

The idea of the Côtes du Rhône Villages started in 1953, when the INAO determined that four Rhône communities were making wine worthy of carrying a higher status than the ordinary 'Côtes du Rhône' label, now often referred to as Côtes du Rhône *générique*. These communities – Gigondas, Cairanne, Chusclan and Laudun – were not considered sufficiently good to be allowed to join the select band of full *appellation* wines – Châteauneuf-du-Pape, Côte-Rôtie, Cornas and so on – but were clearly superior to the mass of wines sold under the simple 'Côtes du Rhône' title. Rules were therefore laid down governing the grape varieties that they would be permitted to use; the minimum alcohol strength of their red wines had to rise from 11 per cent to 12.5 per cent; less wine per hectare was to be made.

The four communities complied with these regulations and, in return, were allowed to sell their wine as 'Côtes du Rhône Cairanne', for instance. In this way it was hoped that a definite and recognizable identity would be promoted for each village. In 1955 Vacqueyras joined the group, followed in 1957 by Vinsobres. In 1967 it was decided to give all the communities a common title: the example of the Beaujolais was heeded, and the Côtes du Rhône Villages came into official being.

In 1992 there were sixteen communities allowed to put their village name on the label, along with Côtes du Rhône Villages. An important distinction is that from 1984 a further fifty-four communities have been allowed to produce Côtes du Rhône Villages wine, but they are not allowed to show their name on the label. Centralized, accurate statistics are not a Rhône speciality, but a rough indication of their relative size is that the sixteen big-name Villages – led by Cairanne – account for around 4,300 hectares, while the fifty-four anonymous Villages account for around 650 hectares. Both are allowed to harvest

42 hectolitres of wine per hectare. There is, however, a world of difference between Cairanne and an anonymous community's wine, and this promotion of the fifty-four does not favour Cairanne.

Such distinctions are nonplussing for buyers. The authorities seem to love to create little mezzanine layers in the hierarchy, as if they are more – or totally – on the side of the growers rather than lending thought to the people who buy the wine: no drinkers, no wine. So there are differently priced Côtes du Rhône Villages on the market, and a Cairanne red from Domaine Alary will, and should, cost more than a straight Côtes Villages from part of a small community in the Drôme. But try explaining all the many intricacies to the general public – over to you, Messieurs of the INAO . . . and could we have an English language translation as well, please? It might be a good idea now that the Rhône is exporting over 425,000 hectolitres in bottle these days.

The most recent promotion to full Villages status was Beaumes-de-Venise for its red wines in 1976. All growers are permitted to sell their wine under their own Village name, providing it all comes from that Village. When an owner has vineyards that run into a neighbouring community, as may happen with growers at Rasteau and Cairanne, or Sablet and Beaumes, for instance, and the wine is blended, this has the legal right to be sold as 'Côtes du Rhône Villages' without the name attachment. Of the founder members, Gigondas was raised to full *appellation* status in 1971, while a relative new-comer, Vacqueyras, was also moved up to sole *appellation* status in 1989 – perhaps fortunate to take precedence over other Villages. The next obvious candidate for promotion – some would say this is overdue – is Cairanne, while during the 1980s marked improvement came from Sablet and Séguret. Generally the impulse for such improvement comes from private growers, but in the case of Cairanne there is a strong band of private growers and a very good, well-run Cave Co-opérative.

Since all wine made in excess of the 42 hectolitres per hectare has to be sold as ordinary *vin de pays* – café wine – there is still a temptation for some growers to choose to ignore the Villages category and just supply Côtes du Rhône *appellation* wine which receives a 52-hectolitre-per-hectare allowance: this means another 10 hectolitres of wine sold at *appellation* rates. But during the 1980s a greater differential between Villages and Rhône *générique* wines emerged to slow this trend, and in the early 1990s the makings of a quality hierarchy are starting to emerge. But it is a long road, and *vignerons* must still debate among themselves how much actual advantage full *appellation* status brings. Lirac and Gigondas are not broadly known wines, and the Syndicats des Vignerons are compelled to mount extensive and regular promotions and public relations campaigns that bring only very gradual rewards.

The 1992 list of Villages was:

Beaumes-de-Venise (other than the Muscat)
Cairanne
Chusclan
Laudun
Rasteau (wines other than the *vin doux naturel*)
Roaix
Rochegude
Rousset-les-Vignes
Sablet
St-Gervais
St-Maurice-sur-Eygues
St-Pantaléon-les-Vignes
Séguret
Valréas
Vinsobres
Visan

CAIRANNE

Sixteen kilometres north-east of Orange is the tiny village of Cairanne, the top community included in the Côtes du Rhône Villages category. It is set on the top of a gently rising hillock and, with its raised bell-tower dominating the straggling village rooftops, is easily visible for miles around on the surrounding plain. From Cairanne the view once more emphasizes the marked contrast that exists between the southern and northern Côtes du Rhône: the vineyards cover a massive area, stretching south for 10 kilometres towards Gigondas, and then another 10 kilometres west towards Rochegude. Their only interruption comes from the occasional little village or row of hills – otherwise it is a land completely given over to the vine and to the wind.

The open spaces of the wine plain south of Cairanne are an easy prey for the legendary *mistral* wind, and it is hard to imagine a more desolate scene than when it is blowing as hard as it can through these exposed vineyards. In winter it is freezing; fully muffled workers toil unhappily over the vines, striving to keep both footing and sanity intact as the wind buffets them. The French have a word, *énervant*, that they use often when talking about the *mistral*: it is not chosen lightly, for the wind really does sear the nerves, particularly when it has been blowing non-stop for three days and nights.

Cairanne is one of the older villages of the Vaucluse *département*, although it is not known when wine was first made there. The discovery of a neolithic cemetery near the village indicates that there was a habitation there from at least 2000 BC, and traces of a Roman *castrum* have also been found in the vicinity. With wine being made by the Roman centurions resident at Gigondas, it is not improbable that other parts of the region also held vineyards, although undoubtedly on a very limited scale.

By the fourteenth century village decrees mention vineyards, and at the start of the fifteenth century there are known to have been over 130,000 vine plants – which would work out at 40 hectares or so these days. Little else is known about Cairanne's vinous past around this time, for in the sixteenth century the village became fully involved in the wars of religion, due probably to its advantageous setting on the top of a small hill. Rival armies fought constantly for its possession, and in 1589 the whole village was even held to ransom for 35,000 *écus* (a lot of money, so the locals say) by the Huguenot general Lesdiguières; this gentleman was no mean dealer, since the following year he had turned on his tracks and was holding Huguenot communities to ransom.

In the nineteenth century Cairanne's wine had a good reputation, for the asking price per hectolitre in 1817 was quoted as 35 francs, higher than Châteauneuf-du-Pape at 30 francs and considerably higher than all neighbours such as Rasteau, Roaix and Ste-Cécile-les-Vignes. The vineyard then amounted to about 142 hectares, and expansion of it has continued ever since, particularly since the First World War. This thriving wine area is now distinguished by its progressive and well organized Cave Co-opérative and a collection of very good and reliable private *domaines*. The Co-opérative and most of the private cellars stand near the D8 road in what is known as the new village; the old village on top of the hill was largely abandoned in the years following the wars of religion and, sadly, has never been restored.

The Cave des Coteaux de Cairanne was founded in 1929 and has 250 subscribers who contribute a total of around 6 million litres of wine every year. It is one of the larger, but also one of the best, Co-opératives in the Rhône Valley; its director, M. Lacrotte, and his technical assistant, M. Coulouvrat, are set on establishing the name of Cairanne both inside and outside France and are therefore continuing the forward-looking policy that the Cave has long held: all their Villages wine, generally around 1.4 million litres a year, is bottled by them, for instance. When the Co-opérative started bottling some of their wine in 1957, ripples of scepticism went all around the tradition-conscious Côtes du Rhône. Such a view only started properly to change in the early 1980s, with *viticulteurs* becoming aware of the extra revenues they could generate from home-bottling with a recognizable name and *domaine* stamp on their wine.

Almost half the Cairanne vineyards are planted on the clayey slopes north-east of the village, and from this *quartier* comes the best wine – fine and rounded. The *garrigues* area south of the village accounts for another 35 per cent of the vines; this is a stony, meagre soil that manages to support only vines, lavender and the odd juniper tree. It extends down towards the village of Travaillan and the lonely Plan de Dieu plain, as well as across to Gigondas and the Montmirail mountains. Wines from the *garrigues* are normally high in alcohol degree, very coloured and tannic, and need three or four years' ageing to acquire a certain finesse.

A combination of these two wines is what is most usually sold as Cairanne, and the result of the blend is highly successful. Richly coloured, often resembling the attractive brightness of black cherries, the red wine of Cairanne has a bouquet of rich, burnt spices and blackcurrant fruit flavours. With some bottle-age – perhaps half a dozen years in good or strong vintages like 1985, 1989 or 1986 – its bouquet will develop a spicy complexity that is more profound and aromatic than any of the other Villages wines – sub-Gigondas and superior to Vacqueyras. A big, mouth-filling wine, it is nevertheless a shade less forceful and 'wild-tasting' when young than its neighbour Vacqueyras, to which it is often compared. The best examples from private *domaines* come from the Alary family at L'Oratoire St-Martin, Daniel Brusset's Domaine des Travers, Corinne Couturier's Domaine Rabasse Charavin, Jean Calatayud's Domaine du Grand-

Chêne, the Domaine Richard and the Domaine l'Ameillaud of Rieu-Hérail. In line with accepted local thinking, which includes Michel Coulouvrat of the Co-opérative, these *domaines* are stepping up the incidence of Syrah and Mourvèdre in their vineyards, while the Cinsault decreases a little. So, while Grenache remains the majority grape at between 65 and 70 per cent of the vineyard, extra colour, depth and elegance are being gradually brought to the reds via the Syrah and Mourvèdre.

From around the mid-1980s more *domaines* have experimented with the use of new oak for both red and white – not only the Cave Co-opérative, but also the free spirit Daniel Brusset, the Alary family for their pure white Marsanne, and the brothers Berthet-Rayne, for example. There is a healthy impetus in the *appellation* with different growers trying different methods and *cépages*, and it will be a crime if Cairanne does not receive full *appellation* status by 1994.

The orthodox red wines settle down after three or four years, and the best *cuvées* will drink well for around eight years. The presence of greater proportions of Syrah and Mourvèdre may alter the way Cairanne red ages during the 1990s but the *vignerons*' prime aim is elegance rather than longevity in their wines.

At the other end of the scale, the Co-opérative has followed current taste with its Cairanne Primeur, a fresh wine made in the Beaujolais style for production on the market by around the middle of November. Average production runs to around 500,000 litres; fermentation never exceeds three days. Because this is not one of their leading 'prestige' wines, the *vignerons* tend to make use of their less good vineyards, near the River Aigues, for it.

A little reasonable rosé is also made, although it is no way the equal of the red wine. Like the red, it is predominantly made from the Grenache Noir. Like many of the Vauclusian rosés, it can be rather heady. Meanwhile, the sign of a progressive *appellation* is its attitude to white wine, and several *domaines* have stepped up their commitment of time and money to try to dominate this often elusive subject. The excellent Domaine des Travers white is stimulated by the presence of Bourboulenc; the Alary family at L'Oratoire St-Martin have Marsanne and Roussanne in place since the 1980s, while another successful white producer, Corinne Couturier, follows more closely the Co-opérative's white-grape line-up with Clairette and Bourboulenc. The Co-opérative makes 150,000 litres of white each year, most of it as Côtes du Rhône *générique*, and includes Ugni

Blanc and Marsanne with its Grenache Blanc and Clairette.

These whites are improving year on year. The introduction of different white grape varieties, a greater dedication and mastery of their vineyard cultivation and date of harvesting, and much-improved vinification methods have all contributed to this advance. Vinified at low temperatures after a brief period of settling, they are bottled early as a rule. Like many of the new breed of southern whites, they are fresh and zesty when young, but they carry throughout their life a most appealing fullness and weight that sustain them and give them greater all-round class than any whites previously made in this region. Tasting the valiant efforts of the Cave Co-opérative in the mid-1970s, the continual impression of the whites was then one of bitter, rather oxidized flavours whose flatness made them very dull indeed.

In terms of quantity, Cairanne is easily dominated by its Cave Co-opérative, but there are some very interesting and thriving private *domaines*. A selection of these:

DOMAINE DE L'ORATOIRE ST-MARTIN

This 17-hectare *domaine* was split in 1983 and is now run by Bernard Alary's son Frédéric; another 19 hectares – the Domaine Alary – are under the control of Daniel and Denis Alary. Bernard Alary recalled that his family had always lived at Cairanne but had had a surprising number of different occupations. 'Cairanne had its own silk factory between 1860 and 1890, and my great-grandfather was a large-scale silkworm breeder,' he said. 'He also extensively cultivated the *garance* plant, which makes red dye, and at that time had no vines at all. One day nylon was invented, which was a blow for his silkworms, and then the French army gave up using red trousers. My grandfather was left totally high and dry and as a result went back to the vineyards, which he had given up when the silk trade was going so well. You can see from all this that the face of the countryside has been constantly evolving over the last hundred years.'

This is one of the best Côtes du Rhône Villages *domaines*. Over the years its red wine has always been thorough and full; in the 1970s it was largely shaped by a high presence of the Grenache, but this has now reduced to around 60 per cent, with increased support from the Syrah, Mourvèdre and Cinsault. The special Cuvée Prestige is made from pre-First World War Grenache, and is aged for a couple of years in cask before release. It is a complex, deep-tasting wine which after about five or six years produces an array of spicy and exotic flavours on the palate. It is a restrained, old-fashioned sort of Rhône, with a dryness and depth in it that many of the modern Rhônes have set aside in pursuit of fruit and elegance. A strong but well-balanced wine, it is well worth seeking out in very good years like 1985 and 1989. The *domaine*'s other red Cairanne, as well as the rosé and the clean, fresh white wine (contributions here from Roussanne and Marsanne) are also good, soundly made wines.

Alary, Bernard et Frédéric
    Domaine de l'Oratoire St-Martin   84290 Cairanne

DOMAINE BRUSSET

Daniel took over from his father André during the 1980s, and has made something of a name for himself with his pursuit of detail in improving his wines. The *domaine* now has over 45 hectares, including some plots near the Dentelles de Montmirail at Gigondas. Daniel Brusset is prepared to vinify his different grape varieties apart; for his Cairanne reds the base grape is Grenache, around the 60 per cent mark, with support from Syrah, Mourvèdre and Cinsault. There is more Mourvèdre – about 25 per cent – in the Cuvée des Templiers, which is only made in the best vintages like 1985, 1988 and 1989. The Coteaux des Travers is a more direct style of wine, with greater earthiness and sheer fullness in it, and both are capable of showing well over the course of about eight to ten years.

These very good reds – which include the Hauts-de-Montmirail Gigondas, a strong, robust wine with great extract – are supported by a series of whites whose vinification clearly acts as a great challenge for Daniel Brusset. He relies on the Clairette, the Bourboulenc and the Ugni Blanc and is concerned to maintain liveliness in the wines, which leads him to block the malolactic. The Clairette accounts for the major part of his Cairanne *blanc*: pale and fresh when young, this possesses enough 'stuffing' to allow a steady development over three years, and in vintages like 1990 showed great local *typicité* and character. The complexity of wines like these points to Daniel Brusset's talent.

Daniel Brusset also makes one of the better rosés of the *appellation*, a powerful wine marked by the presence of some Mourvèdre.

Brusset, Daniel
　　Domaine Brusset　　　　　　84290 Cairanne

DOMAINE RABASSE-CHARAVIN

The Rabasse-Charavin family, long established at Cairanne, produce extremely good red and white wines. The property is run by Corinne Couturier, the daughter of Abel Rabasse-Charavin, who is a very talented wine-maker. There are 23 hectares spread between Cairanne (8 hectares, mostly on slopes), Rasteau (8 hectares) and Mondragon, where the vines can produce Rhône Villages without a commune name attached.

Their full-bodied Villages reds reflect the presence of juice from old, low-yielding Grenache supported most prominently by the Syrah; in the past a pure Syrah Côtes du Rhône has been made, as well as a 20 per cent Syrah, 80 per cent Grenache Cuvée d'Estevenas which carries an abundance of juicy fruit in it. The normal Cairanne red is a solid wine that leans towards the elegant style sought by younger growers; but, as with all the Couturier wines, there is a strong presence of fruitiness in it, which can make it delicious to drink after four or five years.

The Rasteau red contains a greater proportion of Mourvèdre, and is often their most spectacular wine, containing more depth and extract than the Cairannes, and in a vintage like 1988 possessing exceptional balance.

The *domaine*'s white is made mainly from Bourboulenc and Clairette and is a wine that shows well over four or five years.

Couturier, Corinne
　　Domaine Rabasse-Charavin　　84290 Cairanne

DOMAINE DE L'AMEILLAUD

This 30-hectare estate has part of its vines producing Cairanne and part producing straight Côtes du Rhône. Historically there have been some aged Carignan vines contributing to the depth and guts of the Côtes red.

The style of the wines is for deep, well-extracted reds which are capable of living for up to ten years. Well scented, the Cairanne is excellent to drink when it still contains much of its power and extra complexity – in the 1985 and 1986 this was after about six years.

The reds are aged in cask for between six and eighteen months, and this is a *domaine* to look out for.

Also within the same group of production are the Domaine Le Château with 10 hectares of slope vines and the 22-hectare Domaine la Béraude, both of which are at Cairanne. Some of these wines are sold off in bulk.

Domaine de l'Ameillaud
    SCEA Domaines Rieu-Hérail   84290 Cairanne

Leading Growers at Cairanne

Alary, Bernard et Frédéric
   Domaine de l'Oratoire
   St-Martin   84290 Cairanne
Alary, Daniel et Denis
Aubert, Max
   Domaine de la Présidente
   Château de Galliffet   84290 Ste-Cécile-les-Vignes
Beaumet, Père et Fils
   Domaine de St-Andéol
Berthet-Rayne, Michel et André
Brusset, Daniel
   Domaine des Travers
Calatayud, Jean
   Domaine du Grand-Chêne
La Cave des Coteaux de Cairanne
Couturier, Corinne   84290 Cairanne
   Domaine Rabasse-Charavin
Delubac, André
   Domaine de la Fauconnière
Grignan, Raoul
   Domaine du Grand-Jas
Jullian–Gap
   Domaine d'Aeria
Pierrefeu, Gérard, et Fils
   Domaine Le Plaisir
Plantevin, A.

Domaine de la Gayère
Rabasse-Charavin
   Les Coteaux St-Martin
Richaud, Marcel
   Le Bon Clos
Rieu-Hérail, SCEA Domaines
   Domaine de l'Ameillaud
Zanti-Cumino
   Domaine du Banvin

84290 Cairanne

CHUSCLAN

The famed rosé village of Chusclan stands in unexpectedly green countryside north of Laudun and 11 kilometres west of Orange. Its vineyards are on the narrow plain that runs north between the west bank of the Rhône and the Laudun hills as far as Bagnols-sur-Cèze. The River Cèze, full only after the torrential rains of early spring, runs right past the village, and as a result the countryside around Chusclan has unaccustomed luxury in its colour.

Chusclan was one of the first four villages to be named in a decree of 1953 that permitted it to use its village name on its wine, in addition to the usual 'Côtes du Rhône' title. The area that is now allowed to make Chusclan, in fact, extends over the neighbouring communities of Orsan, Bagnols-sur-Cèze, Codolet and St-Étienne-des-Sorts, but none of these four in any way matches the quality of the wines that come from Chusclan itself.

Wine relics have been found that date from the first to the fifth century AD, so it is reasonable to suppose that wine was being made at Chusclan by the Romans, even if there was no particularly large encampment around the village. Later on it was the Church, in the form of a Benedictine community, that assured Chusclan's prosperity as a wine-producing community. The monks' priory, which has since disappeared, supported a good-sized vineyard from the tenth century up until the Revolution, and in 1550 the parish register described the village vineyards as covering 80 hectares.

At the same time, the local aristocratic family, the Counts of Grignan, also owned a renowned vineyard at Chusclan. The Grignans, a powerful and politically very nimble family, succeeded in having their wine served at the royal table for many years. A clever concession was made to the monarchy by naming a section of their vineyard the 'King's Garden', and the practice was also established that whenever a ruling monarch was travelling in the area, he should be presented with several barrels of Chusclan. It is unlikely that the wine then being made was rosé; the one firm record of the Grignans' sly approach speaks of a present of four casks of white Chusclan given to Louis XIII when he was visiting Pont St-Esprit, 16 kilometres away, in 1629. Antiquity also mentions a sweet dessert wine of Chusclan, but precise references to it are untraceable, and the *vignerons* themselves are unaware of its existence.

An export trade was started at an early date, most probably due to the initiative of the Grignan family. In 1748 some wine was sent off to two Dutch merchants, and in 1788 there was a dispatch to England: in both cases the quantity sold is not known. Then, in 1811, a memorandum from the Academy of the Gard (probably in Nîmes) speaks of trading with Germany, Russia, Denmark and Sweden. In most instances the port of embarkation was Sète, 130 kilometres away on the Mediterranean coast.

Chusclan has therefore known a quietly prosperous past, which seems to have reached its summit around the time of the Napoleonic Wars. In 1812 the wine of Chusclan was fetching the highest price of any of the Gard *département* communities, Tavel and Lirac included. And in 1813 its vineyards numbered 400 hectares, not far off the plantation of the late 1960s.

At the start of the twentieth century, however, Chusclan seemed to be marking time; it lacked a bottling and sales outlet for its wine. This was corrected in 1939, when M. Joseph Rivier founded the Cave Co-opérative de Chusclan. Now 137 members cultivate about 800 hectares of *appellation* vines, under the guidance of M. Rivier's successor, M. Jean Grangeon. The vineyard surface area has been increasing as wooded land has been cleared and vines, notably white-grape carriers, have been planted. Currently in vogue are the Grenache Blanc, Bourboulenc, Roussanne and Syrah.

While Chusclan's past fame has been founded on its rosé, this is now only a small part of the total production – around 10 per cent. In the early 1970s rosé accounted for over 40 per cent. The trend away from drinking rosé throughout a meal and towards white followed by red is seen by the growers of Chusclan as the reason for this decline, but it is not much comfort when their main export market, already well established, was the United States. Now they are having to join in a battle for shelf space with any amount of broadly similar reds.

The best rosé, the Cave's Cuvée de Marcoule, comes in an attractive flute-shaped bottle. The wine is made by the *saignée* method, with a maceration whose length depends on the harvest conditions. 'In 1986, when it was so hot, we only macerated for four hours,' commented M. Grangeon. 'In colder harvests we will leave the grapes to macerate for up to twenty hours or so.' The juice is fermented in concrete vats at 15–18°C and the pressed juice is added to ensure better colour and body. After the malolactic has occurred, bottling will start around the first days of March.

Made mainly from the Grenache and the Cinsault, Chusclan rosé is a delightful wine, superior in its class to the red, and it is sad that it should be overlooked by wine drinkers in general. The Co-opérative make their rosé to be drunk fresh and young, when all its fruit and youthful vigour can be amply enjoyed. It has a pleasing pink-orange colour, an agreeable roundness and a surprisingly clean, dry aftertaste. Occasionally it can be a little too heady, with around 14° alcohol by volume, and this can slightly unbalance the wine's general harmony. None the less, the best Chusclan *cuvées* outclass all the other Côtes du Rhône Villages rosés and can stand with pride within reach of those of Tavel and Lirac.

The red wine is made from the customary selection of Côtes du Rhône grapes, led by the Grenache, Syrah and Mourvèdre, with the Cinsault, Carignan and a purely local name for the Vaccarèse grape found at Châteauneuf-du-Pape, the Camarèse. Some of the red wine is produced by *macération carbonique*, but no solely *macération* wines are sold. The rest of the red is fermented for about five days, and aged in cask for just three or four months. The basic wine is light and can be uninspiring; the 1988 Domaine de la Baranière, for instance, was very pale and thin, and unworthy of this normally sound Co-opérative. The Seigneurie de Gicon is more marked by Syrah and is a fair wine; the Co-opérative's top *cuvée*, La Cuvée du Père Bridayne, which is named after one of Louis XIV's courtiers born at Chusclan, spends longer in cask and has more guts in it.

White wine has only been made since the mid-1970s, and now forms about 7 per cent of the total production. It is made from the Grenache Blanc, Bourboulenc, Clairette and Ugni Blanc, with some young Roussanne added since the late 1980s. This is fresh and full-tasting; the Roussanne has helped to add extra aromas and finesse to what is already a correct, sound wine.

There are few private growers – only three of the local estates bottle a part of their wine as Chusclan. The red Villages from Jean-Claude Chinieu's Domaine de Lindas is well spoken of; this is made from 60 per cent Grenache, 30 per cent Syrah and 10 per cent Cinsault, and is bottled within its first year. The white is pure Clairette.

Leading Growers at Chusclan

Broche, Francis
    Le Vieux Manoir de Maransan   30200 Bagnols-sur-Cèze
Cave Co-opérative de Codolet   30200 Codolet
Cave Co-opérative d'Orsan   30200 Orsan
Cave des Vignerons de St-Étienne
    des-Sorts   30200 St-Étienne-des-Sorts
Caves des Vignerons de Chusclan   30200 Chusclan
Chinieu, Jean-Claude
    Domaine de Lindas   30200 Bagnols-sur-Cèze
Rieu, Bernard
    Domaine des Rieux   30200 Orsan

LAUDUN

Laudun is one of the four oldest Côtes du Rhône Villages, having been allowed to use its name on its wine since 1953, when Gigondas (now a full *appellation*), Cairanne and Chusclan were similarly promoted. It is also one of the Gard *département*'s oldest vineyards, for amphorae dating from 300 to 200 BC have been found on the plateau of Camp de César immediately behind and above the village. Admittedly, these could have contained olive oil, but it is noticeable that around Laudun the vine has always been much more commonly cultivated than the olive.

The village is set against the hillside formed by the plateau cliff, and its vineyards spread out around and below it. The communities of St-Victor-la-Coste and Tresques are also permitted to share the Laudun *appellation*; two good private *domaines* exist at St-Victor, but apart from the Domaine de Fabre, the wine of Tresques often fails to match that from Laudun itself. These are real 'backwater' villages that lie in the rambling, deserted hills south and west of Laudun; it requires a definite detour to visit either of them, and the uninhibited wide-eyedness of the locals when they see a stranger speaks for itself. But the inhabitants of this side of the Rhône are, as the French phrase so tellingly insinuates, '*un peu différents*'. Let an extract from the majestic pen of Gerald Asher, a king of wine writers with his monthly column in America's *Gourmet* magazine, explain:

Protest and individual involvement are not new on this side of the Rhône. In the religious wars of the sixteenth century it was Protestant territory, and in 1876 Jules Guyot, the eminent viticulturalist, doubtless with the horrors of the Paris Commune fresh in his mind, complained bitterly and exceptionally of the insolence of the labourers on the west bank of the Rhône. 'It is painful to see the exploitation of the landowners by their workers,' he said in his *Étude des Vignobles de France*, a work of several volumes otherwise concerned solely and entirely with technical matters of viticulture.

What particularly upset Guyot was the independence with which Gard farm-workers, even in summer, delayed starting their day's work until half past seven in the morning in order first to work elsewhere for three or four hours. He complained that they would then quit at five in the afternoon so that they could work at some other task in the evening. At length he railed against them and at their self-assurance. 'Each one thinks himself knowledgeable and capable,' he chided.

And that is probably what they did think. In 1889, on the square in front of their new village offices, they dedicated a monument not to saints, war heroes, or their betters, but to the idea of a rational world. The obelisk, commemorating Galileo Galilei and Isaac Newton, is still there. It displays on its four faces a hymn to science inscribed in the form of the metric measures of length, area and volume. ('A metre is 1/40,000,000 part of the circumference of the globe,' it begins.) On its fourth side is a list of the members of the village council who had caused the obelisk to be erected.[1]

But wine was something that these rural thinkers had been crafting out of their rocky, sparse countryside for several centuries before the

[1] Gerald Asher, Wine Journal, *Gourmet*, July 1990.

St Victor-la-Coste obelisk. Probably the first organized wine-making at Laudun originated with the building of a medieval castle at the village, and in 1375 wine was sent from Laudun, via Codolet on the Rhône, to the papal cellars in Avignon. The date of this castle, which has long since disappeared, is not known, and the next reference to the wine surfaces in a local document of 1557. In this a M. Olivier de Serres is reported as describing 'the old Château of Laudun in Languedoc' as producing '*très-excellent vin*'. Obviously, the aristocratic family inhabiting it had useful contacts overseas, for in 1561 a shipment of *vin de Laudun* was sent to a customer in Rome.

Thereafter the village wine continued to grow steadily in stature and renown. During the reign of King Henry IV (1589–1610), royal prospectors were sent to the South of France to seek out suppliers of silk for the ladies of the Court; there was then a flourishing silk trade at Laudun, but the prospectors found themselves equally charmed by the country wine and consequently returned to Paris laden with both commodities. Much of the wine at this time was white, and very highly regarded, for when King Louis XIII visited the region in 1629, he was presented with a barrel of white Laudun.

During the eighteenth century the wine's success naturally encouraged an enlargement of the vineyards, and in a register of 1774 Laudun was deemed to be the region's second largest producer of wine – after Roquemaure, but ahead of Tavel, for instance. By 1800 its vineyards totalled 710 hectares and were mainly situated on the slopes immediately around the village. The plain below that runs eastwards was reserved for cereal plantation. Even then it was the white wine that continued to draw praise, and in 1816 the respected chronicler A. Jullien gave it warm mention in one of his books. By strange contrast, the red wine was barely ever spoken of, for the 1892 *Dictionnaire géographique et administratif de la France* also only mentioned the 'light, sparkling white wines of Laudun' in its brief description of the Gardois wines.

Today Laudun is quite a big, bustling place, since many of the nearby factory workers live there. Some of its old-world Provençal charm has therefore been lost, as the core of the old village is surrounded by an abrupt ring of modern houses. Wine and industry seem more or less compatible, however, and the village vineyards are still well cultivated.

Laudun's red, rosé and white wines are made mainly by three Caves Co-opératives (two near Laudun and one at St-Victor) and by a small but growing handful of good private growers. The white wine, now made from a broader selection of white grapes that includes Viognier in places and greater amounts of Bourboulenc in addition to Clairette, Grenache Blanc and Roussanne, is well thought of; it is unquestionably one of the best of the southern Rhône whites, behind only the leading names at Lirac and Châteauneuf-du-Pape. It is marked by a pleasing freshness and a soft, simple aroma that lingers well over its first two or three years. Pale to the eye, it is a wine that seems to seek colder, more northerly origins, and the difference between it and equivalent Villages whites made on the east bank of the Rhône must come from the lighter soil around Laudun, as well as a low percentage of Grenache Blanc.

There is not a lot of white Laudun, however. The very good Cave des Quatre Chemins, which has over 280 members with vines in about twenty local *communes*, makes four or five times more red than white; its annual production of around 5,000 hectolitres of white far exceeds any amounts from the handful of small growers, so this is a wine that will never be easy to find. It bases its whites on a mix of Clairette, Grenache Blanc, Ugni Blanc, Roussanne and Bourboulenc, which are stainless steel-fermented at around 18°C.

When they come from a good supplier, the reds of Laudun are very good; they have a bright red–purple colour and are generally well balanced, with a nicely constituted combination of fruit and spicy flavours. They have lightened up over the past fifteen years; wines from the early 1970s were more raw and dense than those made by the Co-opératives and several of the private *domaines* these days. In its time the Domaine Pelaquié red was a veritable giant of a wine, but the consensus now is more for approachable wines whose fruit predominates over sterner tannic features. Some of the producers are using new oak, while it is also interesting that these Gardois growers have remained more faithful to the Carignan vine – old ones by now – than many other Villages: this generally adds a little gutsy severity to a wine early on. The most notable vinifiers at Laudun are the Domaine Pelaquié, the Cave des Quatre Chemins and the Domaine de Serre-Biau of M. Faraud, who is also a restorer of Romanesque chapels. The top *cuvées* of Pelaquié and Serre-Biau – the latter receiving six to twelve months' cask-ageing – are wines that will drink well up to about seven or eight years old. Lesser *cuvées* whose structure centres more on fruit extract should be drunk earlier. The Quatre Chemins Cave give their top red *cuvées*, which are made from a mix of mainly Grenache, Syrah, Cinsault and Carignan, a little cask-ageing in seasoned 50-hl *foudres*.

For Luc Pelaquié, his grandfather's death in 1976 marked the end of an era of a near-legendary red wine made under the guidance of old M. Joseph Pelaquié. Joseph was with the Cave Co-opérative of St-Victor for fifty-five years, having co-founded it in 1921; his successors skipped a generation, and the brothers Luc and Emmanuel took over, Luc working more on cellar matters than his brother. Alas, Emmanuel died in the late 1980s, so that Luc is now on his own. Luc recalls that his grandfather instructed him and his brother to make their Laudun red in precisely the old manner. Thus there would be a fermentation in contact with the skins for at least a month, as had been the practice in Châteauneuf-du-Pape when M. Pelaquié was a young man. Then, after anything from two to four years in cask, the wine would emerge with an enormous colour and extremely high tannin content, which, according to M. Pelaquié senior, would allow it to live for forty to fifty years '*sans aucun problème*'.

His grandsons changed the style of vinification to be more in keeping with current-day attitudes, and undertook a massive replanting programme in their vineyard, which has risen to a size of 65 hectares. Luc is justifiably proud of his white wine, which at a little over 10 per cent of the total production makes Domaine Pelaquié the largest proportional producer of white at Laudun. The *appellation* laws support his contention that the Clairette is fundamental to the making of good white here, since 'It is the one grape that provides the wine with most of its character.' The fresh, elegant Pelaquié *blanc* is made up of about 65 per cent Clairette, with support from Grenache Blanc and Bourboulenc, and a smattering of Roussanne, Marsanne and Viognier. 'We are different from the growers over in the Vaucluse with our attachment to the Clairette,' he states; 'Apart from the Viognier and the other grapes of the northern Rhône, here we have always had much the same line-up of white wines, led by the Clairette. My grandfather was a great supporter of the Clairette.'

About 300 hectolitres of white a year are made at Domaine Pelaquié, and although Luc advises drinking it as a fresh, young wine, he is aware that some vintages – he quotes his 1980 *blanc* – will stay on well over seven years or more. This is supported by the author's drinking of a 1972 Pelaquié *blanc* in England in late 1985; this held a bold straw colour and a very appealing, mostly floral bouquet, which turned more nutty with air. The palate was half-way between a rich dry white and a fine sherry, with plenty of dried apricot fruit: a very good drink, even at that age.

For the reds Grenache is the basic vine, accounting for around 60 per cent of the plantation, backed up by the Syrah, Mourvèdre, Cinsault and Counoise. An added task is that of bringing together, or fusing, the wines of different plots that make up the total vineyard. Although all the vines are on slopes, some grow on sandy soil, others on a combination of sand and clay and others on a gravelly topsoil. The Pelaquié reds are full-bodied but in the best vintages like 1986 and 1988 have a balance that makes them excellent to drink around the five-year mark.

Not a lot of rosé is made at Laudun, but the best of it is very good, almost on a par with better-known Chusclan. The Cave des Quatre Chemins make a typically light, fresh, zippy rosé, while the Domaine Estournel offers a rounder, more heavily extracted rosé. The Domaine Estournel of Rémy Estournel, the Domaine de Fabre of Anne-Marie Lafont and the Château Saint-Maurice of André Valat are three properties whose red wines are worth monitoring during the first half of the 1990s, since they are making serious efforts on these wines. The Estournel red relies on Grenache, Cinsault, Mourvèdre, Carignan and Syrah, while the Domaine de Fabre red is made from Grenache, Syrah and Cinsault. The Château Saint-Maurice red is made from mainly Grenache, Syrah and Cinsault, and has improved since the early 1980s.

Leading Growers at Laudun

Cave Co-opérative de St-Victor-la-Coste	30290 St-Victor-la-Coste
Cave des Quatre Chemins 'Le Serre de Bernon'	30290 Laudun
Cave des Vignerons de Laudun	30290 Laudun
Domaine Chambon	
GAEC Faraud, et Fils	30290 St-Victor-la-Coste
Domaine de Serre-Biau	
GAEC Michel	
Domaine St-Pierre	30300 Tresques
Estournel, Rémy	
Domaine Estournel	

Lafont, Anne-Marie
   Domaine de Fabre   30300 Tresques
Pelaquié, Luc
   Domaine Pelaquié   30290 St-Victor-la-Coste
Rousseau, Alexis
   Domaine Rousseau
Valat, André, et Fils   30290 Laudun
   Château de St-Maurice
   d'Ardoise

ROAIX AND SÉGURET

Roaix and Séguret are two very attractive medieval villages, both lying near the River Ouvèze that runs southwards past Gigondas and across the Plan de Dieu plain. Linked since 1960 by a communal Cave Co-opérative near Séguret, they received the Villages *appellation* in 1967.

The Ouvèze Valley is an old wine-producing area and was mentioned as such by Pliny in Book XIV of his *Natural History*, written around AD 77. Vine-growing was certainly an active pastime in the medieval era, for Séguret's local grandee, the Comte de Toulouse, was a noted vineyard owner in the thirteenth century. Very little else is recorded in later history about the making of wine at these villages, although we know that in 1817 only 18 hectares of vines were formally declared as giving a harvest at Roaix; while Séguret had nearly 80 hectares of vines, the value per hectolitre was noticeably higher at Roaix – 28 francs as opposed to 20 francs. Mind you, the wine of Gigondas was going for only 22 francs a hectolitre in that year, so surely there must be hope for these small vineyards in the next century!

Nowadays the vineyards of both villages are generally grouped into small plots, as several of the *vignerons* also cultivate a wide range of fruit and vegetables; since the early 1980s there has been a slow move towards greater autonomy by some vineyard owners, most of them with vines within Séguret. In the early 1990s there are over half a dozen now making and selling their own wine. The way has been led by the excellent Domaine de Cabasse of Nadine Latour, which is also a very peaceful *auberge* for travellers in this picturesque part of the Vaucluse. Other prominent names are the Château La Courançonne of Gérard Meffre and the quite good Fernand Chastan wine from the Domaine de la Garancière. Séguret is also the usual source for the Paul Jaboulet Aîné Côtes du Rhône Villages red, with two suppliers regularly used. This is bought in wine form and receives no wood-ageing.

Séguret gives perhaps the best general view of the main southern Côtes du Rhône vineyards, for it is a village almost precisely sculpted into a rocky hillside that faces due west towards Orange. In summer the plain below becomes an enormous stretch of green that contains the leading Villages and Côtes du Rhône *domaine* wines of the Vaucluse *département*.

The red wine of the Cave Co-opérative that reaches the bottle – most of its sales are in bulk – is made up of around 65 per cent Grenache, with the difference taken by Syrah, Mourvèdre and Cinsault. Stored for around eighteen months in vats before bottling, this is not a particularly distinguished wine, lacking in true depth and regional character. A better idea of the wine of these two villages can be gained from the private *viticulteurs*.

Nadine Latour came to wine through the unusual route of teaching economics in a technical college in Paris. After the death of her father, she came to Séguret in 1962, and set about improving her wine knowledge through studies at both Montpellier and Beaune. With her sister Hélène, who had also been a teacher, she spent the years 1964–70 grouping together all the different plots their father had left them. The most notable distinction was between the vineyards grouped around her *domaine* (the cellars and the *auberge*) and those at higher ground in the Vallon des Noisetiers, behind the village.

The Cabasse 25 hectares are situated on the border of Séguret and Sablet. The soil is quite sandy and light lower down, while higher up it is more red and stony, which suits the Syrah. The mix is around 60 per cent Grenache, with major support from the Syrah and the Mourvèdre and a final grouping of Carignan, Picpoul, Clairette and Cinsault. In her grandmother's time the Domaine de Cabasse had sold off its harvest to intermediaries, but Nadine Latour moved to making the wine herself in 1970, and by 1976 was acceding to the wishes of friends and bottling a little. The estate has progressed from there, and is now the leading exporter and flag-waver for Séguret.

The red wines of Domaine de Cabasse are representative of the style for this small area: they are usually coloured a dark red, with a touch of black cherry depth in them. The bouquet is not exuberant when young, and after two or three years displays more ripe or stewed fruit aromas than a blatant garden fruit aroma carried by a Gard *département* wine or the earthy, more dark raspberry fruit of a neighbour like Cairanne. On the palate there is greater acidity than with many of the Vaucluse neighbours, a pleasant, peppery fruit backed by some occasionally austere tannins. It is not a wine that appeals to all regular Rhône drinkers, since it has a finer, less mouth-filling side to it that some tasters may call *in extremis* a bit stringy. But it is a cleaner-finishing wine than many Rhône Villages, and is excellent to drink around four or five years old from vintages like 1989 or 1986. It also possesses discreet but firm powers of ageing, and a 1980 Cabasse Séguret drunk in 1992 showed mature but still rich and pleasant flavours, with no blatant sign of oxidation.

Of the whites, a very good example is made by the Château La Courançonne under a *blanc de blancs* title. This has the typical weight of a Vaucluse white, but carries a delightful ripe bouquet with a greengage fruit depth on the palate. Clean and extended on the finish, this is well worth looking out for. The Meffre *domaine* formerly sold its Séguret as the Fiole du Chevalier d'Elbène, but now appears to have simplified matters by using the simple Courançonne title.

A little rosé is made by estates like Domaine de Cabasse and Florimond Lambert, and the overall standard is fair: these come in a straightforward, hearty style.

The wines of Séguret have edged forward in quality over the past ten years. There is no reason why the private *domaines* from both Séguret and Roaix should not justifiably become better known during the 1990s, and therefore provide good-value red and white wines for those in the know.

Leading Growers at Roaix and Séguret

Cave Co-opérative de Roaix-Séguret	84110 Séguret
Chassagne, Jean-Claude	84110 Sablet
Chastan, Fernand	
Domaine de la Garancière	84190 Gigondas
Durand et Fils	
Domaine de l'Éoune	
Domaine St-Claude	84110 Roaix
Lambert, Florimond	

Latour, Nadine
  Domaine de Cabasse
Liautaud, Jean } 84110 Séguret
  Domaine du Sommier
Meffre, Frères et Fils
  Château La Courançonne   84150 Violès
Quinquin, Jean-Louis   84110 Séguret

ROCHEGUDE

Rochegude lies in dense vine country 8 kilometres south-east of the industrial town of Bollène. Easily recognizable from a distance because of the outline of its elegant seventeenth-century château – now a luxury hotel – the village appears to stand guard over the massively arranged rows of vines that line up in every direction before it. The vines are 70 per cent Grenache, with the complement made up principally of Cinsault, Carignan, Syrah and Mourvèdre, and the roughly 800 hectares of vineyards reach out across a short plain towards Suze-la-Rousse in the north and Ste-Cécile-les-Vignes in the east.

In the last century a different style of wine from today's red table wine was responsible for bringing the village a certain fame. The Marquis d'Aquéria imported some vine plants (which varieties are not specified) from Jerez and commenced making a white wine that would be sold when six years old; so famous did it become that Thomas Jefferson is said to have sent George Washington a few bottles.

Today it is the Cave Co-opérative, formed only in 1958, that bears the main responsibility for harbouring the village's reputation. There is one private *domaine*, the Domaine de Roquevignan of M. Pierre Bourret, which has a commercial link with the respected *négociant* house of Pascal, and which looks after the raising and bottling of a large part of the wine made from its 55 hectares. The red is made three-quarters from Grenache and is vinified in progressive form, without destalking and crushing, and a twelve-day *cuvaison* precedes a short three-month stay in cask for the top-of-the-range Villages red. There is a substantial Syrah presence in M. Bourret's wine, which makes it a little more solid than the red wines of the Cave Co-opérative.

Around 35,000 hectolitres of wine are made every year, and under the Villages denomination, granted in 1966, only red can be sold as Rochegude Villages. The Co-opérative style is for well-scented reds that are pleasantly soft and marked by a gentle fruitiness. The Cuvée du Président is just such a wine, perhaps helped by the destalking of the grapes before fermentation: this is made from 75 per cent Grenache, 15 per cent Carignan and 5 per cent each of Syrah and Cinsault. The Co-opérative offer other *cuvées* which have selected grape mixes or varying degrees of exposure to cask. One of the challenges faced by the Co-opérative is that of working with the fruit brought in by 280 subscribers who live across a range of twenty-seven different communities around Rochegude: this makes for a very dispersed spread of vineyards, vines and soils – and maturities.

Of the other *cuvées* offered by the Co-opérative, the lightest is the Cuvée Le Boulidou; and the most cask-aged, with a few months in young oak, is the obviously named Cuvée Vieillie en Fûts de Chêne. This contains less Carignan than the Cuvée du Président, but is still based on three-quarters Grenache.

Rochegude red is good, middle-ground Rhône Villages wine, but it is not one of those *appellations* on the move whose name should be noted for the 1990s. Some ordinary white and fair rosé Côtes du Rhônes are made, but these are no more than average in quality.

Leading Growers at Rochegude

Bourret, Pierre
Domaine de Roquevignan } 26790 Rochegude
Cave Co-opérative Vinicole
  de Rochegude

SABLET

Sablet is decidedly upwardly mobile, and is definitely a name to watch during the 1990s. From being a sleepy backwater with a very average Cave Co-opérative in the early 1970s, it progressed through the 1980s into an *appellation* infused by new, younger talent and innovators who have wrenched the quality of its red and white wines markedly upwards.

The neighbour of Séguret and Gigondas, it is a classic old fortified village. Extending away from its neat Romanesque bell-tower, which incongruously tells the right time, its winding, concentric streets and tunnelled archways lead through to splendid views on every side: the singularly shaped Dentelles Mountains, the long green ridge of umbrella pines that ends in the bumpy hillocks above Séguret, and the massive Plan de Dieu wine plain. Promoted to Villages status in 1974, Sablet lives by its wine: under his counter the butcher has almost as good a collection of wines from the local *domaines* as has the village tasting *caveau*, while even the litter bins exhort passers-by to drink the wines of Sablet!

Sablet used to be a papal possession and by the early sixteenth century was producing wine on a steady basis. By 1833 176 hectares around the village contained vines, but the main local products were then the olive and the *garance* dye plant. Most of the wine was drunk by the villagers themselves.

The village gained prominence in the late nineteenth century, when a M. François-Frédéric Leydier of Sablet invented a machine for grafting American vine root-stock on to French vines. This helped to halt phylloxera, which was then at its height, and M. Leydier's vice-like machine became a widespread bestseller.

As its name implies, Sablet is surrounded by mainly sandy ground. The success of the local vines on such sandy soil led to new plantations and experiments being tried along the Camargue coast west of Marseille, and today the Camargue produces large quantities of very respectable wine in addition to its traditional rice.

Sablet's Cave Co-opérative, 'Le Gravillas', was founded in 1935 and makes an acceptable red Villages wine. For long the centre of vinous attraction, it has been surpassed in recent years by the blossoming of several private *domaines* that have started to produce better, more stylized wine. Certainly one of the more unusual is the Domaine de Verquière of the Chamfort family. Now run by son Bernard, this is a *domaine* that now varies the practice of Louis Chamfort *père* of ageing his Sablet Villages wine for five or even seven years in cask before bottling. For example, in early 1982 M. Chamfort was still selling his 1975 and the 1983 was only released after five years' ageing. While these wines held a strong extract from the presence of Grenache, Mourvèdre and Cinsault, the cask-ageing obviously marked them violently towards a dried cedar or tar flavour. They were singular wines – for the Chamforts believe in the ageing possibilities of Sablet reds. Under Bernard, bottling occurs earlier, particularly for a stylish red Vacqueyras and a more robust earthy Rasteau red. In a big year like 1983 the prolonged cask-ageing works well with the ripe, tannic harvest, and it is years like this, 1989 and 1990, that show up the *domaine*'s work in its best light.

M. Chamfort *père* did much to secure Sablet's Villages promotion by busily researching the community's past history, which he freely admits has not been exactly action-packed! Between them, sons Bernard and Denis now look after around 50 hectares of vines spread around Sablet. The core Sablet vineyard is 15 hectares, but there are also holdings at Violès that contribute to a sound Côtes du Rhône, and a Rasteau *vin doux naturel* completes the line-up.

Another of the original *viticulteurs* is Charles Roux of the Château du Trignan. With his son André he has been a great mover of convention and apathy in local wine circles; the Château du Trignan makes red Villages from not only Sablet, but also Rasteau – the Sablet is more marked by Syrah, the Rasteau more by Mourvèdre with the Grenache. Like several other growers such as the excellent Jean-Pierre Cartier and the gifted Jean-Marc Autran, the *domaine* makes a Gigondas as well as a Sablet.

Over the years the Trignan vinification has included *macération carbonique* methods, which first started in 1962. The red Sablet has usually been a light red, strawberry-fruited wine suitable for drinking before about four years old, but it has become a little firmer recently. Likewise, the red Gigondas – made from one-third each of Grenache, Syrah and Mourvèdre – is a very successful, well-balanced wine with good depth in it. And André Roux also vinifies a very fine and stylish, citrus-flavoured Côtes du Rhône *blanc de blancs*.

In the second half of the 1980s M. Roux took on a Georges Duboeuf-style idea of going around different *domaines* in the Rhône selecting and bottling wines which are sold under the label of Charles Roux, *négociant*. This is a *domaine* whose progress should always be monitored – the wine is good, and the family are interesting.

One of the bright newer talents is Jean-Marc Autran of Domaine de Piaugier, a 25-hectare estate that makes Sablet reds, Gigondas and straight Côtes du Rhônes. He took over the vinification of his father Marc's estate in 1984 and has gained a strong Paris-based following from the wine press there, being named the Gault-Millau *Vigneron* of the Year 1990. Marc *père* looks after the vines, which suits father and son well: Jean-Marc was never interested in selling off his wine in bulk. The Sablet *cuvée* Montmartel in a vintage like

1989 was a big, tannic wine with a well-extracted fruit essence at its centre; it will show openly around 1994 and is capable of running for nine years or so. Jean-Marc has changed his father's vinification methods by neither destalking nor crushing the harvest on reception, while he has also increased the plantation of Mourvèdre. Nevertheless, Marc had a sure hand as a vinifier as is witnessed by his 1983 Côtes du Rhône *rouge*, an upright but warm wine with plenty of style about it: it was drinking well in 1992, and can run towards around 1997. The dense, promising Piaugier wines are well worth seeking out.

Jean-Marc Autran's buddy and contemporary is another 'new-wave' *vigneron*, Christian Bonfils of the 40-odd hectare Domaine de Boissan, who has taken over from his father, Hubert. The red Sablet is made primarily from Grenache, with support from the Mourvèdre, the presence of which is very much *de rigueur* for many of these young growers. Again, the reds here are dark, well extracted and drink very well around the age of four to seven years.

In the future more excitement is likely to be provided by the young growers – still under thirty years old – tackling white wine vinification. Christian Bonfils makes a white Côtes du Rhône from 40 per cent Clairette, 40 per cent Bourboulenc and 20 per cent Grenache Blanc, which shows that superior, clean-tasting whites are more likely to be a regular feature of growers' work here in years to come.

Like both the Domaine de Boissan and the Domaine de Piaugier, the Cave Co-opérative makes Sablet and red Gigondas, and in similar vein its top *cuvées* receive some cask-ageing. The Gravillas reds are light and pleasant, but in the past have lacked the style and concentration that the private *domaines* have clearly shown the vicinity to be capable of. In all probability the advance of the *vignerons* bottling their own production will stir the Co-opérative to greater efforts. Meanwhile other private *domaines* to note are the Grangeons' Domaine du Parandou (Sablet and Gigondas), René Bernard's solid, straightforward Sablet and the Domaine Roumanille Sablet of Paul Roumanille, made from a modern mix of *cépages*, with just 65 per cent Grenache supported by 15 per cent Syrah and 10 per cent each of Cinsault and Mourvèdre. Jean-Pierre Cartier of Gigondas fame is another top name here, and he has a dedicated following for his very good white Sablet, made from Bourboulenc, Roussanne and a little Clairette, as well as his rich, dark and almost tarry red Sablet that contains one-third Syrah.

Leading Growers at Sablet

Arène, Luc
    Domaine de la Marsanne
 Autran, Marc et Jean-Marc
    Domaine de Piaugier
 Bernard, René
 Bonfils, Christian
    Domaine de Boissan
 Cave Co-opérative Le Gravillas
	84110 Sablet

Cartier, Jean-Pierre Domaine Les Goubert	84190 Gigondas

Chamfort, Bernard et Denis
    Domaine de Verquière
 Chassagne, Jean-Claude
    Domaine du Pourra
 Chauvin Frères
    Domaine Le Souverain
	84110 Sablet

Gaudin, Roland Domaine du Terme	84190 Gigondas

Grangeon, Denis
    Domaine du Parandou
 Roumanille, Paul
    Domaine Roumanille
	84110 Sablet

Roux, Charles et André Château du Trignon	84190 Gigondas

ST-GERVAIS

Five kilometres or so north-west of Bagnols-sur-Cèze is the village of St-Gervais, which was promoted to Côtes du Rhône Village status in May 1974. It is an unassuming little community, made up of a clutter of tiny, light brown houses all built out of the local soft stone; some of the streets are said by the locals to be the width of a car, but the scarred walls testify to the trapping of all larger models. Bordered to the north by the outhills of the Ardèche, this somnolent village looks out across the short valley of the Cèze. There, a winding line of trees denotes the curling progress of the river, and the light green colours of the vines form a simple contrast with the dark green hills beyond the river. It is a world that could come from an artist's canvas, and odd splashes of red are occasionally added to it by fields of gently waving poppies.

St-Gervais's past has gone largely unrecorded, but *département* archives mention the fact that wine was being made there around the seventeenth century. By 1789 the local aristocrat, the Marquis de Guasc, was reported even to be bottling some of his wine, but this practice was terminated shortly afterwards when he ended up on the guillotine.

Today most of the vineyards run down from the hills behind the village and on to the river's edge. As is normal for this part of the Gard *département*, they are subjected to extremes of both heat and wind. In summer the *mistral* wind can be so violent that fierce flurries of dust coil constantly over the vines. Tractor drivers take to wearing thick goggles for protection against the dust, looking for all the world like pioneer aviators.

Altogether there are around 240 hectares of *appellation* vines, mainly Grenache and Cinsault. A lot of replanting has been undertaken since the early 1960s as the growers have worked hard to attain their Village status, and now there are very few low-grade or common vines to be found in the local clay–limestone soil.

Most of the wine is made by the village Cave Co-opérative, with only two private *domaines*. The Co-opérative, founded in 1924, groups together 158 members – not a bad number for a village of only 500 inhabitants! In winter it is sometimes almost deserted, as most of the *vignerons* are out pruning their vines.

There is a commendable tradition of long service here at the Co-opérative; the previous *directeur*, the charming M. Henri Roux, had been with the Co-opérative since 1953 before his retirement in the mid-1980s. The current manager, M. Pradier, has continued the export drive that started with shipments to Belgium and Holland during the 1970s. The Co-opérative red and rosé wines are generally pretty good, although their greatest fault is that they can be too light-bodied. Some of the wine is made by *macération carbonique* and this heightens the light, almost fluffy texture of some of the *cuvées*. Like many Gard red wines, they never have the concentration or guts that the more earthy wines of the east bank possess – this is a question of soil and of lower levels of Grenache and higher levels of Cinsault.

The best *cuvées* are supple, well coloured with a cherry hue and agreeably fruity, with a suggestion of blackcurrants: these reds should be drunk before they are five years old.

A respectable white is also made by the Co-opérative, founded on Grenache Blanc, Cinsault and Bourboulenc. This sells as straight Côtes du Rhône.

However, the greatest fame that St-Gervais achieves is generated in international and local circles by one of the best of all Côtes du Rhône Villages *domaines*, the Guy Steinmaier Domaine Ste-Anne. Burgundian by origin, Steinmaier has brought on this *domaine* steadily through the last twenty years. In the early 1970s it was a curiosity property, since at that time the making of Rhône Villages by entirely *macération carbonique* methods was unusual. The Ste-Anne reds of the early to mid-1970s were pleasant, fruit-filled wines suitable for drinking within about four years.

But since then the vineyard has matured, and so has M. Steinmaier's son Alain, who is now in charge. One of the *domaine*'s best-known claims to fame among Rhône enthusiasts is its production of a very good – for the southern Rhône – Viognier white, from vines that were planted in the early 1980s. But their St-Gervais reds have gained tremendously in breeding, finesse and substance, and are now in a league of their own among the red Villages wines of the Gard, compared with Laudun, Chusclan and the Co-opérative at St-Gervais. They are also better than many of the red Liracs.

The Domaine Ste-Anne red is Mourvèdre-based – over half comes from this fashionable grape – and is supported by one-third Syrah . . . and only around 15 per cent Grenache. This carries a good, even and firm red colour which retains an attractive clarity even after around five years. The bouquet is sleek and elegant, showing touches of vanilla and berry fruit aromas, while the overriding impression on the palate is the intense fruit extract, very much as if the fruit comes from the very centre of the grape – it is not an easy sensation to describe but is very marked and sits nicely alongside a lovely balance and length of finish.

Here is an exceptional wine, one that drinks very well after five or six years, but which is well capable of showing over ten to twelve years. It is skilfully made, so that years like 1986 are great successes, as well as prominent years like 1985, 1988 and 1989.

Another *cuvée* of red is offered by this 26-hectare *domaine*, the Cuvée Notre-Dame-des-Cellettes: this is more traditionally composed of around 60 per cent Grenache, with a double support of 20 per cent each from the Syrah and the Mourvèdre.

M. Steinmaier has never leaned towards cask-ageing and has always pursued the extraction of as much fruit as possible from his grapes. In this he and his sons are remarkably successful. Meanwhile their whites, with their plantations of Roussanne, Marsanne and Viognier all maturing nicely, are very successful, with single-grape Côtes du Rhônes made from the Viognier; occasionally the Roussanne on its own provides the white Villages.

In company with experts like Paul Avril and François Perrin from Châteauneuf-du-Pape, Guy Steinmaier has done much to put the Mourvèdre on the map as an international vine, and this *domaine* is a must for enthusiasts or collectors.

Leading Growers at St-Gervais

Cave Co-opérative de St-Gervais
GAEC Les Frères Pailhon
   Domaine le Baine   } 30200 St-Gervais
Steinmaier, Guy, Jean et Alain
   Domaine Ste-Anne

ST-MAURICE-SUR-EYGUES

St-Maurice-sur-Eygues is a tiny, nondescript village, with a token fountain plonked down in its middle, that lies half-way along the main N94 road from Bollène to Nyons. Most of the community's life revolves around its Cave Co-opérative, which has 180 members. The River Eygues flows just south of the village, and most of the vineyards are situated on short slopes that line the northern part of the Eygues valley. As usual, the majority of the vines are Grenache, and can form as much as 80 per cent of the total plantation.

The wines of St-Maurice are generally of a reasonable quality, with signs of some improvement in the early 1990s under Co-opérative director Paul Rouvier. In the 1970s the Co-opérative was keen on placing its Villages wines in cask and provided a rather woody, stewed version of Rhône red. By the early 1980s greater sophistication of approach was applied, so that the Villages red received just three months' cask-ageing and the special *cuvée* several months more. Now the style is graded according to exposure to cask.

The basic red Villages is typical of its region, being made from around three-quarters Grenache and one-quarter Syrah. Like the St-Maurice reds over the years, it is an agreeable cherry red colour and shows an easy strawberry style fruitiness on the palate: these wines from this part of the Drôme are quite distinct in style from the Vaucluse reds further south, certainly more delicate in texture, and good to drink without any airs or to-do within their first four years.

The other layers of the Co-opérative wine depend a little on *cépage* selection and wood exposure. The Cuvée de Prestige Marquis de la Charce is made from around 70 per cent Grenache, topped up with 15 per cent each of Syrah and Mourvèdre, although in some years there is less Mourvèdre. This is a more solid, keeping wine than the standard *cuvée*, as is the Grande Réserve, a Grenache–Syrah wine that spends some time in young oak. This in turn is marked by its vinification, with the introduction of vanilla flavours from the new oak. Both these wines are sound enough, and may gain in refinement during the next years.

A small amount of light Villages rosé is made, mainly from Grenache and Cinsault, and some white Côtes du Rhône from around two-thirds Ugni Blanc and one-third Clairette: this is not yet one of the front runners among the improving band of southern Rhône whites.

Just one *domaine* bottles its own St-Maurice red, the Domaine de Deurre, which since 1987 has been revamped by Jean-Claude Valayer and his *œnologue* son Hubert. Their red St-Maurice is made from 85 per cent Grenache and 15 per cent Syrah, and it will be interesting to chart the development of this wine and this *domaine*, which also makes a red Vinsobres, over the coming years.

Leading Growers at St-Maurice-sur-Eygues

Cave des Coteaux de St-Maurice-sur-Eygues	26650 St-Maurice-sur-Eygues
Valayer, Jean-Claude et Hubert Domaine de Deurre	26110 Vinsobres

ST-PANTALÉON-LES-VIGNES AND ROUSSET-LES-VIGNES

The villages of St-Pantaléon-les-Vignes and Rousset-les-Vignes are the two most north-easterly Côtes du Rhône Villages and are set against a ring of forbidding mountains that separate them from the early Alpine settlements south of Die. The countryside at the foot of these mountains is suddenly verdant, for it is criss-crossed by a network of life-giving mountain streams. Many *vignerons* are therefore able to grow all their own vegetables and occasionally sell them further afield to regional markets.

As the village names imply, it is the vine that is predominant. But there is a discreet change of climate, away from the hotter, more Mediterranean style to a more breezy, temperate year – with the effect of making the wines somewhat lighter and finer than the full-bodied Vaucluse reds.

Until 1948 both villages made a wine known as Haut Comtat, but in that year the denomination was changed to the straightforward title of 'Côtes du Rhône'. In 1969, St-Pantaléon was promoted to Villages status, and Rousset followed suit in 1972. Now both wines are vinified at the Cave Co-opérative of St-Pantaléon founded in 1960 and presided over since 1973 by the affable M. René Bernard. All the wine that the 220 members want bottled goes on to the Cellier des Dauphins bottling centre at Tulette.

Most of the vines are grown on flat clay and limestone ground all around the two communities. In places there are plots of vines on sloping land, and these grow on a mainly gravelly surface. Some 60 per cent of the vines are Grenache, and these are followed in importance by the Carignan, the Cinsault, the Syrah (on the increase) and the Mourvèdre. The Carignan is not used in the Villages wines, while M. Bernard interestingly gave the view that the Mourvèdre was not at its best in these vineyards near the Alpine foothills.

Around 200,000 litres, which represents the best wine from the two Villages, is bottled every year. This leaves the Cave Co-opérative with little sales or export latitude in promoting the name of these two Villages: most of the wine still serves local requirements in cubitainer or basic litre form. But as one has clearly seen, such suppliers are disappearing or upgrading as consumers move to drinking less and better wine. St-Pantaléon and Rousset will change in the same way, but will be at a disadvantage through having started the upgrading process late.

A gradual expansion of the range of *appellation* wines occurred during the 1980s, so that both St-Pantaléon and Rousset red Villages are offered, as well as red, white and rosé Côtes du Rhône and red Coteaux du Tricastin. The vinification process is carefully graded, with different *cépages* vinified apart, and crushing and destalking occurring before a ten-day *cuvaison*. The Villages reds receive cask-ageing nowadays – a departure from the practice of the 1970s, when it was only the straight Côtes du Rhône that was placed in some of their 200 Burgundian casks. These Villages red wines are never very dark-coloured – very much a local characteristic – and are soft in style. Their fruitiness is sweeter and more like garden fruit jam than the more berry fruit shown by Villages wines further south and across the Eygues. With cask exposure, there is a little more substance than previously, but these are still wines to be drinking before they are around six or seven years old. They are a suitable accompaniment for white meats – veal or pork, for example. The ubiquitous gastronome Curnonsky was acquainted even with the wine of St-Pantaléon, and in one of his diaries he praised it highly.

The Côtes du Rhône reds are sound, while the rosés have improved in the last few years. Some white Côtes du Rhône has been made since the late 1970s, from Grenache Blanc, Clairette and a little Bourboulenc, but it is only fair in quality.

The Cave Co-opérative is the only producer in these two villages bottling any of the local wine on the spot. There are four private growers in St-Pantaléon, but they send their wine to merchants, while all the growers in Rousset belong to the Co-opérative.

Leading Grower at St-Pantaléon-les-Vignes and Rousset-les-Vignes

Union des Producteurs de
   St-Pantaléon-les-Vignes et   26230 St-Pantaléon-les-Vignes
   Rousset-les-Vignes

SÉGURET *see* ROAIX and SÉGURET

VALRÉAS

Strategically placed on the top of a hill, and protected by a ring of mountains to the north, east and south, Valréas is on the N541 road, about 25 kilometres east of Donzère and the Rhône. It is a compact town, built within the confines of a circular boulevard and against the slope of its hillside. At the top of the hill stand a fine twelfth-century church and a renovated eighteenth-century château. The church possesses a splendid organ, originally built in 1506, on which young enthusiasts are allowed to practise freely, and some of its oldest corner towers are respectfully dedicated to St Vincent, the patron of wine growers.

Valréas used to be one of four villages that formed a papal enclave inside France from 1317 until 1791; even today the four villages – Valréas, Grillon, Richerenches and Visan – have maintained their separate identity, for all are officially situated in the Vaucluse *département* even though they are completely surrounded by the *département* of the Drôme. This represents quite an anomaly for the French administration, which ever since the establishment of the Code Napoléon has organized its *départements* to be neatly adjacent to one another: in this case, however, history and precedent have prevailed.

During the fourteenth century the Popes resident in Avignon were given to casting rapacious looks over the surrounding countryside, and whenever possible land acquisitions were made at suitably nominal prices. Consequently, in 1317 the sharp-minded Pope John XXII retrieved the extravagant Dauphin of France from financial ruin by paying him 6,000 *livres* for the village of Valréas. In 1320 Pope John continued his good work and succeeded in actually being given Richerenches: this usefully extended his property outside Avignon and gave him another source of wine, for the Knights Templar had for 200 years been making wine from their base there.

By 1383 the papacy had bought the other two villages of Visan and Grillon and found itself with a 200-square-kilometre enclave conveniently situated about 65 kilometres from Avignon – a very useful fallback if ever trouble should arise in the papal city. The wisdom of this acquisition was amply demonstrated a little later, when the papacy returned definitively to Rome and yet the papal enclave remained intact on French territory, an undoubted bugbear to successive French monarchs. It was not until 1791 that the enclave finally returned to French hands, following the victory of the revolutionary army from Avignon over the gathered enclave forces at Sarrians, near Carpentras.

Wine has long been made at Valréas and in its early days was largely the responsibility of the Church. A statement by the Bishop of Vaison-la-Romaine in 1262 mentioned the vines of Valréas, and later documents of 1298 and 1316 point to the quite extensive cultivation of the vine around the village. By the start of the nineteenth century Valréas had become one of the largest wine-making communities of the Vaucluse *département*, with its vineyards covering nearly 535 hectares.

Today Valréas makes wine – and cardboard boxes. Almost half the town works in the carton industry, which originated in the last century when boxes were needed for transporting the silk thread that was produced locally on an extensive scale. And the inhabitants still possess a strong sense of an identity apart: in 1974 they formed a grouping known as the Union of Wine Growers of the Enclave des Papes. This is a centre that bottles Cave Co-opérative and private *domaine* wine from anywhere within the old papal territory. There is a strict rule that no outside wine is allowed, as the *vignerons* are anxious to emphasize their separate nature.

The Valréas vineyards now cover over 1,500 hectares, and all the important Côtes du Rhône grape varieties are included in the plantation. Many of the vines grow on gentle inclines, rather than full slopes, and it is noticeable that the soil can change quite sharply from one plot to the next. Generally, there is a mixture of clay and limestone, with a sprinkling of rounded pebbles on the surface. This sparse ground is ideal for vines, as well as for olive trees and lavender plants, which are grown in lesser numbers.

Valréas possesses a well-known Cave Co-opérative founded back in 1928 with an annual production then of all wine of just 9,900 hectolitres. The figure today has risen past the 100,000-hectolitre mark, of which about half qualifies for Côtes du Rhône *générique* and under 10 per cent for Valréas Villages. The granting of the Villages status in 1966 served as a great boost to the 500 members, who over the past dozen years have been encouraged to undertake 'progressive' replanting in their vineyards – meaning that plants like the Syrah, the Cinsault and a little Mourvèdre are more in favour than the Carignan. The local favourite of these 'improver' vines is the Syrah, which is thought to marry well with the Grenache in these slightly cooler climes than further south on the hotter, more baked plains and slopes of the Vaucluse. The red wine of the Cave Co-opérative 'La Gaillarde' fits into the category of reasonably made wines from large-scale sources that are quite frequently available in the southern Rhône. The emphasis is on early drinkability, with a soft, cleanly fruited wine suitable for drinking under five years of age.

Valréas has a number of thriving wine *domaines* that are helping to spread the *appellation*'s name to a wider public, of which the most interesting is undoubtedly Le Val des Rois, owned by M. Romain Bouchard, who comes from the famous Burgundian family that has been making wine since 1681. 'The trouble was that there were too many of us,' said M. Bouchard, a lean, very courteous man in his sixties, whose ruddy-brown face testifies to an outdoor life in the vineyards. 'I was the first of the family to leave Burgundy, and until 1964 actually grew oranges in southern Morocco, which I expect raised a few eyebrows at home! When I came back to France, I did a brush-up wine course near Lausanne and bought this *domaine*, Le Val des Rois. Most of the vines were over fifty years old, so I replanted from scratch using the Grenache, Syrah and Cinsault at a novel distance of 3 metres apart, so that I could work the slopes with machinery. Given the relative height of my vines and their largely clay subsoil, I've found that they have handled the dry years of the late 1980s and early 1990s better than those sited in the full glare of the plain. On the very highest vineyards, at 400 metres, I also have a little Gamay, and am very pleased with the result – these vines have given a wine with an enormous blackcurrant aroma.'

M. Bouchard is similar to another great innovator and standard-bearer for his *appellation*, Guy Steinmaier of St-Gervais. An after-noon in their company would be a treat indeed, for quite apart from the excellence of both men's wines, the angle of their thinking and their perception of wine-making would make for a fascinating exchange of ideas.

M. Bouchard's Val des Rois *domaine* covers 15 hectares and runs alongside the Vinsobres property that now belongs to Thierry Bouchard, his brother. He regards wine as just as much an intellectual as an agricultural challenge and calls himself the 'Provençal surgeon from a Burgundian family'. By this he means that his vinification process runs along Burgundian lines, whereas in the vineyards he generally follows the local customs. Hence he destalks all the grapes but does not crush them, and then has a three- to five-day *cuvaison* with its *chapeau* immersed. His Villages wine from Valréas may spend up to one year in enamel-lined vats before bottling; he has given up ageing it in wood, seeking a very steady evolution of the young fruit flavours, and will go as far as making a rendezvous to drink a bottle of any of his best vintages like 1990, 1989, 1986 or 1985 after ten years.

M. Bouchard's Domaine du Val des Rois red Valréas is a wine whose raspberry-style fruit is accentuated within a surround of great balance and length. Like Steinmaier, he has captured the art of providing sensuous, approachable and elegant wines from soil and climates that usually deliver robust, more rough-and-tumble wines. And he has done it in the most modest way possible, with no fancy marketing and no fanfares, just solid hard work topped up with a sense of humour and a determination to have his wines respected. The Val des Rois is made from roughly one-quarter Syrah and three-quarters Grenache, and has a ripe flavour and inspiring fruit bouquet when drunk after around five years. But it is a wine that also drinks well, with a racy fruitiness and a shade more evident tannin, after only two or three years.

M. Bouchard thinks that there lies a very subtle difference between the wines of Valréas and Vinsobres, where he used also to own a property. He described it in the following way: 'I believe this difference is most apparent in the respective wines' fruit. A Valréas seems to me vaguely evocative of flowers on its bouquet, while a Vinsobres red wine has more a suggestion of blackcurrants. But at source I consider that it is perhaps the grape variety that plays a more important role here in the constitution of the wine than does the soil make-up.'

A little Valréas rosé is made in addition to the red wine, and this is good for relaxed summer drinking, being a shade superior to many local offerings. Other private *domaines* worth noting are the Ferme de la Verrière of Pierre Rosati – a fresh, promising white and a red Valréas aged for two years in *foudres*; and the Domaine de la Fuzière of Léo Roussin, who has always been a producer of old-fashioned, rather advanced-tasting reds from his 21-hectare property. These are still formed around 70 per cent Grenache, but destemming has been introduced, making the wines a little fresher.

The Domaine des Grands Devers of René Sinard is a notable producer, whose Valréas is made to the tune of 90 per cent from the Grenache; it is stored in vat for over a year before bottling, and is a very good, rich wine capable of drinking well over six to eight years. A well balanced, firmly fruited Côtes du Rhône Syrah and a sound rosé are also made from this 25-hectare estate. Lastly, the Domaine de la Prévosse is the producer of red Valréas that in part is vinified by a *macération carbonique* process, but which then receives a stay in vat and a stay in *foudres*. It therefore comes more in the ripe, advanced tasting style of wine which some drinkers would find woody; again, this is a wine dominated to about 80 per cent by the Grenache. Henri Davin also owns the Château de Montplaisir, a 5-hectare property in addition to his 20 hectares, and this will be a name to look out for since Syrah and Mourvèdre are being planted on it alongside the Grenache. This family also make a little Rhône white from the Clairette and the Bourboulenc, as do the Domaine Mireille et Vincent, and the commitment to white wine mastery at Valréas may well increase and improve during the 1990s.

Leading Growers at Valréas

Bonnefoy, Albert et Annie
   Notre Dame des Vieilles
Bouchard, Romain
   Le Val des Rois
Cave Co-opérative
   La Gaillarde
Davin, Henri, et Fils
   Domaine de la Prévosse
   Château de Montplaisir
Domaine Mireille et
   Vincent   84600 Valréas
Gras, André
   Domaine de St-Chétin
Laurent, Maurice
Pouizin, Denis
   Domaine du Séminaire
Rosati, Pierre
   Ferme de la Verrière
Roussin, Léo
   Domaine de la Fuzière

Sayn, André
  Cours de la Recluse
Sinard, René
  Domaine des Grands Devers

84600 Valréas

VINSOBRES

Vinsobres is a typically dormant little brown Provençal village, full of narrow streets, gossiping old-timers and softly flowing fountains. Situated about 30 kilometres east of Bollène along the course of the Eygues Valley, it is one of the more senior Côtes du Rhône Villages, having been allowed to use its own name on its wine since 1957. Its main point of activity lies in its two Caves Co-opératives; these stand some way out of the village, which is thereby deprived of the motions of everyday life, though this matters little to the inhabitants of Vinsobres, who nearly all work in the vineyards anyway.

Vinsobres is an old wine village. Around the fourth century AD Vinsobrium is thought to have been in the hands of the Vocontii tribe, who would make wine from the sloping fields around the village. References to this wine, and the fact that it was later mostly made by the Church and the local *seigneur*, appear in local documents throughout the Middle Ages; then, in 1633, the Bishop of Vaison-la-Romaine, one Monseigneur de Suarès, came up with a quotation that has never been forgotten by the grateful people of Vinsobres, so conveniently suited is it to the world of twentieth-century advertising. The Bishop's words were:

> *Vin Sobre ou Sobre Vin*
> *Prenez le Sobrement.*[1]

What is most noticeable about this saying is that it only rhymes when spoken in a strong Provençal accent, whereby the final words become 'vaing' and 'sobremaing'!

During the eighteenth century the vineyards extended to as many as 210 hectares, a figure that held constant and even rose slightly before the attack of phylloxera, which was apparently more severe than normal at Vinsobres. Vineyard reconstruction did not begin on

[1] Sober Wine or Wine of Sobriety,
  Take it soberly.

any scale until 1905, but it gradually accelerated and today plantation has reached the healthy size of around 1,300 hectares, spread chiefly over an 8-kilometre strip either side of the River Eygues.

The older Cave Co-opérative, the 'Vinsobraise', was founded in 1949 and now has 300 members, who contribute towards an average total of 80,000 hectolitres of wine, from ordinary table wine up, every year. Over three-quarters of this wine is red, and most of it is sold by the Cellier des Dauphins bottling and marketing centre at Tulette, 15 kilometres away. Usually it passes under the ordinary 'Côtes du Rhône' label, without the 'Vinsobres'; the wine dedicated to the Vinsobres Villages title is drawn from plantations on slopes and the plateau which is at around an altitude of 450 metres. It is largely Grenache-based, with support from the Syrah and the Carignan. This receives a brief stay in wood before bottling by the Cellier des Dauphins, and has improved its quality in recent years, showing greater length on the palate than previously. The Co-opérative also produces white Rhône from Clairette and Ugni Blanc and a rosé from Grenache, Cinsault and Syrah.

In 1959 a second Co-opérative, the Cave du Prieuré, was formed. This concerns itself solely with ageing and selling the Vinsobres Villages wine, some of which is exported to Switzerland, Germany, Belgium and Britain. The Co-opérative takes in the wine from its ninety-five *vigneron* members, some of whom also belong to the 'Vinsobraise', around Easter after the harvest and ages it in both large and small casks. These wines can sometimes taste rather stewed, as if they have either been in the wood for too long or have been made from unpromising parts of the harvest.

The Cave du Prieuré also acts for several private growers in ageing and bottling their Vinsobres Villages production – an example is Denis Vinson of Domaine du Moulin who makes consistently good, gently styled red Vinsobres. However, it is curious that what is probably the best *domaine* at Vinsobres makes no Vinsobres Villages wine at all, and restricts itself merely to straight Côtes du Rhône. M. Claude Jaume's Vinsobres used to be rich, thorough wine, but the 1974 change in the *appellation* laws stopped him from making it. He explained: 'Before I could make 35 hectolitres per hectare of Villages wine that would obviously fetch higher Villages rates, as well as being able to sell excess production up to 50 hectolitres as Côtes du Rhône *générique*: so, 35 hectos of Villages and 15 hectos of *générique*. The change of law meant that I could only sell any excess above the Villages quantity – which has now been raised to 42 hectos – as *vin de pays*, for which I get much less money. I therefore prefer to produce a full 52 hectos per hectare and sell it all as full *appellation* Rhône *générique* wine, and be done.'

M. Jaume's attitude is one that is both understandable and common in the southern Rhône Valley. The rules do not seem to be encouraging quality in this instance, for it is with the more indifferent wine-makers that extra production of Côtes du Rhône *générique* becomes out of place in an area already bursting at the seams with this class of wine.

M. Jaume has worked in an impeccable, modern cellar since 1981 and his 35-hectare *domaine* provides a well-extracted red Rhône which has been strengthened by some extra Mourvèdre in the last few years. It is aged for six to twelve months in wood, and is a very good, clean and full wine, as is his rosé, made by the *saignée* method.

Another front-rank property is the Domaine les Aussellons which is split between 17 hectares at Vinsobres and 13 hectares producing Côtes du Rhône from Villedieu. M. Ézingeard varies the vinification of his Vinsobres according to the nature of the vintage, so that lighter years are not placed in cask. The reds are stored in vat for several months so that their release in bottle comes usually after around two years or more. The main *cépage* is the Grenache, but the *domaine* also uses notable amounts of Syrah and Carignan. These are very thorough wines, with a deep fruitiness and substance working well together to make them good to drink around the age of five to eight years or so.

M. François Vallot's Domaine du Coriançon is another sound source for Vinsobres. This is one of the larger *domaines* dedicating itself to the production of Villages wine – 60 hectares all told, which are led by the Grenache (65 per cent), with support from the Syrah, Cinsault and Mourvèdre. The Coriançon red Vinsobres is a solid and elegant wine which receives around a year in cask.

Leading Growers at Vinsobres

Benôit-Ézingeard
    Domaine les Aussellons   84110 Villedieu
Bouchard, N.
    Domaine de la Bicarelle   26110 Vinsobres
La Cave du Prieuré

Cave Co-opérative
  'La Vinsobraise'
Durma, Fernand
  Domaine St-Vincent
Valayer, Hubert
  Domaine de Deurre
Vallot, François   26110 Vinsobres
  Domaine du Coriançon
Vallot, Xavier
  Domaine des Escoulaires
Vinson, Denis
  Domaine du Moulin

VISAN

Inside the Enclave des Papes and 22.5 kilometres north-east of
Orange is the charming old village of Visan. Once noted for its
château, which was destroyed in the sixteenth-century wars of
religion, the medieval village stands on a small hill a little apart from
most of today's habitation. A series of narrow stone archways leads
into the sandy-coloured upper part of the village, where stands a
cluster of crooked old houses, some festooned with climbing wistaria
and vine plants, others connected to one another by shaky-looking
overhead passages. These circular streets and neat archways are
impressive reminders of the well-guarded prosperity of former ages,
when first one single family owned the whole village, which was then
divided between the Baux and Dauphin families. By the fourteenth
century it was the Church that possessed most of the village, including
its already flourishing vineyards.

It is thought that wine-making extends even further back in history,
for when the Cave Co-opérative was being built in 1937, several
coins, pots and jars dating from the time of Augustus and Hadrian
were unearthed. It is not certain that these pots and jars were used
for wine, of course, but the local *vignerons* typically have no doubts
about it!

By 1250 a village winepress was spoken of in contemporary
archives, and at roughly the same time the church of Notre Dame
des Vignes was built near the road to St-Maurice-sur-Eygues. Tucked
away in a tiny grove of evergreens in the middle of a vineyard, the

church undoubtedly drew its name from its location. Even today it has a deep significance for the local wine-making community, and every year on 8 September there is a pilgrimage to it. Three Masses are celebrated, and there is a general blessing of the vineyards. Out of respect for the pilgrimage, the *vignerons* of Visan never do any work on that day, and many of them take part in the service and the carefree buffet that follows.

Wine-making at Visan for many years revolved almost entirely around the village Cave Co-opérative. Although this was not founded until 1937, wine had been made on its premises for forty years previously. In 1897 the local Delaye family decided to expand their cellars in order to cater for a larger production and took over a site on the edge of the village. By 1912 the private cellars were extremely well equipped, with novel glass-lined vats being used for fermentation and storage of young wine and the old wooden barrels serving to mature all the red wine. Sales outlets were no problem, since M. Delaye ran a successful restaurant in the suburbs of Paris; by the outbreak of the First World War his *vin des Côtes du Rhône* had become very popular in the capital.

Before 1937 most of the local growers had started to send their grapes to M. Delaye, and when he died in that year a group of eighty-eight of them bought the Cave from his widow. The cellars were once more expanded, and today there are 370 contributors to the Co-opérative, which is directed by the capable M. Jean Ordener, who has been with the Co-opérative for twenty-five years.

Since the 1988 harvest the Co-opérative has worked with a new *cuverie* to make their wine; on average around 20,000 hectolitres of Visan Villages are made each year, and around 70,000 hecto-litres of straight Rhône. This is out of a total production of around 120,000 hectos, and it is noticeable that the proportion of top wine has grown from about one-tenth to one-sixth over the past ten years.

M. Ordener commented on their vinification process: 'We select carefully all the harvested grapes according to which part of the vineyard they have come from. You see, we use most of the slope grapes for our Villages wines: these are generally riper and more healthy than the grapes from the plain vines. Our members have increased their planting of Syrah and Mourvèdre in recent years – the Syrah was very much the vine of the 1970s and the Mourvèdre the vine of the 1980s, while we have been taking out much of our

Cinsault, which we feel gives a *vin de primeur* rather than one that deserves to age.'

The Visan Co-opérative is therefore set on producing wines of greater substance and durability, and the Visan red is now composed of around 70 per cent Grenache, supported by 15 per cent each from the Syrah and the Mourvèdre. A further change comes from the Co-opérative's rejection of *macération carbonique* methods that were tried in the late 1970s. Now there is an eight-day *cuvaison* of the different varieties, with the Mourvèdre only assembled near bottling. The wine was not put into wood until the 1989 vintage, and normally emerges with a typical middling colour and a pleasant strain of fruit running through it. Visan reds are not big, vigorous wines and tend towards a style of rounded fruit with a touch of heat on the finish. The Co-opérative reds improved in the late 1980s, but some *cuvées* still miss the mark, with rather fuzzy flavours on the palate.

Starting with the 1989 vintage, the Co-opérative has an 800-hectolitre capacity for wood-ageing – *pièces* that are rotated every two years and *foudres* of 30-hectolitre capacity. The wine is spending around a year or so in cask before bottling, and this treatment has given their Visan Cuvée Saint-Vincent red more depth and tannic overlay.

The Co-opérative makes a small amount of white wine, from the Grenache Blanc, Clairette and Bourboulenc grapes; sold as the Baron des Adrets under a straight Rhône bottling, this has never delivered the goods, often being drinkable but lacking in freshness and vigour.

Since the second half of the 1970s the Co-opérative has been put on its mettle by two *domaines* that have aimed to bottle as much as possible of their very good wine. The Domaine de Cantharide is owned and run by Janine Roux, a lady in her thirties who shows great stamina in raising a son and working the 16-hectare property outside Visan on sloping ground. A visit is marked by the presence of a wandering turkey that follows and often menaces newcomers around the vineyard, only ceasing hostilities at the cellar entrance.

Janine Roux first explained how she had started up the *domaine* after emerging from pruning the vineyards in the teeth of a savage January *mistral* gale; the fact that she was at the time five months pregnant seemed not to slow her down in the slightest. 'I designed the cellar in 1977 and decided to start bottling some of our harvest straight away. I didn't want to get too carried away with bottling all the crop, especially in indifferent years like 1981, when the wines lacked acidity, so we bottle maybe three-quarters of our wine. The vineyard runs all around the little chapel of Notre Dame des Vignes, which I think should bring us some good luck, and our vines extend as far as the line of low hills that separate Visan from the Eygues Valley.

'Our soil here is mainly clay, and my husband and I have both found that grapes grown on this soil don't seem to lend themselves to the *macération carbonique* process. We undertake a traditional fermentation, with no destalking and a very light crushing just to break the grape skins a little. We vinify in stainless steel tanks and leave the wine in vats for about eighteen months before bottling.'

Some experiments with wood have been done by Janine Roux and her husband M. Laget. Their main wines are still formed around the Grenache, although some *cuvées* contain as much as 40 per cent Syrah with it, while others are more marked by the presence of the Mourvèdre. The best wines hold a firm mauve colour when young, have a gentle fruit bouquet and a good raspberry-type fruit on the palate. They are more solid than many at Visan, but their substance is refined rather than heavy. This is a *domaine* whose wines, including some fair white and rosé, are worth looking out for.

The other noted *domaine*, Clos du Père Clément, is owned by M. Henri Depèyre and his sons, who displayed a rare reluctance, bordering on total suspicion, to answer any questions about their neatly laid-out property. Their smart *domaine* house is 300 years old, and its varnished doors and shutters point to a recent restoration, while the vineyards, set in a mainly clay soil, carry a rose at the end of each row. Their 20 hectares of vineyards were planted in stages from 1972 onwards, and now they bottle all their Visan Villages, which is mostly red wine. Like the Domaine de la Cantharide, they ferment in stainless steel tanks, but only put their ordinary Côtes du Rhône *générique* in cask; the Villages red, the Cuvée Notre Dame, is stocked in underground concrete vats for two years before being released for sale.

The Père Clément reds carry a firm fruitiness that, as with the Cantharide wines, resembles raspberries, but there is also the presence of tannin at the end to invest a little more punch. Both these *domaine* Visan reds are good to drink around the five-year mark.

All the Visan red wines reflect the strong heat that is generated in the local countryside during the summer months and consequently carry an alcohol degree that runs from 12.5–14°. However, in the hands of skilful *vignerons* who select the time of picking carefully, and can control vinification with modern *pigeage* equipment and the use of stainless steel, Visan shows again that the Villages of the Rhône are an area of wine-making potential as we move through the 1990s.

Leading Growers at Visan

Cave Co-opérative
  'Les Coteaux de Visan'
Depèyre Père et Fils
  Clos du Père Clément   84820 Visan
Domaine de Costechaude
Laget-Roux
  Domaine de la Cantharide

Côtes du Rhône Villages Vintages

1955   Excellent.

1956   Poor.

1957   Very good.

1958   Good. Wines that were generally well balanced.

1959   Only mediocre. The wines tended to be too light.

1960   Mediocre. Undistinguished, light-bodied wines.

1961   Excellent; full-bodied, sound wines.

1962   Good; the wines were lighter than the 1961s, and so unfortunately suffered by unfair comparison.

1963   Very poor.

1964   Very good. Strong, tannic wines.

1965   Poor.

1966   Good. The wines were supple and well balanced.

1967   Excellent. A really strong-bodied vintage, the wines had abundant bouquet and great all-round charm.

1968   Very poor. Light wines.

1969   Very good. Sound, appealing wines.

1970   Excellent. Very full wines, with ample bouquet and strong appeal.

1971   A very good vintage. Pleasant, quite full wines that were better in the Gard *département* than in the Vaucluse or the Drôme.

1972   Generally a good year. The red wines were quite rich and possessed good balance.

1973   A mediocre vintage. The wines tended to be unevenly coloured and lacking in fullness.

1974   An average year. The wines were generally lacking in colour, and were sometimes low in alcohol content. The Gard *département* wines were on the whole a shade better than the others.

1975   Poor. Both the reds and the whites suffered from lack of balance and lightness of colour.

1976   Good. The red wines developed quite well, although they possessed less staying power than was at first thought likely. The Vaucluse Villages reds were notably full-blown, with big alcoholic extract.

1977   Poor. Most of the reds were lightly coloured and deficient in flavour, despite there being only a small harvest.

1978   Very good indeed. The vintage was successful throughout the Villages area, with the growers around Vacqueyras, Cairanne and the best *générique* growers from the Drôme *département* obtaining some really full-blooded *cuvées* of big, slow-maturing wine. The odd bottle of Vacqueyras or Rasteau could still provide a pleasant surprise, with aged cedar aromas and pepper flavours now to the fore.

1979   Very good in most of the Côtes du Rhône area. The Vaucluse *département* came up with the best wines, which were a little more gentle than the firmer, stronger 1978s. They are weakening now. The vintage was a bit less successful in the Gard *département*, where the wines were sometimes rather light.

1980   A variable vintage. There were some very good wines made by the better growers who were careful to sort their harvest, but there was also an excess of low-end of the market wine that was pale and weak. The leading *domaines* in the Vaucluse and Drôme succeeded in making well-balanced wines with good richness and follow-through, while the Gard *département* growers' wines were marked by an agreeable harmony that made them good to drink early. Some of the Vaucluse reds have aged well into the 1990s.

1981   A vintage that was good in parts, with better wines made in the southern part of the Villages – Sablet, Beaumes-de-

Venise and even Cairanne – than elsewhere, for example Visan and Vinsobres. Ripening was difficult to achieve in some places because of the indifferent summer, and many of the reds were lean. The best *cuvées* were very good; austere initially, they straightened out really well after five or six years. Drink up surviving bottles.

1982   Moderate. A year of major impact on Rhône growers, which affected future thinking and accelerated the modernization of many cellars. The first 'big heat' year of the 1980s caught out many of the growers, and, particularly in the Vaucluse, there were many 'got-up' wines – stewed, jammy and unconvincing on the palate. The Gard wines were also rather pale and cooked.

1983   Very good indeed. There were some excellent, full-bodied and darkly coloured reds made all over the Rhône Villages. Tannin levels were high in the Vaucluse, providing strong, chewy reds that can still show well in the early 1990s. There were some excellent reds made in the Gard, with a notable, elegant Domaine St-Anne St-Gervais from Guy Steinmaier – way above the run of Villages wines. The whites, when successful as from Domaine Pelaquié at Laudun, were firm and good to drink over around six years.

1984   A fair vintage. A late flowering led to a late harvest, and the composition of many of the wines in the Vaucluse – villages like Séguret and Cairanne – was affected by *coulure* on the Grenache. The wines were medium-bodied and rather spare, although colour levels were sound enough. The reds should be drunk up. Some early drinking whites were made by the better producers – their acidity early on was appealing.

1985   Very good. Ripe, voluptuous reds were made. In a way, this was a seminal vintage. It marked the first concerted progression by the Rhône Villages reds towards a generous but more elegant style of wine. The rounded and pleasant tannins of the vintage contributed, as did the growing mastery of the *vignerons* to work with very ripe fruit after yet another very hot summer and autumn. There were success stories all over the region, with wines that held great appeal early on, but which had the fullness to keep going for eight years or more. They are good to drink sooner rather than later to best enjoy the plump fruitiness. The whites were good on the most part, well rounded and attractive for early consumption. Sound rosés as well.

1986   Good to very good. The reds were more sharply tannic than the 1985s, and growers had to pre-sort their harvest more than in 1985. Some of the Vaucluse reds are a little hard – there are some very stern Vacqueyras reds around – but, once again, it was a year to back the good grower – hence excellent work by the likes of Steinmaier at St-Gervais, Romain Bouchard at Valréas, Corinne Couturier at Rasteau, and Roger Combe at Vacqueyras. These often robust wines are likely to be near their peak around 1992–4. In the more northerly areas, such as Visan, some uneven, rather over-alcoholic wines were made. It was a good year for whites, with the Lauduns showing especially well, while some very good rosés were made from villages like Rasteau.

1987   Fair. The variable summer weather made life more difficult than usual for growers becoming used to nature delivering nearly 'ready-made' grapes. Some of the reds are thin and rather mean-tasting on the palate: they lack structure and were good simply for early consumption. The better growers worked soundly with the crop, and produced some gentle wines which are worth drinking until around 1993. The whites were more successful, cast in a fresh and lively vein with some well extracted fruit. They, too, should show well until around 1993. Fair for the rosés, some of which were a bit hard.

1988   Good to very good. The reds were generally well coloured and held firm tannins. It was an excellent year for the classic, hard-core *appellations* like Cairanne and Rasteau, with the good work of the new wave at Sablet coming through. These reds need a little time to settle their tannins, and will provide well-balanced drinking when five years old or so. The Gard reds were also well extracted and successful, as usual marked by some agreeable finesse. It was a good year for white Rhônes, with growers able to extract firm fruit and fairly rich bouquets from their wines. Some decent rosés were also made.

1989　A uniformly good vintage throughout the region with the proviso that the second consecutive year of drought made some of the Vaucluse tannins quite severe in the reds. The well selected red *cuvées* are rich above all – really ripe and thorough, and they have good rounded strength on the palate. According to their place of origin, they will provide great drinking from three years old up to around ten years old. An excellent year for the whites, which have more marked bouquets than the 1988s, and great depth and length on the palate. The rosés were full and good for drinking in their first three years.

1990　Very good indeed. The reds are very rich and dense after another hot summer, but the odd rainfall near harvest-time brought an extra roundness to the crop, making *vignerons'* lives easier. The reds have more sustained flavours and colours than the 1989s and they are also likely to open up more slowly than them – their bouquets are less prominent at a young stage but have great promise for the future. Look out for the wines from growers in progressive Villages like Cairanne, Sablet and Valréas. The whites are full, fresh and clean and they, too, will need a little time to develop their aromas on the bouquet. The rosés are a shade behind the more generous 1989s.

17

Côtes du Rhône

Côtes du Rhône is the best-known wine in the lower Rhône Valley because, quite simply, it accounts for around 85 per cent of all the *appellation* wine made between Vienne and Avignon. This represents the region's backbone but not its pennant. Most Côtes du Rhône is an unpretentious country wine that is sometimes very good, sometimes very bad but nearly always pretty drinkable. It is also the wine of the small grower – the farmer whose family have long tilled their own little plot of ground, producing vegetables, fruit and staple family needs, as well as a little wine to wash it all down.

Such small growers today put their trust in their local Caves Coopératives, which since the 1920s have directly aided the fortunes of the many little 'Clochermerle'-type villages all over southern France. The Co-opérative has at the same time become an important social unit, a forum and point of contact for the whole community, and, according to its far-sightedness, a prestigious link with the outside world, be it in France or overseas.

Among the whole range of Co-opératives, which in the Rhône Valley number sixty-six, there are a handful that are very good, a lot that are respectable and nowadays very few that produce very poor wine: this is itself a definite advance over the last twenty years. The very good Co-opératives, such as those at Gigondas, Tavel, Cairanne, St-Désirat, Rasteau, Ste-Céciles-les-Vignes (Caveau Chantecôtes) and Laudun, are often rightly known for their principal *appellation* or Villages wine, but they serve a valuable purpose in helping to break down the consumer's somewhat natural resistance to wines that come from one mass source, as they inevitably must when emanating from a Cave Co-opérative.

Meanwhile, since the mid-1960s there has been a perceptible change in attitude in many Co-opératives, which have made themselves much more efficiently organized than ever before. Qualified wine chemists are employed in the more prominent Co-opératives, and marketing and sales know-how seems to have risen directly in proportion to the quality of the wine. Some of the visible results of this for the consumer are specially selected *cuvées*, young-cask-aged wines and fresher tasting whites.

The Côtes du Rhône *appellation* differs from the Villages in that it is less demanding over how much wine may be made per hectare, how much alcohol the wine must contain and what grapes should be allowed to be grown. Thus the Côtes du Rhône (called locally the *appellation générique*) is permitted to produce a maximum of 52 hectolitres per hectare, whereas the Villages are restricted to 42 hectolitres per hectare. Obviously, the less wine that is drawn from a given unit of land, the more concentrated and better it will be.

Plain Côtes du Rhône wines need only contain 11 per cent alcohol by volume, while the Villages are fixed at 12.5 per cent for the red wines and 12 per cent for the rosés and the whites. There is, of course, nothing to stop the *vigneron* from making a wine of naturally higher degree: one of the best ways of doing this is by growing higher-grade vines like the Grenache or the Syrah, which are the backbone grapes of the southern and northern Rhône respectively. Thus growers making red wine in the Villages category must use a maximum of 65 per cent Grenache and a minimum of 25 per cent of one, two or all three of the Syrah, Cinsault and Mourvèdre, all of which are regarded as 'improver' grape varieties. No such demand is made of the *générique* growers, who must merely conform to growing a wide selection of vines termed 'noble' as opposed to hybrid, at the same time restricting their Carignan plantation to under 30 per cent (10 per cent for the Villages); the Carignan is the mass-producing vine found all over the Midi and Languedoc regions of France. Its wines can be hard and sharp-tasting unless they come from very old vines, in which case they can contribute some backbone to a blend of different grape varieties.

The laws on vineyard plantation are sensible and well balanced, for it takes decades first to change country people's outlook and then to enact such a change when as complicated and extended a task as replanting a vineyard is considered. In such circumstances room has still been left for the individual who may wish to pursue his hunch or his whim over what vine goes well in what soil, so that a Côtes du Rhône *générique* can still be made from grapes such as the Picpoul,

Roussanne or Viognier if it is white, or from the Gamay, Pinot Noir or Terret Noir, for instance, if it is red. Decreeing that a minimum total of 25 per cent should come from three good-quality grapes in the making of Villages red wine is likewise intended to reflect on growers who will also be making *générique* wines. They do not have to grow all three grapes, however; not every grower may agree that the Syrah is necessarily suited to the southern Rhône valley, with particular reference to parts of the Vaucluse *département*, for example.

During the 1980s one development of particular excitement occurred in the southern Rhône, which was the progress made in white wine-making. In the 1970s, most whites from this area were frankly unpalatable, with a few notable exceptions where forward-thinking *domaines* like the Château de l'Estagnol were taking the whole subject – vines, vineyards, cellar equipment, vinification – seriously.

During the 1980s, as cool-fermentation techniques came to be the norm, controlled by better cellar installations, so growers turned to revising the composition of their vineyards. More Clairette, more Bourboulenc, the appearance of much more Roussanne, which had hardly been sighted before, even some Viognier along with some Marsanne: out went much humdrum Ugni Blanc, as well as the often coarse Grenache Blanc, whose greatest sin was its proneness to early oxidation.

Now this is a region from which we can expect a whole host of stimulating white wines, which can be mercifully free of the dreary, ordinary tastes of much Chardonnay and Sauvignon which have been forced in massive quantities on wine drinkers around the world. There are outbreaks of the use of young oak, and all in all we are in for a fascinating decade marking the advance of the notoriety of Côtes du Rhône *blanc*.

Côtes du Rhône rosés remain very much a hit-and-miss affair. Here much depends on the geography of their place of origin, the selection of grapes used in them, and the skill of their vinifier. Some of these wines are still sub-red; in other words, they are poor versions of light red wine, and do not carry a predominant fruitiness or a measured grapiness, the latter along the lines of a traditional Tavel. The Gard *département* remains the best area for rosés, although the cooler climes of parts of the Drôme can also provide interesting rosés.

Below are mentioned a random cross-section of Côtes du Rhône *domaines, négociants* and Cave Co-opératives. It is not intended to be comprehensive, with the area constantly evolving and changes in ownership, bottling practices and vineyard plantation also occurring on a perpetual basis. Since the early 1970s there has been a gratifying advance in the number of *vignerons* prepared to undertake their own vinification and bottling, and although some fairly awful surprises are in store for the dedicated investigator, many good discoveries can be made. The choice now, in the early 1990s, is so much larger that importers should have no justification for not quoting a good private Côtes du Rhône *domaine* on their list. While the Vaucluse *département* still produces the richest, most complex wines with great depth of flavour and punch, the Gard *département vignerons* have been the most active in recent years in combining a new independence from the Cave Co-opératives or the *négociants* with a concerted drive to make their own wines individually and, if necessary, to sell them collectively. The style of the Gardois reds will never make them world-beaters, for they lack the all-embracing sturdiness and potential complexity of the reds from across the Rhône, but their softness and balance ensure that there is a ready audience for them among people who prefer to drink lighter wines in the Beaujolais vein.

The best Côtes du Rhône comes from the *domaines*, here a heartening trend has been the number of good Chateauneuf-du-Pape *domaines* who now own 'Côtes' vineyards – Beaurenard, Mont-Redon, la Gardine, to name but a few. Excellent suppliers are also the top-class *propriétaire-négociant* houses such as Paul Jaboulet, Guigal or the Perrin brothers of Châteauneuf-du-Pape, whose whole range of wines is known to be reliable. However, such wine is not always easy to find, partly because some *domaines* produce only limited quantities of wine, partly because wine traders and importers prefer in this modern age to deal with just one source of supply for their Rhône Valley wines, one for their Bordeaux region wines and so on. Thus in addition to the *domaines*, the *négociants* listed are all based in the Côtes du Rhône region and sell by the bottle directly to the consumer. Their wine is certainly on average more *soigné*, truer tasting and more satisfying than in the 1970s and much of the 1980s. Much Côtes du Rhône that is available throughout the world today will obviously not be mentioned in this brief report: it is bought by merchants all over France and Europe, shipped to them in bulk-carrying tankers or lorries and does, occasionally, emerge in the bottle with its composition a little altered. 'Go to the source' must be the cry: those *négociants* that are based in the Rhône Valley itself provide easily the best wine in this category. Failing such a supplier, it is best and simplest to purchase Côtes du Rhône from one's best-known, most reputable local shipper.

DOMAINES

Both the style of vinification and the finished wine vary substantially from one place to another when considering such a large category as Côtes du Rhône *générique*. For this reason the *domaines* have been subdivided by *département*.

The Ardèche Département

This is still a young area for *domaine*-bottled Côtes du Rhône wines. M. Herberigs has been bottling for nearly twenty years and makes a steady, quite well-balanced red wine. For a long time he was the only grower in the area to be making and bottling and selling his wine, but in the past ten years he has been joined by a handful of keen growers, mainly around the attractive village of St-Marcel-d'Ardèche, which lies equidistant between Pont-St-Esprit and Bourg-St-Andéol. Also worth noting is the wine of M. Rodolphe Goossens of Domaine de l'Olivet near Bourg-St-Andéol. Unfiltered and briefly aged in cask, it presents an interesting combination of fruit and backbone that is rather unusual for this region of normally light wines. M. Goossens relies on the Clairette not only for his white, but also has about one-third in his red, to provide greater elegance. The region has also been given extra impetus since the early 1980s through the investment and presence of the Burgundy house of Louis Latour, who make an interesting, fresh and light Chardonnay from the Ardèche.

On the Co-opérative front, the trend has been to plant *cépages* that are not traditionally associated with the Rhône, such as the Pinot Noir, Cabernet Sauvignon, Merlot and Chardonnay. The Vignerons Ardèchois is a leading exponent of some of these light, often value for money country wines. At the top end of their range they make and sell in bottle Coteaux du Vivarais (q.v.).

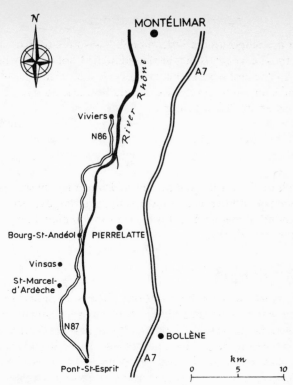

Ardèche Département

LEADING CÔTES DU RHÔNE DOMAINES IN THE ARDÈCHE
DÉPARTEMENT

Charmasson Roger	
Goossens, Rodolphe	07700 Bourg-St-Andéol
Domaine de L'Olivet	
Grangaud, Alain	
Domaine des Amoureuses	07700 Vinsas
Herberigs, Gilbert	
Château de Rochecolombe	07700 Bourg-St-Andéol
Sabatier, Jacques	
Le Plan de Lage	
Saladin, Louis et Paul Terrasse, R.	07390 St-Marcel-d'Ardèche
Domaine du Roure	
Thibon, Jean-Pierre	
Mas de Libian	

The Drôme Département

BRÉZÈME

An unusual intermediary *appellation* was created in 1974, when Brézème was granted its own Côtes du Rhône *appellation* – not as part of the Côtes du Rhône Villages, but as Brézème, Côtes du Rhône. This provides red wines made from the Syrah, whose style reflects its situation between the northern and southern Rhône areas. Livron-sur-Drôme is about 20 kilometres south of Valence on the east bank of the Rhône, and only a few kilometres to the east one is at Crest and plunging into the highland territories and fast-flowing streams of Die and the pre-Alps.

The principal grower, unearthed with great enthusiasm by British Rhône wine importer Robin Yapp, is Jean-Marie Lombard. He had been a member of the Co-opérative at Loriol, having developed his vine plantation in the mid-1960s, after only cultivating fruit trees. Along with the four other small growers at Brézème, M. Lombard's custom had been to send his wine to the Co-opérative.

But discoveries are part of the opium of the wine world, and M. Lombard was originally discovered by Gérard Chave of Hermitage together with a French restaurateur and wine writer. Apparently white wine had been made here around 1850, under the Château de la Roulière, but the habit then was to leave it a very long time in cask and drink it with a maderized taste. Phylloxera then destroyed the vineyard, and it was only gradually reconstituted during this century, with a white Haut Brézème made from Marsanne and Roussanne before the Second World War.

The Brézème from Jean-Marie Lombard comes from only a little over 2 hectares of vines, with the Syrah growing in soil marked by some deposits of Alpine stones. The style of M. Lombard's basic Brézème is robust, sometimes with a fruitiness that is a little austere: in character it is somewhere near a red Crozes-Hermitage without having so much class and length. This wine, the Cuvée Réservée, is suitable to drink around four or five years old. Since 1989 both it and the next quality wine, the Cuvée du Grand Chêne, have had the harvest destalked and destemmed upon reception, with M. Lombard aiming to make a more supple wine.

The Grand Chêne, as its name implies, is aged in oak casks for eighteen months to two years. It has a firm depth, but is often a very 'straight' wine, probably because of its length in wood, which tends to mark it. The top quality is the Cuvée Eugène de Monicault, which is 20 per cent destalked and aged mostly in new oak. This is a firmly styled Syrah wine, leaning towards the old-fashioned fullness of the Rhône of the 1970s. It is thorough and full on the palate, and is a wine that needs time to settle and soften – this is suitable to drink between five and ten years old.

M. Lombard has planted a mere quarter-hectare of Marsanne and Roussanne, so perhaps there will be even more curiosity in the future from this unexpected source. Of recent years at Brézème, 1982, 1985, 1986 and 1990 have been the best.

Lombard, Jean-Marie,   26250 Livron-sur-Drôme

CAVE JAUME

M. Claude Jaume is an intelligent, ambitious man of around fifty who was one of the first Rhône *générique* growers totally to modernize his cellars in the late 1970s. His vineyard covers 35 hectares, and he concentrates now more on red wine than before, considering that the Eygues Valley is most suited to this. In former times the Jaume family also owned several olive groves, for in the dry and very sunny Eygues Valley area the olive tree and the vine are able to flourish side by side on the gentle slopes that flank the river. The very severe weather of 1956 unfortunately killed off many of the olive trees, however, and now the *vignerons* tend their much reduced olive groves only as a very minor sideline.

M. Jaume has invested his future in the latest equipment for his cellar – stainless steel fermenting tanks and horizontal presses that can be set with great accuracy – and is making one of the best, most drinkable and most consistent Côtes du Rhône reds to be found in the Valley. The emphasis is on balance and a fruity, accessible style which is cleverly backed by the tannin and alcohol lent by the presence of around 15 per cent Syrah. His wines should really be drunk by the time they are three or four years old, with just a little attention given to the fact that they reflect the abnormally temperate climate of the area through an alcohol degree that varies between 13–14°.

Jaume, Claude et Nicole
   Cave Jaume   26490 Vinsobres

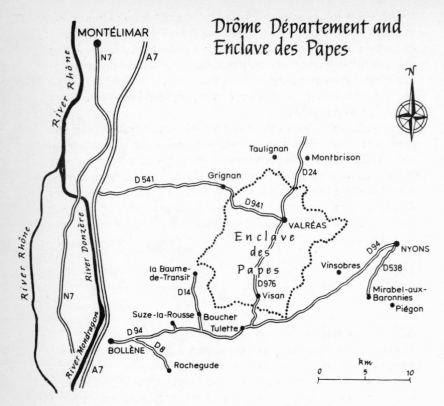

Drôme Département and
Enclave des Papes

CHÂTEAU DE L'ESTAGNOL

Just north of Suze-la-Rousse and its commanding twelfth-century castle, which now houses the Université du Vin, is the Château de l'Estagnol. Its 85-hectare vineyard stands in ground that over the years has been cleared of woody thickets and briars to make way for vine plantation and harvesting by machine in the modern way. The vineyard is divided up into plots which are all interconnected by tracks cut through the woods and scrub.

This is novel country for the vine. Until 1936, when M. Chambovet bought the property, the main local products were barley, wheat and sunflowers. Now it is the Grenache that is predominant, along with five other traditional Rhône vines.

Four-fifths of the wine is red, of which a small part is made by the *macération carbonique* process. The rest is fermented for five days and then left to age in wood for a few months, a reduction in the tendency in the mid-1970s to age in cask for eighteen months. It is generally a very sound wine, although the change in style has not necessarily benefited it, placing it more on a par with many correctly made but not inspiring wines that come under the Côtes du Rhône title. Nevertheless, it is well balanced and supple and should be drunk before it is four years old.

The white wine, made entirely from the Bourboulenc grape, is one of the best white Côtes du Rhônes to be found, although reliance on only the Bourboulenc is now unusual, given the success of varieties like the Roussanne during the 1980s. Fruity, with a light, almost petrol-smelling bouquet, it is crisp-tasting and well-constructed; it should be drunk within two years of the harvest and is an excellent partner for seafood. The rosé is the least eminent of the three wines but reflects credit on its *domaine* by always being well vinified.

SIAP
    Château de l'Estagnol   26130 Suze-la-Rousse

CHÂTEAU LA BORIE

The splendid Château La Borie stands among woods and vines 3 kilometres north of Suze-la-Rousse. Once the possession of the Princes of Orange, it is today owned by M. Émile Bories, whose name, curiously enough, bears absolutely no connection with the property.

M. Bories arrived in France from Algeria in 1963 and boldly decided to replant almost the whole of the château's vineyard. Seven different vines were used, including initially the Alicante, of Spanish origin, and the Counoise, more often found at Châteauneuf-du-Pape, where it has a strong following among leading wine-makers such as Baron Le Roy. Great emphasis was placed on the Syrah, and it constitutes over one-fifth of the 70 hectares of vines.

The Château La Borie red wine is vinified in the traditional way, although it is never actually aged in cask. The best is bottled within the year following the harvest; it usually straightens out a little afterwards and is perfect to drink when two or three years old. The presence in it of at least one-third Syrah is well illustrated by the strong colour, and the wine's general harmony and length of finish place it among the leading Côtes du Rhône wines.

Bories, Emile
   Château La Borie   26130 Suze-la-Rousse

DOMAINE A. MAZURD ET FILS

The Mazurd family own 75 hectares of vineyards extending through the villages of Tulette, Bouchet, Visan and Valréas and are a typical case of a grower leaving a Co-opérative in order to branch out on his own – in the case of the Mazurds, with great success.

The Mazurd cellars are on the edge of Tulette, a nondescript place that looks south to the Aigues Valley and a long tree-topped ridge of hills that partially hide the vast presence of Mont Ventoux. It is open vine country with, as usual, the emphasis on the Grenache; this accounts for 70 per cent of the Mazurd vines, the difference being made up of 10 per cent Syrah, 10 per cent Cinsault and 10 per cent Carignan and Mourvèdre. Some of their Grenache vines are over seventy years old, and, according to M. Mazurd, they provide an ideal backbone to his wines.

The Mazurds perform an unusual vinification for their red wines, which account for 95 per cent of their total production. Starting with uncrushed *raisins entiers* entering carbonic gas-filled vats, they undertake a rapid *macération carbonique* fermentation and then place the wine for racking purposes in concrete vats. Maturing is completed over the course of anything from one to two or more years in cask, depending on whether M. Mazurd is making a Côtes du Rhône or a Côtes du Rhône Villages and on whether it is his Grenache–Syrah blend (called Mazurka) or his 100 per cent Grenache (titled Cuvée St-Quenize).

The red wines of Domaine Mazurd are very successful, for they show an alluring fruitiness which is backed by a substantial finish. In this respect their style is more reminiscent of a strong-bodied Vinsobres wine, which should be drunk in winter with stews or hot meat dishes: good country wine to suit good country food would be an apt description for them. They are not particularly long-lived, five years being a typical maximum longevity.

Domaine Mazurd, A., et Fils   26130 Tulette

DOMAINE DU PETIT BARBARAS

This is a first-rate *domaine* owned by M. R. Feschet, who, like his neighbour M. Mazurd, was a member of two Caves Co-opératives, in this case those of Suze-la-Rousse and the Costebelle at Tulette, until building his cellars in 1976.

The Feschets own over 30 hectares of vines on the stony-topped, clay-soil plateau that runs due east of Suze-la-Rousse beside the main D94 road. The vines are principally Grenache and Cinsault, backed up by Syrah with a little very old Carignan, and obviously do well at this higher than usual exposure, around 150 metres.

Ninety per cent of the wine is red; cask-aged for six to twelve months, it is full-bodied and attractive. Bright purple in colour, it has a richness of flavour and a strong blackcurrant-inspired taste that stand up well to the tannins and spicy aftertastes that the wine leaves when drunk before it is three years old. A very good wine to accompany roast beef or autumn game birds, it is well worth while looking out for. A little white is made, from Grenache, Bourboulenc, Marsanne and Ugni Blanc.

Feschet, R., et Fils
  Domaine du Petit Barbaras   26130 Bouchet

DOMAINE DE LA TAURELLE

At the top end of the Eygues Valley, and set against a charming backdrop of fruit trees and lavender plants, is the Domaine de la Taurelle. The local village, Mirabel-aux-Baronnies, is one of those settlements perching on a hillock, distinguished by the church and its spire at the top and by the circle of stone-walled houses protecting it at the bottom.

The vineyards stand at over 240 metres here, and most of the trees bear witness to the force of the *mistral* wind, their trunks bent in a variety of theatrical-looking poses but all in the same direction. Mme Roux and her friendly son, Christophe, cultivate 20 hectares of vines on slopes running away from their well-sited *domaine*, the varieties in order of importance being Grenache, some of it over sixty years old, Syrah, Carignan and Cinsault. They make traditionally styled red Côtes du Rhône, which is stored in vat for around two years before bottling, with cask-ageing no longer used to help the wine to develop its potential. Cherry-coloured, it is a wine of firm power and tannin in strong vintages such as 1990, 1988 and 1983, while in years like 1985 and 1986 most notable are its balance and softness of flavour, which seems most to resemble apricots or plums. The Rouxs recommend that their red wine should be drunk before it is five or six years old; they also make a little white, from Bourboulenc, Clairette and Grenache Blanc, and rosé, which are of secondary interest.

Roux, Mme, et Fils
   Domaine de la Taurelle   26480 Mirabel-aux-Baronnies

DOMAINE DES TREILLES

This is a very attractive *domaine* whose restored soft-stone manor house has belonged to the Rey-Mery family since 1772. It stands beside the D10 road running from Valréas to Montbrison and is one of the most northerly Côtes du Rhône *domaines* in the lower half of the Rhône Valley.

M. Rey is one of the jokers of the area, an instantly likeable man with a broad tweed cap tilted spectacularly over his left ear and an anecdote always at the ready. An ex-rugby player for Valréas ('They carried me off in my last match after I had played most of the game with a broken shoulder – feel it, feel it!'), he retired when he was thirty-nine, since when all his activities have been channelled into looking after his 23-hectare vineyard as well as his asparagus and olive tree plantations. Eighty per cent of their vines are Grenache, with 15 per cent Syrah and Clairette; Cinsault and Carignan making up the complement. They grow on a mixture of sandy and stony ground near the *domaine* and running into the Valréas *appellation* area, but, like other growers, M. Rey is no longer interested in making Villages wine if he is to be limited to 42 hectolitres per hectare for it. His normal crop is about 50 hectolitres per hectare, and he prefers to make all his wine as Côtes du Rhône *générique*, with its *appellation* price, as a result.

The red wine receives just under a year's ageing in cask in the *domaine*'s pre-Revolution vaulted cellars, and much of it is bottled. Full-blooded and well marked by the strong presence of the Grenache, with an alcohol degree generally around 13.5°, it bears a bright purple hue and displays ample fruit on both bouquet and palate. The scent is, in fact, almost akin to violets, a description that M. Rey would gladly accept about his wine, since he is convinced that it is anyway capable of bestowing life-giving properties on people and animals. 'My grandmother lived until she was nearly 100, and my mother lived well into her nineties. Then take the case of our dog. He used to suffer from epileptic fits until one day he licked up some wine that had spilt into a bronze pan. Now we give him a daily ration of wine in this bronze pan, and he has never had another epileptic fit.' In the face of such evidence, there is only one recommendation – try the wine of Domaine des Treilles!

M. Rey

Rey, R., et Mery
    Domaine des Treilles   26230 Montbrison-sur-Lez

LES ASSEYRAS

Robert Blanc is a keen *vigneron* who looks after 19 hectares of vines split into two properties, one of them near his house above Tulette and the other inside the Valréas vineyard area. Based on 90 per cent Grenache, with support from the Syrah, Carignan and just a little Cinsault, he makes mainly Côtes du Rhône *générique* with a small proportion of Villages for good measure.

M. Blanc has been bottling his wine since the mid-1970s and is used to giving it a quick three-month stay in 225-litre casks before release. He feels that the quality is enhanced by his vines being in large part on slopes and by there being a substantial amount of old Grenache plants as well. Certainly, he is succeeding in making an excellently fruity and soft style of wine, whose steady red colour and hint of tannin are more evocative of a Gard *département* wine. His Côtes du Rhône is preferable to his Villages (which can be a little too pitchy or 'cooked') and is good for drinking with white meats or poultry.

Blanc, Robert
    Les Asseyras   26130 Tulette

OTHER CÔTES DU RHÔNE DOMAINES IN THE DRÔME DÉPARTEMENT

Bérard, Père et Fils
    Domaine de la Berardière   26130 Tulette
Bourret, Pierre
    Domaine de Roquevignan   26130 Rochegude
Couston et Monnier
    Domaine de la Tour Couverte   26130 Tulette
Domaine La Serre du Prieur
Domaine Ste-Marie   } 26130 Suze-la-Rousse
Estève, Jean-Pierre
    Domaine du Bois Noir   26130 La Baume-de-Transit
Gautier, Jean
    Château de Lignane   26130 Suze-la-Rousse
Ginies, Gilbert   26480 Piégon
Laurent, Philippe et Michel
    Domaine Gramenon   26230 Montbrison-sur-Lez
Monteillet, Jean-Luc
    Domaine de Moutine   26230 Grignan
Pinet, Joseph
    Domaine Chastelle   26230 Taulignan
Pradelle, R. et Fils
    Domaine du Jas   26130 Suze-la-Rousse
Le Terroir St-Rémy   26130 La Baume-de-Transit

Tourtin, M-J
    Domaine Louis Tourtin   26130 Rochegude
Trutat, Bruno
    Les Davids   26250 Livron-sur-Drôme

The Gard Département

CHÂTEAU DE BOUSSARGUES

Set in over 200 hectares of woodlands just off the main D6 road that runs west of Bagnols-sur-Cèze to Alès, the Château de Boussargues has 25 hectares of vineyards that were planted in the early 1970s by Mme Chantal Malabre. The attractive château has been very well restored, having been in the family for about eighty years, and the Malabre-Constants also cultivate asparagus as well as keeping several hives of bees.

The principal vines are the Grenache, Cinsault, Syrah, Clairette and Ugni Blanc, and vinification is commenced by using *raisins entiers* in order to endow the wine with as much fruitiness as possible. The red, rosé and white Côtes du Rhône are all bottled for early drinking, and Mme Malabre is keen on selling her wine as far afield as she can, having relied on bulk sales to *négociants* until 1981. The Boussargues red is a typical Gard wine, with an innocuous fruitiness and pleasant accessibility that make it sound and worth drinking within about five years. The rosé is dry and fruity.

Malabre-Constant, Chantal
    Château de Boussargues   30200 Colombier

CHÂTEAU DE DOMAZAN AND CAVEAU DU CHÂTEAU DE DOMAZAN

The 30-hectare Château de Domazan vineyards are run by M. Christian Chaudérac, a lean, grey-haired but athletic-looking man in his early forties. The Chaudéracs have been at Domazan for many years, and their *domaine* dates back to the fourteenth century; sacked during the Revolution, its lands were subsequently divided up so that the vineyard accompanying it today is relatively small.

Ninety per cent of their wine is red, made from only 50 per cent Grenache, with a firm concentration on the Syrah (25 per cent of the

Gard Département

plantation) and, typically for the Gard, on the Cinsault (20 per cent). Most of the vines at Domazan are cultivated on a plateau which holds terraces of alluvial stones covering a light topsoil, although near the village entrance there are some sandy *quartiers*.

A commendable *esprit de corps* is detectable at Domazan, where five of the growers have grouped themselves together to form a selling organization called the Caveau du Château. They are all young men who realize the importance of selling to a wide variety of markets, and are regular shippers to Britain, the United States, Belgium and Germany; they refuse to sell in bulk, which is often sought after at giveaway prices by Swiss customers.

The Château de Domazan red wine is bottled one year after the harvest, following storage in concrete vats, and carries a racy wild fruit bouquet that could have come off a hedgerow. Quite pale in colour, its pleasing mixture of fruit and acidity makes it an excellent summer wine for drinking before it is three years old.

The other four members of the Caveau du Château de Domazan are all making wine worthy of attention. There is Jean-Paul Arnaud of Domaine des Roches d'Arnaud, whose wine, red-purple in colour and bearing a bouquet that is herbaceous and surprisingly lingering and complex for the area, has a Mourvèdre-inspired style of firm fruit. There is Daniel Charre of Domaine du Sarrazin, whose wine more typically shows an attacking wild fruit flavour, and whose light balance makes it ideal for drinking within two years of the harvest. There is Serge Gallon of the Mas d'Eole, who makes a light and quite fruity wine, as pale as one would expect from some areas of the Gard. And, finally, there is Louis Reynaud of the 41-hectare Domaine Reynaud, whose Côtes du Rhône is marked by a strong Syrah presence; its soft fruit is well held together by just a trace of tannin.

Arnaud, Jean-Paul
   Domaine des Roches d'Arnaud
Chaudérac, Christian
   Château de Domazan
Charre, Daniel
   Domaine du Sarrazin   } 30390 Domazan
Gallon, Serge
   Mas d'Eole
Reynaud, Louis, et Fils
   Domaine Reynaud

CHÂTEAU DE FAREL

The Château de Farel at Comps, about 18 kilometres south-west of Avignon, is the most southerly *domaine* in the Côtes du Rhône. A 25-hectare property, it is owned by M. Pierre Silvestre, the former Director of the General Union of Côtes du Rhône *Vignerons*, who looks after their interests from Avignon.

The vineyard is based on the Grenache, with the Syrah, Mourvèdre, Cinsault and Carignan also present, and grows in a mainly clay soil which is topped by round alluvial deposit stones. M. Silvestre ferments in a classical manner in concrete vats and, according to the position of his stocks, ages his wine in large oak barrels for a few months before putting it on sale.

Nine-tenths of the wine is red, and although never particularly strong-coloured, it has an agreeable balance and finish. It is best to drink the wine young, while M. Silvestre also produces a sturdier, cask-aged wine called the Grande Réserve. A little rosé and white are also made.

Silvestre, Pierre
    Château de Farel   30300 Comps

DOMAINE DE L'AMANDIER

This is a very well-run *domaine* set beside the main Bagnols to Alès road, on the edge of a tiny hamlet called Carmes. It has about 20 hectares of Côtes du Rhône vines and another 10 hectares of table-wine grape varieties. The Pages family have been making wine at Carmes for over 150 years; Urbain Pages looks after the *domaine* on a day-to-day basis and has been responsible for replanting the vineyard with a relatively low percentage of Grenache and higher than usual quantities of Syrah and Cinsault. He is also experimenting with Cabernet Sauvignon and with Syrah for his *vin de table*, which could give interesting results in years to come. The vines are all trained along wires and are immaculately kept.

Eighty per cent of the wine is red, 10 per cent rosé and 10 per cent white, the last being made from the Ugni Blanc, the Grenache Blanc and the Bourboulenc. Since 1978 the *domaine* has been bottling almost all its wine; the red, made from 50 per cent Syrah, is stored in concrete for one year and in bottle for another year before its release on sale.

As a result, the red wine of Domaine de l'Amandier is ready to drink in the year after it is put on sale; it has quite an attractive, almost sweet, fruitiness and a pleasant length of finish – good but not great wine. The rosé is supple with a clean fruit flavour and is good to drink with spicy Chinese food, while the white, fermented at low temperature in the Pages' stainless steel tanks, is crisp-tasting and should be drunk before it is two years old.

Pages, Urbain
   Domaine de l'Amandier   30200 Carmes

DOMAINE DE COCOL

Hidden at the end of a track among trees in a vale north of Donnat is the 30-hectare Domaine de Cocol. Its proximity to the River Cèze allows the owner, M. Jean-Paul Sabot, to cultivate pear and apple trees as well as his vines. Since the late 1950s M. Sabot, a smiling and healthy-looking man in his early fifties, has been gradually replanting his vineyard, so that it is now based on no more than 30 per cent Grenache, a total of 35 per cent being accounted for by the Syrah and the Cinsault. M. Sabot also grows the Picpoul, Bourboulenc and Clairette for his white wine.

His cellar is distinguished by eight large barrels that are unusually shaped – long and rather flat, with a slight tapering at one end only. M. Sabot, obviously proud of them, explained: 'The barrels belonged to the French Railways and were used for transporting wine all over France on the goods wagons of the SNCF. That is why they are this curious shape, so they wouldn't fall off on the railway. The largest holds 20,500 litres and the smallest 14,000 litres, and my father bought them off the SNCF in 1947. Despite opposition from the young *œnologue* advising me, I am using them to age my wine for ten months or so.'

M. Sabot would sell his wine to *négociants* until the 1980 vintage. Bottling now plays a much larger part in his operations. His wine reflects its *raisin entier* fermentation and its Gard *département* origins, showing a bright red cherry colour and a softness on the palate that sustains the initial fruity attack. Like most of its neighbouring wines, it is best drunk before it is three or four years old.

Sabot, Jean-Paul
    Domaine de Cocol   30200 Donnat

DOMAINE LE HAUT CASTEL

Two or three kilometres north-west of Bagnols-sur-Cèze is the Domaine Le Haut Castel. The smart pale stone *domaine* and its cellars are at the top of a small hillside and look out over the vineyards and the peaceful Cèze Valley that lies beyond.

Since the 1970s the size of the vineyard has almost doubled, to reach 25 hectares, some of which lie within the Chusclan *appellation* area. However, the Arène family feel the same way as many growers in the Rhône Valley in choosing not to make Villages wine with its lower permitted quantity per hectare, so that any extra wine must be sold off as *vin de pays*. They are therefore happy to make red, rosé and white Côtes du Rhône *générique*; most of the wine is red, and its soundness speaks well for M. Arène's old-style vinification methods, which include a roughly one-year ageing in cask, reduced from two years formerly. Generally rich and well balanced, the wine has a firm purple colour and a substantial, long finish. It has always been one of the best wines of the region. Also popular with the *domaine*'s British and Dutch customers is the white wine. Made from the Clairette, Grenache Blanc, Picpoul and Bourboulenc, this is bottled in the spring following the harvest.

Arène, Augustin
    Domaine Le Haut Castel   30200 Bagnols-sur-Cèze

DOMAINE DES MOULINS

M. André Payan, the owner of the 40-hectare Domaine des Moulins at Saze, is an intense, bearded man who typifies the new zeal to be found among young wine growers in the Gard *département*. His *domaine* has been in the family for over fifty years, but he has modified the composition of the vineyards since his father's day so as to accommodate as much as 40 per cent Syrah, of which he is a great fan.

The vineyards run between Saze and Domazan and are distinguished by the deposits of smooth round stones that lie on top of compacted clay soil. M. Payan completes his vineyard with extensive planting of Grenache (40 per cent) and with Mourvèdre, Cinsault, Clairette and Carignan.

In the past few years his attitude towards his red wine has changed, in part prompted by demand from his customers, so that he admits that he is now making a softer, less robust style of wine. The accent is on fruit, and he feels that the Syrah is a grape admirably suited to achieving this. The Moulins red wine, generally a steady purple, certainly lives up to M. Payan's intentions, for a wild raspberry scent is followed by a lingering fruitiness on the palate whose fresh style is very appealing.

The *domaine* red and rosé have been bottled since the 1980 vintage, and the enterprising M. Payan has justly earned himself an extensive overseas clientele, thanks to his fruity and uncomplicated wine that is delicious to drink at any time, in not always moderate quantities. M. Payan also has a commercial link with Georges Duboeuf, which helps broaden distribution.

Payan, André
   Domaine des Moulins   30650 Saze

DOMAINE DE LA RÉMÉJEANNE

This 25-hectare vineyard is run by M. Rémy Klein, whose father François arrived in the Gard in 1961 from Morocco, where he had managed a 1,000-hectare wine *domaine*. Having done his studies at agricultural college in Morocco, François had been keen to experiment in an area of France that he considered underrated in viticultural terms – very much the same sort of reaction felt by the ex-Algerian residents who are now making wine at Lirac.

M. Klein's vineyards are very spread out, in some fifty plots, and are mainly composed of Grenache (40 per cent) and Syrah (25 per cent), backed up by Cinsault, Carignan and Counoise, which thrive in his largely sandy ground. *Cuvées* of the red wine like Les Genévriers (65 per cent Grenache, 30 per cent Cinsault) are made partly by *macération carbonique*, partly by a standard vinification.

After a five- to seven-day fermentation in concrete, M. Klein stores his wine once again in concrete for eighteen months to two years and, after bottling, does not release it for another four or five months. It shows very good rich fruit, with a typical Gardois softness and elegance. Well constructed and possessing good depth, it has great charm and is ideal to drink until it is about five or six years old. M. Klein has made white Rhone since 1983 from the Bourboulenc and Ugni Blanc. The *domaine* also grows asparagus, cherries and figs. This is now one of the best Gardois Côtes du Rhône *domaines* – keep an eye open for its wine.

Klein, Rémy
    Domaine de la Réméjeanne   30200 Cadignac

DOMAINE DE LA ROUETTE

A 17-hectare property, this *domaine* belongs to the Guigue family, who have been wine-makers since the seventeenth century. This does not stop them from using modern vinification methods, and the white and rosé are fermented under controlled temperature in stainless steel tanks. The rosé, light and inoffensive, is certainly the better of the two wines.

The red wine is made from about 45 per cent Grenache, supported by Syrah, Cinsault and Mourvèdre, and the Guigues like to vinify this by *macération carbonique* in underground concrete vats. The wine is then aged for a year or two in barrel, the length of stay being determined by the weight of demand for the *domaine* wine at any one time. Lightly styled but attractively fruity, it represents good middle-range Côtes du Rhône in the noticeably soft style of Gard wines.

Guigue, Père et Fils
    Domaine de la Rouette   30650 Rochefort-du-Gard

MAS CLAULIAN

St-Alexandre, the first community south of Pont-St-Esprit, is an attractive circular village whose appearance gives the hint of fortified Provençal villages to be found further down the valley. As one stands surrounded by pine-clad hillsides and vineyards and with scattered olive trees growing in the rolling countryside, the pulse quickens at the prospect of Provence not far away.

The Herbouze family arrived in St-Alexandre from Morocco in 1962, and their 14-hectare vineyard has been built partly on pine-covered woodland that was cleared to create today's terraces. Claude Herbouze, an enterprising man in his early forties, is now making the *domaine* red wine on the basis of uncrushed grapes, which he leaves to macerate in enamel-lined or concrete vats. Headed by the Grenache and the Syrah, his wine is then stored in vats for one to two years before it is bottled. It has a respectable quality, with a sound red colour and fruity attack on the palate, which indicates that it is good for drinking before it is four years old.

The Herbouzes are concentrating their sales efforts on France, for they work on their own and do not find it easy to sell in bottle further afield. As it is, the Herbouzes rely on Claude's sister-in-law in Brittany to hold a little stock for them, and this family aid has helped them sell to a wider public.

Herbouze, Claude
    Mas Claulian   30130 St-Alexandre

OTHER CÔTES DU RHÔNE DOMAINES IN THE GARD DÉPARTEMENT

Allauzen
    Château de Valpinson   30130 St-Alexandre
Barrière, Jacques et Patrick
    Domaine du Vieux Colombier 30200 Sabran
Broche, Francis
    Vieux Manoir de Maranson   30200 Bagnols-sur-Cèze
Castan, Mesmin
    Domaine de la Valériane   30390 Domazan
Castay et Johannet
    Domaine de Signac   30200 Bagnols-sur-Cèze
Castor Gérard
    Domaine St-Nabor   30630 Cornillon
Chinieu, Jean-Claude
    Domaine de Lindas   30200 Bagnols-sur-Cèze
Coste, Pierre
    Domaine de Laplagnol   30130 Pont St-Esprit
De Serésin, Père et Fils
    Domaine de Bruthel   30200 Sabran

Fabre, Georges
   Domaine des Romarins   30390 Domazan
Granier, Françoise
   Domaine de la Croze   30150 Roquemaure
Imbert-Cadignac, Père et Fils
   Domaine de Lascamp   30200 Cardignac
Juls, Joel
   Château du Bresquet   30200 St-Nazaire
Mathieu, Jacques
   Mas des Séraphin
Merger, Lucien   } 30390 Domazan
   Domaine des Boumianes
Payan, Achille
   Domaine du Cabanon   30650 Saze
Riqué, Pierre
   Domaine de Roquebrune   30130 St-Alexandre
Pons, Dominique
   Domaine des Cèdres   30200 St-Nazaire
Poudevigne, André
   Domaine de la Crompe   30390 Domazan
Riot Frères
   Domaine des Riots
Robert, Alain, et Fils
   Vieux Manoir de Frigoulas   } 30200 St-Michel-d'Euzet
Sabatier, Roger
   Domaine de l'Espéran
Simon, Francis
   Domaine du Moulin du
     Pourpré   30200 Sabran
Tarsac, Jacques
   Domaine St-Jacques   30200 St-Michel-d'Euzet
Valat, André
   Château St-Maurice-l'Ardoise 30290 Laudun
Verda et Fils
   Domaine Cantegril-Verda   30150 Roquemaure

The Vaucluse Département

CHÂTEAU DE FONSALETTE

This 11-hectare *domaine* is the reclusive Jacques Reynaud's second property after the highly rated Château Rayas at Châteauneuf-du-Pape. Quality, which used to be consistently top-class, has been less regular since the death of Louis Reynaud in 1980, but Fonsalette can still provide excellent one-off drinking in both red and white. The price of these wines bears greater resemblance to good Hermitage than to Côtes du Rhône, but when at their best, the red and the white are challenging, and highly unusual for the region.

The *domaine* was built up between 1945 and 1955, as M. Reynaud *père* experimented to see which vines were best suited to Fonsalette's terrain. Eventually he decided upon the Grenache, Syrah and Cinsault for the red wine, and the Grenache Blanc, Clairette and Chardonnay for the white.

Vaucluse vineyards and Mont Ventoux

The Grenache was largely planted in 1945, while the Syrah mostly dates from 1960, with partial additions since. The rough proportion by 1992 was 50 per cent Grenache, 35 per cent Cinsault and 15 per cent Syrah. The whites are split – again roughly – 50 per cent Grenache Blanc, and 25 per cent each of Clairette and Chardonnay; the last-named was planted around 1965. The red wine can contain a high proportion of Cinsault, especially as M. Reynaud now regularly produces a pure Syrah *cuveé*, which he admits sells very quickly – like *'le petit pain'*.

These wines, and the more recent La Pialade, which is a second-string Fonsalette Côtes du Rhône, are vinified at M. Reynaud's Château Rayas cellars. The single *cuvées* of Cinsault and Syrah are often exemplary when tasted from cask within the first year, the Cinsault containing a depth hard to encounter elsewhere, and the Syrah a lively, true fruitiness that many southern Rhône Syrahs fail to achieve.

The Syrah is planted in two different soils; what M. Reynaud calls his Syrah I grows in more gravelly, sticky soil, while his Syrah II is in lighter, less clayey soil. Tasting the two side by side is instructive; the 1990 Syrah I in cask was very dark, with plenty of black elements in the colour; the bouquet after nine months was warm, with discreet dark fruit aromas. The palate was a docile form of the Syrah – neither stringy as can be the case with this grape in the southern Rhône, nor big and blackstrap as is the norm for many northern Rhônes of Syrah origin. The Syrah II was dark black, and the bouquet contained the wild, racy berry aromas of the northern Rhône. There was good depth and plenty of *cassis* fruit on the palate, with a more striking, vibrant feel to it than the Syrah I. The *assemblage* of the two produces one of the best Rhône Syrahs from outside the granite-based slopes of the north; but at its best, it is still nearer a very good St-Joseph than a Hermitage.

The red Fonsalette stays about a year in cask – just the same as Rayas – while the white receives about nine months in cask – again like Rayas. Both the red Fonsalette and the Syrah *cuvée* can be utterly delicious, as happened with the startling 1979, the good 1985 and the promising 1989 Fonsalettes. Irregularities do occur, however, between tastings in the cellars and in bottle, as well as between different bottles labelled the same.

At its best, the red Fonsalette, with its deep purple colour and overwhelming sensation of blackcurrants on both bouquet and palate, is a magical wine, and bears a fruitiness and refinement that brings to mind such wines as good Fixin or Gévrey-Chambertin. It

Vaucluse Département

can live for fifteen years or even more. The 1979, for instance, was still moving strongly when last drunk in 1991. The dark red held traces of ruby, while there were excellent damson and dried fruit aromas on the nose – very firm and well extracted. The palate had held together its deep flavours very tightly and was very long – plenty of future still rests with this wine. The 1981 carried in, held out good fruit and structure and drank well after only four or so years, while the 1985 was more rounded, the 1983 more firm. All three held a little less all round extraction than the 1979, but are very good none the less.

The 1987 Fonsalette was a good effort for the year – a delicate wine, its texture on the palate is a little jammy and it should be drunk before around 1994. The 1989 Fonsalette is a heady wine, near enough 14.8°, which shows through in part on the bouquet. There is a tremendous tannic surge on the palate, and while some ripe fruits come through, this is a wine to lock away until at least 1995 before review. Its guts could give it a long and interesting development. The 1990 Fonsalette red promises very well; the separate grapes tasted apart were all well extracted, with plenty of colour and core fruit, and the Grenache side of the wine was very well worked and controlled. This will also be a big wine.

The single-*cuvée* Syrah is a wine that developed in depth and flamboyance during the 1980s and has moved away from long spells in the cellar prior to bottling. The rather hard 1980, for instance, was not bottled until the autumn of 1984. By and large it is good to drink within the first six to ten years to capture its essence of fruit; it can clearly live longer, however, and transform itself into a more sober, sit-down wine.

The Côtes du Rhône La Pialade is the lightest of M. Reynaud's reds; in 1989, for instance, it bore correct length and softness of fruit on the palate, with a paleish red colour: a fair, but not impressive wine.

The white Fonsalette can hit the heights, but one never quite knows when or which bottle. In a year like 1976 it was quite outstanding. A bottle drunk in 1990 was still lively, with only a hint of maderization developing on the bouquet after prolonged exposure to air. Possessing great length, it is a wine that can still show well when it is twenty-five years old.

A year like 1983 was also excellent: by 1991 the colour had turned to a pale straw, but as with many of Jacques Reynaud's wines, it changed and blossomed after half an hour's opening, with the bouquet showing impressive all-round appeal and depth of aroma – citrus fruit and sometimes nuttiness. The palate bore great finesse, and an unusual softness and elegance for a southern white. This wine, for example, can be drunk out towards 1999. The 1990 Fonsalette *blanc* is promising, with great length on the palate that runs into a satisfying, chewy finish. It needs time to work itself out, but should be delicious after six to ten years.

Generally a system of prior tasting or advice from an utterly reliable importer is advised before purchase. Certainly these are wines from one of France's most curious twentieth-century wine dynasties, and given that Jacques Reynaud has no heirs and no-one receiving tutelage, the leading Fonsalettes should be searched out while they still come from such an extraordinary source.

Reynaud, Jacques
    Château de Fonsalette   84290 Lagarde-Paréol

CHÂTEAU GOURDON

Two or three kilometres north of Bollène is the striking Château Gourdon, built in 1780 and distinguished by its one lonely spire. Owned by Mme Sanchez-Gauchet, her son and daughter, it has a 45-hectare vineyard based on 60 per cent Grenache, 20 per cent Cinsault, 15 per cent Syrah and 5 per cent Mourvèdre and Carignan. These grow on a light, partly sandy soil, which is also suitable for the extensive asparagus cultivation that the family undertakes. Indeed, they believe that the asparagus is a crop ideal for resting land between taking out and planting vines.

Château Gourdon appears in red and rosé Côtes du Rhône; the red is vinified traditionally with storage for one year in concrete vats, and about three months in cask, before being put on sale. Only about half the production is bottled, and this is sound enough: its sturdiness and the tannin hiding behind the early suggestion of fruit mean that it is suitable to drink when it is three or four years old.

Sanchez et Gauchet
    Château de Gourdon   84500 Bollène

CHÂTEAU DU GRAND MOULAS

This is an enterprising young *domaine* whose cellars are set in the unlikely surroundings of Mornas, a huddled little village that stands right on the main N7 road between Bollène and Orange. It is owned by the Ryckwaert family, who are of Flemish origin but who in reality are almost nomadic, having been in Algeria from 1820 until the early 1960s, when they arrived in France.

The *domaine* is run by two brothers, Yves, who looks after sales and finance, and Marc, who is responsible for the viticulture. Both are in their early forties and have their time fully spent directing their wine and fruit interests. Yves explained more about how the *domaine* had started to make wine: 'We left Algeria with virtually no money, so that although we had grown vines and fruit there, we couldn't consider starting up a vineyard with all the necessary cellar installations. Instead we chose to go into low-investment fruit trees – apples and pears – of which we now have 65 hectares and an export-oriented business.

'Having banked a little money, our father bought just over 50 hectares of heavily wooded, sloping country at Uchaux, just behind the Château de St-Estève, in fact. We had a tremendous task clearing this land and have now managed to increase from 23 hectares to 30 hectares. The problem is that much of this land is simply too ravinous and too dense to clear to our satisfaction.'

Marc continued: 'We originally planted 66 per cent Grenache and the rest Syrah, and we made our first wine from these vines in 1978: we've added Mourvèdre since then. There is a slight problem with the vineyards lying 11 kilometres from our cellars here at Mornas, but we spread the grapes out in 400-kilogram fruit crates so that they are not crushed during transportation. Then we ferment virtually unbroken grapes, starting with an extended maceration in stainless steel tanks, and are at present bottling the regular wine six months after the harvest.'

Grand Moulas Côtes du Rhône succeeds in fulfilling its makers' objectives, for it is admirably fruity, with a fresh but not superficial tang to it which denotes the presence of one-third Syrah. As the Ryckwaerts decide when to harvest according to the acid and not the sugar levels in their grapes, they tend to restrict the alcohol degree to some extent, which is of great importance in a wine of this nature. Thus their Côtes du Rhône is generally around 12°. It is a wine of such a summery disposition that it drinks well lightly chilled.

Grand Moulas also produces a Côtes du Rhône Villages, and, since 1989, a pure Syrah Cuvée Clos L'Écu which is very highly regarded. There is also a little white now made at the *domaine*. Yves Ryckwaert is also very proud of his *eau-de-vie* made from pears, something which they distil after they have the apple harvest out of the way.

Ryckwaert, M.
    Château du Grand Moulas   84350 Mornas

CHÂTEAU MALIJAY

Château Malijay is one of the most resplendent of all Côtes du Rhône *domaines*. Situated about 8 kilometres east of Orange, it stands in the middle of some prolific wine-producing country, near the villages of Jonquières and Violès. An old château was built on the site around the eleventh century, but this was almost completely destroyed towards the end of the eighteenth century. A new château was then constructed, using stones from the old building, by the Seigneur Baron de Malijay. The Baron also kept up the estate vineyards, which had been cultivated from the fifteenth century onwards.

The cellars here are modern, efficient and on a large scale. The vats are stainless steel; the wine is closely and scientifically looked after; and bottling is performed under sterilization so as to prevent the entry of any foreign bacteria into the wine.

The vineyards cover 185 hectares and are mainly composed of Grenache, Cinsault, Muscardin, Counoise and Syrah, with more recent Mourvèdre and Clairette. The château's average annual production is very high – around 9,000 hectolitres – and the style of both the red and the rosé is extremely light. For those seeking easy, simple wines Château Malijay red is par for the course: very pale, it has adequate fruit on the bouquet and just enough length to give it some appeal. It should ideally be drunk before it is about two years old. The rosé is a good, clean wine, whose lightness is no hindrance. Drunk chilled, within the year following the harvest, it will liven up a summer's afternoon.

The wine of Malijay has always been widely exported – so widely, in fact, that the author has actually sipped Malijay *rouge* while the guns and cannons fired off around him during a *coup d'état* (*manqué*) in the South American republic of Surinam.

Chavarnac, Henri
    Château Malijay   84150 Jonquières

CHÂTEAU DE ST-ESTÈVE

Eight kilometres north of Orange, in rolling wooded countryside, is the Château de St-Estève. The 250-hectare estate has belonged to the Français family since 1804, but it was not until the start of this century that any vines were grown on it. Even then its principal occupations continued to be its forestry, sheep farming and silk-worm rearing.

In 1953 M. Gérard Français-Monier, a former French diplomat, decided to do away with his 20 hectares of common vines and to increase the whole vineyard to what is today 60 hectares of nothing but noble, and at times unusual, Rhône vines. These are led in orthodox fashion by the Grenache, followed by the Syrah, Cinsault and Mourvèdre, but for the whites St-Estève has caught the following of enthusiasts through its plantation in 1981 of Viognier – initially just 1 hectare and now 4 hectares – to go with the Grenache Blanc, Roussanne, Clairette and Bourboulenc. There is a pure Viognier white Rhône now made by St-Estève in addition to a very good white Rhône produced from the other varieties. These whites are fermented at low temperatures after a prior overnight maceration in their whole form, and have sound depth on the palate and a lasting freshness, making them suitable to drink within three years. The Viognier is still in a fairly experimental stage, with the 1989 receiving part fermentation in new oak, part in stainless steel: this is a wine to watch, and the likelihood is that if it is successful, there will be more cuttings of Viognier either jetting off to California or being taken from the Calera vineyards there, as Viognier is one vine a lot of innovators dearly love to master, even more than the Pinot Noir.

M. Français has cereal interests elsewhere, and the estate is run entirely by his intelligent and progressive-thinking son Marc, who with his spectacles and corduroy trousers looks every inch the thoughtful *vigneron*. Vineyard techniques are modern: since 1983 they have partly harvested by machine, while they also ensure a safer, faster development of young vines through the use of protective coverings, which were introduced some years before many growers had adopted them.

The red, rosé and white Rhônes are very cleanly vinified, and their high quality is firm evidence of the Français's up-to-date policies. In his search for broader frontiers in his wine-making, Marc Français harvested some of his Viognier two weeks later than usual in 1991, and vinified it in two-year-old Nevers casks. With an alcohol degree of around 15°, this is a wine that evoked the more intense Viognier scents and flavours that used to be the norm thirty or so years ago – very much in keeping with Gérard Chave's thinking on the matter when he makes his equally tiny amount of Viognier from Hermitage.

The principal red wine, the Grande Réserve, used to receive six months' ageing in cask; it is generally about half Syrah, half Grenache, has good style and is less overtly robust than in the 1970s and early 1980s. It is a wine to drink between three and seven years old. The Tradition red is a more supple, rounded wine, while the rosé, made by *saignée*, is sound but less inspiring than the best reds and whites.

Français-Monier
   Château de St-Estève   84110 Uchaux

DOMAINE DE LA CHAPELLE

This seventeenth-century *domaine* stands on a small plateau overlooking Châteauneuf-de-Gadagne, a quiet village nearly 10 kilometres east of Avignon. The vineyard was acquired in 1955 by M. Marcel Boussier, a short, affable man in his early seventies, who was determined to produce the good wine he knew the country around Châteauneuf-de-Gadagne to be capable of. Châteauneuf-de-Gadagne had possessed a respected vineyard as far back as the fourteenth century but had subsequently fallen sharply from prominence. With its stony soil strongly resembling that of Châteauneuf-du-Pape, M. Boussier saw no reason why he should not be able to make wines of a very high standard.

From their 10 hectares of vines, headed by nearly 50 per cent Grenache, Marcel and his art college-educated son, Claude, concentrate on making wine of as high a quality as possible. They vinify the red wine in the traditional way, ageing it in cask for eighteen months. It is generally a very powerful wine, possessing a deep colour and bouquet to match, and is best drunk when it is about three years old; in this way it will have rounded out and cast aside some of its high initial tannin content.

About one-tenth of the wine is rosé, and this is bottled one year after the harvest. Fresh and well scented when tasted from the vat *chez* Boussier, it suffers from not being bottled earlier.

Boussier, Claude
    Domaine de la Chapelle   84470 Châteauneuf-de-Gadagne

DOMAINE DE L'ESPIGOUETTE

Many of the 20 hectares of the Domaine de l'Espigouette are sited on the vast open space of the Plan de Dieu, and with no Cave Coopérative at Violès, many of the local growers choose to vinify and bottle their own wine.

M. Edmond Latour is one such man; grey-haired and friendly, he has been bottling his wine since the mid-1970s. He is helped by his son, who has attended wine school at Mâcon, and together they make their red wine based on the Grenache, Cinsault and Syrah, which are fermented together rather than being assembled vat by vat at a later stage.

Their red Côtes du Rhône is somewhat pale-coloured but carries an interestingly spicy bouquet, something like the *goût de terroir* in a wine like Cairanne. The fruit on the palate is similar to plums, and its subdued nature indicates that the wine should be drunk before it is three years old.

White and rosé wines are also made at Domaine de l'Espigouette, but neither is exceptional.

Latour, Edmond
    Domaine de l'Espigouette   84150 Jonquières

DOMAINE DE LA GIRARDIÈRE

Louis Girard left the Cave Co-opérative at Rasteau and undertook his first bottling with the 1979 vintage. His red Côtes du Rhône is made mainly from Grenache, of which there are some very old plants growing on his 20–hectare vineyard. Fermented traditionally, it is a deep rich red, with a powerful blackcurrant inspired bouquet. On the palate there is a good balance of tannin and acidity, and the wine's concentrated fruit flavour makes it suitable for considered wintertime drinking.

The Girard family also make a little Rasteau *vin doux naturel* from their Grenache vines, and this too is very good. It displays a surprising finesse, and the bouquet is particularly striking, with aromas such as marzipan in evidence.

Girard, Louis
    Domaine de la Girardière   84110 Rasteau

DOMAINE MARTIN

Formerly called the Vignoble du Plan de Dieu, this 35-hectare property has been in the Martin family since 1905. It stands just outside Travaillan, on the edge of the vast stony plain known as the Plan de Dieu, and the *domaine*'s vines are split into small lots that grow all around the village; their terrain is the same throughout – the massive bed of small stones that has been nurturing vines on and off since the thirteenth century.

During the 1970s Jules Martin's sons, Yves and René, introduced the Syrah to the vineyard, and this now forms 10 per cent of the plantation. The Grenache accounts for 60 per cent, the Cinsault for 10 per cent and the Mourvèdre for 5 per cent, while the remainder of the vineyard is composed of Carignan, Grenache Blanc and Clairette.

The style of their red wine is therefore full-bodied, with a rich earthiness and depth of colour that can remind one of red Gigondas. René, the brother in charge of vinification, ferments their red for about a week, and it is then matured in oak. His wine is lighter than that of his father Jules, and nowadays he estimates that the *domaine*'s best vintages, such as 1985 and 1989, should be drunk up to five years old.

A little rosé is made, and now that this is bottled less than a year after the harvest, it is more able to display a pleasant freshness. The Martins also make some white wine – only 6,500 bottles a year, but it is a well-balanced, clean and fruity drink. First made in the 1980 harvest, it is something which the sons are keen to develop as they continue to reduce the Carignan plantation in the vineyard.

Jules Martin, who first bottled the family wine in 1952, has now retired, but a good *vigneron* is hard to keep down, and he can be seen in the neighbourhood making deliveries to local customers. He leaves the commercial side of the *domaine* to Yves; married to a Rasteau girl whose dowry was some Grenache vines from that village, he also makes a Rasteau *vin doux naturel*.

Martin, Jules, et ses Fils
    Domaine Martin   84150 Travaillan

DOMAINES MEFFRE

The Gigondas company of Gabriel Meffre, bought out in the early 1990s, has been the largest owner of *appellation* vines in France. It is the proprietor of altogether six Côtes du Rhône *domaines*: the Domaines du Plan de Dieu, La Meynarde and St-Jean at Travaillan, the Domaine de l'Abbaye de Prébayon and the Domaine du Bois des Dames at Violès, and the Château de Ruth at Ste-Cécile-les-Vignes. The wines of all six *domaines* are good and fairly regular, the best probably being the Château de Ruth; they fill the need for middle-range Côtes du Rhône but lack the individuality to be something exceptional.

Domaines Meffre   84190 Gigondas

DOMAINE MITAN

This small but very good *domaine* of 10 hectares is near the village of Vedène, about 10 kilometres from Avignon. It is very much a one-man show, with M. Mitan looking after everything himself, from the vineyards, to the cellars, to the sales of his wine.

The vineyards are set on clayey slopes and are composed of four vines, the Grenache, Cinsault, Syrah and Mourvèdre. M. Mitan makes his wine on traditional lines, and after a year's ageing in oak it bears a strong colour and agreeable richness of flavour. It also possesses a softness and finesse that are unusual for wines of the Côtes du Rhône *générique* category.

Less than one-quarter of the wine is rosé, and this too is well made. Its strong pink colour and fullness of taste make it reminiscent of one of the good Gard *département* rosés such as Chusclan.

Mitan, Frédéric
    Domaine Mitan   84270 Vedène

DOMAINE DES RICHARDS

An 18-hectare *domaine*, whose vineyard is made up of Grenache, Syrah, Carignan and Ugni Blanc, this property has belonged to the Combe family for three generations. Like some of their neighbours, they ceased selling their wine in bulk to *négociants* in the early part of the 1970s and are now bottling a successful, richly flavoured Côtes du Rhône red. Vinified along traditional lines, this is aged in approximately 1,500-litre barrels for one year and is very good: darkly coloured, with a touch of black cherries in its aspect, the wine has a raspberry-inspired bouquet of fine depth. There is the flavour of wild raspberries on the palate which continues into a long follow-through, and the Domaine des Richards red should ideally be drunk when it is three years old, when extra softness has been gained.

The Combe family, not to be confused with the affable Roger Combe at Vacqueyras, are rather suspicious of foreign visitors and would only release the additional information that they make 10 per cent rosé and 5 per cent white wine.

Combe, Pierre
Domaine des Richards   84150 Violès

DOMAINE STE-APOLLINAIRE

This 15-hectare property is set on slight slopes at a height of about 300 metres on the outskirts of the attractive little village of Puyméras, which lies enclosed by the foothills of the Low Alps about 8 kilometres north-east of Vaison-la-Romaine.

Puyméras is surrounded by vines and fruit trees, the latter bent and looking south with one regard in deference to the incessant *mistral* wind. Local articles dating back to 1380 speak of vines being grown in the village, while in the fifteenth century more than 250,000 plants (about 80 hectares in modern terms) were said to have been cultivated at Puyméras.

Frédéric Daumas and his wife are a young couple dedicated to planting and tending their vineyards and making their wine by what they term 'bio-dynamic' methods. Thus, rather in the guise of followers of Rudolph Steiner, they will look at the cosmos before replanting vines and will study the lunar cycles before pruning them for instance. This is not as way out as it may sound when one takes into account how important the lunar cycle was considered to be in the last century among merchants in Bordeaux trying to decide when was the most propitious moment for bottling their wine. The pressure exerted through the position of the moon in relation to the earth was regarded as capable of altering bottle levels: less wine would be needed to fill a bottle when the moon was full, for instance.

M. Daumas relies on the Grenache and the Syrah as his principal vines, and the Syrah makes its presence well felt in his Cuvée d'Apolline Côtes du Rhône. Although not heavily coloured, it carries bags of tannin behind the initial fruit and is a wine good for drinking until it is five years old. Like the *domaine*'s *cuvée* of pure Syrah, which has a soaring fruit sensation on the palate, it must be opened at least two hours in advance of drinking, and even then may not be capable of throwing off its locked-up gases and early mustiness.

Daumas, Frédéric
    Domaine Ste-Apollinaire   84110 Puyméras

DOMAINE ST-MICHEL

This 12-hectare *domaine* is in the charming, almost perfectly restored hamlet of Uchaux, remarkable for the neatness and symmetry of its soft Provençal stone dwellings. Uchaux lies north of Orange on the way to Rochegude and is surrounded by vineyards and thickly wooded countryside. The better vineyards are on the sloping ground at Uchaux, where the soil is predominantly sandy, although most *domaines* such as St-Michel also have plots on the clay soil plain below.

M. Nicolas relies on just three vines – the Grenache for half his plantation and the Syrah and the Cinsault for a quarter each. He likes to vinify his grapes in uncrushed or *raisin entier* form, and after a rapid fermentation of a week or so he stores his wine in concrete for about two years. He has been bottling part of his crop since 1981 and is happy with this move away from dependence on *négociants*.

He makes only red wine, which, bright red in colour, carries a respectable bouquet and a reasonable length of finish. It is an honest example of correct Côtes du Rhône.

Nicolas, Jean
    Domaine St-Michel   84110 Uchaux

DOMAINE ST-PIERRE

The 25 hectares of vines belonging to this *domaine* are spread out over Violès, Gigondas and Vacqueyras, the result of intermarriages over three generations. It is the property of M. Jean-Claude Fauque, a very keen and ambitious grower who has a penchant for fast sports cars – not quite the *vieille France* picture of the country wine grower!

M. Fauque depends on 80 per cent Grenache, plus Syrah, and a little help from some very old Carignan plants, to make his red Côtes du Rhône. This is vinified traditionally and spends one year in cask. It is a very good wine indeed: bright purple, the bouquet shows the *goût de terroir* characteristics of the better wines from this part of the Vaucluse, recalling damp truffles; the depth of fruit and tannin indicate a well-structured and superior wine that is suitable for drinking before its fourth birthday.

The *domaine* also makes quite a good Gigondas and a less appealing Côtes du Rhône rosé. Its future appears to be in good hands, with M. Fauque's son having studied at wine school in Bordeaux.

Fauque, Jean-Claude
    Domaine St-Pierre   84150 Violès

DOMAINE DU VIEUX CHÊNE

This 30-hectare *domaine* has its vineyards split into three holdings, around the villages of Travaillan, Sérignan and on the Plan de Dieu. It is run by two brothers Jean-Claude and Dominique Bouche; Jean-Claude, a wiry-looking, thoughtful man in his early forties, is a biology and chemistry graduate of Marseille University and admits that it took him a few years to go into wine, because 'I didn't want to spend the rest of my life driving a tractor for eight hours a day.' He then graduated from the Montpellier wine school and soon discovered how wrong his conception of wine-making had been.

He is now completely involved in the subject and has the unbridled attitude of a young, well-educated man. The *domaine*'s vines are mainly Grenache (about 75 per cent), with 15 per cent Syrah; the difference is made up with Mourvèdre. The grapes are fed into the stainless steel vats by way of a conveyor belt so that they enter almost completely uncrushed; following an extended maceration and fermentation at controlled temperatures, the wines are stored for about fifteen months in concrete vats until bottling.

The Bouche brothers made their first wine in 1978, before which date their father had been sending the grapes to the Cave Co-opérative at Sérignan. They make two differently styled Rhône Villages *cuvées* every year, the fresher, almost strawberry-flavoured one being called Les Capucines, and the sturdier, more traditional one entitled Haie aux Grives. The latter is perhaps more interesting, with greater complexity in its red-black colour and more length provoked by the higher Syrah content. Of course, the brothers would suggest purchasing both wines at once, so that the Capucines could be happily drunk while the Haie aux Grives was getting itself ready to be drunk. Both are good wines, and it is worth keeping an eye open for them.

During the 1980s the brothers moved into making white wine, some of it 'mere' *vin de pays*. The varieties in the *vin de pays* include Roussanne and Viognier and it is worth looking out for.

Bouche, Jean-Claude et Dominique
  Domaine du Vieux Chêne   84150 Camaret

PLAN DEÏ

This curiously named *domaine* represents around 20 hectares of what used to be the 109-hectare Château La Meynarde, which was dispersed in 1979, when Gabriel Meffre bought the major portion of 45 hectares plus the Meynarde name. The vines run across the Plan de Dieu, notable for its immense size and for its heaps of small alluvial stones, and are made up of 15 hectares of Grenache, some of which supply a pure old-vines Grenache *cuvée*, the Cabassole, plus support from Mourvèdre, Counoise, Cinsault and Bourboulenc.

Jean-Marie Lobreau is an innovator who likes to present to the public different styles of wine. He was an early devotee of the Mourvèdre in these parts, and he now produces as many as half a dozen different wines. The top of the range is the red Côtes du Rhône Villages, in which the Mourvèdre dominates over the Grenache. The Côtes du Rhône reds are Plan Deï, his original wine made up of 60 per cent Grenache, 25 per cent Mourvèdre and 15 per cent Counoise, and La Vignonnerie, also his first *cuvée*, which is a lighter, earlier style of wine. Two pure Grenache *cuvées* were instituted during the 1980s – the Rouvières and Cabassole.

The grapes are fermented at no more than 20°C in stainless steel, and the finishing touches are added by a stay of several months in oak; the fresh La Vignonnerie *cuvée* does not go into wood. The other reds are well coloured, with due tannic support, and a solid structure. All are cleanly made and should be drunk around the four- to seven-year mark. M. Lobreau is also making white from Bourboulenc and Clairette, and very successful it is too, with a hint of oak in it.

Lobreau, Jean-Marie
  Plan Deï   84150 Travaillan

SOCIÉTÉ DES GRANDS VINS DE CHÂTEAUNEUF-DU-PAPE ET DES CÔTES DU RHÔNE

This sizeable company owns several *domaines* in Châteauneuf-du-Pape and the Côtes du Rhône, the most famous being the Château des Fines Roches at Châteauneuf-du-Pape. The Côtes du Rhône wines in general tend to lack flair and can be very humdrum, the sort of wine that raises false hopes when found on a supermarket shelf at an interesting price. This is very sad because some years ago the quality of the *domaine* wines used to be very fine. Today the firm's two leading Côtes du Rhône *domaines* are the Château du Bois de la Garde and the Château du Prieuré St-Joseph.

SGVC   84230 Châteauneuf-du-Pape

OTHER CÔTES DU RHÔNE DOMAINES IN THE VAUCLUSE DÉPARTEMENT

Alessandrini, Vincent
  Domaine Bois Lauzon   84100 Orange
d'Arnaudy, J.-P.
  Château de La Serre   84800 L'Isle-sur-la-Sorgue
Autard, Paul
  Domaine Autard   84350 Courthézon

Barbaud, Jean-Paul
    Domaine des Favards   84150 Violès
Biscarrat, François
    Domaine de la Guicharde   84430 Derboux
Biscarrat, Louis
    Château du Grand-Prébois   84100 Orange
Bonnet, Gérard
    La Bastide St-Dominique   84350 Courthézon
Boyer et Fils
    Domaine de Bel-Air   84150 Violès
Brun, Pierre
    Domaine de la Cambuse   84110 Villedieu
Charasse, Claude et Associés
    Domaine de St-Claude   84110 Vaison-la-Romaine
Combe, Pierre
    Domaine de Tenon   84150 Violès
Coulon, Paul et Fils
    La Ferme Pisan   84110 Rasteau
Damoy, Julien
    Domaine de la Renjarde   84100 Sérignan
Daniel, Guy
    Domaine La Bastide
    St-Vincent   84150 Violès
Daniel, Patrick
    Château La Croix Chabrière   84500 Bollène
Daussant, Eric
    Domaine de Grant Plantier   84270 Vedène
Deforge, La Veuve de Jean
    Domaine Jean Deforge   84470 Châteauneuf-de-Gadagne
Farjon, Albert
    Les Grands Rois   84290 Ste-Cécile-les-Vignes
Faurous, Henri et Fils
    Domaine Le Grand Retour   84150 Travaillan
Garagnon, Paul
    Domaine du Gros-Pata   84110 Vaison-la-Romaine
Gargani, R.
    La Fauconnière   84290 St-Romain-de-Mallegarde
Gleize, André
    Vignoble Gleize   84150 Violès

Gonnet, Cohendy et Fils
  Domaine La Berthète   84150 Camaret
Groiller, M.
  Domaine de Boilauzon   84150 Travaillan
Guichard, A.   84430 Mondragon
Jaume, Alain
  Domaine Grand Veneur   84110 Orange
Jullien, et Fils
  Domaine de l'Aigaillons   84190 Suzette
Martin, Hélène, et Fils
  Domaine de Grangeneuve   84150 Jonquières
Maurizot, Charles
  Domaine Les Roures du Plan
  de Dieu   84150 Travaillan
Meffre, Gérard
  Château La Courançonne   84150 Violès
Merle, François, et Fils
  Château de Beaulieu   84100 Orange
Michel, Eric, et Fils
  Domaine du Cros de la Mure   84430 Mondragon
Perrin, Pierre
  Le Coudoulet de Beaucastel   84350 Courthézon
Plumet, Marie-Pierre
  Domaine La Tissote   84430 Mondragon
Pradier, Bernard
  Château d'Hugues   84100 Uchaux
Sahuc, Abel
  Domaine de la Grand' Ribe   84290 Ste-Cécile-les-Vignes
Saurel, S.
  Domaine de la Combe Dieu   84 La Baumette
Serguier, Yves, et Fils
  Clos Simian   84110 Uchaux
Thompson, Nick
  Domaine La Beraude   84290 Cairanne
Tramier, Monique
  Domaine de la Grangette
  St-Joseph   84150 Violès

NÉGOCIANTS

BELLICARD

Founded at Mâcon in 1889, this house moved a large part of its business to Avignon in 1920. It owns no vineyards, and although its wine is bought shortly after the harvest – in November – none is actually brought to the company cellars until the following spring. Half the wine is from Caves Co-opératives, and half from small *vignerons*.

Their two best-selling wines are the Côtes du Rhône *générique* and Tavel. The red Côtes du Rhône is a very good wine, well coloured and full-flavoured, with just a hint of *macération carbonique* about it. The Tavel rosé is generally a sound wine with adequate fruit in it, but can sometimes be a little hard or metallic.

DOMAINES MICHEL BERNARD

This is not a pure, orthodox *négociant* organization. It is a collection of independent growers formed in 1980 primarily to bottle but also to help with raising wine and selling it.

Michel Bernard himself is the owner of the 5-hectare Châteauneuf-du-Pape Domaine de la Serrière, which is in the north-east of the *appellation* towards Orange. The red is a Grenache-dominated wine, with Syrah support, and is correct – it is sound, middle-range Châteauneuf with fair depth and authenticity, the sort of wine to drink around seven to ten years old. This forms one of the single-*domaine* names within the grouping, while others include the Domaine de la Vialle and the Domaine des Trois Plantiers.

The quality of the other southern Rhône wines from this grouping, which include Côtes du Rhône and Tavel, is sound and reliable. The northern Rhône wines include a reliable Crozes-Hermitage red.

Domaines Michel Bernard   84110 Orange

LE CELLIER DES DAUPHINS

Founded in 1967, the Cellier des Dauphins at Tulette acts as a bottling and marketing centre for ten local Caves Co-opératives. These are the Co-opératives of Ste-Cécile-les-Vignes (Cécilia), Nyons,

Rochegude, St-Maurice-sur-Eygues, St-Pantaléon-les-Vignes, Suze-la-Rousse, Tulette (Costebelle), Tulette (Nouvelle), Vaison-la-Romaine and Vinsobres.

This is a go-ahead, very commercial operation. It has always been in the front rank of promoting the Rhône to a wider audience outside the restrictions of the region and has always thought 'big' on projects. In 1974 it first mounted a large publicity campaign in leading French magazines and newspapers, getting away from the old folklore approach to wine and introducing a bit of urban chic into pictures of single people arriving to dinner with their bottle of Cellier des Dauphins tucked behind their back: it may sound oldish-hat today, but it wasn't nearly twenty years ago. This bold policy extended in 1991 to placing advertising billboards in a Moscow football stadium for a televised European Cup game involving Marseille. The Cellier des Dauphins bottle, engraved with its letters, is another hallmark that has been laid down.

During the 1980s other projects have included the Cellier's involvement in setting up the University of Wine at the Château of Suze-la-Rousse. This runs courses for enthusiasts, has laboratories and offers help to local *vignerons*, and is a big step forward for the Rhône region. The Cellier has also extended to having an ageing cellar in the twelfth-century Cistercian Abbey of Bouchet.

So, all in all, this is one of the most interesting commercial stories of the Rhône over the past twenty years. On the wine production front, the tally is large. Around 3,500 local *vignerons* are represented here; the member *caves* make around 740,000 hectolitres of wine each year, of which over half is Côtes du Rhône. The reds are sound enough, but as with big production source wines, they can lack character and style. They have improved since the 1970s, however, and are more regular in quality. The rosés are a little hard from time to time, and it is better to seek out a smaller local supplier for them. The whites are straightforward, commercial wines, but they could well be upgraded during the 1990s.

Le Cellier des Dauphins   26130 Tulette

DAVID ET FOILLARD

This *négociant-éleveur* company was founded in the Beaujolais in 1826 and now possesses a subsidiary that deals in all the wines of the southern Côtes du Rhône. These are headed in volume by the cheaper wines from the whole area – Côtes du Rhône, Côtes du Ventoux and Coteaux du Tricastin. A considerable quantity is exported, and the wines are generally of a quite reasonable standard. The company co-owns Château La Nerthe at Châteauneuf-du-Pape.

David, T., et Foillard, L.   84700 Sorgues

A. OGIER ET FILS

Founded in 1824, this *négociant-éleveur* company is situated in the town of Sorgues, near Châteauneuf-du-Pape. It deals in all the *appellation* wines of the Côtes du Rhône and buys them immediately after the harvest, in mid-October. The various wines are then left to mature in their modern cellars, for a duration of two or three years for the Hermitages and the Châteauneuf-du-Papes.

The quality of the wines is constant without being startling. The Côtes du Rhône is a sound wine, but it lacks the individuality of the best *domaines*. The house's Châteauneuf-du-Pape is probably its leading wine.

Ogier is now one of three companies owned by the Berger Group – the other two are Caves Bessac and Malbec.

A. Ogier et Fils   84800 L'Isle-sur-la-Sorgue

SOCIÉTÉ NOUVELLE DES VINS FINS SALAVERT

Founded at Bourg-St-Andéol in 1840, Salavert deals in all the main wines of the Côtes du Rhône and its neighbouring wine regions, such as the Côtes du Ventoux, Côtes du Vivarais and Côtes de Provence. The various wines are bought during the year following the harvest, and are aged and bottled in the company's underground cellars near the Rhône.

Although the company's reputation used to be based upon its fine Rhône wines, such as Hermitage and Châteauneuf-du-Pape, it has recently turned its attention more towards the cheaper wines of the Rhône Valley and Provence. These are generally very soundly made and represent good value for money. At the same time Salavert continues to produce worthy fine wines, its Châteauneuf-du-Pape being particularly notable.

Société Nouvelle des
   Vins Fins Salavert   07700 Bourg-St-Andéol

LA VIEILLE FERME

This branded wine is successfully produced by Jean-Pierre Perrin, whose family owns the Château de Beaucastel at Châteauneuf-du-Pape. Formerly made from grapes bought from Côtes du Rhône vineyards, it is now composed of grapes and wine bought in the Côtes du Lubéron area for the white and the Côtes du Ventoux (q.v.) for the red. Both the red and the white are very reliable, well-priced wines that give great pleasure if drunk before about four years old.

Perrin, Jean-Pierre
   La Vieille Ferme   84100 Orange

OTHER CÔTES DU RHÔNE NÉGOCIANTS

Abbaye de Bouchet	26130 Bouchet
Barbier, Léon, et Fils	84230 Châteauneuf-du-Pape
Boissy et Delaygue	07130 Cornas
Brotte, Jean-Pierre	84230 Châteauneuf-du-Pape
Du Peloux et Cie	84350 Courthézon
Garnier, Camille	30200 Bagnols-sur-Cèze
Malbec, Eugène	84230 Châteauneuf-du-Pape
Meffre, Éts. G.	84190 Gigondas
Mouret, Michel	84340 Entrechaux
Paul-Étienne, Père et Fils	07130 St-Péray
Revol, Léon	26600 Tain-l'Hermitage
Sirop, Pierre	84110 Vaison-la-Romaine

LEADING CÔTES DU RHÔNE CAVES CO-OPÉRATIVES

With sixty-six Caves Co-opératives spread out in the Ardèche, Drôme, Gard and Vaucluse *départements*, there is obviously an enormous selection of different Côtes du Rhône *génériques* from which to choose – in theory. For despite a tremendous advance in commercial awareness and the commitment to bottle their wine, it is curious what a restricted number and variety of Co-opératives have their wine represented overseas, for instance. One feels that there are still pockets of caution and perhaps complacency that make the Co-opératives' managements consider it easier to supply a regional audience or passing trade, and not bother with large-scale export drives – in bottle, at least.

Since the 1970s much better cellar equipment has appeared in many of the large cellars of Co-opératives. This means not just stainless steel and temperature-controlled vats, but also upgraded barrels, including new oak at progressive Co-opératives like Sainte-Cécile-les-Vignes' Caveau Chantecôtes. Thinking about grape varieties has also changed, noticeably in the attitude towards growing more refined *cépages*, with perhaps lower yields and lower alcohol in their wines; the Mourvèdre immediately springs to mind, as a replacement for the Grenache. And white wine is fast becoming a challenge that big enterprises wish to master: here again, more planting, more Bourboulenc and less Grenache and Ugni Blanc.

Particularly recommended among this mass of producers are three Co-opératives who do not make sole *appellation* wine like Gigondas or Côtes du Rhône Villages, those of Puyméras and of Villedieu in the Vaucluse and of Vénéjan in the Gard.

Puyméras's Côtes du Rhône area is 850 hectares, which stand at between 330 and 550 metres altitude. Set largely on clay-limestone soil, the reds are made up of around 65 per cent Grenache, 15 per cent Cinsault, 10 per cent Carignan, 7 per cent Syrah and 3 per cent Mourvèdre. The presence of the last two *cépages*, creeping into the listings, shows a typical Rhône vineyard evolution of the 1980s and into the 1990s. The white wine is made from around 50 per cent Grenache Blanc, 45 per cent Clairette and 5 per cent Ugni Blanc.

Fermentation of the reds has remained constant for several years, and after a brief six-day *cuvaison*, the different *cuvées* are assembled and remain for four to six months in cask before bottling. These are extremely well made, authentic Côtes du Rhône reds; they are full-bodied, develop good aromas after three or four years and are extremely satisfying to drink with winter food. The whites are cool-fermented, bottled in the spring and are fresh and well made as well: they are good to drink within about three years, and have a nice mix of fresh flavours with some underlying substance.

Perhaps high altitude is the secret, for the neighbouring Co-opérative of Villedieu also draws its grapes from vineyards about

250 metres up and makes a very good job of vinifying them. Marginally less impressive than the wine of Puyméras, their Côtes du Rhône red is also traditional, with some ageing in cask, and although not an abundantly fruity wine, has an interesting complexity of spicy and tannic flavours. Their white wine is also very respectable; made mainly from the Bourboulenc and the Grenache Blanc with minor support from the Clairette, its fruitiness would have even more zest with just a little more acidity.

Vénéjan is about 4 kilometres north-east of Bagnols-sur-Cèze and is as pretty a Provençal village as one could wish to encounter: cobbled stone streets with wistaria tumbling down the outside of the soft stone houses in cascades of pale blue and a finely restored twelfth-century chapel on a small hillside. The Co-opérative bottles some red, white and rosé every year, and its red is of major interest. Pale, with touches of pink at the top, it displays a satisfying soft blackcurrant fruit, which has charm and balance enough to mould in well with the wine's acidity. It makes an attractive summer wine, one that drinks well within its first two years but which can evolve gently over several years if left alone.

There follows a list of the principal Caves Co-opératives making Côtes du Rhône red, white and rosé.

Cave Co-opérative Agricole du Nyonnais	26110 Nyons
Cave Co-opérative Costebelle	26130 Tulette
Cave Co-opérative des Coteaux	30210 Fournes
Cave Co-opérative de St-Hilaire-d'Ozilhan	30210 St-Hilaire d'Ozilhan
Cave Co-opérative de Tresques	30330 Tresques
Cave Co-opérative de Vénéjan	30200 Vénéjan
Cave Co-opérative La Vigneronne	84110 Villedieu
Cave Co-opérative des Vignerons	30200 Bagnols-sur-Cèze
Cave Co-opérative des Vignerons	84110 Vaison-la-Romaine
Cave Co-opérative Vinicole	84310 Monères

Cave Co-opérative Vinicole Cécilia	84290 Ste-Cécile-les-Vignes
Cave Co-opérative Vinicole La Suzienne	26130 Suze-la-Rousse
Cave des Vignerons	30300 Cavillargues
Cave des Vignerons du Duché de Gadagne	84470 Châteauneuf-de-Gadagne
Cave des Vignerons Réunis Caveau Chantecôtes	} 84290 Ste-Cécile-les-Vignes
Co-opérative Vinicole Comtadine Dauphinoise	84110 Puyméras
Co-opérative Vinicole Les Coteaux du Rhône	84100 Sérignan-du-Comtat
Co-opérative Vinicole des Coteaux de Tulette	26130 Tulette
Les Vignerons du Castelas	30650 Rochefort-du-Gard

Other Wines and Liqueurs

―――――

AIGUEBELLE

Aiguebelle liqueur comes from a Trappist abbey set in some remote hills 16 kilometres south-east of the nougat town of Montélimar. It is not one of France's best known liqueurs, and its popularity has always been fairly localized around its region of production. Its similarity to the more celebrated, more widely marketed Green Chartreuse may have contributed to this, for both are made on a secret, herb-based formula, and both are green liqueurs.

In 1137 the abbey of Notre Dame d'Aiguebelle was founded by the monks of an expanding Trappist order whose seat was in the Champagne country. The Trappist philosophy of life is rigid; industry and dedication are all-important, and the monks' day is consequently divided into four strictly defined stages: prayer, work, reading or study, and reception. From the very beginning, opportunities for outside industry were limited at Aiguebelle since the surrounding countryside was particularly craggy and non-productive. Thus for many years, throughout the Middle Ages and beyond, the monks were able only to eke out the most primitive rural existence. The abbey was then abandoned at the time of the French Revolution, but shortly afterwards, in 1815, some enterprising Swiss Trappists arrived to restart the community with greater energy than ever before.

So successful were the Swiss monks that by the start of the twentieth century Aiguebelle found itself barely able to support the dependencies that had sprung up since 1815. Unfortunately, a steady source of income – and wine – had been forfeited during the Revolution, when the abbey lost its land holdings at Gigondas and Vacqueyras in the Vaucluse *département*. The spartan nature of the country around continued to rule out any serious agricultural exploitation, so the brothers were compelled to find another source of income, somehow or other.

The solution lay in the monastic archives, which contained old 'elixir' recipes dating from different times during the abbey's existence. Father Aelred, a large, benign monk who arrived at Aiguebelle in 1958, proceeded to explain how the Aiguebelle Trappists had decided to use their recipe: 'In olden days, the Fathers here would make up a very potent elixir that was at least 60° Guy Lussac. Local plants like sage, verbena and rosemary were macerated and then distilled, and the fiery mixture would be drunk in the main by the inhabitants of the abbey. At that time each monastery would have a specialist herbalist, who would be charged with creating a magic recipe, the contents of which, of course, remained a closely guarded secret. Early in the twentieth century the Fathers decided to go back through our archives and came up with an old elixir recipe. This formed the basis of a liqueur that they resolved to produce commercially. In view of the fact that they couldn't be agricultural, they became industrial instead!'

At first, the precise ingredients of the magic formula eluded the Fathers. By 1930, however, a suitable composition had been perfected: a mixture of thirty-five Provençal plants and roots were to make up the Green Liqueur of Aiguebelle. Soon afterwards twenty other liqueurs were devised, notably a Yellow Liqueur that was, in fact, a sweeter cousin of the Green. All these were made on quite a large scale, and the range of choice was broadened by the subsequent production of *eau-de-vie* brandies, such as *framboise* (raspberry) and *mirabelle* (plum). In 1960 the monks started to make concentrated fruit syrups as well, and these have now come to form nine-tenths of the business.

The Green and Yellow Liqueurs are the two most important of the abbey's selection of liqueurs and brandies. They are composed of root plants, cloves, herbs and flowers that come from as far afield as the Equatorial regions. About eight of the sixty white-robed monks occupy themselves with the distillery, and first macerate the plants and flowers in neutral alcohol spirit. This mixture is then distilled very slowly for twelve hours in copper stills and is afterwards left to stabilize in glass-lined vats for around eighteen months. Before bottling there is a small addition of sugar syrup to provide a little extra sweetness: the Yellow Liqueur receives a larger dose than the Green.

The Aiguebelle Green Liqueur is a sweet, quite smooth drink that seems to possess traces of mint in its flavour. A certain aromatic spiciness comes out in the aftertaste, and the liqueur is also believed by some supporters to have outstanding restorative qualities. The Yellow Liqueur, which is made from about twenty-five assorted plants, is sweeter still and carries less diversity of flavour. Among the other liqueurs, the apricot is outstanding.

Consumption of the liqueurs has fallen away since the Second World War, when a peak was attained through the presence in France of the combined American forces. Many southern French bars have a bottle on their shelves, but it is usually dust-covered and hidden behind rows of Aiguebelle fruit syrups. For the Trappist monks, however, the Green Liqueur carries a special importance and a special memory, since it was that which originally enabled them to increase their contacts and aid as far abroad as Hong Kong, the United States and Brazil.

Distillerie d'Aiguebelle   26230 Grignan

CHÂTILLON-EN-DIOIS

The wine-producing region of Châtillon-en-Diois is very restricted, with vineyards covering no more than 70 hectares. It is centred on a dozen villages and hamlets to the south and east of Die, and all the wine – red, white and rosé – is made by the Cave Co-opérative of Die.

In 1974 Châtillon-en-Diois was promoted from *VDQS (Vin Délimité de Qualité Supérieure)* status to full *appellation contrôlée*. As a result the red and rosé wines have to be three-quarters composed of the Gamay Noir grape, with one-quarter coming from the Syrah and Pinot Noir grape varieties. The white wines also bear a Burgundian slant and must be made from the Aligoté and Chardonnay grapes, of which around 10 hectares have been planted.

The principal vine-growing communities are Châtillon-en-Diois, Menglon, St-Romain and Laval d'Aix. All are in the beautiful, wild, mountainous countryside that follows the river Drôme as it runs south of Die and on to the most southerly wine-producing village, Poyols, which is 19 kilometres from Die.

Every year a total of about 300,000 litres of wine is made. These undergo a brief vinification, with a rapid fermentation and bottling early in the new year. Unfortunately, the wines are all thoroughly nondescript, the red in particular failing to live up to its noble Gamay-Syrah-Pinot 'breeding'. Often very pale, weak and watery, it possesses little intrinsic charm or character; it merely remains a point of amazement that such a wine can have been considered worthy, on its own, of qualifying for the highest accolade in French viticulture – full *appellation* status.

Cave Co-opérative de Die   26150 Die

CLAIRETTE DE DIE

About 65 kilometres south-east of Valence, the old town of Die nestles easily into the first Alpine mountain ranges. Beside it the River Drôme runs on a steady course towards the Rhône, and the green, poplar-lined Drôme Valley exactly traces the 1,200 hectares of vineyards of Clairette de Die. These extend for 56 kilometres on either bank, all the way from Aouste, 3 kilometres east of Crest, up to Luc-en-Diois, 19 kilometres south-east of Die.

As the vineyards go east, the countryside becomes steadily more Alpine. Little chalets that stand away from the sleepy villages are dwarfed by the high mountains looming over them; sudden patches of luscious, dark green grass are cropped by grazing goats, and at the foot of the hillsides tight little clumps of pine trees add extra colour to the vivid scene.

Wine has probably been made in the region of Die for almost 2,000 years, since there was a lengthy reference to a local wine in Chapter 9 of Pliny's *Natural History (c.* AD 77). Here Pliny criticized the thirteen known varieties of sweet wine then found in Greece and the Roman Empire, some of them, he said, being products of art and not of Nature, while others were guilty of being given mixtures devised to make them simulate honey. One, known as honey wine, even received salt and honey in its must, thereby producing a very rough flavour. The star wine, for Pliny, was the natural form of 'Aigleucos' or sweet wine then being made by the Vocontii people. 'In order to make it,' Pliny wrote, 'they keep the grape hanging on the tree for a considerable time, taking care to twist the stalk.' When Pliny was writing the capital town of the Vocontii was called Dea Augusta; today it is Die.

The wine Pliny referred to is sparkling today but is still made by natural methods, with no addition of any substance or liquid to give it its bubbles. It goes by the title of Clairette de Die *Tradition*, or *Demi-Sec*. Meanwhile another sparkling wine is now made, along formal champagne lines, and this sells as Clairette de Die *Brut*. Unlike the *Tradition*, which is made from the Clairette and Muscat grapes, the *Brut* comes solely from the low-scented Clairette grape, and has less individual style about it. Finally, there is a little still dry white wine of quite reasonable quality, made generally from the Clairette. This was Die's main wine until 1926, when the first sparkling wine experiments took place.

Because the wine region is so long, the composition of the vineyards is very varied, and the *Tradition* wines from different ends of the *appellation* can vary very widely in character. The most common soil elements are limestone and clay, while the rock soil base becomes progressively harder the nearer one is to Die and the high Alps. This seems to suit the Muscat more than the Clairette, but in recent years it has been the latter whose plantation has increased. This is because it is a hardier vine than the Muscat, and because the more neutral-tasting *Brut* wine is easier to sell than the *Tradition*. The Muscat used at Die is the *petits grains* variety, which is also found at Beaumes-de-Venise and which gives the *Tradition* its strong, flowery bouquet.

Growers differ over how much Muscat should be included in the *Tradition* wine, however. The Cave Co-opérative of Die makes about three-quarters of all Clairette de Die, and its *Tradition* is composed of half Muscat and half Clairette. By contrast, the next largest wine house, Buffardel Frères, prefers a combination of three-quarters Clairette and one-quarter Muscat. Smaller *vignerons* sometimes rely on three-quarters Muscat and only one-quarter Clairette. For the drinker there is one easy answer – personal taste. Those who like the strongly scented Muscat will choose the third type of wine.

The *vendanges* generally commence in late September and can continue nearly into November, by when the grapes are usually very ripe and sugary. On arrival at the cellar, the harvest is crushed, pressed, and the juice is run off into isothermal vats that are cooled to a temperature of $-3°C$. The liquid is left to settle for forty-eight hours and is then put through a centrifuge machine in order to rid it of all loose particles. Finally, it is filtered lightly, which removes the largest yeast cells and delays the start of fermentation.

This is the broad technique used in making the *Tradition*, where the principal idea is to ferment the wine extremely slowly, even to the point of filtering it when fermentation seems to be going too fast. Thus by the time the wine is bottled in January, there is still some unfermented sugar left in it, and it is the subsequent fermentation of this sugar inside the bottle that makes the wine sparkling. By prolonging the alcoholic fermentation for such a long time, the growers are able to achieve their sparkling wine without having to add any yeasts or extra sugar.

Clearly, the small *vignerons* do not possess the Cave Co-opérat-ives's isothermal vats, so instead they filter their wine a little more often in order to spin out its fermentation. They too start bottling around the month of February; by law all Clairette de Die *Tradition* must therefore spend at least four months in the bottle, to make sure that all fermentation is completely finished before the wine is released for sale. In reality most growers leave their *Tradition* for about six months, while the *Brut* must by law always spend nine months in bottle before being disgorged.

The final operation in the elaboration of the *Tradition* sparkling wine is the *dégorgement*, or removal of the deposits gathered in the bottle during the second stage of fermentation. The wine is filtered under carbon dioxide pressurization so that all its natural gas will be carefully preserved. It is then rebottled, and left for a month or two to settle down; consequently, it is always something over one year old when first put on sale.

This is the oldest sparkling wine at Die, for the *Brut* did not appear until the early 1960s. The latter is vinified just like champagne, with the addition of sugar and yeasts in order to make it sparkling, and with a *remuage*, or turning of the bottles, in order to clear the wine of its deposits. Less distinctively flavoured than the *Tradition*, the *Brut* has proved an easier wine to market, and has quickly come to account for around 40 per cent of all Clairette de Die; its promotion has been notably supported by Buffardel Frères, a house which is run by two brothers born in the Champagne country.

The difference in style between the two sparkling wines is startling. The *Brut* is usually paler and much less scented and fully flavoured; because of this it is simpler to drink than the *Tradition*, and a well-chilled bottle can disappear very rapidly on a warm summer's afternoon. The *Tradition* is the more interesting wine, however. It is often called *Demi-Sec*, and this description gives some idea of its basic style. Slightly lime-yellow coloured, it is a wine of appealing richness and roundness, whose flavours resemble apples or gooseberries; a good bottle has a long, just very partly sweet aftertaste. It is not a 'quaffing' wine like the *Brut*, but a glass or two is ideal as the introduction to a good meal.

Production of Clairette de Die has increased steadily over the years to around 6 million bottles, and one of the main reasons for this is the impetus given to the region by its ambitious Cave Co-opérative. Founded in 1951, this now has a well-organized international sales network, and farmers have therefore been persuaded to enlarge their vine holdings. For many years Clairette de Die was pretty well unknown beyond the south of France, and so there existed little incentive to plant vineyards on a more widespread scale.

Other leading producers include Buffardel Frères and the CUMA (Co-opérative for the Use of Agricultural Materials). Buffardel Frères is possibly the best house in Clairette de Die, and its wines are always thoroughly consistent and well balanced. In exceptional years they give their wine a vintage, as in Champagne, and this *tête de cuvée* represents Clairette de Die at its very best. Otherwise all the wine is sold without a vintage, so that the wine of different years can be blended together to form a uniform style.

CUMA is a looser organization than either the Co-opérative or Buffardel Frères and consists of about thirty small farmer-*vignerons* who broke away from the Co-opérative in 1967. Each man makes and sells his own wine individually but shares out all equipment, be it for vineyards, wheat, maize or sunflowers; for the vines this includes caterpillar-track tractors that are used on the slopes and all vineyard spraying tools, as well as a mobile filtering machine. The standards of all the growers are generally very good, although some have taken to using plastic tops instead of corks to stopper their bottles. The effect on the wine is somewhat dubious, since the plastic 'breathes' less than a cork. Among these smaller growers, prominent producers include Pierre Salabelle, Georges Poulet, René Aubert, Jean-Claude Vincent, Henri Grangeron and Archard-Vincent. All make wine of very good quality, although like most Clairette de Die it is not intended for long keeping, three years being an average lifespan.

Leading Clairette de Die Growers

Archard, Claude	26150 Barsac-par-Die
Andrieux, Albert	26340 Saillans
Archard-Vincent	26150 Ste-Croix
Aubert, René	26340 Aurel-par-Saillans
Banet, Georges	26340 Saillans
Barnier, Maurice Barnier, Yvon	} 26150 Pontaix
Bec, Martial	26340 Aurel-par-Saillans
Buffardel Frères	26150 Die
Carod, A.	26340 Vercheny
Cave Co-opérative de Die	26150 Die
Decorse, Fernand	26150 Barsac-par-Die
Girard Fils	26150 Die
Grangeron, Henri	26150 Ste-Croix
Granon, Michel	26150 Pontaix
Long, André	26150 Barsac par Die
Marcel, Émile	26150 Ponet-St-Aubin-par-Die
Marcel, René	26150 Pontaix
Poulet, Élie	26340 Vercheny
Poulet, Georges Poulet, Roger	} 26150 Pontaix
Raspail, Georges	26340 Aurel-par-Saillans
Salabelle, Pierre Truchefaud, André Vincent, Jean-Claude	} 26150 Barsac-par-Die

COSTIÈRES DE NÎMES

This wine area near Nîmes started life in 1950 as the Costières du Gard VDQS (*V in Délimitée de Qualité Supérieure*) region – a producer of light red table wines that were somewhere on the lines of the Côtes du Ventoux reds with a little more body in them.

In 1986, Costières du Gard was promoted to full *appellation* status and in 1989 the area was given more precise definition by a change of name to Costières de Nîmes. By 1990, it was accepted as part of the French Rhône Valley grouping of wines, although it retains its own identity and marketing office from Nîmes rather than Avignon.

The full *appellation* zone covers much of the land between the two ancient Roman cities of Nîmes and Arles. From its most northerly point, the commune of Sernhac, to its most southerly, near the commune of Le Cailar, is a distance of about 30 kilometres. Altogether, twenty-four communes are included in the area, with Vauvert the unofficial capital, and a total of around 10,000 hectares planted.

The vines permitted for the red wine are Carignan, Grenache, Mourvèdre, Syrah and Cinsault, with some provisos attached to the quantity allowed of each of these. Neither the Carignan nor the Cinsault can by law exceed 50 per cent of the finished wine; the Grenache must form at least 25 per cent (this was raised from 15 per cent with the 1990 harvest); the Mourvèdre and the Syrah must, together or separately, make up 5 per cent of the total, rising to 15 per cent by the 1995 harvest. The rosé of Costières de Nîmes must be made from the same *cépages*, with a softening proviso that allows the inclusion of up to 10 per cent white grape varieties in the wine.

Serious efforts are therefore being made to upgrade the vineyard plantation and to strengthen the final red wine. The growing conditions are similar to those found in the southern Côtes du Rhône, with plenty of *mistral* wind and, in summer, sudden localized storms. In this open, sweeping countryside, summer temperatures can rise easily above the 40°C mark, and controlling the ripeness of their grapes is one of the growers' most consistent tasks.

Over such an extended area there is no one soil type; the mark of alluvial deposits – sandy-coloured stones smaller than those at Châteauneuf-du-Pape – appears in much of the region, with subsoils ranging from a thick sand to a red clay whose local term is *gapan*; there is also present a solid chalk, called *taparas*, which acts as a stop on water filtration after any rainfall. Consequently, this is an area used to drought during the maturing process.

The white wines can be made from 'principal' grape varieties – Clairette, Grenache Blanc, Bourboulenc and Ugni Blanc – with support from 'complementary' varieties – Marsanne, Roussanne, Maccabéo and Rolle, the last-named a synonym for the Malvoisie: this last group must not exceed 50 per cent of the plantation. The Ugni Blanc must not exceed 50 per cent, a figure that drops to 40 per cent in 1995, while the presence of at least two 'principal' grape varieties is obligatory.

As with the red, efforts are being made to upgrade the white wine plantation, centring on the reduction of the bland Ugni Blanc and the insertion of vines with greater liveliness of fruit, such as the Roussanne.

Nevertheless, this remains a dense production area by Rhône standards; southern Rhône *appellations* like Lirac permit a yield of 42 hectolitres per hectare, the Côtes du Rhône allowance is 52 hectolitres, but the Costières de Nîmes yield is set at 60 hectolitres a hectare.

Reflecting the greater inclination of southern French wine growers to bottle their own wine, there are now over 70 Costières de Nîmes bottlers. Eighteen of these are traditional Caves Co-opératives, such as those at Bellegarde, only 12 kilometres north-west of Arles, and at Vauvert, in the south-west of the *appellation*. Three prominent large *domaines* are the Château de la Tuilerie, the Château de Campuget, which has another property, the Domaine de l'Amarine, within the same ownership of 170 hectares, and the 50-hectare, progressive Château Guiot.

The Château de la Tuilerie is a 70-hectare estate run energetically and professionally by Mme Chantal Comte. Pierre-Yves Comte is the head of the Serres Group, an industrial organization whose activities include packaging, farming and distribution interests in countries like Spain and Martinique, as well as in France.

Sixty-five per cent of the Tuilerie wine is red, 15 per cent rosé and 20 per cent white. The reds and rosés are made from Syrah, Grenache, Cinsault and Carignan, the whites from Grenache Blanc and Rolle.

Much of the vineyard is covered by the typical Rhône stone deposits, which in this area is called *gress*.

The Château de la Tuilerie has an avant-garde approach both to its wine-making and its commercial policy. The red wine is totally destalked and Mme Comte likes to work with *raisins entiers* to extract as much fruit as possible. The different grape varieties are vinified apart and the top *cuvée*, the Cuvée Éole, spends up to twenty months in new Bordelais *barriques* before bottling about two years after the harvest. The standard *cuvées* are bottled from nine months after the harvest onwards. The white crop spends a night in the fridge before going into the *pressoir* at 4°C; it is fermented at up to 18°C, and has a good reputation for being crisp and clean – a wine to drink in its first two or three years.

Like the white, the rosé is bottled around the month of April, after a *saignée* vinification.

Reflecting their packaging interests, the Comtes use a Bordelais bottle for their wines with artists' paintings on the labels.

The reds of La Tuilerie are among the progressive wines of Costières; already the wine is well known abroad, with 70 per cent of the production exported. With the château Japanese-owned, the number one overseas market is Japan, which since 1983 has taken regular amounts of red, white and rosé.

Selected Growers at Costières de Nîmes

Cave Co-opérative de Bellegarde	30127 Bellegarde
Cave Co-opérative de Generac	30510 Generac
Cave Co-opérative de Ledenon	30210 Remoulins
Cave Co-opérative de Milhaud	30540 Milhaud
Cave Co-opérative de Rodilhan	30230 Rodilhan
Cave Co-opérative de Sernhac	30210 Remoulins
Cave Co-opérative de Vauvert	30600 Vauvert
Château Beaubois	30600 Beauvoisin
Château Boissy d'Anglas	30600 Gallician
Château de Campuget	30129 Manduel
Château Fonteuil	30600 Gallician
Château Guiot	30800 St-Gilles
Château Roubaud	30600 Gallician
Château de Rozier	30129 Manduel
Château St-Louis-la-Perdrix	30127 Bellegarde
Château des Tourelles	30300 Beaucaire
Château de la Tuilerie	30000 Nîmes
Domaine de l'Amarine	30129 Manduel
Domaine de Beauchêne	30800 St-Gilles
Domaine de Contevall	30600 Gallician
Domaine de Dévèze	30000 Nîmes
Domaine du Haut Plâteau	30129 Manduel
Domaine de Mourier	30000 Nîmes
Domaine de Rapatel	30128 Garons
Domaine des Sources Mas Carlot	} 30127 Bellegarde
Mas Du Notaire	30600 Gallician
Sica des Sept Collines	30000 Nîmes

COTEAUX DU TRICASTIN

The Coteaux du Tricastin is the wine region that has expanded most quickly near the Côtes du Rhône, and since the late 1950s its vineyards have increased from almost nothing to nearly 2,200 hectares. They are set in parched countryside east of the Rhône between Montélimar and Bollène, with their centre at Les Granges-Gontardes, a hamlet near Donzère.

The *appellation* is covered by thirteen Caves Co-opératives and twenty-five private growers, only about half of whom actually bottle their wine. The rest sell to *négociants*.

Tricastin's main areas of production are Les Granges-Gontardes, La Baume-de-Transit, Roussas, Malataverne, Allan, Valaurie, Donzère and Grignan. All are tiny, very quiet communities that in some cases had become almost derelict before the increase in vine-growing. Les Granges-Gontardes, for instance, was a village that had lost its school, its shop and almost all its inhabitants to the nearby factories until some enthusiastic wine growers arrived in 1964. The three or four families that went there at that time had been French settlers in Algeria, forced to leave the country after the granting of independence. Receiving favourable terms from the public authorities and agricultural banks, they proceeded to reclaim much of the wooded countryside around Donzère and Les Granges-Gontardes.

This land was generally poor and mostly supported thick masses of small oaks, pine bushes and lavender plants. It was also a renowned centre for black truffles, which have a definite preference for the sturdy little oak trees of the Tricastin. Even the truffle industry was in sharp decline, however. Before 1900 the local yield had been around 2,000 tonnes a year; after the First World War, many young men never returned to continue the tradition, and now the average annual yield is no more than 100 tonnes.

In 1964 Coteaux du Tricastin was promoted to *VDQS* (*Vin Délimité de Qualité Supérieure*) status, and at the same time large-scale replantation commenced on ground that had not held vines since phylloxera. The choice of vines was made with almost scientific care and precision; some of the vineyards were model examples, their vines being selected according to various climatic and soil factors that had been closely analysed.

The pattern that emerged copied the general format of Château-neuf-du-Pape, particularly because many of the new vineyards had been created on similarly stony ground. In places no earth at all is visible among the vines, and the effect of such ground – to give the grapes extra heat – is just as at Châteauneuf-du-Pape. Accordingly, the vines chosen were the Grenache (50–60 per cent), the Cinsault (about 15 per cent), the Syrah (about 20 per cent), the Mourvèdre and the Carignan. The latter, a high producer, was to be planted as little as possible.

Around Tricastin the *mistral* wind reaches some of its fastest speeds – over 100 kph on occasions – and this directly influences the working of the vineyards. Thus the vines have to be trained against strong 1.2-metre stakes that need to be firmly hammered into the stone-covered ground. When snow is in the offing – and it is not un-common – the *vigneron* can do very little to protect his vineyards: any straw put down among the vines is promptly blown away by the *mistral*.

The *vendanges* last from around mid-September into October, and the red wines are generally given only a brief vinification; after crushing and destalking, the grapes are fermented for four to six days, and most of the wine is then stored in concrete vats for several months before bottling. The wine sold off in bulk to *négociants* all over France will leave the cellars more quickly, however, normally within three or four months of the harvest.

The best-known *domaines* at Tricastin are two of the oldest: the Domaine de la Tour d'Elyssas, with its two *crus*, Le Devoy and Les Echirousses, and the Domaine de Grangeneuve at Roussas. The Domaine de la Tour d'Elyssas was started in 1966 by the late M. Pierre Labeye and became immediately memorable for its vast 15-metre-high circular tower that housed the fermenting vats in spectacular style next to the cellars. The locals had never seen anything like it, but, alas, M. Labeye's futurism was undone by one of the world's recessions, and the 105-hectare property was put into the hands of the receiver in late 1981, though it is still making wine.

The *domaine* sells about 200,000 bottles a year, including the two *crus* already mentioned, a pure Syrah wine and some rosé. Most interesting is the Syrah wine, since it has greater depth and length of finish than either of the light-styled *crus*. Nevertheless, all are good drinking wines; they should not be kept for more than about three years.

The Domaine de Grangeneuve at Roussas and the Domaine des Lones at St-Paul-les-Trois-Châteaux are owned by Mme Odette Bour, a widow who is helped by her two attractive daughters in the running of the properties. Repatriates from Algeria, the Bours planted their vineyards in 1965 and started bottling their wine in 1974; the Grangeneuve wine comes from about 100 hectares of vines made up of 50 per cent Grenache, 30 per cent Syrah and 20 per cent mixed between Cinsault, Mourvèdre and Carignan, the last-named grape being used in the rather unimpressive rosé. Their red wine – 95 per cent of their production – is the best at Tricastin, one that fully justifies the decision in 1974 to award full *appellation* status to this area. It carries a deeper red colour than the wine of Elyssas and greater profundity of flavour. Certainly the presence of more Syrah than usual is evident, for this is the most complex and best perfumed wine in the *appellation*. It is fermented in stainless steel after the grapes have been crushed in the normal way and goes out for sale about a year after the harvest. Its tannin level is then still quite pronounced, and it is better to drink the wine when it is between two and three years old.

There is generally an interesting concentration of flavour and extract in the best Tricastins; other *domaines* to note are the Domaine du Serre Rouge of the Brachet family, the Château La Décelle with an excellent Syrah *cuvée*, and the Domaine St-Luc of Ludovic Cornillon, who used to be a ladies' hairdresser: as Jacques Dupont of the Gault Millau wine magazine wittily put it – 'at least one can be sure his vines are well pruned'.

Meanwhile the style of most Tricastin wines resembles that of the nearest Côtes du Rhône wines from Suze-la-Rousse and Rochegude, which are themselves soft and easy to drink. Only rarely are these wines aged in wood – some *cuvées* from the Domaine de la Tour d'Elyssas and the Cellier des Templiers Cave Co-opérative at Richer-enches spend a few months in cask – and with more and more private *domaines* beginning to bottle their wine, a greater variety of approach will no doubt be noted in the coming years.

Barely 5 per cent of the annual production is rosé, and this is noticeably inferior to the red wine. A tiny amount of white wine is also made, based on the Grenache Blanc, Clairette, Picpoul, Bourboulenc and Ugni Blanc, but it is only of passing interest.

The years 1985, 1988, 1989 and 1990 were by and large good ones at Tricastin. As a rule the wines of Tricastin are made to be drunk before they are two or three years old, although the best *cuvées*, aged in cask or made from pure Syrah, can live for up to six years.

In the 1990s the main problem facing this *appellation* will be its *rentabilité*, or viability. The growers face the same overheads as those in the Côtes du Rhône, but the fetching price of Tricastin in bulk can be 50 per cent lower than Côtes du Rhône. Should Tricastin become part of the Côtes du Rhône?

The alternative, already adopted by growers like Jean-Pierre Forge of Domaine de l'Orgeat at Monboucher-sur-Jabron and the well-regarded Domaine du Rieu-Frais of Jean-Yves Liotaud at Ste-Jalle, is to step outside the mainstream system, much as many modern-thinking wine-growers have in Italy. They make single varietal wines from grapes like Cabernet Sauvignon, Syrah, Chardonnay and Viognier; M. Liotaud's 20-hectare *domaine* produces its wines under the Coteaux des Baronnies *appellation*.

Leading Growers in the Coteaux du Tricastin

Almoric	26 Allan
Berthet, Paul	84290 Cairanne
Berthet-Rayne, Père et Fils	26290 Donzère
Bour, Mme Odette	
Domaine de Grangeneuve	26230 Roussas
Boyer, Philip	26130 Suze-la-Rousse
Brachet, Jean et Fils	
Domaine du Serre Rouge	26230 Valaurie
Cave Co-opérative Le Cellier	
des Templiers	84600 Richerenches
Cave Co-opérative Vinicole de	
Rochegude	26130 Rochegude
Co-opérative Vinicole	
La Suzienne	26130 Suze-la-Rousse
Les Caves de Montbrison	26230 Montbrison
Le Cellier des Dauphins	26130 Tulette
Cornillon, Ludovic	
Domaine St-Luc	26130 La Baume-de-Transit
Domaine de la Tour d'Elyssas	26290 Les Granges-Gontardes
Estève, Jean-Pierre	
Domaine du Bois Noir	26130 La Baume-de-Transit
Étienne, Gaston et Fils	
Domaine Ste-Agnes	26 Malataverne
Feschet, Robert	26130 Bouchet

Jalifier, Jacques
   Domaine de Raspail   26130 La Baume-de-Transit
Pommier, Hubert
   Domaine La Curate   26 Malataverne
Roth-Morel
   Les Estubiers   26290 Les Granges-Gontardes
Roux, Mme Renée   26130 La Baume-de-Transit
Seroin, A.M. et H.
   Château La Décelle   26130 St-Paul Trois Châteaux
Le Terroir St-Rémy   26130 La Baume-de-Transit
Truffaut, Pierre   26 Malataverne
Vergoby Frères   26290 Les Granges-Gontardes

CÔTES DU VENTOUX

The extensive Côtes du Ventoux vineyards, numbering around 7,000 hectares, are situated along the southern flank of the massive Mont Ventoux (1,770 metres), and are mostly spread out over several communities that run in two lines across the south of the mountain. The upper line, composed of Caromb, Bédoin and Flassan, is nearest the mountain and is separated from the other villages, Mazan, Mormoiron, and Villes St-Auzon, by a sweeping 8-kilometre-wide valley that contains row upon row of wine grapes, table grapes and cherry trees. North of these, near Malaucène, Beaumont-du-Ventoux also makes a little Côtes du Ventoux as do Pernes-les-Fontaines, St-Didier and Apt further south below Carpentras.

The Ventoux countryside possesses an unrestrained natural beauty, and its villages are some of the least changed of the Vaucluse *département* that runs east of the Rhône. The area has a long-established tradition as a centre of table-grape growing, with the Muscat eating grape a speciality, but it has attracted greater attention through its red, rosé and white wines, which were promoted to full *appellation contrôlée* status in 1974.

The style of these wines is surprisingly out of keeping with those from the nearby Côtes du Rhône vineyards, for they are invariably much lighter in colour and flavour. The grapes used in the wines' making are much the same as usual – Grenache, Carignan (maximum 30 per cent), Cinsault, Syrah and Mourvèdre – but they are in places grown at altitudes of 400 metres or more. While these grapes will not ripen up as well as those growing down on the plain, they cannot be considered responsible for the wines' lightness. It may be more a question of the soil composition and/or the vinification. The soil varies sharply all over the *appellation* area, ranging between gravel, sand, clay and chalk.

The vinification of the Ventoux wines can be somewhat contentious. Many of the *vignerons* have always made their wine *en café* and see no good reason why they should change. Vinification *en café* consists of a speedy, forty-eight-hour fermentation, a brief rest period in the vat and an early release for sale. Wines made in this way live up to their title: they are very pale, barely darker than rosé, low in alcohol (the minimum degree is 11°) and have no tannins or depth to make them anything other than good for swigging back on a shaded café terrace. 'Uncomplicated' is how some connoisseurs might describe them, but sadly this seems to miss the point. Wines of a similar nature are made in many parts of Languedoc and the Midi, and in the one-night vinification form they are so one-dimensional and boring that it is surprising they were considered worthy of their own *appellation* as long ago as 1974.

The sixteen Caves Co-opératives account for around 90 per cent of the wine. There are only around twenty private growers, and their wines are interesting, for as much as anything they show the differences in the mentality of the growers: one of the most thoughtful wine-makers in Ventoux is certainly Jean-Pierre Perrin, who, as the son of the late and very respected M. Jacques Perrin of Château de Beaucastel at Châteauneuf-du-Pape, has had a first-class grounding in wine-making. Jean-Pierre sells a branded wine called La Vieille Ferme, and talked about its origins and current composition: 'The Vieille Ferme as a property does not exist; I am merely a *négociant* buying grapes and young wines that I blend together in my cellars near Jonquières in order to make one uniform red wine. I used to buy grapes from the Côtes du Rhône in order to make a Vieille Ferme Côtes du Rhône but switched to the Côtes du Ventoux in 1976 when grape prices in the Rhône rose too steeply. Since then I have never been back to the Rhône.

'The Ventoux provides me with grapes that are ideal for making a fresh wine for good early drinking; the only problem, in fact, is that the grapes produce wines that seem to oxidize quite young. Strangely, it is the tannins that oxidize, unlike Côtes du Rhône, in which it is the alcohol that oxidizes first.'

M. Perrin started the Vieille Ferme in 1971, with the intention of making what he called an 'everyday wine', and so successful has his marketing technique been that he is now selling 800,000 bottles a year, of which almost half go abroad, mainly to the United States, Britain and Germany. His Vieille Ferme red Ventoux is a wine that shows up well the inclusion of up to 30 per cent Syrah, since it carries an attractive bright colour and crisp, clean fruitiness that becomes soft and appealing by its third year. It is certainly one of the best wines in the *appellation*, a long way ahead of some of the abominations produced by the indifferent Co-opératives.

Another man who makes better wine than most of the Co-opératives is an English exile, Malcolm Swan, who cultivates around 17 hectares of vines near Mormoiron. He renounced the world of advertising for his vineyard and took over the Domaine des Anges in 1973. His red wine is made from the Grenache, Syrah, Carignan and Cinsault grapes, partly traditionally and partly by *macération carbonique*. His early vintages were made in the style of fresh, easy-to-drink *cuvées*; but cash, or lack of it, is a great brake on man's ambitions, and that is why his 30-hectare property is still not fully planted with vines – and that is why Mr Swan still yearns to make some strong, keeping wines here.

His method is sound, however, and the colour and body of his wine are strong enough to place it in the top three of the *appellation*, and far above much of the wine found in the majority of the Co-opératives, which have an alarming tendency to harvest every single grape and quite a bit of their foliage too. The Domaine des Anges red has improved steadily over the past ten years as the vineyard has grown up, and now is solid, well extracted and very good to drink around three years old. There are slight traces of tannin in it, which show the resisters in some of the Co-opératives what the region can do with an open mind, effort and skill.

Another excellent producer, operating since only 1988, is Claude Fonquerle of the Château de Valcombe, a 15-hectare *domaine* at St-Pierre-de-Vassols which lies between Bédoin and Caromb. The red is made from 80 per cent Grenache and 10 per cent Cinsault and Syrah, the Syrah entering the vats in the *raisin entier* form to extract extra fruitiness. The wine has good depth, and in a strong and successful vintage like 1989 takes about three years to shake off some of its tannin and more raw edge. There is vibrant fruitiness in it, and it is light years ahead of most of the Ventoux wines – again, it is helped by its depth and substance. M. Fonquerle also makes rosé (70 per cent Cinsault, 30 per cent Grenache) and white (30 per cent Grenache Blanc, 30 per cent Ugni Blanc and 40 per cent Bourboulenc). These, like the good, full reds and whites of Christian Gélys Domaine de Champ-Long at Entrechaux are well worth seeking out.

One of the other private growers, M. Guy Rey of Aubignan, makes a wine similar in style to Mr Swan's, and it too is perfectly drinkable without being very exciting. A fourth grower, M. Paul Coutelen of Flassan, has a different approach in that he ferments his wine for a week and then ages it in a cask for about one year. This sounds very fine, but, as mentioned by Jean-Pierre Perrin, the red wine of Ventoux has a natural tendency to oxidize early and seems unable to resist such ageing. As a result, many of M. Coutelen's wines have a perceptible 'woody' taste that overruns all their fruit and flavour. Paul Jaboulet of Hermitage, finally, is another very reliable supplier of good, more substantial Côtes du Ventoux. Among the Co-opératives, Mormoiron's Les Roches Blanches is one of the best, and innovative as well. It has been producing a good pure Syrah *cuvée* now for some years. Other Co-opératives emerging as makers of sound wines are St-Didier's La Courtoise and the Cave de Lumières at Goult.

About a quarter of the wine is rosé, although in some vintages the colour of some of the reds is barely darker than that of the rosés. They are vinified with just a rapid stay on the skins to extract some colour and can prove quite satisfactory, the Co-opératives of Bédoin, Mormoiron and St-Didier producing some of the best – attractive, featherweight wines that should be drunk well chilled; they go well with Chinese food. A very little white wine is made too, generally from the Clairette, Ugni Blanc and Bourboulenc grapes. It is not an interesting wine, although the Cave Co-opérative of Mazan makes a respectable *cuvée*.

Estate-bottled Côtes du Ventoux is not very easy to find, since several of the Co-opératives are unwilling to take on the extra burden of bottling and selling much of their own wine. Consequently, the wine is sold mainly to *négociants* inside and outside France and as a result may often reach its final destination with an unusually strong, attractive dark red colour. The best thing that can happen to Ventoux in the early 1990s is that more and more Co-opératives beef up their wines and move away from the 'one-night wine' tag.

Leading Growers in the Côtes du Ventoux

Cave Co-opérative d'Apt	84400 Apt
Cave Co-opérative de Canteperdrix	84380 Mazan
Cave Co-opérative des Coteaux du Mont Ventoux	84410 Bédoin
Cave Co-opérative de la Montagne Rouge	84570 Villes-St-Auzon
Cave Co-opérative Les Roches Blanches	84570 Mormoiron
Cave de Lumières	84220 Goult
Cave Vinicole La Pernoise	84210 Pernes-les-Fontaines
Cave Vinicole St-Marc	84330 Caromb
Co-opérative Intercommunale La Courtoise	84210 St-Didier
Co-opérative Vinicole de Beaumont-du-Ventoux	84340 Beaumont-du-Ventoux
Co-opérative Vinicole du Lubéron	84 Maubec
Combe, Philippe Domaine de Tenon	84150 Violès
Coutelen, Paul	84 Flassan
Fonquerle, Claude Château de Valcombe	84330 St-Pierre-de-Vassols
GAEC Aymard	84200 Carpentras
Gély, Christian Domaine de Champ-Long	84340 Entrechaux
Maubert, et Fils Domaine de la Verrière	84220 Goult
D'Ollone Domaine de Champaga	84330 Le Barroux
Quiot, J. Château du Vieux-Lazaret	84230 Châteauneuf-du-Pape
Rey, Guy Domaine St-Sauveur	84190 Aubignan
Ribas, Augustin	84330 Caromb
Soulard, J. Domaine Ste-Croix	84220 Gordes
Swan, Malcolm Domaine des Anges	84570 Mormoiron

CÔTES DU VIVARAIS

The Côtes du Vivarais wine area is set in the Ardèche *département*, on the west side of the Rhône. It is a wild, picturesque region, whose natural wonders have always been better known than its wine; the centrepiece is the giant canyon of the Ardèche – 'les Gorges de l'Ardèche' – that runs in a jagged line south-east to join up with the Rhône near Pont-St-Esprit. All around there are woods and little hamlets, interspersed by sudden-plunging caves and grottoes, some of the deepest in France. Beside them race fast-flowing streams and rivers full of delicious trout and pike.

The Ardèche's natural beauty and unchanged way of life have over the years brought it wide popularity as a holiday region. As a result, its unpretentious country wines have become considerably better-known. The best of them are the Côtes du Vivarais and some of the top Ardèche *vin de pays* made from grapes like the Syrah and the Cabernet Sauvignon, which have proliferated since the early 1980s in the hands of producers like Les Vignerons Ardèchois at Ruoms (planters of Sauvignon Blanc, Merlot, Cabernet Sauvignon as well as Rhône varieties) and La Cévenne Ardèchoise at St-Didier-sous-Aubenas (producers of pure Merlot, Pinot Noir, Chardonnay and Viognier among others).

The Côtes du Vivarais runs to around 850 hectares; it has no 'capital' town of its own and is made up of a collection of scattered villages that run in a broad circle around the Gorges de l'Ardèche: Viviers is the most northerly point, and Pont St-Esprit the most southerly. The principal vineyards lie around Orgnac, St-Remèze, St-Montan, Vinezac, Ruoms, Barjac and Gras. All possess their own Caves Co-opératives.

Until the trend to planting much higher grade vines from all over France started, most of the local wine here was sold as straight-forward *vin de consommation courante*. This is made from a mixture of 'noble' and hybrid grapes, its production per hectare is high (about 75 hectolitres), and it is usually drunk a few months after the harvest, at a price dictated by its alcohol strength. Light and ordinary, it is the sort of wine found in the fridge of any French café.

The Vivarais wines are more regulated, according to both grape variety and volume of yield. They follow the general pattern of the Côtes du Rhône *générique* wines, however, and are made from a combination of grapes headed by the Grenache, Cinsault, Syrah and Carignan. Sometimes a little Gamay is included.

The red and rosé wines must contain at least 11° alcohol by volume, and their production is restricted to around 4,500 litres per hectare. The Caves Co-opératives who make them have no false pretensions about their wines: they seek to make light, refreshing wines that are easy to drink and easy to understand. Consequently, fermentation is brief, for between four and eight days, and the red wine is normally bottled before the start of the summer. When well vinified, it is an agreeably fruity wine, one that should be drunk rather than sipped and which benefits from being served chilled. The rosés are less good as a rule, sometimes tasting hard and metallic, while the white wine of Vivarais is often overshadowed by the light but clean-tasting Ardèche Chardonnays of producers like Louis Latour, the top-class Burgundy house whose interest in the Ardèche goes back to the late 1970s.

Two private growers distinguish themselves here, and have been early suppliers of estate-bottled Vivarais, thereby helping the name to gain greater profile. Christian Gallety produces Côtes du Vivarais from 10 hectares planted with about half Grenache, supported by young plantations of Syrah, which replaced his Cinsault, Carignan and Clairette. These grow in clay soil covered in broken stones, and the style of the wine is direct – fruit is sought through *macération carbonique*. M. Gallety's white is made from 100 per cent Clairette.

Hervé Boulle makes some Côtes du Vivarais and Coteaux de l'Ardèche, much of which is contracted to go to the Netherlands.

About 35,000 hectolitres of Côtes du Vivarais wines are made every year, and the best Co-opératives are at Orgnac l'Aven, St-Didier and Ruoms, while one of the best *négociants* for these simple country wines is Salavert at Bourg-St-Andéol.

Leading Growers in the Côtes du Vivarais

Boulle, Hervé
Brunel, Léon   }   07700 St-Remèze
    Domaine du Belvezet
Cave Co-opérative de Vallon
    Pont d'Arc   07150 Vallon Pont d'Arc
Cave Co-opérative des Coteaux   07110 Vinezac

Cave Co-opérative d'Orgnac l'Aven	07150 Orgnac
Co-opérative Vinicole	07220 St-Montan
La Cévenne Ardèchoise	07200 St-Didier-sous-Aubenas
Les Vignerons Ardèchois	07120 Ruoms
Marron, André	07150 Vallon Pont d'Arc

Appendices

═══════

APPENDIX 1. The 'Appellation Contrôlée' Laws

Note: 1 hectolitre (hl) per hectare = approximately 54 bottles per acre.

In years of abundant harvest the *appellations* have until 1992 been permitted to submit wine in excess of the maximum yield to a tasting panel, which decides whether the quality is sufficiently high for the extra wine to be allowed *appellation contrôlée* status. Thus, for instance, Côte-Rôtie has been permitted to sell up to 15 per cent above its 40 hectolitres per hectare limit, Condrieu up to 10 per cent above. Known as the *droit de dérogation*, this is set to be dropped in favour of applications for extra *appellation* wine on an individual, or *domaine-by-domaine* basis. While the intention is to ensure controlled yields and therefore continuing quality as France faces a drop in the consumption of fine wines, an individual application system sounds like a recipe for anarchy.

BEAUMES-DE-VENISE

Vin doux naturel, or sweet fortified wine allowed.
Maximum yield: 30 hl per hectare.
Minimum degree: 15° of natural alcohol.

CHÂTEAU-GRILLET

White wine only allowed.
Maximum yield: 37 hl per hectare.
Dérogation: 10 per cent.
Minimum degree: 11°.

CHÂTEAUNEUF-DU-PAPE

Red and white wines allowed.
Maximum yield: 35 hl per hectare.
Minimum degree: 12.5°.

CONDRIEU

White wine only allowed.
Maximum yield: 37 hl per hectare.
Dérogation: 10 per cent.
Minimum degree: 11°.

CORNAS

Red wine only allowed.
Maximum yield: 40 hl per hectare.
Dérogation: 10 per cent.
Minimum degree: 10.5°.

CÔTE-RÔTIE

Red wine only allowed.
Maximum yield: 40 hl per hectare.
Dérogation: 15 per cent.
Minimum degree: 10°.

CÔTES DU RHÔNE

Red, white and rosé wines allowed.
Maximum yield: 52 hl per hectare.
Minimum degree: 11°.

CÔTES DU RHÔNE VILLAGES

Red, white and rosé wines allowed.
Maximum yield: 42 hl per hectare.
Minimum degree: 12.5° for the red wines; 12° for the white and rosé
wines.

CROZES-HERMITAGE

Red and white wines allowed.
Maximum yield: 40 hl per hectare.
Dérogation: 15 per cent.
Minimum degree: 10°.

GIGONDAS

Red and rosé wines allowed.
Maximum yield: 35 hl per hectare.
Minimum degree: 12.5°.

HERMITAGE

Red and white wines allowed.
Maximum yield: 40 hl per hectare.
Dérogation: 15 per cent.
Minimum degree: 10.5° for the red wines; 11° for the white wines;
14° for the *vin de paille*.

LIRAC

Red, rosé and white wines allowed.
Maximum yield: 35 hl per hectare.
Dérogation: 20 per cent.
Minimum degree: 11.5°.

RASTEAU

Vin doux naturel, or sweet fortified wine allowed.
Maximum yield: 35 hl per hectare.
Minimum degree: 15° of natural alcohol.

ST-JOSEPH

Red and white wines allowed.
Maximum yield: 40 hl per hectare.
Dérogation: 15° per cent.
Minimum degree: 10°.

ST-PÉRAY

Sparkling and still white wines only allowed.
Maximum yield: 45 hl per hectare.
Dérogation: 15 per cent.
Minimum degree: 10° for still wines; 9° for sparkling wines.

TAVEL

Rosé wine only allowed.
Maximum yield: 48 hl per hectare.
Dérogation: 15 per cent.
Minimum degree: 11°.

VACQUEYRAS

Red, rosé and white wine allowed.
Maximum yield: 35 hl per hectare.
Minimum degree: 12.5°.

APPENDIX 2. Table of Vineyard Surface Areas

(In hectares, to the nearest hectare)

VINEYARD	1971	1973	1982	1989
Côtes du Rhône (including Côtes du Rhône Villages)	30,224	33,579	36,538	46,600
Beaumes-de-Venise VDN	158	185	233	—
Château-Grillet	1.7	2.7 (1977)	3	3.8 (1991)
Châteauneuf-du-Pape	2,950	3,080	3,077	3,315
Condrieu	12	12	14	40
Cornas	53	75	67	65
Côte-Rôtie	70	72	102	135
Crozes-Hermitage	454	550	903	1,050
Gigondas	946	990	1,154	1,181
Hermitage	123	123	123	125
Lirac	250	717	617	763
Rasteau VDN	135	135	111	—
St-Joseph	97	122	245	540
St-Péray	56	56	48	65
Tavel	660	720	759	946

APPENDIX 3. Declaration of the Crop (*Récolte*) for all Côtes du Rhône 'Appellations'

(In hectolitres)

Region	1970	1971	1972	1973	1974
Beaumes-de-Venise	4,403	4,441	3,403	5,172	5,113
Château-Grillet	65	47	28	84	87
Châteauneuf-du-Pape	91,700	92,792	71,398	98,472	80,499
Condrieu	138	142	66	206	122
Cornas	1,787	1,022	1,145	2,029	1,586
Côte-Rôtie	2,355	1,562	1,428	2,927	1,831
Côtes du Rhône	1,167,216	1,047,947	1,154,487	1,363,784	1,260,761
Côtes du Rhône Villages	68,882	115,496	69,283	154,506	70,277
Crozes-Hermitage	19,542	13,203	19,768	27,997	21,044
Gigondas	31,250	26,850	26,634	30,601	26,753
Hermitage	5,576	3,128	3,356	4,108	3,859
Lirac	14,644	16,786	13,870	24,404	11,724
Rasteau VDN	3,718	3,096	2,723	2,803	2,335
St-Joseph	3,145	1,821	1,962	4,093	4,310
St-Péray	1,453	1,458	1,183	1,447	1,716
Tavel	24,734	26,983	21,841	28,055	28,722

Region	1975	1976	1977	1978	1979
Beaumes-de-Venise	3,294	5,185	4,604	6,922	6,304
Château-Grillet	40	87	63	29	97
Châteauneuf-du-Pape	62,660	93,333	86,466	90,398	98,873
Condrieu	105	176	115	96	298
Cornas	810	1,424	1,354	1,551	1,854
Côte-Rôtie	1,468	2,132	2,108	3,077	4,128
Côtes du Rhône	991,638	1,514,862	1,538,189	1,538,346	1,504,386
Côtes du Rhône Villages	79,394	68,728	65,241	109,263	133,482
Crozes-Hermitage	17,748	20,014	17,584	27,106	34,387
Gigondas	17,503	27,729	23,166	31,416	33,946
Hermitage	2,022	3,304	3,159	3,136	4,895
Lirac	10,704	10,077	10,741	16,175	21,843
Rasteau VDN	1,722	2,363	1,087	3,099	5,087
St-Joseph	2,188	4,684	3,812	5,726	8,492
St-Péray	880	1,447	1,646	1,061	1,423
Tavel	19,971	28,426	29,161	30,624	34,788

Region	1980	1981	1983	1984	1985
Beaumes-de-Venise	7,562	6,597	1,627	9,267	10,459
Château-Grillet	116	75	85	114	53
Châteauneuf-du-Pape	101,033	86,394	137,385	79,878	109,319
Condrieu	363	310	181	622	499
Cornas	1,894	1,718	2,132	1,699	1,731

Côte-Rôtie	3,378	4,185	4,460	3,516	2,631
Côtes du Rhône	1,697,963	1,411,450	970,499	1,722,751	2,020,000
Côtes du Rhône Villages	101,420	118,982	163,801	134,510	143,904
Crozes-Hermitage	40,783	33,541	44,556	38,222	39,509
Gigondas	37,116	30,460	43,948	32,172	39,866
Hermitage	4,582	4,093	3,658	3,999	4,340
Lirac	20,088	17,183	24,796	17,197	16,299
Rasteau VDN	4,120	3,896	8,944	2,726	3,373
St-Joseph	8,426	10,272	15,044	12,411	13,542
St-Péray	1,981	2,053	2,681	2,003	1,810
Tavel	35,411	30,098	19,633	36,552	38,642

Region	1986	1987	1988	1989	1990
Beaumes-de-Venise	9,462	9,834	10,705	—	
Château-Grillet	91	97	57	78	158
Châteauneuf-du-Pape	104,727	94,867	106,914	106,597	105,447
Condrieu	894	822	688	1,183	1,711
Cornas	2,858	2,615	2,420	3,082	3,059
Côte-Rôtie	3,803	4,092	4,984	6,952	4,461
Côtes du Rhône	1,998,663	2,007,369	2,059,696	2,225,709	2,109,201
Côtes du Rhône Villages	221,000	178,250	147,010	153,746	203,946
Crozes-Hermitage	41,161	40,026	44,290	51,148	49,517
Gigondas	37,622	35,273	36,993	40,838	41,281
Hermitage	4,340	6,180	5,010	5,373	5,361
Lirac	20,353	21,162	19,198	18,837	22,084
Rasteau VDN	896	884	949	—	—
St-Joseph	17,531	18,303	17,613	22,203	22,833
St-Péray	2,789	3,167	2,097	2,626	2,784
Tavel	38,343	41,212	41,127	38,175	41,658
Vacqueyras				9,500	26,355

APPENDIX 4. Exports

A. Côtes du Rhône Exports

Year	Volume (hectolitres)	Value (francs)
1965	122,278	34,094,000
1968	170,204	46,307,000
1969	185,380	55,256,000
1970	191,416	73,623,000
1971	231,029	89,415,000
1972	271,897	123,064,000
1973	352,256	169,569,000
1974	364,598	160,649,000
1975	418,025	171,485,000
1976	368,637	198,164,000
1977	374,907	254,756,000
1978	392,685	313,467,000
1979	451,804	354,042,000
1980	516,282	377,274,000
1981	602,365	462,039,000
1982	541,900	553,910,000
1983	584,293	590,687,000
1984	599,134	661,157,000
1985	605,186	737,253,000
1986	667,403	803,190,000
1987	685,086	856,919,000
1988	669,749	889,425,000
1989	673,465	938,722,000
1990	619,776	932,961,000
1991	632,512	907,915,000

B. French Appellation Wine Exports

		Volume in hectolitres		
Region	*1976*	*1978*	*1980*	*1990*
Anjou (Loire)	211,658	190,283	188,397	233,018
Beaujolais	328,942	384,991	474,918	581,429
Burgundy	388,114	434,314	354,019	514,964
Côtes du Rhône	368,637	392,685	516,282	619,776
Alsace	129,351	172,086	166,207	336,283
Bordeaux	1,072,280	1,072,280	1,230,500	1,802,963
Others (AC except Champagne)	247,951	383,774	502,498	1,394,856
Provence				111,139
Muscadet				238,722

C. Leading Côtes du Rhône Export Countries (volume in hectolitres)

Years	Switzerland	Belg/Lux	UK	Netherlands	West Germany	Canada	USA	Denmark	Sweden	Japan	EEC
1951	11,573	4,445	1,738	391	6,620	—	957	—	29	—	
1959	18,841	8,508	1,999	1,591	18,962	292	4,540	1,150	1,422	71	
1961	26,375	10,749	2,141	2,114	16,749	550	6,639	2,833	2,909	40	
1966	50,071	19,319	7,550	4,223	19,534	1,127	12,852	4,191	5,257	59	
1971	93,027	28,304	14,613	7,111	25,398	3,827	22,825	10,736	5,802	419	
1976	137,974	49,685	24,213	26,409	31,365	9,734	24,049	22,748	17,187	906	
1981	177,303	104,351	55,043	61,327	68,235	21,965	24,005	36,781	20,192	1,458	
1985	153,583	76,224	82,953	75,832	66,749	37,517	32,264	25,150	12,515	3,478	
1986	163,437	87,626	95,614	94,779	79,755	33,564	26,204	20,464	15,631	5,423	
1987	162,882	91,957	99,485	95,887	87,483	32,325	23,094	25,614	16,137	4,933	
1988	137,247	92,805	111,048	93,345	92,115	26,484	23,651	23,499	14,435	8,291	
1989	158,891	90,546	109,021	89,212	81,455	34,314	22,794	17,018	14,147	7,416	392,233
1990	137,585	95,854	108,459	81,172	83,175	26,290	22,833	12,192	11,591	6,429	376,328
1991	138,552	92,266	117,216	94,072	83,834	23,811	19,159	12,632	8,677	4,979	404,735

APPENDIX 5. Calendar of Wine Fairs Held in the Region of the Côtes du Rhône

Around 20 January: Orange (Vaucluse) – tasting competition of young wines. Gold, silver and bronze medals are given, and the Foire acts as a guide to the quality of the new vintage.

Around 20 January: Ampuis (Rhône) – public fair of the wines of Côte-Rôtie, with some wines of Condrieu present as well.

Around 25 April: Châteauneuf-du-Pape (Vaucluse) – *fête* of St Marc (patron of the village).

Around end of April: Tavel (Gard) – *fête* of St Vincent (patron of *vignerons*).

Around end of May: Vacqueyras (Vaucluse) – *fête* of the Côtes du Rhône Villages.

Around end of May: Roquemaure (Gard) – public fair of the wines of the *cru* of Lirac.

Around July/August: Orange (Vaucluse) – permanent exhibition in the grottoes of the Antique Theatre of the wines of the Côtes du Rhône.

Around end of July: Côtes du Rhône Villages fair. Held in a different village every year.

Around 15/25 September: Châteauneuf-du-Pape (Vaucluse) – *Ban des Vendanges*.

Around 3rd Sunday in September: fair and wine competition at Tain-l'Hermitage.

Around mid-November: Vaison-la-Romaine (Vaucluse) – tasting of Côtes du Rhône *primeur* wines.

Around 7 December: Cornas (Ardèche) – public fair of the wines of the Syrah and Roussette.

APPENDIX 6. Other Labels ('Sous Marques') used by leading Côtes-du-Rhône Négociants

M. Chapoutier: Delapine
Delas Frères: Forrestier
Paul Jaboulet Ainé: Jaboulet-Isnard and André Passat
Pascal: Charles Pax

Glossary

═══

APPELLATION D'ORIGINE CONTRÔLÉE   The certificate of authenticity of wines of a high quality: such wines must conform to certain strict rules in order to merit the status. The word *appellation* by itself often refers to a specific vineyard area – e.g. Côte-Rôtie, Tavel, Gigondas, etc.

BAN DES VENDANGES   Public proclamation of the start of the harvest.

BARRIQUE   The name commonly used in Bordeaux for their small ageing-casks of about 220 litres

BENEAU   A grape harvest holder, made either of wood or, more commonly, plastic.

BIGOT   A special hoe used in the northern Rhône vineyards.

BONBONNE   A large glass jug, stoppered with a flat, wide cork, used for holding bulk drinking wine. An average capacity is 10–15 litres.

BOULES   The steel balls that are used in the target game of *pétanque*; also the name of the game itself.

CAVISTE   A cellar worker.

CHALAIS   Dried stone terrace.

CHAPEAU   The top of fermenting grapes, mainly skins and pips.

CLAIE   A straw or cane mat. Often used in making *vin de paille* (q.v.)

CLIMAT   A named section within a vineyard.

CÔTE   Slope; when used to designate a wine, as in Côtes du Rhône or Côtes de Beaune, the word usually refers to the most basic quality of wine made in its region.

COTEAU   Hillside; *demi-coteau* is a gentle incline, and is a term often used in the sweeping southern Côtes du Rhône wine area.

COULURE   Malformation of the fruit at the time of flowering, often in May. The vine's bunches remain partially formed. The Grenache suffers especially.

CRU   Growth; in the Côtes du Rhône it commonly describes a grower's best wine.

CUVE   A vat.

CUVÉE   After *assemblage*, or the assembly of different vats, a final integrated wine. *Tête de cuvée* represents the very best wine which a grower makes in any one year.

DÉROGATION   The right to sell under the full *appellation contrôlée* label wine that is in excess of the statutory quantity allowed.

EAU-DE-VIE   Distilled alcohol spirit. *Eau-de-vie de marc* refers to the spirit taken from the distilled grape *marcs* (q.v.) left over after fermentation.

ÉGRAPPAGE   The destalking of the grapes prior to fermentation.

FOUDRE   A large cask used for maturing the wine.

FOULAGE   The crushing of the grapes before fermentation.

GÉNÉRIQUE   Generic, or a wine of the most basic *appellation contrôlée* category, such as Côtes du Rhône.

GIBIER   Game, as in birds and beasts. A tasting term to denote a 'high' smell.

GOÛT DE TERROIR   Literally, earthy taste. It really means a profound, very 'thick' flavour in a wine that is thought to be drawn from the soil composition of its vineyards.

GRAIN   A single grape.

INAO   Institut National des Appellations d'Origine. The State-sponsored body which manages the *appellation* system in France.

INOX   Stainless steel.

LIEU-DIT   A place name within the vineyards of an *appellation*, often derived from an historical anecdote or legend.

LIQUEUR DE TIRAGE   A blend of sugar and yeasts, which is added to wine at the moment it is bottled to encourage a further fermentation.

MAISON DU VIN   A wine house: it often indicates an owner of vineyards who doubles as a merchant in other wines.

MAÎTRE DE CHAI   A cellar master.

MARC   The crushed leftovers of the pulp after it has been pressed. It is composed mainly of skins, pips and stalks and is often distilled to produce grape-flavoured spirit.

MÉTHODE CHAMPENOISE   Wine that is made sparkling through the application of the pure champagne-making process.

MÉTIER   Profession or craft.

MUID   An old term for a Rhône Valley barrel of 675 litres capacity. Also used in Burgundy.

MUTAGE   The addition of alcohol spirit to a wine. It is performed with such fortified wines as Rasteau and Beaumes-de-Venise.

NATURE   A still wine.

NÉGOCIANT   A wine merchant.

NÉGOCIANT-ÉLEVEUR   A merchant who buys grapes and/or wine. The wine is left in his cellars to mature until ready for sale.

OUILLAGE   The topping up of a cask following the evaporation of its wine.

PARCELLE   A plot of land within a vineyard – usually belonging to a small-holder.

PÉPIN   A grape pip.

PÉTANQUE   The very popular French game of bowls, played with small metal balls.

PICHET   A short wooden stump used for immersing the *chapeau* (q.v.) during fermentation.

PIÈCE   A barrel of 225 litres' capacity. It can be used for primary fermentation, but more commonly serves to age the wine.

PIGEAGE   The immersion of the *chapeau* of skins and pips in the juice during a vat's fermentation. Increasingly done by machine rather than manually.

PORTEUR   A carrier of the harvest.

POURRITURE   Rotting of the grapes.

PRIMEUR   A short-lived wine that is made by an abbreviated vinification process. It is released for sale in the middle of November, and also passes under the name of *vin nouveau*.

PROPRIÉTAIRE-NÉGOCIANT   A vineyard owner who supplements his wine-holding by buying other people's grapes or wine.

PROPRIÉTAIRE-RÉCOLTANT   A vineyard owner who makes nothing but his own wine.

PUPITRE   A wooden holder in which bottles of wine made by the *méthode champenoise* (q.v.) accumulate their deposit around the neck of the bottle.

QUARTIER   A section of a vineyard.

RAISIN ENTIER   A whole, uncrushed grape. A term used when the grapes are not crushed before fermentation.

RANCIO   A wine that shows 'age' on its taste.

RAPÉ   The discard, or rejected portion of the grape harvest. Such over-ripe or under-ripe grapes can be made into a wine of the same name, subject to a special tasting.

REMONTAGE   The pumping of the bottom of a vat of wine over the top or *chapeau* during its fermentation. This helps to keep the *chapeau* cool and aids colour extraction.

REMUAGE   The 'turning' of bottles of sparkling wine made by the traditional champagne method. It acts to lodge any deposits in the neck of the bottle.

ROBE   The general appearance of a wine; not only its colour but also its lustre or brilliance.

SOMMELIER (SOMMELIÈRE)   A wine waiter or waitress.

SOUS-BOIS   A tasting term describing an advanced stage in the evolution of the bouquet of principally Syrah and Mourvèdre wines. Literally, like damp leaves in an autumn forest, or the slightly rotting smell when lifting up a long-untouched piece of wood.

SYNDICAT DES VIGNERONS   A wine-growers' union.

TONNEAU   A wine barrel of no specific dimension.

TONNELIER   A cooper.

TRIAGE   A qualitative sorting of the grape harvest.

VENDANGE(S)   The grape harvest. The word is used in both the singular and plural form.

VENDANGEUR   A grape picker.

VIGNERON   A wine grower.

VIN DE CAFÉ   A light simple wine, often pale in colour, which when red may have only been exposed to the grape skins for up to a day.

VIN DE GARDE   A long-lived wine, one suitable for laying down.

VIN DÉLIMITÉ DE QUALITÉ SUPÉRIEURE   Literally, a delimited wine of superior quality. This is the category below *appellation contrôlée*, and the wine-making rulings, although similar in form, are accordingly less demanding.

VIN DE MÉDECINE   A 'booster' wine that is used to fill out a weak wine.

VIN DE PAILLE   Literally, 'straw wine'. It is a white wine made from grapes that are left to dry out completely before fermentation.

VIN DE TABLE   Table wine – a wine that bears no particular name and, often, no particular quality.

VIN DE TOUS LES JOURS   An everyday drinking wine.

VIN DOUX NATUREL   Literally, a sweet fortified wine. The *naturel* is therefore a slight misnomer.

VIN MOUSSEUX   Sparkling wine.

VIN ORDINAIRE   Ordinary wine, like *vin de table* the most basic category of wine that exists in France.

VRAC   Goods that are transported in bulk. In the wine world the term refers to wines that have not been bottled before they are moved around.

Bibliographical Note

There isn't a lot of choice on the Rhône – not surprisingly for such a recently 'discovered' region. But two works in English are definitely *sérieux*. Of a more commercial nature, there is Robert M. Parker Jr's *The Wines of the Rhône Valley and Provence* (Simon & Schuster, 1987). Robert Parker is now a well-known figure in the wine world for his commentaries and scores out of 100 on all sorts of wines. But the Rhône is, I suspect, where a substantial part of his heart lies, and his enthusiasm for the wines and the area comes through strongly. It is light on areas that do not especially appeal to Mr Parker, like Tavel, but particularly strong in the northern Rhône.

Robert W. Mayberry, also an American and whose pseudonym in the southern Rhône is 'the Professor', is the author of *Wines of the Rhône Valley: A Guide to Origins* (Rowman & Littlefield, 1987). This is more of an intellectual exercise, the sort of book that will appeal to the purist, and has extensive comment on grape varieties and their tasting sensations. It covers the southern Rhône more strongly than the north.

Index

Note: names in brackets refer to the *appellation* where a given *cuvée* comes from; italicized names in brackets refer to the *appellation* where a given *lieu-dit* is located.

Word-by-word alphabetical order ignoring Château, Clos, Domaine, de, de la, des, du, La, Le, Les.

INDEX